POLITY AND ECOLOGY IN
FORMATIVE PERIOD COASTAL OAXACA

POLITY and ECOLOGY

IN FORMATIVE PERIOD COASTAL OAXACA

EDITED BY

ARTHUR A. JOYCE

UNIVERSITY PRESS OF COLORADO
Boulder

© 2013 by University Press of Colorado

Published by University Press of Colorado
5589 Arapahoe Avenue, Suite 206C
Boulder, Colorado 80303

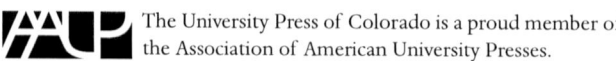 The University Press of Colorado is a proud member of
the Association of American University Presses.

The University Press of Colorado is a cooperative publishing enterprise supported, in part,
by Adams State University, Colorado State University, Fort Lewis College, Metropolitan State
University of Denver, Regis University, University of Colorado, University of Northern Colorado,
Utah State University, and Western State Colorado University.

∞ This paper meets the requirements of the ANSI/NISO Z39.48-1992 (Permanence of Paper).

Polity and ecology in formative period coastal Qaxaca / edited by Arthur A. Joyce.
    p. cm.
  Includes bibliographical references and index.
  ISBN 978-1-60732-202-3 (hardcover : alk. paper) — ISBN 978-1-60732-212-2 (ebook)
1. Indians of Mexico—Mexico—Oaxaca (State)—Antiquities. 2. Indians of Mexico—Mexico—
Verde River Valley (San Luis Potosí)—Antiquities. 3. Indians of Mexico—Mexico—Oaxaca
(State)—Politics and government. 4. Indians of Mexico—Mexico—Verde River Valley (San Luis
Potosí)—Politics and government. 5. Indigenous peoples—Ecology—Mexico—Oaxaca (State)
6. Indigenous peoples—Ecology—Mexico—Verde River Valley (San Luis Potosí) 7. Excavations
(Archaeology)—Mexico—Oaxaca (State) 8. Excavations (Archaoelogy)—Mexico—Verde River
Valley (San Luis Potosí) 9. Oaxaca (Mexico : State)—Antiquities. 10. Verde River Valley (San Luis
Potosí, Mexico)—Antiquities. I. Joyce, Arthur A.
  F1219.1.O11P65 2012
  972'.7401—dc23
                        2012041736

Design by Daniel Pratt

22   21   20   19   18   17   16   15   14   13   10   9   8   7   6   5   4   3   2   1

To Donald Brockington,
pioneer of Oaxaca coast archaeology

CONTENTS

FIGURES

TABLES

employ their diverse expertise toward a comprehensive reconstruction of Formative period archaeological and paleoecological developments in this underappreciated Pacific coastal region of Mesoamerica.

Joyce himself was introduced to the Río Verde region of the Oaxaca coast as a graduate student participant in a 1986 project involving archaeological reconnaissance and some small-scale excavation. Previously noteworthy mainly as the locus of a Postclassic and early colonial period statelet at Tututepec, the region at the time was gaining renewed attention not so much for its own achievements but as an exemplar of a hinterland region conquered by an emergent Late Formative period Zapotec empire, the capital of which lay a couple of hundred miles to the northeast in the highland Valley of Oaxaca. His interest stimulated in part by the conquest hypothesis, Joyce returned to the Río Verde region in 1988 for his doctoral dissertation project. Along with his excavations at several sites and construction of a regional ceramic chronology, Joyce joined with Raymond Mueller, a specialist in physical geography and soil science, for a geomorphological analysis of the Río Verde's changing hydrology. Collectively their objective was to elucidate the river's impact on the development and expansion of maize agriculture and human settlement.

A chapter in this volume by Mueller, Joyce, Aleksander Borejsza, and Michelle Goman reports on the updated results of their geomorphological research into the effects of anthropogenic and natural highland erosion on agricultural growth and population on the lower Río Verde floodplain. Their conclusions are enhanced by the results of recent paleoecological analyses of sediment cores drawn from one of the region's coastal lagoons, the formation of which was found to be owed in part to deposition from the highland erosion. As discussed in a chapter by Goman, Joyce, and Mueller, the estuarine lagoons came to serve as new sources of food. The results of microbotanical, archaeozoological, odontometric, and osteological analyses of materials recovered from lagoon and floodplain cores and archaeological excavations provide valuable insights into the dietary record of the Río Verde's Formative period inhabitants, including their adoption of maize agriculture, as well as their health and disease.

What became the most controversial facet of Joyce's original Río Verde archaeological research was his conclusion that the region did not fall victim to imperialism, contrary to what others had interpreted as epigraphic evidence to that effect found on stone carvings at Monte Albán, the Zapotec capital, and from the widespread adoption of a grayware pottery style emanating from the highland state. In this volume a chapter by Andrew Workinger, drawing on data from his excavations at the Río Verde site of San Francisco de Arriba, and another by Marc Levine comparing Río Verde's local grayware with that of the Monte Albán variety, have, in my opinion, pretty much put the question to rest. Workinger evaluates the "world system" concept of core domination of peripheral regions against other models of interregional interaction and finds it defi-cient in accounting for archaeological evidence from the lower Río Verde, not only for the Formative but for a later time period when Teotihuacan reigned as an influential Mesoamerican power. Congruently, Levine concludes that the Late Formative adoption of a grayware ceramic tradition in the Río Verde region was not a marker of Zapotec conquest. Rather, as a locally distinctive pottery variant related to—and perhaps, I would add, initially imitative of—its highland progenitor, Río Verde grayware is shown to exemplify a Oaxaca-wide cluster of shared values and interregional relationships.

Also in the manner of interdisciplinary research, several other chapters delve into questions about local Formative period developments within the lower Río Verde region. A multifaceted study of 156 burials recovered from six local sites provides insights into changing human diet, disease, physical pathol-ogies, and ideology. The research reported in a chapter by Sarah Barber, Joyce, Arion Mayes, José Aguilar, and Michelle Butler, while revealing evidence of growing socioeconomic inequality over time, shows Formative period Río Verde burial practice to be distinctively autochthonous, further rebutting spec-ulation from outside researchers about Zapotec conquest. Additional evidence of the region's autonomous growth of sociopolitical inequality comes from a chapter by Joyce, Levine, and Barber summarizing the results of excavations at Río Viejo, the region's principal civic-ceremonial center during the Terminal Formative. The size and complexity of a mammoth acropolis at the site indi-cated the need and ability to recruit construction labor from surrounding com-munities; its violent destruction and abandonment less than two hundred years later suggests the fragility of the political centralization that this labor con-scription implied.

In another chapter, focusing on excavations at a couple of outlying archae-ological sites, Barber aptly elaborates on the expressed ambivalence toward regional political centralization. Among other things, her analysis reveals how, until the closing stages of the Formative period, Río Verde elite personages lim-ited their articulation of fealty to the Río Viejo center in favor of emphasizing local community affiliation. Adding a different perspective, a chapter by Guy Hepp and Joyce summarizes the iconographic analysis of Formative period fig-urines, musical instruments, and ceramic appliqués and discusses their utility as expressions of social identity, ritual activity, and religious ideology.

As bookends to this insightful volume, Joyce's introduction and the con-cluding chapter by Christopher Pool summarize and elaborate on results of the past quarter century of integrated interdisciplinary research in the Río Verde region. In his preamble to the chapters that follow, Joyce provides his readers with a brief outline of archaeological research in the region, reviews his collab-orators' studies of settlement and sociopolitical development along with their research into ecological change, population growth, and the development of social inequality, and considers the impact of regional political centralization as the Formative period wound down. Toward the end of his introduction he briefly outlines the agency-based, poststructural models that have guided much of the research reported in this volume. Pool's final chapter broadens the perspective by comparing sociopolitical developments in the lower Río Verde region with contemporaneous polities at Zapotec Monte Albán in the Valley of Oaxaca and Olmec Tres Zapotes on the Gulf Coast. The comparison highlights the similarities and differences through which each balanced the often conflicting pull between communal and hierarchical sociopolitical practices. As a whole, the ten chapters in this volume stand as a tribute to Joyce's initiative in organizing the collaborative effort that has generated this research and to the fine work he and his colleagues have produced in return. Readers will be rewarded with a rich and comprehensive synopsis of Formative period archaeological developments in this important hinterland region of Mesoamerica.

ROBERT N. ZEITLIN
BRANDEIS UNIVERSITY

POLITY AND ECOLOGY IN
FORMATIVE PERIOD COASTAL OAXACA

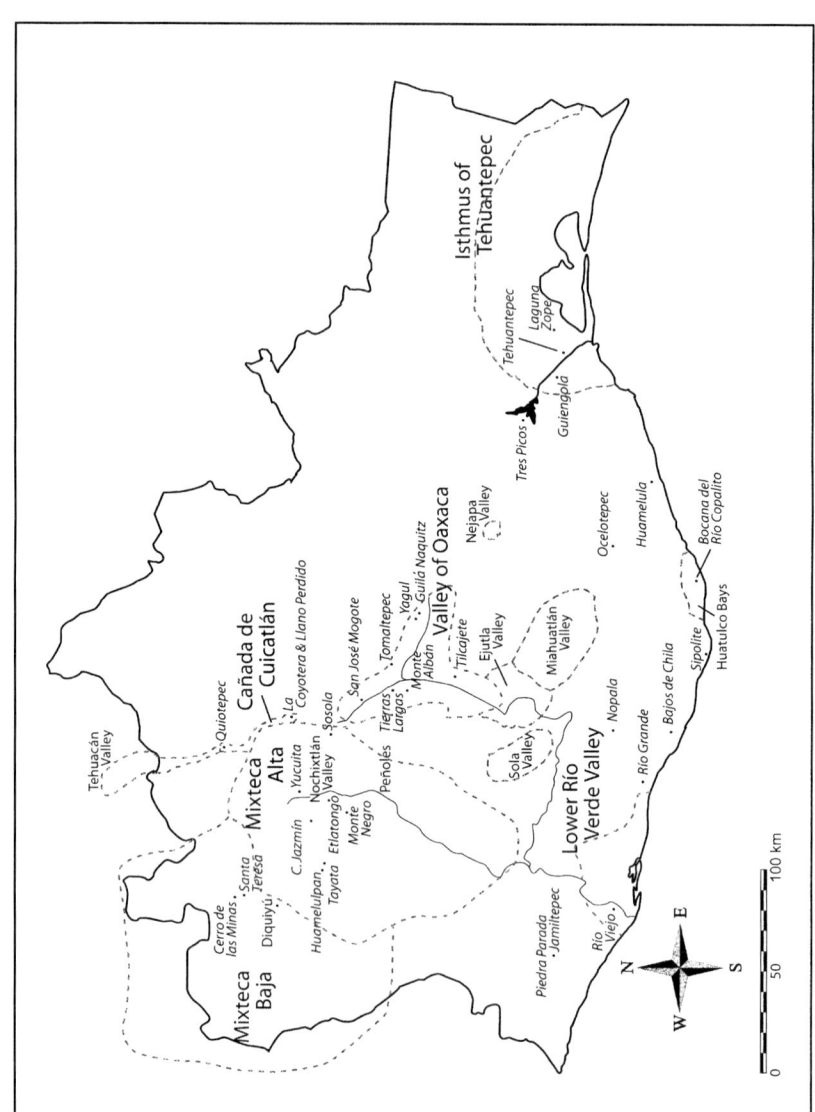

FIGURE 1.1. Map of the state of Oaxaca showing geographical regions and archaeological sites mentioned in the book.

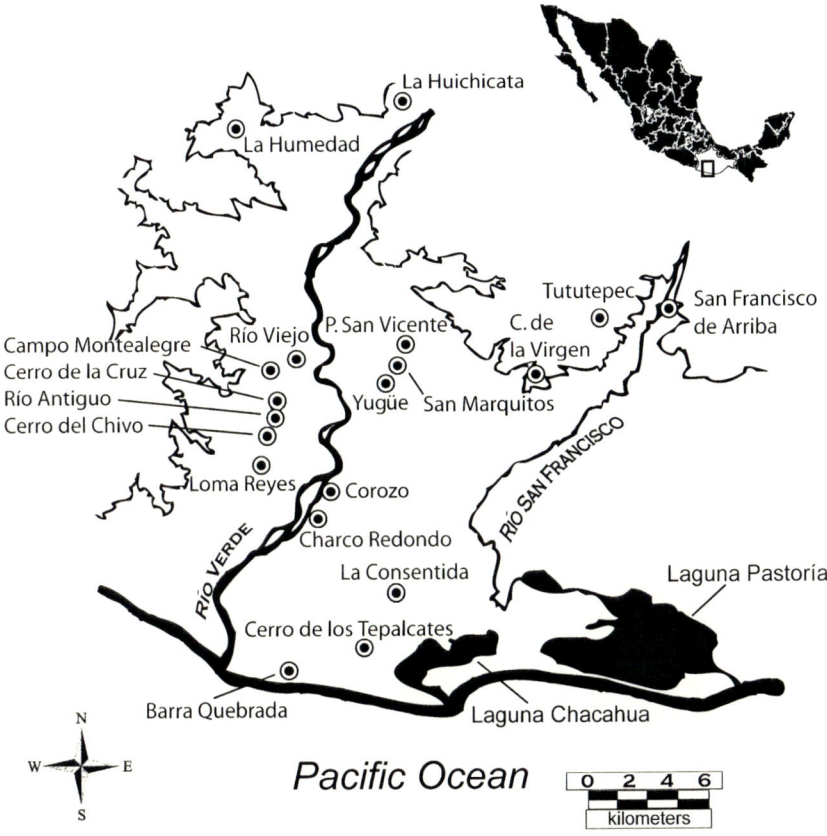

FIGURE 1.2. Map of the lower Río Verde Valley showing archaeological sites mentioned in the book.

that the region was a center of prehispanic population and social complexity, especially in the later Formative period. The chapters provide empirically oriented studies that trace Formative period developments from the earliest known evidence of a human presence in the region during the Archaic period to the collapse of Río Viejo, the region's first centralized polity, at ca. AD 250. This period saw the earliest agricultural settlements in the region as well as the origins of sedentism and early village life. The Early/Middle Formative witnessed major changes in the lower Verde's floodplain and in environments along the coast that expanded the productivity of subsistence resources. Social complexity emerged by the Late Formative, although we suspect future research will show that hereditary inequality began by the Middle Formative. By the Terminal Formative period an urban center had developed at the site of Río Viejo, which became the dominant community in the valley. Centralized

FIGURE 1.4. Donald Brockington excavating at Piedra Parada Jamiltepec (courtesy of Donald Brockington).

MA thesis, which represent the first archaeological excavations on the Oaxaca coast (Figure 1.4).

Following the survey by De Cicco and Brockington (1956), research shifted to the eastern coast with survey and excavation projects in the southern Isthmus of Tehuantepec (Delgado 1965; Wallrath 1967) and Brockington's (1966) dissertation research at Sipolite near Puerto Angel. Brockington then directed the 1969–1970 Oaxaca Coast Project, which involved a more extensive survey from the Oaxaca-Guerrero border to Salina Cruz. Brockington and his colleagues (1974; Brockington and Long 1974) recorded 128 sites and completed test excavations at 13 of these. The lower Río Verde Valley had the greatest density of sites in the region, with 38 recorded during Brockington's project.

The goals of these initial archaeological investigations on the Oaxaca coast were necessarily aimed at basic issues of chronology, culture history, and the recording of sites. Specialized studies included descriptions of ceramics, especially from the central and eastern coast, by J. Robert Long (1974) and Margaret Houston (1974). María Jorrín (1974) described carved stones, which included monuments in the lower Río Verde Valley from the sites of Río Viejo, Charco Redondo, Tututepec, La Huichicata, and La Humedad, as well as petroglyphs from Cerro de los Tepalcates. By the late 1960s, Brockington was also beginning to address questions involving interregional interaction, especially with the Oaxacan highlands and the Maya. Brockington (1983, 29) found that ceramic evidence for interaction with the Valley of Oaxaca was strongest during the Terminal Formative and Early Classic periods, especially in the central coast around the site of Bajos de Chila, although he concluded that "Monte Albán never dominated the Coast at any time." Houston (1974) argued that Terminal Formative Gralisa pottery from the central coast was imported at Monte Albán.

During the 1970s and early 1980s, research on the Oaxaca littoral focused on the eastern coast, especially the southern Isthmus of Tehuantepec. Peterson and Macdougall (1974) carried out a study of the Postclassic fortress of Guiengola in the southern isthmus. In the early 1970s, Robert and Judith Zeitlin carried out a survey and excavation project along the lower reaches of the Río los Perros in the southern isthmian region. The Zeitlins constructed a detailed ceramic sequence for the region (J. Zeitlin 1978; R. Zeitlin 1979) and carried out studies of changes in interregional interaction, settlement, and subsistence (J. Zeitlin 1978; R. Zeitlin 1978, 1990, 1993).

Following the Zeitlins' project in the southern isthmus, there was little archaeological research in the Oaxaca coast region for the next thirteen years. Roberto Zárate (1986) described three carved stones from the coast, while Méndez (1975) conducted preliminary archaeological investigations in the coastal Huave zone of the southern isthmus. More recent research along the eastern coast of Oaxaca includes Robert Zeitlin's excavations at the large Formative period site of Laguna Zope (R. Zeitlin 1993) and Judith Zeitlin's excavation of a Late Postclassic/early colonial barrio at Tehuantepec (J. Zeitlin 1994, 2005). In the Huatulco Bays area archaeologists from the Mexican Instituto Nacional de Antropología e Historia (INAH) have carried out archaeological survey and test excavations (Fernández and Gómez 1988) along with excavations at the site of Bocana del Río Copalito (Matadamas 2009). Other projects include rescue excavations at the site of Río Grande (Zárate 1995), research on carved stones at Nopala (Arnaud 2003), and survey and test excavations at the site of Huamelula in the Chontal region (Kroefges 2004).

In 1986 research resumed in the lower Verde region with a collaborative project involving archaeologists from the United States and INAH. This was the Río Verde Archaeological Project (RVAP), a pilot study directed by David Grove, Marcus Winter, Susan Gillespie, and Raul Arana. The directors of the 1986 project also provided my introduction to the lower Verde region since I was a graduate student on the project. The RVAP was designed to examine the Archaic to Formative transition with regard to settlement, resource utilization, exchange, and the development of social complexity (Gillespie 1987; Grove 1988; Joyce and Winter 1989). The lower Verde was chosen for investigation because of its ecological similarity to the environments of early villages known elsewhere in Mesoamerica. Like the lower Río Verde Valley, regions such as the Gulf coast and the Soconusco have a diverse ecology including rivers, fertile floodplains, and large estuaries (Pool, Chapter 10). The RVAP carried out a regional site reconnaissance that recorded seventy-one sites and conducted test excavations at six sites. Surprisingly, the project recovered little evidence of settlement prior to the Middle Formative. The data suggested, however, that the region experienced rapid population growth and increasing social complexity during the Late/Terminal Formative. Comparison of ceramic styles and monumental art suggested that the region had been inhabited by Chatino speakers until the arrival of Mixtecs in the Postclassic (Joyce and Winter 1989; also see Urcid 1993; Joyce 2010; Joyce et al. 2001).

In 1988 I returned to the Oaxaca coast for my dissertation project, the Río Verde Formative Project, which examined the effects of ecology and interregional interaction on Late/Terminal Formative social change. The project included large-scale horizontal excavations at Cerro de la Cruz, excavation of five deep trenches at Río Viejo, test excavations at two other sites, and a program of geomorphological research in the floodplain (Joyce 1991a, 1991b, 1994; Joyce and Mueller 1992; Joyce et al. 1995, 1998). The geomorphological research, directed by Raymond Mueller, indicated that a major change in the hydrology of the lower Río Verde occurred during the Formative period, which probably increased agricultural productivity and may have made the region more attractive for human settlement (Joyce and Mueller 1992; Mueller et al., Chapter 3). Studies of interregional interaction focused on relations with the Valley of Oaxaca, since Joyce Marcus (1983) had suggested, based on epigraphic data, that the lower Verde might have been conquered by Monte Albán during the Terminal Formative. The 1988 project also resulted in the construction of a ceramic chronology for the region (Figure 1.5), which has been continuously refined (see Barber 2005; Forde 2006; Hedgepeth 2009; Joyce 1991a; Joyce et al. 1998, 2001; Levine 2007; Workinger 2002).

Oaxacan archaeologists have traditionally used uncalibrated dates when reporting the age range of ceramic phases. The calibrated dates were converted using OxCal 4.1 (Bronk Ramsey 2009). Throughout the book uncalibrated dates are used, although both uncalibrated and calibrated dates are provided when specific radiocarbon determinations are reported in the text and in tables. In this volume we use the median of the calibrated radiocarbon ages. The median age is preferred over traditional intercept-based methods as these are overly sensitive to minor changes in the mean of the radiocarbon date (Telford et al. 2004). Ceramic phases have not yet been defined for the Early Formative and the early Middle Formative in the lower Río Verde Valley.

Investigation of the effects of environmental change and interregional interaction on social developments in the lower Verde continued in the 1990s and 2000s. These projects included further large-scale excavations at the urban center of Río Viejo (Figure 1.6) as well as test excavations at another seven sites. In addition, Andrew Workinger (2002, Chapter 7) conducted block excavations

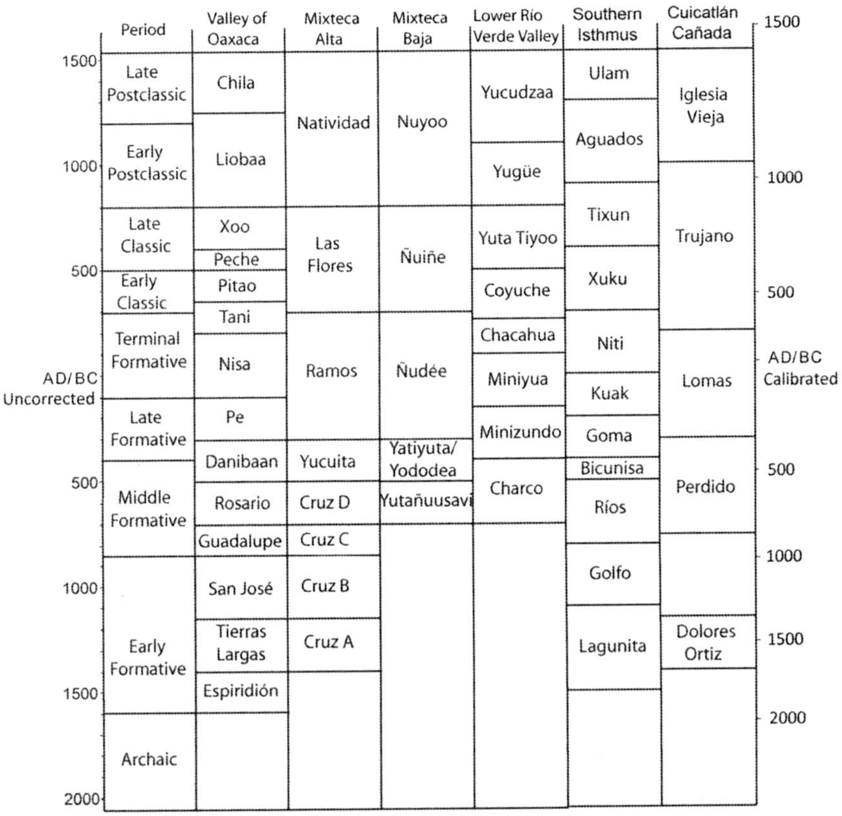

Period	Valley of Oaxaca	Mixteca Alta	Mixteca Baja	Lower Río Verde Valley	Southern Isthmus	Cuicatlán Cañada
Late Postclassic	Chila	Natividad	Nuyoo	Yucudzaa	Ulam	Iglesia Vieja
Early Postclassic	Liobaa			Yugüe	Aguados	
Late Classic	Xoo / Peche	Las Flores	Ñuiñe	Yuta Tiyoo	Tixun	Trujano
Early Classic	Pitao / Tani			Coyuche	Xuku	
Terminal Formative	Nisa	Ramos	Ñudée	Chacahua / Miniyua	Niti / Kuak	Lomas
Late Formative	Pe			Minizundo	Goma	
	Danibaan	Yucuita	Yatiyuta/Yododea		Bicunisa	Perdido
Middle Formative	Rosario	Cruz D	Yutañuusavi	Charco	Ríos	
	Guadalupe	Cruz C				
	San José	Cruz B			Golfo	
Early Formative	Tierras Largas	Cruz A			Lagunita	Dolores Ortiz
	Espiridión					
Archaic						

FIGURE 1.5. Ceramic chronologies in Oaxaca (after Joyce 2010: Figure 1.6).

at San Francisco de Arriba in 1997 and 1999 to investigate questions of interregional interaction. Marc Levine's (2002, Chapter 8) study of Late and Terminal Formative ceramics showed that lower Verde pottery is stylistically distinct from highland ceramics and that an increase in serving wares in the Terminal Formative suggests a rise in feasting practices. Regional full-coverage surveys now span 152 km² of the lower Verde region, providing an excellent picture of changes in settlement and sociopolitical organization (Joyce 2005; Joyce et al. 2001, 2004; Workinger 2002). The research on interregional interaction has not supported the hypothesis of Marcus and Flannery (1996) that parts of the lower Verde region were incorporated into a Terminal Formative Monte Albán empire (Joyce 1993, 2003; Levine, Chapter 8; Workinger 2002, Chapter 7; Workinger and Joyce 2009; Zeitlin and Joyce 1999). The research has focused attention on Teotihuacan, the southern Isthmus of Tehuantepec, and the Mixteca Alta along with the Valley of Oaxaca as important interaction partners during the lower Verde's prehispanic history.

9

FIGURE 1.6. Excavations on the acropolis at Río Viejo in 2000.

Since the 1990s, the lower Verde research has been moving beyond questions of interregional interaction and environmental change. Excavations on the acropolis at Río Viejo by Joyce and Barber (Joyce 2006, 2008; Joyce and Barber 2011; Joyce et al. 2010, Chapter 5) as well as horizontal excavations at the sites of Yugüe and Cerro de la Virgen by Barber (2005, Chapter 6) have examined political authority at the end of the Formative period. Our research indicates that regional political authority during the Terminal Formative was tenuous (Barber 2005; Barber and Joyce 2007; Joyce 2008, 2010, 186–196). The abandonment and burning of the civic-ceremonial center of the Río Viejo polity, located on its massive acropolis, along with the demographic decline of the city at ca. AD 250 show that Terminal Formative political centralization was short-lived.

Geomorphological research has continued in the lower Río Verde Valley (Joyce and Mueller 1997, Mueller et al., Chapter 3) as well as in the highland valleys of Oaxaca, Nochixtlán, and Ejutla, which make up most of the Verde's upper drainage basin (Mueller and Pou 2008; Mueller et al. 2012). The research suggests that human land use in the highlands triggered geomorphic changes that may have affected the entire drainage. The data indicate that population growth and agricultural expansion in the highlands during the Early Formative period accelerated anthropogenic erosion into the drainage basin. Sediment carried down the drainage system to the coast triggered major shifts in the geomorphology of the lower valley, including changes in river morphology and the expansion of the Río Verde's agriculturally productive floodplain (Joyce and Mueller 1997; Mueller et al., Chapter 3). Paleoecological studies by Michelle Goman and colleagues (Goman et al. 2005, 2010, Chapter 2) show that coastal environments were also affected by the increased sediment load carried down from the highlands. Sediment cores extracted from Laguna Pastoría, a coastal estuary, show that sediment carried down the Río Verde contributed to the formation of bay barriers and therefore the creation of the coastal estuaries by 450 BC. The estuaries are highly productive ecosystems rich in populations of fish, shellfish, and waterfowl (Rodríguez et al. 1989). Archaeofaunal studies suggest that people took advantage of the estuaries since brackish-water fish and shellfish increased in frequency in midden deposits at the end of the Formative (Fernández 2004). Alec Christensen's (1998) odontometric research suggests that coastal ecology provided people with diets that had a significant selective effect, reducing the size of the dentition relative to highland populations. Melmed's (2006) bioarchaeological research shows that inhabitants of the region enjoyed varied diets and general good health (also see Mayes and Barber 2008), although congenital syphilis was present in the region by the first few hundred years AD (Mayes et al. 2009).

Although this volume focuses on Formative period research in the lower Río Verde Valley, there has also been important work on the Classic and Postclassic periods. Survey and excavation data demonstrate that after a period of political fragmentation in the Early Classic, the city of Río Viejo reemerged and once again became the dominant political center in the region during the Late Classic (Joyce 2008, 229–234, 2010, 239–247). Río Viejo collapsed at ca. AD 800, and excavations on the site's acropolis show that during the Early Postclassic it was occupied by commoners (Joyce et al. 2001). Excavations of Early Postclassic residences have examined political change, domestic economy, and exchange (Arnaud et al. 2009; Hedgepeth 2009; Joyce et al. 2001; King 2003, 2008). Research on the Late Postclassic imperial center of Tututepec has synthesized archaeological and ethnohistorical evidence, including indigenous histories recorded in the Mixtec codices (Forde 2006; Joyce et al. 2004; Levine 2007, 2011). Javier Urcid has studied the iconography and epigraphy of carved stone monuments (1993; Urcid and Joyce 1999, 2001), and Heather Orr (2001) has examined pictographs from Piedra San Vicente.

The interdisciplinary research in the lower Río Verde Valley has therefore yielded evidence for more than 3,500 years of cultural developments and achievements. The research has focused on the Formative period, which is examined in detail in this volume. In the next two sections of this chapter, I provide a brief summary of Formative period cultural and environmental change to contextualize the studies that follow. My discussion introduces the chapters in the volume as part of a general overview of the Formative period in the region. The final chapter by Christopher Pool provides a broader Mesoamerican context for the lower Rio Verde research.

EARLY SETTLEMENT AND SOCIAL COMPLEXITY

Survey and excavation data indicate that the lower Río Verde Valley was only sparsely inhabited before the late Middle Formative period Charco phase (700–400 BC). As discussed by Goman and colleagues in Chapter 2, the earliest evidence for a human presence in the region comes from a sediment core extracted from Laguna Pastoría along the coast, which indicates a short period of land clearance for shifting horticulture in the vicinity of the estuary from ca. 2110 to 1560 BC, which included the planting of domesticated maize (Goman et al., Chapter 2). Human impact is not evident again in the coastal cores until the Middle Formative when land clearance is more extensive, probably representing the establishment of maize-based agricultural systems. The paleoecological data are consistent with archaeological evidence that the lower Río Verde region may have been only sporadically occupied until the Middle Formative. The earliest archaeological sites discovered thus far in the region date to the Early Formative period (1600–700 BC), although only three sites from this period covering a total of 5 ha have been discovered. Two of the sites are located near the salt flats north of the coastal estuaries, suggesting a different settlement pattern than later in the Formative when communities were oriented toward the Río Verde's floodplain and piedmont.

The only site to have yielded primary deposits from the Early Formative is La Consentida, located about 1 km north of the salt flats and estuaries. The site covers 2.6 ha and is dominated by several mounds reaching elevations of 5 m above the surrounding floodplain. Excavations in 1988 by Joyce (1991a, 116–117) and in 2009 by Hepp (Hepp 2011a, 2011b; Hepp and Joyce, Chapter 9) exposed occupational surfaces, hearths, and burials as well as numerous samples of obsidian flakes, pottery, and figurines. Uncalibrated radiocarbon dates from three charcoal samples range from 1408 BC to 1532 BC, dating the site to the beginning of the Early Formative period. The data suggest that a small number of sedentary communities were present in the region during the Early Formative.

The low population levels indicated for the Early Formative and the beginning of the Middle Formative are somewhat surprising given that the southern Pacific coast of Mexico and Guatemala includes some of the earliest evidence for sedentary villages and the origins of social complexity in Mesoamerica. In the southern Isthmus of Tehuantepec and the Soconusco coast of Chiapas archaeological research has shown that large sedentary communities, some with populations of perhaps 2,000 people, had developed by the Early Formative (Love 1999; R. Zeitlin 1979). One of these communities, Paso de la Amada, in the Mazatán region of the Soconusco, grew to 140 ha (Clark 2004; Lesure 1997). Excavations at Paso de la Amada exposed monumental architecture, including the earliest ball court yet discovered in Mesoamerica as well as a huge public plaza and elite residence. Another of these precocious villages is Laguna Zope, located only 220 km east of the lower Río Verde Valley (R. Zeitlin 1979).

In the lower Río Verde Valley evidence for communities on the scale of Paso de la Amada and Laguna Zope do not occur until the late Middle Formative period Charco phase (700–400 BC). By the Charco phase, population had increased with the occupational area in the full-coverage survey reaching 64 ha. A regional center developed at Charco Redondo, which grew to 62 ha, making it one of the largest Middle Formative sites in Oaxaca. Deep test excavations have recovered Chaco phase deposits at the sites of Charco Redondo, Río Viejo, Cerro de la Cruz, Corozo, and San Francisco de Arriba. Paleozoological analysis of a midden excavated at Corozo suggests a focus on freshwater and brackish fish from the river (Fernández 2004). Further excavation of Charco phase sites is needed to say more about the period, but the size of the regional center suggests the emergence of social complexity. By the late Middle Formative period hereditary status distinctions are evident in other regions of Oaxaca, including at San José Mogote in the Valley of Oaxaca and probably at sites like Tayata, La Providencia, Etlatongo, and Yucuita in the Mixteca Alta (Blanton et al. 1999, 36–42; Blomster 2004; Joyce 2010, 110–128, 160–161).

One factor that probably contributed to Formative period social developments in the lower Río Verde Valley is environmental change, particularly during the Early and Middle Formative periods (Goman et al. 2005, Chapter 2; Joyce et al. 1998; Joyce and Mueller 1992, 1997; Mueller 1991; Mueller et al., Chapter 3). Paleoenvironmental research in the valleys of the upper drainage basin of the Río Verde indicates that highland erosion increased the sediment load and discharge of the river, which had a major impact on lowland environments. New data, discussed in Chapter 3 by Mueller and colleagues, provide a more precise chronology for lowland environmental change. They show that major changes in floodplain and coastal environments in the lower valley occurred during the Early/Middle Formative and were likely triggered by erosion in the Río Verde's upper drainage basin, resulting at least in part from agricultural and demographic expansion in the highlands. As discussed by Mueller and colleagues, paleoenvironmental research in the lower valley indicates a major shift in the form and position of the river during the Early Formative. Data from cores in the floodplain show an increase in flooding and sediment load that triggered a shift from meandering to more braided river conditions. More important for human populations was an expansion of the Río Verde's agriculturally productive floodplain. Evidence from sediment cores in the coastal lagoons suggests that the increase in sediment carried by the river also accelerated the formation of bay barrier features along the coast (Goman et al. 2005, Chapter 2).

Although it is tempting to argue that the ecological changes contributed to population growth in the region after 700 BC, we have not yet established a strong causal link between environmental change and demographic expansion. A causal connection is suggested, however, by studies of human diet in the region, although more data are needed to confirm the patterns. Specifically, archaeofaunal studies suggest a shift toward estuarine resources during the end of the Formative period and into the Classic (Fernández 2004, 128), while isotope and trace element studies on human bone suggest an increase in the consumption of maize and/or estuarine resources (Taylor et al. 2009).

The Late and Terminal Formative periods in Oaxaca and in many areas of Mesoamerica were a time of population growth, rising social complexity, and the development of urban centers that were the political seats of regional polities (Balkansky 1998a; Balkansky et al. 2004; Joyce 2010; Kowalewski et al. 2009; Pérez et al. 2011; Winter 2007a, 2007b; R. Zeitlin 1993). In Oaxaca the earliest urban center emerged at the very end of the Middle Formative at the hilltop site of Monte Albán, which came to dominate the Valley of Oaxaca and perhaps some nearby regions (see below). Urban and proto-urban centers also arose within a few hundred years after the founding of Monte Albán at Yucuita, Monte Negro, Huamelulpan, Cerro Jazmín, and Etlatongo in the Mixteca Alta; Cerro de las Minas and Diquiyú in the Mixteca Baja; and Laguna Zope and Tres Picos in the southern Isthmus of Tehuantepec. These urban centers have evidence of monumental buildings and powerful leaders, although significant interregional variation in political organization is evident (Balkansky et al. 2004; Joyce 2010, 161–195; Winter 2004). Long-distance exchange increases at this time, and there is an expansion of interpolity warfare, at least in the Oaxacan highlands (Joyce 2010; Levine, Chapter 8; Marcus and Flannery 1996; Winter 1984).

In the lower Río Verde Valley considerably more is known about the Late Formative than earlier time periods, and as in other regions trends toward urbanization and rising social complexity are evident. The regional survey indicates a significant expansion in population during the Late Formative Minizundo phase (400–150 BC), with the occupational area in the full-coverage survey increasing from 64 ha to 299 ha. Settlement was distributed between the piedmont (43.2%), floodplain (36.4%), and secondary valleys (20.4%). Charco Redondo continued as a demographic and presumably a political center, growing to 70 ha. Population at San Francisco de Arriba exploded from 1 ha in the Middle Formative to 95 ha in the Late Formative, making it one of the largest communities in Oaxaca at the time. Block excavations by Workinger (2002, 171–222) at San Francisco de Arriba show that much of the site's massive public acropolis was constructed at this time, indicating the mobilization of a large labor force, presumably by emerging social elites. The size and monumentality of San Francisco de Arriba suggest that it was approaching urban scale.

Excavations at the site of Cerro de la Cruz in 1988 provide data on social practices and the architectural layout of a Minizundo phase community as well as evidence for emerging status differences (Joyce 1991a, 1991b, 1994). Cerro de la Cruz lies approximately 4 km west of the Río Verde and occupies about 1.5 ha of a low flat spur extending from a large rocky hill in the floodplain. Most of the work at the site involved a 300 m^2 exposure of Minizundo phase residential terraces. Settlement on the terraces was dense, with buildings usually placed within 5 m of one another. Construction of the terraces at Cerro de la Cruz and other Minizundo phase sites represent communal building projects. Four probable low-status residences (Structures 6, 9, 10, and 11) were characterized by stone foundations, earthen floors, simple burials beneath floors, and small cooking features. Burials from the site yielded remains from 115 individuals, most of which were dated stratigraphically to the Minizundo phase.

The work at Cerro de la Cruz focused on the upper terrace, where excavations revealed a granite flagstone patio surrounded by stone foundations of five structures (Structures 1–5; Figure 1.7). The granite flagstone patio included a large hearth (F1) intruded into its surface that far exceeded the volume of typical cooking features associated with residences. Three of the structures surrounding the patio (Structures 2, 3, and 4) were small (approximately 3 m × 3 m each) storage rooms with their floors deliberately sunken beneath the level of the patio. A thin organic deposit in Structure 2 contained over 1,000 fragments of charred maize (Woodard 1991, 869). Structure 5 was only partially excavated, but it appears to have been a residence, based on the presence of probable cooking features. The large hearth and storerooms suggest that ritual feasting

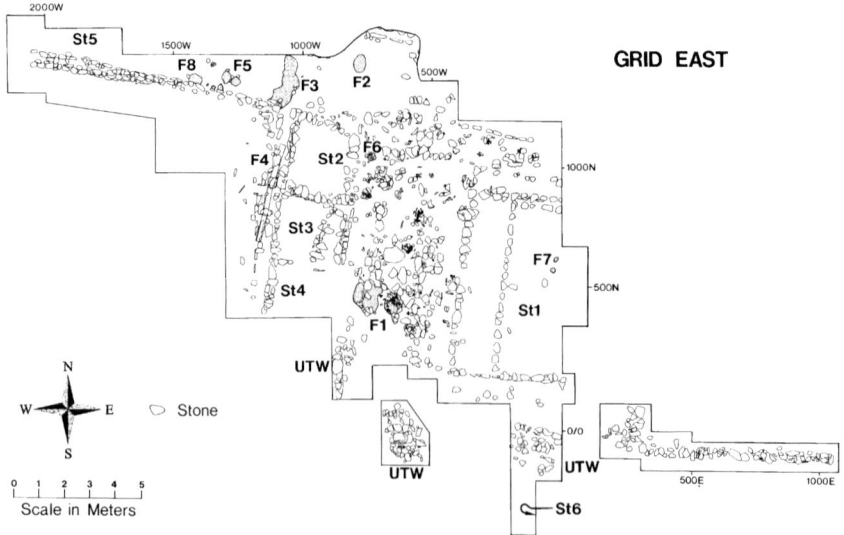

FIGURE 1.7. Plan of the upper terrace complex at Cerro de la Cruz (after Joyce 1991b: Figure 4). © Society for American Archaeology. Reprinted by permission from *Latin American Antiquity* Volume 2, Number 2.

carried out on the patio brought together multiple households and perhaps the entire community. Similar large cooking features with charred remains of edible plants, animal bones, and shellfish have been recovered in Minizundo phase deposits at Río Viejo and Yugüe (Barber 2005, 292, 2009; Joyce 1991a, 364, Fernández 2004, 126–130). Evidence for feasting at Río Viejo also includes an organic deposit containing charred maize as well as 286 seeds, possibly of zapote or avocado, discovered at the base of a well-made stone retaining wall, probably part of a low platform that may have been a public building (Joyce 1991a, 365). Given the relatively modest status distinctions and indications that authority was more communal than exclusionary (see below), I suspect that Minizundo phase feasting resembled Dietler's (2001) empowering feasts rather than patron-role or diacritical feasts that require social settings with well-established political hierarchies.

Evidence from Structure 1 in the patio complex at Cerro de la Cruz suggests other forms of communal ceremony. As discussed by Barber and colleagues in Chapter 4, mortuary data from Structure 1 indicate that it was a public cemetery (also see Joyce 1991a, 1994). There were forty-nine individuals, including forty-two adults, interred beneath the floors and along the walls of Structure 1.[1] An additional nine individuals were interred along the interior of a terrace wall associated with the patio complex. None of the burials recovered from the upper terrace were accompanied by offerings. The lack of offerings suggests that these individuals were non-elites, although the high proportion of adults suggests that some type of achieved status was required for interment in the cemetery. The burials associated with the patio complex occurred over the course of several generations, as shown by the frequent instances of later burials having disturbed earlier ones. Claims that the cemetery associated with Cerro de la Cruz Structure 1 was actually the result of a massacre (Balkansky 1998b, 470; Redmond and Spencer 2006, 375–377; Spencer 2007) have been strongly refuted (see Barber et al., Chapter 4; Joyce 2003; Joyce et al. 2000; Workinger and Joyce 2009). As discussed by Barber and colleagues (Barber 2005; Barber et al., Chapter 4), the discovery of Terminal Formative cemeteries at Yugüe and Charco Redondo shows that communal cemeteries were a long-term tradition in Formative period coastal society.

Emerging status differences were suggested by mortuary data from Structure 8 at Cerro de la Cruz, exposed on the lower terrace. A total of fifteen individuals were recovered from beneath four floors constructed sequentially in Structure 8, a probable residence. These burials included all four of the Minizundo phase interments with definite grave offerings, suggesting that these people had higher status than those from other parts of the site. The most elaborate burial offering was a sash of forty-five carved marine shells found with an adult male (Figure 1.8).

Another indication of status differences was the discovery of hundreds of sherds from vessels imported into the lower Río Verde Valley from the Oaxaca Valley, the Mixteca Alta, and an as yet unidentified region (as determined by INAA, ICP, and petrographic analyses; see Banker and Joyce 1991; Joyce 1991c; Joyce et al. 2006; Workinger 2002, 345–369). These sherds were recovered at Cerro de la Cruz, Río Viejo, and San Francisco de Arriba in contexts with other evidence of public ritual activity or high status, indicating that they were imported as social valuables (Joyce 1991a, 517–519; Joyce et al. 2006; Workinger 2002, 389–390; Chapter 7). The establishment of long-distance exchange relations and the acquisition of exotic goods through these networks were means through which people set themselves apart from others (see below).

Overall, the data for the Late Formative show the presence of two large, nucleated sites at San Francisco de Arriba and Charco Redondo. The construction of monumental architecture at these sites (Butler 2011; Workinger 2002) implies the mobilization of labor by elites. Evidence for social inequality based on mortuary and residential data, however, is rather limited (Joyce 1991a, 1991b, 1994, 2010, 180–186). Much stronger evidence indicates practices that foregrounded communal identity rather than strong status distinctions. Evidence for ritual feasting, communal cemeteries, and collective labor used to build public structures indicates the construction of socially meaningful places tied to the identity of corporate groups consisting of multiple households and perhaps entire communities (Barber 2005, 95–101; Chapter 6; Barber and Joyce

FIGURE 1.8. Burial with carved shell sash in Structure 8 at Cerro de la Cruz (after Joyce et al. 1998: Figure 3.11).

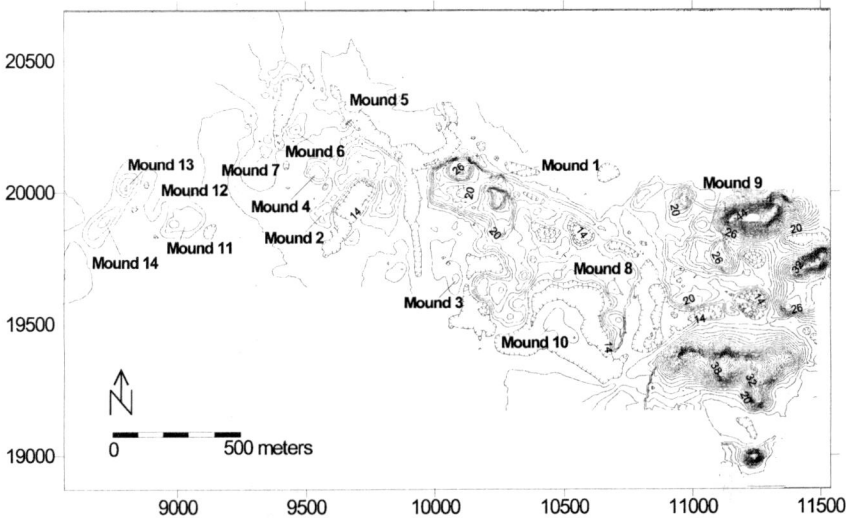

FIGURE 1.9. Plan of Río Viejo showing mounded architecture, including the Mound 1 acropolis (after Joyce et al. 2001: Figure 3; with kind permission of Spinger Science+Business Media).

2007; Barber et al., Chapter 4; Joyce 2008, 2010, 180–186; Pool, Chapter 10). In the case of the complex around Structure 1 at Cerro de la Cruz, shared pasts were a component of communal identity with burials and sequential rebuildings referencing history and the ancestors. Throughout the region, communal practices such as feasting and the creation of public buildings and spaces appear to have been locally focused.

POLITICAL CENTRALIZATION AND COLLAPSE

Formative period political centralization culminated during the Terminal Formative with the emergence of an urban center at Río Viejo (Joyce 2005, 2006, 2008, 2010). Río Viejo increased in size from 25 ha in the Late Formative to 225 ha by the early Terminal Formative (Figure 1.9). Regional population grew through this period based on the area occupied in the survey zone, which increased from 299 ha in the Late Formative Minizundo phase (400–150 BC) to 446 ha in the early Terminal Formative Miniyua Phase (150 BC–AD 100) and to 699 ha by the late Terminal Formative Chacahua phase (AD 100–250). Other large communities that may have been tied to Río Viejo through political, religious, and economic relations include San Francisco de Arriba, Charco Redondo, Cerro de la Virgen, and Tututepec. These sites ranged in size from about 60 ha to 72 ha, and all had monumental public spaces and probably powerful individuals and families.

Researchers in the Oaxacan highlands assert that the lower Río Verde Valley was conquered and incorporated into an empire dominated by the rulers of the Oaxaca Valley polity of Monte Albán (Balkansky 1997, 222; 1998b, 470–471; Marcus and Flannery 1996, 201–202; Redmond and Spencer 2006; Sherman et al. 2010; Spencer 2007). The Monte Albán imperialism argument was first proposed by Marcus (1976, 1983) based on her interpretation that the imagery on carved slabs set into the walls of Building J at Monte Albán represented conquered places. Marcus's interpretation of the Building J slabs as well as preliminary evidence from several regions led Marcus and Flannery (1996, 206) to argue that the areas conquered and administered by Monte Albán reached 20,000 km². These arguments led to research in several regions that were believed to have been part of the Monte Albán empire, including the lower Río Verde (Joyce 1991a, 1991b). With the exception of the Tilcajete site complex in the Valley of Oaxaca (Spencer and Redmond 2006), however, the evidence thus far does not support imperial conquest of other regions, and this is especially true for the lower Río Verde Valley, despite years of research investigating the problem (Joyce 1991a, 1991b, 2003, 2011; Workinger 2002; Workinger and Joyce 2009; Zeitlin and Joyce 1999). Scholars have also raised issues with Marcus's interpretation of carved stone monuments at Monte Albán (e.g., Urcid 1994, 2008; Whittaker 1980; Workinger and Joyce 2009).

As discussed by Levine (Chapter 8) and Workinger (Chapter 7), research in the lower Verde region has contradicted the hypothesis that the region was incorporated into an empire centered at Monte Albán (Joyce 1991a, 2003; Joyce et al. 2000; Levine 2002, Chapter 8; Pool, Chapter 10; Workinger 2002, Chapter 7; Workinger and Joyce 2009; Zeitlin and Joyce 1999). We cannot eliminate the possibility of occasional raiding by highland groups, although we have yet to discover data supporting this scenario. The data show that there are no indications of warfare, settlement shifts to defensible piedmont locations, or the presence of Zapotec administrators. Río Viejo covered 225 ha by the Terminal Formative, and since Monte Albán was only 416 ha, the lower Verde would have been a formidable opponent to Zapotec expansion. In addition, the lower Verde lies 150 km southwest and about a week's hard travel through the mountains by foot from Monte Albán, which would have created logistical difficulties for imperial armies or administrators (Barber et al. 2011). Ceramics were imported from the Valley of Oaxaca into the lower Río Verde Valley during the Minizundo phase, indicating exchange relations, although imports from elsewhere were more common (see above). Except for the diffusion of some highland grayware pottery styles, there is little evidence for interaction between the Oaxaca Valley and the lower Río Verde Valley during the Miniyua phase (Levine, Chapter 8).

Although the evidence indicates that the lower Río Verde region was not conquered by Monte Albán, warfare in the highlands may have disrupted exchange routes to the coast (Joyce 1993, 73). Elaborate ceramics imported from the highlands decreased during the Terminal Formative, and there also seems to be a decline in the importation of obsidian (Joyce 1991a; Joyce et al. 1995; Levine, Chapter 8; Workinger 2002). In response, people in the lower Río Verde may have established stronger ties to the southern Isthmus of Tehuantepec, as indicated by an increase in ceramics imported from that region (Barber 2005; Workinger 2002, 357–358; Chapter 7).

Rather than domination of the region by Monte Albán, the evidence shows continuity in cultural practices. During the Terminal Formative feasting, caching, mortuary rituals, and the construction of public buildings and spaces continued to reproduce community identity as they had done in the Late Formative (Barber and Joyce 2007). For example, an early Terminal Formative Miniyua phase cemetery was discovered at Charco Redondo by Michelle Butler during a pilot study in summer 2009 (Barber et al., Chapter 4; Butler 2011). This cemetery appears similar to the earlier one at Cerro de la Cruz in that only adults have been recovered thus far. In contrast to the Cerro de la Cruz cemetery, however, the one at Charco Redondo includes interments with modest offerings and two slab-lined graves.

Evidence from several sites indicates an expansion in the scale of communal practices (Barber 2005; Barber and Joyce 2007; Joyce 2010, 186–195; Joyce and Barber 2011). For example, as discussed by Marc Levine in Chapter 8 (also see Levine 2002), analysis of early Terminal Formative Miniyua phase ceramics shows a significant increase in the proportion of fancy serving vessels in non-elite ceramic inventories, perhaps indicative of an increase in ritual feasting. Likewise, studies of Formative figurines in the lower Río Verde Valley suggest their use in public ceremonies both in households and in more accessible, suprahousehold settings (Hepp 2009; Hepp and Joyce, Chapter 9). Imagery on Terminal Formative figurines suggests that ritual feasting and other ceremonies at times involved shamanistic transformations into divine beings, probably by socially prominent people. The burial of a possible Chacahua phase ritual specialist interred with an elaborate bone flute was excavated at Yugüe (see below and Barber 2005; Barber and Olvera 2012; Barber et al. 2009, Chapter 4).

The association of feasting and communal mortuary ceremonies identified for the Late Formative at Cerro de la Cruz continued in the Terminal Formative as shown by the results of Sarah Barber's (2005) horizontal excavations at Yugüe, a floodplain site on the east side of the river that she discusses in Chapter 6. The site is dominated by a huge mixed-use platform supporting both residences and public buildings that measures approximately 300 m × 150 m and reached 10 m at its highest point. Yugüe was first occupied during the Late Formative and grew to 10 ha by the Terminal Formative. During the Miniyua phase, people constructed a public building on the site's ceremonial center (Substructure 1; Barber 2005, 150–206). Feasting is indicated by a cooking feature just outside of the public building that included three large jars, burned on their exterior surfaces; one still contained whole shells of estuarine mussels. Middens containing sherds, ash, bone, and estuarine shells resulted from a number of distinct feasting events. Three Miniyua phase burials were recovered in the fill of the building on Substructure 1.

During the late Terminal Formative Chacahua phase, Substructure 1 was the location of a communal cemetery (Barber et al., Chapter 4). Although she exposed slightly less than a 7 m² area of the cemetery, Barber (Barber 2005; Barber et al., Chapter 4) recovered the remains of at least forty-one individuals, both male and female. Like the Cerro de la Cruz cemetery, the one from Yugüe included earlier burials disturbed by later ones. Unlike the earlier cemetery, the one at Yugüe included people of varying status levels and a broader range of ages.

Additional evidence for the repetitive use of community ceremonial spaces is in the form of ritual caches used to dedicate the construction of public buildings. During the Miniyua phase, Chatinos placed a cache of twenty ceramic vessels in the fill of the public building on Substructure 1 at Yugüe (Barber 2005, 164–165, Chapter 6). By the Chacahua phase, at least fifty cylindrical vessels were cached sequentially in Substructure 1, perhaps as a way to "feed" the sacred structure, much like burials in Mesoamerican cosmology were viewed as a way of feeding the gods (Monaghan 1990, 1995). At San Francisco de Arriba, people left ritual caches similar to those at Yugüe in the fill of different building phases of the site's acropolis (Workinger 2002, 185–214). One cache, however, was much grander than the others, consisting of 356 greenstone beads, 27 rock crystal beads, 109 beads of an unidentified stone, 2 greenstone bird head pendants, 2 rock crystal pendants, fragments of iron ore, 9 locally produced miniature grayware jars, and disarticulated animal bone.

Major communal works projects during the Terminal Formative included the construction of monumental buildings at Río Viejo and at least nine other sites, including Charco Redondo, San Francisco de Arriba, Cerro de la Virgen, and Yugüe (Barber 2005, 117–118; Joyce 1991a, 393; 2005, 20–23; Workinger 2002, 147–230). The scale of monumental construction was considerable, even at some smaller sites such as Yugüe (Barber, Chapter 6), with most consisting of large mixed-use platforms that supported both residences and public buildings. People probably built these huge platforms in part to raise living surfaces off the floodplain and protect residences from seasonal flooding that was increasing in intensity due to highland erosion and perhaps increased El Niño frequencies (Goman et al. 2005, 257; Joyce and Mueller 1997, 90; Mueller et al., Chapter 3). At Cerro de la Virgen monumental constructions included a probable ceremonial precinct that contained a public plaza measuring approximately 2,800 m² surrounded by a ball court and several possible high-status residences (Barber 2005, 138–140).

The largest monumental building in the region was the Mound 1 acropolis at Río Viejo, which was the civic-ceremonial center of the site. The construction and early history of this massive architectural complex is examined more fully by Joyce and colleagues in Chapter 5. With an estimated volume of 560,050 m³, Mound 1 was one of the largest structures ever built in prehispanic Oaxaca. The platform supports two large substructures each at least 17 m high, along with five smaller buildings, a plaza, and a sunken patio. Evidence discussed in Chapter 5 suggests that the acropolis was built almost entirely during the late Terminal Formative. Excavations show that one of the substructures (Structure 2) supported a large stepped platform rising at least 16 m above the floodplain. On the summit of the platform, excavations revealed remnants of an elaborate, though poorly preserved adobe building, probably a temple. As explained by Joyce and colleagues, energetics estimates and analyses of building techniques suggest that the acropolis required large labor forces that were probably drawn from Río Viejo and other communities in the region.

Participation of commoners in the construction of the acropolis as well as the rituals carried out there would have acted as practices of affiliation that constituted new social formations and contributed to the creation of a corporate identity centered on the symbols, institutions, and rulers at Río Viejo. As discussed by Levine (2002), reliance on the tortilla as inferred by the earliest comals in the region may have allowed people to more easily transport food while working on communal labor projects outside of their home community. Joyce and colleagues (Chapter 5) argue that construction of the acropolis was sponsored by rulers struggling to expand their influence beyond the community of Río Viejo to a broader region through the scaling-up of communal practices, including the construction of monumental buildings and large-scale public ceremonies (also see Barber 2005, 309–314; Barber and Joyce 2007; Joyce 2006, 85–88; 2008, 24–29; 2010, 186–195; Pool, Chapter 10). It is not clear, however, if people from the entire region were engaged physically and symbolically in practices of affiliation centered on Río Viejo and its politico-religious institutions and authorities.

A variety of data indicate that more powerful rulers emerged and social inequality increased during the Terminal Formative (Barber 2005, 284–321; Chapter 6; Barber and Joyce 2007; Barber et al., Chapter 4; Joyce 2005, 19–23; 2006, 86–88; 2008, 223–228). For example, most people interred in the Yugüe cemetery did not have offerings or were accompanied by a few ceramic vessels or beads made of greenstone or shell. One interment, however, was discovered with two remarkable objects indicating high status and perhaps a special ritual role. As discussed by Barber and colleagues in Chapter 4, this burial (Yugüe Burial B14-I16) was a male aged fifteen to seventeen, interred wearing a plaster-backed iron-ore mirror and holding an intricately incised bone flute made from a deer femur (Figure 1.10; also see Barber 2005, 186–191; Barber and Olvera

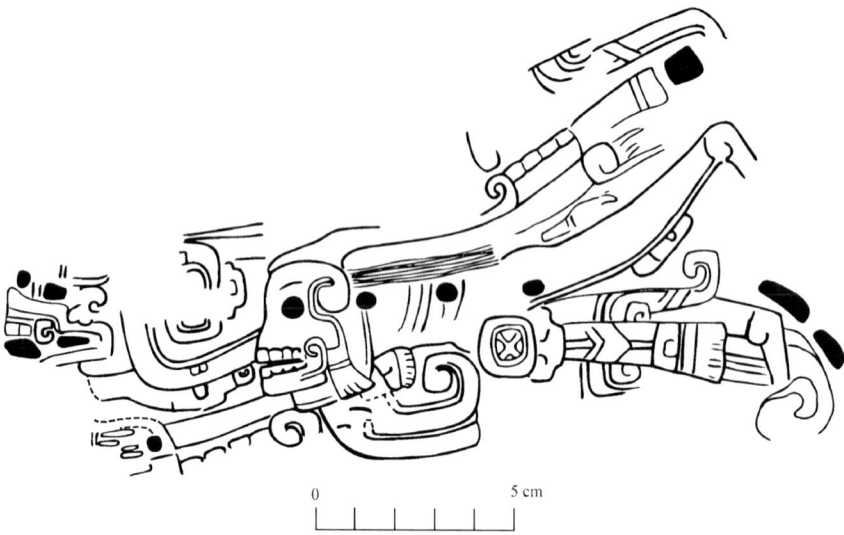

FIGURE 1.10. Imagery on the Terminal Formative bone flute from Burial B14-I16 in the Yugüe cemetery (after Barber et al. 2009: Figure 4).

2012; Barber et al. 2009: Figure 5; Mayes and Barber 2008). Luxury goods like iron ore and greenstone, recovered in caches and as burial offerings, were obtained through networks of interregional exchange among Mesoamerican nobles. The scale of Terminal Formative monumental buildings, especially Río Viejo's acropolis, also suggests that rulers had considerable power to mobilize labor, although perhaps not without exacerbating social divisions (Joyce et al., Chapter 5).

Evidence for social inequality also comes from the excavation of a high-status residence at Cerro de la Virgen (Barber 2005, 234–270; Chapter 6). Cerro de la Virgen is located on a hill that rises 200 m above the coastal plain approximately 14 km north of the Pacific Ocean. The site was one of the largest communities in the region during the Chacahua phase, with settlement covering 60 ha and dozens of residential terraces. The high-status residence excavated by Barber (2005, Chapter 6) was built on a large terrace near the summit of the hill and was spatially associated with the monumental public plaza mentioned above. The residence consisted of several rooms with stone benches surrounding a patio. The overall area of the house was 476 m² including the patio, which measured 13 m × 13 m, making this residence far larger and more elaborate than typical Late/Terminal Formative residences in Oaxaca (Elson 2006, 56; Robles 1988; Winter 1974).

Despite increasing inequality and the development of regional political affiliations and identities, distinctions between nobles and commoners were not emphasized in public settings (Barber, Chapter 6; Barber and Joyce 2007, 235–236; Joyce 2008, 227–228). We argue that the consumption of socially valued goods in burials and caches along with the construction of monumental buildings contributed to status inequality and regional authority, but were practices that transformed hierarchy into expressions of traditional communal principles. Social valuables obtained through long-distance exchange linked lower Verde nobles to elites in other parts of Mesoamerica and contributed to the creation of a noble identity. The use of such materials in community rituals, particularly caches in public buildings, however, transformed these objects from prestige items that embodied high status into inalienable objects that materialized corporate identities (Barber et al. n.d.). By obtaining the exotic items through which collective pasts were celebrated, nobles would have become pivotal and powerful community members. Likewise, monumental buildings, constructed with voluntary labor, emphasized corporate action and identity. Evidence for the celebration of rulers and rulership has not been found, such as monuments depicting rulers, elaborate tombs that differentiated the burials of elites from commoners, or the presence of palaces that combined public space with the residence of the ruler. Public social practices therefore appear to have continued to materialize social relations as corporate, while restraining expressions of exclusionary authority. Practices that tied social identity to regional political authority were scaled-up versions of earlier communal practices that revolved around public spaces and ceremonies such as feasting and mortuary rituals associated with the patio complex at Cerro de la Cruz. Corporate forms of rulership are evident in the Mixteca Alta at sites like Yucuita, Huamelulpan, Monte Negro, and Cerro Jazmín; communal authority may also have existed alongside more hierarchical leadership at Monte Albán (Balkansky et al. 2004; Joyce 2010, 141–146, 177–179; Pérez et al. 2011).

The evidence suggests that despite an emerging regional power at Río Viejo, local community affiliations remained strong. Ceremonial centers at other sites in the region exhibit considerable variability in construction techniques and materials as well as architectural form and use, arguing against the presence of architectural, political, and ritual principles imposed by the rulers of Río Viejo. As discussed by Barber in Chapter 6, local elites, such as the young man interred at Yugüe, appear to have been more closely tied to their local communities than to regional authorities at Río Viejo. Likewise, evidence from the region's Formative period cemeteries suggests that communal affiliations were becoming more inclusive with children as well as adults and persons of high-status and/or special social roles as well as commoners buried in cemeteries by the Chacahua phase (Barber et al., Chapter 4).

The emergence of regional political authority at Río Viejo with simultaneous continuities in strong local community affiliations suggest that attempts by Río Viejo's nobility to expand their influence created points of tension in

Terminal Formative social and political relations (Barber, Chapter 6; Barber and Joyce 2007; Joyce 2008, 2010, 194–196; Joyce et al., Chapter 5; Pool, Chapter 10). I see at least two intersecting fracture points within Terminal Formative society: along status lines and between local communities and the incipient regional authorities at Río Viejo. For example, social contradictions and tensions are suggested by the scale of supracommunity practices of affiliation, especially the construction and use of Río Viejo's acropolis, and paradoxically the simultaneous evidence for the continuation and increasing inclusivity of traditional communal practices and identities. The construction of Río Viejo's acropolis as well as rituals carried out there drew both nobles and commoners alike away from traditional sites of social interaction tied to their local communities. Levine (Chapter 8) argues that elaborate grayware pottery symbolized broader supracommunity affiliations and were used in practices involving the sharing of food and drink, such as ritual feasting, where these new social and political relations were negotiated.

There is also evidence for points of tension surrounding increasing inequality and the emergence of regional political authorities at Río Viejo. Even though local leaders were still tied to their communities, as shown by the excavations at Yugüe, Cerro de la Virgen, and Charco Redondo (Barber 2005, Chapter 6; Barber and Joyce 2007; Barber et al., Chapter 4; Joyce 2010, 186–195), they were also increasingly distinguishing themselves from others through mortuary practices, prestige goods, and elaborate residences. Nobles were involved in wider interregional networks of exchange and interaction, creating distance from commoners. There is reason to believe that the ritual transformation of inequality into an ideology of communalism was not completely closed, providing openings for discursive penetration. Tensions surrounding social inequality and newer forms of political authority may have been negotiated in the context of mortuary and caching ceremonies as seen in the cemeteries at Yugüe and Charco Redondo (Barber et al., Chapter 4) and the impressive caches at Yugüe and San Francisco de Arriba (Barber 2005, Chapter 6; Barber and Joyce 2007; Workinger 2002).

Despite the emergence of Río Viejo as a powerful political center at the end of the Formative, the evidence suggests that authority in the region was not singular. It is likely that newer, more regional, hierarchical forms of authority existed alongside traditional, community-based, less hierarchical leadership. Rather than unified under a singular regional polity, we argue that political relations among communities were dynamic and negotiated (Barber 2005, Chapter 6; Barber and Joyce 2007; Barber et al., Chapter 4; Joyce 2008; Joyce et al., Chapter 5; Pool, Chapter 10). I suspect that while Río Viejo was the most powerful political center, people of other communities had considerable independence and were able to strategically strengthen ties with or create distance from rulers and ruling institutions at Río Viejo. The collapse of regional authority at ca. AD 250, followed by a period of political fragmentation in the Early Classic period (AD 250–500), shows that the newer, more hierarchical forms of authority were indeed tenuous and short-lived.

AFTERMATH: THE COLLAPSE OF TERMINAL FORMATIVE POLITICAL AUTHORITY

The evidence from the lower Río Verde Valley demonstrates that the early urban polity centered at Río Viejo was not stable or long lasting, although causes of its collapse are not clear (Joyce 2005, 2008, 234–240; 2010, 195–196). At about AD 250 Río Viejo's acropolis was abandoned. Burned adobes and floor areas suggest that the elaborate public building on Structure 2 was destroyed by fire, and evidence from other areas of the acropolis shows that this destruction event was widespread (Joyce and Barber 2011). The settlement data also indicate a dramatic disruption in regional sociopolitical organization. Río Viejo decreased in size from 200 ha in the late Terminal Formative to 75 ha in the Early Classic Coyuche phase (AD 250–500). Several other large Terminal Formative floodplain sites with mounded architecture, including Yugüe, declined significantly in size or were abandoned. Elsewhere in Oaxaca many of the early urban centers also collapsed at the end of the Formative period, including Yucuita, Huamelulpan, Monte Negro, Cerro Jazmín, and Cerro de las Minas (Balkansky 1998a; Balkansky et al. 2004; Kowalewski et al. 2009; Pérez et al. 2011; Winter 1994b, 2007a). At Monte Albán there is evidence for internal political conflict at the end of the Formative period (Joyce 2010, 155–159; Urcid 1994; Urcid and Joyce 2011). Unlike many of the urban centers in the Mixteca and the lower Río Verde Valley, however, the rulers of Monte Albán successfully consolidated power and the city continued as a powerful political center until the end of the Classic period.

A regional survey in the lower Río Verde region shows a shift to defensible piedmont locations. During the Early Classic, the region contained perhaps as many as eight first-order centers of roughly equivalent size. There is little evidence for monumental building activities, suggesting that leaders were unable to mobilize large labor forces as they did in the Terminal Formative. The data indicate that the lower Río Verde Valley was occupied by multiple, perhaps competing polities. The scale of political influence was far reduced from the Terminal Formative, when Río Viejo was the single dominant center in the region, and from the Late Formative, when two first-order centers were present.

The data suggest that some form of conflict led to Early Classic political fragmentation in the lower Río Verde Valley (Joyce 2003, 64–68; 2008, 229–230; 2010, 239–241). It is not clear whether this conflict involved local political factions or whether an outside power conquered the region. Excavation data from the Early Classic Coyuche phase indicate interaction with the powerful central Mexican polity of Teotihuacan (Joyce 2003, 64–68; Workinger, Chapter 7). In particular, obsidian studies, including neutron activation analyses, have shown that 80 percent of the 356 pieces of obsidian excavated from Early Classic contexts was from Pachuca (Joyce et al. 1995, 10–11; Workinger 2002, 325–329). This is the highest proportion known for a region outside of the central Mexican highlands. While the data for Teotihuacan contacts are intriguing, at present plausible models of Early Classic interaction range from conquest to increased reciprocal exchange (Joyce 2003, 64–70; Workinger 2002, 394–402; Chapter 7).

Another factor in the collapse could have been social tension over divergent forms of authority and practices that increasingly drew people away from their traditional communities, leading to the rejection of regional rulers and ruling institutions by local elites and commoners (Barber 2005; Barber and Joyce 2007; Joyce 2005, 22–24; 2008, 228–230; 2010, 194–196). Conflict with neighboring polities and/or with distant powers could have exacerbated these tensions.

After the destruction and abandonment of the acropolis this important political and religious building was left to slowly disintegrate for 250 years. It is interesting to speculate why the acropolis was not rebuilt or reoccupied during the Early Classic since flat elevated surfaces are ideal locations on which to live in the hot, lowland climate of the Oaxaca coast. If the Terminal Formative polity collapsed due to factional competition, it could have symbolized a failed political system. Another possibility is that foreign conquerors could have seen the acropolis as a symbol of a defeated enemy, and its reoccupation, a potential expression of resistance. By the Late Classic Yuta Tiyoo phase (AD 500–800), a powerful centralized polity had reemerged at Río Viejo, although political authority at this time was much more exclusionary, with rulers celebrated in carved monuments and little evidence for large-scale communal projects (Joyce 2008).

The past twenty-five years of archaeological research in the lower Río Verde Valley demonstrate that the region experienced a series of important social and cultural transformations during the Formative period. As discussed by Christopher Pool in the final chapter of this volume, the lower Río Verde shares general similarities in Formative period historical developments with other regions of Mesoamerica. Pool compares the Formative period in the lower Río Verde Valley to two other regions: the Valley of Oaxaca and the lower Papaloapan Basin on the Gulf coast. As in all complex societies, the people of these regions were faced with the problems of addressing the inherent tensions between hierarchical and collective interests. As insightfully discussed by Pool, regional political authority in each of these regions at the end of the Formative had to balance emerging hierarchy with a public emphasis on communal symbols and practices. Pool's comparative study shows that the history of the Terminal Formative Río Viejo polity differed from the contemporaneous Monte Albán and Tres Zapotes polities. At Monte Albán communal and hierarchical interests were effectively balanced in the face of ongoing conflict with competing polities in the valley and perhaps beyond. At Tres Zapotes in the lower Papaloapan Basin, rulers had to deal with a legacy of exclusionary rulership that continued to create factional tensions among elites throughout the region. Negotiations of regional political authority in all three regions were complex and tenuous as shown by their subsequent histories. Río Viejo collapsed suddenly and perhaps violently at ca. AD 250, while Tres Zapotes began a protracted decline in political prominence. At Monte Albán tensions between communal and elite interests also reached a climax at the very end of the Formative, as earlier architecture and monumental art was dismantled or destroyed (Joyce 2010, 159). As discussed by Pool, however, the result was a further consolidation of political authority by Monte Albán's rulers.

A BRIEF NOTE ON THEORY

Most of the archaeological research in the lower Río Verde Valley has been informed by theories of practice, power, and identity that are drawn from poststructural and feminist perspectives (for broader summaries of these approaches in archaeology see Hutson 2010; Joyce 2010, 17–34; Joyce and Lopiparo 2005; Pauketat 2001). These theories assert that the dynamics of social life result from the recursive relationship between the practices of people and the broader social relations, cultural schema, and material conditions that together constitute society and culture. Practice is socially embedded because human activity cannot be considered apart from cultural ideas, rules, and material relations. In Giddens's (1979) well-known formulation, structure is thus both the medium and the outcome of the reproduction of practices. From this perspective, people's subjectivities – their beliefs, knowledge, dispositions, and identities – are constructed and transformed through social practice and the people, places, and objects that are encountered and experienced daily (Hutson 2010). Places and things in turn come to take on or objectify ideas, including aspects of identity.

As discussed in several chapters of this book, identity in the Formative period lower Río Verde Valley was objectified in the material world of monumental buildings, clay figurines, ceramic vessels, exotic imported goods, and the ways in which people were interred at death. For example, Hepp and Joyce (Chapter 9) discuss how figurines objectified social distinctions based on age and gender. Levine (Chapter 8) argues that grayware ceramic styles found in the lower Río Verde region and throughout much of Oaxaca reflect the expansion of interregional affiliations and shared practices. Barber (Chapter 6) and Joyce and colleagues (Chapter 5) show how community identity and status distinctions were objectified in the divergent styles and uses of public buildings like the acropolis at Río Viejo.

Several chapters also show the ways in which social practice reproduced or changed the social relations, cultural schema, and material conditions that constituted Formative period society and culture in the lower Río Verde Valley. As discussed by Joyce and colleagues in Chapter 5, probably the most far-reaching attempt to alter social relations in the region involved the sponsorship by Río Viejo's rulers of the construction of the site's massive acropolis at the end of the Formative period. Attempts such as this to strategically transform society, however, often have unanticipated consequences, as exemplified by the political collapse at the end of the Formative period. Social and political relations in the lower Verde were affirmed and at times altered in the performance of ceremonies ranging from the burial of the dead (Chapter 4) to ritual feasts (Chapter 6), through communal projects like the construction of monumental buildings (Chapter 5), and by the acquisition of exotic trade items used to enhance status distinctions (Chapter 7). While often mischaracterized as an idealist position, the material world is fundamental to poststructural and feminist approaches making relevant ecological as well as social and cultural perspectives; hence ecology has also been a focus of research in the region, as represented by the chapters in the volume by Goman and colleagues (Chapter 2) and Mueller and colleagues (Chapter 3).

The chapters in this volume demonstrate that lower Río Verde Valley society consisted of people of varied interests, identities, and world views distinguished along dimensions such as gender, status, occupation, and community affiliation. Social distinctions such as these mean that lower Verde society, like all societies, was not an integrated and coherent system, but rather was fragmented and contested to varying degrees. As discussed by Joyce and colleagues (Chapter 5) and Barber (Chapter 6), political relations at the end of the Formative period involved complex negotiations among varied social actors. Attempts by rulers at Río Viejo to extend their influence and authority over the region as a whole may have created points of social tension with commoners and elites in outlying communities, possibly leading to the collapse of the Río Viejo polity at ca. AD 250. As discussed by Pool (Chapter 10), similar tensions may have played a role in Formative period social change in other regions of Mesoamerica.

The chapters show that research in the lower Río Verde Valley has progressed beyond problems of chronology and culture history that of necessity framed the initial work in the region (Brockington 1966; Grove 1988; Joyce and Winter 1989). As this book demonstrates, researchers have begun to address theoretically significant questions of broad relevance, such as the origins and spread of agriculture, the social negotiation of complex political formations, the effects of long-distance trade and interaction, the macroregional effects of landscape change, and prehispanic ideology and political power. These and many more questions remain; yet as summarized here, the past twenty-five years of research in the lower Río Verde Valley have provided a comprehensive understanding of the Formative period archaeology of this important and long-neglected region of Oaxaca.

ACKNOWLEDGMENTS

I would like to thank John Clark and Jeff Blomster, who were reviewers for the entire volume, and Sarah Barber, who provided comments on this chapter. I would also like to thank the people of the lower Río Verde Valley for their friendship and assistance through the years as well as the Instituto Nacional de Antropología e Historia, especially the presidents of the Consejo de Arqueología: Lorena Mirambell, Mari Carmen Serra Puche, Norberto González Crespo, Joaquín García-Bárcena, Roberto García Moll, and Nelly Robles García. I would like to thank the directors of the Centro INAH Oaxaca, María de la Luz Topete, Ernesto González Licón, Eduardo López Calzada, Enrique Fernández Dávila, and Nelly Robles García, who have supported my research in the lower Río Verde Valley. Funding for my archaeological and paleoenvironmental field research in Oaxaca has been provided by grants from the following organizations: National Science Foundation (grants BCS–0923909, BCS–0096012, BCS–0508078, BNS–8716332, and BCS–1123388), NASA (NNX08AO31G), Foundation for the Advancement of Mesoamerican Studies (#99012), National Geographic Society (grant 3767–88), Wenner-Gren Foundation (GR. 4988), Vanderbilt University Research Council and Mellon Fund, Fulbright Foundation, H. John Heinz III Charitable Trust, Explorers Club, Sigma Xi, University of Colorado (CARTSS, CRCW, Dean's Small Grant, Norton Fund, and Innovative Grant Program), and Rutgers University. I would like to thank Guy Hepp for indexing and proofreading the volume.

NOTE

1. This total includes one burial that was in a disturbed area of the site, but probably associated with the Structure 1 cemetery. In previous analyses of the cemetery this interment was omitted, but since it is likely to have been part of the cemetery, we include it in the analysis presented in Chapter 4.

REFERENCES CITED

Arnaud, Laura, Arthur A. Joyce, and Marc N. Levine. 2009. Río Viejo, Operación A, excavaciones horizontales. In "El proyecto Río Verde," ed. Arthur A. Joyce and Marc N. Levine, 20–80. Report submitted to the Consejo de Arqueología, Instituto Nacional de Antropología e Historia, Mexico City.

Arnaud Bustamante, Laura. 2003. "Análisis iconográfico de las piedras grabadas de los Santos Reyes Nopala, Juquila, Oaxaca." Licenciatura thesis, Escuela Nacional de Antropología e Historia, Mexico City.

Balkansky, Andrew K. 1997. *Archaeological Settlement Patterns of the Sola Valley, Oaxaca, Mexico.* PhD dissertation, Department of Anthropology, University of Wisconsin at Madison. Ann Arbor, MI: University Microfilms.

Balkansky, Andrew K. 1998a. "Urbanism and Early State Formation in the Huamelulpan Valley of Southern Mexico." *Latin American Antiquity* 9 (1): 37–67. http://dx.doi.org/10.2307/972127.

Balkansky, Andrew K. 1998b. "Origin and Collapse of Complex Societies in Oaxaca (Mexico): Evaluating the Era from 1965 to the Present." *Journal of World Prehistory* 12 (4): 451–93. http://dx.doi.org/10.1023/A:1022870516264.

Balkansky, Andrew K., Verónica Pérez Rodríguez, and Stephen A. Kowalewski. 2004. "Monte Negro and the Urban Revolution in Oaxaca, Mexico." *Latin American Antiquity* 15 (1): 33–60. http://dx.doi.org/10.2307/4141563.

Banker, Sherman, and Arthur A. Joyce. 1991. "Appendix 4: Petrographic Analysis of Ceramics: Río Verde Formative Project." In *Formative Period Occupation in the Lower Río Verde Valley, Oaxaca, Mexico: Interregional Interaction and Social Change*, by Arthur A. Joyce, 883–910. PhD dissertation, Department of Anthropology, Rutgers University, New Brunswick, NJ. Ann Arbor, MI: University Microfilms.

Barber, Sarah B. 2005. *Heterogeneity, Identity, and Complexity: Negotiating Status and Authority in Terminal Formative Coastal Oaxaca.* PhD dissertation, Department of Anthropology, University of Colorado, Boulder. Ann Arbor, MI: University Microfilms.

Barber, Sarah B. 2009. Excavaciones de prueba en el valle inferior del Rió Verde. In "El proyecto Río Verde," ed. Arthur A. Joyce and Marc N. Levine, 228–321. Final report to the Consejo de Arqueología, Instituto Nacional de Antropología e Historia, Mexico City.

Barber, Sarah B., and Arthur A. Joyce. 2007. "Polity Produced and Community Consumed: Negotiating Political Centralization in the Lower Río Verde Valley, Oaxaca." In *Mesoamerican Ritual Economy*, ed. E. Christian Wells and Karla L. Davis-Salazar, 221–44. Boulder: University Press of Colorado.

Barber, Sarah B., and Mireya Olvera. 2012. "A Divine Wind: The Arts of Death and Music in Ancient Oaxaca." *Ancient Mesoamerica* 23(1): 9–24.

Barber, Sarah B., Gonzalo A. Sanchez Santiago, and Mireya Olvera. 2009. "Sounds of Death and Life in Mesoamerica: The Bone Flutes of Ancient Oaxaca." *Yearbook of Traditional Music* 41: 40–56.

Barber, Sarah B., Devin White, and Allison Matos. 2011. "Modeling Coastal Exchange in Precolumbian Oaxaca." Paper presented at the 76th Annual Meeting of the Society for American Archaeology, Sacramento, CA.

Barber, Sarah B., Andrew Workinger, and Arthur Joyce. N.d. "Situational Inalienability and Social Change in Formative Period Coastal Oaxaca." In *Inalienable Possessions in the Archaeology of Mesoamerica*, ed. Brigitte Kovacevich and Michael G. Callaghan. Washington, DC: American Anthropological Association, under review.

Berlin, Heinrich. 1947. *Fragmentos desconocidos del códice de Yanhuitlán y otras investigaciones mixtecas.* Mexico City: Antigua Librería Robredo.

Bevan, Bernard. 1934. "Travels with a Donkey in Mexico." *National Geographic* 66: 756–88.

Blanton, Richard E. 1978. *Monte Albán: Settlement Patterns at the Ancient Zapotec Capital.* New York: Academic Press.

Blanton, Richard E., Gary M. Feinman, Stephen A. Kowalewski, and Linda M. Nicholas. 1999. *Ancient Oaxaca.* Cambridge: Cambridge University Press. http://dx.doi. org/10.1017/CBO9780511607844.

Blomster, Jeffrey P. 2004. *Etlatongo: Social Complexity, Interaction, and Village Life in the Mixteca Alta of Oaxaca, Mexico.* Belmont, CA: Wadsworth/Thomson Learning.

Brockington, Donald L. 1957. "Piedra Parada: A Comparative Study of a Site in Jamiltepec, Oaxaca." MA thesis, Mexico City College, Mexico City.

Brockington, Donald L. 1966. *The Archaeological Sequence from Sipolite, Oaxaca, Mexico.* Archives of Archaeology 28. Madison: Society for American Archaeology and University of Wisconsin Press.

Brockington, Donald L. 1983. "The View from the Coast: Relationships between the Coast and Valley of Oaxaca." *Notas Mesoamericanas* 9: 24–31.

Brockington, Donald. L., Maria Jorrín, and J. Robert Long. 1974. *The Oaxaca Coast Project Reports: Part I.* Vanderbilt University Publications in Anthropology 8. Nashville, TN: Vanderbilt University.

Brockington, Donald L., and J. Robert Long. 1974. *The Oaxaca Coast Project Reports: Part II.* Vanderbilt University Publications in Anthropology 9. Nashville, TN: Vanderbilt University.

Bronk Ramsey, Christopher. 2009. "Bayesian Analysis of Radiocarbon Dates." *Radiocarbon* 51 (1): 337–60.

Butler, Michelle M. 2011. Excavaciones en Charco Redondo, 2009. In "El proyecto Río Verde: Informe técnico de la temporada de 2009," ed. Sarah B. Barber and Arthur A. Joyce, 185–221. Final report submitted to the Consejo de Arqueología, Instituto Nacional de Antropología e Historia, Mexico City.

Caso, Alfonso, Ignacio Bernal, and Jorge R. Acosta. 1967. *La cerámica de Monte Albán.* Memorias del Instituto Nacional de Antropología e Historia No. 13. Mexico City: INAH.

Christensen, Alexander F. 1998. "Colonization and Microevolution in Formative Oaxaca, Mexico." *World Archaeology* 30 (2): 262–85. http://dx.doi.org/10.1080/0043824 3.1998.9980410.

Clark, John E. 2004. "Mesoamerica Goes Public: Early Ceremonial Centers, Leaders, and Communities." In *Mesoamerican Archaeology,* ed. Julia Hendon and Rosemary Joyce, 43–72. Oxford: Blackwell.

De Cicco, Gabriel, and Donald L. Brockington. 1956. *Reconocimiento arqueológico en el suroeste de Oaxaca.* Informe No. 6. Mexico City: Dirección de Monumentos Prehispánicos, Instituto Nacional de Antropología e Historia.

Delgado, Agustín. 1965. *Archaeological Reconnaissance in the Region of Tehuantepec, Oaxaca, Mexico.* Papers of the New World Archaeological Foundation No. 18. Provo, UT: Brigham Young University.

Dietler, Michael. 2001. "Theorizing the Feast: Rituals of Consumption, Commensal Politics, and Power in African Continents." In *Feasts: Archaeological and Ethnographic Perspectives on Food, Politics, and Power,* ed. Michael Dietler and Brian Hayden, 65–114. Washington, DC: Smithsonian Institution Press.

Elson, Christina M. 2006. "Intermediate Elites and the Political Landscape of the Early Zapotec State." In *Intermediate Elites in Pre-Columbian States and Empires*, ed. Christina M. Elson and R. Alan Covey, 44–67. Tucson: University of Arizona Press.

Fernández, Deepika. 2004. "Subsistence in the Lower Río Verde Region, Oaxaca, Mexico: A Zoological Analysis." MA thesis, Department of Archaeology, University of Calgary, Calgary, Alberta.

Fernández Dávila, Enrique, and Susana Gómez Serafin. 1988. *Arqueología de Huatulco, Oaxaca*. Mexico City: Collección Cientifica, Serie Arqueología, Instituto Nacional de Antropología e Historia.

Forde, Jaime E. 2006. *Ideology, Identity, and Icons: A Study of Mixtec Polychrome Pottery from Late Postclassic Yuca Dzaa (Tututepec), Oaxaca, Mexico*. MA thesis, Department of Anthropology, University of Colorado, Boulder. Ann Arbor, MI: University Microfilms.

Gamio, Lorenzo. 1967. "Zona arqueológica de Cola de Palma, Pinotepa Nacional, Oaxaca." *Boletín del INAH* 28: 25–28.

Giddens, Anthony. 1979. *Central Problems in Social Theory*. Berkeley: University of California Press.

Gillespie, Susan D. 1987. "Excavaciones en Charco Redondo 1986." Report submitted to the Centro Regional de Oaxaca. Instituto Nacional de Antropología e Historia, Oaxaca.

Goman, Michelle, Arthur A. Joyce, and Raymond G. Mueller. 2005. "Stratigraphic Evidence for Anthropogenically Induced Coastal Environmental Change from Oaxaca, Mexico." *Quaternary Research* 63 (3): 250–60. http://dx.doi.org/10.1016/j.yqres.2005.02.008.

Goman, Michelle, Arthur Joyce, Raymond Mueller, and Larissa Paschyn. 2010. "Multi-Proxy Paleoecological Reconstruction of Prehistoric Land Use History in the Western Region of the Lower Río Verde Valley, Oaxaca, Mexico." *Holocene* 20 (5): 761–72. http://dx.doi.org/10.1177/0959683610362811.

Grove, David C. 1988. "Archaeological Investigations on the Pacific Coast of Oaxaca, Mexico, 1986." Report submitted to the National Geographic Society, Washington, DC.

Hedgepeth, Jessica. 2009. "The Domestic Economy of Early Postclassic Río Viejo, Oaxaca, Mexico: Daily Practices and Worldviews of a Commoner Community." MA thesis, Department of Anthropology, University of Colorado, Boulder.

Hepp, Guy D. 2009. *Formative Period Figurines of Coastal Oaxaca, Mexico: Ancient Mesoamerican Ceramic Iconography from the Lower Rio Verde Valley*. Saarbrücken: VDM Verlag Dr. Müller.

Hepp, Guy D. 2011a. "The Material Culture of Early Sedentism in Coastal Oaxaca: Probable Early Formative Ceramics from La Consentida." Paper presented at the 76th Annual Meeting of the Society for American Archaeology, Sacramento, CA.

Hepp, Guy D. 2011b. Excavaciones en La Consentida, 2009. In "El proyecto Río Verde: Informe técnico de la temporada de 2009," ed. Sarah B. Barber and Arthur A. Joyce, 146–184. Final report submitted to the Consejo de Arqueología, Instituto Nacional de Antropología e Historia, Mexico City.

Houston, Margaret S. 1974. "Gralisa Ceramic Group: A Graphite-and-Red Painted Pottery from the Coast of Oaxaca." MA thesis, Department of Anthropology, University of North Carolina, Chapel Hill.

Hutson, Scott R. 2010. *Dwelling, Identity, and the Maya: Relational Archaeology at Chunchucmil*. Lanham, MD: AltaMira Press.

Jorrín, Maria. 1974. "Stone Monuments." In *The Oaxaca Coast Project Reports: Part I*, ed. Donald L. Brockington, Maria Jorrín, and J. Robert Long, 23–81. Vanderbilt University Publications in Anthropology No. 8. Nashville, TN: Vanderbilt University.

Joyce, Arthur A. 1991a. *Formative Period Occupation in the Lower Río Verde Valley, Oaxaca, Mexico: Interregional Interaction and Social Change*. PhD dissertation, Department of Anthropology, Rutgers University. Ann Arbor, MI: University Microfilms.

Joyce, Arthur A. 1991b. "Formative Period Social Change in the Lower Río Verde Valley, Oaxaca, Mexico." *Latin American Antiquity* 2 (2): 126–50. http://dx.doi.org/10.2307/972274.

Joyce, Arthur A. 1991c. "Appendix 5: Trace Element Data from Ionic-Extraction Analysis of Ceramics: Río Verde Formative Project." In *Formative Period Occupation in the Lower Río Verde Valley, Oaxaca, Mexico: Interregional Interaction and Social Change*, by Arthur A. Joyce, 910–15. PhD dissertation, Department of Anthropology, Rutgers University, New Brunswick, NJ. Ann Arbor, MI: University Microfilms.

Joyce, Arthur A. 1993. "Interregional Interaction and Social Development on the Oaxaca Coast." *Ancient Mesoamerica* 4 (1): 67–84. http://dx.doi.org/10.1017/S0956536100000791.

Joyce, Arthur A. 1994. "Late Formative Community Organization and Social Complexity on the Oaxaca Coast." *Journal of Field Archaeology* 21: 147–68.

Joyce, Arthur A. 2003. "Imperialism in Pre-Aztec Mesoamerica: Monte Albán, Teotihuacan, and the Lower Río Verde Valley." In *Ancient Mesoamerica Warfare*, ed. M. Kathryn Brown and Travis M. Stanton, 49–72. Walnut Creek, CA: AltaMira Press.

Joyce, Arthur A. 2005. "La arqueología del bajo Río Verde." *Acervos* 7 (29): 16–36.

Joyce, Arthur A. 2006. "The Inhabitation of Río Viejo's Acropolis." In *Space and Spatial Analysis in Archaeology*, ed. Elizabeth C. Robertson, Jeffrey D. Seibert, Deepika C. Fernández, and Marc U. Zender, 83–96. Albuquerque: University of New Mexico Press; Calgary: University of Calgary Press.

Joyce, Arthur A. 2008. "Domination, Negotiation, and Collapse: A History of Centralized Authority on the Oaxaca Coast Before the Late Postclassic." In *After Monte Albán: Transformation and Negotiation in Oaxaca, Mexico*, ed. Jeffrey Blomster, 219–54. Boulder: University Press of Colorado.

Joyce, Arthur A. 2010. *Mixtecs, Zapotecs, and Chatinos: Ancient Peoples of Southern Mexico*. Malden, MA: Wiley-Blackwell Press.

Joyce, Arthur A. 2011. "Debating Warfare in Late Formative Oaxaca." Paper presented at the symposium Conflict, Conquest, and the Performance of War in Pre-Columbian America, Dumbarton Oaks, Washington, DC.

Joyce, Arthur A., and Sarah B. Barber. 2011. "Excavating the Acropolis at Río Viejo, Oaxaca, Mexico." *Mexicon* 33 (1): 15–20.

Joyce, Arthur A., Sarah B. Barber, Marc N. Levine, and Hal Baillie. 2010. "The Acropolis at Río Viejo, Oaxaca, Mexico: Political Implications of Its Initial Construction, Use, and Abandonment." Paper presented at the 75th Annual Meeting of the Society for American Archaeology, St Louis, MO.

Joyce, Arthur A., Laura Arnaud Bustamante, and Marc N. Levine. 2001. "Commoner Power: A Case Study from the Classic Period Collapse on the Oaxaca Coast."

Journal of Archaeological Method and Theory 8 (4): 343–85. http://dx.doi.org/10.10
23/A:1013786700137.

Joyce, Arthur A., J. Michael Elam, Michael D. Glascock, Hector Neff, and Marcus Winter. 1995. "Exchange Implications of Obsidian Source Analysis from the Lower Río Verde Valley, Oaxaca, Mexico." *Latin American Antiquity* 6 (1): 3–15. http://dx.doi.org/10.2307/971597.

Joyce, Arthur A., and Raymond G. Mueller. 1992. "The Social Impact of Anthropogenic Landscape Modification in the Río Verde Drainage Basin, Oaxaca, Mexico." *Geoarchaeology* 7 (6): 503–26. http://dx.doi.org/10.1002/gea.3340070602.

Joyce, Arthur A., and Raymond G. Mueller. 1997. "Prehispanic Human Ecology of the Río Verde Drainage Basin." *World Archaeology* 29 (1): 75–94. http://dx.doi.org/10.1080/00438243.1997.9980364.

Joyce, Arthur A., Hector Neff, Mary S. Thieme, Marcus Winter, J. Michael Elam, and Andrew Workinger. 2006. "Ceramic Production and Exchange in Late/Terminal Formative Period Oaxaca." *Latin American Antiquity* 17 (4): 579–94. http://dx.doi.org/10.2307/25063073.

Joyce, Arthur A., and Marcus Winter. 1989. "Investigaciones arqueológicas en la cuenca del Río Verde inferior, 1988." *Notas Mesoamericanas* 11: 249–62.

Joyce, Arthur A., and Marcus Winter. 1996. "Ideology, Power, and Urban Society in Prehispanic Oaxaca." *Current Anthropology* 37 (1): 33–86. http://dx.doi.org/10.1086/204473.

Joyce, Arthur A., Marcus Winter, and Raymond G. Mueller. 1998. *Arqueología de la costa de Oaxaca: Asentamientos del periodo Formativo en el valle del Río Verde inferior.* Estudios de Antropología e Historia No. 40. Oaxaca: Centro INAH Oaxaca.

Joyce, Arthur A., Andrew Workinger, Byron Hamann, Peter Kroefges, Maxine Oland, and Stacie King. 2004. "Lord 8 Deer 'Jaguar Claw' and the Land of the Sky: The Archaeology and History of Tututepec." *Latin American Antiquity* 15 (3): 273–97. http://dx.doi.org/10.2307/4141575.

Joyce, Arthur A., Robert N. Zeitlin, Judith F. Zeitlin, and Javier Urcid. 2000. "On Oaxaca Coast Archaeology: Setting the Record Straight." *Current Anthropology* 41 (4): 623–25. http://dx.doi.org/10.1086/317385.

Joyce, Rosemary A., and Jeanne Lopiparo. 2005. "Postscript: Doing Agency in Archaeology." *Journal of Archaeological Method and Theory* 12 (4): 365–74. http://dx.doi.org/10.1007/s10816-005-8461-3.

King, Stacie M. 2003. *Social Practices and Social Organization in Ancient Coastal Oaxacan Households.* PhD dissertation, Department of Anthropology, University of California, Berkeley. Ann Arbor, MI: University Microfilms.

King, Stacie M. 2008. "Interregional Networks of the Oaxacan Early Postclassic: Connecting the Coast and Highlands." In *After Monte Albán: Transformation and Negotiation in Oaxaca, Mexico,* ed. Jeffrey Blomster, 255–91. Boulder: University Press of Colorado.

Kowalewski, Stephen A., Andrew K. Balkansky, Laura R. Stiver Walsh, Thomas J. Pluckhahn, John F. Chamblee, Verónica Pérez Rodríguez, Verenice Y. Heredia Espinoza, and Charlotte A. Smith. 2009. *Origins of the Ñuu: Archaeology in the Mixteca Alta, Mexico.* Boulder: University Press of Colorado.

Kowalewski, Stephen, Gary Feinman, Laura Finsten, Richard Blanton, and Linda M. Nicholas. 1989. *Monte Albán's Hinterland, Part II: Prehispanic Settlement Patterns in Tlacolula, Etla, and Ocotlán, the Valley of Oaxaca, Mexico*. Memoirs of the University of Michigan Museum of Anthropology No. 23. Ann Arbor: University of Michigan Museum.

Kroefges, Peter C. 2004. *Sociopolitical Organization in the Prehispanic Chontalpa de Oaxaca, Mexico: Ethnohistorical and Archaeological Perspectives*. PhD dissertation, Department of Anthropology, the University at Albany, State University of New York, Albany. Ann Arbor, MI: University Microfilms.

Lesure, Richard. 1997. "Early Formative Platforms at Paso de la Amada, Chiapas, Mexico." *Latin American Antiquity* 8 (3): 217–35. http://dx.doi.org/10.2307/971653.

Levine, Marc N. 2002. "Ceramic Change and Continuity in the Lower Río Verde Region of Oaxaca Mexico: The Late Formative to Early Terminal Formative Transition." MA thesis, Department of Anthropology, University of Colorado, Boulder.

Levine, Marc N. 2007. *Linking Household and Polity at Late Postclassic Period Yucu Dzaa (Tututepec), a Mixtec Capital on the Coast of Oaxaca, Mexico*. PhD dissertation, Department of Anthropology, University of Colorado, Boulder. Ann Arbor, MI: University Microfilms.

Levine, Marc N. 2011. "Negotiating Political Economy at Late Postclassic Tututepec (Yucu Dzaa)." *American Anthropologist* 113 (1): 22–39. http://dx.doi.org/10.1111/j.15 48-1433.2010.01304.x.

Long, J. Robert. 1974. "The Late Classic and Early Postclassic Ceramics from the Eastern Portion of the Coast." In *The Oaxaca Coast Project Reports: Part 2*, ed. Donald L. Brockington and J. Robert Long, 39–98. Vanderbilt University Publications in Anthropology No. 9. Nashville, TN: Vanderbilt University.

Love, Michael. 1999. "Ideology, Material Culture, and Daily Practice in Pre-Classic Mesoamerica: A Pacific Coast perspective." In *Social Patterns in Pre-Classic Mesoamerica*, ed. David C. Grove and Rosemary A. Joyce, 127–54. Washington, DC: Dumbarton Oaks Research Library and Collection.

Maler, Teoberto. 1883. "Notes sur la basse Mixtéque." *Revue d'ethnologie* 2: 154–61.

Marcus, Joyce. 1976. "The Iconography of Militarism at Monte Albán and Neighboring Sites in the Valley of Oaxaca." In *Origins of Religious Art and Iconography in Preclassic Mesoamerica*, ed. Henry Nicholson, 125–39. Los Angeles: UCLA Latin American Center Publications.

Marcus, Joyce. 1983. "The Conquest Slabs of Building J, Monte Albán." In *The Cloud People. Divergent Evolution of the Zapotec and Mixtec Civilizations*, ed. Kent V. Flannery and Joyce Marcus, 106–8. New York: Academic Press.

Marcus, Joyce, and Kent V. Flannery. 1996. *Zapotec Civilization*. London: Thames and Hudson.

Martínez Gracida, Manuel. 1910. "Los indios oaxaqueños y sus monumentos arqueológicos, Civilización mixteco-zapoteco." Five unpublished volumes in the Biblioteca Pública Central del Estado de Oaxaca, Oaxaca.

Martínez López, Cira, Robert Markens, Marcus Winter, and Michael D. Lind. 2000. *Cerámica de la fase Xoo (Epoca Monte Albán IIIB–IV) del valle de Oaxaca*. Contribución No. 8 del Proyecto Especial Monte Albán 1992–1994. Oaxaca: Centro INAH Oaxaca.

Matadamas Díaz, Raúl. 2009. "Copalita, Huatulco: La transición al período Clásico en la costa de Oaxaca." Paper presented at the 5th Mesa Redonda de Monte Albán, Oaxaca, Mexico.

Mayes, Arion T., and Sarah B. Barber. 2008. "Osteobiography of a High Status Burial from the Lower Río Verde Valley of Oaxaca, Mexico." *International Journal of Osteoarchaeology* 18 (6): 573–88. http://dx.doi.org/10.1002/oa.1011.

Mayes, Arion, Anamay Melmed, and Sarah B. Barber. 2009. "Stigmata of Congenital Syphilis on a High Status Juvenile at Yugüe, Oaxaca, Mexico." *Dental Anthropology* 22 (3): 73–84.

Melmed, Anamay. 2006. "Health, Diet, and Behavior in Prehistoric Oaxaca." MA thesis, Department of Anthropology, San Diego State University, San Diego.

Méndez, Enrique. 1975. "Arqueología del area Huave." MA thesis, Escuela Nacional de Antropología e Historia, Mexico City.

Monaghan, John. 1990. "Sacrifice, Death, and the Origins of Agriculture in the Codex Vienna." *American Antiquity* 55 (3): 559–69. http://dx.doi.org/10.2307/281286.

Monaghan, John. 1995. *The Covenants with Earth and Rain.* Norman: University of Oklahoma Press.

Muehlenpfordt, E.A.E. 1984. *Los palacios de los Zapotecos en Mitla.* Mexico City: Universidad Nacional Autónoma de México.

Mueller, Raymond G. 1991. "Appendix 2: Technical Report on the Geomorphological Research of the Río Verde Formative Project." In *Formative Period Occupation in the Lower Río Verde Valley, Oaxaca, Mexico: Interregional Interaction and Social Change,* by Arthur A. Joyce, 788–839. PhD dissertation, Department of Anthropology, Rutgers University, New Brunswick, NJ. Ann Arbor, MI: University Microfilms.

Mueller, Raymond G., Arthur A. Joyce, and Aleksander Borejsza. 2012. "Alluvial Archives of the Nochixtlán Valley, Oaxaca, Mexico: Age and Significance for Reconstructions of Environmental Change." *Palaeogeography, Palaeoclimatology, Palaeoecology* 321–322 (2012): 121–136.

Mueller, Raymond G., and Lucia Pou. 2008. "The Nochixtlán Valley: A Report of Background Information and Results of Fieldwork." Manuscript in possession of the authors.

Orr, Heather. 2001. "The Pictographs of Piedra San Vicente, Coastal Oaxaca, México." Report submitted to the Foundation for the Advancement of Mesoamerican Studies, Crystal River, FL.

Pauketat, Timothy R. 2001. "Practice and History in Archaeology." *Anthropological Theory* 1 (1): 73–98.

Peñafiel, Antonio. 1890. *Monumentos del arte mexicano antiguo: Ornamentación, mitología, tributos y monumentos.* 3 vols. Berlin: A. Asher and Company.

Pérez Rodríguez, Verónica, Kirk C. Anderson, and Margaret K. Neff. 2011. "The Cerro Jazmín Archaeological Project: Investigating Prehispanic Urbanism and Its Environmental Impact in the Mixteca Alta, Oaxaca, Mexico." *Journal of Field Archaeology* 36 (2): 83–99. http://dx.doi.org/10.1179/009346911X12991472411321.

Peterson, David A., and Thomas B. Macdougall. 1974. *Guiengola: A Fortified Site in the Isthmus of Tehuantepec.* Vanderbilt University Publications in Anthropology 10. Nashville, TN: Vanderbilt University.

Piña Chan, Román. 1960. "Algunos sitios arqueológicos de Oaxaca y Guerrero." *Revista Mexicana de Estudios Antropológicos* 116: 65–76.

Redmond, Elsa M., and Charles S. Spencer. 2006. "From Raiding to Conquest: Warfare Strategies and Early State Development in Oaxaca, Mexico." In *The Archaeology of Warfare: Prehistories of Raiding and Conquest*, ed. Elizabeth N. Arkush and Mark W. Allen, 336–93. Gainesville: University Press of Florida.

Robles García, Nelly M. 1988. *Las unidades domésticas del Preclásico Superior en la Mixteca Alta*. BAR International Series 407. Oxford: British Archaeological Reports.

Rodrigo Alvarez, Luis. 1998. *Geografía general del estado de Oaxaca*. 3rd ed. Oaxaca: Carteles Editores.

Rodríguez, Adolfo C., Gabriel Narváez C., Antonio Hernández M., Jorge Romero P., Bernardo C. Solano S., Francisco L. Anaya A., Nicolás Dillanes R., and José de los Santos Castro C. 1989. *Caracterización de la producción agrícola de la región costa de Oaxaca*. Pinotepa Nacional: Universidad Autónoma Chapingo.

Sherman, R. Jason, Andrew K. Balkansky, Charles S. Spencer, and Brian D. Nicholls. 2010. "The Expansionary Dynamics of the Nascent Monte Albán State." *Journal of Anthropological Archaeology* 29 (3): 278–301. http://dx.doi.org/10.1016/j.jaa.2010.04.001.

Spencer, Charles S. 2007. "Territorial Expansion and Primary State Formation in Oaxaca, Mexico." In *Latin American Indigenous Warfare and Ritual Violence*, ed. Richard J. Chacon and Rubén G. Mendoza, 55–72. Tucson: University of Arizona Press.

Spencer, Charles S., and Elsa M. Redmond. 2006. "Resistance Strategies and Early State Formation in Oaxaca, Mexico." In *Intermediate Elites in Pre-Columbian States and Empires*, ed. Christina M. Elson and R. Alan Covey, 20–43. Tucson: University of Arizona Press.

Spores, Ronald. 1993. "Tututepec: A Postclassic-Period Mixtec Conquest State." *Ancient Mesoamerica* 4 (1): 167–74. http://dx.doi.org/10.1017/S0956536100000845.

Tamayo, Jorge L. 1964. "The Hydrography of Middle America." In *Handbook of Middle American Indians*, Vol. 1: *Natural Environment and Early Cultures*, ed. Robert C. West, 84–121. Austin: University of Texas Press.

Taylor, Sarah R., Arthur A. Joyce, Mathew Sponheimer, and Sarah B. Barber. 2009. Dieta y agricultura en el valle del Río Verde inferior: Basado en análisis de microdesgaste dental e isótopos estables. In "Estudios alimenticios y de ADN de dientes humanos del valle del Río Verde inferior, Oaxaca, México," ed. Arthur A. Joyce, 3–31. Report submitted to the Consejo de Arqueología, Instituto Nacional de Antropología e Historia, Mexico City.

Telford, Richard J., Einar Heegaard, and H.J.B. Birks. 2004. "The Intercept Is a Poor Estimate of a Calibrated Radiocarbon Age." *Holocene* 14 (2): 296–98. http://dx.doi.org/10.1191/0959683604hl707fa.

Urcid, Javier. 1993. "The Pacific Coast of Oaxaca and Guerrero: The Westernmost Extent of Zapotec Script." *Ancient Mesoamerica* 4 (1): 141–65. http://dx.doi.org/10.1017/S0956536100000833.

Urcid, Javier. 1994. "Mound J at Monte Albán and Zapotec Political Geography during Period II (200 BC–AD 200)." Paper presented at the 59th Annual Meeting of the Society for American Archaeology, Anaheim, CA.

Urcid, Javier. 2008. "The Writing Surface as a Cultural Code: A Comparative Perspective of Scribal Traditions from Southwestern Mesoamerica." Paper presented at the Symposium Scripts and Notational Systems in Pre-Columbian America, Dumbarton Oaks, Washington, DC.

Urcid, Javier, and Arthur A. Joyce. 1999. "Monumentos grabados y nombres calendáricos: Los antiguos gobernantes de Río Viejo, Oaxaca." *Arqueología* 22: 17–39.

Urcid, Javier, and Arthur A. Joyce. 2001. "Carved Monuments and Calendrical Names: The Rulers of Río Viejo, Oaxaca." *Ancient Mesoamerica* 12 (2): 199–216. http://dx.doi.org/10.1017/S0956536101122108.

Urcid, Javier, and Arthur A. Joyce. 2011. Formative Period Transformations of Monte Albán's Main Plaza and Their Political Implications." Paper presented at the 76th Annual Meeting of the Society for American Archaeology, Sacramento, CA.

Wallrath, Mathew. 1967. "Excavations in the Tehuantepec Region." *Transactions of the American Philosophical Society*, n.s. 57 (2).

Whittaker, Gordon. 1980. *The Hieroglyphics of Monte Albán*. PhD dissertation, Department of Anthropology, Yale University, New Haven, CT. Ann Arbor, MI: University Microfilms.

Winter, Marcus. 1974. "Residential Patterns at Monte Alban, Oaxaca, Mexico." *Science* 186, no. 4168 (Dec. 13): 981–87. http://dx.doi.org/10.1126/science.186.4168.981. Medline:17843045.

Winter, Marcus. 1984. "Exchange in Formative Highland Oaxaca." In *Trade and Exchange in Early Mesoamerica*, ed. Kenneth G. Hirth, 179–214. Albuquerque: University of New Mexico Press.

Winter, Marcus. 1989. *Oaxaca: The Archaeological Record*. Mexico City: Minutiae Mexicana.

Winter, Marcus, ed. 1994a. *Monte Albán: Estudios recientes*. Contribución No. 2 del Proyecto Especial Monte Albán 1992–1994. Oaxaca: Centro INAH Oaxaca.

Winter, Marcus. 1994b. "The Mixteca Prior to the Late Postclassic." In *The Mixteca-Puebla Concept in Mesoamerican Archaeology*, ed. Henry B. Nicholson and Eloise Quiñones Keber, 201–21. Culver City, CA: Labyrinthos.

Winter, Marcus, ed. 1995. *Entierros humanos de Monte Albán*. Contribución No. 7 del Proyecto Especial Monte Albán 1992–1994. Oaxaca: Centro INAH Oaxaca.

Winter, Marcus. 2004. "Monte Albán: Su organización e impacto político." In *Estructuras políticas en el Oaxaca antiguo*, ed. Nelly M. Robles García, 27–59. Mexico City: Instituto Nacional de Antropología e Historia.

Winter, Marcus. 2007a. *Cerro de las Minas: Arqueología de la Mixteca Baja*. 2nd ed. Oaxaca: Centro INAH Oaxaca.

Winter, Marcus. 2007b. "Recent Archaeological Investigations of Preclassic Occupations in the Southern Isthmus of Tehuantepec." In *Archaeology, Art, and Ethnogenesis in Mesoamerican Prehistory: Papers in Honor of Gareth W. Lowe*, ed. Lynneth S. Lowe and Mary E. Pye, 193–207. Papers of the New World Archaeological Foundation 68. Provo, UT: Brigham Young University.

Woodard, S. Justine. 1991. "Appendix 3: Paleobotanical Study Río Verde Formative Project." In *Formative Period Occupation in the Lower Río Verde Valley, Oaxaca, Mexico: Interregional Interaction and Social Change*, by Arthur A. Joyce, 840–82. PhD dissertation, Department of Anthropology, Rutgers University, New Brunswick, NJ. Ann Arbor, MI: University Microfilms.

Workinger, Andrew. 2002. *Coastal/Highland Interaction in Prehispanic Oaxaca, Mexico: The Perspective from San Francisco de Arriba.* PhD dissertation, Department of Anthropology, Vanderbilt University, Nashville, TN. Ann Arbor, MI: University Microfilms.

Workinger, Andrew, and Arthur A. Joyce. 2009. "The Scope of Conflict in Formative Oaxaca." In *Blood and Beauty: Organized Violence in the Art and Archaeology of the Americas*, ed. Heather Orr and Rex Koontz, 3–38. Los Angeles: Cotsen Institute Press.

Zárate Morán, Roberto. 1986. "Tres piedras labradas en la región Oaxaqueña." *Cuadernos de Arquitectura Mesoamericana* 7: 75–77.

Zárate Morán, Roberto. 1995. "El Corozal, un sitio arqueológico en la costa del Pacífico de Oaxaca." *Cuadernos del Sur* 10: 9–36.

Zeitlin, Judith F. 1978. "Changing Patterns of Resource Exploitation, Settlement Distribution, and Demography on the Southern Isthmus of Tehuantepec, Mexico." In *Prehistoric Coastal Adaptations*, ed. Barbara L. Stark and Barbara Voorhies, 151–77. New York: Academic Press.

Zeitlin, Judith F. 1994. "Precolumbian Barrio Organization in Tehuantepec, Mexico." In *Caciques and Their People*, ed. Joyce Marcus and Judith F. Zeitlin, 275–300. Anthropological Paper No. 89. Ann Arbor: Museum of Anthropology, University of Michigan.

Zeitlin, Judith F. 2005. *Cultural Politics in Colonial Tehuantepec.* Stanford, CA: Stanford University Press.

Zeitlin, Robert N. 1978. "Long-Distance Exchange and the Growth of a Regional Center on the Southern Isthmus of Tehuantepec, Mexico." In *Prehistoric Coastal Adaptations: The Economy and Ecology of Maritime Middle America*, ed. Barbara L. Stark and Barbara Voorhies, 183–210. New York: Academic Press.

Zeitlin, Robert N. 1979. *Prehistoric Long-Distance Exchange on the Southern Isthmus of Tehuantepec, Mexico.* 2 vols. PhD dissertation, Department of Anthropology, Yale University, New Haven, CT. Ann Arbor, MI: University Microfilms.

Zeitlin, Robert N. 1990. "The Isthmus and the Valley of Oaxaca: Questions about Monte Albán Imperialism in the Pacific Lowlands." *American Antiquity* 55 (2): 250–61. http://dx.doi.org/10.2307/281646.

Zeitlin, Robert N. 1993. "Pacific Coastal Laguna Zope: A Regional Center in the Terminal Formative Hinterlands of Monte Albán." *Ancient Mesoamerica* 4 (01): 85–101. http://dx.doi.org/10.1017/S0956536100000808.

Zeitlin, Robert N., and Arthur A. Joyce. 1999. "The Zapotec-Imperialism Argument: Insights from the Oaxaca Coast." *Current Anthropology* 40 (3): 383–92. http://dx.doi.org/10.1086/200029.

PALEOECOLOGICAL EVIDENCE for EARLY AGRICULTURE and FOREST CLEARANCE IN COASTAL OAXACA

Michelle Goman, Arthur A. Joyce, and Raymond G. Mueller

The intensive paleoecological analysis of lake and wetland sediments in Mesoamerica has provided important evidence of the origins and development of agriculture and the manipulation of the landscape by prehistoric groups (e.g., Deevey 1978; Jones and Voorhies 2004). This evidence not only complements the archaeological data but can temporally extend the record of human land use to periods of time for which no archaeological remains have been discovered for a region (e.g., Goman and Byrne 1998; Horn 2006; Jones 1994; Leyden 2002). The paleoecological record has also played an important role in the development and refinement of models of the geography and chronology of maize domestication and diffusion (e.g., Blake 2006; Dull 2006; Piperno 2006a). This chapter presents the first paleoecological evidence of early maize domestication in lowland Oaxaca and discusses changes in land use during the Late Archaic and Formative periods.

Two rival theoretical models have evolved to explain the origins of maize domestication in Mesoamerica (MacNeish and Eubanks 2000; Piperno 2006b). The Highland or Tehuacán model posits that maize was domesticated in the highlands of Mexico resulting from the hybridization of two wild relatives of maize (Mangelsdorf et al.

DOI: 10.5876/9781607322023.c02

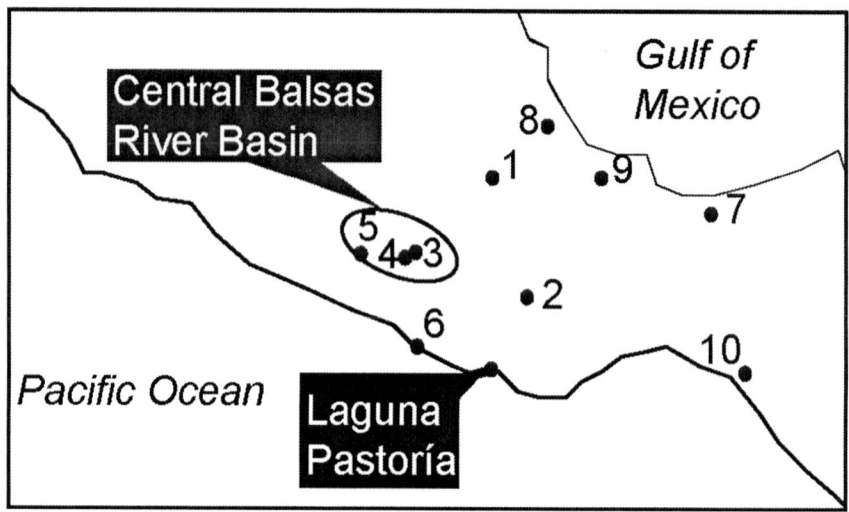

FIGURE 2.1. Map of sites of earliest published claims for maize (*Zea mays* subsp. *mays*) macro- and microfossils in Mexico mentioned in the text. *1*, Tehuacán, Puebla; *2*, Guilá Naquitz Cave, Oaxaca; *3*, Xihuatoxtla, Guerrero; *4*, Iguala Valley, Guerrero; *5*, El Venancio, Guerrero; *6*, Laguna Tetitlán, Guerrero; *7*, San Andrés, Tabasco; *8*, Laguna Catarina, Veracruz; *9*, Laguna Pompal, Veracruz; *10*, Pijijiapan, Chiapas.

1967). This hypothesis was supported by the findings of morphologically primitive corn cobs from the highland cave site of Coxcatlán in the Tehuacán Valley, Puebla (Smith 1967). In the alternate argument, known as the Lowland or Río Balsas model, a single genetic mutation of *Zea mays* subsp. *parviglumis* (Balsas teosinte) is thought to have occurred (Doebley 1990; Iltis 1983).

Recent genetic evidence indicates that maize was indeed domesticated from a single event that arose in Balsas teosinte approximately 9,000 years ago (Benz 2006; Matsuoka et al. 2002; also see Pool, Chapter 10). This annual grass has a modern range that is limited to the Río Balsas drainage of Guerrero (Doebley 1984; 1990; Figure 2.1). The Río Balsas drainage region therefore offers a compelling location for the domestication of maize and the possible corroboration of the Lowland model; however, it is conceivable that paleo-distributions of the grass at the beginning of the Holocene may have differed (Doebley 1990; Piperno et al. 2007).

Accelerator mass spectrometry (AMS) age analysis and new phytolith data from Guilá Naquitz Cave in the highlands of Oaxaca (Piperno and Flannery 2001) shed further light on the issue of the location of maize domestication. Two primitive-looking maize cobs originally found during the 1966 excavations of Guilá Naquitz (Smith 1986) were directly dated by AMS and returned ages of approximately 4300 cal BC (3450 ^{14}C yr BC; Piperno and Flannery 2001).

This age places them as the oldest specimens of maize cobs found, to date, in Mesoamerica, significantly older than the cobs found in the Tehuacán Valley (Long et al. 1989). If the early Holocene range of the Balsas teosinte differed markedly from today, then it is possible that the highlands of Oaxaca might have been the locus of maize domestication. However, based on the detailed phytolith studies of soil samples from Guilá Naquitz, Piperno and Flannery (2001) suggest that this was not the case. While phytoliths of grasses and other plants were common, no phytoliths attributable to teosinte or maize were present in deposits that ranged between ca. 10,670–5840 cal BC (8700–5030 ^{14}C yr BC; zones B through E), but maize phytoliths were present in the youngest zone (A), thought to date to ca. cal AD 690 (AD 620 ^{14}C yr). These data indicate that maize was introduced to highland Oaxaca.

Recent microbotanical evidence from the heart of the Balsas Valley appears to have put the long debate to rest as starch grain and phytolith evidence from the Archaic cave site of Xihuatoxtla place the presence of domesticates during the seventh millennium cal BC (Piperno et al. 2009; Ranere et al. 2009). With the identification of the ancestral hearth of maize domestication in Guerrero, the question remains of when and how domesticated maize diffused throughout Mesoamerica. In this chapter we summarize the paleoecological evidence for early maize within southern Mexico and present the first paleoecological evidence of lowland maize cultivation in Oaxaca. In order to facilitate comparisons between regions, we report calibrated AMS dates since only calibrated dates are available for many studies of early maize.

PALEOECOLOGICAL EVIDENCE FOR EARLY MAIZE AGRICULTURE IN SOUTHERN MEXICO

While the early Holocene range of Balsas teosinte may have been more expansive given our current understanding of paleoclimate conditions (Piperno 2006b), and common in lower-elevation tropical areas (Piperno et al. 2007), today Balsas teosinte has a highly restricted distribution. The plant prefers elevations of between 500 and 1800 m above sea level, with mean annual temperature ranges from 20 to 25°C and mean annual precipitation from 1250 to 2000 mm (Doebley 1990; Matsuoka et al. 2002); thus isolating it to the central parts of the Río Balsas drainage.

Given the history and association of teosinte with studies of early domestication, it is perhaps surprising that until recently no paleoecological work had been undertaken in the Balsas drainage (Hastorf 2009). However, Piperno and colleagues' (2009) work at the Archaic cave site of Xihuatoxtla, located in the central Balsas, rectifies this gap. They used starch grain and phytolith analyses to document the presence of maize by 6750 cal BC (5970 ^{14}C yr BC) extracted from residue on Archaic period grinding stones (Ranere et al. 2009).

Paleoecological analysis from multiple lake sites in the Iguala Valley of the central Balsas found *Zea* pollen was important at Laguna Ixtacyola by ca. 5290 cal BC (4340 ^{14}C yr BC) during the Mesoamerican Middle Archaic period (Piperno et al. 2007). While *Zea* pollen cannot be categorically ascribed to maize (Holst et al. 2007), the associated supporting evidence is strong, in particular weedy disturbance taxa, primarily ragweed-type pollen (*Ambrosia* spp.), and microscopic charcoal, indicating that forest disturbance by humans was occurring, most likely for shifting horticulture. The presence of humans is also confirmed by the recovery of artifacts from excavations undertaken at the lake's edge (Piperno et al. 2007).

At Laguna Tuxpan, Guerrero, excavations at the shoreline found a rich phytolith but poorly preserved pollen record. Although age assessment of the deposit is problematic, with age inversions possibly caused by the percolation and subsequent contamination by humic acids, or from erosion and redeposition of older dried sediments to the location, maize cob phytoliths and probable maize leaf phytoliths occur between 8000 and 3950 cal BC (8050–3050 ^{14}C yr BC; Piperno et al. 2007). Phytoliths from the fruit rinds of squash (*Cucurbita* spp.) are also found within the same deposits. Importantly, phytoliths associated with the leaves and fruitcases of teosinte are absent. Although pollen was poorly preserved, a *Zea* grain 87 μm long was also recovered; although size cannot be reliably used to differentiate between teosinte and domesticated maize pollen, the large grain size and associated evidence suggest that it is maize pollen (Holst et al. 2007).

The data from the Balsas region provides the earliest paleoecological evidence for maize-based agriculture and indicates that this was occurring by at least 5290 cal BC (4340 ^{14}C yr BC). The data from Ixtacyola and Tuxpan as well as evidence from other sites in the Balsas region, such as Chaucles (Piperno et al. 2007) and Venancio (Piperno 2006a), indicate that maize domestication and forest clearance for horticulture were well under way by ca. 2550 cal BC (2280 ^{14}C yr BC) during the Late Archaic. On the coast of Guerrero at Laguna Tetitlán the identification of *Zea mays* pollen indicates that maize was cultivated in the region by the Early Formative (1220 ± 280 ^{14}C yr BC, 1450 cal BC; González-Quintero and Mora-Echeverría 1978).

San Andrés, located in modern-day Tabasco on the Gulf of Mexico, currently provides the second-oldest regional data point for maize within Mesoamerica. *Zea* pollen grains larger than 70μm and with distinctive characteristics of domesticated maize have been identified from estuarine sediments dating to 5050 cal BC (4250 ^{14}C yr BC; Pope et al. 2001). The maize pollen is accompanied by additional disturbance indicators such as peaks in other grass pollen as well as peaks in microscopic charcoal. Sluyter and Dominguez (2006) have disputed the age of the maize pollen from San Andrés suggesting that bioturbation may have affected the integrity of the record. Careful reanalysis of the record as well as new phytolith evidence from the region indicates that this is not the case (Pohl et al. 2007). Indeed, the phytolith data indicate that teosinte and *Tripsacum* were lacking at the site, providing further supporting evidence that the domestication of maize happened elsewhere in the tropics.[1]

Sluyter (1997) identified maize in lagoon deposits dating to ca. 6,000 years ago in Veracruz. Sluyter and Dominguez (2006), however, reanalyzed this result and suggested that this age was too old by approximately 1,500 years, based on a newly acquired AMS date of pollen. This younger age is comparable to an age for maize pollen obtained from the sediments of Laguna Pompal in the Tuxtlas highlands of Veracruz (Goman and Byrne 1998). Maize pollen and agricultural disturbance indicators are found in the lowermost sediments of Pompal and date to 2880 cal BC (2300 ^{14}C yr BC); since the basal sediments contain maize, the domesticate must have been introduced to the region at an earlier date and at lower, more environmentally suitable elevations (Goman and Byrne 1998) and thus supports the early maize data from Tabasco (Pohl et al. 2007).

New multi-proxy paleoecological evidence from the Pacific coastal low-lands of Chiapas at Pijijiapan places forest clearance and early maize cultivation at ca. 4550 cal BC (3840 ^{14}C yr BC; Kennett et al. 2010). Several sediment cores were examined from low-energy coastal wetlands for phytoliths, pollen, and macroscopic charcoal. Phytoliths from maize leaves and cobs were present in near basal sediments. Many of the phytoliths were burned, indicating human-set fires for land clearance. Similar to the Tabasco record, phytoliths of teosinte were absent, and thus the large *Zea* pollen grains identified at the site are likely from maize. Regionally, increased forest clearance and agricultural expansion occurs about 2050 cal BC (1760 ^{14}C yr BC; Kennett et al. 2010).

In summary, maize appears to have been domesticated in the vicinity of the Río Balsas drainage of modern Guerrero sometime between 9,000 and 7,000 years ago. From there the new crop diffused outward, spreading south-ward and into the Gulf lowlands presumably via the Isthmus of Tehuantepec. Geographically, therefore, Oaxaca, surrounded by regions with evidence for early maize cultivation, must have acted as an important conduit for disper-sal to the rest of Mexico and beyond. This is confirmed by the antiquity of the early maize cobs excavated from the highland rock-shelter site of Guilá Naquitz (Flannery 1986; Piperno and Flannery 2001; Smith 1986). However, little is known about the chronology of early maize introduction to the coastal lowlands of Oaxaca. In the next section we present paleoecological evidence for prehistoric maize, initial forest clearance, and agriculture from the Oaxacan estuarine site of Laguna Pastoría.

PALEOECOLOGICAL EVIDENCE FOR PREHISTORIC MAIZE CULTIVATION IN LOWLAND COASTAL OAXACA

Paleoecological field and laboratory work concentrating on the region of the lower Río Verde Valley of Oaxaca commenced in AD 2000 and continues today (e.g., Goman et al. 2005, 2010). Multiple sediment cores were raised from floodplain locations west of the Río Verde as well as from a coastal lagoon site approximately 23 km to the east of the mouth of the river (see Figure 1.2). The paleoecological record from the floodplain sites is generally younger (ca. Classic period to the present[2]) and is discussed elsewhere (Goman et al. 2010). This chapter focuses on the paleoecological record from the coastal lagoon which encompasses the last ca. 5,000 years.

LAGUNA PASTORÍA

Laguna Pastoría (16°00'N 97°35'W) is a brackish microtidal (tidal amplitude variations of 1 m or less) lagoon approximately 9 km long, with depth varying but with a 3 to 4 m maximum. The lagoon is protected from the Pacific Ocean by a roughly east-west trending bay barrier (Contreras 1988; Lankford 1977), which is about 500 m wide and 2 to 4 m high. Low scrub vegetation (cacti, thorny bushes, small trees, and palms) grows on the barrier. A diverse array of mangroves (*Rhizophora mangle, Laguncularia racemosa, Conocarpus erectus,* and *Avicennia germinans*) fringe the lagoon. Immediately behind the bay barrier, discrete mangrove islands have formed.

METHODS

Sediment cores were retrieved using a Livingstone corer at Laguna Pastoría (Figure 2.2). The sediment cores were X-radiographed and analyzed continuously for magnetic susceptibility analysis prior to cutting open for stratigraphic description. Magnetic susceptibility assesses the concentration of magnetic minerals within sediments and as such can be used to determine changes in sediment composition or erosional processes (Nowaczyk 2001). Core lithostratigraphy was described using standard stratigraphic techniques, including hand-testing of grain size and description by Munsell colors. An archival section of each sediment core was retained.

In order to reconstruct the regional vegetation history, pollen analysis was undertaken. An exotic spore (*Lycopodium*) was added to each pollen sample at the beginning of processing as a control and to enable calculation of fossil pollen concentration (Stockmarr 1971), which followed standard techniques (Faegri and Iversen 1989). Thirty-two samples were processed for pollen analysis. Pollen was counted using an Olympus BX51 with 10X and 40X objectives.

FIGURE 2.2. Michelle Goman and Arthur Joyce using a Livingstone corer at Laguna Pastoría. The authors are standing on a raft platform affectionately named *The Titanic. Left,* The authors initiate the core drive; *right,* Core device with core ready to be extruded.

Fossil pollen was identified using published keys (Bartlett and Barghoorn 1973; Lozano-García and Hernández 1990) and personal reference collections. *Zea mays* grains were identified by size and pore structure during regular counts and during scans of slides. Eighty-nine different pollen and spore taxa were identified. The relative amount of microscopic charcoal was qualitatively assessed at each level. Charred grass cuticles and charred grass phytoliths were also identified during pollen counts and scans (Wooller 2002).

RESULTS

The stratigraphy from Core LP1 and a second core (LP2) from Laguna Pastoría provided data on the history of coastal landforms along the lower Río Verde Valley (Goman et al. 2005). Here we focus on the record from LP1, which provides the longest paleoecological record in the region with basal materials dating to ca. 2900–2680 cal BC (2263 ^{14}C yr BC; see Table 2.1). While most of the core is composed of estuarine sediments, three distinct shell hash layers and two sand layers are embedded within the estuarine material (Figure 2.3). The abrupt upper and lower contacts of these layers, as revealed through examination of the X-radiographs, are indicative of high-energy deposition most likely caused by storm surges associated with hurricanes (Goman et al. 2005). Changes in type of storm surge deposit, from disarticulated shells to sand layers reflect changes in coastal geomorphology marking the formation of the bay barrier (Figure 2.3). A thick sand layer between 231 and 249 cm indicates that the bay barrier was in place by ca. 400–210 cal BC (340 ^{14}C yr BC; Table 2.1). Prior to this, as indicated by the environmental requirements of the mollusk species

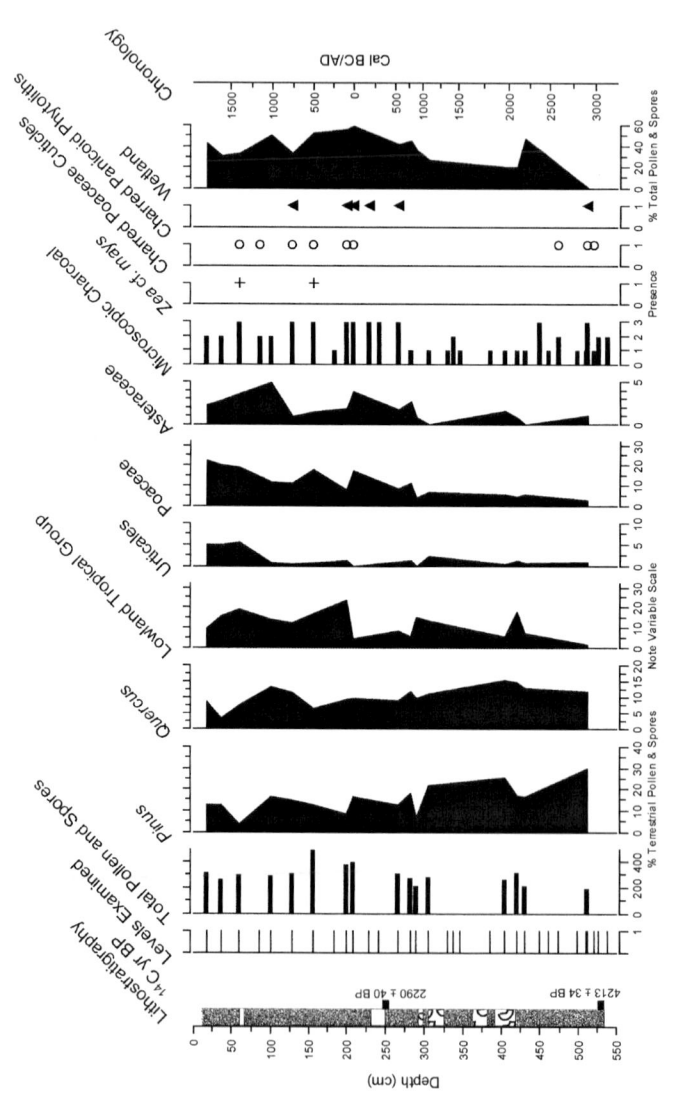

FIGURE 2.3. Summary pollen diagram for Laguna Pastoría. The Urticales group includes the following: *Trema, Cecropia, Ficus,* and diporate to six-porate, psilate, to scabrate undifferentiated Urticales types. The Lowland Tropical Group (LTG) includes: *Bursera, Ilex,* Sapindaceae, Leguminosae, and Palmae. The wetland taxa comprise mangles (*Rhizophera* and *Avicennia*) and Cyperaceae. The microscopic charcoal is a qualitative representation of charcoal presence.

TABLE 2.1. AMS radiocarbon data from Laguna Pastoría

Lab No.[a]	Site and Depth (cm)[b]	Material	$\delta^{13}C$	^{14}C yr BP	^{14}C yr BC	Calibrated Range BC (2σ)[c]	Midpoint of Range BC
Beta 168001	LP1 231	Organic Sediment	–20.6 ‰	2290 ± 40	340	400–210	305
AA 42080	LP1 534	Organic Sediment	–27.6 ‰	4213 ± 34[d]	2263	2900–2680	2790

[a] Radiocarbon assays by Beta Analytic Inc. and NSF-Arizona AMS Lab.
[b] These depths do not take into account core compaction. Decompacted depths are 249 cm and 536 cm respectively.
[c] Rounded to the nearest decade.
[d] Represents the average of three individual measurements.

identified from the shell hash layers and from archaeological data (Joyce 1991a, 495–497; Joyce, Chapter 1) an open bay system existed at what is now Laguna Pastoría. Some of the mollusk species in the shell hash layers live in depths up to 90 m, indicating that at this time the bay barriers had not yet formed and that deepwater shells could by pushed into shallow-water areas by storm surges. Archaeological data from Barra Quebrada on the bay barrier also confirm that the barrier formed toward the end of the Formative period, with people first occupying the site during the Miniyua phase (150 BC–AD 100). The formation of the bay barrier system as well as floodplain alluviation and alteration of the morphology of the lower Río Verde was the result of the complex interregional effects of soil erosion in the highlands of Oaxaca (Goman et al. 2005; Joyce and Mueller 1997, Mueller et al. 2012, Chapter 3).

A high degree of pyritization has occurred within the core sediments, particularly in those below the thick sand layer. Pyritization is a common type of fossilization whereby skeletal and sometimes soft tissue is replaced or coated with the mineral pyrite. This occurs during decomposition if all available oxygen is consumed, certain types of bacteria can reduce sulfate to sulfide to produce energy (instead of oxidizing organic carbon), which combines with iron to produce pyrite. Authigenic pyrite is, therefore, an indicator of anaerobic, sulfidic diagenesis (Berner 1970). Its presence in the lower section of the core likely reflects the dominant anaerobic and geochemical processes at the time when the more open bay existed. Determining the geochemical mechanism behind the reduction in pyrite production above the sand layer is beyond the scope of this chapter. However, a geomorphic change to a shallower tidally controlled lagoonal system, such as would have occurred following bay barrier development, may have removed the necessary environment for pyrite formation, namely anaerobic conditions as well as the presence of sufficient sedimentary organic matter, iron content, and dissolved sulfate. Thus any change in these criteria could have resulted in the overall absence of pyrite in the sediments above the thick sand layer.

Unfortunately, a consequence of the deposition of authigenic pyrite is that pollen preserved in the sediment core is typically of poor quality and identification of small taxa is particularly problematic, as they may be totally pyritized and not even identifiable as pollen (Figure 2.4; Delcourt and Delcourt 1980). Half of the thirty-two slides examined had sufficient identifiable pollen and spores to enable a count, with a minimum of at least 200 grains and whenever possible counts of 300 or more (Figure 2.3), although there may be a biasing in counting toward larger grains because of the pyritization. The majority of levels containing sufficient pollen to enable a count were located in the section of the core above the thick sand layer. It is important to acknowledge, therefore, that interpretation of the pollen record from the sparsely represented lower sections may be problematic.

Due to the limitations of the pollen preservation we present a summary pollen diagram displaying the major pollen groupings (Figure 2.3). Two groups represent wind-pollinated tropical trees and shrubs from the lowland tropical forests of Oaxaca: the Urticales and Lowland Tropical Group (LTG). The Urticales group combines taxa from the Moraceae, Urticaceae, and Ulmaceae families, which can be difficult to differentiate to genus or family level. The pollen for this tropical forest grouping typically has two to six pores and has either a smooth (psilate) or slightly bumpy surface (scabrate). Some taxa, such as *Trema, Cecropia,* and *Ficus* (e.g., pumpwood and fig), are identified, but because of low numbers are graphed within the Urticales grouping. The Lowland Tropical Group (LTG) includes a diverse array of taxa, including *Bursera, Ilex,* Sapindaceae, Leguminosae, and Palmae (e.g., gumbo-limbo, pea, and palm family) and is also graphed as a group (Byrne and Horn 1989; Goman and Byrne 1998).

Overall the temperate tree taxon *Pinus* and *Quercus* (pine and oak respectively) are indicative of greater regional pollen rain from the highlands and to a lesser extent the piedmont regions (Woodard 1991). These taxa show declining percentage abundance toward the present. Pine in particular shows a half-fold decline beginning ca. AD 750 (AD 770 ^{14}C yr).[3] The overall decline in temperate taxa with time is likely indicative of extraregional forest clearance. In contrast, the herbaceous taxa show an almost inverse pattern to the temperate taxa, with Poaceace (grasses) and Asteraceace (members of the sunflower family and typical weedy agricultural associates) dramatically increasing at this time; this likely reflects land clearance for agriculture. Disappointingly, maize pollen was rarely found in the core. Two large grass pollen grains (> 70 μm), consistent with the lower size range for maize (Holst et al. 2007), were identified at two levels in the younger, upper section of the core (dating to the Late Classic and Postclassic). Maize pollen was not identified from the lower and older depths. This result is perhaps not surprising, however, as maize pollen does not travel great distances from its source (Raynor et al. 1972) and

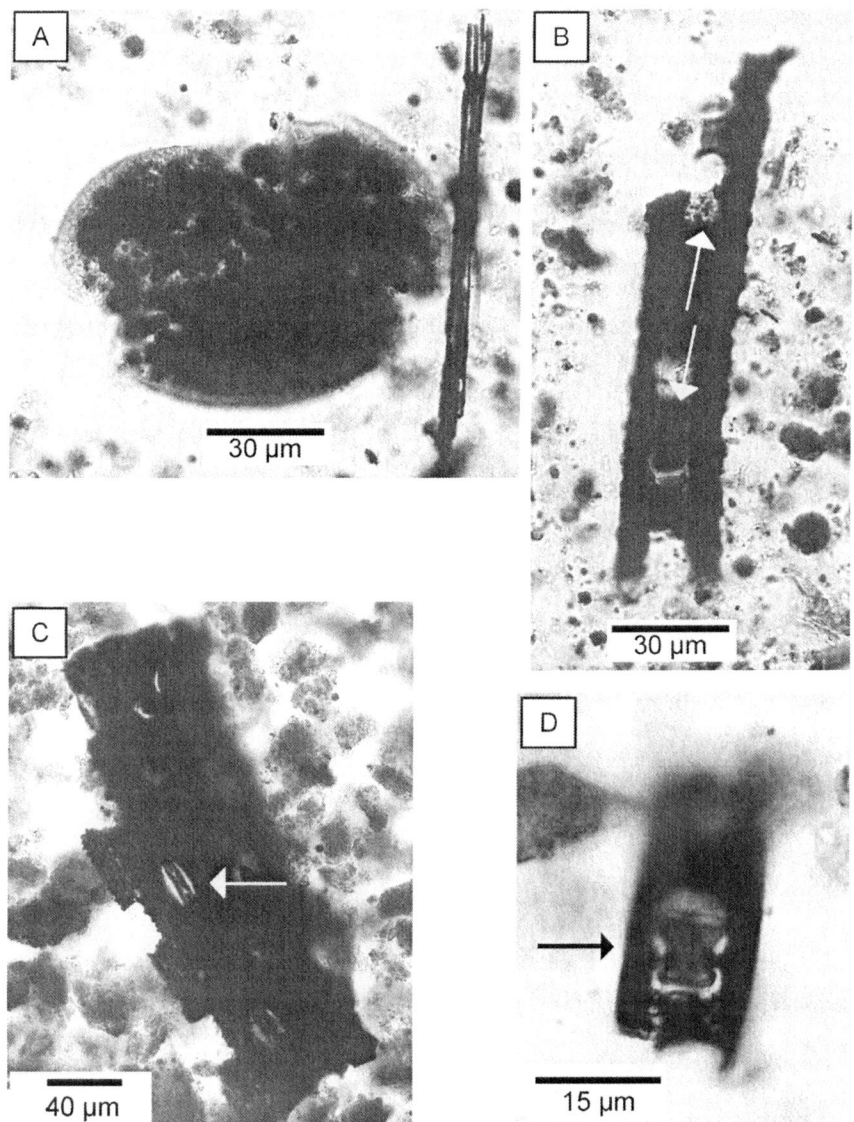

FIGURE 2.4. Microfossils from Laguna Pastoría. *A,* Highly pyritized pine pollen grain (*left*) and long, thin piece of charcoal (*right*). *B,* Panicoid-type grass charcoal from 512 cm; lower arrow indicates dumbbell-shaped silica body (phytolith), and upper arrow points to void left by dumbbell-shaped silica body. *C,* Grass charcoal from 200 cm; arrow indicates cuticle. *D,* Panicoid-type grass charcoal from 200 cm; arrow indicates dumbbell-shaped silica body.

the archaeological record indicates that the lower Río Verde Valley was only sparsely settled until the Middle Formative (Joyce 2005, 17–18; 2010, Chapter 1).

Microscopic charcoal fragments, an indicator of regional biomass burning (Patterson et al. 1987), were identified throughout the record, but only a qualitative analysis was undertaken because of the compounding problem of pyritization. Charred grass cuticles and the remains of burnt phytoliths (actual phytoliths or the void left by a phytolith) were identified, and all levels were scanned for these microfossils (Figures 2.3 and 2.4). The clearing of land by burning in preparation for seeding (a practice that persists today in the region) probably produced these microfossils, which were likely derived from grasses, possibly maize. These charred microfossils therefore provide important evidence for the early cultivation of maize in the region.

The oldest paleoecological evidence for maize cultivation is found in the near basal sediments of Pastoría at 512 cm (ca. 2830 cal BC; 2110 ^{14}C yr BC). This level contained considerable amounts of microscopic charcoal, including the piece shown in Figure 2.4b, which holds the remains of a charred dumbbell-shaped phytolith that surprisingly survived the hydrofluoric acid stage of sample preparation, as well as the void left by a dumbbell-shaped feature. Dumbbell-shaped phytoliths are characteristic of panicoid grasses such as maize (William Middleton, personal communication, 2008; Wooller 2002). While we cannot categorically say the phytoliths came from maize, their burnt nature as well as the presence of charred grass cuticles and microscopic charcoal in general attests to the presence of human agency for land clearance, most likely for maize-based shifting cultivation.

Following this early evidence for horticulture, microscopic charcoal is not important in the record, and the associated grass microfossils are generally absent until about ca. 266 cm and above. Qualitative analysis of the distribution of microscopic charcoal within the core indicates that it is much more prevalent in samples younger than ca. 535 cal BC (450 ^{14}C yr BC), and charred grass microfossils are found in nearly every level until about cal AD 1400 (AD 1410 ^{14}C yr). This is associated with the increased presence of grass pollen as well as pollen of weedy disturbance taxa and thus indicates the onset of significant agricultural disturbance within the lower Río Verde. Indeed, the palynological data complements the full coverage regional survey and excavation program (Joyce 2005, 2010), which indicates a major demographic expansion beginning in the Middle Formative (700–400 BC).

The vegetation is undoubtedly responding to the impacts of agricultural activity by the Middle Formative period. Pressure on vegetation is sustained until the modern period, although there appears to have been slight regional forest recovery during the Classic (AD 250–800) or perhaps the Early Postclassic period (AD 800–1100), as exhibited by increases in pine, oak, and the LTG as well as an absence of charred panicoid phytoliths. Interestingly, evidence for maize (pollen and charred microfossils) drops out of the record at the end of the Postclassic, probably as a result of the demographic collapse and major land use changes resulting from the Spanish Conquest.

Changes in the percentage importance of the Urticales and the LTG, while driven primarily by land clearance for agriculture, also appear to reflect changes in coastal morphology. Relatively low percentages of the two tropical groupings are seen for the early part of the record, but both display a near doubling in importance by approximately 2,000 years ago (Figure 2.3). While the tropical taxa would have been significantly impacted by lowland clearance, the formation of the bay barrier protecting Laguna Pastoría would have been in place by this time, creating preferred habitats for the tropical taxa. We therefore interpret the dramatic increases in the tropical taxa as reflecting colonization of the barrier by thorny scrub vegetation and palms, which dominate the LTG. The hypothesized late Holocene development of the barrier island is further supported by the increasing importance of wetland taxa (*Rhizophera* and Cyperaceae), indicating the expansion of calm water areas suitable for wetland plants (Goman et al. 2005).

DISCUSSION

Coastal regions such as the Gulf coast lowlands, the Costa Grande of Guerrero, and the Soconusco provide some of the earliest data for the cultivation of maize and early sedentism in Mesoamerica (e.g., Kennett et al. 2010; Neff et al. 2006; Pohl et al. 2007; Pope et al. 2001; Voorhies 2004). In these regions access to marine and estuarine resources such as fish, shellfish, and waterfowl provided important sources of animal protein (Blake et al. 1992; Clark 1991, 16; Coe and Diehl 1980, 390; Kennett et al. 2004; VanDerwarker 2006, 194–195; Voorhies 2004; Voorhies et al. 1991). Tropical and semitropical climates coupled with the floodplains of large rivers also provided ideal habitats for early maize cultivation. Indeed, paleoecological evidence from Pacific coastal regions indicates that maize farming was well established by 2050 BC (e.g., Kennett et al. 2010; Jones and Voorhies 2004; Neff et al. 2006), although stable isotope analysis of human bone from the Mazatán coastal region of Chiapas indicates that maize was not a major dietary component until the Middle Formative (Blake et al. 1992).

The finding of the charred panicoid grass phytoliths in the near basal material from Pastoría (512 cm), while not conclusive, does indicate that maize-based horticulture was occurring within the region of the lagoon at about 2830 cal BC (2110 ^{14}C yr BC). The evidence, however, indicates that prehistoric groups favored the area for only a short period of time during the Late Archaic, as pollen of maize, elevated microscopic charcoal levels, and associated charred microfossils disappear from the record by ca. 2070 cal BC (1560 ^{14}C yr BC). The absence of disturbance indicators between 2070 and 540 cal BC (1560 –535 ^{14}C yr BC), following the initial early evidence for land clearance and maize, is therefore at first surprising in light of the evidence and persistence of maize cultivation through time to the east in Chiapas (Kennett et al. 2010).

However, given our understanding of the history of regional landscape changes in the environs of the Río Verde, it is perhaps to be expected that the lower Verde was not a major center of population during the Archaic or Early Formative periods. Geomorphological research in the floodplain of the lower Río Verde indicates an increase in alluviation and a shift from more meandering to more braided river conditions during the Early/Middle Formative period (1600–400 BC) due to erosion in the Verde's upper drainage basin (Joyce and Mueller 1992, 1997; Joyce et al. 1998; Mueller et al. 2012, Chapter 3). These data indicate that the floodplain of the lower Verde was smaller and less fertile prior to the shift in the fluvial system. The lower Río Verde Valley therefore may not have been as agriculturally productive during the Archaic and Early Formative as it was later in the prehispanic era and continues to be today.

Evidence from the Laguna Pastoría sediment core also indicates that coastal resources would have been more difficult to exploit for the occupants of the lower Río Verde prior to ca. 550 cal BC The earliest sediments at Pastoría were likely deposited in an open bay at some distance from the paleo-coastline, prior to the formation of the bay barrier. This hypothesis is supported by the poor preservation and significant pyritization of pollen grains between 3,000 and 5,000 years old and the change in preservation associated with the formation of the bay barrier and increases in wetland taxa following the formation of the back-barrier estuaries. It is possible that the environment in the vicinity of the ancestral bay was not as attractive to prehistoric settlers as the modern setting would indicate. Using the modern high-energy wave environment of the Oaxacan coastline as an analogue for conditions in the bay, it is reasonable to assume that offshore coastal resources would have been more difficult to exploit than resources within protected estuaries. Today, even with motorized launches, it is often difficult for fishing people along this part of the coast to navigate through the strong surf, especially during the rainy season. Fish bones from the offshore marine environment are rare in archaeobotanical samples from the Middle Formative to the Early Classic (Fernández 2004).

The hypothesis that marine and estuarine resources were less available prior to the formation of the bay barrier is supported by preliminary data from a test excavation at the Early Formative period site of La Consentida, located about 1 km north of the present-day salt flats (Joyce 2005, 17; Winter n.d.; Figure 1.2). The site covers 2.6 ha and is dominated by several mounds reaching elevations of 5 m above the surrounding plain. The test pit exposed an occupational surface but yielded almost no shell or fish bone, and, interestingly, no paleobotanical remains of maize were found in flotation samples examined from the site (Woodard 1991). Further test excavations in 2009 by Hepp (2011; Hepp and Joyce, Chapter 9) recovered animal bone, including fish, and some shell. While study of the faunal samples is pending, recent radiocarbon analysis securely places the site occupation in the Early Formative period.

Only when the bay barrier formed, by 550 cal BC (450 ^{14}C yr BC), and quieter estuarine conditions developed do we see an improvement in pollen preservation and significant evidence for extensive maize-based agriculture. At the same time, Fernández's (2004, 135–137) preliminary archaeofaunal study shows a regional trend toward increasing utilization of estuarine resources, which is consistent with the formation of the estuaries at the end of the Formative. Trace element studies of human long bones from Late/Terminal Formative burials show dietary inputs of marine/estuarine resources, although the data indicate a largely terrestrial (agricultural) diet (Joyce 1991b, 137–138). Interestingly, the first pollen grain identified as maize in the Laguna Pastoría cores occurs at approximately cal AD 490 (AD 570 ^{14}C yr); this coincides with a possible Classic period expansion in settlement near the estuaries (Joyce 1991a, 420–439; Joyce et al. 1999, 2009; Workinger 2002).

Perhaps early horticulturalists favored the lower Río Verde Valley? However, archaeological evidence for early occupations, let alone early land use, from the floodplain region of the Río Verde is also elusive. No Archaic sites have been found in the region, including within several small rock shelters that have been surveyed (Joyce 2005; Joyce, Chapter 1). Only three archaeological sites covering a total of 5 ha have been discovered that date to the Early Formative (1600–700 BC). Two of the sites are located near the salt flats north of the coastal estuaries, suggesting a different settlement pattern than later in the Formative when communities were oriented toward the Río Verde's floodplain and piedmont. By the Middle Formative Charco phase (700–400 BC) the settlement data show a major expansion in regional population, with the occupied area in the full-coverage survey zone increasing to 64 ha. A regional demographic center developed at Charco Redondo, which grew to 62 ha, making it one of the largest Middle Formative sites in Oaxaca (Joyce 2005, Chapter 1). Regional population continued to increase through the remainder of the Formative, reaching 699 ha by the Chacahua phase (AD 100–250). During the Miniyua phase (150 BC–AD 100), an urban center emerged at the site of Río Viejo in the floodplain west of the river.

Paleobotanical remains identified from flotation samples at several archaeological sites in the valley, including the partial remains of a cob, indicate that maize was being eaten by the Minizundo phase (400–150 BC; Woodard 1991). Several lake-core records obtained from remnant oxbows in the floodplain regrettably do not provide insight into the Archaic and Early Formative periods, but rather record much later, predominantly Classic period, agricultural land use (Goman et al. 2010).

The extent of landscape change in the region, especially floodplain alluviation, could complicate the search for early agricultural evidence and its impacts (Joyce and Mueller 1992, 519; Mueller et al., Chapter 3). The growing body of evidence drawn from the paleoecological, geomorphological, and archaeological data sets, however, indicates that the lower Río Verde Valley was not as attractive for settlement until dramatic landscape changes had significantly altered the geomorphic evolution of the valley by the Late Formative. The paleoecological proxy data obtained from the basal sediments of Laguna Pastoría suggest that Archaic and Early Formative peoples were using the region near what was then a bay for subsistence, and possibly agriculture, but it was not until after the formation of the bay barrier and the coincident changes in the lower Verde floodplain that we see significant evidence for prehistoric agriculture and population growth, whether from migration or increased fecundity (Joyce 2005; Joyce and Mueller 1992, 1997). Stable isotope data from human teeth suggest that maize increased as a component of the diet from the Late Formative to the Postclassic (Taylor et al. 2009). The evidence is accumulating to suggest that ecological changes contributed to population growth in the region after 700 BC, although we need to establish additional causal links between environmental change and demographic expansion.

The paleoecological data from Laguna Pastoría indicate that the Oaxacan coastline was used by shifting horticulturalists or incipient agriculturalists in the Late Archaic period. The timing of cultivation and land clearance in the region is, however, a millennium or more younger than paleoecological evidence from sites in the Gulf coast. While more evidence is needed, this finding suggests that maize agriculture initially dispersed out of the Río Balsas region toward the Gulf of Mexico, rather than agriculturalists moving down the Río Balsas drainage toward the Pacific coast. Our studies continue in the Río Verde drainage, and we are confident that paleoecological analysis of recently collected sediment cores will enhance our understanding of the history of maize agriculture as well as regionally based anthropogenic landscape change.

ACKNOWLEDGMENTS

We would like to thank Don Thieme, Cristina Peterson, and the people of San José del Progesso for their hospitality during our fieldwork. We would also like to thank the Instituto Nacional de Antropología e Historia, especially the president of the Consejo de Arqueología, Joaquín García-Bárcena, as well as the director of the Centro INAH Oaxaca, Eduardo López Calzada, who granted permission and supported this research. Much of this research was undertaken at Cornell University, where Goman was a member of the research faculty in the Department of Earth and Atmospheric Sciences. Jonathan Hendricks identified the mollusks in the Pastoría cores. Christine Nelson kindly provided the use of her X-radiography facilities. Dennis Kent and Luca Lanci (Rutgers University) facilitated magnetic susceptibility data collection. This research was funded by a National Science Foundation grant (BCS-0096012) to Arthur Joyce and by an Association of American Geographers grant-in-aid to Michelle Goman.

NOTES

1. The term "teosinte" describes all species and subspecies in the genus *Zea*. Maize (*Z. mays* subsp. *mays*) is the only member of *Zea* that is not a teosinte. *Tripsacum* is the closet wild relative to the genus *Zea*. Paul Mangelsdorf, in the 1930s, suggested that domesticated maize was the result of a hybridization event between an unknown wild maize and *Tripsacum*. However, careful phenotypic studies and genetic analyses have shown that maize is closely related to *Zea mays* subsp. *parviglumis* (Benz 2006; Matsuoka et al. 2002).

2. The radiocarbon and calibrated ages of archaeological periods and phases defined by ceramics can be found in Figure 1.5.

3. Dates listed that fall outside of the two radiocarbon ages are based on extrapolations assuming constant rates of deposition.

REFERENCES CITED

Bartlett, Alexandra S., and Elso S. Barghoorn. 1973. "Phytogeographic History of the Isthmus of Panama during the Past 12,000 Years." In *Vegetation and Vegetational History of Northern Latin America*, ed. Alan K. Graham, 203–94. New York: Elsevier Scientific Publishing Company.

Benz, Bruce F. 2006. "Maize in the Americas." In *Histories of Maize: Multidisciplinary Approaches to the Prehistory, Linguistics, Biogeography, Domestication and Evolution of Maize*, ed. John Staller, Robert Tykot, and Bruce Benz, 9–20. New York: Elsevier Scientific Publishing Company.

Berner, Robert A. 1970. "Sedimentary Pyrite Formation." *American Journal of Science* 268 (1): 1–23. http://dx.doi.org/10.2475/ajs.268.1.1.

Blake, Michael. 2006. "Dating the Initial Spread of *Zea mays*." In *Histories of Maize: Multidisciplinary Approaches to the Prehistory, Linguistics, Biogeography, Domestication and Evolution of Maize*, ed. John Staller, Robert Tykot, and Bruce Benz, 55–72. New York: Elsevier Scientific Publishing Company. http://dx.doi.org/10.1016/B978-012369364-8/50256-4.

Blake, Michael, Brian S. Chisholm, John E. Clark, Barbara Voorhies, and Michael W. Love. 1992. "Prehistoric Subsistence in the Soconusco Region." *Current Anthropology* 33 (1): 83–94. http://dx.doi.org/10.1086/204038.

Byrne, Roger, and Sally Horn. 1989. "Prehistoric Agriculture and Forest Clearance in the Sierra de Los Tuxtlas Veracruz, Mexico." *Palynology* 13 (1): 181–93. http://dx.doi.org/10.1080/01916122.1989.9989360.

Clark, John E. 1991. "The Beginnings of Mesoamerica: Apologia for the Soconusco Early Formative." In *The Formation of Complex Society in Southeastern Mesoamerica*, ed. William R. Fowler Jr., 13–26. Boca Raton, FL: CRC Press.

Coe, Michael D., and Richard A. Diehl. 1980. *In the Land of the Olmec: The Archaeology of San Lorenzo Tenochtitlán*, vol. I. Austin: University of Texas Press.

Contreras, Francisco. 1988. *Las lagunas costeras mexicanas.* 2nd ed. Mexico City: Ecodesarrollo, Secretaria de Pesca.

Deevey, Edward S. 1978. "Holocene Forests and Maya Disturbance near Quexil Lake, Petén, Guatemala." *Polskie Archiwum Hydrobiologii* 25: 117–29.

Delcourt, Paul A., and Hazel R. Delcourt. 1980. "Pollen Preservation and Quaternary Environmental History in the Southeastern United States." *Palynology* 4 (1): 215–31. http://dx.doi.org/10.1080/01916122.1980.9989209.

Doebley, John F. 1984. "Maize Introgression into Teosinte: A Reappraisal." *Annals of the Missouri Botanical Garden* 71 (4): 1100–1112. http://dx.doi.org/10.2307/2399247.

Doebley, John F. 1990. "Molecular Evidence and the Evolution of Maize." In *New Perspectives on the Origin and Evolution of New World Domesticated Plants,* ed. Peter K. Bretting, 6–28. Lawrence, KS: Allen Press. Supplement to *Economic Botany* 44.

Dull, Robert. 2006. "The Maize Revolution: A View from El Salvador." In *Histories of Maize: Multidisciplinary Approaches to the Prehistory, Linguistics, Biogeography, Domestication and Evolution of Maize,* ed. John Staller, Robert Tykot, and Bruce Benz, 357–65. New York: Elsevier Scientific Publishing Company.

Faegri, Knut, and Johannes Iversen. 1989. *Textbook of Pollen Analysis.* New York: John Wiley and Sons.

Fernández, Deepika. 2004. Subsistence in the Lower Río Verde Region, Oaxaca, Mexico: A Zoological Analysis. MA thesis, Department of Archaeology, University of Calgary, Calgary, Alberta.

Flannery, Kent V., ed. 1986. *Guilá Naquitz: Archaic Foraging and Early Agriculture in Oaxaca, Mexico.* New York: Academic Press.

Goman, Michelle, and Roger Byrne. 1998. "A 5000-Year Record of Agriculture and Tropical Forest Clearance in the Tuxtlas, Veracruz, Mexico." *Holocene* 8 (1): 83–89. http://dx.doi.org/10.1191/095968398670396093.

Goman, Michelle, Arthur Joyce, and Raymond Mueller. 2005. "Stratigraphic Evidence for Anthropogenically Induced Coastal Environmental Change from Oaxaca, Mexico." *Quaternary Research* 63 (3): 250–60. http://dx.doi.org/10.1016/j.yqres.20 05.02.008.

Goman, Michelle, Arthur Joyce, Raymond Mueller, and Larissa Paschyn. 2010. "Multiproxy Paleoecological Reconstruction of Prehistoric Land-Use History in the Western Region of the Lower Río Verde Valley, Oaxaca, Mexico." *Holocene* 20 (5): 761–72. http://dx.doi.org/10.1177/0959683610362811.

González-Quintero, Lauro, and Jesús Mora-Echeverría. 1978. "Estudio arqueológico-ecológico de un caso de explotación de recursos litorales en el Pacífico Mexicano." In *Arqueobotánica (Métodos y Aplicaciones),* ed. Fernando Sánchez Martínez, 51–66. Colección Científica, núm. 63. México City: INAH.

Hastorf, Christine. 2009. "Rio Balsas Most Likely Region for Maize Domestication." *Proceedings of the National Academy of Sciences of the United States of America* 106, no. 13 (Mar. 31): 4957–58. http://dx.doi.org/10.1073/pnas.0900935106. Medline:19321745.

Hepp, Guy. 2011. "The Material Culture of Early Sedentism in Coastal Oaxaca: Probable Early Formative Ceramics from La Consentida." Paper presented at the 76th Annual Meeting of the Society for American Archaeology, Sacramento, CA.

Holst, Irene, J. Enrique Moreno, and Dolores R. Piperno. 2007. "Identification of teosinte, maize, and Tripsacum in Mesoamerica by using pollen, starch grains, and
phytoliths." *Proceedings of the National Academy of Sciences of the United States of
America* 104, no. 45 (Nov. 6): 17608–13. http://dx.doi.org/10.1073/pnas.0708736104.
Medline:17978176.

Horn, Sally. 2006. "Pre-Columbian Maize Agriculture in Costa Rica, Pollen and Other
Evidence from Lake and Swamp Sediments." In *Histories of Maize: Multidisciplinary
Approaches to the Prehistory, Linguistics, Biogeography, Domestication and Evolution of
Maize*, ed. John Staller, Robert Tykot, and Bruce Benz, 367–80. New York: Elsevier
Scientific Publishing Company.

Iltis, Hugh H. 1983. "From Teosinte to Maize: The Catastrophic Sexual Transmutation."
Science 222, no. 4626 (Nov. 25): 886–94. http://dx.doi.org/10.1126/science.222.46
26.886. Medline:17738466.

Jones, John G. 1994. "Pollen Evidence for Early Settlement and Agriculture in Northern Belize." *Palynology* 18 (1): 205–211. http://dx.doi.org/10.1080/01916122.1994.99
89445.

Jones, John G., and Barbara Voorhies. 2004. "Human and Plant Interactions." In *Coastal
Collectors in the Holocene: The Chantuto People of Southwest Mexico*, ed. Barbara Voorhies, 300–343. Gainesville: University Press of Florida.

Joyce, Arthur A. 1991a. *Formative Period Occupation in the Lower Río Verde Valley, Oaxaca,
Mexico: Interregional Interaction and Social Change*. PhD dissertation, Department
of Anthropology, Rutgers University, New Brunswick, NJ. Ann Arbor, MI: University Microfilms.

Joyce, Arthur A. 1991b. "Formative Period Social Change in the Lower Río Verde
Valley, Oaxaca, Mexico." *Latin American Antiquity* 2 (2): 126–50. http://dx.doi.org
/10.2307/972274.

Joyce, Arthur A. 2005. "La arqueología del bajo Río Verde." *Acervos* 7 (29): 16–36.

Joyce, Arthur A. 2010. *Mixtecs, Zapotecs, and Chatinos: Ancient Peoples of Southern Mexico*.
Malden, MA: Wiley-Blackwell Press.

Joyce, Arthur A., and Raymond Mueller. 1992. "The Social Impact of Anthropogenic
Landscape Modification in the Río Verde Drainage Basin, Oaxaca, Mexico." *Geoarchaeology* 7 (6): 503–26. http://dx.doi.org/10.1002/gea.3340070602.

Joyce, Arthur A., and Raymond G. Mueller. 1997. "Prehispanic Human Ecology of the
Río Verde Drainage Basin, Mexico." *World Archaeology* 29 (1): 75–94. http://dx.doi.
org/10.1080/00438243.1997.9980364.

Joyce, Arthur A., Maxine Oland, and Peter Kroefges. 2009. Recorrido regional de
superficie. In "El proyecto Río Verde," ed. Arthur A. Joyce and Marc N. Levine,
322–53. Final report submitted to the Consejo de Arqueología, Instituto Nacional
de Antropología e Historia, Mexico City.

Joyce, Arthur A., Marcus Winter, and Raymond G. Mueller. 1998. *Arqueología de la costa
de Oaxaca: Asentamientos del periodo formativo en el valle del Río Verde inferior*. Estudios de Antropología e Historia No. 40. Oaxaca: Centro INAH Oaxaca.

Joyce, Arthur A., Andrew Workinger, Scott Hutson, Stacie King, Neil Ross, Michael
Swanton, Karolo Aparicio, Brant Schwartz, Brigham Golden, Billiana Miteva,
Matthew Dudgeon, and Nicole Falcoust. 1999. Recorrido regional de superficie.
In "El proyecto patrones de asentamiento del Río Verde," ed. Arthur A. Joyce,

5–36. Final report submitted to the Consejo de Arqueología, Instituto Nacional de Antropología e Historia, Mexico City.

Kennett, Douglas J., Dolores Piperno, John G. Jones, Hector Neff, Barbara Voorhies, Megan Walsh, and Brendan J. Culleton. 2010. "Pre-Pottery Farmers on the Pacific Coast of Southern Mexico." *Journal of Archaeological Science* 37 (12): 3401–11. http://dx.doi.org/10.1016/j.jas.2010.07.035.

Kennett, Douglas J., Barbara Voorhies, José Iriate, John G. Jones, Dolores Piperno, María Teresa Ramírez Herrera, and Thomas A. Wake. 2004. "Avances en el proyecto Arcaico-Formativo: Costa de Guerrero." Report submitted to the Consejo de Arqueología, Instituto Nacional de Antropología e Historia, Mexico City.

Lankford, Robert R. 1977. "Coastal Lagoons of Mexico: Their Origin and Classification." In *Estuarine Processes*, ed. Martin L. Wiley, 182–215. New York: Estuarine Research Federation, Academic Press.

Leyden, Barbara W. 2002. "Pollen Evidence for Climatic Variability and Cultural Disturbance in the Maya Lowlands." *Ancient Mesoamerica* 13 (1): 85–101. http://dx.doi.org/10.1017/S0956536102131099.

Long, Austin, Bruce F. Benz, Douglas J. Donahue, A. J. Timothy Jull, and Laurence J. Toolin. 1989. "First Direct AMS Dates on Early Maize from Tehuacán, Mexico." *Radiocarbon* 31 (3): 1035–40.

Lozano-García, María, and Enrique Martínez Hernández. 1990. *Palinología de los Tuxtlas: Especies arbóreas.* UNAM Publicaciones Especiales No. 3. Mexico City: Instituto de Biología.

MacNeish, Richard S., and Mary W. Eubanks. 2000. "Comparative Analysis of the Río Balsas and Tehuacán Models for the Origin of Maize." *Latin American Antiquity* 11 (1): 3–20. http://dx.doi.org/10.2307/1571668.

Mangelsdorf, Paul C., Richard S. MacNeish, and Walton C. Galinat. 1967. "Prehistoric Wild and Cultivated Maize." In *Prehistory of the Tehuacán Valley*, vol. 1, ed. Douglas Byers, 178–200. Austin: University of Texas Press.

Matsuoka, Yoshihiro, Yves Vigouroux, Major Goodman, J. Sanchez G., Edward Buckler, and John Doebley. 2002. "A Single Domestication for Maize Shown by Multilocus Microsatellite Genotyping." *Proceedings of the National Academy of Sciences of the United States of America* 99, no. 9 (Apr. 30): 6080–4. http://dx.doi.org/10.1073/pnas.052125199. Medline:11983901.

Mueller, Raymond G., Arthur A. Joyce, and Aleksander Borejsza. 2012. "Alluvial Archives of the Nochixtlán Valley, Oaxaca, Mexico: Age and Significance for Reconstructions of Environmental Change." *Palaeogeography, Palaeoclimatology, Palaeoecology* 321–322 (2012): 121–136.

Neff, Hector, Deborah M. Pearsall, John G. Jones, Bárbara Arroyo, Shawn K. Collins, and Dorothy E. Freidel. 2006. "Early Maya Adaptive Patterns: Mid-Late Holocene Paleoenvironmental Evidence from Pacific Guatemala." *Latin American Antiquity* 17 (3): 287–315. http://dx.doi.org/10.2307/25063054.

Nowaczyk, Norbert R. 2001. "Logging of Magnetic Susceptibility." In *Tracking Environmental Change Using Lake Sediments*, Volume 1: *Basin Analysis, Coring, and Chronological Techniques*, ed. William M. Last and John P. Smol, 155–70. Dordrecht, The Netherlands: Kluwer Academic Publishers.

Patterson, William A., III, Kevin J. Edwards, and David J. Maguire. 1987. "Microscopic Charcoal as a Fossil Indicator of Fire." *Quaternary Science Reviews* 6 (1): 3–23. http://dx.doi.org/10.1016/0277-3791(87)90012-6.

Piperno, Dolores R. 2006a. "Quaternary Environmental History and Agricultural Impact on Vegetation in Central America." *Annals of the Missouri Botanical Garden* 93 (2): 274–96. http://dx.doi.org/10.3417/0026-6493(2006)93[274:QEHAAI]2.0.CO;2.

Piperno, Dolores R. 2006b. "The Origin of Plant Cultivation and Domestication in the Neotropics." In *Behavioral Ecology and the Transition to Agriculture*, ed. Douglas J. Kennett and Bruce Winterhalder, 137–66. Berkeley: University of California Press.

Piperno, Dolores R., and Kent V. Flannery. 2001. "The Earliest Archaeological Maize (*Zea mays* L.) from Highland Mexico: New Accelerator Mass Spectrometry Dates and Their Implications." *Proceedings of the National Academy of Sciences of the United States of America* 98 , no. 4 (Feb. 13): 2101–3. http://dx.doi.org/10.1073/pnas.98.4.2101. Medline:11172082.

Piperno, Dolores R., Jorge E. Moreno, Jose Iriarte, Irene Holst, Matthew Lachniet, John G. Jones, Anthony J. Ranere, and Ronald Castanzo. 2007. "Late Pleistocene and Holocene Environmental History of the Iguala Valley, Central Balsas Watershed of Mexico." *Proceedings of the National Academy of Sciences of the United States of America* 104, no. 29 (Jul. 17): 11874–81. http://dx.doi.org/10.1073/pnas.0703442104. Medline:17537917.

Piperno, Dolores R., Anthony J. Ranere, Irene Holst, Jose Iriarte, and R. Dickau. 2009. "Starch Grain and Phytolith Evidence for Early Ninth Millennium B.P. Maize from the Central Balsas River Valley, Mexico." *Proceedings of the National Academy of Sciences of the United States of America* 106, no. 13 (Mar. 31): 5019–24. http://dx.doi.org/10.1073/pnas.0812525106. Medline:19307570.

Pohl, Mary E., Dolores R. Piperno, Kevin O. Pope, and John G. Jones. 2007. "Microfossil Evidence for Pre-Columbian Maize Dispersals in the Neotropics from San Andres, Tabasco, Mexico." *Proceedings of the National Academy of Sciences of the United States of America* 104, no. 16 (Apr. 17): 6870–75. http://dx.doi.org/10.1073/pnas.0701425104. Medline:17426147.

Pope, Kevin, Mary E. Pohl, John G. Jones, David L. Lentz, Christopher von Nagy, Francisco J. Vega, and Irvy Quitmyer. 2001. "Origin and Environmental Setting of Ancient Agriculture in the Lowlands of Mesoamerica." *Science* 292, no. 5520 (May 18): 1370–73. http://dx.doi.org/10.1126/science.292.5520.1370. Medline:11359011.

Ranere, Anthony J., Dolores R. Piperno, Irene Holst, Ruth Dickau, and José Iriarte. 2009. "The Cultural and Chronological Context of Early Holocene Maize and Squash Domestication in the Central Balsas River Valley, Mexico." *Proceedings of the National Academy of Sciences of the United States of America* 106, no. 13 (Mar. 31): 5014–18. http://dx.doi.org/10.1073/pnas.0812590106. Medline:19307573.

Raynor, Gilbert S., Eugene C. Ogden, and Janet V. Hayes. 1972. "Dispersion and Deposition of Corn Pollen from Experimental Sources." *Agronomy Journal* 64 (4): 420–27. http://dx.doi.org/10.2134/agronj1972.00021962006400040004x.

Sluyter, Andrew. 1997. "Regional, Holocene Records of the Human Dimension of Global Change: Sea-Level and Land-Use Change in Prehistoric Mexico." *Global and Planetary Change* 14 (3–4): 127–46. http://dx.doi.org/10.1016/S0921-8181(96)00007-0.

Sluyter, Andrew, and Gabriela Dominguez. 2006. "Early Maize (*Zea mays* L.) Cultivation in Mexico: Dating Sedimentary Pollen Records and Its Implications." *Proceedings of the National Academy of Sciences of the United States of America* 103, no. 4 (Jan. 24): 1147–51. http://dx.doi.org/10.1073/pnas.0510473103. Medline:16418287.

Smith, C. Earle. 1967. "Plant Remains." In *The Prehistory of the Tehuacán Valley: Environment and Subsistence*, ed. Douglas S. Byers, 220–55. Austin: University of Texas Press.

Smith, C. Earle. 1986. "Preceramic Plant Remains from Guilá Naquitz." In *Guilá Naquitz: Archaic Foraging and Early Agriculture in Oaxaca, Mexico*, ed. Kent V. Flannery, 265–74. New York: Academic Press.

Stockmarr, Jens. 1971. "Tablets with Spores Used in Absolute Pollen Analysis." *Pollen et Spores* 8: 615–21.

Taylor, Sarah R., Arthur A. Joyce, Mathew Sponheimer, and Sarah B. Barber. 2009. Dieta y agricultura en el valle del Río Verde inferior: Basado en análisis de microdesgaste dental e isótopos estables. In "Estudios alimenticios y de ADN de dientes humanos del valle del Río Verde inferior, Oaxaca, México," ed. Arthur A. Joyce, 3–31. Report submitted to the Consejo de Arqueología, Instituto Nacional de Antropología e Historia, Mexico City.

VanDerwarker, Amber M. 2006. *Farming, Hunting, and Fishing in the Olmec World*. Austin: University of Texas Press.

Voorhies, Barbara, ed. 2004. *Coastal Collectors in the Holocene: The Chantuto People of Southwest Mexico*. Gainesville: University Press of Florida.

Voorhies, Barbara, George H. Michaels, and George M. Riser. 1991. "An Ancient Shrimp Fishery in South Coastal Mexico." *National Geographic Research and Exploration* 7 (1): 20–35.

Winter, Marcus. N.d. "Excavaciones en La Consentida, 1988." Manuscript in possession of the author.

Wooller, Matthew J. 2002. "Grass Cuticles from Lacustrine Sediments: A Review of Methods Applicable to the Analysis of Tropical African Lake Cores." *Holocene* 12 (1): 97–105. http://dx.doi.org/10.1191/0959683602hl524rr.

Woodard, S. Justine. 1991. "Appendix 3: Paleobotanical Study Río Verde Formative Project." In *Formative Period Occupation in the Lower Río Verde Valley, Oaxaca, Mexico: Interregional Interaction and Social Change*, by Arthur A. Joyce, 840–82. PhD dissertation, Department of Anthropology, Rutgers University, New Brunswick, NJ. Ann Arbor, MI: University Microfilms.

Workinger, Andrew. 2002. *Coastal/Highland Interaction in Prehispanic Oaxaca, Mexico: The Perspective from San Francisco de Arriba*. PhD dissertation, Department of Anthropology, Vanderbilt University, Nashville, TN. Ann Arbor, MI: University Microfilms.

THREE

ANTHROPOGENIC LANDSCAPE CHANGE AND THE HUMAN ECOLOGY OF THE LOWER RÍO VERDE VALLEY

Raymond G. Mueller, Arthur A. Joyce, Aleksander Borejsza, and Michelle Goman

Environmental degradation caused by human land use is often viewed as a problem of the modern industrial age. Recent research in Europe, the Near East, and Mesoamerica, however, has yielded evidence for anthropogenic landscape change dating back thousands of years (Redman 1999). In Mesoamerica evidence of land clearance for agriculture is present in lake and estuarine cores since the mid-Holocene (Dunning et al. 2002; Kennett et al. 2010; Lesure 2008; Neff et al. 2006; Piperno et al. 2007), with increasingly significant ecological changes triggered by agricultural practices accompanying the growth of large sedentary populations in the first millennium BC (e.g., Borejsza et al. 2011; Dunning et al. 2002; Heine 2003; Metcalfe et al. 1989; Park et al. 2010; Velez et al. 2011). Research indicates significant land degradation and a reduction in soil fertility in some regions. In many of them the large-scale development of soil and water conservation technologies, especially terraces, seems to have been spurred by prior anthropogenic erosion (Borejsza et al. 2008; Córdova and Parsons 1997; Dunning and Beach 1994; Fisher et al. 2003; Flannery 1983; Kirkby 1972; Spores 1969). Land degradation has been implicated in major cultural changes in Mesoamerica, especially the collapse of Classic Maya polities in the ninth and tenth centuries AD (Aimers 2007: Table 1).

DOI: 10.5876/9781607322023.c03

Despite the increasing research focus on human impact, debate continues over the timing and nature of anthropogenic landscape change and its effects on prehispanic peoples (e.g., Fisher 2005; Metcalfe et al. 2007). In this chapter we discuss and update the results of long-term interdisciplinary research on the environmental and social effects of anthropogenic landscape change in the Río Verde drainage basin in the southern Mexican highlands and coast of Oaxaca. Our research involves an interdisciplinary collaboration of archaeologists, geologists, and paleoecologists designed to examine anthropogenic landscape change and its impact on human populations along the Río Verde.

The majority of research on prehispanic human impact on the environment has focused on landscape degradation resulting from local land use. Our research is different in that we take a macroregional perspective by examining the effects of prehispanic agriculture in the upper drainage basin of the Verde on people and environments in the lower valley more than 150 km downstream (Goman et al. 2005, 2010, Chapter 2; Joyce 1991a, 1991b; Joyce and Mueller 1992, 1997; Joyce et al. 1998; Mueller and Joyce 2007; Mueller et al. 2012; Mueller and Pou 2008). Previous interdisciplinary projects indicated that erosion in the highlands triggered ecological changes in the lowlands, including a modification of stream channel dynamics that resulted in alluviation and expansion of the lower Verde's floodplain. Although the causes of highland erosion are difficult to untangle, settlement and land use data as well as geomorphological research point to human impact as a likely contributor. We hypothesized that the expansion of the lower Verde's floodplain (Joyce and Mueller 1992), as well as related changes in coastal landforms (Goman et al. 2005), could have significantly affected the abundance and distribution of resources available to human populations. This chapter discusses recent geomorphological research that clarifies the chronology of environmental change in the lower valley as well as archaeological evidence suggesting possible effects on human populations. First we review the physiographic properties of the drainage basin and summarize research on the history of natural and anthropogenic erosion in the highland valleys of the upper drainage basin. We then consider how highland erosion affected environments and people in the lower valley. The geomorphological research complements recent paleoecological studies (Goman et al. 2005, 2010, Chapter 2) that together contribute to a complex model of the macroregional effects of prehispanic anthropogenic landscape change.

THE RÍO VERDE FLUVIAL SYSTEM

The Río Verde is one of the largest rivers on the Pacific coast of Mesoamerica in terms of both drainage area and discharge (Álvarez 2003; Tamayo 1964; Figure 3.1). The upper drainage basin of the Verde, which is the major zone of sediment production, consists largely of the Valley of Oaxaca and the Nochixtlán

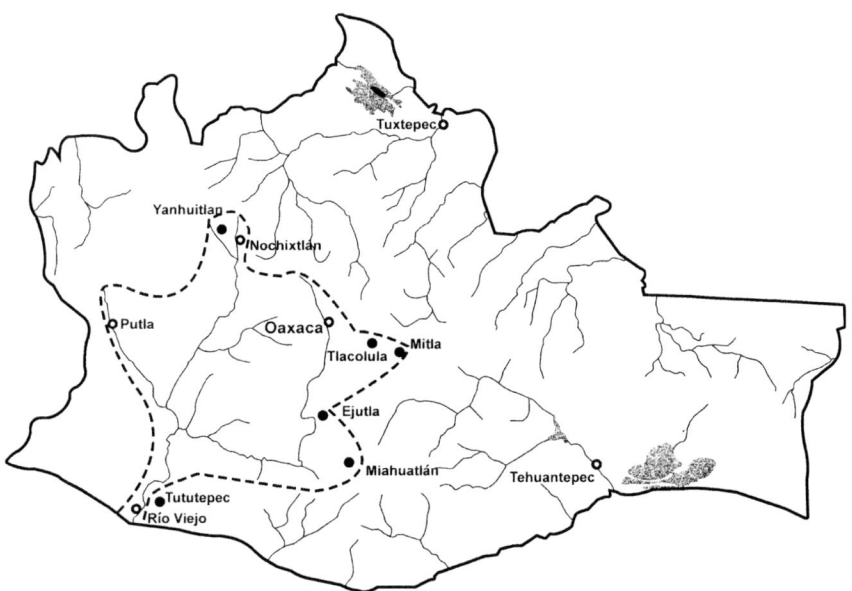

FIGURE 3.1. Map of the Río Verde drainage basin, Oaxaca.

Valley. The Valley of Oaxaca lies at an elevation of 1500 to 1700 m above sea level, while the Nochixtlán Valley varies from 2000 to 2500 m. Mean annual temperature in the highland valleys is about 16 to 20°C and average annual rainfall, which is strongly seasonal, varies from about 600 to 1000 mm. The lower Río Verde Valley is the major zone of deposition for the drainage system. The coastal climate is hot and humid with mean temperatures ranging from 25 to 28° C and mean annual rainfall between 1000 and 2000 mm near sea level (Rodríguez et al. 1989).

Intervening sections of the drainage basin that link the highland and low-land valleys pass through the Sierra Madre del Sur in narrow, deep canyons with steep gradients. This means that the Verde system has little opportunity for depositing the sediment exported from the highland valleys until the stream gradient decreases near the coast. Even within that coastal reach, the valley quickly narrows in the upstream direction (Figure 3.2). Topographic cross sections from the present channel to an absolute elevation of 200 m above sea level were made for three locations along the lower Río Verde. At Río Viejo, 15 km along the river from the coast, the floodplain has a width of 6 km. The floodplain widens considerably just below this point. At Piedra Blanca, only 35 km from the coast, the floodplain has already narrowed to slightly over 1 km in width. At Paso de la Reyna, 50 km from the coast the floodplain has narrowed to less than 1 km in width. The physiographic characteristics of the drainage basin thus mean that environments in the lower valley are sensitive

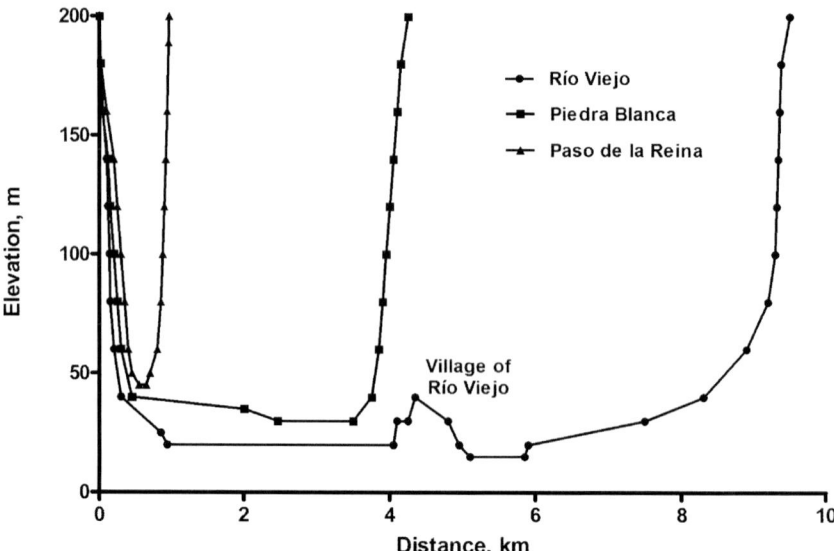

FIGURE 3.2. Topographic cross sections of the Río Verde at Río Viejo, Piedra Blanca, and Paso de la Reyna showing the width of the floodplain and channel elevation.

to changes in geomorphic variables in the highland valleys, especially sediment production (Bridge 2003; Schumm 1977, 1981; Strahler 1980).

In the early stages of our research we attempted in vain to find a spatially more proximate reason for the channel modifications observed in the local stratigraphic record. Despite the proximity of the coast, we are reasonably confident that base-level changes due to fluctuations in relative sea levels were insignificant within the time frame of documented human occupation of the area. Holocene sea levels are estimated to have stabilized by 4000 BC in neighboring Chiapas (Voorhies 2004) and to the north in Nayarit (Curray et al. 1969), and there are no local landforms in Oaxaca to suggest otherwise. Neither are we aware of any geologically recent tectonic deformation of the lower or middle reaches of the system that would be of a magnitude sufficient to transform the sedimentation style of the river. Thus, we have gradually shifted our attention to the possibility that land-use patterns in the Oaxaca and Nochixtlán valleys had a significant impact on landforms and hydrology in the lower Río Verde Valley.

EVIDENCE FOR HIGHLAND EROSION

We have carried out geomorphological research in the upper drainage basin of the Río Verde designed to investigate periods of highland erosion that could have triggered environmental changes in the lower valley (Joyce and Mueller 1992, 1997; Mueller et al. 2012; Mueller and Pou 2008). In the highlands we took advantage of the fact that most streams have deeply incised channels that expose long stratigraphic sequences. Only limited auger coring is thus required. Our research has involved the study of sequences exposed along such reaches in the Nochixtlán, Oaxaca, and Ejutla valleys. We have focused on the Nochixtlán Valley, given the great lateral extent of current stream incision, the great thickness of late Quaternary alluvial sequences, as well as the presence of several generations of erosional landforms on the slopes.

In Nochixtlán we have examined stratigraphic exposures along the Ríos Grande, Yanhuitlán and Yucuita, and their tributaries. Well over 100 km of stream courses were surveyed, and forty-one locations were examined in detail and described. The most numerous alluvial sequences of Holocene age consist of vertically stacked overbank deposits. These may be separated into discrete units by erosional unconformities and by paleosols that mark periods of relative floodplain stability. Many paleosols are very weakly developed and circumscribed to short reaches of the fluvial system. They cannot be used to make inferences about drainage-wide environmental change, but in view of their short residence times, they provide excellent targets for radiocarbon dating. Others show signs of more advanced structural development and horizon differentiation, particularly in the form of coats of translocated clay (argillans) and secondary carbonates. The A horizons of both types of paleosols provided the samples for the thirty-eight radiocarbon assays on which our alluvial chronology for Nochixtlán rests at the moment. Samples were also collected for soil geochemistry as well as phytolith and isotopic studies, which are currently under way.

The results of our research in Nochixtlán, coupled with previous and ongoing studies concerned with environmental change (Cook 1949; Kirkby 1972; Pérez et al. 2011; Smith 1976; Spores 1969) as well as demography and land use (e.g., Balkansky et al. 2000; Kowalewski et al. 2009; Spores 1972, 1974), allow us to summarize valley-wide trends that could have had significant effects on the behavior of the entire fluvial system of the Río Verde. Causal factors are still difficult to disentangle, and we are certainly not in a position to quantify sediment transfers through the system at different times in the past, but prehispanic human impacts in Nochixtlán can be relatively well documented (see Figure 1.5 for ceramic periodizations for both the lower Río Verde and the Mixteca Alta, which encompasses the Nochixtlán Valley).

At present we condense and simplify the complex alluvial stratigraphic record of the Nochixtlán Valley into six cycles of aggradation, separated by widespread incision events. We refer to them as fill cycles numbered 0 through 5, whereby 0 corresponds to the modern floodplains. Each cycle reflects the cumulative effect of hillslope erosion and, to a lesser extent, the reworking of alluvium previously stored upstream. Cycle 5 is likely very ancient and has not yet been dated. Cycle 4 precedes a period of stream incision at ca. 10,200 BC and thus predates any evidence of human presence known from Oaxaca (Flannery 1986; Flannery and Spores 1983; Joyce 2010). Cycle 3, initiated by this incision, began with the formation of rather peculiar soils that hint at the alternation of contrasting climatic conditions during the last stages of the North American deglaciation. They roughly correspond to the Paleoindian period, the end of which in Oaxaca is usually put at ca. 8000 BC. No sites of this period have yet been discovered in Nochixtlán.

The stratigraphy of the remainder of fill cycle 3 suggests a shift toward relatively warm and semiarid Holocene climates similar to those of today. This time span corresponds to most of the Archaic (8000–1600 BC). Archaeological evidence from this period suggests that population densities in the highlands were low (Flannery 1986; Flannery and Spores 1983; Winter et al. 2008). People were forager-farmers living in small, mobile groups. They were still experimenting with horticulture, and domesticates probably constituted only a small proportion of the diet. Only two Archaic period sites have been discovered in Nochixtlán (Lorenzo 1958; Mueller and Joyce 2004), both of which were exposed in the river cuts. These data lead us to conclude that anthropogenic slope erosion must have been very limited. The deposits of cycle 3 account for a major portion of the alluvium stored in the valley to this day. This suggests that the mid-Holocene climate did not allow the development of a vegetation cover dense enough to stem natural slope erosion, and that sediment delivery to the streams was significant well before the advent of sedentary agriculture, contrary to some previous interpretations. On the other hand, the large volume of cycle 3 alluvium in Nochixtlán may mean that stream discharge was insufficient to export it farther downstream.

The incision separating fill cycles 3 and 2 seems to have propagated gradually up the fluvial system of the Nochixtlán Valley between 3200 and 1700 BC. It is not yet clear what triggered it. Cycle 2 lasted until ca. AD 1100 and thus encompasses the entire Formative period as well as the Las Flores phase (AD 300–800). The Cruz A and B phases in the Nochixtlán Valley (1500–850 BC) mark the period of initial sedentism as well as population growth and an increasing commitment to agriculture as a subsistence strategy (Blomster 2004; Spores 1984, 18–19; Winter 1989a). For instance, during Cruz A (1500–1150 BC), the site of Yucuita grew to a village covering perhaps 20 ha with a population estimated at 200 (Winter 1982, 10; 1984, 188), although most communities were in the 1 to 3 ha range with perhaps a few dozen people (Spores 1972). Throughout the highlands of Oaxaca the earliest Formative communities were usually located on low piedmont spurs adjacent to humid, agriculturally productive land on the valley floors, which was probably the focus of agriculture (Joyce 2010, 70–104). By the Ramos phase (300 BC–AD 300), early urban centers were coalescing in the Nochixtlán Valley (see Figure 1.1), including Yucuita, Etlatongo, Monte Negro, and Cerro Jazmín (Joyce 2010, 160–179; Kowalewski et al. 2009; Pérez et al. 2011). All of the early urban centers were located on the tops of hills or mountains, and their location promoted the agricultural colonization of the low and middle piedmont (see Marcus and Flannery 1996, 146–147). Archaeological surveys suggest a doubling of population in the Nochixtlán Valley between the Cruz and Ramos phases (Spores 1972). Population growth and agricultural expansion resumed in the Las Flores phase, during which the number of sites tripled with respect to the Ramos phase.

Several of the described shifts in settlement patterns are of a kind that one would expect to accelerate hillslope erosion and sediment delivery to streams. Land clearance in the vicinity of the earliest villages would have made the soil more erodible, even in areas of relatively low relief. Shifts to higher elevations and higher slope gradients would have involved taking under cultivation progressively more marginal soils and extending the range of lands exploited for fuelwood. The gullying of slopes unprotected by vegetation would have increased drainage density (Kirkby 1972) and thus augmented both sediment delivery to the trunk streams and their peak discharges. There is some archaeological evidence that the inhabitants of the Nochixtlán Valley attempted to actively manage these transfers of water and sediment from a very early stage. In several cuts we observed remnants of the retaining walls of cross-channel terraces, in stratigraphic positions that suggest an age between the Cruz and Las Flores phases. The dating of paleosols associated with one such wall placed its construction and use between 890 and 780 BC. This would be the earliest stratigraphically constrained example of the so-called *lama-bordo* systems, which consist of long flights of stone and rubble-faced cross-channel terraces that trap sediment and slow the flow of water (Flannery 1983, 330–331; Pérez 2006; Spores 1969, 561–564; Figure 3.3). Based on survey evidence, Kowalewski and colleagues (2009, 290) also suggest that *lama-bordos* may have begun as early as Cruz D (700–500 BC). Their later proliferation may have been a form of adaptation to anthropogenic erosion (Joyce and Mueller 1997; Kirkby 1972; Kowalewski et al. 2009, 300; Spores 1969). The development and function of hillside terracing is more difficult to document archaeologically. Again, in the near absence of stratigraphic evidence, we can only speculate on the basis of settlement surveys that they began to be built in large numbers at least as early as the Ramos phase. In sum, we believe that by the end of the Formative, the Nochixtlán Valley and probably other valleys in the Oaxacan highlands had already become anthropogenic landscapes characterized by dense urban settlements surrounded by rural communities with farm fields on the valley floors, and residential as well as agricultural terraces covering many hillslopes.

We would imagine that the general impact of this transformation on the fluvial system would have been to increase the flux of water and sediment

FIGURE 3.3. *Lama-bordo* terrace system in the Nochixtlán Valley. Reprinted from Mueller et al. 2012: Figure 7, with permission from Elsevier).

(Joyce and Mueller 1997, 83). It would have been accelerated not only by higher rates of sediment delivery from the slopes, but also by more rapid runoff from bare or eroded slopes and by repeated failures of both hillslope and cross-channel terraces. The stratigraphic record contains several hints that these processes were indeed operating. The alluvium of fill cycle 2 is on average coarser-grained than that of cycle 3, while the paleosols are fewer, less developed, and separated by thicker packets of sediment with no signs of pedogenic modification. All of these can be taken as indicators of higher stream energy and a faster pace of floodplain aggradation. Charcoal is also noticeably more common, and likely derived from farming activities. In comparison to the fill of cycle 3, that of cycle 2 is less commonly preserved along the stream reaches surveyed, and extremely fragmented. This may be due to several factors, among which we would like to stress two. One possibility is that many reaches, especially those in headwater areas, actually underwent more than one cut-and-fill cycle in the time span of cycle 2 of our synthetic scheme. This would have been the case, for example, if short-term local changes in land use forced the repeated collapse and rebuilding of *lama-bordos*. The other possible explanation of the relative scarcity of cycle 2 sediment is that most of what was delivered to streams ended up being carried beyond the Nochixtlán Valley.

Returning to the strictly archaeological record, the end of fill cycle 2 coincides with the social upheaval and population decline that accompanied the collapse of Classic-period cities and ruling dynasties after ca. AD 800 (Joyce 2010; Kowalewski et al. 2009; Spores 1984; Winter 1989a). Unfortunately, difficulties with identifying diagnostic ceramics have meant that throughout highland Oaxaca this period is not well understood and has been the focus of considerable debate (Marcus and Flannery 1990; Markens 2004, 2008; Martínez López et al. 2000; Winter 1989b). It seems likely, however, that it involved a degree of political unrest and fragmentation as well as population loss (Kowalewski et al. 2009, 345–346; Winter 1989b). If this led to a neglect in the maintenance of terraces, then a major pulse of sediment could have been generated by the failure of retaining walls and gullying of terrace fills. A shift toward more arid climatic conditions has been documented in other parts of Mesoamerica (Curtis et al. 1996; Hodell et al. 2005; Metcalfe and Davies 2007) at this time, which makes the assessment of causality an even more daunting task.

All we can affirm at the moment is that some of the coarsest and thickest alluvial packets were deposited at roughly that time, followed by the incision that ends fill cycle 2. What is most remarkable is that the incision was propagated all the way to the lowest-order tributaries within a very short window of time between AD 1000 and 1150. This in itself implies (like any incision event) that an enormous volume of previously stored alluvium was exported out of the Nochixtlán Valley. Fill cycle 1 and the incision that created the modern floodplains encompass the apogee of population density of the later Natividad phase (see Pérez et al. 2011) and the profound demographic and economic upheavals that followed the Conquest, but our field knowledge and chronological control of the relevant deposits are too fragmentary to merit discussion in this chapter.

Even though additional research is obviously needed to refine our understanding of the timing, magnitude, and causes of geomorphic change, we can affirm with a reasonable degree of confidence that large volumes of sediment were being exported from Nochixtlán toward the middle and lower reaches of the Río Verde as early as the Formative period, and that the process was driven in large measure by the land use strategies implemented by sedentary farmers. Limited data from the valleys of Oaxaca and Ejutla point to a similar pattern (Joyce and Mueller 1997). In the next section we consider how all of this would have affected environments in the lower valley and present new evidence clarifying the timing of major changes there.

LANDSCAPE CHANGE IN THE LOWER VALLEY

Given the physiographic characteristics of the drainage basin discussed above, we hypothesized that anthropogenic erosion in the highland valleys could have

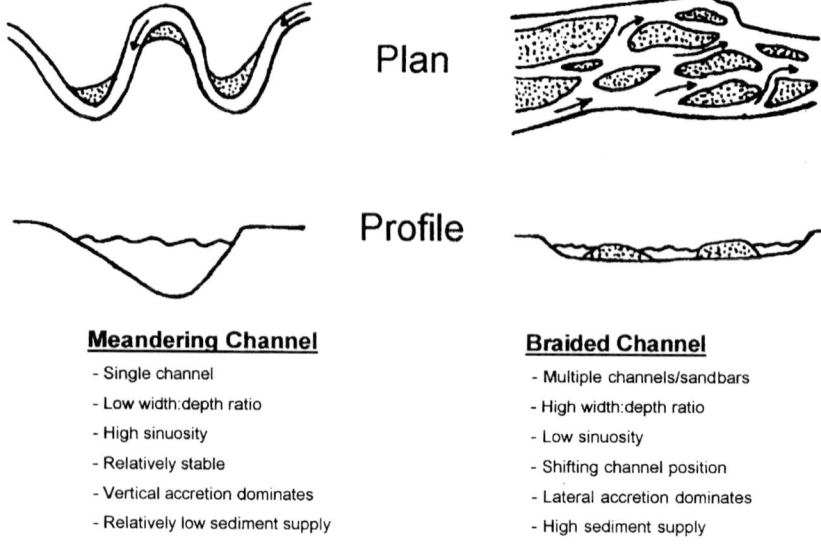

FIGURE 3.4. Common attributes of meandering and braided river channels (after Joyce and Mueller 1997: Figure 5; reprinted by permission of the publisher, Taylor & Francis Ltd.: http://www.tandf.co.uk/journals).

triggered significant environmental changes in the lowlands (Joyce 1991b; Joyce and Mueller 1992, 1997; Joyce et al. 1998; Mueller 1991). An increase in sediment load and discharge leaving the upper basin would be felt as far as the lowermost reach of the Río Verde. Discharge, which increased in the highlands because of higher drainage density and higher rates of runoff from eroded slopes, would be the parameter most rapidly transferred to the lower valley (see Blum 2007, 633). The increase would be expressed in the values of both mean and peak discharge, and would thus also augment the seasonal range of discharge. The larger sediment loads would also gradually reach the lower valley, promoting higher rates of deposition across the floodplain. The coupled effects of higher discharge and sediment supply from upstream would result in the deposition of larger-grained alluvium and more severe rainy-season flooding. Larger floods would spread sediment over a wider area, thereby expanding the active flood-plain. If the magnitude of change exceeded geomorphic thresholds controlling channel morphology, we would eventually expect to see a shift from a more meandering to a more braided pattern (Bridge 2003, 141–219; Knighton 1998, 205–36; Knox 1977; Nelson 1966; Figure 3.4). This would involve a decrease in channel sinuosity and an increase in its width-depth ratio. Braided channels also tend to be less stable than meandering ones and migrate across floodplains at a greater rate (Eaton et al. 2010).

Our geomorphological research has yielded several lines of stratigraphic evidence that conforms to the scenario hypothesized above (Goman et al. 2005; Joyce 1991a, 1991b; Joyce and Mueller 1992, 1997; Joyce et al. 1998; Mueller 1991, Mueller et al. 1999). Fieldwork included the excavation of transects of auger cores and test pits across the floodplain, the collection of stratigraphic data from archaeological excavations, the coring of wetlands in coastal estuaries, and sampling of surface sediments. The subsurface testing of the Río Verde floodplain distinguished three general sediment types indicative of different depositional environments: (1) lateral accretion deposits consisting of coarse multimineral sands resulting from high-energy deposition within the river channel; (2) vertical accretion deposits consisting of fine silts, clayey silts, and silty clays resulting from moderate- to low-energy overbank deposition; and (3) lacustrine deposits resulting from low-energy deposition of dense organic-rich clays within oxbow ponds. For radiocarbon dating we targeted contexts in which sediments of Type 3 overlay those of Type 1. In this situation the date is assumed to approximate the moment when a lateral channel shift turned the former thalweg into an oxbow or backswamp with no channelized flow. The date thus provides a minimum age for the channel in its active phase. The distribution and stratigraphic relationships of the three sediment types across the floodplain and their association with abandoned channels visible in air photos and on the surface allowed us to distinguish two distinct depositional regimes during the Holocene in the lower Río Verde Valley.

The best example of the earlier depositional regime is a meandering channel, designated C.1, which runs along the western edge of the floodplain up to 5.5 km from the present position of the river (Figure 3.5). Auger cores extracted from C.1 adjacent to the archaeological site of Loma Reyes show that, following its abandonment, this reach of the channel became an oxbow pond that gradually filled with dense lacustrine clays (Figure 3.6). The lower contact of the clay clearly outlined the cross section of the channel, which is 8 m deep and 405 m wide, consistent with a meandering pattern. Samples from the base of the clay, immediately above channel sands, yielded radiocarbon dates of 4427 and 4240 BC for the time of abandonment of the channel (see Table 3.1 for uncalibrated and calibrated dates and ranges for all lower Río Verde Valley radiocarbon dates discussed in this chapter). A date obtained farther up one of the cores indicates that the oxbow was not infilled until after 1372 BC.

The different channels to the east of C.1 correspond to the more recent depositional regime. They generally have surface and subsurface characteristics indicating a higher width-depth ratio than C.1, closer to that of the current river. These would be consistent with more braided channels, though the size and spacing of our cores meant that we were not able to distinguish individual braids or identify any of the sedimentary structures typically associated with the bars separating them. A test pit excavated in channel C.4

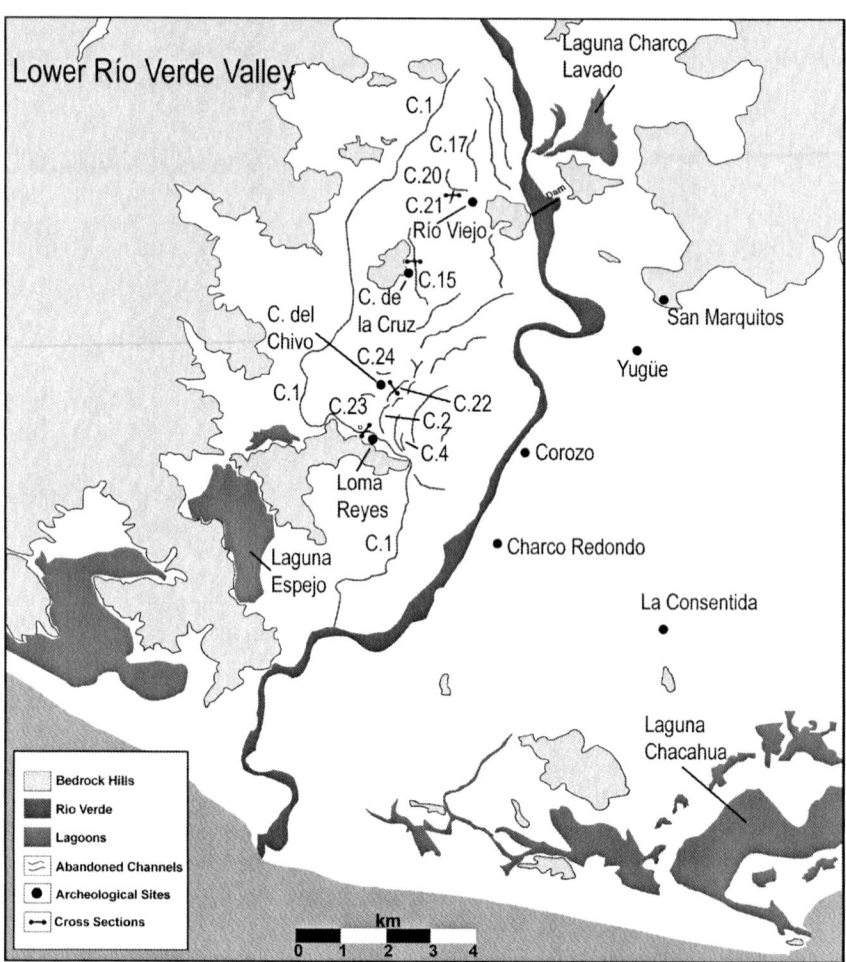

FIGURE 3.5. Map of the lower Río Verde Valley showing locations of abandoned channels and archaeological sites mentioned in the text. The numbering of channels (C = channel) follows the order of exploration and does not imply anything about their age (after Joyce 1991a: Figure 2).

recovered waterlogged wood from the channel sands that yielded a radiocarbon date of AD 1740, demonstrating that only a few hundred years ago the river was located there, approximately 2 km from its present position. These data indicate that the river has been migrating back and forth across the floodplain in the vicinity of Loma Reyes since the shift in depositional regimes, producing a palimpsest of abandoned channels.

Farther north the river movement has been more constrained by spurs of the piedmont and a series of isolated hills that protrude from the floodplain.

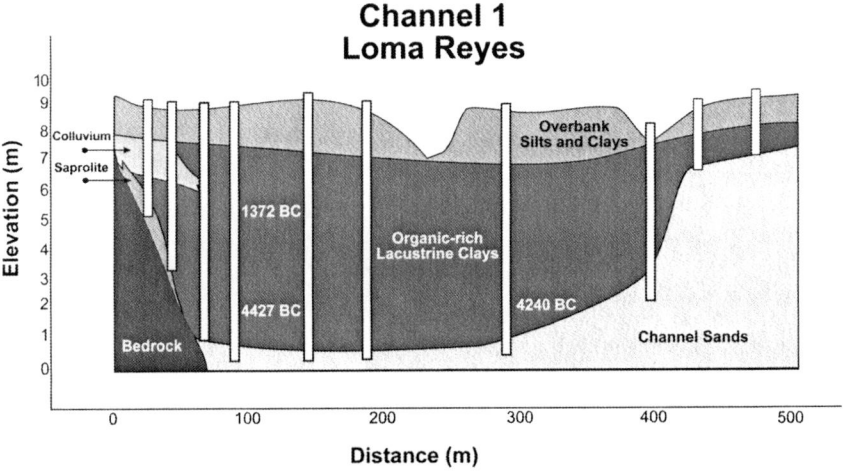

FIGURE 3.6. Stratigraphic cross section of channel C.1 at Loma Reyes showing stratigraphy, auger core locations, and radiocarbon dates.

A transect extending northeast from the archaeological site of Cerro de la Cruz revealed up to 7 m of overbank deposits, suggesting that a channel has remained stable in this area for a considerable period of time. East of the modern channel (Joyce 1991a; Joyce et al 1998; Joyce and Mueller 1992; Mueller 1991) we have found little evidence of lateral movements of the river in the form of abandoned channels. At the same time, surface soil profiles east of the river tend to be better developed, suggesting little recent vertical accretion. It thus seems that the Río Verde has rarely shifted east of its modern course.

The modern river channel, which was braided before the construction of a dam in 1992, and the mid-Holocene meandering C.1 channel thus constitute the end members, in both space and time, of a sequence of morphological change. It is to be pointed out, however, that relative distance between these two cannot be used as a simple guide to the age of abandoned channels. We have also documented several channels of intermediate age and in a few instances can positively affirm that they also display an intermediate morphology.

One of the earliest dated channels, C.23, was discovered in a deep auger core at the archaeological site of Cerro del Chivo. A radiocarbon date at the base of the lacustrine clays burying the channel sands yielded an age of 2231 BC. Since prehispanic structures covered portions of the channel, it was impossible to trace its cross section. The same problem was encountered with neighboring channel C.24, whose abandonment was dated in an analogous fashion to shortly before 1492 BC.

C.21 is one of several abandoned channels visible at the large archaeological site of Río Viejo, which was a regional political center during the Miniyua,

TABLE 3.1. Lower Río Verde Valley radiocarbon dates referred to in this chapter. Calibrated using IntCal04 curve in CALIB 5.1 beta. See Stuiver and Reimer (1993) for previous version of program. The calibrated figures are rounded to the nearest 10 years.

Lab No.	Site/Channel	Material	Method	$\delta^{13}C$	^{14}C yr BP	^{14}C yr BC/AD	Calibrated Range BC/AD (2σ)	Midpoint of Range
AA41208	Loma Reyes/C.1	lacustrine clay	AMS	−17.6	3322 ± 47	1372 BC	1740–1500 BC	1620 BC
Beta 85027	Loma Reyes/C.1	lacustrine clay	LS	NA	6190 ± 70	4240 BC	5310–4960 BC	5140 BC
AA41207	Loma Reyes/C.1	lacustrine clay	AMS	−18.6	6377 ± 50	4427 BC	5470–5230 BC	5350 BC
Beta 26220	Loma Reyes/C.4	waterlogged wood	LS	NA	210 ± 70	AD 1740	AD 1520–1950[a]	AD 1740
AA37672	Cerro de la Cruz/C.15	lacustrine clay	AMS	−24.8	2785 ± 70	835 BC	1120–810 BC	970 BC
AA37670	Río Viejo/C.21	lacustrine clay	AMS	−22.4	3401 ± 51	1451 BC	1880–1540 BC	1710 BC
AA37675	Cerro del Chivo/C.22	buried levee soil	AMS	−20.3	2750 ± 46	800 BC	1000–810 BC	910 BC
AA37674	Cerro del Chivo/C.23	lacustrine clay	AMS	−21.8	4181 ± 86	2231 BC	2930–2490 BC	2710 BC
AA41206	Cerro del Chivo/C.22	organic-rich clay	AMS	−11.2	2324 ± 39	374 BC	510–230 BC	370 BC
AA37673	Cerro del Chivo/C.24	lacustrine clay	AMS	−18.3	3442 ± 44	1492 BC	1880–1640 BC	1760 BC

[a] Range suspect due to impingement on the end of the calibration data set.

Note: AMS = accelerator mass spectrometry; LS = liquid scintillation; NA = not available.

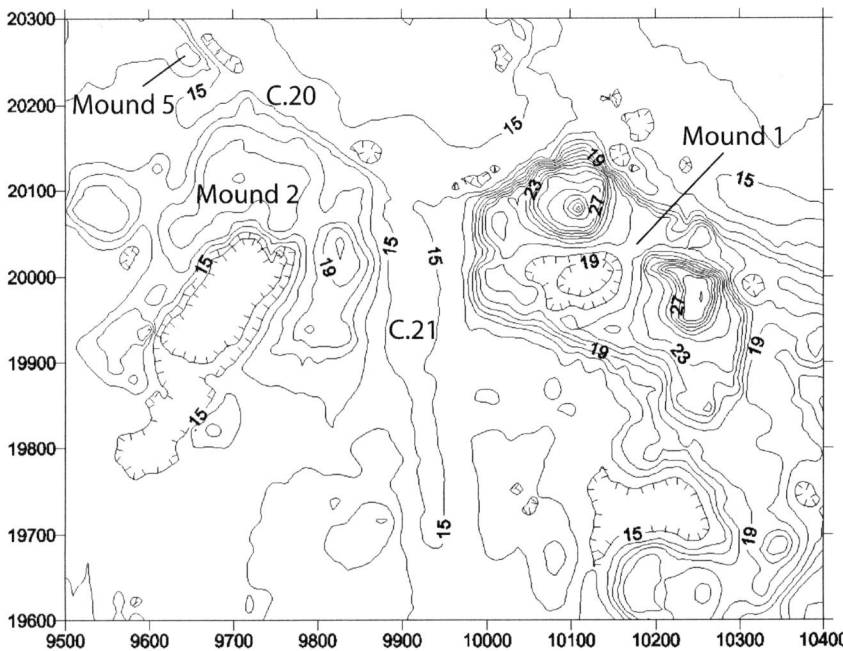

FIGURE 3.7. Topographic map of the center of Río Viejo showing channel C.21 and prehispanic structures (after Joyce and Goman 2012: Figure 11A).

Chacahua, and Yuta Tiyoo phases (Joyce 2008, Chapter 1). C.21 is almost identical in age to C.24, and the two may represent different reaches of the same channel. C.21 lies between two prehispanic structures, Mound 1 and Mound 2 (Figure 3.7). The lacustrine deposits that have filled in the abandoned channel average some 3 m of organic-rich clays. In the transect shown in Figure 3.8 they total as much as 5 m, but this represents the accumulation in two superimposed oxbows of different age. The width of the channel is at least 125 m but cannot be determined precisely because it disappears beneath Mound 2. C.21 is thus much shallower than C.1 and possibly approaches its width. A sample of basal clays yielded a radiocarbon date of 1451 BC consistent with the proposed direction of morphological change. At Río Viejo C.21 is cut into by another channel, C.20. It is younger by at least 2,000 years, as it also cuts into the base of Mound 5.

Another pair of almost contemporaneous channel reaches are C.15 and C.22, located in the vicinity of the archaeological sites of Cerro de la Cruz and Cerro del Chivo, respectively. Cerro de la Cruz has occupations that range from the Charco to the Yuta Tiyoo phases. The settlement is located on a spur that extends into the floodplain from a large hill (Joyce 1994). One side of the channel is bounded by the bedrock base of the hill. C.15 conforms to what

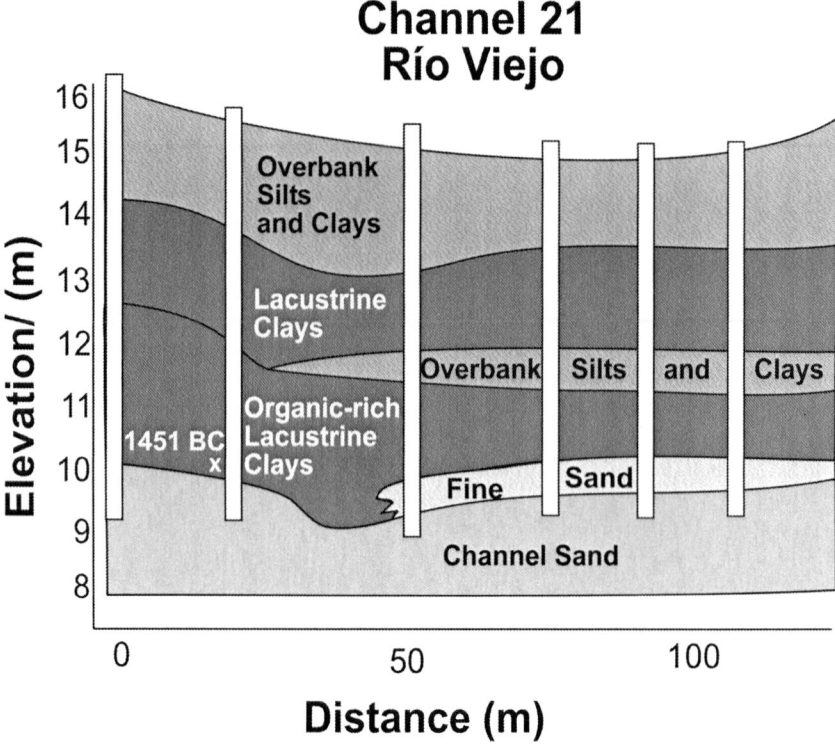

FIGURE 3.8. Stratigraphic cross section of channel C.21 at Río Viejo showing stratigraphy, auger core locations, and radiocarbon dates.

we would expect in the transitional stage of changes in channel morphology (Figure 3.9). The measured dimensions are a width of 250 m and a depth of slightly more than 4 m, giving a significantly higher width-depth ratio than C.1 (compare with Figure 3.6). Note, however, that the ratio was still sufficiently low (i.e., the channel was sufficiently deep) to allow the formation of an oxbow pond following channel abandonment. A basal sample of the lacustrine clays yielded a radiocarbon date of 835 BC.

C.22 was the only channel at Cerro del Chivo that was relatively unobstructed by prehispanic structures and could be traced for a considerable length in air photos. Like the other two channels in the area, however, it had been abandoned by the time the site was occupied in the Miniyua phase. Immediately southeast of the site we trenched a levee of C.22 (Figure 3.10). The excavation exposed a paleosol formed on the levee that had sufficient organic content to provide a radiocarbon determination, which returned a date of 800 BC. C.22 remained active after this date, burying this soil under another sediment package added to the levee. It was the first channel in our sequence that was so

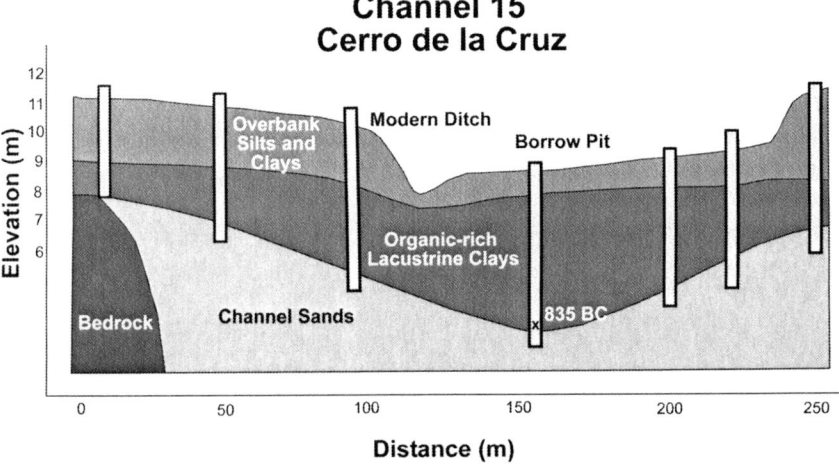

FIGURE 3.9. Stratigraphic cross section of channel C.15 at Cerro de la Cruz showing stratigraphy, auger core locations, and radiocarbon dates.

broad and shallow that it did not form an oxbow pond after abandonment and did not accumulate lacustrine clays. Nonetheless, the silty clay deposits that filled in the inactive channel were organic enough to return a date of 374 BC, which approximates the moment of channel abandonment. The series of channels east of Loma Reyes (C.2 to C.12) seem to belong to the same morphological type as C.22 in that they did not convert to oxbow ponds. Paleosols more recent than the ones of the C.22 levee have not been discovered in the vicinity and seem to be rare along the lower Río Verde in general. This suggests that the changes in channel morphology were accompanied by reduced floodplain stability. This in turn would be consistent with the presence of braided channels that migrated laterally at a rapid rate, truncating or removing any soils that may have formed in the more distal portions of the floodplain.

The alluvial stratigraphy of the lower Río Verde floodplain thus contains evidence for a transition in channel morphology that involved an increase in the width-depth ratio, likely accompanied by the replacement of meanders by ever more braided reaches. The first stages of this transition may have been under way near 1500 BC, but marked changes have so far been documented only for channels younger than 800 BC. This would correspond to the first half of fill cycle 2 in the highlands, which is the time span when we think that erosion was first accelerated by agriculture to a significant degree and a great amount of sediment was exported downstream. This in itself could have provoked changes in several parameters of the fluvial system, as described above, and induced the shift in channel morphology. If at the same time farmers undertook large-scale clearance of the lower Río Verde floodplain (as seems

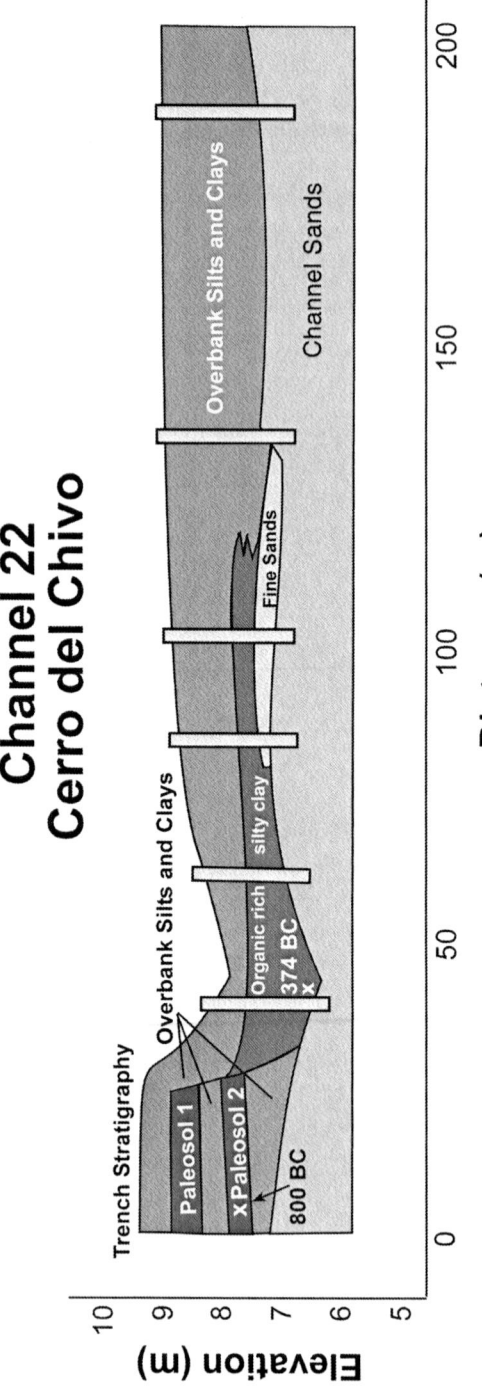

FIGURE 3.10. Stratigraphic cross section of Channel C.22 at Cerro del Chivo showing stratigraphy, auger core and trench locations, and radiocarbon dates.

likely; see next section), they would have rendered channel banks less stable. This would have increased local sediment supply and facilitated lateral channel migration. Both factors are known to contribute significantly to the development of braided channels. A powerful positive feedback loop of local origin would thus have been set in place, because a mature closed-canopy forest would no longer be able to develop on the unstable floodplain, while the more open secondary vegetation communities would attract farmers because of the relative ease of clearance.

Another line of evidence that supports this scenario and helps to establish its time frame comes from the coastal estuaries (Goman et al. 2005, Chapter 2). Two sediment cores were extracted from Laguna Pastoría, located some 10 km east of Laguna Chacahua (Figure 3.5). They yielded a record of major hurricane strikes for the Late Holocene and indications of a shift in coastal morphology from an open bay to an enclosed lagoon following the formation of a bay barrier. The cores were dominated by organic muds with discrete beds of coarse shell and sand. Deposits older than 450 BC included periodic high-energy facies consisting of mollusks that had been transported from depths of up to 90 m and mixed with shallow-water species. More recent strata included several sand deposits, indicating the presence and accessibility of a local sand source that was previously absent. It seems that the mollusk deposits in the lower section of the core were the result of the mobilization of deepwater mollusks during major storm surges prior to the formation of the bay barrier. The shift to sand deposits resulted from the mobilization of sand during major hurricanes following the formation of the bay barrier and the closing off of the bays. The data thus indicate that the bay barriers had formed by ca. 450 BC. The major sediment source for the formation of the bay barriers is alluvium carried down the Río Verde and discharged into the Pacific Ocean. Long shore currents, which run from west to east, then deposited the sediment along the coast and thus formed the bay barriers. The stratigraphic evidence from the Laguna Pastoría cores is consistent with bay barrier formation by the Minizundo phase. Archaeological evidence from the site of Barra Quebrada (Figure 1.2) shows that people began colonizing the bay barrier during the ensuing Miniyua phase (150 BC–AD 100; Winter and Joyce 1987). Sediment deposited at Barra Quebrada at this time suggests, however, that the bay barrier was periodically overwashed by storms until ca. AD 100.

Overall, the geomorphological evidence from the lower Río Verde Valley is limited to the Middle to Late Holocene and so does not allow us to draw any conclusions about the effects of the earlier cut-and-fill cycles documented for the Nochixtlán Valley (cycles 5 through 3). The data from the lower valley indicate major environmental changes during the Charco phase and the preceding (and as yet unphased) part of the Formative, including increased alluviation and an expansion of the floodplain as well as the formation of the bay barrier and back-barrier estuaries. Their timing corresponds to the first half of fill cycle 2 in the Nochixtlán Valley and thus suggests that anthropogenic erosion in the highlands may have been a significant causal factor. Geomorphic conditions in the Nochixtlán Valley remained dynamic through the remainder of the prehispanic period. The sedimentological evidence from the lower valley does not indicate major geomorphic changes after the Minizundo phase, but the continued supply of large amounts of sediment may have helped to maintain the braided channel patterns despite the inherently low gradient of the coastal reach of the Río Verde, and to assure the permanence of the bay barrier.

IMPLICATIONS OF LANDSCAPE CHANGE FOR RESOURCE AVAILABILITY IN THE LOWER VALLEY

The shift in depositional regimes and the formation of the bay barrier have major implications in terms of the distribution and productivity of resources important to human populations in the lower valley (Goman et al. 2005, 2010, Chapter 2; Joyce and Mueller 1992, 1997; Joyce et al. 1998). The lower Río Verde Valley today is one of the most productive agricultural regions in Oaxaca with abundant rainfall combined with a broad floodplain (Rodríguez et al. 1989). Our paleoenvironmental research suggests, however, that the lower valley was considerably less productive under the earlier depositional regime. Prior to the Minizundo phase, it is likely that both the river and its floodplain were smaller and less productive. Floods depositing alluvium that replenished and maintained soil fertility were both less frequent and less extensive. The position of the river hugging the western edge of the valley at the base of the piedmont would have left the eastern part of the coastal plain without a dependable freshwater source. Before the formation of the bay barriers at ca. 450 BC, the coast was more of an open embayment, limiting the abundance and accessibility of marine and estuarine species. Even today the high-energy wave environment found along the Río Verde's coast makes it difficult for fishing communities to penetrate through the waves into the open ocean with the aid of gasoline-powered motors, particularly during the rainy season.

Our recent research in the floodplain and coastal estuaries demonstrates that the period of major environmental change in the region dates to ca. 1800–400 BC. The modern depositional regime was therefore in place by the Minizundo phase (400–100 BC). By this time, the river had shifted from its mid-Holocene meandering form to a more braided pattern and migrated across a great width of the lower valley, except in areas obstructed by bedrock. Frequent river migration could have precluded the establishment of closed-canopy forest and eased land clearance for agriculture. Agricultural productivity would have gradually increased as sediment was eroded from the highland valleys and deposited along the lowland floodplain. Organic matter derived from land clearance and soil erosion in the highlands would have been carried down the Río Verde, contributing to greater agricultural fertility in the lowlands. As the river migrated east across the floodplain, it would have left oxbow ponds in abandoned channels like C.15 and C.21. Oxbow ponds today are productive microenvironments supporting populations of fish and waterfowl. When the Río Verde floods each summer, fish populations in the oxbow ponds are replenished. Bones of mojarra (*Diapterus* sp.) and catfish (*Ictalurus* sp.), which are found in the oxbow ponds, are common in midden deposits dating to the Late/Terminal Formative (Fernández 2004; Joyce 1991b). Even abandoned channels that are completely infilled are attractive habitats for farming since their soils are more humid and closer to the water table, allowing for year-round cultivation.

In addition to the expansion of the floodplain, formation of the bay barrier and estuaries increased the environmental productivity of the region (Goman et al. 2005). Estuaries are among the most productive ecosystems in the world (Odum 1953, 364–366; Voorhies 2004, 12). The estuaries in the lower Verde region, such as Laguna Pastoría and Laguna Chacahua, are important environments in the modern subsistence economy as people exploit fish, shellfish, and waterfowl (Alfaro and Sánchez 2002). Infilled lagoons resulting from coastal progradation are also utilized as areas to render salt (Grove 1988). Archaeological and ethnohistorical data show that prehispanic populations exploited the estuaries for key sources of protein, such as fish, shellfish, and waterfowl, as well as salt and ornamental shell (Fernández 2004; Joyce 1991a, 1991b, 1993). That estuarine resources were highly valued is indicated by early colonial period documents stating that Pedro de Alvarado (born Ixtac Quiautzin), ruler of the region from 1522 to 1547, claimed ownership of lagoons for fishing and salt works among his most valued resources (Fernández de Recas 1961).

THE HUMAN RESPONSE TO ECOLOGICAL CHANGE IN THE LOWER RÍO VERDE VALLEY

The increasing productivity of the floodplain and coastal estuaries since the Minizundo phase created more attractive environments for people living in the lower Río Verde Valley. The subsequent Miniyua and Chacahua phases were a time of population growth and increasing social complexity, including the emergence of an urban center at Río Viejo (Barber and Joyce 2007; Joyce 2005, 2008, 2010, Chapter 1; Joyce et al., Chapter 5). Although this period of dramatic cultural change follows immediately after the regional environmental shifts, it is difficult to establish how the social and ecological changes may have been causally related. Recent research, however, indicates several ways in which people were responding to Formative period landscape change (also see Goman et al. 2010, Chapter 2).

The expansion of the floodplain and the formation of the back-barrier estuaries would have increased the productivity of the most important subsistence resources in the region. Maize grown on the floodplain as well as estuarine resources such as fish, shellfish, and waterfowl are r-selected resources, which have been identified as important in the development of complex societies (Clark and Blake 1994; Hayden 1990, 1995). R-selected resources are characterized by rates of replacement and population densities that make them difficult to overexploit (however, see Kennett et al. 2008). These resources create the types of "intensifiable habitats" that allow for resource surpluses and the expansion of population that are necessary for escalating competition by incipient elites during the development of social complexity. Clark and Blake (1994) do not assert that intensifiable habitats with abundant r-selected resources are the sole cause of social complexity, but these resources appear to be an important material factor.

Archaeological and paleoecological research shows that the lower Río Verde Valley supported only small populations during the Archaic period and the pre-Charco phase of the Formative (Goman et al., Chapter 2; Joyce 2005, 2010). Although no Archaic period sites have thus far been discovered in the region, paleoecological evidence from the sediment core extracted from Laguna Pastoría indicates a short period of maize-based horticulture in the vicinity of the estuary between ca. 2110 and 1560 BC. Agricultural signals are not in evidence again in the coastal cores until the Charco phase. Only three Early Formative period sites have been discovered in the region, and they total only 5 ha. Two of the sites are located near the salt flats north of the coastal estuaries approximately 5 km from the present-day river and possibly even farther from the position of the river at the time of their earliest occupation.

Regional archaeological data demonstrate a major demographic expansion beginning in the Charco phase (Joyce 2005, 2010, 180–181; Chapter 1). The occupational area in the full-coverage survey zone increased from 5 to 64 ha, with most people living at the site of Charco Redondo on the floodplain of the Río Verde (Figure 1.2). Regional population continued to increase through the remainder of the Formative, with the occupational area in the survey zone reaching 699 ha by the Chacahua phase (AD 100–250). During the Miniyua phase an urban center emerged at the site of Río Viejo on the floodplain west of the river. The site grew to cover 225 ha. Mortuary and residential evidence from multiple sites in the region indicates that social inequality increased between the Minizundo and Chacahua phases (Barber 2005, Chapter 6; Joyce 1991a, 1991b, 1994, 2005, 2010, 180–195; Chapter 1).

Resource surpluses were mobilized in the construction of massive monumental architecture as well as in the observance of communal ceremonies, including ritual feasting, mortuary rituals, and the emplacement of impressive ceremonial caches (Barber, Chapter 6; Barber and Joyce 2007; Barber et al., Chapter 4; Joyce 2010; Workinger 2002). The scale of monumental construction was considerable, even at some smaller sites, with most consisting of large mixed-use platforms that supported both residences and public buildings. For example, the mixed-use platform at Yugüe measured approximately 300 m × 150 m and reached 10 m at its highest point (Barber, Chapter 6). The largest monumental building in the region was the Mound 1 acropolis at Río Viejo with an estimated volume of 455,050 m³ by the end of the Formative (Joyce et al., Chapter 5). Excavations on the acropolis indicate that it supported ceremonial architecture during the Chacahua phase. Within a century or two after its construction, however, the acropolis was abandoned and burned. During the Coyuche phases the region fragmented politically, although regional authority reemerged in the subsequent Yuta Tiyoo phase.

We attribute most of the social changes at the end of the Formative to social and cultural factors such as the negotiation of political authority and the development of new principles and practices that created broader social and political affiliations (Barber 2005, Chapter 6; Barber and Joyce 2007; Joyce 2005, 2008, 2010, Joyce et al., Chapter 5; Workinger 2002). The increase in environmental productivity and the creation of intensifiable habitats, however, would have supported population growth and the generation of surpluses in both resources and labor. In addition, a growing body of evidence indicates that people altered their subsistence practices to more intensively focus on maize-based agriculture and estuarine resources.

Pollen, phytolith, and charcoal evidence from sediment cores in estuaries and freshwater ponds in the region indicate the resumption of maize-based agriculture on the floodplain by the Charco phase (Goman et al., Chapter 2). Macrobotanical remains of maize have been recovered from midden deposits in Minizundo phase archaeological sites (Woodard 1991). A fine-grained paleoecological study (Goman et al. 2010) based on sediment cores from the west side of the lower Río Verde's floodplain showed a close correspondence between population growth at the end of the Formative period and into the Classic, and indicators of intensive agriculture (i.e., magnetic susceptibility, micro and macroscopic charcoal, pollen, and stable carbon isotopes). The data are consistent with an expansion in maize-based agriculture in the latter part of the Formative. A recent stable carbon isotope study of human teeth, primarily from Minizundo and Chacahua phase deposits, suggests a significant increase in maize consumption over this period (Taylor et al. 2009). A preliminary analysis of dental microwear concurs with the isotope results, although the sample size was too small to yield statistically significant differences. These data indicate an increasing reliance on maize at the end of the Formative as the agricultural fertility of the floodplain improved.

Archaeofaunal analyses suggest an increasing reliance on estuarine resources at the end of the Formative. Faunal remains show an increase in the proportion of estuarine shellfish in midden deposits from the Charco to the Coyuche phase (Fernández 2004). In summarizing the results of the faunal study, Fernández (2004, 140) states that "resource procurement changed from terrestrial and riverine, to estuarine and littoral." Midden samples from Cerro de la Cruz and Río Viejo show that estuarine species such as snook (*Centropomus* sp.) and sea catfish (*Arius* sp.) were an important source of high-quality protein by the Late Formative, while open-ocean species were exploited infrequently. By the Early Classic period, shellfish largely replace fish. Analyses of Ba/Sr ratios from human long bones show that marine/estuarine resources were significantly greater in the diets of coastal people relative to a highland control sample (Joyce 1991b, 137–138). Evidence for the greatest consumption of marine/estuarine resources comes from the site of Barra Quebrada, located on the bay barrier adjacent to the coastal estuary system. Although people in the region exploited estuarine resources like fish and shellfish from the estuaries, the archaeological and bone chemistry data indicate that the focus of subsistence was agricultural. Animals exploited from the estuaries, however, may have provided an important source of high-quality protein in human diets. A biocultural study of skeletal remains from the Chacahua phase cemetery at Yugüe suggests that coastal populations enjoyed a mixed diet, rich in carbohydrates, iron, and protein, that resulted in an overall pattern of good health (Melmed 2006).

Although the data indicate that Formative period environmental change in the lower Río Verde Valley had a largely positive impact on human populations, there are indications that the increased severity of flooding during the Formative period may have created problems for people living on the floodplain. Probable high-energy flood deposits have been noted in stratigraphy dating to the Minizundo phase at Río Viejo (Joyce 1991a, 360–361). At Río Viejo we also noted frequent incidents of raising and rebuilding the level of houses between the Minizundo and Chacahua phases (Joyce 1991a, 392; Workinger and Joyce 1999). We suspect that the construction of massive residential and mixed-use platforms at that time at many sites in the lower Verde's floodplain was probably in part a response to increasing rainy-season flooding and the need to elevate residences above floodwaters during years of severe inundations. These platforms constituted a form of landscape capital (Erickson 1999; Fisher 2005), which required major labor investments to construct, but provided benefits to succeeding generations. Today many communities in the region, such as Río Viejo, Charco Redondo, and Yugüe, continue to occupy these ancient platforms. The environmental changes of the Formative period therefore provided both risks and benefits to people in the lower Río Verde Valley.

CONCLUSIONS

The results of our interdisciplinary research along the Río Verde show that erosion in the highlands had both local and macroregional effects. In the Nochixtlán Valley the transformation of the landscape wrought by sedentary farmers was a mixed blessing for the environment and its long-term productivity. Anthropogenic erosion degraded many slopes, but at the same time it helped to improve and maintain farmland on the valley floor, especially in the form of the very productive *lama-bordo* systems. The increased flux of sediment and water transferred down the drainage to the coast had a largely positive effect as the agriculturally productive floodplain expanded and the rate of bay barrier formation accelerated, creating the back-barrier estuaries. The expansion of the floodplain and the formation of the estuaries created highly productive, intensifiable habitats that contributed to population growth and the generation of resource surpluses during the later Formative. Subsistence and dietary data show people relying to a greater extent on maize agriculture in the floodplain and the exploitation of estuarine fish and shellfish. Increased flooding was not entirely beneficial, as major floods would have periodically damaged communities and destroyed crops. As in the highlands, people in the lowlands responded to these environmental problems through technological innovations such as the construction of platforms that elevated living surfaces on the floodplain. Our ongoing interdisciplinary research will continue to tease apart the complex relationships between land use, environment, and human ecology along the Río Verde drainage basin. Although many questions remain, our research is increasingly revealing the complex effects of land use on the environments and people of the entire Río Verde drainage over the past 4,000 years.

ACKNOWLEDGMENTS

We would like to thank the Instituto Nacional de Antropología e Historia for permission to carry out the research in Oaxaca, especially the presidents of the Consejo de Arqueología during our projects: Lorena Mirambell, Mari Carmen Serra Puche, Norberto González Crespo, Joaquín García-Bárcena, and Roberto García Moll. Funding for this research was provided by grants from the following organizations: National Science Foundation (grants BCS-0923909, BCS-0096012, and BNS-8716332), National Geographic Society (grant 3767-88), Wenner-Gren Foundation (GR 4988), Vanderbilt University Research Council and Mellon Fund, Fulbright Foundation, H. John Heinz III Charitable Trust, Explorers Club, Sigma Xi, University of Colorado Innovative Grant Program, and Rutgers University. We would also like to thank Naomi Levin for comments on the manuscript.

REFERENCES CITED

Aimers, James J. 2007. "What Maya Collapse? Terminal Classic Variation in the Maya Lowlands." *Journal of Archaeological Research* 15 (4): 329–77. http://dx.doi.org/10.1007/s10814-007-9015-x.

Alfaro, Mara, and Gustavo Sánchez, eds. 2002. *Chacahua: Reflejos de un parque.* Mexico City: CONANP and Plaza y Valdés.

Álvarez, Luis Rodrigo. 2003. *Geografía general del estado de Oaxaca.* 4th ed. Oaxaca: Carteles Oaxaca.

Balkansky, Andrew K, Stephen A. Kowalewski, Verónica Pérez Rodríguez, Thomas J. Pluckhahn, Charlotte Smith, Laura R. Stiver, Dmitri Beliaev, John F. Chamblee, Verenice Y Heredia Espinoza, and Roberto Santos Pérez. 2000. "Archaeological Survey in the Mixteca Alta of Oaxaca, Mexico." *Journal of Field Archaeology* 27 (4): 365–89. http://dx.doi.org/10.2307/3092718.

Barber, Sarah. 2005. *Heterogeneity, Identity, and Complexity: Negotiating Status and Authority in Terminal Formative Coastal Oaxaca.* PhD dissertation, Department of Anthropology, University of Colorado, Boulder. Ann Arbor, MI: University Microfilms.

Barber, Sarah B., and Arthur A. Joyce. 2007. "Polity Produced and Community Consumed: Negotiating Political Centralization in the Lower Río Verde Valley, Oaxaca." In *Mesoamerican Ritual Economy,* ed. E. Christian Wells and Karla L. Davis-Salazar, 221–44. Boulder: University Press of Colorado.

Blomster, Jeffrey P. 2004 *Etlatongo: Social Complexity, Interaction, and Village Life in the Mixteca Alta of Oaxaca, Mexico.* Belmont, CA: Wadsworth/Thomson Learning.

Blum, Michael D. 2007. "Large River Systems and Climate Change." In *Large Rivers: Geomorphology and Management,* ed. A. Gupta, 627–59. Chichester, West Sussex: Wiley.

Borejsza, Aleksander, Charles D. Frederick, and Richard G. Lesure. 2011. "Swidden Agriculture in the *tierra fría*? Evidence from Sedimentary Records in Tlaxcala." *Ancient Mesoamerica* 22(1): 91–106.

Borejsza, Aleksander, Isabel Rodríguez López, Charles D. Frederick, and Mark D. Bateman. 2008. "Agricultural Slope Management and Soil Erosion at La Laguna, Tlaxcala, Mexico." *Journal of Archaeological Science* 35 (7): 1854–66. http://dx.doi.org/10.1016/j.jas.2007.11.024.

Bridge, John S. 2003. *Rivers and Floodplains: Forms, Processes and Sedimentary Record.* Oxford: Blackwell Publishing.

Clark, John E., and Michael Blake. 1994. "The Power of Prestige: Competitive Generosity and the Emergence of Rank Societies in Lowland Mesoamerica." In *Factional Competition and Political Development in the New World,* ed. Elizabeth M. Brumfiel and John W. Fox, 17–30. Cambridge: Cambridge University Press. http://dx.doi.org/10.1017/CBO9780511598401.003.

Cook, Sherburne F. 1949. *Soil Erosion and Population in Central Mexico.* Ibero-Americana, vol. 34. Berkeley: University of California Press.

Córdova, Carlos E., and Jeffrey R. Parsons. 1997. "Geoarchaeology of an Aztec Dispersed Village on the Texcoco Piedmont of Central Mexico." *Geoarchaeology* 12 (3): 177–210. http://dx.doi.org/10.1002/(SICI)1520-6548(199705)12:3<177::AID-GEA1>3.0.CO;2-#.

Curray, Joseph R., Frans J. Emmel, and Parry J.S. Crampton. 1969. "Holocene History of a Strand Plain, Lagoonal Coast, Nayarit, Mexico." In *Lagunas costeras,* ed.

Augustine Ayala-Castenares and Fred B. Phleger, 63–100. Mexico City: UNAM, UNESCO.

Curtis, Jason H., David A. Hodell, and Mark Brenner. 1996. "Climate Variability on the Yucatan Peninsula (Mexico) during the Past 3500 Years, and Implications for Maya Cultural Evolution." *Quaternary Research* 46 (1): 37–47. http://dx.doi.org/10.1006/qres.1996.0042.

Dunning, Nicholas P., and Timothy Beach. 1994. "Soil Erosion, Slope Management, and Ancient Terracing in the Maya Lowlands." *Latin American Antiquity* 5 (1): 51–69. http://dx.doi.org/10.2307/971902.

Dunning, Nicholas P., Sheryl Luzzadder-Beach, Timothy Beach, John G. Jones, Vernon L. Scarborough, and T. Patrick Culbert. 2002. "Arising from the Bajos: The Evolution of a Neotropical Landscape and the Rise of Maya Civilization." *Annals of the Association of American Geographers. Association of American Geographers* 92 (2): 267–83. http://dx.doi.org/10.1111/1467-8306.00290.

Eaton, Brett C., Robert G. Millar, and Sarah Davidson. 2010. "Channel Patterns: Braided, Anabranching, and Single-Thread." *Geomorphology* 120 (3–4): 353–64. http://dx.doi.org/10.1016/j.geomorph.2010.04.010.

Erickson, Clark L. 1999. "Neo-Environmental Determinism and Agrarian 'Collapse' in Andean Prehistory." *Antiquity* 73: 634–42.

Fernández, Deepika. 2004. "Subsistence in the Lower Río Verde Region, Oaxaca, Mexico: A Zoological Analysis." MA thesis, Department of Archaeology, University of Calgary, Calgary.

Fernández de Recas, Guillermo de. 1961. *Cacicazgos y nobiliario indígena de la Nueva España*. Mexico City: Instituto Bibliográfico Mexicano.

Fisher, Cristopher T. 2005. "Demographic and Landscape Change in the Lake Pátzcuaro Basin, Mexico: Abandoning the Garden." *American Anthropologist* 107 (1): 87–95. http://dx.doi.org/10.1525/aa.2005.107.1.087.

Fisher, Christopher T., Helen P. Pollard, Isabel Israde-Alcántara, Victor H. Garduño-Monroy, and Subir K. Banerjee. 2003. "A Reexamination of Human-Induced Environmental Change within the Lake Pátzcuaro Basin, Michoacán, Mexico." *Proceedings of the National Academy of Sciences of the United States of America* 100, no. 8 (Apr. 15): 4957–62. http://dx.doi.org/10.1073/pnas.0630493100. Medline:12671066.

Flannery, Kent V. 1983. "Precolumbian Farming in the Valleys of Oaxaca, Nochixtlán, Tehuacán, and Cuicaltán: A Comparative Study." In *The Cloud People: Divergent Evolution of the Mixtec and Zapotec Civilizations*, ed. Kent V. Flannery and Joyce Marcus, 323–38. New York: Academic Press.

Flannery, Kent V., ed. 1986. *Guilá Naquitz: Archaic Foraging and Early Agriculture in Oaxaca, Mexico*. New York: Academic Press.

Flannery, Kent V., and Ronald Spores. 1983. "Excavated Sites of the Oaxacan Preceramic." In *The Cloud People: Divergent Evolution of the Zapotec and Mixtec Civilizations*, ed. Kent V. Flannery and Joyce Marcus, 20–26. New York: Academic Press.

Goman, Michelle, Arthur Joyce, and Raymond Mueller. 2005. "Stratigraphic Evidence for Anthropogenically Induced Coastal Environmental Change from Oaxaca, Mexico." *Quaternary Research* 63 (3): 250–60. http://dx.doi.org/10.1016/j.yqres.2005.02.008.

Goman, Michelle, Arthur Joyce, Raymond Mueller, and Larissa Paschyn. 2010. "Multi-Proxy Paleoecological Reconstruction of Prehistoric Land Use History in the

Western Region of the Lower Río Verde Valley, Oaxaca, Mexico." *Holocene* 20 (5): 761–72. http://dx.doi.org/10.1177/0959683610362811.

Grove, David C. 1988. "Archaeological Investigations on the Pacific Coast of Oaxaca, Mexico, 1986." Report submitted to the National Geographic Society, Washington, DC.

Hayden, Brian. 1990. "Nimrods, Piscators, Pluckers, and Planters: The Emergence of Food Production." *Journal of Anthropological Archaeology* 9 (1): 31–69. http://dx.doi.org/10.1016/0278-4165(90)90005-X.

Hayden, Brian. 1995. "Pathways to Power: Principles for Creating Socioeconomic Inequalities." In *Foundations of Social Inequality*, ed. T. Douglas Price and Gary M. Feinman, 15–86. New York: Plenum Press.

Heine, Klaus. 2003. "Paleopedological Evidence of Human-Induced Environmental Change in the Puebla-Tlaxcala Area (Mexico) during the Last 3,500 years." *Revista Mexicana de Ciencias Geológicas* 20: 235–44.

Hodell, David A., Mark Brenner, and Jason H. Curtis. 2005. "Terminal Classic Drought in the Northern Maya Lowlands Inferred from Multiple Sediment Cores in Lake Chichancanab (Mexico)." *Quaternary Science Reviews* 24 (12–13): 1413–27. http://dx.doi.org/10.1016/j.quascirev.2004.10.013.

Joyce, Arthur A. 1991a. "Formative Period Social Change in the Lower Río Verde Valley, Oaxaca, Mexico." *Latin American Antiquity* 2 (2): 126–50. http://dx.doi.org/10.2307/972274.

Joyce, Arthur A. 1991b. *Formative Period Occupation in the Lower Río Verde Valley, Oaxaca, Mexico: Interregional Interaction and Social Change*. PhD dissertation, Department of Anthropology, Rutgers University, New Brunswick, NJ. Ann Arbor, MI: University Microfilms.

Joyce, Arthur A. 1993. "Interregional Interaction and Social Development on the Oaxaca Coast." *Ancient Mesoamerica* 4 (1): 67–84. http://dx.doi.org/10.1017/S0956536100000791.

Joyce, Arthur A. 1994. "Late Formative Community Organization and Social Complexity on the Oaxaca Coast." *Journal of Field Archaeology* 21: 147–68.

Joyce, Arthur A. 2005. "La arqueología del bajo Río Verde." *Acervos* 7 (29): 16–36.

Joyce, Arthur A. 2008. "Domination, Negotiation, and Collapse: A History of Centralized Authority on the Oaxaca Coast Before the Late Postclassic." In *After Monte Albán: Transformation and Negotiation in Oaxaca, Mexico*, ed. Jeffrey Blomster, 219–54. Boulder: University Press of Colorado.

Joyce, Arthur A. 2010. *Mixtecs, Zapotecs, and Chatinos: Ancient Peoples of Southern Mexico*. Malden, MA: Wiley-Blackwell.

Joyce, Arthur A., and Michelle Goman. 2012. "Bridging the Theoretical Divide in Holocene Landscape Studies: Social and Ecological Approaches to Ancient Oaxacan Landscapes." *Quaternary Science Reviews* 55: 1–22.

Joyce, Arthur A., and Raymond G. Mueller. 1992. "The Social Impact of Anthropogenic Landscape Modification in the Río Verde Drainage Basin, Oaxaca, Mexico." *Geoarchaeology* 7 (6): 503–26. http://dx.doi.org/10.1002/gea.3340070602.

Joyce, Arthur A., and Raymond G. Mueller. 1997. "Prehispanic Human Ecology of the Río Verde Drainage Basin." *World Archaeology* 29 (1): 75–94. http://dx.doi.org/10.1080/00438243.1997.9980364.

Joyce, Arthur A., Marcus Winter, and Raymond G. Mueller. 1998. *Arqueología de la costa de Oaxaca: Asentamientos del periodo formativo en el valle del Río Verde inferior.* Estudios de Antropología e Historia 40. Oaxaca: Centro Regional Oaxaca, Instituto Nacional de Antropología e Historia.

Kennett, Douglas J., Dolores R. Piperno, John G. Jones, Hector Neff, Barbara Voorhies, Megan K. Walsh, and Brendan J. Culleton. 2010. "Pre-Pottery Farmers on the Pacific Coast of Southern Mexico." *Journal of Archaeological Science* 37 (12): 3401–11. http://dx.doi.org/10.1016/j.jas.2010.07.035.

Kennett, Douglas J., Barbara Voorhies, Thomas Wake, and Natalia Martinez. 2008. "Human Impacts on Marine Ecosystems in Guerrero, Mexico." In *Human Impacts on Marine Environments*, ed. Torben C. Rick and Jon M. Erlandson, 103–24. Berkeley: University of California Press.

Kirkby, Michael J. 1972. *The Physical Environment of the Nochixtlán Valley, Oaxaca.* Vanderbilt University Publications in Anthropology 2. Nashville, TN: Vanderbilt University.

Knighton, David. 1998. *Fluvial Form and Process: A New Perspective.* London: Arnold.

Knox, John C. 1977. "Human Impacts on Wisconsin Stream Channels." *Annals of the Association of American Geographers* 67 (3): 323–42. http://dx.doi.org/10.1111/j.1467-8306.1977.tb01145.x.

Kowalewski, Stephen A., Andrew K. Balkansky, Laura R. Stiver Walsh, Thomas J. Pluckhahn, John F. Chamblee, Verónica Pérez Rodríguez, Verenice Y. Heredia Espinoza, and Charlotte A. Smith. 2009. *Origins of the Ñuu: Archaeology in the Mixteca Alta, Mexico.* Boulder: University Press of Colorado.

Lesure, Richard G. 2008. "The Neolithic Demographic Transition in Mesoamerica? Larger Implications of the Strategy of Relative Chronology." In *The Neolithic Demographic Transition and Its Consequences*, ed. Jean-Pierre Bocquet-Appel and Ofer Bar-Yosef, 107–38. New York: Springer. http://dx.doi.org/10.1007/978-1-4020-8539-0_6.

Lorenzo, José Luis. 1958. *Un sitio precerámico en Yanhuitlán, Oaxaca.* Mexico City: Dirección de Prehistoria, Instituto Nacional de Antropología e Historia.

Marcus, Joyce, and Kent Flannery. 1990. "Science and Science Fiction in Postclassic Oaxaca: Or, 'Yes Virginia, There Is a Monte Albán IV.'" In *Debating Oaxaca Archaeology*, ed. Joyce Marcus, 191–205. Anthropological Papers Museum of Anthropology 84. Ann Arbor: University of Michigan.

Marcus, Joyce, and Kent Flannery. 1996. *Zapotec Civilization.* London: Thames and Hudson.

Markens, Robert. 2004. *Ceramic Chronology in the Valley of Oaxaca, Mexico, during the Classic and Postclassic Periods and the Organization of Ceramic Production.* PhD dissertation, Department of Anthropology, Brandeis University, Waltham, MA. Ann Arbor, MI: University Microfilms.

Markens, Robert. 2008. "Advances in Defining the Classic-Postclassic Portion of the Valley of Oaxaca Ceramic Chronology: Occurrence and Phyletic Seriation." In *After Monte Albán: Transformation and Negotiation in Oaxaca, Mexico*, ed. Jeffrey Blomster, 49–94. Boulder: University Press of Colorado.

Martínez López, Cira, Robert Markens, Marcus Winter, and Michael D. Lind. 2000. *Cerámica de la fase Xoo (época Monte Albán IIIB–IV) del Valle de Oaxaca.* Contribución

No. 8 del Proyecto Especial Monte Albán 1992–1994. Oaxaca: Centro Regional Oaxaca, Instituto Nacional de Antropología e Historia.

Melmed, Anamay. 2006. "Health, Diet, and Behavior in Prehistoric Oaxaca." MA thesis, Department of Anthropology, San Diego State University, San Diego.

Metcalfe, Sarah, and Sarah Davies. 2007. "Deciphering Recent Climate Change in Central Mexican Lake Records." *Climatic Change* 83 (1–2): 169–86. http://dx.doi.org/10.1007/s10584-006-9152-0.

Metcalfe, Sarah E., Sarah J. Davies, John D. Braisby, Melanie J. Leng, Anthony J. Newton, Nicola L. Terrett, and Sarah L. O'Hara. 2007. "Long and Short-Term Change in the Pátzcuaro Basin, Central Mexico." *Palaeogeography, Palaeoclimatology, Palaeoecology* 247 (3–4): 272–95. http://dx.doi.org/10.1016/j.palaeo.2006.10.018.

Metcalfe, Sarah E., F. Alayne Street-Perrott, Roy B. Brown, P. E. Hales, R. Alan Perrott, and F. M. Steininger. 1989. "Late Holocene Human Impact on Lake Basins in Central Mexico." *Geoarchaeology* 4 (2): 119–41. http://dx.doi.org/10.1002/gea.3340040203.

Mueller, Raymond G. 1991. "Appendix 2: Technical Report on the Geomorphological Research of the Río Verde Formative Project." In *Formative Period Occupation in the Lower Río Verde Valley, Oaxaca, Mexico: Interregional Interaction and Social Change*, by Arthur A. Joyce. PhD dissertation, Department of Anthropology, Rutgers University, New Brunswick, NJ. Ann Arbor, MI: University Microfilms.

Mueller, Raymond G., and Arthur A. Joyce. 2004. "Buried Archaic Sites in the Nochixtlán Valley, Oaxaca, Mexico." Paper presented at the 69th meeting of the Society for American Archaeology, Montreal, Canada.

Mueller, Raymond G., and Arthur A. Joyce. 2007. "Environmental Degradation and Erosion Related to Demographic Changes: Nochixtlán Valley, Oaxaca, Mexico." Paper presented at the 72nd Annual Meeting of the Society for American Archaeology, Austin, TX.

Mueller, Raymond G., Arthur A. Joyce, and Aleksander Borejsza. 2012. "Alluvial Archives of the Nochixtlán Valley, Oaxaca, Mexico: Age and Significance for Reconstructions of Environmental Change." *Palaeogeography, Palaeoclimatology, Palaeoecology*, 321–322 (2012): 121–136.

Mueller, Raymond G., Billiana Miteva, and Arthur A. Joyce. 1999. Estudios geomorfológicos. In "El proyecto patrones de asentamiento del Río Verde," ed. Arthur A. Joyce, 120–29. Informe final entregado al Consejo de Arqueología, Instituto Nacional de Antropología e Historia, Mexico City.

Mueller, Raymond G., and Lucia Pou. 2008. "The Nochixtlán Valley: A Report of Background Information and Results of Fieldwork." Manuscript in possession of the authors.

Neff, Hector, Deborah M. Pearsall, John G. Jones, Bárbara Arroyo, Shawn K. Collins, and Dorothy E. Freidel. 2006. "Early Maya Adaptive Patterns: Mid-Late Holocene Paleoenvironmental Evidence from Pacific Guatemala." *Latin American Antiquity* 17 (3): 287–315. http://dx.doi.org/10.2307/25063054.

Nelson, James G. 1966. "Man and Geomorphic Process in the Chemung River Valley, New York and Pennsylvania." *Annals of the Association of American Geographers* 56 (1): 24–32. http://dx.doi.org/10.1111/j.1467-8306.1966.tb00541.x.

Odum, Eugene P. 1953. *Fundamentals of Ecology*. Philadelphia: W. B. Saunders.

Park, Jungjae, Roger Byrne, Harald Böhnel, Roberto Molina Garza, and Mariaelena Conserva. 2010. "Holocene Climate Change and Human Impact, Central Mexico: A Record Based on Maar Lake Pollen and Sediment Chemistry." *Quaternary Science Reviews* 29 (5–6): 618–32. http://dx.doi.org/10.1016/j.quascirev.2009.10.017.

Pérez Rodríguez, Verónica. 2006. "States and Households: The Social Organization of Terrace Agriculture in Postclassic Mixteca Alta, Oaxaca, Mexico." *Latin American Antiquity* 17 (1): 3–22. http://dx.doi.org/10.2307/25063034.

Pérez Rodríguez, Verónica, Kirk C. Anderson, and Margaret K. Neff. 2011. "The Cerro Jazmín Archaeological Project: Investigating Prehispanic Urbanism and Its Environmental Impact in the Mixteca Alta, Oaxaca, Mexico." *Journal of Field Archaeology* 36 (2): 83–99. http://dx.doi.org/10.1179/009346911X12991472411321.

Piperno, Dolores R., J. Enrique Moreno, J. Iriarte, Irene Holst, Matthew Lachniet, John G. Jones, Anthony J. Ranere, and R. Castanzo. 2007. "Late Pleistocene and Holocene Environmental History of the Iguala Valley, Central Balsas Watershed of Mexico." *Proceedings of the National Academy of Sciences of the United States of America* 104, no. 29 (Jul. 17): 11874–81. http://dx.doi.org/10.1073/pnas.0703442104. Medline:17537917.

Redman, Charles L. 1999. *Human Impact on Ancient Environments.* Tucson: University of Arizona Press.

Rodríguez, Adolfo C., Gabriel Narváez C., Antonio Hernández M., Jorge Romero P., Bernardo C. Solano S., Francisco L. Anaya A., Nicolás Dillanes R., and José de los Santos Castro C. 1989. *Caracterización de la producción agrícola de la región costa de Oaxaca.* Pinotepa Nacional: Universidad Autónoma Chapingo.

Schumm, Stanley A. 1977. *The Fluvial System.* New York: Wiley.

Schumm, Stanley A. 1981. "Evolution and Response of the Fluvial System, Sedimentological Implications." *Society of Economic Paleontologists and Mineralogists Special Publications* 31: 19–29.

Smith, C. Earle, Jr. 1976. *Modern Vegetation and Ancient Plant Remains of the Nochixtlán Valley.* Vanderbilt University Publications in Anthropology 16. Nashville, TN: Vanderbilt University.

Spores, Ronald. 1969. "Settlement, Farming Technology, and Environment in the Nochixtlan Valley." *Science* 166, no. 3905 (Oct. 31): 557–69. http://dx.doi.org/10.1126/science.166.3905.557. Medline:17778189.

Spores, Ronald. 1972. *An Archaeological Settlement Survey of the Nochixtlán Valley, Oaxaca.* Vanderbilt University Publications in Anthropology 1. Nashville, TN: Vanderbilt University.

Spores, Ronald. 1974. *Stratigraphic Excavations in the Nochixtlán Valley, Oaxaca.* Vanderbilt University Publications in Anthropology 11. Nashville, TN: Vanderbilt University.

Spores, Ronald. 1984. *The Mixtecs in Ancient and Colonial Times.* Norman: University of Oklahoma Press.

Strahler, Arthur N. 1980. "Systems Theory in Physical Geography." *Physical Geography* 1: 1–27.

Stuiver, Minze, and Paula J. Reimer. 1993. "Extended 14C Database and Revised CALIB Radiocarbon Calibration Program." *Radiocarbon* 35: 215–30.

Tamayo, Jorge L. 1964. "The Hydrography of Middle America." In *Handbook of Middle American Indians*, Vol. 1: *Natural Environment and Early Cultures*, ed. Robert C. West, 84–121. Austin: University of Texas Press.

Taylor, Sarah R., Arthur A. Joyce, Mathew Sponheimer, and Sarah B. Barber. 2009. Dieta y agricultura en el valle del Río Verde inferior: Basado en análisis de micro-desgaste dental e isótopos estables. In "Estudios alimenticios y de ADN de dientes humanos del valle del Río Verde inferior, Oaxaca, México," ed. Arthur A. Joyce, 3–31. Report submitted to the Consejo de Arqueología, Instituto Nacional de Antropología e Historia, Mexico City.

Velez, Maria I., Jason H. Curtis, Mark Brenner, Jamie Escobar, Barbara W. Leyden, and Marion Popenoe de Hatch. 2011. "Environmental and Cultural Changes in Highland Guatemala Inferred from Lake Amatitlán Sediments." *Geoarchaeology* 26 (3): 346–64. http://dx.doi.org/10.1002/gea.20352.

Voorhies, Barbara, ed. 2004. *Coastal Collectors in the Holocene: The Chantuto People of Southwest Mexico*. Gainesville: University Press of Florida.

Winter, Marcus. 1982. *Guía zona arqueológica de Yucuita*. Oaxaca: Centro Regional Oaxaca, Instituto Nacional de Antropología e Historia.

Winter, Marcus. 1984. "Exchange in Formative Highland Oaxaca." In *Trade and Exchange in Early Mesoamerica*, ed. Kenneth G. Hirth, 179–214. Albuquerque: University of New Mexico Press.

Winter, Marcus. 1989a. *Oaxaca: The Archaeological Record*. Mexico City: Minutiae Mexicana.

Winter, Marcus. 1989b. "From Classic to Post-Classic in Pre-Hispanic Oaxaca, Mexico." In *Mesoamerica after the Decline of Teotihuacan, AD 700–900*, ed. Richard A. Diehl and Janet C. Berlo, 123–30. Washington, DC: Dumbarton Oaks.

Winter, Marcus, and Arthur A. Joyce. 1987. "Excavaciones en Barra Quebrada, 1986: Un informe preliminar." Report submitted to the Centro Regional Oaxaca, Instituto Nacional de Antropología e Historia, Oaxaca.

Winter, Marcus, Cira Martínez López, and Robert Markens. 2008. "Early Hunters and Gatherers of Oaxaca: Recent Discoveries." Paper presented at the 73rd Annual Meeting of the Society for American Archaeology, Vancouver.

Woodard, S. Justine. 1991. "Appendix 3: Paleobotanical Study; Río Verde Formative Project." In *Formative Period Occupation in the Lower Río Verde Valley, Oaxaca, Mexico: Interregional Interaction and Social Change*, by Arthur A. Joyce, 840–82. PhD dissertation, Department of Anthropology, Rutgers University, New Brunswick, NJ. Ann Arbor, MI: University Microfilms.

Workinger, Andrew. 2002. *Coastal/Highland Interaction in Prehispanic Oaxaca, Mexico: The Perspective from San Francisco de Arriba*. PhD dissertation, Department of Anthropology, Vanderbilt University, Nashville, TN. Ann Arbor, MI: University Microfilms.

Workinger, Andrew, and Arthur A. Joyce. 1999. Excavaciones arqueológicas en Río Viejo. In "El proyecto patrones de asentamiento del Río Verde," ed. Arthur A. Joyce, 51–119. Report submitted to the Consejo de Arqueología and the Centro INAH Oaxaca, Instituto Nacional de Antropología e Historia, Mexico City.

FORMATIVE PERIOD BURIAL PRACTICES and CEMETERIES

SARAH B. BARBER, ARTHUR A. JOYCE, ARION T. MAYES, JOSÉ AGUILAR, AND MICHELLE BUTLER

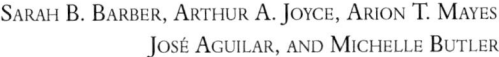

The lower Verde has an extensive, well-studied sample of human remains that spans the Late to Terminal Formative periods (400 BC–AD 250). The 156 individuals securely dated to the Late/Terminal Formative periods have been excavated or identified at six sites (Figure 4.1; see Barber 2005, 2009; Butler 2011; Joyce 1991a, 1991b, 1999; Joyce et al. 1998: Figure 1.2). Taken together, this burial sample represents domestic and public contexts, covers the entire demographic spectrum, and includes individuals of varying social statuses. Continuity and change through time in burial practices provide insight into shifting social relations as communities became increasingly hierarchical and regional political relations became increasingly centralized. The burials from the lower Verde attest to these changes and also provide information on health (e.g., Mayes et al. 2009; Melmed 2006), nutrition (Joyce 1991b; Taylor et al. 2009), human biology (Christensen 1998a, 1998b), and a variety of social and economic relations (e.g., Barber and Joyce 2007; Joyce 1991b, 1994; King 2006; Mayes and Barber 2008).

Drawing conclusions about social organization using mortuary data is a complex and often problematic process (i.e., Binford 1971; Carr 1995; Chesson 2001a; Goldstein 1981; R. Joyce 1999; Meskell

DOI: 10.5876/9781607322023.c04

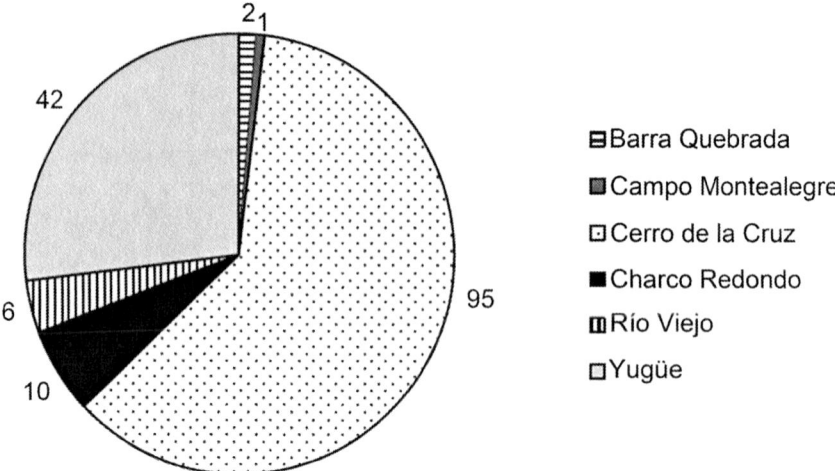

FIGURE 4.1. Distribution of Formative period human remains by site.

1999, 2000; Saxe 1970). Our approach is based on the premise that burial practices were part of broader social relationships that encompassed the living, the dead, material culture, and the spatial setting in which human remains were located. There is considerable ethnographic, ethnohistoric, and archaeological evidence demonstrating that human interaction did not end with death in pre-Columbian Mesoamerica (i.e., Flannery and Marcus 1976; Gillespie 2001a; Greenberg 1981; Hendon 2000; Houston et al. 2006; Joyce 2000; Lind and Urcid 1983, 2010; McAnany 1995; Monaghan 1995; Urcid 2005; Vogt 1976; Watanabe 1992). As Monaghan (1995, 158) observes for modern Mixtecs, "People maintain an ongoing relationship with the dead in a manner similar to the way they maintain relationships with . . . other members of the community." The terms of social relationships altered when individuals died, but the dead continued to have responsibilities within their social networks and to affect events in the mundane world. The physical remains of deceased individuals were understood to be animate, imbued with the living essence either of a specific individual or of a collectivity to which an individual belonged (Geller 2004; Gillespie 2001b, 71; Houston et al. 2006, 57–101; Urcid 2005). The locations in which the dead were placed as well as the items adorning or accompanying their bodies could be similarly animate (i.e., Barber and Olvera 2012; Greenberg 1981; Houston et al. 2006; Mock 1998; Stuart 1998; Taube 1998). Mortuary practices thus were based on decisions made with input from and in reference to a variety of socially relevant beings.

While many of these decisions are invisible to archaeology, approaching human remains and associated material culture as animate entities with agentive capacities transforms burials from the discarded physical matter of once-living people into active elements of ancient social groups. Burial location, body positioning, and grave goods were not passive reflections of identities and statuses, either of the dead during their lives or their still-living kin. Instead, burial practices emerged from the formation and reassertion of social relationships. As such, they provide insight into social groups and the terms by which these groups were defined (Chesson 2001b; R. Joyce 1999).

We begin, therefore, with a detailed discussion of how human remains were emplaced by ancient people. To facilitate discussion here and enable future use of these data by other scholars, we describe burial practices by ceramic phase and by site. We briefly discuss population health and pathologies and conclude with a diachronic assessment of continuity and change in burial practices over time. A detailed examination of the burial data from the lower Verde demonstrates changing definitions of social groups, including local communities, status groups, gender categories, and age. The way in which members of different social groups interacted clearly altered over time; inequality became more openly expressed and community membership became more inclusive.

LATE FORMATIVE PERIOD BURIAL PRACTICES

The largest sample of human remains for the pre-Columbian sequence dates to the Minizundo phase (400–150 BC), representing a total of ninety-one individuals. The bulk of the sample ($n = 86$ individuals) derives from excavations at Cerro de la Cruz, a small site situated on the west side of the Verde's floodplain only a few kilometers from Río Viejo (Joyce 1991a; Joyce et al. 1998). Another five individuals have been recovered from Río Viejo itself. Because they were deeply buried, Minizundo phase burials from Río Viejo have limited contextual information. We discuss the burial evidence from each site separately before summarizing Late Formative burial practices as a whole.

BURIAL PRACTICES AT CERRO DE LA CRUZ

Seventy-six of the eighty-six burials at Cerro de la Cruz were concentrated in three areas of the site: forty-nine were interred below or near a series of small superimposed public buildings collectively referred to as Structure 1, another nine individuals were buried in fill near a buried terrace wall, and eighteen were buried below and around the various phases of residential Structure 8 (Figure 4.2).[1] Ten additional individuals were buried in a residential area below the lower terrace wall. Of these last, seven were associated with probable domestic Structures 9, 10, and 11.

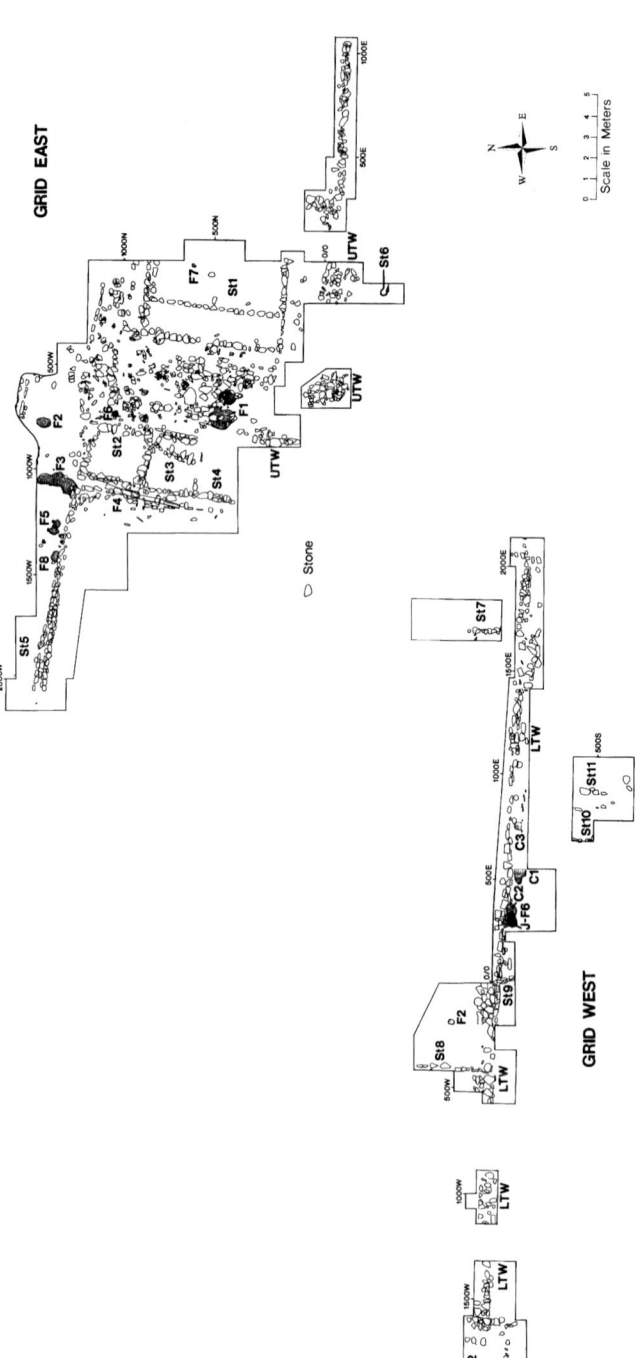

FIGURE 4.2. Plan view of the Cerro de la Cruz excavations (after Joyce 1994: Figure 3; published with permission from Maney Publishing: www.maney-publishing.com/journals/jfa and www.ingentaconnect.com/content/maney/jfa).

Structure 1

As Joyce discusses in Chapter 1 (see also Joyce 1991a, 1991b, 1994), Structure 1 was a small public structure that, in its later phases, was part of a complex of features that included a flagstone patio, several small storage buildings, and a possible residence. The area consisted of a terrace with a retaining wall running along its southern and western edges (the Upper Terrace Wall, or UTW; see Figure 4.2). This portion of the site had seen considerable modification, with evidence for an earlier retaining wall defining a smaller terrace and four construction episodes defining earlier iterations of Structure 1 itself. Most of the individuals ($n = 49$) were buried beneath the floor or along the foundation walls of Structure 1 and were associated with either the penultimate or final renovation of the structure (Figure 4.3). Since only small portions of the first three construction phases of Structure 1 were exposed in the excavations, it is possible that additional burials were associated with these versions of the building.

These burials represented continuous interment over a span of decades, if not a century or more. Joyce (1994, 158) has estimated that renovations of Structure 1 may have been undertaken as infrequently as every 75 years, meaning that interments may have spanned a period of up to 150 years since they pertain to the final two construction episodes. Stratigraphic relationships and damage caused to earlier burials by subsequent interments indicate that many distinct burial events are represented. For instance, there are between six and twenty-one chronologically discrete burial events in the interior of Structure 1 (Joyce 1991a, 733).

The most notable characteristic of the upper terrace burials was their homogeneity (Joyce 1991a: Appendix 1). Adults predominated ($n = 42$, 86%), with only seven (14%) subadults present (Table 4.1). There was an almost even distribution of males and females present among those individuals that could be sexed: fourteen male, eleven female. There were at least twenty-eight (57%) primary interments and four (8%) likely secondary interments, the rest ($n = 17$, 35%) were sufficiently disarticulated that they could either have been heavily disturbed primary burials or secondary burials. Although most of the primary burials were in an extended supine position ($n = 21$, 75%), a small percentage were extended on their right ($n = 3$, 11%) or left ($n = 2$, 7%) sides. The majority of the burials were oriented on cardinal directions, following the orientation of nearby architecture, regardless of whether they were inside or outside a structure. Most burials were parallel to the nearest foundation or retaining wall, although several beneath the floor of Structure 1 were interred perpendicular to a low wall that divided the building into two rooms (see Figure 4.3). There was no identifiable correlation between body position and orientation and age, sex, time period, or burial location. There were no grave offerings clearly associated with the Structure 1 and upper terrace burials.

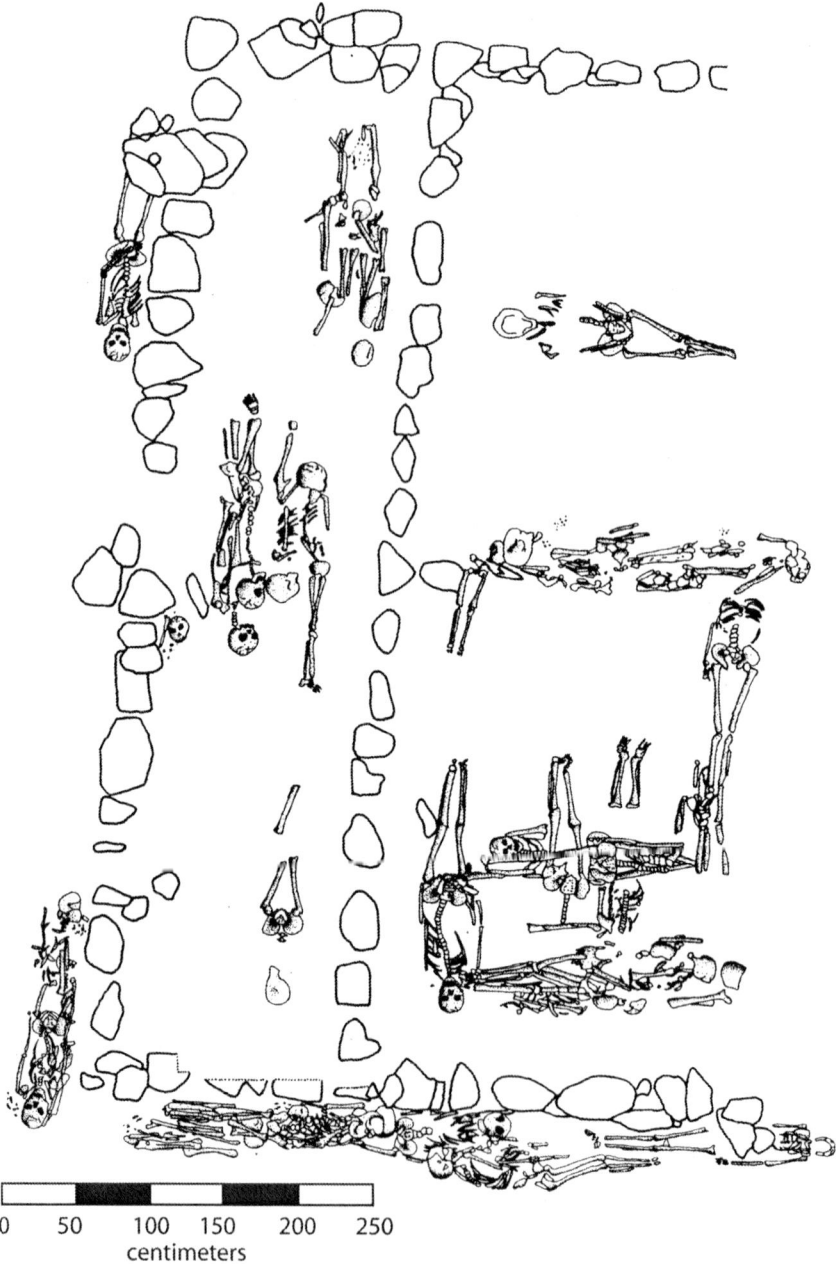

FIGURE 4.3. Plan view of Structure 1, Cerro de la Cruz, showing burials (after Joyce 1994: Figure 9; published with permission from Maney Publishing: www.maneypublishing.com/ journals/jfa and www.ingentaconnect.com/content/maney/jfa).

TABLE 4.1. Age groups for Minizundo phase burials

Age Group	Structure 1		Upper Terrace Wall		Structure 8		Lower Terrace Wall	
	n	%	n	%	n	%	n	%
Infant (birth–1 yr)	1	2	—	—	2	10	3	30
Child (2–10 yrs)	5	10	—	—	10	55	1	10
Adolescent (11–20 yrs)	1	2	1	11	1	5	2	20
Adult (> 20 yrs)	8	16	1	11	0	0	1	10
Young Adult (20–35 yrs)	26	53	4	45	4	25	3	30
Middle Adult (36–45 yrs)	7	15	3	33	1	5	—	—
Old Adult (> 45 yrs)	1	2	—	—	—	—	—	—
Total	49	100	9	100	18	100	10	100

Note: Subadult age categories for all tables are adapted from Scheuer and Black (2000: 468–469). Where age ranges were given for a particular individual, the center of the age range was used for the tally (e.g., an individual aged 3 to 8 was counted as a 5-year-old). For those adults whose ages were determined only to the youngest possible year (e.g., "35+" or "20+"), the individual's age was treated as the age given plus one year. So "35+" adults were counted as "Middle Adults."

Upper Terrace Wall

Nine individuals were interred in fill held back by an earlier terrace retaining wall located near Structure 1 (UTW–1st; Joyce 1991a, 209, 740–744). These burials, which postdate the use of the UTW–1st, were located underneath what became the southwest corner of the patio fronting Structure 1. The burials near the UTW–1st were densely stacked one atop the other and had been interred during six separate burial events. Like the Structure 1 burials, the majority of those near the UTW–1st were adult ($n = 8$, 89%; Table 4.1). Unlike the Structure 1 burials, they were predominantly male—six of seven sexed individuals (86%). Four of the burials (45%) were primary single interments, including the one subadult present in the group. There were four (45%) secondary burials, two of which were arranged around the primary interment of an adult female. The extended supine position was most common ($n = 4$, 44.5%), but one young adult male was interred extended on his right side (11%). Primary interments were oriented to cardinal directions. Body position and orientation did not correlate with age, sex, time period, or burial location. One middle adult male may have been interred with a gray obsidian flake.

Structure 8 and the Lower Terrace

Structure 8 was a residence built on the lower terrace. Structure 8 had been renovated three times during the Minizundo phase, as evidenced by four floors separated by narrow fill layers (Joyce 1991a, 225). The eighteen

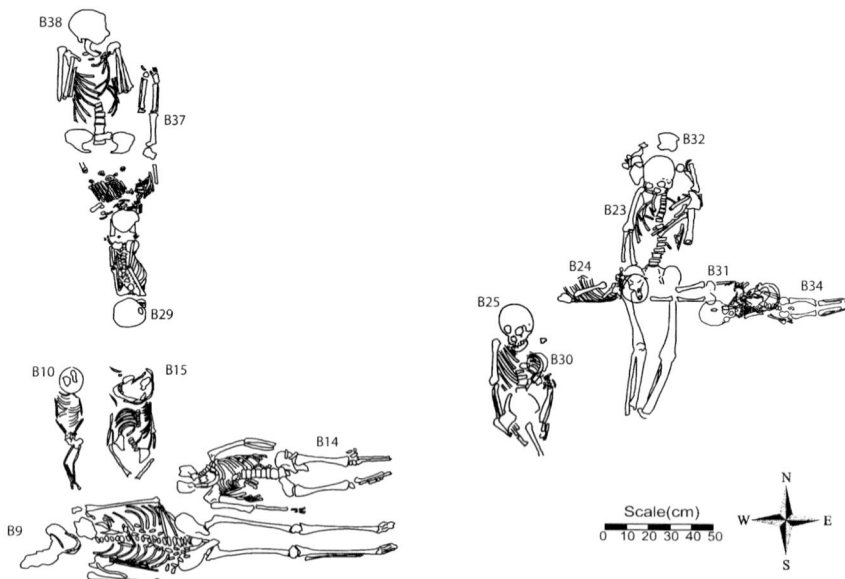

FIGURE 4.4. Plan view of Structure 8, Cerro de la Cruz, showing burials.

individuals buried around the residence were emplaced beneath the interior floors ($n = 15$) and in fill on the exterior of the western foundation wall ($n = 3$; Figure 4.4). The burials around Structure 8 were interred over an extended period of time that spanned the use-life of the residence. Unlike the Structure 1 burials, those around Structure 8 were weighted toward juveniles and included a range of grave offerings (Joyce 1991a, 751–760). Infants and children composed 72 percent of the sample ($n = 13$; Table 4.1). Of the five adults present, three were identified as female and two as male. Following the pattern observed at Structure 1, extended supine body position was most common ($n = 12$; 67%). However, a wider range of body positions was observed at Structure 8, with individuals also placed in a flexed position on their back ($n = 1$), left ($n = 1$), and right ($n = 1$) sides. There was one prone individual. There were no clear secondary burials near Structure 8. Bodies were positioned on cardinal directions either parallel or perpendicular to the residence's foundation walls. Body position and orientation did not correlate with age, sex, time period, or burial location.

Mortuary offerings were present among the burials from Structure 8. Four individuals could be associated unequivocally with grave goods: three adults and a child (Table 4.2). Four others—all young children or infants—were possibly interred with offerings. The possible offerings either could not be definitively associated with any one individual, as in the case of a grayware jar located in the dense jumble of bones beneath the third floor of Structure 8

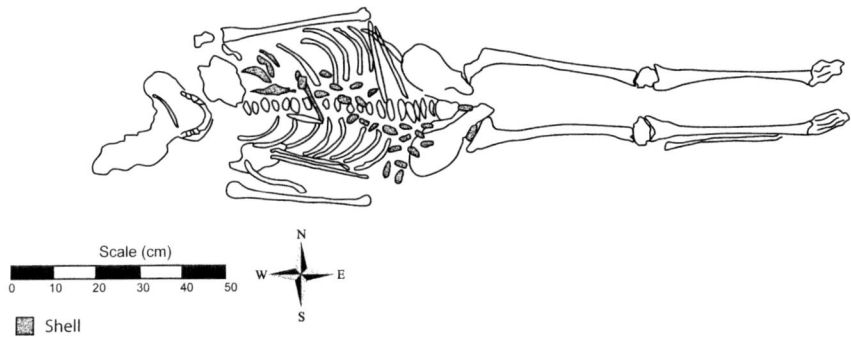

Scale (cm)

0 10 20 30 40 50

Shell

FIGURE 4.5. Burial 13–Individual 9, Cerro de la Cruz, showing the shell sash.

(Joyce 1991a, 753), or were located such that they may have been redeposited as part of the burial fill, as in the animal bones and obsidian flake found near three of the child burials (Joyce 1991a, 757, 761). The four burials with clearly defined offerings were located beneath the last two floors of Structure 8. As Table 4.2 demonstrates, offerings were generally modest and took a wide range of forms that did not correlate with age or sex. The two most elaborate mortuary items were an *olivella* and *pleuroploca* shell sash worn by an adult male (Figure 4.5) and a canine-tooth necklace worn by a child. Both burials pertain to the second construction episode of the residence.

The child burial, Burial 22–Individual 37 (B22-I37; 2.5–3.5 years at death), also included a ceramic bowl and was accompanied by a second child aged 3.5–4.5 years old at death (B22-I29).[1] The latter individual was unusual in that it was in an extended, prone position. B22-I29 is the only prone interment currently known for the Minizundo phase although prone positions are found in later burials in the region. The position of the burial, along with the placement of the individual's arms, which appear to be pulled behind the back, led Joyce (1991a, 758) to speculate that it could have been a sacrificial victim interred as an offering with B22-I37. The tight positioning of this individual's bones (Figure 4.6), observed during recent osteological investigation, suggests that the arm position may have been due to wrapping or swaddling of the entire body rather than binding of just the wrists. At least two other individuals may have been similarly wrapped. One was a child (B15-I40) interred on its side, with its arms positioned toward the back as if they had fallen that way postmortem. The other was an infant (B13-I15). In addition, there is no evidence for status differences between the two individuals based on their skeletons. Both children had serious health problems from infancy, with B22-I29 showing stress in the form of linear enamel hypoplasias (LEH) during gestation and infancy and B22-I37 suffering from a possibly infectious disease severe enough to affect whole tooth-crown development. While human sacrifice cannot be ruled out,

TABLE 4.2. Burials with offerings, Structure 8

Burial No.	Individual No.	Sex	Age	Position	Construction Phase	Offering
BA3	23	F	25–35	Supine	3rd	2 basalt axes and animal bone
12	38	F	30	Flexed dorsal	3rd	1 bowl and an animal tooth
13	9	M	27–35	Supine	2nd	Sash of 45 notched shells
22	37	NA	2.5–3.5	Supine	2nd	1 bowl, necklace of 22 canine teeth, and possibly 1 child sacrifice (B22-I29)

we suggest that the new information on context and pathology reduces the likelihood that B22-I29 was a sacrificial victim.

Below the Lower Terrace Wall

A final set of ten individuals was interred in association with domestic structures located just downhill and south of the site's lower terrace wall (Joyce 1991a, 763–768). Of these, five individuals were interred near residential Structure 9, although it was not possible to determine whether the burials were inside or outside of the building. Two more were buried beneath the floor of a heavily disturbed residential structure (Structure 11). One burial (B5-I7) predated the construction of the residential structures uncovered in this area of the site (Joyce 1991a, 766–768). Two more burials were interred in fill overlying the lower terrace wall. As with the burials around Structure 8, juveniles predominated in this area of Cerro de la Cruz with 60 percent of individuals under the age of 18 and 40 percent under the age of 11 (Table 4.1). Two of the adults were possibly males. One burial beneath the floor of Structure 9 consisted of an adolescent female (14–15 years) next to an infant (less than 8–10 months). This joint burial may represent a mother and child, indicating that adult responsibilities were shouldered prior to the achievement of developmental adulthood. Body position was more diverse among this group of burials and included: flexed ($n = 2$; one each right and left sides), extended side ($n = 5$; three on the right and two on the left sides), and extended supine ($n = 1$). Only one burial of a juvenile may have been a secondary interment. Most bodies were positioned along cardinal directions either parallel or perpendicular to nearby walls. Body position and orientation did not correlate with age, sex, time period, or burial location. One adult burial included animal bone as an offering.

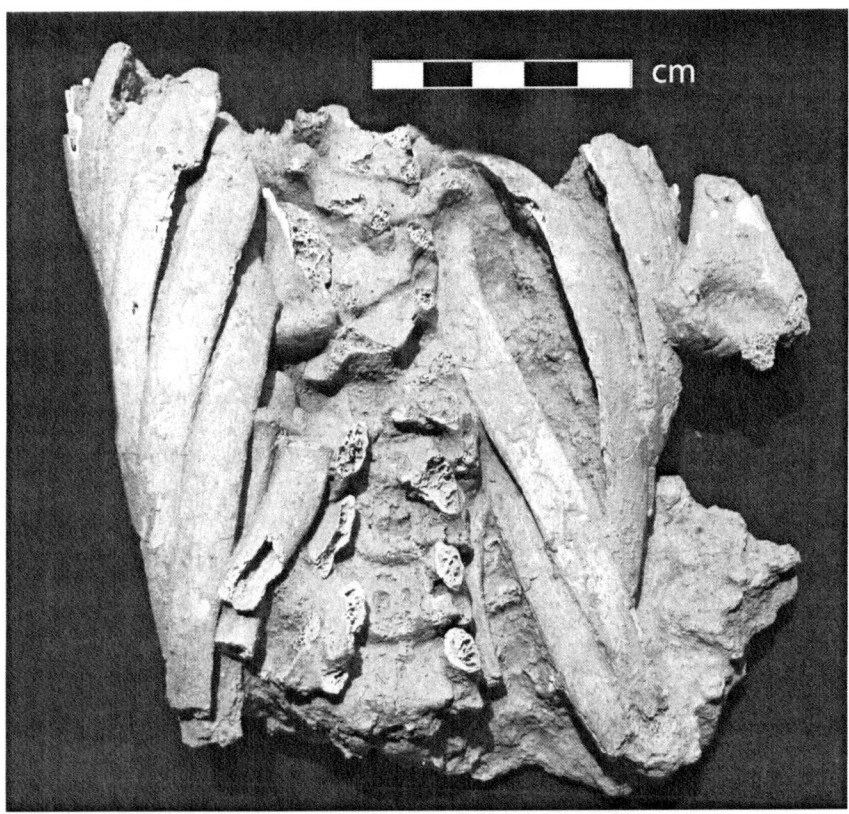

FIGURE 4.6. Tight positioning of ribs and arms on B22-I37.

Summary

There is a higher proportion of adults (69%) in the Cerro de la Cruz burial sample than expected based on age distributions in other large pre-Columbian burial samples (i.e., Storey 1985: Table 5). The overrepresentation of adults is largely due to the fact that most of the sample derives from Structure 1 and the UTW–1st, where adults made up 86 percent of buried individuals (Joyce 1991a, 253–257, Appendix 1). The adult-dominated age profile from the Structure 1 cemetery and along the UTW–1st, however, resembles the Early Formative cemetery from the Valley of Oaxaca site of Tomaltepec (Whalen 1981, 50; Figure 1.1). When burials from the residential and public spaces at Cerro de la Cruz are considered together (Table 4.3), the demographic curve begins to approach a more normal distribution. Both the demographic profile and the number of interred individuals around Structure 1 demonstrate that these burials represent a supradomestic social group. Although precise ages could

TABLE 4.3. Age groups, Cerro de la Cruz

Age Group	Minizundo Phase Total		Upper Terrace		Residential Areas	
	n	%	n	%	n	%
Infant (birth–1 yr)	6	7	1	2	5	18
Child (2–10 yrs)	16	18	5	8	11	39
Adolescent (11–20 yrs)	4	5	1	2	3	10
Subadult (< 20 years)	1	1	1	2	0	0
Adult (> 20 yrs)	10	12	9	15	1	4
Young Adult (20–35 yrs)	37	43	30	52	6	21
Middle Adult (36–45 yrs)	11	13	10	17	1	4
Old Adult (> 45 yrs)	1	1	1	2	1	4
Total	86	100	58	100	28	100

not be determined for some individuals with poorly preserved remains, the presence of several mature and old adults suggests that the Cerro de la Cruz population was relatively healthy. Age was clearly an important social distinction given that children and infants were buried almost exclusively near residences (see also King 2006). Of the six preadolescents buried near Structure 1, two (33%) were secondary, three (50%) possibly secondary, and only one (17%) was a confirmed primary interment for an individual under the age of 11. Of all those categorized as subadults on the upper terrace, only three (37%) were confirmed primary interments and at least one of those individuals was possibly considered an adult culturally, if not developmentally. Thus many adults became part of the social group whose members were buried on the upper terrace at the time they died, or just after, while juveniles rarely did so. Most of the juveniles who were placed on the upper terrace were interred elsewhere first. Perhaps they underwent changes in their social position after death before joining the group abiding in the area near Structure 1.

There was greater flexibility in the location of adult burials, since adults of all ages were interred near residences or near public architecture. The near absence of secondary burials in domestic contexts (one possible subadult south of the lower terrace) and their presence on the upper terrace further supports the notion that social position and relationships changed for certain individuals after death. While most juveniles remained part of their domestic groups, some adults ($n = 5$) and juveniles ($n = 3$) must have been moved to collective burial facilities like Structure 1 at some point after they died. The presence of adults beneath house floors may represent different stages in the transition to death rather than permanent burial places (see also R. Joyce 1999, 23).

TABLE 4.4. Sex ratios, Cerro de la Cruz

	Male		Female		Undetermined	
Context	n	%	n	%	n	%
Structure 1 and Upper Terrace	20	34	12	21	26	45
Structure 8	2	10	3	15	15	75
South of Lower Terrace	2	25	1	13	5	62
Total	24	28	16	19	46	53

Except in the case of the burials along the UTW–1st, sex ratios were largely equal. Poor preservation meant that less than half (47%) of all buried individuals could be sexed, but there were slightly more males present (60%) in cases where sex could be determined (Table 4.4). Given that females and males were found in all excavated contexts, it seems likely that the disparity is a result of preservation rather than evidence for differences in burial location between the sexes. In the case of the UTW–1st burials, males overwhelmingly predominated. The bias toward males probably had social significance. Some personal characteristic of these individuals may have influenced their burial location. Or, given that multiple domestic or kin groups were using the upper terrace for burial, the location and male bias may have resulted from social distinctions between these groups. It may also indicate that different domestic or kin groups, while involved in the general practice of collective burial on the upper terrace, chose to define and access deceased individuals in unique ways.

There were two patterns in body positioning: extended supine burial position was preferred, and bodies were oriented to cardinal directions. While most individuals were in an extended supine position, a number of other positions were observed (Table 4.5). The dead, like the buildings they were buried in or near, were situated in reference to the cardinal directions. As with other areas of Mesoamerica (i.e., Ashmore and Sabloff 2002; Joyce 2009; Kowalewski et al. 1991, 37; Sugiyama 2004, 102–103; Tolstoy 1989), there seems to have been general recognition of a celestially defined social landscape. Other aspects of body position were not standardized, but all individuals were oriented to the primary axes that defined socialized spaces.

The dead were a fundamental component of such spaces, as evidenced by the repeated use of certain locations for burial. Nearly all burials were placed in reference to other burials and architecture. Many individuals were part of either multiple primary burials or one of a sequence of interments set one atop the other. Since the excavations at Cerro de la Cruz were focused on architecture, the association evident between burials and structures is to some degree an artificial result of the sampling strategy. Nonetheless, ancient burial practices definitively referenced architecture. Most individuals (60%) were located beneath the interior floor of a structure, with a significant minority (20%)

TABLE 4.5. Body position by age, Cerro de la Cruz

Position	Inf.	Ch.	Adol.	A	YA	MA	OA	n	%
Supine	5	5	4	4	18	2	—	38	44
Extended left side	—	1	—	—	3	—	—	4	5
Extended right side	1	—	—	—	4	1	1	7	8
Extended prone	—	1	—	—	—	—	—	1	1
Extended unknown	—	—	1	—	—	—	—	1	1
Flexed left	—	—	1	—	—	1	—	2	2
Flexed right	—	2	—	—	2	—	—	4	5
Flexed supine	—	—	—	—	—	—	1	1	1
Undetermined	3	5	1	4	14	1	—	28	33
Total	9	14	7	8	42	5	1	86	100

Note: Inf. = Infant; Ch. = Child; Adol. = Adolescent; A = Adult; YA = Young Adult; MA = Middle Adult; OA = Old Adult.

positioned immediately next to a structural foundation wall on the exterior of a building. Even the nine burials located beneath the southwest corner of the patio near Structure 1 were set next to a buried retaining wall.

Status inequality was also evident in the burials of Cerro de la Cruz (Joyce 1991a, 1994). Members of the household that built and inhabited Structure 8 distinguished themselves from others at Cerro de la Cruz through the inclusion of grave offerings and items of personal adornment in some burials. This inequality was hereditary since these burials were associated with two different floors of the structure. Each of the four burials was located in a separate grouping, suggesting some separation in time between the interments associated with the same building phase. Furthermore, one of the individuals with an offering was no more than 8 years in age. How inequality intersected with other social phenomena such as political authority or economic interaction is unclear given the modesty of the grave goods and the small number of individuals interred with offerings. The placement of the four individuals accompanied by offerings inside a residence, however, suggests a level of exclusivity for the inhabitants of Structure 8 not evidenced elsewhere at the site. Knowledge of and access to these dead was limited to those people who lived in and used the dwelling. The relative status of other individuals buried at the site remains unclear. The emphasis on uniformity on the upper terrace may have precluded the presence of distinguishing items regardless of status in life. So those burials may not represent individuals of lower status (Joyce 1994, 159). Indeed, the many adults among the Structure 1 burials suggest that these were individuals of higher esteem or social position regardless of whether they had greater access to material resources.

TABLE 4.6. Age groups for Minizundo phase burials, Río Viejo

Age Group	n	%
Fetal (< 40 weeks in utero)	0	0
Infant (birth–1 yr)	0	0
Child (2–10 yrs)	2	40
Adolescent (11–20 yrs)	0	0
Adult (> 20 yrs)	0	0
Young Adult (20–35 yrs)	1	20
Middle Adult (36–45 yrs)	2	40
Old Adult (> 45 yrs)	0	0
Total	5	100

TABLE 4.7. Burial offerings, Río Viejo

Burial No.	Individual No.	Sex	Age	Position	Comments
9	9	M	35+ years	Extended left	1 conch shell
	10	—	25+ years	Extended left	A granite stone and animal bones
	11	—	3–6 years	Flexed right	Necklace of 20 perforated snail shells
10	12	—	6–9 years	Left side	Small worked stone (possible offering)

BURIAL PRACTICES AT RÍO VIEJO

Minizundo phase human remains from Río Viejo consist of five individuals recovered from a single trench (Joyce 1991a, 779–781). Due to extensive Terminal Formative and Classic period construction at the site, the Minizundo phase materials were deeply buried. Available evidence suggests that these burials were associated with domestic contexts in what would have been a Minizundo phase village. The demographic profile of the burials follows a normal curve, with children and adults present but no adolescents (Table 4.6). Bodies were positioned on the left or right side in either an extended or flexed position. There was no predominant body orientation. Body position and orientation did not correlate with age, sex, or burial location. Three of the five individuals had clearly identifiable grave goods, and a fourth was likely interred with a modest offering (Table 4.7). Minizundo phase grave goods at Río Viejo were modest, however, with the most elaborate offering probably consisting of a necklace of small, perforated snail shells accompanying a child.

MINIZUNDO PHASE SUMMARY

The total Minizundo phase burial sample consists of ninety-one individuals interred in both domestic and public architectural spaces. While the small size of the Río Viejo sample in comparison with that of Cerro de la Cruz makes comparison between the two sites difficult, several patterns across the two sites are apparent. First, the practice of using the same physical location for repeated burial is evident at both sites. Three of the five individuals from Río Viejo were emplaced in the same stratum in close physical proximity, and none of the five were more than 2 m from any other individual (Joyce 1991a). Second, bodies were again oriented to the cardinal directions. The importance of certain celestial axes was regionally shared. Finally, heritable, ascribed status inequality is apparent (see Joyce 1994). Inequality was probably ascribed at the scale of the household at this time since both adults ($n = 5$) and juveniles ($n = 3$) in residential areas were interred with offerings. The kinds of items present in Minizundo phase burials included personal adornments like jewelry or elaborate clothing as well as tools and pottery. With the possible exception of a single obsidian flake at Cerro de la Cruz, only locally available resources were present in graves.

EARLY TERMINAL FORMATIVE PERIOD BURIAL PRACTICES

The burial sample from the early Terminal Formative period Miniyua phase (150 BC–AD 100) is currently the smallest. It consists of twenty-two individuals from the sites of Barra Quebrada ($n = 2$), Cerro de la Cruz ($n = 4$), Charco Redondo ($n = 10$), Río Viejo ($n = 1$), and Yugüe ($n = 5$). Because of its small size and limited contextual data, the entire sample will be discussed together. The burials from Cerro de la Cruz were eroding from the modern ground surface (Joyce 1991a, 768–771). The burials from Barra Quebrada (Winter and Joyce 1987) and Río Viejo (Christensen 1999) were from domestic contexts. Those from Yugüe were interred in a public structure (Barber 2005, 159–164, 386–389), and it is likely that those from Charco Redondo were as well (Butler 2011). The Miniyua phase sample covers ages ranging from infant through adult, with adults composing the majority (71%) of the sample (Table 4.8). All of the Charco Redondo, Barra Quebrada, and Río Viejo burials were adult. The Yugüe burials showed the greatest diversity in age, including two infants, a child, and an adult. Both sexes were represented among the adults at Charco Redondo. The Río Viejo individual was male, and those from Yugüe and Barra Quebrada could not be sexed. Burial position and orientation varied considerably (Table 4.8). The Charco Redondo burials were prone: one extended and two with flexed legs. The most prevalent position overall was extended on the left side ($n = 4$, 40%). Given the small sample size, it was not possible to determine if body position and orientation correlated with age, sex, or burial location.

Offerings were present in burials at four of the five sites (Table 4.9), although the Barra Quebrada burials were only partially excavated, and so

TABLE 4.8. Body position by age, Miniyua phase

Position	Fet.	Inf.	Ch.	A	YA	n	%
Supine	—	—	—	2	—	2	20
Prone Flexed	—	—	—	1	—	1	10
Prone Extended	—	—	—	—	1	1	10
Extended Left	—	—	1	3	—	4	40
Flexed Right	—	1	—	1?	—	2	20
Total	—	1	1	7	1	10	100

Note: Fet. = Fetal; Inf. = Infant; Ch. = Child; A = Adult; YA = Young Adult.

offerings may have been present. Despite the small sample size, 64 percent ($n = 7$) of the fully excavated burials included offerings. These tended to be relatively modest, ranging from single greenstone beads in the mouths of individuals at Río Viejo (Workinger and Joyce 1999, 79) and Charco Redondo to small coarse brownware vessels. Offerings were predominantly associated with adults (86%), but one juvenile also had offerings. Two burials, at Cerro de la Cruz (B4-I6) and Charco Redondo (B9-I9), had granite slabs lining the grave. At Charco Redondo an adult male (B9-I9) interred in a flexed prone position had granite slabs surrounding the lower half of the body and the cranium (Figure 4.7). Large sherds from a coarse brownware jar were also set among the slabs—whether as part of the grave lining or from a damaged offering vessel is not clear.

Several general observations may be made about the Miniyua phase burial sample. Age appears to have been an important principle determining burial location. Miniyua phase burials are again dominated by adults because collective adult burial was undertaken at Charco Redondo. The Charco Redondo individuals were part of a larger, partially excavated cemetery that consisted of at least ten adult individuals interred close together or one atop the other. The Charco Redondo burials, like those from Yugüe, were presumably beneath the floor of a communal structure. At both sites burials were interred near other individuals. At Charco Redondo burials were oriented to an axis of 25 degrees east of north, and at Yugüe they were oriented 15 degrees east of north (Barber 2005, 386–387); both orientations represent a change from the Minizundo phase. Diversity in body position is evident based on the five different positions documented. While there were no clear secondary burials, the Yugüe adult was in extremely fragmentary condition that indicated some kind of postmortem exposure or processing (Figure 4.8). Status differences between individuals are evidenced by a high percentage of individuals with grave offerings. Nonetheless, there is actually less diversity in offerings from the preceding Late Formative,

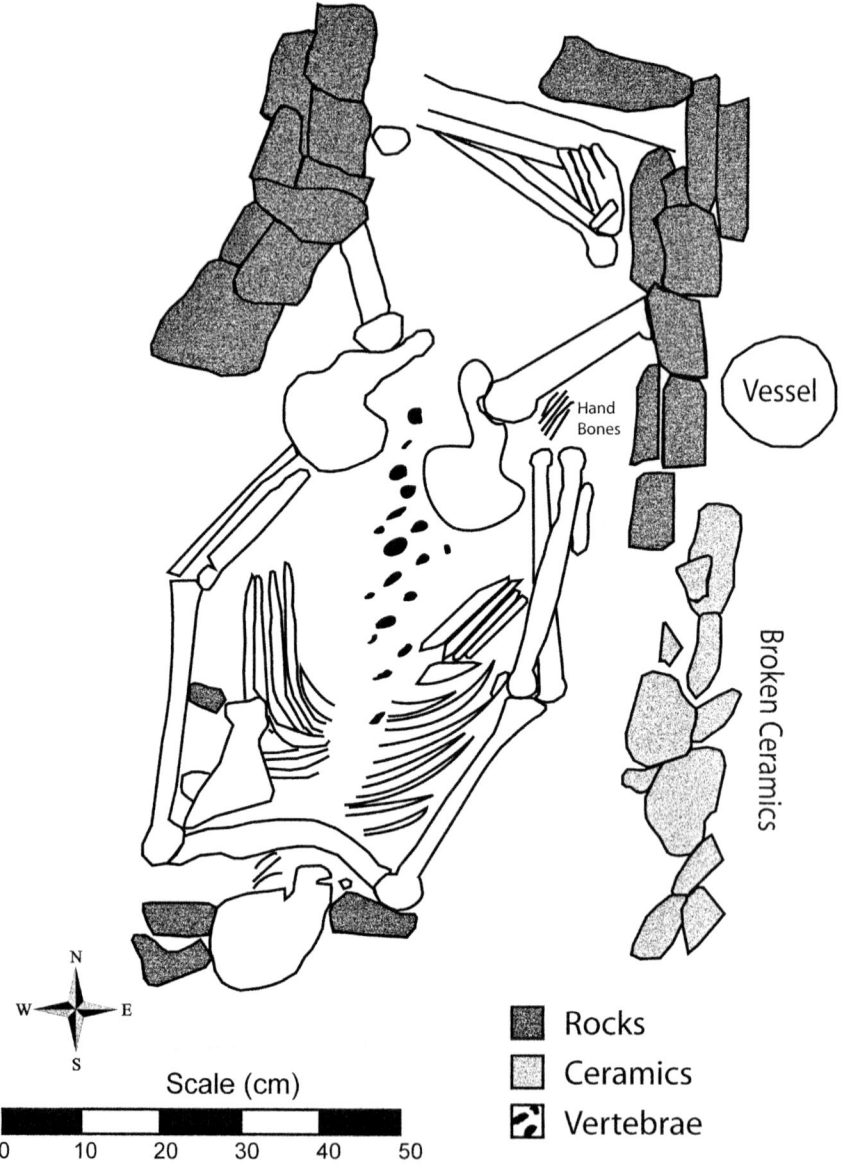

Hand Bones

Vessel

Broken Ceramics

N
W — E
S

Scale (cm)

| 0 | 10 | 20 | 30 | 40 | 50 |

Rocks
Ceramics
Vertebrae

FIGURE 4.7. B9-I9, Charco Redondo, showing the prone, flexed position and the stone and ceramic lining to the burial pit.

although this is likely a function of sample size. Similar offerings occurred at different sites, with locally made coarse brownware jars and bowls present in all but one (87%) burial with offerings.

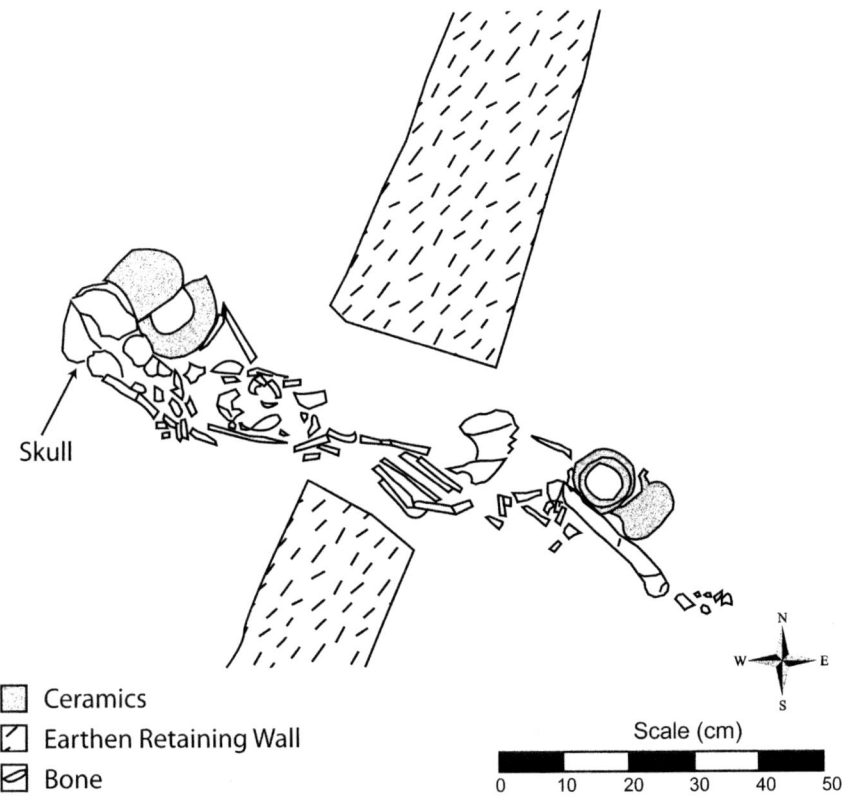

Skull

Ceramics
Earthen Retaining Wall
Bone

Scale (cm)

0   10   20   30   40   50

FIGURE 4.8. B6-I6, Yugüe, showing offerings and fragmentary condition of bones.

LATE TERMINAL FORMATIVE PERIOD BURIAL PRACTICES

The late Terminal Formative period Chacahua phase (AD 100–250) burial sample ($n = 43$) is derived from a cemetery at the site of Yugüe ($n = 41$; Barber 2005, Chapter 6), an adult next to a retaining wall at Yugüe (Barber 2005), and one adult in fill at the site of Campo Montealegre (Barber 2009).[2] The Yugüe cemetery, or Burial Area 1 (BA1), was located at the summit of Yugüe's 10 m tall mixed-use platform in an area used for collective ritual and interment throughout the Terminal Formative (see Barber, Chapter 6). Because it was just below the modern ground surface, BA1 could not be associated with any nearby superstructures due to sediment loss from erosion. However, the west and south limits of BA1 were abrupt and formed a clear right angle, suggesting that the burials had been emplaced beneath the floor of a now-lost superstructure (see Barber, Chapter 6: Figure 6.5). The remnants of one superstructure and several low substructural platforms were found in the vicinity of BA1. As with the Structure 1 burials at Cerro de la Cruz and probably the Charco

TABLE 4.9. Burial offerings, Miniyua phase

Site	Burial No.	Individual No.	Sex	Age	Position	Comments
Río Viejo	20	23	M	Adult	Supine	Greenstone bead in mouth
Yugüe	5	5	—	5	Partial, left side	Coarse brownware jar with fine brownware bowl lid
Yugüe	6	6	—	Adult	Extended left	4 coarse brownware jars: 2 at the head, 2 next to the femora
Cerro de la Cruz	8	49	—	18+	Extended left	Red-slipped coarse brownware bowl and possibly a notched *olivella* shell
Cerro de la Cruz	4	6	—	20+	Extended left	Red-slipped coarse brownware bowl; granite slab lining
Cerro de la Cruz	4	8	—	Adult	Supine	Worked granite disk (15 cm in diameter) and red-slipped coarse brownware bowl
Charco Redondo	9	9	M	28+	Prone flexed	Greenstone bead in mouth and coarse brownware cylindrical bowl; partial granite slab lining

Redondo burials, the Yugüe interments took place over a period of time. All but four individuals had been disturbed by later burials, and some were likely secondary burials.

BA1 manifested greater demographic diversity than earlier burial samples but showed standardization in body position and orientation. The Yugüe sample follows a normal mortality curve. Juvenile mortality was highest among individuals younger than 7 years of age (Mayes and Barber 2008, 584). Where sex could be ascertained, both sexes were present, although females ($n = 7$, 70%) were more common than males ($n = 3$, 30%). The practice of side burial caused severe taphonomic changes to both crania and pelvises such that only ten of the nineteen (53%) adults and adolescents in the sample could be sexed. There was a pattern in burial position and orientation (Table 4.10). Three adults were buried on their right sides with their heads to the west. The youngest individual interred in this position (B14-I16) was a male between 15 and 17 years of age at death. Four juveniles, one female holding an infant, and one adult male were placed perpendicular to the remaining adults, on their left sides with their heads to the south. Only three adults and one infant were fully articulated; all other individuals had been disturbed by subsequent interments. Most likely those individuals lacking a pelvis and lower extremities ($n = 5$) were emplaced in an extended position like the intact individuals, but there is no way to confirm this assertion. Similar to the cemetery at Cerro de la Cruz, many sections of BA1 contained mixed collections of bone that were a result of either cul-

TABLE 4.10. Body position, Chacahua phase, Yugüe

Head to:	Inf.	Ch.	Ado.	A	YA	MA	OA	n	%
West	—	—	1	—	1	1	—	3	14
South	2	2	—	—	—	1	1	6	27
Disarticulated	1	2	—	7	3	—	—	13	59
Total	3	4	1	7	4	2	1	22	100

Note: Inf. = Infant; Ch. = Child; Adol. = Adolescent; A = Adult; YA = Young Adult; MA = Middle Adult; OA = Old Adult.

tural disturbance or secondary burial. Based on long bones of fully or partially articulated individuals, bodies were oriented in reference to an approximate azimuth of 15 degrees east of north for juveniles and a few adults ($n = 4$) and 15 degrees north of west for adults ($n = 3$).

Inequality was evident in the form of associated funerary objects ($n = 2$; 6%) and dental modification ($n = 2$; 6%; Table 4.11). Offerings or cultural modification of dentition were found with individuals of all ages and both sexes. While most offerings at Yugüe were modest, one individual was interred with two unusual items. B14-I16, the adolescent male interred as an adult, was holding an incised deer femur flute and wearing a plaster-backed iron ore pectoral (Barber 2005, Chapter 6; Barber and Olvera 2012; Mayes and Barber 2008). This individual was likely a local elite and a ritual specialist with the ability to contact entities living in the underworld or the celestial realm (Barber and Olvera 2012). Two adult females showed evidence for pyrite incrustations in their upper incisors. Although others have found that dental modification was not necessarily an indicator of high status in pre-Columbian Mesoamerica (Krejci and Culbert 1995), iron pyrite is sufficiently rare in the lower Río Verde Valley that it was likely a socially valued material in the Terminal Formative period. There is only one other example of iron pyrite from pre-Columbian archaeological contexts in the region: a few fragments from a cache at San Francisco de Arriba (Workinger 2002, 193). Six individuals, five adults and a child, had pebbles beneath their skulls. The pebbles were intentionally placed because the fill of the burial area was well sorted. Since only one of these individuals had other associated offerings, the pebbles were probably not related to status inequality.

Several additional burial offerings were present in the fill of BA1. These included a lidded coarse brownware cup, an incised grayware jar, and three miniature grayware jars. Because of the level of disturbance, it was not possible to determine with whom these items were associated. The cup and jar, however, were next to the legs of B14-I16 and probably were grave offerings for that individual.

Several patterns are evident in the Yugüe burial sample. Collective burial was an important principle in the Chacahua phase. Excavations elsewhere on

TABLE 4.11. Burial offerings and dental modification, Chacahua phase

Burial No.	Individual No.	Sex	Age	Position	Comments
8	8	F	40–50	Extended left	Pyrite incrustations in upper incisors
11	12	—	6	Partial, left side	String of 29 greenstone and white stone or shell beads, anthropomorphic greenstone pendant
14	16	M	15–17	Extended right	Plaster-backed iron ore mirror, incised deer femur flute
28	32	F	30–40	Secondary?	Circular impressions in incisors for incrustations

the Yugüe platform did not uncover burials, indicating that proximity to other individuals and association with certain physical spaces were significant when locating interments (Barber 2005). While too large to represent a single domestic group, BA1 manifested a normal mortality curve for a preindustrial population. Children under age 7 and adults made up the majority of the sample. Males and females were both present. Nonetheless, age was a significant social distinction. As the orientation of B14-I16 indicates, adulthood was achieved by the adolescent years. No juveniles were buried in the northwest-southeast orientation characteristic of adults, although one adult female with a child and one adult male were buried in the southwest-northeast orientation shared by juveniles. This pattern suggests that age was more relevant than gender in defining burial position. Individuals of varying social statuses were also present. At least one ritual specialist was interred in BA1 (B14-I16). And yet there were also two young adults in the cemetery without grave offerings whose joints showed evidence of heavy labor (Mayes and Barber 2008, 585). The grave goods at Yugüe included a mix of both local and imported goods. Iron ores and greenstone beads and pendants were likely imported from the highlands. Limestone for plaster is rarely encountered in the lower Río Verde Valley and may also have been imported. The pottery was locally produced.

HEALTH, DISEASE, AND PATHOLOGIES

Of the entire lower Verde skeletal population, only the eleven individuals from Yugüe with greater than 25 percent of the skeletal elements present and four individuals from Cerro de la Cruz have received detailed paleopathological analysis (Mayes and Barber 2008; Mayes et al. 2009; Melmed 2006). Dental pathologies were examined for an additional two individuals from Yugüe (170 teeth; Mayes and Barber 2008, 583; Melmed 2006: Table 6). At Yugüe three individuals dated to the early Terminal Formative period and eight to the late

FIGURE 4.9. Example of the plastic distortion common in the human remains of the lower Río Verde Valley.

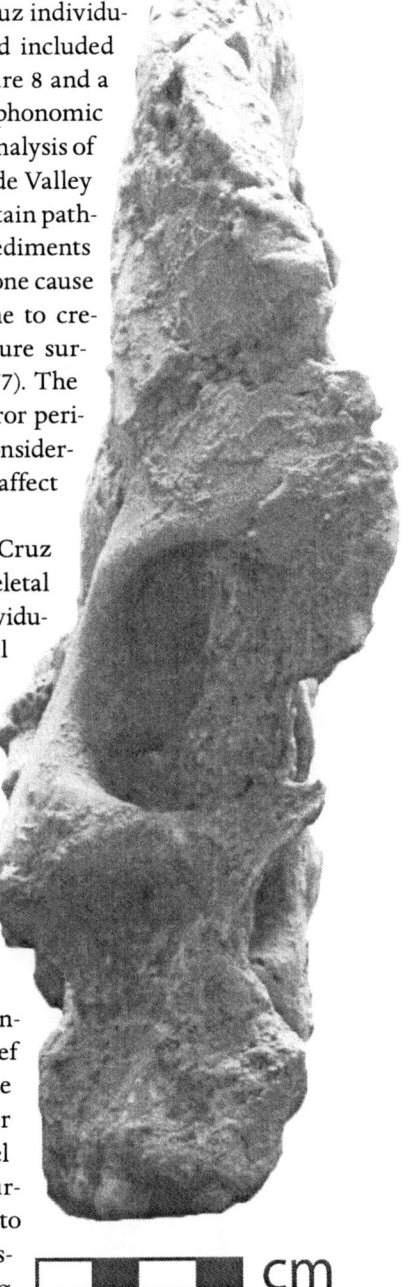

Terminal Formative. The Cerro de la Cruz individuals were all Late Formative in date and included three individuals buried beneath Structure 8 and a fourth buried near Structure 9. Severe taphonomic processes complicate paleopathological analysis of skeletal remains from the lower Río Verde Valley and may have limited the visibility of certain pathological conditions. The heavy, clayey sediments characteristic of most of the floodplain zone cause warping (Figure 4.9) and adhere to bone to create a cement-like coating that can obscure surface features (Mayes and Barber 2008, 577). The resultant crushing of bone can also mirror perimortem trauma, requiring careful consideration of all possible processes that could affect the bone before and after death.

One individual in the Cerro de la Cruz sample manifested antemortem skeletal pathologies while all four studied individuals evinced dental pathologies. Burial 12—Individual 38 (B12-I38) was an older (45–50) female with a well-healed head injury (a depression fracture on the left parietal bone), osteoarthritis, osteophytosis, periodontal disease, and periostitis. The degenerative changes were due to the individual's advanced age. Interestingly, while sick at the time of death (Figure 4.10), her dentition shows she was relatively healthy during development, with one slight linear enamel hypoplasia indicating a brief physiological disturbance around the age of four. The dentition of the other three individuals revealed linear enamel hypoplasias indicative of biological disturbances during development. In addition to the two children from Structure 8 (discussed above), the dentition of a young

cm

FIGURE 4.10. Cross section of femur (B12-I38) showing a second outer layer of enlarged poros-ity under compact bone. This swollen shaft-within-shaft appearance is consistent with severe periostitis caused by infection.

female aged 14–15 years at death (B10-I16) showed several brief physiological disruptions during development. These began around 1.5 years of age and most likely corresponded with the introduction of food into her diet; they ended around age 5, when she was probably fully weaned. Otherwise, this individual appeared to be very healthy.

In contrast to the Cerro de la Cruz sample, there were only two types of bone pathologies evident in the Terminal Formative skeletal collection: degen-erative joint disease and iron deficiency anemia (Melmed 2006, 42). There was no evidence for infection, tumors, or trauma (Melmed 2006, 69). Dental pathologies, on the other hand, indicate periods of physiological stress, one instance of congenital syphilis, and several instances of dental modification (Mayes et al. 2009; Melmed 2006, 71–76). Most individuals studied had linear

TABLE 4.12. Age groups by time period

	Minizundo Phase		Miniyua Phase		Chacahua Phase	
Age Group	n	%	n	%	n	%
Fetal (< 40 weeks *in utero*)	—	—	—	—	1	3
Infant (birth–1 yr)	6	7	2	14	4	14
Child (2–10 yrs)	18	20	2	14	6	20
Adolescent (11–20 yrs)	5	5	—	—	1	3
Adult (> 20 yrs)	10	11	9	65	10	33
Young Adult (20–35 yrs)	38	42	1	7	4	14
Middle Adult (36–45 yrs)	13	14	—	—	3	10
Old Adult (> 45 yrs)	1	1	—	—	1	3
Total	91	100	14	100	30	100

enamel hypoplasias indicating weaning and post-weaning stress between the ages of 2.5 and 4 years (Mayes and Barber 2008, 583; Melmed 2006, 73). At the same time, the number of dental caries was low, suggesting that riverine, estuarine, and marine proteins made up a larger proportion of the diet than that of contemporaneous inland populations (Melmed 2006, 73), which is consistent with trace element analyses of human bone (Joyce 1991b, 136–138) and archaeofaunal data (Fernández 2004). Overall, Formative period populations appear to have been relatively healthy. Only one individual in the collection shows evidence for trauma (Cerro de la Cruz B12-I38), but that trauma was not a cause of death. Future research on the Cerro de la Cruz skeletal collection is necessary to identify patterns in health over time.

CONTINUITY AND CHANGE IN BURIAL PRACTICES

Formative period burial practices in the lower Río Verde Valley provide evidence for continuity and change in a variety of social relationships. Of particular interest is the persistence and significance of supradomestic social groups through at least the end of the Formative. Collective burial in public spaces was an enduring pattern in the lower Río Verde Valley, one that distinguishes the region from other areas of Oaxaca. This practice concentrated many individuals from multiple households in specific physical locations and created accessible public places where the living and the dead could interact. We see the creation of these less restricted and intergenerationally shared spaces as fundamental to the formation of local community identities, which were social groups embedded in local history and place (Barber 2005, Chapter 6; Barber and Joyce 2007; Joyce 2010, 181–195). While community identities persisted throughout the Formative, burial evidence shows that this type of social group became increasingly inclusive over time (Table 4.12). In the Minizundo phase, community membership was age-restricted and may, in some instances, have been achieved after death. There were only eight subadults buried on the upper terrace at Cerro de la Cruz, and at least two of these were secondary burials. Uniformity was emphasized, with no other distinctions between individuals such that even durable items of personal adornment were excluded. Community affiliation superseded domestic, gender, and probably status affiliations.

The age-exclusivity and social uniformity of community membership broke down in the Terminal Formative. At Charco Redondo collective burial in community facilities remained exclusive to adults in the Miniyua phase. However, some individuals were distinguished from others based on offerings or elaboration of the burial pit. At Yugüe age restrictions were not evident and offerings were present in some Miniyua phase burials. Nonetheless, individual and status distinctions at both sites were deemphasized since burial offerings were relatively generic. In other words, during the Miniyua phase, the communally interred dead lacked items that referenced personal status or individual responsibilities, unlike domestic burials from the Minizundo phase. By the Chacahua phase, community membership had become inclusive rather than exclusive. In the Yugüe cemetery individuals of all ages were interred together, and some individuals were distinguished not just by burial offerings but also by personal adornment. Some of these latter were clearly personal possessions that pertained to specific individuals' status, skills, or responsibilities, particularly the bone flute and mirror (Barber and Olvera 2012; Mayes and Barber 2008).

Collective burial in public facilities served to create community ancestry. In many other parts of Late and Terminal Formative period Mesoamerica, the dead were affiliated with their households except in specialized cases (i.e., Gillespie 2001b; Hammond 1995, 1999; R. Joyce 1999; McAnany et al. 1999; Urunuela and Plunket 2002; Winter 1995). The high proportion of adults, sometimes adult males (Urunuela and Plunket 2002, 30), in domestic burials elsewhere is generally understood to indicate ancestor worship (i.e., McAnany 1995) as well as the significance of households as the primary social group through which generational continuity and property rights were assured (Buikstra and Charles 1999; Gillespie 2001b; McAnany 1995; McAnany et al. 1999). The community burials of the lower Verde suggest that group continuity, ancestry, and perhaps land tenure were articulated at a larger scale in the Formative period, at the level of the community or of multihousehold factions within a community.

The spatial redundancy of burials supports the notion that identities were defined by both ancestry and geography throughout the Formative. The relationship between people and the built environment was pronounced. Of the

156 Formative period individuals whose remains have been collected or identified through archaeological excavation, the vast majority were buried close to architectural features. The association is not an outcome of sampling bias: penetrating excavations beyond the limits of earthen platforms have been undertaken at eighteen sites, including Yugüe, Río Viejo, and Charco Redondo (Barber 2008, 2009; Gillespie 1987; Joyce 1991a; Workinger 2002; Workinger and Joyce 1999). While these excavations have recovered the remains of middens, roasting pits, and occupational surfaces, they have not recovered burials. Formative period burial sites represented locations where the living, the dead, and the landscape intersected, embedding the history of social groups in significant places (i.e., Watanabe 1990, 139). Placing the dead beneath or near important architectural elements like foundation walls or floors literally built people into buildings, socializing the landscape and clearly defining who was and was not affiliated with a particular geographical area. Indeed, association with a specific location was more relevant than the physical integrity of bodies. This is most explicit at Yugüe, where only four (11%) of the thirty-six excavated Chacahua phase individuals were fully articulated. A similar pattern is evident at Cerro de la Cruz, where fourteen (29%) of the Structure 1 interments were complete or nearly complete. Relations within domestic and supradomestic groups also had a spatial component. In the Minizundo phase proximity to buildings probably pertained to individuals' position within a collectivity. As previously observed, all burials with offerings at Cerro de la Cruz were inside the Structure 8 residence. In the Chacahua phase, age and certain gender roles had a spatial component. Children and an adult female buried with a child were oriented differently than adults. To be a certain kind of person was to be in a certain place.

Age and status inequality were persistently distinguished in burial practices over time. Age remained an important aspect of social identity throughout the pre-Columbian era, with age-related burial patterns evident through the Early Postclassic (King 2006). However, the place of children in households and communities shifted. Juveniles predominated in the domestic burials of Cerro de la Cruz, indicating that they were members of their households at or near birth but that they were segregated from larger-scale corporate groups. By the Chacahua phase, however, group membership began at or before birth, even though age continued to distinguish children from adults. The social attainment of adulthood occurred concomitant with puberty since individuals between the ages of 12 and 15 were treated as adults in death at both Cerro de la Cruz and Yugüe. Status inequality was expressed more openly at the end of the Formative period. In the Late Formative expressions of status inequality were restricted to private, residential spaces. In the Terminal Formative inequality was publicly pronounced between community members. Miniyua phase burials in public architecture at Yugüe and Charco Redondo included modest offerings, differentiating some members of the community from others based on status inequality. This pattern continued into the Chacahua phase, when individuals with unusual skills or higher social position were interred in community facilities. The public visibility of high status furthermore suggests that inequality had become entrenched by the Chacahua phase (Barber et al. n.d.). Rather than restricting status distinctions to exclusive residential contexts, as occurred in the Minizundo phase, inequality in the Chacahua phase was central to community group definition. Individuals with special knowledge and skills became a collective resource, legitimizing inequality in terms that had once been used to define uniformity (Barber and Joyce 2007; Barber et al. n.d.).

The items that accompanied the dead indicate changes in large-scale socio-economic networks. While materials like obsidian and ceramics had been imported into the lower Río Verde Valley since the Early Formative period (see Hepp 2011; Workinger, Chapter 7), they were not incorporated into burials during the later Formative. Their absence from burials probably indicates that imported items were more appropriately used and accessed by the living. In the Chacahua phase, however, socially valuable imported items like iron ores and plaster began to appear in buried deposits (Barber 2005; Barber et al. n.d.). The presence of these items may indicate changes in long-distance exchange relations such that certain social groups now had greatly increased access to imported valuables. It also could indicate sumptuary restrictions: use of these materials was so closely linked to specific individuals (or kinds of individuals) that the materials remained with a person after death.

LOWER VERDE BURIAL PRACTICES IN REGIONAL PERSPECTIVE

Burial practices in the lower Río Verde Valley in the Formative period were distinct from those of neighboring areas and do not indicate the presence or influence of highland Zapotecs or Mixtecs in the region. Most strikingly, the kind of collective, public burial found in the lower Río Verde Valley is uncommon in the Oaxaca highlands (cf. Sherman et al. 2010, 292–293). Only three possible cemeteries are known for the entire pre-Columbian sequence in the far more intensively studied Valley of Oaxaca (Urcid 2005, 29). Two date to the Early Formative period—from the sites of Tomaltepec (Whalen 1981) and San José Mogote (Flannery and Marcus 1983, 55). A third possible cemetery dates to the Early Classic from the site of Yagul (Urcid 2005, 29). While the two Early Formative cemeteries consisted of individuals from multiple domestic groups, the burials were located away from occupation areas and were not placed beneath or near architecture.

Beyond these three examples, the overwhelming majority of burials in the Valley of Oaxaca were situated near or beneath residential architecture

(Barber and Joyce 2006; Blomster 2011, 119; Urcid 2005, 29–30; Winter 1974, 1995, 3). Even in the Early Formative period burials at the site of Tierras Largas were associated with residences and consisted of small groups of adults and juveniles that likely represented domestic groups (Winter 1972: Table 34, 235). By the Middle Formative, the practice of burying the dead in supradomestic groups had largely ceased (Blomster 2011, 115; Drennan 1976). At Tomaltepec, for instance, adults were buried in residential contexts after 800 BC (Whalen 1988, 261). From the Late Formative period until the end of the Classic period, a characteristic and enduring highland Zapotec burial pattern developed: adults and juveniles were interred beneath residential floors or along walls, with a small number of adult males and females interred in tombs or slab-lined graves (Barber and Joyce 2006; Blomster 2011, 123; Martínez López 2011, 319; Urcid 2005, 32–33; Winter 1974, 1995, 3). As Martínez López (2011, 340) demonstrates, there is considerable change in the uses, offerings, and even occupants of Zapotec tombs over the course of the Formative. Nonetheless, the association between adult and juvenile inhumations and residences remains stable for over 1,000 years.

In the Mixteca Alta and Baja regions of northwestern Oaxaca, residential burial was also the most common practice. At the Late Formative site of Monte Negro, however, burials and tombs were located beneath both residences and temples (Acosta and Romero 1992; Joyce 2010, 168–173). The temple interments were mostly older adults, indicating that age-related status differences were as important at Monte Negro as they were in the lower Río Verde Valley at this time (Joyce 2010, 167). Both juvenile and adult burials were recovered from residential contexts at the site of Huamelulpan, including a tomb containing multiple individuals that is reminiscent of the Valley of Oaxaca pattern (Gaxiola 1984, 60–64). While there are few data from the Mixteca Baja, excavations at Cerro de las Minas revealed eight residential interments (Joyce 2010; Winter and Montague 1991). Looted tombs have also been reported from the public plaza at the site of Santa Teresa (Winter 2005).

CONCLUSIONS

The Formative period burial practices of the lower Río Verde Valley represent a distinct regional tradition within pre-Columbian Oaxaca. The persistence of collective burial in association with public buildings or spaces indicates a unique coastal practice that appears to have developed separately from burial traditions in the Oaxaca highlands. The transition from the Minizundo phase to Miniyua phase marked a significant shift in regional political relations as Río Viejo became the seat of a regional polity (Joyce 2008, 2010, Chapter 1; Joyce et al., Chapter 5). The regional variety in Miniyua phase burial practices, which encompass many body positions, differences in treatment of children, and some public access to higher-status individuals, may have been part of the process whereby people valley-wide redefined a variety of social relationships. Communal affiliations were being maintained in reference to new, external political forces while individual and domestic status was being asserted in terms of both local and regional networks. Future research on Miniyua phase burials will provide valuable insight into these processes. By the Chacahua phase, the definitions of various social groups were significantly different than they had been in the Minizundo phase. Communities were more inclusive of both children and elites. Neither youth nor high status precluded corporate group membership. Barber and colleagues have postulated elsewhere (Barber 2005; Barber and Joyce 2007; Barber et al. n.d.) that expanding membership in these groups would have provided more frequent opportunities to maintain and redefine local social relationships in the face of external pressures. Nonetheless, inequality had become more pronounced by the Chacahua phase. Elites retained their access to and use of certain highly valuable items in death, remaining distinct from fellow community members despite being interred with them.

The end of the Formative period coincided with a major shift in political and economic organization in the lower Río Verde Valley. By the Early Classic, Río Viejo had lost much of its population and valley-wide political authority had disintegrated (Joyce 2003, 2008, 2010). Political restructuring was accompanied by significant changes in local and regional social relationships. These changes, while still poorly understood, are evident in burial practices. Some of the valley's most elaborate burials date to the Early Classic, suggesting that inequality became increasingly pronounced over time. Imported goods from central Mexico and other coastal areas begin to appear as funerary offerings (Joyce 2003). Unsurprisingly, the dead were part of this shifting political, economic, and social landscape.

ACKNOWLEDGMENTS

We would like to thank the Instituto Nacional de Antropología e Historia for sanctioning the excavations and analysis on which this chapter is based. We are particularly indebted to the presidents and members of the Consejo de Arqueología; current and former directors of the Centro INAH-Oaxaca, including María de la Luz Topete, Ernesto González Licón, Enrique Fernandez Dávila, and Eduardo López Calzada; and Dr. Sergio López Alonso, director of physical anthropology at the Centro INAH-Oaxaca. Funding for archaeological field research in the lower Río Verde Valley was provided by grants from the following organizations: National Science Foundation (BNS-8716332, BCS-0096012, BCS-0202624), Foundation for the Advancement of Mesoamerican Studies (#02060), the Association of Women in Science, the Women's Forum

Foundation of Colorado, National Geographic Society (grant 3767-88), Wenner-Gren Foundation (GR 4988), Vanderbilt University Research Council and Mellon Fund, Fulbright Foundation, H. John Heinz III Charitable Trust, Rutgers University, Sigma Xi, Colorado Archaeological Society, the University of Colorado at Boulder, the San Diego State University College of Arts and Letters, the San Diego State University Research, Scholarship, and Creative Activity Grant, the Explorers Club Exploration Fund, and the University of California–Riverside CHASS Humanities Research Grant. We would also like to thank Alex Christensen, María Rosado, and Alicia Herrera Muzgo Torres for carrying out the preliminary bioarchaeological analyses on burials from Cerro de la Cruz and Río Viejo.

NOTES

1. The ages of four individuals from Cerro de la Cruz reported here differ slightly from those initially published by Joyce (1991a: Appendix 1) and are based on a recent, more detailed osteological analysis by Arion Mayes.

2. There was also one likely late Terminal Formative burial uncovered at Río Viejo (Workinger and Joyce 1999, 83–84) and another at Barra Quebrada (Winter and Joyce 1987).

REFERENCES CITED

Acosta, Jorge R., and Javier Romero. 1992. *Exploraciones en Monte Negro, Oaxaca: 1937–1938, 1938–1939, y 1939–1940*. Mexico City: Instituto Nacional de Antropología e Historia.

Ashmore, Wendy, and Jeremy Sabloff. 2002. "Spatial Orders in Maya Civic Plans." *Latin American Antiquity* 13 (2): 201–16. http://dx.doi.org/10.2307/971914.

Barber, Sarah B. 2005. *Heterogeneity, Identity, and Complexity: Negotiating Status and Authority in Terminal Formative Coastal Oaxaca*. PhD dissertation, Department of Anthropology, University of Colorado, Boulder. Ann Arbor, MI: University Microfilms.

Barber, Sarah B. 2008. "Proyecto Río Verde, 2003: Informe final." Final report submitted to the Consejo de Arqueología, Instituto Nacional de Antropología e Historia, Mexico City.

Barber, Sarah B. 2009. Excavaciones de prueba en el valle inferior del Río Verde. In "El proyecto Río Verde," ed. Arthur A. Joyce, 228–321. Final report submitted to the Consejo de Arqueología, Instituto Nacional de Antropología e Historia, Mexico City.

Barber, Sarah B., and Arthur A. Joyce. 2006. "When Is a House a Palace? Elite Residences in the Valley of Oaxaca." In *Palaces and Power in the Americas*, ed. Jessica J. Christie and Patricia J. Sarro, 211–55. Austin: University of Texas Press.

Barber, Sarah B., and Arthur A. Joyce. 2007. "Polity Produced and Community Consumed: Negotiating Political Centralization in the Lower Río Verde Valley, Oaxaca." In *Mesoamerican Ritual Economy: Archaeological and Ethnological Perspectives,* ed. E. Christian Wells and Karla L. Davis-Salazar, 221–44. Boulder: University Press of Colorado.

Barber, Sarah B., and Mireya Olvera. 2012. "A Divine Wind: The Arts of Death and Music in Ancient Oaxaca." *Ancient Mesoamerica* 23(1): 9–24.

Barber, Sarah B., Andrew Workinger, and Arthur Joyce. N.d. "Situational Inalienability and Social Change in Formative Period Coastal Oaxaca." In *Inalienable Possessions in the Archaeology of Mesoamerica*, ed. Brigitte Kovacevich and Michael G. Callaghan. Washington, DC: American Anthropological Association, under review.

Binford, Lewis. 1971. "Mortuary Practices: Their Study and Their Potential." In *Approaches to the Social Dimension of Mortuary Practices*, ed. James A. Brown, 6–29. Memoirs, vol. 25. Washington, DC: Society for American Archaeology.

Blomster, Jeffrey P. 2011. "Bodies, Bones, and Burials: Corporeal Constructs and Enduring Relationships in Oaxaca, Mexico." In *Living with the Dead: Mortuary Ritual in Mesoamerica*, ed. James L. Fitzsimmons and Izumi Shimada, 102–60. Tucson: University of Arizona Press.

Buikstra, Jane E., and Douglas K. Charles. 1999. "Centering the Ancestors: Cemeteries, Mounds, and Sacred Landscapes of the Ancient North American Midcontinent." In *Archaeologies of Landscape*, ed. Wendy Ashmore and A. Bernard Knapp, 201–28. Malden, MA: Blackwell Publishers.

Butler, Michelle. 2011. Excavaciones en Charco Redondo, 2009. In "El proyecto Río Verde: Informe técnico de la temporada de 2009," ed. Sarah B. Barber and Arthur A. Joyce, 185–221. Final report submitted to the Consejo de Arqueología, Instituto Nacional de Antropología e Historia, Oaxaca.

Carr, Christopher. 1995. "Mortuary Practices: Their Social, Philosophical-Religious, Circumstantial, and Physical Determinants." *Journal of Archaeological Method and Theory* 2 (2): 105–200. http://dx.doi.org/10.1007/BF02228990.

Chesson, Meredith S., ed. 2001a. *Social Memory, Identity, and Death: Anthropological Perspectives on Mortuary Rituals*. Archeological Papers of the American Anthropological Association, vol. 10. Arlington, VA: American Anthropological Association.

Chesson, Meredith S. 2001b. "Social Memory, Identity, and Death: An Introduction." In *Social Memory, Identity, and Death: Anthropological Perspectives on Mortuary Rituals*, ed. Meredith S. Chesson, 1–10. Archeological Papers of the American Anthropological Association, vol. 10. Arlington, VA: American Anthropological Association.

Christensen, Alexander F. 1998a. *Biological Affinity in Prehispanic Oaxaca*. PhD dissertation, Department of Anthropology, Vanderbilt University, Nashville, TN. Ann Arbor, MI: University Microfilms.

Christensen, Alexander F. 1998b. "Colonization and Microevolution in Formative Oaxaca, Mexico." *World Archaeology* 30 (2): 262–85. http://dx.doi.org/10.1080/0043824 3.1998.9980410.

Christensen, Alexander F. 1999. Apéndice 3: Los restos humanos. In "El proyecto patrones de asentamiento del Río Verde," ed. Arthur A. Joyce, 487–94. Final report submitted to the Consejo de Arqueología, Instituto Nacional de Antropología e Historia, Mexico City.

Drennan, Robert D. 1976. *Fábrica San José and Middle Formative Society in the Valley of Oaxaca*. Prehistory and Human Ecology of the Valley of Oaxaca, vol. 4, Memoirs of the University of Michigan Museum of Anthropology No. 8. Ann Arbor: University of Michigan.

Fernández, Deepika. 2004. "Subsistence in the Lower Río Verde Region, Oaxaca, Mexico: A Zoological Analysis." MA thesis, Department of Archaeology, University of Calgary, Calgary, Alberta.

Flannery, Kent V., and Joyce Marcus. 1976. "Formative Oaxaca and the Zapotec Cosmos." *American Scientist* 64: 374–84.

Flannery, Kent V., and Joyce Marcus. 1983. "The Growth of Site Hierarchies in the Valley of Oaxaca: Part I." In *The Cloud People: Divergent Evolution of the Zapotec and Mixtec Civilizations*, ed. Kent V. Flannery and Joyce Marcus, 53–64. New York: Academic Press.

Gaxiola, Margarita. 1984. *Huamelulpan: Un centro urbano de la Mixteca Alta*. Mexico City: Colección Científica, Instituto Nacional de Antropología e Historia.

Geller, Pamela L. 2004. *Transforming Bodies, Transforming Identities: A Consideration of Pre-Columbian Maya Corporeal Beliefs and Practices*. PhD dissertation, Department of Anthropology, University of Pennsylvania, Philadelphia. Ann Arbor, MI: University Microfilms.

Gillespie, Susan D. 1987. "Excavaciones en Charco Redondo, 1986." Report submitted to the Centro Regional de Oaxaca, Instituto Nacional de Antropología e Historia, Oaxaca.

Gillespie, Susan D. 2001a. "Personhood, Agency, and Mortuary Ritual: A Case Study from the Ancient Maya." *Journal of Anthropological Archaeology* 20 (1): 73–112. http://dx.doi.org/10.1006/jaar.2000.0369.

Gillespie, Susan D. 2001b. "Body and Soul among the Maya: Keeping the Spirits in Place." In *Social Memory, Identity, and Death: Anthropological Perspectives on Mortuary Rituals*, ed. Meredith. S. Chesson, 67–78. Archeological Papers of the American Anthropological Association, vol. 10. Arlington, VA: American Anthropological Association.

Goldstein, Lynne. 1981. "One-Dimensional Archaeology and Multi-Dimensional People: Spatial Organization and Mortuary Analysis." In *The Archaeology of Death*, ed. Robert Chapman, Ian Kinnes, and Klava Randsborg, 53–69. Cambridge: Cambridge University Press.

Greenberg, James B. 1981. *Santiago's Sword: Chatino Peasant Religion and Economics*. Berkeley: University of California Press.

Hammond, Norman. 1995. "Ceremony and Society at Cuello: Preclassic Ritual Behavior and Social Differentiation." In *The Emergence of Lowland Maya Civilization: The Transition from the Preclassic to the Early Classic*, ed. Nikolai Grube, 49–59. Acta Mesoamericana, vol. 8. Mèockmèuhl, Germany: A. Saurwein.

Hammond, Norman. 1999. "The Genesis of Hierarchy: Mortuary and Offeratory Ritual in the Pre-Classic at Cuello, Belize." In *Social Patterns in Pre-Classic Mesoamerica*, ed. David C. Grove and Rosemary Joyce, 49–66. Washington, DC: Dumbarton Oaks Research Library.

Hendon, Julia A. 2000. "Having and Holding: Storage, Memory, Knowledge, and Social Relations." *American Anthropologist* 102 (1): 42–53. http://dx.doi.org/10.1525/aa.2000.102.1.42.

Hepp, Guy. 2011. "The Material Culture of Early Sedentism in Coastal Oaxaca: Probable Early Formative Ceramics from La Consentida." Paper presented at the 76th Annual Meeting of the Society for American Archaeology, Sacramento, CA.

Houston, Stephen D., David Stuart, and Karl A. Taube. 2006. *The Memory of Bones: Body, Being, and Experience among the Classic Maya.* Austin: University of Texas Press.

Joyce, Arthur A. 1991a. *Formative Period Occupation in the Lower Río Verde Valley, Oaxaca, Mexico: Interregional Interaction and Social Change.* PhD dissertation, Department of Anthropology, Rutgers University, New Brunswick, NJ. Ann Arbor, MI: University Microfilms.

Joyce, Arthur A. 1991b. "Formative Period Social Change in the Lower Río Verde Valley, Oaxaca Mexico." *Latin American Antiquity* 2 (2): 126–50. http://dx.doi.org/10.2307/972274.

Joyce, Arthur A. 1994. "Late Formative Community Organization and Social Complexity on the Oaxaca Coast." *Journal of Field Archaeology* 21: 147–68.

Joyce, Arthur A., ed. 1999. "El proyecto patrones de asentamiento del Río Verde." Final report submitted to the Consejo de Arqueología, Instituto Nacional de Antropología e Historia, Mexico City.

Joyce, Arthur A. 2000. "The Founding of Monte Albán: Sacred Propositions and Social Practices." In *Agency in Archaeology*, ed. Marcia-Anne Dobres and John Robb, 71–91. London: Routledge.

Joyce, Arthur A. 2003. "Imperialism in Pre-Aztec Mesoamerica: Monte Albán, Teotihuacan, and the Lower Río Verde Valley." In *Ancient Mesoamerican Warfare*, ed. M. Kathryn Brown and Travis W. Stanton, 49–72. Walnut Creek, CA: AltaMira Press.

Joyce, Arthur A. 2008. "Domination, Negotiation, and Collapse: A History of Centralized Authority on the Oaxaca Coast Before the Late Postclassic." In *After Monte Albán: Transformation and Negotiation in Oaxaca, Mexico*, ed. Jeffrey Blomster, 219–54. Boulder: University Press of Colorado.

Joyce, Arthur A. 2009. "The Main Plaza of Monte Albán: A Life History of Place." In *The Archaeology of Meaningful Places*, ed. Brenda Bowser and María Nieves Zedeño, 32–52. Salt Lake City: University of Utah Press.

Joyce, Arthur A. 2010. *Mixtecs, Zapotecs, and Chatinos: Ancient Peoples of Southern Mexico.* Malden, MA: Wiley-Blackwell.

Joyce, Arthur A., Marcus Winter, and Raymond G. Mueller. 1998. *Arqueología de la costa de Oaxaca: Asentamientos del periodo Formativo en el valle del Río Verde inferior.* Estudios de Antropología e Historia No. 40. Oaxaca: Centro INAH Oaxaca.

Joyce, Rosemary A. 1999. "Social Dimensions of Pre-Classic Burials." In *Social Patterns in Pre-Classic Mesoamerica*, ed. David C. Grove and Rosemary Joyce, 15–48. Washington, DC: Dumbarton Oaks Research Library.

King, Stacie M. 2006. "The Marking of Age in Ancient Coastal Oaxaca." In *The Social Experience of Childhood in Ancient Mesoamerica*, ed. Tracy Ardren and Scott R. Hutson, 169–200. Boulder: University Press of Colorado.

Kowalewski, Stephen A., Gary Feinman, Laura Finsten, and Richard Blanton. 1991. "Pre-Hispanic Ballcourts from the Valley of Oaxaca." In *The Mesoamerican Ballgame*, ed. Vernon Scarborough and David Wilcox, 25–44. Tucson: University of Arizona Press.

Krejci, Estella, and T. Patrick Culbert. 1995. Preclassic and Classic Burials and Caches in the Maya Lowlands. In *The Emergence of Lowland Maya Civilization: The Transi-*

tion from the Preclassic to the Early Classic, ed. Nikolai Grube, 103–16. Acta Meso-americana, vol. 8. Mèockmèuhl, Germany: A. Saurwein.

Lind, Michael, and Javier Urcid. 1983. "The Lords of Lambityeco and Their Nearest Neighbors." Notas Mesoamericanas 9: 78–111.

Lind, Michael, and Javier Urcid. 2010. The Lords of Lambityeco: Political Evolution in the Valley of Oaxaca During the Xoo Phase. Boulder: University Press of Colorado.

Martínez López, Cira. 2011. "El origen y desarollo de las tumbas en Monte Albán y sus implicaciones sociopoliticas." In Monte Albán en la encrucijada regional y discipli-naria, ed. Nelly M. Robles García and Ángel I. Rivera Guzmán, 315–44. Mexico: Instituto Nacional de Antropología e Historia.

Mayes, Arion, and Sarah B. Barber. 2008. "Osteobiography of a High Status Burial from the Lower Río Verde Valley of Oaxaca, Mexico." International Journal of Osteo-archaeology 18 (6): 573–88. http://dx.doi.org/10.1002/oa.1011.

Mayes, Arion, Anamay Melmed, and Sarah B. Barber. 2009. "Stigmata of Congenital Syphilis on a High Status Juvenile at Yugüe, Oaxaca, Mexico." Dental Anthropology 22 (3): 73–84.

McAnany, Patricia Ann. 1995. Living with the Ancestors: Kinship and Kingship in Ancient Maya Society. Austin: University of Texas Press.

McAnany, Patricia Ann, Rebecca Storey, and Angela K. Lockard. 1999. "Mortuary Ritual and Family Politics at Formative and Early Classic K'axob, Belize." Ancient Mesoamerica 10 (1): 129–46. http://dx.doi.org/10.1017/S0956536199101081.

Melmed, Anamay. 2006. "Health, Diet, and Behavior in Prehistoric Oaxaca." MA the-sis, Department of Anthropology, San Diego State University, San Diego.

Meskell, Lynn. 1999. Archaeologies of Social Life: Age, Sex, Class et cetera in Ancient Egypt. Social Archaeology. Oxford: Blackwell.

Meskell, Lynn. 2000. "Writing the Body in Archaeology." In Reading the Body: Repre-sentations and Remains in the Archaeological Record, ed. Alison E. Rautman, 13–24. Philadelphia: University of Pennsylvania Press.

Mock, Shirley Boteler, ed. 1998. The Sowing and the Dawning: Termination, Dedication, and Transformation in the Archaeological and Ethnographic Record of Mesoamerica. Albuquerque: University of New Mexico Press.

Monaghan, John. 1995. The Covenants with Earth and Rain: Exchange, Sacrifice and Rev-elation in Mixtec Society. Norman: University of Oklahoma Press.

Saxe, Arthur A. 1970. Social Dimensions of Mortuary Practices. PhD dissertation, Depart-ment of Anthropology, University of Michigan, Ann Arbor. Ann Arbor, MI: Uni-versity Microfilms.

Scheuer, Louise, and Sue Black. 2000. Developmental Juvenile Osteology. San Diego: Aca-demic Press.

Sherman, R. Jason, Andrew K. Balkansky, Charles S. Spencer, and Brian D. Nicholls. 2010. "The Expansionary Dynamics of the Nascent Monte Albán State." Journal of Anthro-pological Archaeology 29 (3): 278–301. http://dx.doi.org/10.1016/j.jaa.2010.04.001.

Storey, Rebecca. 1985. "An Estimate of Mortality in a Pre-Columbian Urban Popula-tion." American Anthropologist 87 (3): 519–35. http://dx.doi.org/10.1525/aa.1985.87.3 .02a00010.

Stuart, David. 1998. "'The Fire Enters His House': Architecture and Ritual in Clas-sic Maya Texts." In Function and Meaning in Classic Maya Architecture, ed. Stephen

D. Houston, 373–426. Washington, DC: Dumbarton Oaks Research Library and Collection.

Sugiyama, Saburo. 2004. "Governance and Polity at Classic Teotihuacan." In *Mesoamerican Archaeology: Theory and Practice*, ed. Julia A. Hendon and Rosemary A. Joyce, 97–123. Malden, MA: Blackwell.

Taube, Karl. 1998. "The Jade Hearth: Centrality, Rulership, and the Classic Maya Temple." In *Function and Meaning in Classic Maya Architecture*, ed. Stephen D. Houston, 427–78. Washington, DC: Dumbarton Oaks Research Library and Collection.

Taylor, Sarah R., Arthur A. Joyce, Matthew Sponheimer, and Sarah B. Barber. 2009. Dieta y agricultura en el valle del Río Verde inferior: Basado en análisis de microdesgaste dental e isótopos estables. In "Estudios alimenticios y de ADN de dientes humanos del valle del Río Verde inferior, Oaxaca, México," ed. Arthur A. Joyce, 3–31. Final report submitted to the Consejo de Arqueología, Instituto Nacional de Antropología e Historia, Mexico City.

Tolstoy, Paul. 1989. "Coapexco and Tlatilco: Sites with Olmec Materials in the Basin of Mexico." In *Regional Perspective on the Olmec*, ed. Robert J. Sharer and David C. Grove, 85–121. Cambridge: Cambridge University Press.

Urcid, Javier. 2005. *Zapotec Writing: Knowledge, Power, and Memory in Ancient Oaxaca*. Coral Gables, FL: Foundation for the Advancement of Mesoamerican Studies. http://www.famsi.org/zapotecwriting/.

Uruñuela, Gabriela, and Patricia Plunket. 2002. "Lineages and Ancestors: The Formative Mortuary Assemblages of Tetimpa, Puebla." In *Domestic Ritual in Ancient Mesoamerica*, ed. Patricia Plunket, 21–30. Los Angeles: Cotsen Institute of Archaeology, University of California.

Vogt, Evon Zartman. 1976. *Tortillas for the Gods: A Symbolic Analysis of Zinacantecan Rituals*. Cambridge, MA: Harvard University Press.

Watanabe, John M. 1990. "From Saints to Shibboleths: Image, Structure, and Identity in Maya Religious Syncretism." *American Ethnologist* 17 (1): 131–50. http://dx.doi.org/10.1525/ae.1990.17.1.02a00080.

Watanabe, John M. 1992. *Maya Saints and Souls in a Changing World*. Austin: University of Texas Press.

Whalen, Michael E. 1981. *Excavations at Santo Domingo Tomaltepec: Evolution of a Formative Community in the Valley of Oaxaca, Mexico*. Prehistory and Human Ecology of the Valley of Oaxaca, vol. 6, Memoirs of the University of Michigan Museum of Anthropology 12. Ann Arbor: University of Michigan.

Whalen, Michael E. 1988. "Small Community Organization during the Late Formative Period in Oaxaca." *Journal of Field Archaeology* 15: 291–306.

Winter, Marcus. 1972. "Tierras Largas: A Formative Community in the Valley of Oaxaca, Mexico." PhD dissertation, Department of Anthropology, University of Arizona, Tucson.

Winter, Marcus. 1974. "Residential Patterns at Monte Alban, Oaxaca, Mexico." *Science* 186, no. 4168 (Dec. 13): 981–87. http://dx.doi.org/10.1126/science.186.4168.981. Medline:17843045.

Winter, Marcus. 1995. "Introduccion." In *Entierros humans de Monte Albán*, ed. Marcus Winter, 2–10. Contribucion No. 7 del Proyecto Especial Monte Albán 1992–1994. Oaxaca: Centro INAH Oaxaca.

Winter, Marcus. 2005. "La cultura Ñuiñe de la Mixteca Baja: Nuevas aportaciones." In *Pasado y presente de la cultura mixteca*, ed. Reina Ortiz Escamilla and Ignacio Ortiz Castro, 77–115. Huajuapan de León, Oaxaca: Universidad Tecnológica de la Mixteca.

Winter, Marcus, and Arthur A. Joyce. 1987. "Excavaciones en Barra Quebrada, 1986: Un informe preliminar." Report submitted to the Centro INAH Oaxaca, Instituto Nacional de Antropología e Historia, Oaxaca.

Winter, Marcus, and Antonia Montague. 1991. Excavaciones menores en depósitos de la fase Ñudée, ladera sur (Areas E y J). In "Exploraciones arqueológicas en Cerro de la Minas, Mixteca Baja, Oaxaca. Temporadas 1987–1990, informe preliminar," ed. Marcus Winter, 134–39. Report on file Centro INAH Oaxaca, Instituto Nacional de Antropología e Historia, Oaxaca.

Workinger, Andrew. 2002. *Coastal/Highland Interaction in Prehispanic Oaxaca, Mexico: The Perspective from San Francisco de Arriba*. PhD dissertation, Department of Anthropology, Vanderbilt University, Nashville, TN. Ann Arbor, MI: University Microfilms.

Workinger, Andrew, and Arthur A. Joyce. 1999. Excavaciones arqueológicas en Río Viejo. In "El proyecto patrones de asentamiento del Río Verde," ed. Arthur A. Joyce, 51–119. Final report submitted to the Consejo de Arqueología, Instituto Nacional de Antropología e Historia, Mexico City.

PLACE-MAKING AND POWER IN THE TERMINAL FORMATIVE

Excavations on Río Viejo's Acropolis

ARTHUR A. JOYCE, MARC N. LEVINE, AND SARAH B. BARBER

Archaeological research in the lower Río Verde Valley shows that a centralized polity first developed in the region during the Terminal Formative period (150 BC–AD 250). The region experienced significant population growth at this time with the area occupied in the regional survey zone increasing from 299 ha in the Late Formative Minizundo phase (400–150 BC) to 699 ha by the late Terminal Formative Chacahua phase (AD 100–250). Social inequality also increased, as shown by evidence from mortuary offerings, domestic architecture, ceremonial caches, and monumental buildings (Barber 2005, Chapter 6; Joyce 2005, 2006, 2008, 2010, 186–195). The most powerful community in the region during the Terminal Formative was the urban center of Río Viejo (Joyce 2005, 2008, 2010). Río Viejo increased in size from 25 ha in the Minizundo phase to 225 ha by the early Terminal Formative Miniyua phase, with a slight decrease in area to 200 ha by the Chacahua phase. During the Chacahua phase a massive public acropolis was constructed at Río Viejo and became the civic-ceremonial center of the polity. Although monumental public buildings were built at San Francisco de Arriba and Charco Redondo as early as the Minizundo phase (Butler 2011; Workinger 2002), these structures were dwarfed by the construction of the

DOI: 10.5876/9781607322023.c05

FIGURE 5.1. Río Viejo Mound 1, photographed from 1 km to the southwest (after Joyce et al. 1998: Lámina 4.5).

acropolis at Río Viejo, which we have designated Mound 1 (Figure 5.1). In its final form, the acropolis covered an area of 350 m × 200 m and supported two large superstructures rising to at least 17 m above the floodplain (designated Structures 1 and 2, respectively) as well as a large plaza, a sunken patio, and several smaller buildings.

Excavations in 2000 and 2009 provide evidence of the construction history and use of Río Viejo's acropolis (Figure 5.2). In this chapter we present a detailed discussion of the acropolis excavations and their implications for political relations during the Terminal Formative. We will show that the construction of the acropolis required a massive mobilization of labor and represented a huge communal labor project. These practices, which had been important in the constitution of community identities since at least the Minizundo phase, may have been co-opted and expanded in scale by rulers. An outcome of the construction and use of the acropolis was the creation of broader regional affiliations and forms of social interaction that enhanced the authority of the rulers of Río Viejo, if only briefly (Barber 2005, Chapter 6; Barber and Joyce 2007; Joyce 2005, 2006). Although there still is much work to be done to fully comprehend the significance of this massive structure, we suggest that the acropolis was an exercise in place-making. We define place-making as the process by which human actions and history become embedded in the landscape, providing a physical and temporal anchor for social identities (Ashmore 2002; Basso 1996; Pred 1984). The construction and use of socially meaningful places through architecture can transform social identity by reordering space as well as people's experiences and associations with those places (A. Joyce 2009; R. Joyce 2004). We argue that the construction and use of the acropolis material-

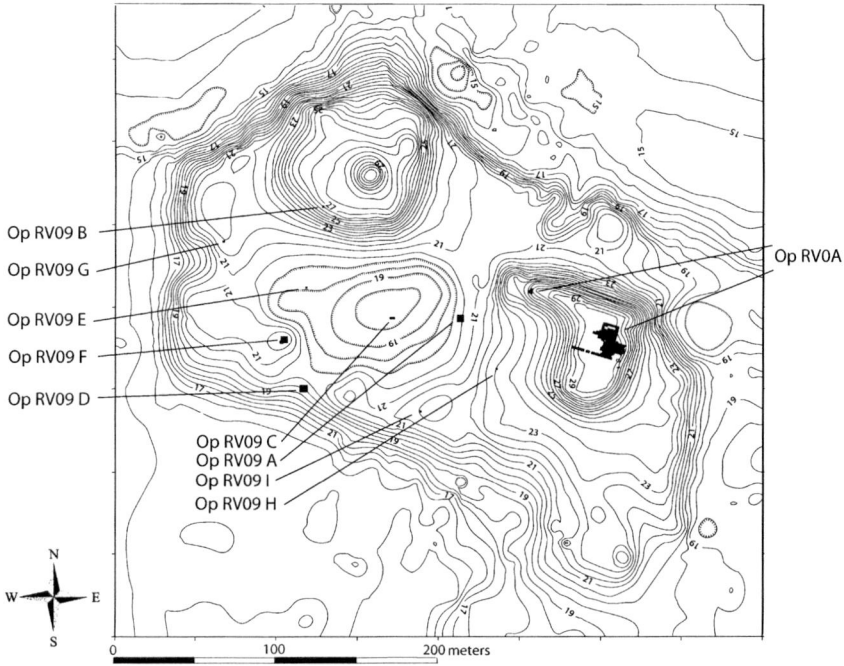

FIGURE 5.2. Plan of Río Viejo Mound 1 showing locations of the 2000 and 2009 excavations (after Joyce and Barber 2011: Figure 3).

ized a new corporate identity centered on the ruling institutions of Río Viejo. The evidence indicates, however, that regional political authority was tenuous, contested, and relatively short-lived. At ca. AD 250 the acropolis was burned and abandoned, and the broader Río Viejo polity collapsed, probably as a result of political conflict and instability within the region.

THE ACROPOLIS EXCAVATIONS

Excavations were carried out on the Mound 1 acropolis as part of a long-term study of the origins and development of centralized political authority in the lower Rio Verde Valley (Joyce 2005, 2008, 2010). Survey, excavation, and mapping at the site of Río Viejo were carried out in 1988, 1994, 1995, 2000, and 2009 with excavations on the acropolis during the latter two field seasons (Joyce 1991a; Joyce and Barber 2011; Joyce and Levine 2009; Joyce et al. 1998; Workinger and Joyce 1999). Test units at the base of the acropolis were excavated in 1988 and 1994.

The 2000 excavations focused on Mound 1, Structure 2, which is located on the eastern portion of the Río Viejo acropolis (Joyce et al. 2001; Joyce and

Levine 2009). Structure 2 rises 10 m above the surface of the Mound 1 platform (29.6 m above sea level; Figure 5.2). Horizontal excavations covering 242 m² (Río Viejo 2000 Operation A, abbreviated hereafter as Op. RV0A) revealed three construction phases of Structure 2 dating to the Chacahua (Structure 2-sub2), Yuta Tiyoo (Structure 2-sub1), and Yugüe (Structure 2) phases. The terminal occupation on Structure 2 consisted of a series of houses dating to the Early Postclassic Yugüe phase (AD 800–1100). Underlying the Early Postclassic houses were remnants of Late Classic architecture. Only the upper 1.1 m of deposits in the Structure 2 excavations dated to the Classic and Postclassic periods, however. In an area of 55 m² we penetrated into Terminal Formative deposits through excavations that reached up to 3.2 m below the modern ground surface.

The 2009 research consisted of two transects of excavations, one running east–west and the other north–south across the southern half of the acropolis. In total, nine operations were carried out consisting of block excavations up to 4 m × 4 m as well as smaller test units. Excavations penetrated to as much as 5.2 m below the modern ground surface. Most operations were located over anomalies detected by a ground-penetrating radar survey carried out in 2008 (Barber 2009).

TERMINAL FORMATIVE STRATIGRAPHY AND CONSTRUCTION HISTORY

The excavations indicate that most of the acropolis was built during the late Terminal Formative Chacahua phase (AD 100–250). Test excavations on the southern end of Structure 1 (Op. RV09 B) and at the base of Structure 1 on the far western end of Mound 1 (Op. RV09 G), however, indicate that this part of the acropolis may have been built as early as the late Miniyua phase (150 BC–AD 100). Op. RV09 B penetrated to a depth of 3.5 m below the current ground surface (23.9 m asl), while Op. RV09 G went to a depth of 2.4 m (19.6 m asl); with the exception of the upper 0.5–0.8 m, both of these operations consisted of fill with redeposited sherds from the Miniyua phase. The results from Op. RV09 B on Mound 1 were revealing in that the fill consisted largely of alluvial sediment with few artifacts. The composition of the fill indicates that the sediment was mined from the floodplain near the acropolis. The scarcity of redeposited ceramics in the fill suggests that there had been little settlement in this area prior to the mining.

Data from most of the remaining operations (Op. RV0A and Ops. RV09 A, D, F, H, and I) indicate that most of the acropolis was built during the Chacahua phase with all but the upper 1–2 m of the acropolis completed at this time. An exception to the general pattern of construction comes from excavations in the sunken patio. Ops. RV09 C and E show that the sunken patio was built during the Late Classic Yuta Tiyoo phase (AD 500–800). Op. RV09 C was placed in the center of the sunken patio and penetrated to a depth of 5.2 m below the current ground surface (the operation was terminated at the water table and never reached the base of the acropolis). The Op. C excavations exposed more than 4 m of Late Classic construction fill that was likely deposited over a relatively short period to create the sunken patio. In fact, the Op. C excavations found that the construction fill of Mound 1 extends at least 2 m below the modern surface of the floodplain, which means that alluviation has raised the ground surface considerably since the acropolis was first built (see also Joyce and Mueller 1992). Op. RV09 E was located on what appeared to have been a step or bench at the western end of the sunken patio and penetrated through 5.0 m of Late Classic deposits; the lowest 0.7 m of deposits consisted of probable Chacahua phase fill, although few diagnostic ceramics were recovered. Since we did not reach deposits predating the acropolis in any of the excavations, we still do not know the original height of the building.

Terminal Formative period structure fill varied considerably from unconsolidated basket loads to a variety of forms of what we have termed "structured fill." Structured fill is defined as fill that is comprised of sediment carefully mixed prior to being deposited, often using unfired adobe blocks and occasionally fired bricks of various sizes. Because the adobes were not fired, some appear in the stratigraphic profiles as amorphous shapes and others cannot be easily distinguished from the surrounding sediment. A micromorphological analysis by Paul Goldberg (2009) confirmed that these strata indeed represented the eroded remains of adobe blocks sometimes cemented together by a calcareous mortar. The network of structured fill served as an architecturally sound foundation that did not require the use of interior stone cells or other interior walls for additional stability, although occasionally clayey cells containing unconsolidated sediment were used. The structured fill is thus distinct from fill composed of unconsolidated sediment deposited in a haphazard way (e.g., basket loads) or types of cellular fill incorporating interior walls.

Structured fill at Río Viejo included at least four types of organized deposits. Type 1 consisted of puddled adobe made from adobe material that was carefully poured into alternating layers; Type 1 fill occasionally included adobe blocks as well (Figure 5.3a). Type 2 was a less ordered structured fill consisting of variably sized adobes and sometimes fired bricks placed at irregular intervals and surrounded by unconsolidated sediment (Figure 5.3b). The proportion of unconsolidated fill to adobes varied considerably. Type 3 consisted of more formal arrangements of adobes and occasionally fired bricks, sometimes stabilized by a calcareous mortar (Figure 5.3c). Type 4 seems to have involved the use of wooden frames to stabilize the fill. In some areas small cells, probably either puddled adobe or rammed earth, were then filled with loose sediment. Another possible example of the use of a frame was discovered in fill excavated

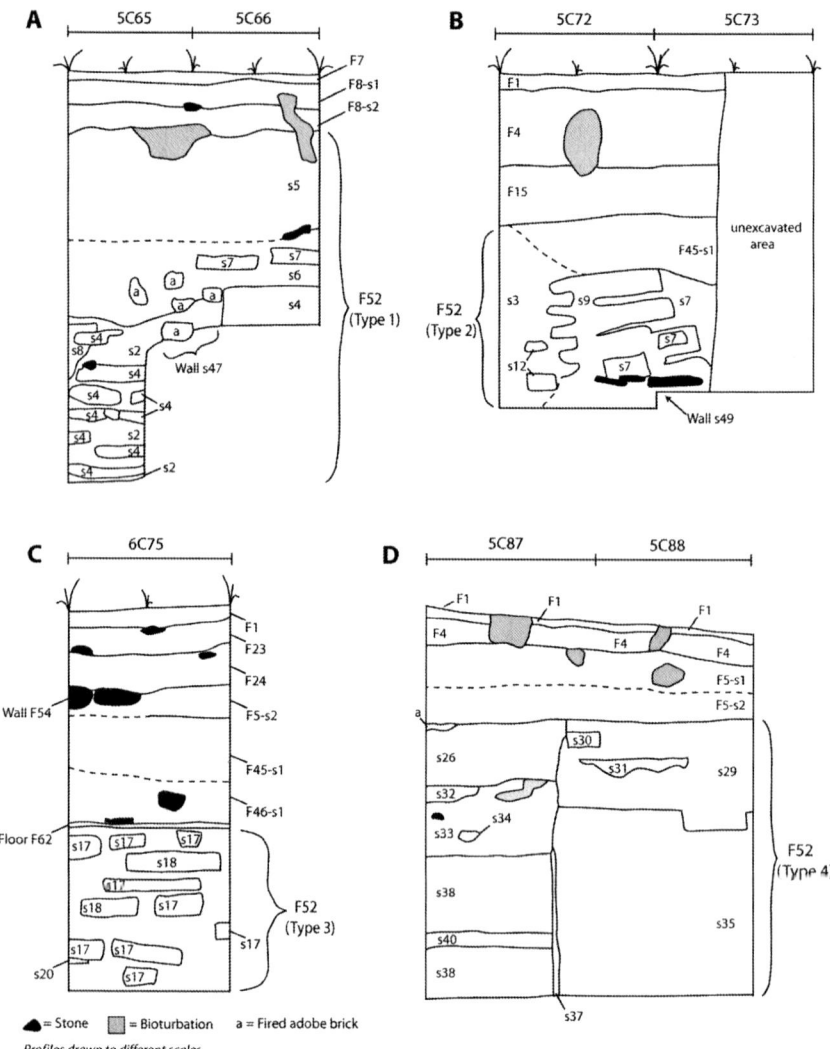

FIGURE 5.3. Profiles of the four types of structured fill from Mound 1, Structure 2-sub2. *A,* Type 1 structured fill; *B,* Type 2 structured fill; *C,* Type 3 structured fill (after Joyce 2006: Figure 3); *D,* Type 4 structured fill. All were found within a major fill episode (F52), which included substrata consisting of adobes (s2, s3, s4, s7, s8, s9, s12, s17, s18, s30, s31, s32, s34, s40) and unconsolidated fill (s5, s6, s26, s29, s33, s35, s38) as well as an ash lens (s20), a thin vertical deposit of silty loam (s37), and a small rock alignment (s49).

in Op. RV0A on Structure 2 (Feature 52). Feature 52, substratum 37 (abbreviated F52-s37) was a curious thin vertical deposit of silty loam found between two fill deposits (F52-s38 and F52-s35; Figure 5.3d). A possible explanation for the odd form of F52-s37 is that strata F52-s38 and F52-s35 were deposited into vertical wooden frames set up on the surface of Structure 2-sub2. The frame would have allowed for the controlled deposition of large blocks of unconsolidated sediment (here the fill included both loose sediment and some adobes) and would have made it possible to more effectively compress and stabilize the fill. After the wooden frames were removed, a small gap was left between the substrata, which was filled by a thin deposit of sediment (F52-s37), probably through natural processes.

Although we suspect that the structured fill observed in the acropolis excavations was not uncommon in ancient Mesoamerica (Figure 1.3), few archaeologists have described the nature of mound fill in detail (also see Daneels 2007, 15, 2008, 2). Similar types of structured fill have been exposed in the interior tunnels of the Pyramid of the Moon at Teotihuacan (Marc Levine, personal observation, 2003). In addition, the "Great Pyramid" at Cholula is reportedly filled with sediments that are so consolidated that excavators tunneled into the mound without using lumber or steel reinforcements to prevent cave-ins (Marquina 1964, 117). It is possible that the Great Pyramid consists of a version of the structured fill observed at Río Viejo (Levine et al. 2004). Drucker and colleagues (1957) describe the complicated layering of clay, adobe blocks, and silts used in the various construction phases at La Venta. While they do not describe fill characteristics in detail, it is clear that sophisticated earthen construction techniques were in use at the site. Careful selection of fill sediment, as well as the use of consolidated gravel retaining walls, is documented at San Lorenzo and surrounding sites dating to the Early Formative (Cyphers and DiCastro 2009; Ann Cyphers, personal communication 2010). Clark (1994, 323, Figure 92) describes Early Formative house platforms at the site of San Carlos in the Mazatán region of Pacific coastal Chiapas constructed using clay walls that retained loose, sandy sediment. Daneels (2007) describes alternating fill blocks of clays and sandy loams used to construct a massive Early Classic pyramid at La Joya, central Veracruz. She argues that the alternating construction styles provided greater stability by controlling the internal pressures of the earthen fill. The different types of structured fill at Río Viejo may have operated in a similar fashion to stabilize the acropolis. Rammed earth or puddled adobe retaining walls were also employed at the Terminal Formative site of Yugüe in the lower Verde.

Low walls or rock alignments and stone slabs were exposed in several areas within the Chacahua phase fill of Structure 2-sub 2 (F52). These substrata within F52 were generally found in isolated areas and did not correlate with extensive surfaces that would have indicated they were associated with floors or superstructures. Nor were the low walls a form of cellular construction technique. Instead, these features appear to have been designed to stabilize the substructure during breaks in construction or may be remnants of small shelters and activity areas used by workers during the long period of construction. For example, F52-s47 was a wall composed of two to three courses of stone and fired bricks that overlay a layer of structured fill (F52-s2; Figure 5.3a). The adobes had inclusions of shell and sand, and some displayed woven mat (*petate*) impressions on their exteriors. The wall was relatively informal, consisting of a variety of materials and lacking any exterior facing. No additional construction materials or features were found associated with F52-s47 that would suggest the presence of a formal structure. The wall is thus interpreted as an interior retaining wall that served to reinforce the west side of Structure 2-sub2, perhaps during a rainy season when building activities probably ceased. Another alignment of stone slabs within the Chacahua phase fill was F52-s49 (Figure 5.3b). The feature does not appear to have been a weight-bearing wall, nor were there any artifacts associated with the feature to provide additional clues revealing its function. F52-s49 may represent an internal division within the fill or an activity area associated with the construction of the acropolis. Other substrata in F52 contain evidence of small activity areas where workers may have rested and cooked meals. There were no artifacts that provided further clues to the use of these features, and similar features were observed in Ops. RV09 D and RV09 G.

STRUCTURE 2-SUB 2: A CHACAHUA PHASE PUBLIC BUILDING

The fill of Structure 2-sub 2 was retained by at least two large east–west-oriented walls composed of broken adobe and fired brick fragments held together with a clayey mortar-like sediment with small amounts of sherds and broken shell. It is likely that the two retaining walls were part of a single building, probably some type of stepped platform. Figure 5.4 provides a hypothetical reconstruction of how these features may have articulated during the Chacahua phase.

Only the top of the northernmost of the two retaining walls (F66) was exposed. F66 was 1 m wide and oriented 105°/285°. The top of the wall reached an elevation of 27.9 m above sea level. Immediately above F66 was a deposit, approximately 0.8 m thick, of unconsolidated fill (F56) containing stone cobbles and a high concentration of adobe and fired brick fragments. Some of the brick fragments displayed polished exteriors painted reddish orange and appeared to be associated with F66. The redeposited painted adobes were probably originally incorporated into a wall from a Chacahua phase superstructure on the surface retained by F66. If this inference is correct, then the presence of painted adobes suggests that it was an architecturally elaborate building.

The second retaining wall (F61) was located 12 m south of F66 and was also roughly 1 m wide, at least 13 m long, and oriented approximately 102°/282°. F61 reached an elevation of 29.1 m above sea level and so was 1.2 m higher than

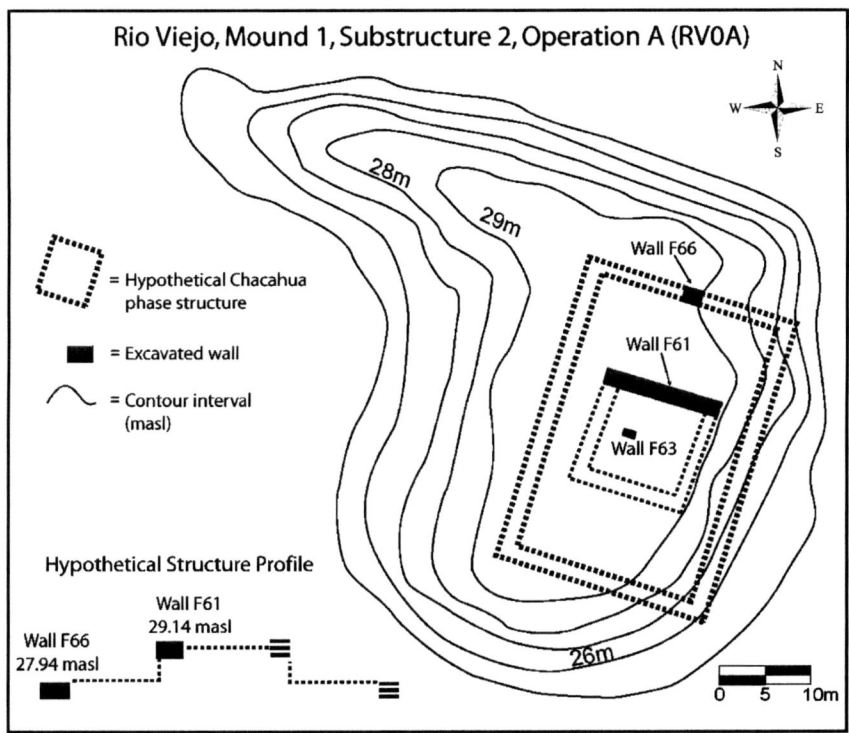

FIGURE 5.4. Hypothetical reconstruction of Mound 1, Structure 2-sub2, the Chacahua phase public building.

the northern wall (F66). F61 retained construction fill to the south, creating what appears to have been the uppermost level of the stepped platform.

Only a handful of poorly preserved and scattered features remain from Chacahua phase floors and superstructures on the surface retained by F61 and at the base of that wall. At the base of F61 to the north, excavations revealed a wall of burned adobes or fired bricks (F65), one course high, and oriented roughly east–west. The wall may have been a foundation for a superstructure. Wall F65 was built on a hard-packed earthen floor extending north from the base of the retaining wall.

South of F61, excavations exposed several areas with remnants of burned floors and adobe wall foundations from superstructures. The largest floor remnant (F62) was exposed across several square meters of the surface retained by F61. The burned floor was probably associated with F63-s1, an adobe wall remnant. A sample of charcoal associated with adobes on the surface of F62 yielded a date of 1573 ± 40 BP or AD 377 (cal AD 406–575; AA40036). The adobe wall, F63-s1, provides the best evidence for a Chacahua phase building

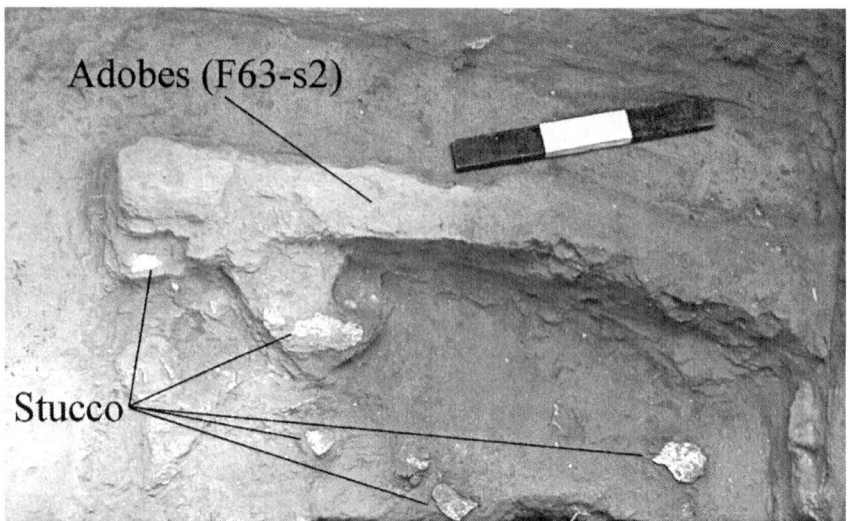

Adobes (F63-s2)

Stucco

FIGURE 5.5. Chacahua phase wall remnant (F63-s2) with fragments of architectural stucco at the base of the wall.

associated with Structure 2-sub2. Stone cobbles and burned adobes formed the core of the poorly preserved wall. The excavations revealed a segment of the wall measuring 1.9 m long × 0.3 m wide and oriented roughly northeast–southwest. F63-s2 represented the eroded and burned remains of the wall's exterior and included fragments of charcoal, daub, and cream-colored, burnished architectural stucco. The stucco fragments were concentrated just east of the adobe wall, suggesting that F63 was the east wall of a superstructure (Figure 5.5). Floor F62 would then have been the interior floor of the building. A second date of 1696 ± 43 BP or AD 254 (cal AD 241–427; AA40037) was recovered from charcoal lying directly on a section of burned floor and sealed by overlying adobes that had fallen from F63 (Figure 5.6). We consider sample AA40037 to be more reliable than sample AA40036 in dating the abandonment and possible destruction of the building because of the former's more secure context and because an uncalibrated date of AD 254 is consistent with the ceramic evidence from the underlying platform. The radiocarbon date and the ceramics in most structural fill deposits correspond to the transition between the late Terminal Formative Chacahua phase and the Early Classic Coyuche phase.

Another foundation wall (F64-s1) of a probable superstructure was exposed 0.4 m south of the retaining wall F61. F64-s1 was a burned adobe wall, one course high and oriented approximately east–west. Only a 1.6 m × 0.3 m section of the wall was exposed by the excavations. The wall was associated with an unburned floor remnant (F59) consisting of compact sediment with two adobe blocks on its surface. Feature F64-s2, which was found overlaying the

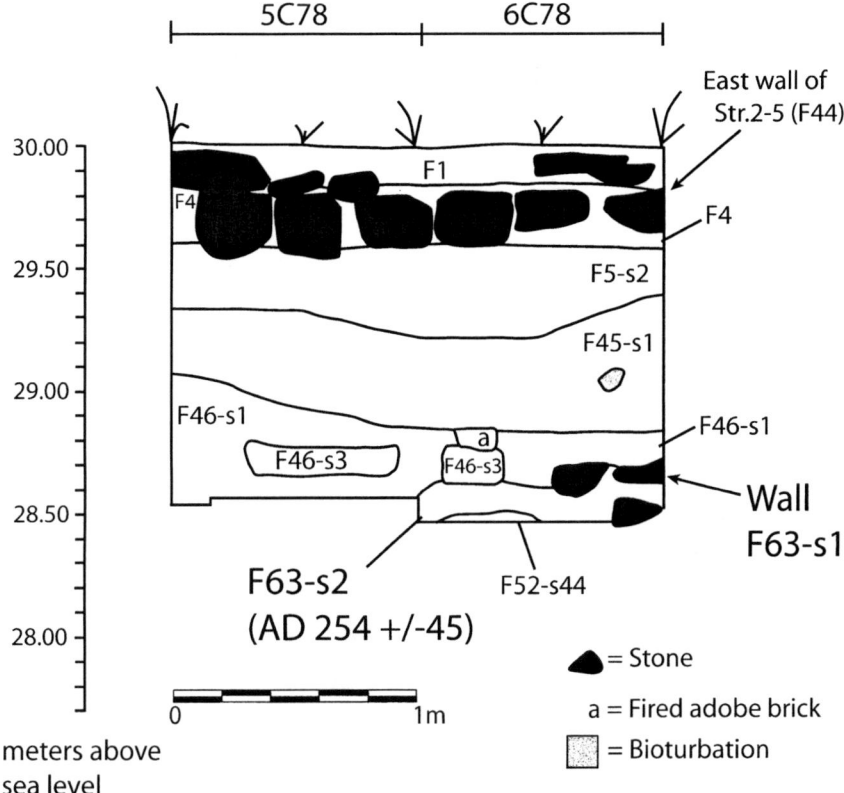

FIGURE 5.6. Profile of a Chacahua phase wall remnant consisting of stones (F63-s1) and adobes (F63-s2). A charcoal sample was recovered overlying a section of burned floor (F62; not visible in profile), which yielded a date of AD 254.

floor (F59), is interpreted as wall fall associated with F64-s1 and included a concentration of carbonized organic material and architectural stucco fragments.

The only stone walls dating to the Chacahua phase (F70, F71) discovered by the excavations on Structure 2 were located approximately 90 m northwest of F66, the northern retaining wall discussed above. The stone walls were revealed in a 3 m² excavation that explored the northwest end of Structure 2 (Figure 5.2). Two stone walls (F70, F71) were exposed that possibly represent the exterior retaining walls of Structure 2-sub2, although their precise relationship to the structure formed by the large adobe retaining walls is unclear. The walls were built over a layer of structured fill (F76). Ceramics recovered from the fill below and behind the wall tentatively date it to the Chacahua phase, although few diagnostic sherds were recovered. The larger of the two walls (F71) was a sloping wall or *talud* oriented 105°/285° and inclined at an angle of

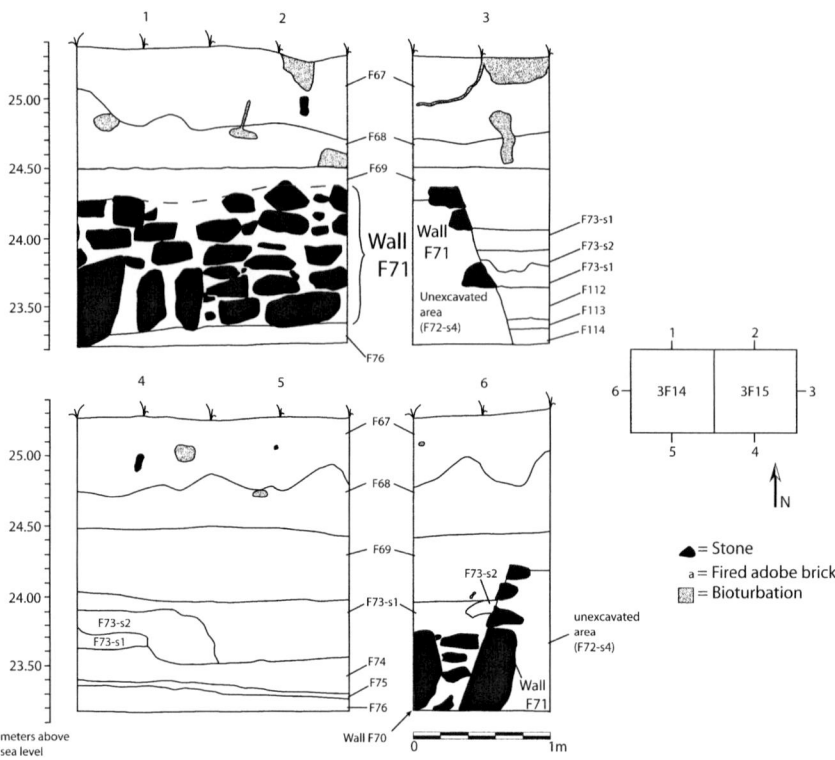

FIGURE 5.7. Profile of a Chacahua phase stone retaining wall (F71) from Mound 1, Structure 2-sub2.

approximately 61° from horizontal. F71 displayed the finest masonry found in the Río Viejo excavations (Figure 5.7) and shares the same orientation as the large adobe retaining wall (F66), suggesting that they may have been part of the same Chacahua phase architectural program. F71 included five courses of stones that were finely worked on their exposed faces. F75 is a probable floor corresponding with the base of Wall F71; the few sherds found within F75 indicate a Chacahua phase date. Wall F70 extended south from the base of F71 at an angle of 15°/195° to F71. The two walls were covered by two distinct fill layers (F74, F73) that through time modified the surface associated with the footing of F70 and F71. Ceramics from these strata suggest they date to the transition between the Chacahua and Coyuche phases (ca. AD 250).

Although the remains of the Chacahua phase version of Structure 2 are meager, they provide some clues regarding the nature of this building. The excavations demonstrate that most of Mound 1, Structure 2, by volume was completed by the end of the Chacahua phase. The large parallel adobe retaining walls (F61, F66) suggest that the Chacahua phase substructure may have been in the form of a stepped platform with at least two levels. The adobe wall remnants recovered from the surface of the upper level of Structure 2-sub2 indicate the presence of one or more superstructures with adobe foundation walls. Fragments of architectural stucco indicate that the building's walls were plastered; no other structures with stucco are known from the entire lower Verde region. The only other stucco known from the region comes from an iron ore mirror recovered from a Chacahua phase high-status burial at the site of Yugüe (Barber 2005, 186–188; Barber et al., Chapter 4; Mayes and Barber 2008).[1] Several painted adobe fragments that were probably from the super-structures were also recovered in the excavations. The rarity of plastered walls and painted adobes in the region and the prominent location of the Chacahua phase building atop Mound 1, Structure 2, indicate that the superstructures were architecturally elaborate. The distribution of stucco fragments suggests that either the stucco-covered building was quite large or that there were addi-tional separate structures. No middens, burials, storage pits, or other features commonly occurring in domestic settings were present in any of the Chacahua phase strata. The complete absence of domestic features or refuse supports our assertion that the superstructure was a public building.

Outside of Structure 2-sub2 there were few examples of Chacahua phase architecture other than construction fill. Several operations (Ops. RV09 A, D, and F) exposed occupational surfaces or earthen floors, often burned, near the top of the Chacahua phase fill. An adobe flagstone pavement was exposed on the surface of a Chacahua phase platform in Op. RV09 F located in the western end of the acropolis. Op. RV09 A, excavated in the area between the sunken patio and Structure 2, exposed a feature consisting of a single course of adobe blocks surrounded by burned or oxidized organic material at about 2 m below ground surface (Figure 5.8). Even though we exposed 6 m^2 of this feature, it was insufficient to clearly determine its function. We suspect that it was a foun-dation wall of a Chacahua phase superstructure or perhaps a fallen adobe wall or pavement, although further work is needed to determine the nature of this feature.

THE ABANDONMENT OF THE ACROPOLIS

The excavations on Río Viejo's acropolis during both field seasons demonstrate that the structure was abandoned at the end of the Chacahua phase and not reoccupied until the Late Classic (also see Joyce 2006, 2008; Levine and Joyce 2009). The evidence also suggests that the acropolis was destroyed by fire and perhaps systematically dismantled, although further research is needed to evaluate this hypothesis. For example, the wall and floor remnants on the sur-face of Structure 2-sub2 were very eroded, but poor preservation does not fully explain the overall scarcity of architectural features. The burned adobes and

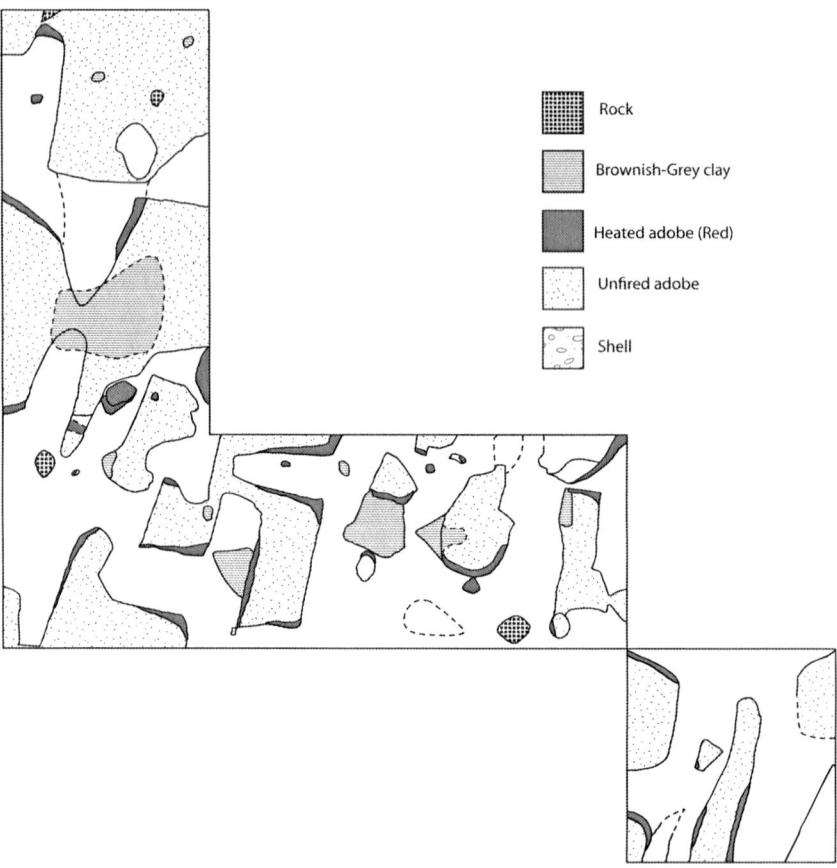

FIGURE 5.0. Adobe feature in Op. RV09 A (after Joyce and Barber 2011. Figure 4).

floor areas demonstrate that Structure 2-sub2 was destroyed by fire at the close of the Chacahua phase, with the radiocarbon date of AD 254 ± 43 offering the best estimate of the age of the burning.

We also discovered evidence for the burning of the acropolis beyond Structure 2-sub2. In Op. RV09 A, ash and oxidation of adobe blocks may have been the result of the burning event dating to the end of the Terminal Formative. We have not been able to infer precisely the cause of the oxidized deposits associated with the adobes in Op. RV09 A (burned wooden beams or a frame of some sort are possibilities). Although Structure 2-sub2 was abandoned at this time, the evidence from Op. RV09 A shows that several thin resurfacing levels and floors were deposited over the adobe feature that likely date to the Chacahua phase. In Op. RV09 D, located at the southern edge of Mound 1, we found fragments of a burned earthen surface. The burned surface was covered by two thin fill layers probably dating to the end of the Chacahua phase. Two burials (Río Viejo B54-I63 and B57-I66) were discovered in the fill deposits. B54-I63 was accompanied by two ceramic vessels dating to the transition between the Chacahua and Coyuche phases. The date of B57-I66 was uncertain, although it may have been Late Classic. Overlying strata consisted of Late Classic fill, indicating a long period of disuse until modification of the area recommenced at least 250 years later. These data suggest that the abandonment of the acropolis may have occurred over the course of a few decades, rather than immediately following the major destruction event, such that some areas of the acropolis (e.g., Ops. RV09 A and D) continued to be used for a short time after the destruction.

Following the Chacahua phase, the acropolis remained unoccupied for approximately 250 years, resulting in erosion and disintegration of most of the adobe superstructure of Structure 2-sub2. Pits dug into Chacahua phase deposits in many of the operations (Op. RV0A; Ops. RV09 D, E, F, and H) also indicate that the acropolis was mined for sediment during the Early Classic period or early in the Late Classic. A hearth that intruded into Chacahua phase structural fill in Op. RV09 F indicates that some sort of cooking activities occurred during the period when the acropolis was mined for sediment. Whether the sediment was just expediently removed for building materials or was seen as having some sort of special significance through its association with an earlier ceremonial building is impossible to know at present. It is also possible that the mining of sediment was associated with the destruction of the acropolis at ca. AD 250 and could have been an act of desecration or decommissioning of the structure.

THE SOCIAL AND POLITICAL
SIGNIFICANCE OF THE ACROPOLIS

The excavations on Mound 1 at Río Viejo show that with the exception of the area of the sunken patio, the acropolis was constructed almost entirely during the Terminal Formative period. The acropolis was easily the largest public construction project for the entire prehispanic period in the lower Río Verde Valley and was one of the largest monumental buildings in ancient Oaxaca. As discussed in this section, a consideration of construction techniques as well as estimates of the labor required to build the acropolis provide important insights into the social significance of this massive building project.

The variability present in fill material, forms of adobes and fired bricks, and techniques in arranging these blocks suggests that the construction of the acropolis may have resulted from the efforts of five or more distinct work groups (e.g., Hastings and Moseley 1975). Each group may have used slightly different materials and strategies to create the stable interior fill (i.e., basket

TABLE 5.1. Estimated volume of selected monumental buildings in the New World

Earthen Mound	Estimated Volume (m³)	Source
Huaca del Sol, Cerro Blanco, Peru	2,000,000	Shimada (1999, 466)
Pyramid of the Sun, Teotihuacan, Mexico	1,170,000	Millon et al. (1965)
Monk's Mound, Cahokia, IL, USA	615,144	Morgan (1999)
Acropolis (Mound 1), Río Viejo, Oaxaca[a]	455,050	—
Mound A, Poverty Point, LA, USA	238,000	Kidder et al. (2006)

[a] Reflects Terminal Formative period acropolis only; the structure was enlarged during the Late Classic period, when it reached 560,050 m³.

loads of unconsolidated fill plus the four types of structured fill). This has important implications for understanding the overall labor investment and social relations surrounding the construction of the Terminal Formative acropolis. For instance, the heterogeneity in structured fill strongly suggests that the acropolis was not built by a permanent work force since we would expect to see greater consistency in construction methods. The degree of variability in construction fill does not appear to be the result of architectural necessity. Instead, we may be seeing the result of a rotation of work groups carrying out their jobs in slightly different ways. Furthermore, we argue that the heterogeneity in mound fill supports the interpretation that the acropolis was completed by temporary laborers who were fulfilling obligations to the community and to the nobility at Río Viejo (Levine et al. 2004).

The results of our excavations allow us to estimate the labor required to construct the Terminal Formative version of the acropolis. To generate such an estimate we must extrapolate the results of excavations completed at present to the remainder of the structure. We also assume that there are no building phases that predate the Terminal Formative. This latter assumption seems reasonable since redeposited ceramics from earlier periods are only rarely found in the acropolis excavations and, based on survey data, the area around the acropolis was not occupied until the early Terminal Formative Miniyua phase.

The total volume of Río Viejo's Terminal Formative period acropolis is estimated at 455,050 m³, based on topographic mapping of Mound 1 (Joyce 1999a, 37–48) with a total station and the excavations carried out in 2000 and 2009 (Joyce 1999b; Joyce and Levine 2009). The volumetric estimate was processed using Surfer software (7.0) and is somewhat larger than previously reported (Joyce 2006, 85; Levine et al. 2004) based on the Op. RV09 C excavations, which found that the acropolis was at least 2 m higher in elevation than previously thought. It should be emphasized that these must be considered minimum estimates since we have yet to determine the original height of the structure. Table 5.1 shows the estimated volume of the Río Viejo acropolis in comparison to several other well-known monumental buildings of the New World.

TABLE 5.2. Labor investment in the construction of the Río Viejo acropolis, expressed in person-days for each step

Task	Step I Excavation of Earth Fill	Step II Transport of Earth Fill	Step II Transport of Water	Step III Adobe Manufacture	Step IV Acropolis Construction	Total
Calculation of person-days[a]	455,050/ 2.6	455,050/ 0.54	63,991/ 0.29	15,800,347/ 20	455,050/ 4.8	NA
Total person-days[b]	175,019	849,427	217,182	790,017	94,802	2,126,447

[a] Numbers are rounded.
[b] Totals are not rounded and thus vary somewhat from numbers in Calculation row.

Following previous energetics-oriented studies of monumental construction in Mesoamerica (e.g., Aaberg and Bonsignore 1975; Abrams 1994; Rosenswig and Masson 2002), we evaluated the labor investment represented by the Río Viejo acropolis in terms of person-days, with a single workday held at a constant of five hours per diem (Erasmus 1965, 283). A five-hour workday involving hard manual labor is consistent with ethnographic observations in tropical settings of Amazonia (Darna Dufour, personal communication 2011). The labor estimates consider four basic steps required for the acropolis construction: (1) procurement of construction materials; (2) transportation of materials to the work site; (3) manufacture of adobes; and (4) the actual construction of the acropolis. The results probably underestimate the true labor investment, as we do not consider person-days required for masonry, finishing work, or the addition of associated superstructures and we must rely on our minimum estimate for the height of the building. The estimates assume that all of the acropolis is made of earthen fill, a conclusion supported by extensive excavations on Mound 1. Furthermore, the excavations suggest that approximately 75 percent of the mound fill is of the structured variety, while the remaining 25 percent consists of loose earthen fill. We also assume that adobes were manufactured (mixed, formed, and sun-dried) in the immediate vicinity of the acropolis. Construction was probably limited to the dry season since it would have been difficult to make adobes during the rainy season. A summary of the energetics analysis, with subtotals of person-days required for each construction step, is presented in Table 5.2.

For Step 1, the excavation of earthen fill with a traditional digging stick, we adopt Erasmus's (1965, 285) rate of 2.6 m^3 per person-days (ppd), resulting in a total of 175,019 person-days (Table 5.2). For Step 2, the transportation of building material to the work site, we used Aaberg and Bonsignore's (1975, 46) formula (also see Abrams 1994, 47; Rosenswig and Masson 2002, 225):

$$\text{Person-days/m}^3 = Q \times 1/(L/V + L/V') \times H$$

The carrying capacity of the container (Q) for hauling fill was estimated at .02 m³, based on an average load of 22 kg (see Aaberg and Bonsignore 1975, 47; Abrams 1994, 48). The distance of the construction materials (L), in this case sediment and water for the production of adobes, was estimated at 350 m. Probable borrow pits for the fill have been identified west of the acropolis in the vicinity of Mound 2 and south of the acropolis adjacent to Mound 8 (Joyce 2010: Figure 7.12). Transport costs would be slightly different if adobes were made in the vicinity of the borrow pits and then transported to the acropolis. Although this seems like a reasonable possibility for the manufacture of adobe blocks, puddle adobe would be easier to mix at the construction site. The kilometers traveled per hour with a load (V) was estimated at 3 km, whereas unloaded return trips (V') were estimated at a rate of 5 km per hour (Aaberg and Bonsignore 1975, 46). Assuming a five-hour workday (H), the resulting calculation for transporting earthen fill was 0.54 m³ ppd, yielding a total of 849,427 person-days (Table 5.2).

Apart from earth, water had to be carried to the acropolis to make adobes, which constituted roughly 75 percent of the acropolis fill, or 341,288 m³. We assume that the water was taken from wells associated with the borrow pits. To estimate the necessary quantity of water, we followed Craig and colleagues' (1998, 252) adobe "recipe" of 3 parts water to 16 parts sediment. Thus, manufacturing adobes with 341,288 m³ of earth would have required approximately 63,991 m³ of water. Using the same transport formula cited above, but assuming a water-carrying capacity of 11 L (.011 m³) for Q, we arrived at a rate of 0.29 m³ ppd.[2] Approximately 217,182 person-days would have been needed to haul water to make the adobes.

Step 3 considered adobe manufacture for the structured fill of the acropolis. Although laborers used various sizes of adobes, the most commonly occurring type recovered in excavations measured 60 × 30 × 12 cm (0.022 m³). Loewe (2009) reports that eighteenth-century Native American laborers in California made adobes measuring half the volume (0.011 m³) of those at Río Viejo at a rate of 40 ppd. Thus, we estimate that Río Viejo laborers made 20 adobes ppd. Given that approximately 75 percent of the acropolis (341,288 m³) was made of adobes with a volume of 0.022 m³ each, the acropolis would have required 15,800,347 adobes, resulting in a significant labor investment of 790,017 person-days.[3]

For Step 4, building the actual acropolis, we used Abrams's (1994, 50) estimated rate of 4.8 m³ ppd. The construction, primarily the placement of adobes and loose fill, would have required an estimated 94,802 person-days. Summing the labor investment associated with construction Steps 1 through 4, we arrive at a grand total of 2,126,447 person-days for the Río Viejo acropolis construction. Table 5.3 translates the total person-days into years needed to erect the acropolis, depending on the number of months worked per annum (one to

TABLE 5.3. Minimum estimates in years for Río Viejo acropolis construction (rounded to nearest year)

Size of Workforce	30-Day Work-Year	60-Day Work-Year	90-Day Work-Year	120-Day Work-Year
100	709	354	236	177
250	284	142	95	71
500	142	71	47	35
1,000	71	35	24	18
5,000	14	7	5	4

four) and the size of the labor force, ranging from 100 to 5,000 people (see Erasmus 1965, 281–283). The energetics study helps translate the great mass of the acropolis into human dimensions and shows that building the structure required a significant mobilization of labor.

Current evidence indicates that the acropolis was built, occupied, and abandoned in less than 200 years, which suggests that it was constructed rapidly, perhaps in just a few years. If this is correct, then based on our energetics study, the construction of the acropolis would have required several thousand people. To assess the labor available solely from the community of Río Viejo, we use formulae developed elsewhere in Mesoamerica to estimate population from a site area (Blanton 1978, 29–30; Blanton et al. 1982, 10–11; Kowalewski et al. 2009, 24–25; Sanders et al. 1979). Given the high density of settlement indicated by surface survey and excavations at the site (Joyce 1991a, 1999b; Joyce and Levine 2009), we use Sanders's (1965, 50) figure of 25–50 people for a "high-density compact village." This yields a figure of 5,000–10,000 people or an average estimated population of 7,500. If we assume that 50 percent of the population was not available to work on the acropolis because they were younger children, elderly, infirm, and those of high status, then the labor force is reduced to an estimated 3,750 people. If women were excluded from working on the acropolis, this would have further reduced the available labor by half. Daily food procurement and processing would have also reduced available labor. In addition, excavations in Mounds 4, 5, and 8 show that construction of several of the massive mixed-use platforms at Río Viejo was begun in the Chacahua phase (Workinger and Joyce 1999), which would have also required significant inputs of labor (evidence from these structures is insufficient to carry out energetics estimates as we have done for Mound 1). Considering all of these factors, as well as the evidence for the involvement of multiple work crews, we think it likely that people from both Río Viejo and from surrounding communities participated in the construction of the acropolis.

The evidence shows that the construction of the acropolis was a massive undertaking requiring a significant degree of planning and organization. The scale of the Terminal Formative acropolis suggests that local leaders had considerable success in mobilizing labor from Río Viejo and probably surrounding communities. Although it is difficult to infer their intentions, the construction of the acropolis may have been sponsored by rulers attempting to expand their influence beyond Río Viejo and nearby communities to the broader region (Barber and Joyce 2007). As has been argued by numerous archaeologists (e.g., Clark 2004; Love 1999), mutual participation in the construction of public buildings and spaces can create a sense of common purpose, pride, group cohesion, and self-perceived community or *communitas*. To the degree that people from other communities participated in the acropolis project, it could have extended this sense of community beyond Río Viejo, creating a broader imagined community and reinforcing the authority of Rio Viejo's rulers. Since the acropolis was likely built and consecrated as a sacred place, participation in its construction also carried greater significance than if it were simply a utilitarian structure. The act of constructing the acropolis was materially inscribed in a highly durable and visible manner since the building could have been viewed from surrounding communities and has persisted for approximately 2,000 years. As shown by our energetics estimates, the acropolis also indexed a massive labor force as well as the new social affiliations involved in its construction.

Following the completion of the acropolis, involvement in activities carried out there would have continued to bring people together. The poor state of preservation makes it difficult to infer in much detail the architectural forms, uses, and cultural significance of Chacahua phase buildings on the acropolis. We believe that the evidence, including the scale of the structure, points to its use as a public space. The stepped platform could have allowed for a degree of restricted access, perhaps reinforcing the ways in which practices on the acropolis differentiated people along status lines. Excavations in Ops. RV09 C and E indicate that the area of the sunken patio was not built until the Late Classic, which suggests that during the Chacahua phase the area eventually covered by the acropolis may have instead consisted of several monumental buildings, perhaps surrounding a large public plaza where communal ceremonies were carried out.[4]

Based on analogies drawn from political centers emerging elsewhere in Mesoamerica at the end of the Formative period, such as Monte Albán's Main Plaza and the Street of the Dead complex at Teotihuacan (Ashmore 1991; Joyce 2010; Love 1999; Pool 2008; Sugiyama 1993), we suggest that the Río Viejo acropolis was a civic-ceremonial center where rulers sponsored politico-religious ceremonies and made political decisions. We suspect that ceremonies carried out on the acropolis involved ritual feasting, emplacement of ceremonial caches, and mortuary rituals in cemeteries since evidence for these practices has been found in public spaces at other Late/Terminal Formative period sites in the region, including Cerro de la Cruz, Yugüe, San Francisco de Arriba, and Charco Redondo (Barber 2005, Chapter 6; Butler 2011; Joyce 1991a, 1991b; Levine 2002; Workinger 2002). The size of the acropolis was far larger than earlier public buildings in the region and implies a scale of ceremonial performance that would have engaged larger audiences drawn from broader areas within the region. Since earlier public buildings at Río Viejo were located in the eastern end of the site, the acropolis also reordered space in the community and region in ways that may have reinforced the association between Río Viejo's rulers and the new collectivities coming together there. We propose that by drawing together larger groups of people, the building of the acropolis as well as the ritual, political, and economic activities carried out there acted as practices of affiliation that constituted new social formations and contributed to the creation of a corporate identity centered on the symbols, institutions, and rulers at Río Viejo. As in other regions of Mesoamerica (Ashmore 1991; Joyce 2009; Love 1999; Ringle 1999; Sugiyama 1993), we hypothesize that the construction and ongoing use of the acropolis was an act of place-making that embedded regional political authority in a particular place that became a prominent focus for collectivities tied to that authority (Barber and Joyce 2007).

Although most researchers have emphasized the integrative effects of large-scale labor projects such as the building of the acropolis, such projects also have the potential to produce unintended consequences, including the accentuation of social divisions and factionalism. Regional evidence suggests to us that the construction and use of the acropolis accentuated social conflicts and tensions while simultaneously bringing together larger social formations. We see at least two intersecting points of tension and potential conflict within Terminal Formative society: along status lines and between local communities and the incipient regional authorities at Río Viejo.

Despite indications that labor was voluntary and that the acropolis was a communal project, Mound 1's construction would have drawn people away from their local communities, leaders, and places of religious devotion and thus may have created a fracture point in Terminal Formative society. Based on current evidence it is not clear if people from the entire region were engaged in the practices of affiliation centered on Río Viejo and its politico-religious institutions and authorities. Ceremonial centers on a smaller scale are found at Yugüe, San Francisco de Arriba, and probably Cerro de la Virgen (Barber 2005, Chapter 6; Workinger 2002). While it is tempting to take a strongly integrationist position and assume that the hierarchy of public buildings and settlements represents an administrative hierarchy through which Río Viejo governed the region as a politically integrated polity, the evidence at present does not support such relationships (Barber 2005, Chapter 6; Joyce 2008, 2010, 191–195). For example, there was considerable variability in construction techniques and materials as well as the architectural form and use of public buildings and spaces in the region, arguing against the presence of architectural, political, and ritual principles imposed by a single centralized, regional authority (cf. Redmond and Spencer 2008). The continuation of ritual feasting, ceremonial caching, and communal cemeteries from the Minizundo phase to the Chacahua phase at many sites indicates the persistence of a strong local community identity despite the emergence of Río Viejo as a focus of supracommunity affiliations (Barber 2005, Chapter 6; Barber and Joyce 2007; Joyce, Chapter 1). Rather than being unified under a singular regional polity with its capital at Río Viejo, we suspect that political relations among communities were more dynamic and negotiated (Barber Chapter 6; Barber and Joyce 2007; Joyce 2008, 2010).

Rising inequality and political power may have been another source of social tension (Barber 2005, Chapter 6; Barber and Joyce 2007; Barber et al., Chapter 4; Joyce 2006, 2008, 2010). Practices like the construction of monumental buildings, mortuary rituals, and ceremonial caching cast inequality and regional authority as expressions of communal history and identity, which communicated an ideology that downplayed emerging hierarchy, suggesting the existence of social tensions along status lines. For example, prestige goods obtained through long-distance exchange linked elites in the lower Verde to elites in other parts of Mesoamerica and contributed to the creation of a noble identity. The use of socially valued goods in communal ceremonies, particularly caches in public buildings, however, transformed these objects from prestige items that embodied high status into offerings that emphasized corporate identities (Barber et al. 2008). Likewise, at many sites in the region monumental buildings were constructed with voluntary labor that emphasized corporate action and identity, rather than exclusionary political authority (Barber 2005; Barber and Joyce 2007; Joyce 2005, 2008, 2010, 189–191).

Mortuary evidence from a Chacahua phase cemetery at Yugüe also suggests a degree of social tension and contradiction along status lines (Barber 2005, Chapter 6). The body of a young nobleman was one of the few interments in the cemetery to remain intact, whereas most others had been badly disturbed by subsequent interments. The body was also marked by an elaborate ornament (i.e., an iron ore mirror) and a prestigious personal object (i.e., an incised bone flute), suggesting acknowledgment of the status of individuals or particular kin groups within the larger community. Yet his body was not interred in a special setting such as a tomb or within a residence, which was common practice in other parts of Oaxaca (Joyce 2010; Winter 1995). Instead, the individual was returned to the corporate body at death by being placed in the communal cemetery. The mortuary evidence from Yugüe suggests that communal affiliations constrained expressions of exclusionary authority and hierarchy.

Based on the data discussed above, we propose that Terminal Formative political relations in the lower Río Verde Valley involved negotiations and tensions between traditional forms of political authority and identity that were more egalitarian and local, and emerging forms of authority that were more hierarchical, exclusionary, and regional. The fate of the acropolis and of Río Viejo as a political center, however, is the most compelling evidence that regional political authority may have been tenuous and contested. The burning and destruction of the acropolis at Río Viejo suggests that social tensions may have been actualized in conflict at ca. AD 250, only a century or two after the initial construction of the structure (Joyce 2006, 2008, 2010, 195–196). After the destruction and abandonment of the acropolis, this important political and religious building, which had taken considerable communal labor to construct and which presumably was an important symbol of the Terminal Formative polity, was mined for raw materials and left to slowly disintegrate for 250 years. It is possible that the mining of sediment from the acropolis was the result of intentional desecration or the decommissioning of the structure. Similar practices have been noted in other regions of Mesoamerica, particularly in the Maya lowlands (Canuto and Andrews 2008; Mock 1998; Navarro Farr et al. 2008). Even if the mining occurred later and was not part of the destruction of the acropolis at the end of the Formative, it indicates that the meanings associated with the building had been profoundly transformed.

The beginning of the Early Classic was marked by political fragmentation in the region as settlement at Río Viejo decreased from 200 ha to 75 ha and other large sites in the floodplain decreased in size or were abandoned. No single community dominated the region in the Early Classic the way that Río Viejo had at the end of the Formative. Settlement shifted toward higher elevations, perhaps for defense, and the construction of monumental architecture may have ceased. Although further research is needed to determine the causes of the political collapse, it is possible that some sort of internal conflict or rebellion led to the destruction and abandonment of Mound 1 as well as the regional political changes that occurred at this time (however, see Joyce 2003). As shown by the histories of other political centers in Late/Terminal Formative period Oaxaca, such as Monte Negro and Yucuita (Balkansky et al. 2004; Joyce 2010, 195–196), experiments in larger-scale political formations were often unstable and short-lived.

CONCLUSIONS

Excavations in 2000 and 2009 show that the acropolis at Río Viejo was built almost entirely during the Terminal Formative period and that the building was one of the largest by volume in ancient Oaxaca. The excavations show that the acropolis was built using a variety of construction techniques, including at least four types of structured fill. Our research draws attention to the great variety and complexity of construction techniques used to build earthen architecture in Mesoamerica. The scale of the construction as well as evidence for the involvement of multiple work crews indicate that the acropolis was a massive project involving the mobilization of labor from Río Viejo and other communities in the region. Additional research is needed to more fully understand the construction techniques and history of the acropolis as well as its political significance. The results of the 2000 and 2009 research demonstrate, however, that the acropolis was a focal point for Terminal Formative political change and for the eventual failure of centralized political authority at ca. AD 250.

We argue that the construction of the acropolis was an act of place-making that materialized novel political relationships and a larger-scale corporate identity. The regional data suggest, however, that ruling institutions did not emphasize the personal or familial power of rulers, but rather focused on nobles as pivotal members of their communities (Barber, Chapter 6). That is, local community identity continued to be important despite the emergence of Río Viejo as a focus of supracommunity affiliations. Rulers at Río Viejo and probably other communities in the valley may have been struggling to negotiate and legitimize rising inequality and political centralization within the context of traditional ideological principles and practices that were more communal, egalitarian, and politically localized. The evidence showing that the acropolis was burned and abandoned at the end of the Terminal Formative indicates that Río Viejo's rulers were unsuccessful in the long term in gaining the necessary consent from commoners and local leaders in order to institutionalize their authority.

ACKNOWLEDGMENTS

Funding for the archaeological research on the acropolis at Río Viejo has been provided by grants from the following organizations: National Science Foundation (BCS–0096012); Foundation for the Advancement of Mesoamerican Studies (#99012); University of Colorado at Boulder CARTSS, CRCW, Norton Anthropology Fund, and Dean's Fund for Excellence; and a University of Central Florida Office of Research and Commercialization in-house grant and a start-up fund to Sarah Barber. We would like to thank the Instituto Nacional de Antropología e Historia and especially the presidents of the Consejo de Arqueología during the 2000 and 2009 projects, Joaquín García-Bárcena and Roberto García Moll, for granting us permission to carry out the research. We thank the Presidente Municipal of Santiago Jamiltepec, who granted us permission to work in the region. We appreciate the friendship and cooperation of the people of the lower Río Verde Valley, especially the owner of the acropolis, Don Roberto Iglesias. We thank Doug Bamforth, Cathy Cameron, Annick Daneels, Gerardo Gutiérrez, Steve Lekson, and Payson Sheets for comments on an earlier draft of this chapter. We also appreciate information on earthen architecture in Mesoamerica provided by John Clark, Ann Cyphers, Annick Daneels, Charles Frederick, and Chris Pool.

NOTES

1. We suspect that the paucity of stucco and plaster in the region results from a lack of available limestone. It is possible that limestone used to make plaster had to be imported and so was highly valued.

2. Though we do not know the size of the containers used to fetch water, we used the volume of a traditional ceramic water jug (5.5L) from Jicayan, a town on the Oaxacan coast. Two of these could have been carried at once, resulting in a total carrying capacity of 11 L.

3. We assume that puddled adobes and rammed earth require similar amounts of labor per volume of construction material.

4. In the energetics study we estimated the area of the possible Terminal Formative plaza based on excavation data and subtracted it from estimates of the size of the acropolis at this time.

REFERENCES CITED

Aaberg, Stephen, and Jay Bonsignore. 1975. "A Consideration of Time and Labor Expenditure in the Construction Process at the Teotihuacán Pyramid of the Sun and the Poverty Point Mound." In *Three Papers on Mesoamerican Archaeology*, ed. John Graham and Robert Heizer, 40–78. Contributions of the University of California Archaeological Research Facility 24. Berkeley: University of California.

Abrams, Elliot. 1994. *How the Maya Built Their World: Energetics and Ancient Architecture.* Austin: University of Texas Press.

Ashmore, Wendy. 1991. "Site-Planning Principles and Concepts of Directionality among the Ancient Maya." *Latin American Antiquity* 2 (3): 199–226. http://dx.doi.org/10.23 07/972169.

Ashmore, Wendy. 2002. "'Decisions and Dispositions': Socializing Spatial Archaeology." *American Anthropologist* 104 (4): 1172–83. http://dx.doi.org/10.1525/aa.2002.104.4 .1172.

Balkansky, Andrew K., Verónica Pérez Rodríguez, and Stephen A. Kowalewski. 2004. "Monte Negro and the Urban Revolution in Oaxaca, Mexico." *Latin American Antiquity* 15 (1): 33–60. http://dx.doi.org/10.2307/4141563.

Barber, Sarah B. 2005. *Heterogeneity, Identity, and Complexity: Negotiating Status and Authority in Terminal Formative Coastal Oaxaca.* PhD dissertation, Department of Anthropology, University of Colorado, Boulder. Ann Arbor, MI: University Microfilms.

Barber, Sarah B. 2009. "Estudio geofisico del bajo Rio Verde: Informe final." Final report submitted to the Consejo de Arqueología, Instituto Nacional de Antropología e Historia, Mexico City.

Barber, Sarah B., and Arthur A. Joyce. 2007. "Polity Produced and Community Consumed: Negotiating Political Centralization in the Lower Río Verde Valley,

Oaxaca." In *Mesoamerican Ritual Economy*, ed. E. Christian Wells and Karla L. Davis-Salazar, 221–44. Boulder: University Press of Colorado.

Barber, Sarah B., Andrew Workinger, and Arthur A. Joyce. 2008. "Who Owns Whom? Inalienable Possessions and Community Identities in the Lower Río Verde Valley, Oaxaca." Paper presented at the 73rd Annual Meeting of the Society for American Archaeology, Vancouver.

Basso, Keith H. 1996. *Wisdom Sits in Places: Landscape and Language among the Western Apache.* Albuquerque: University of New Mexico Press.

Blanton, Richard E. 1978. *Monte Alban: Settlement Patterns at the Ancient Zapotec Capital.* New York: Academic Press.

Blanton, Richard E., Stephen Kowalewski, Gary Feinman, and Jill Appel. 1982. *Monte Alban's Hinterland, Part I: The Prehispanic Settlement Patterns of the Central and Southern Parts of the Valley of Oaxaca, Mexico.* Prehistory and Human Ecology of the Valley of Oaxaca 7, Memoirs of the Museum of Anthropology. Ann Arbor: University of Michigan.

Butler, Michelle M. 2011. Excavaciones en Charco Redondo, 2009. In "El proyecto Río Verde: Informe técnico de la temporada de 2009," ed. Sarah B. Barber and Arthur A. Joyce, 185–221. Final report to be submitted to the Consejo de Arqueología, Instituto Nacional de Antropología e Historia, Mexico City.

Canuto, Marcello A., and Anthony P. Andrews. 2008. "Memories, Meanings, and Historical Awareness: Post-abandonment Behaviors among the Lowland Maya." In *Ruins of the Past: The Use and Perception of Abandoned Structures in the Maya Lowlands*, ed. Travis W. Stanton and Aline Magnoni, 257–74. Boulder: University Press of Colorado.

Clark, John E. 1994. *The Development of Early Formative Rank Societies in the Soconusco, Chiapas, Mexico.* PhD dissertation, Department of Anthropology, University of Michigan, Ann Arbor. Ann Arbor, MI: University Microfilms.

Clark, John E. 2004. "Mesoamerica Goes Public: Early Ceremonial Centers, Leaders, and Communities." In *Mesoamerican Archaeology*, ed. Julia Hendon and Rosemary Joyce, 43–72. Oxford: Blackwell.

Craig, Douglas B., James P. Holmlund, and Jeffrey J. Clark. 1998. "Labor Investment and Organization in Platform Mound Construction: A Case Study from the Tonto Basin of Central Arizona." *Journal of Field Archaeology* 25: 245–59.

Cyphers, Ann, and Anna Di Castro. 2009. "Early Olmec Architecture and Imagery." In *The Art of Urbanism*, ed. William L. Fash and Leonardo López Luján, 21–52. Washington, DC: Dumbarton Oaks Research Library and Collection.

Daneels, Annick. 2007. "La Joya Pyramid, Central Veracruz, Mexico: Classic Period Earthen Architecture." Project grant report submitted to Dumbarton Oaks, Washington, DC.

Daneels, Annick. 2008. "Monumental Earthen Architecture at La Joya, Veracruz, Mexico." Report submitted to the Foundation for the Advancement of Mesoamerican Studies, Crystal River, FL.

Drucker, Philip, Robert Fleming Heizer, and Robert J. Squier. 1957. *Excavations at La Venta, Tabasco, 1955.* Bureau of American Ethnology Bulletin Volume 170. Washington, DC: Government Printing Office.

Erasmus, Charles J. 1965. "Monument Building: Some Field Experiments." *Southwestern Journal of Anthropology* 21: 277–301.

Goldberg, Paul. 2009. Apéndice C: Análisis de laminas delgadas de sedimentos de RV0A. In "El proyecto Río Verde," ed. Arthur A. Joyce and Marc N. Levine, 471–72. Final report submitted to the Consejo de Arqueología, Instituto Nacional de Antropología e Historia, Mexico City.

Hastings, C. Mansfield, and M. Edward Moseley. 1975. "The Adobes of Huaca del Sol and Huaca de La Luna." *American Antiquity* 40 (2): 196–203. http://dx.doi.org/10.2307/279615.

Joyce, Arthur A. 1991a. *Formative Period Occupation in the Lower Río Verde Valley, Oaxaca, Mexico: Interregional Interaction and Social Change.* PhD dissertation, Department of Anthropology, Rutgers University, New Brunswick, NJ. Ann Arbor, MI: University Microfilms.

Joyce, Arthur A. 1991b. "Formative Period Social Change in the Lower Río Verde Valley, Oaxaca, Mexico." *Latin American Antiquity* 2 (2): 126–50. http://dx.doi.org/10.2307/972274.

Joyce, Arthur A. 1999a. Mapeo de sitios. In "El proyecto patrones de asentamiento del Río Verde," ed. Arthur A. Joyce, 37–40. Final report submitted to the Consejo de Arqueología, Instituto Nacional de Antropología e Historia, Mexico City.

Joyce, Arthur A., ed. 1999b. "El proyecto patrones de asentamiento del Río Verde." Final report submitted to the Consejo de Arqueología, Instituto Nacional de Antropología e Historia, Mexico City.

Joyce, Arthur A. 2003. "Imperialism in Pre-Aztec Mesoamerica: Monte Albán, Teotihuacan, and the Lower Río Verde Valley." In *Ancient Mesoamerica Warfare*, ed. M. Kathryn Brown and Travis M. Stanton, 49–72. Walnut Creek, CA: AltaMira Press.

Joyce, Arthur A. 2005. "La arqueología del bajo Río Verde." *Acervos* 7 (29): 16–36.

Joyce, Arthur A. 2006. "The Inhabitation of Río Viejo's Acropolis." In *Space and Spatial Analysis in Archaeology*, ed. Elizabeth C. Robertson, Jeffrey D. Seibert, Deepika C. Fernández, and Marc U. Zender, 83–96. Albuquerque: University of New Mexico Press; Calgary: University of Calgary Press.

Joyce, Arthur A. 2008. "Domination, Negotiation, and Collapse: A History of Centralized Authority on the Oaxaca Coast Before the Late Postclassic." In *After Monte Albán: Transformation and Negotiation in Oaxaca, Mexico*, ed. Jeffrey Blomster, 219–54. Boulder: University Press of Colorado.

Joyce, Arthur A. 2009. "The Main Plaza of Monte Albán: A Life History of Place." In *The Archaeology of Meaningful Places*, ed. Brenda Bowser and María Nieves Zedeño, 32–52. Salt Lake City: University of Utah Press.

Joyce, Arthur A. 2010. *Mixtecs, Zapotecs, and Chatinos: Ancient Peoples of Southern Mexico.* Malden, MA: Wiley-Blackwell Press.

Joyce, Arthur A., and Sarah B. Barber. 2011. "Excavating the Acropolis at Río Viejo, Oaxaca, Mexico." *Mexicon* 33 (1): 15–20.

Joyce, Arthur A., Laura Arnaud Bustamante, and Marc N. Levine. 2001. "Commoner Power: A Case Study from the Classic Period Collapse on the Oaxaca Coast." *Journal of Archaeological Method and Theory* 8 (4): 343–85. http://dx.doi.org/10.1023/A:1013786700137.

Joyce, Arthur A., and Marc N. Levine, eds. 2009. "El proyecto Río Verde." Final report submitted to the Consejo de Arqueología, Instituto Nacional de Antropología e Historia, Mexico City.

Joyce, Arthur A., and Raymond G. Mueller. 1992. "The Social Impact of Anthropogenic Landscape Modification in the Río Verde Drainage Basin, Oaxaca, Mexico." *Geoarchaeology* 7 (6): 503–26. http://dx.doi.org/10.1002/gea.3340070602.

Joyce, Arthur A., Marcus Winter, and Raymond G. Mueller. 1998. *Arqueología de la costa de Oaxaca: Asentamientos del periodo formativo en el valle del Río Verde inferior.* Estudios de Antropología e Historia No. 40. Oaxaca: Centro INAH Oaxaca.

Joyce, Rosemary A. 2004. "Unintended Consequences? Monumentality as a Novel Experience in Formative Mesoamerica." *Journal of Archaeological Method and Theory* 11 (1): 5–29. http://dx.doi.org/10.1023/B:JARM.0000014346.87569.4a.

Kidder, Tristram R., Lee. J. Arco, Anthony L. Ortmann, Timothy Schilling, Caroline Boeke, Rachel Bielitz, Tabitha Heet, Katie A. Adelsberger, Joe Saunders, and Thurman A. Allen. 2006. "Poverty Point Mound A: Final Report of the 2005 Field Season." Manuscript on file at Poverty Point State Historic Site, Pioneer, LA.

Kowalewski, Stephen A., Andrew K. Balkansky, Laura R. Stiver Walsh, Thomas J. Pluckhahn, John F. Chamblee, Verónica Pérez Rodríguez, Verenice Y. Heredia Espinoza, and Charlotte A. Smith. 2009. *Origins of the Nuu: Archaeology in the Mixteca Alta.* Boulder: University Press of Colorado.

Levine, Marc N. 2002. "Ceramic Change and Continuity in the Lower Río Verde Region of Oaxaca Mexico: The Late Formative to Early Terminal Formative Transition." MA thesis, Department of Anthropology, University of Colorado, Boulder.

Levine, Marc N., and Arthur A. Joyce. 2009. Excavaciones profundas en la Estructura 2 del Montículo 1 de Río Viejo. In "El Proyecto Río Verde," ed. Arthur A. Joyce and Marc N. Levine, 81–140. Final report submitted to the Consejo de Arqueología, Instituto Nacional de Antropologia e Historia, Mexico City.

Levine, Marc N., Arthur A. Joyce, and Paul Goldberg. 2004. "Earthen Mound Construction at Río Viejo on the Pacific Coast of Oaxaca, Mexico." Paper presented at the 69th Annual Meeting of the Society for American Archaeology, Montreal.

Loewe, Eric M. 2009. "From the Earth to the Heavens: Economic and Architectural Examination of Adobe Bricks and Brick Making at the Third Mission Santa Clara." *Proceedings of the Society for California Archaeology* 21: 36–43.

Love, Michael. 1999. "Ideology, Material Culture, and Daily Practice in Pre-Classic Mesoamerica: A Pacific Coast Perspective." In *Social Patterns in Pre-Classic Mesoamerica,* ed. David C. Grove and Rosemary A. Joyce, 127–54. Washington, DC: Dumbarton Oaks Research Library and Collection.

Marquina, Ignacio. 1964. *Arquitectura prehispánica.* México City: Instituto Nacional de Antropología e Historia, Secretaría de Educación Pública.

Mayes, Arion T., and Sarah B. Barber. 2008. "Osteobiography of a High Status Burial from the Lower Río Verde Valley of Oaxaca, Mexico." *International Journal of Osteoarchaeology* 18 (6): 573–88. http://dx.doi.org/10.1002/oa.1011.

Millon, Rene, Bruce Drewitt, and James A. Bennyhoff. 1965. "The Pyramid of the Sun at Teotihuacan: 1959 Excavations." *Transactions of the American Philosophical Society* (Philadelphia), vol. 55, pt. 6.

Mock, Shirley B., ed. 1998. *The Sowing and the Dawning: Termination, Dedication, and Transformation in the Archaeological and Epigraphic Record of Mesoamerica.* Albuquerque: University of New Mexico Press.

Morgan, William N. 1999. *Precolumbian Architecture in Eastern North America*. Gainesville: University Press of Florida.

Navarro Farr, Olivia C., David A. Freidel, and Ana Lucia Arroyave Prera. 2008. "Manipulating Memory in the Wake of Dynastic Decline at el Perú-Waka': Termination Deposits at Abandoned Structure M13-1." In *Ruins of the Past: The Use and Perception of Abandoned Structures in the Maya Lowlands*, ed. Travis W. Stanton and Aline Magnoni, 113–46. Boulder: University Press of Colorado.

Pool, Christopher A. 2008. "Architectural Plans, Factionalism, and the Protoclassic-Classic Transition at Tres Zapotes." In *Classic Period Cultural Currents in Southern and Central Veracruz*, ed. Philip J. Arnold and Christopher A. Pool, 121–57. Washington, DC: Dumbarton Oaks; Cambridge, MA: Harvard University Press.

Pred, Allan. 1984. "Place as Historically Contingent Process: Structuration and the Time-Geography of Becoming Places." *Annals of the Association of American Geographers* 74 (2): 279–97. http://dx.doi.org/10.1111/j.1467-8306.1984.tb01453.x.

Redmond, Elsa M., and Charles S. Spencer. 2008. "Rituals of Sanctification and the Development of Standardized Temples in Oaxaca, Mexico." *Cambridge Archaeological Journal* 18 (2): 239–66. http://dx.doi.org/10.1017/S0959774308000279.

Ringle, William M. 1999. "Pre-Classic Cityscapes: Ritual Politics among the Early Lowland Maya." In *Social Patterns in Pre-Classic Mesoamerica*, ed. David C. Grove and Rosemary A. Joyce, 183–223. Washington, DC: Dumbarton Oaks.

Rosenswig, Robert, and Marilyn Masson. 2002. "Transformation of the Terminal Classic to Postclassic Architectural Landscape at Caye Coco, Belize." *Ancient Mesoamerica* 13 (2): 213–35. http://dx.doi.org/10.1017/S0956536102132123.

Sanders, William T. 1965. "The Cultural Ecology of the Teotihuacan Valley: A Preliminary Report of the Results of the Teotihuacan Valley Project." Manuscript on file, Department of Anthropology, Pennsylvania State University, University Park.

Sanders, William T., Robert S. Santley, and Jeffrey R. Parsons. 1979. *The Basin of Mexico: Ecological Processes in the Evolution of a Civilization*. New York: Academic Press.

Shimada, Izuni. 1999. "The Evolution of Andean Diversity: Regional Formations (ca. 500 BCE–CE 600)." In *Cambridge History of Native Peoples of the Americas*, vol. 3, ed. Frank Salomon and Stuart Schwartz, 350–517. Cambridge: Cambridge University Press.

Sugiyama, Saburo. 1993. "Worldview Materialized in Teotihuacán, Mexico." *Latin American Antiquity* 4 (2): 103–29. http://dx.doi.org/10.2307/971798.

Winter, Marcus, ed. 1995. *Entierros humanos de Monte Albán*. Contribución No. 7 del Proyecto Especial Monte Albán 1992–1994. Oaxaca: Centro INAH Oaxaca.

Workinger, Andrew. 2002. *Coastal/Highland Interaction in Prehispanic Oaxaca, Mexico: The Perspective from San Francisco de Arriba*. PhD dissertation, Department of Anthropology, Vanderbilt University, Nashville, TN. Ann Arbor, MI: University Microfilms.

Workinger, Andrew, and Arthur A. Joyce. 1999. Excavaciones arqueológicas en Río Viejo. In "El proyecto patrones de asentamiento del Río Verde," ed. Arthur A. Joyce, 51–119. Final report submitted to the Consejo de Arqueología, Instituto Nacional de Antropologia e Historia, Mexico City.

DEFINING COMMUNITY AND STATUS AT OUTLYING SITES DURING THE TERMINAL FORMATIVE PERIOD

SARAH B. BARBER

The development of a regional polity in the Terminal Formative period (150 BC–AD 250) was inevitably a process that involved people throughout the lower Río Verde Valley (Figure 1.2). For those living in the many midsize and small sites that dotted the valley, the development and maintenance of regional political structures would have created new opportunities and challenges. The expansion of Río Viejo as a political center resulted in regional population movements (Joyce 2005, 2008; Joyce et al., Chapter 5); new economic demands were placed on populations valley-wide (Joyce 2010, 191; Levine, Chapter 8); social and political hierarchies changed as the political authority of Río Viejo's elites expanded (Joyce 2005, 2008, 2010); and ceremonial activities and responsibilities would have shifted with the construction and use of monumental ritual spaces at Río Viejo (Barber and Joyce 2007; Joyce 2005, 2008; 2010, 186–195; Joyce and Barber 2011; Joyce et al., Chapter 5). The manner in which such social changes played out, however, was a result not simply of dictates emanating from Río Viejo, but rather emerged from negotiations between regional political authorities and local populations (Barber 2005; Barber and Joyce 2007; Joyce 2008, 2010).

DOI: 10.5876/9781607322023.c06

In this chapter I consider the local side of those negotiations by reporting the results of excavation in Terminal Formative contexts at two outlying sites: Yugüe and Cerro de la Virgen. In particular, I consider how local community and status identities were constituted through domestic and public ceremonial action. Evidence from both sites indicates that local community affiliation was extensively and publicly reiterated by people of all social positions. Acts defining high status, on the other hand, were conducted primarily in restricted locations like residences and exclusive public spaces. While exclusivity is to be expected in some elite practices, the evidence suggests that public expressions of status inequality were muted. Instead, both elites and commoners at sites outside of Río Viejo prioritized parochial affiliations in public actions.

SOCIAL IDENTITIES IN THE LOWER RÍO VERDE VALLEY

Membership in meaningful collectivities like local communities and status groups is an outcome of social identity formation and maintenance. Social identities exist as practices through which people define themselves, categorize others, and thereby create collectivities that distinguish between group members and nonmembers (Jenkins 1996, 4). While individuals are necessarily involved, social identities are inherently collective and enduring. Social identities cannot exist if they are not recognized by others. They also extend through time and claim continuity with a shared past (Friedman 1994; Bell 1992). Because they manifest through human action, are shared by multiple people, and persist diachronically, social identities have material, spatial, and temporal components (Jenkins 1996, 89). They are therefore amenable to archaeological examination (e.g., Casella and Fowler 2004; Jones 1996; Meskell 2001; Schortman et al. 2001).

Social identities emerge from nondiscursive and discursive practices of definition—acts by which people identify themselves and categorize others. The routines of everyday life among people who interact daily create a collective sense of sameness (Bourdieu 1977, 164). This shared identity, generated through nondiscursive practices of definition, makes social interaction comprehensible and predictable. People may also engage in less quotidian acts that serve as explicit statements of group membership, such as initiation ceremonies or those marking an individual's transition from one social group to another. Such "practices of affiliation" often incorporate a high degree of discursive knowledge in order to make affiliations clear to both group members and non-members (Yaeger 2000, 125). Operationalized for archaeology, social identities are evident in the material remains of practices of definition. What constitutes a practice of definition will depend on the modalities of identity under investigation, as well as the broader historical context of the specific archaeological case (see Barber 2005, Chapters 2–3). Lacking written records, archaeologists must employ analogy with other archaeological and ethnographic examples to generate expectations for the specific social and spatial contexts in which a modality of identity would have manifested. Repetitive actions may also indicate practices of definition since the continuity of social groups over time will result in the reoccurrence of certain events. Regardless, any archaeological study of social identity must begin by demonstrating that a specific collectivity existed in the past to avoid imposing modern categories on ancient societies (Insoll 2007, 4).

The two social groups that are the focus of this chapter have been widely discussed in the anthropological literature of Mesoamerica. Local communities are supradomestic social groups that share a common history and a connection to specific geographic locations (Clark 2004; Cohen 1999; Monaghan 1995; Urban and Schortman 2004; Watanabe 1992; Yaeger and Canuto 2000). People create local communities by undertaking both nondiscursive, everyday practices and more formal practices of affiliation in the same location over multiple generations. While other factors may be involved in definitions of community identity, such as kinship or specific ideals (as in Anderson's [1991] "imagined communities"), local communities are defined here as a place-based modality of social identity. They are archaeologically visible through the repeated use of the same public or accessible domestic spaces by groups of people larger than an individual household.

High-status groups are also supradomestic collectivities, but rather than sharing one or a small number of socially meaningful locations on the landscape, they share a set of privileges or a particular position near the top of a social hierarchy. High-status groups like local elites are defined and maintained by the intergenerational transmission and deployment of exclusive knowledge and valued resources that assure or expand group privileges (see Weber 1968, 305–307). The archaeological visibility of high-status social identity is well documented in the literature of Mesoamerican archaeology (e.g., papers in Chase and Chase 1992). I emphasize changes in the archaeological and social contexts in which practices defining high status took place during the Terminal Formative period.

The ensuing discussion is based on the premises that people act intentionally and that their actions are enabled and constrained by the social groups with which they are affiliated. Because social identities define both group membership and exclusion, affiliations can affect an individual's access to and control of material resources (Schortman and Nakamura 1991; Schortman et al. 2001), knowledge (Joyce 2000), and power networks (Janusek 2004, 16–20). In other words, social identities have a wide range of material and ideological effects on the lived experience of people past and present. It follows that changes in the practices through which people defined modalities of identity would have been the result of intentional choices made in reference to broader social and environmental conditions. Practices defining local community and high-status identities offer insight into actions taken by people at outlying sites in the lower Río Verde Valley to negotiate social and economic changes during the Terminal Formative period. I begin by demonstrating that local communities and high status were modalities of identity in the Terminal Formative and follow with an analysis of how practices of definition changed between 150 BC and AD 250.

YUGÜE AND CERRO DE LA VIRGEN IN THE TERMINAL FORMATIVE PERIOD

The sites of Yugüe and Cerro de la Virgen provide ideal contexts from which to examine changes in the definition of local community and high status in the Terminal Formative period. Both sites had significant Terminal Formative occupations and had been continuously occupied since at least the Minizundo phase (400–150 BC), if not earlier. Both sites were sufficiently large and elaborate to suggest that each was internally stratified. Yugüe, the smaller of the two, was only 9.75 ha in size. However, the core of the site was a 10 m high monumental earthen platform with a footprint of approximately 4.6 ha (A. Joyce 1999). The summit of the platform supported three large substructures that were part of a public ceremonial space (Figure 6.1). At 60 ha in area, Cerro de la Virgen was one of the five largest sites in the valley by the Chacahua phase (AD 100–250; Barber and Joyce 2003; Joyce 2010, 186). While little is known about the Miniyua phase component of the site, the Chacahua phase component probably included a formal public area created by constructing several large terraces and modifying the slopes and peaks of the hill on which the site was located. This space consisted of a central plaza surrounded by probable high-status residences and ceremonial architecture, including a ball court.[1]

Each site was sufficiently different, however, to provide a broad perspective on the lived experience of political centralization in the Terminal Formative. Yugüe was a floodplain site located close to the east bank of the Río Verde and only 4 km from Río Viejo. The presence of redeposited Charco phase (700–400 BC) sherds in Terminal Formative contexts at Yugüe suggests that the site was an old, well-established settlement. Nonetheless, Yugüe was abandoned at the end of the Terminal Formative, not to be reoccupied until the Late Postclassic period (AD 1100–1522). Cerro de la Virgen, on the other hand, was a piedmont site that lined the summit and flanks of a 200 m high hill in the north-central part of the valley. Cerro de la Virgen was 12 km east of Río Viejo and 10 km southwest of the large Terminal Formative site of San Francisco de Arriba (Workinger 2002). While Cerro de la Virgen may have had a Late Formative component based on the presence of redeposited sherds,

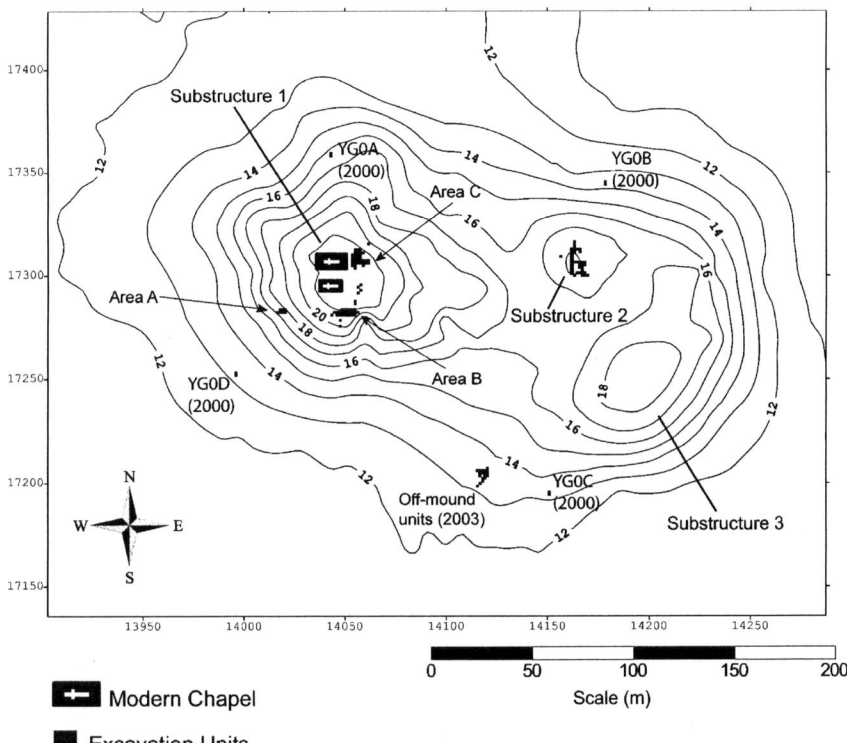

FIGURE 6.1. Topographic map of Yugüe showing substructures and excavated areas (after Joyce 2010: Figure 6.10).

the hill supported only two 3 ha sites during the Miniyua phase (150 BC–AD 100). It grew to its large size in the Chacahua phase, and it became one of eight regional centers in the Early Classic period (AD 250–500) after the collapse of the Terminal Formative Río Viejo polity.

The differences in site size, location, and occupation history make Yugüe and Cerro de la Virgen valuable cases from which to consider the lived experience of political centralization in the lower Río Verde Valley. The archaeological data set from Yugüe derives from block excavations conducted both at the summit and base of the site platform. All three excavation areas (Areas A, B, and C, Figure 6.1) uncovered evidence for supradomestic or "public" ceremony. At Cerro de la Virgen clearing excavation uncovered the remains of a single large residence. Primary contexts recovered included architectural features and several caches. Part of a redeposited midden was also found in building fill. Together, the archaeological data from each site offer insight into domestic and supradomestic social action at outlying sites during the Terminal Formative period.

DEFINING LOCAL COMMUNITY IDENTITY AT YUGÜE

Evidence from excavations at the summit and base of the Yugüe platform mound amply demonstrates that the local community was a modality of identity at the site in the Terminal Formative period. As discussed previously, local communities were collectivities constituted through shared history, place, and practice. Although no Terminal Formative domestic contexts were recovered at Yugüe, which could have attested to the nondiscursive aspects of community identity, there was considerable evidence for a wide range of collective practices of affiliation spanning the entire 400 years of the Terminal Formative period. Block excavations extending over an area of only 126 m² uncovered 175 whole or partial ceramic vessels, at least forty-nine interred individuals, three middens, and several other in-situ deposits. A cemetery and two large, complex caches attested to the repetitive and collective use of the area.

Defining Place Architecturally

Local community identities are ultimately place-based. They are social groups emerging from people's shared connection to a physical location on the landscape. Yugüe's physical location, which had been the site of human habitation since at least the Late Formative, was impressively modified at the beginning of the Miniyua phase with the construction of the site platform. Built entirely of earthen fill set behind clay or mixed clay-silt retaining walls, the platform's final footprint was approximately 300 m long (E–W) by 200 m wide (N–S) with an east–west azimuth lying between 102°/282° and 108°/288° (Barber 2005). The western half of the platform was in place by the beginning of Terminal Formative period based on ceramics and a radiocarbon date from the summit.[2] The eastern portion of the site platform contained primary contexts dating to only the Chacahua phase, indicating that this area did not reach its current height until AD 100 or later. Built over a low outcropping of bedrock, the platform's final volume was between 94,380 and 100,111 m³—a considerable architectural undertaking (Marc Levine, personal communication, 2004).

The expansion and remodeling evident in the platform itself was replicated in the construction of substructures and superstructures on the summit. Substructure 1, at the western summit of the site platform, was modified at least four times and probably more. The earliest preserved version of Substructure 1 (Substructure 1-sub3) was a small stepped platform measuring approximately 3 m long (N–S) and at least 4 m wide (E–W), located in the northeast corner of the substructure (Area C, Figure 6.1; Figure 6.2).[3] Parallel clay retaining walls (F3/F5) oriented to the site azimuth (105°/285°) were connected by a low retaining wall and step (F2) that elevated the western section of Substructure 1-sub3 above the eastern portion. Narrow lines of hardened

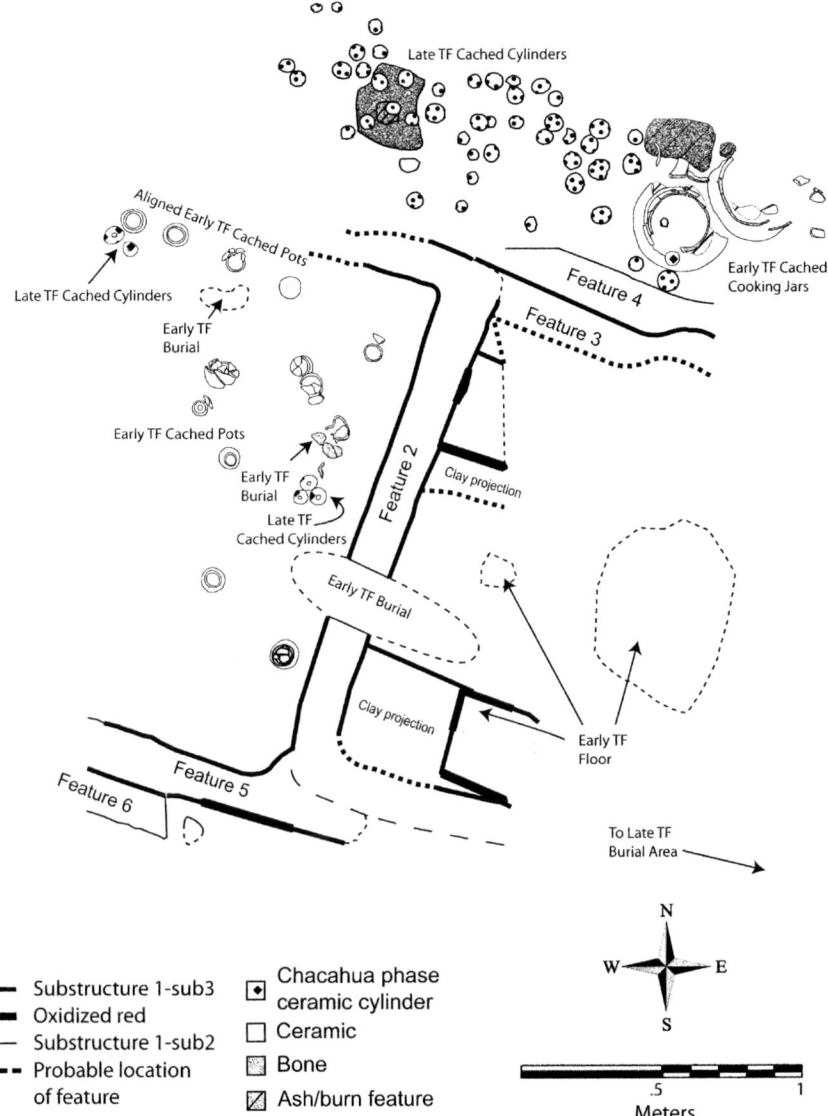

FIGURE 6.2. Plan view of Substructures 1-sub3 and 1-sub2.

clay projected eastward from F2, creating rectangular openings. The bases of these openings were lined with thin layers of hardened carbonates. The outer surfaces of all of the clay retaining walls were oxidized, as were the surfaces of the rectangular openings. It was unclear whether this burning was related to the construction of the structure (perhaps as a means of hardening the clay walls), whether it was related to the subsequent renovation of the structure, or whether it was a result of accidental or intentional burning during the use of the structure. The Miniyua phase burning at Yugüe represents a different phenomenon than the preabandonment Chacahua phase burning at Río Viejo since the burned structure at Yugüe was immediately renovated (see Joyce et al., Chapter 5). The clay walls of Substructure 1-sub2 (F4/F6) were applied directly onto the oxidized surfaces of Substructure 1-sub3. Given the excellent preservation of the oxidized areas, it is unlikely that the walls of Substructure 1-sub3 were exposed to the elements for very long. Substructure 1-sub2 retained the footprint and orientation of Substructure 1-sub3 but created a single elevated surface. A second Miniyua phase substructure may have existed near what is now the southwest corner of Substructure 1 (Area A, Figure 6.1), where a possible clay surface and small offering vessel were found.

At least two additional construction episodes occurred in the Chacahua phase. One was evident only as the poorly preserved remnant of a clay wall located stratigraphically above Substructures 1-sub3 and 1-sub2; the other was a late renovation (or renovations) that created the nearly 1500 m² area of Substructure 1 as it appears today. The north and south sides of the later iterations of Substructure 1 were supported by retaining walls of massive, meter-tall slabs of granodiorite that retained the orientation of the earlier substructures. Later iterations of the substructure supported at least two superstructures, as evidenced by the remnants of an oxidized clay floor in the southeast corner of the substructure (Area B, Figure 6.1). The number and extent of these later renovations remain unclear due to the loss of at least 50 cm of fill across much of Substructure 1 caused by erosion and modern construction.

By the Chacahua phase, Substructure 1 was part of a larger complex of buildings set atop the site platform. To the east, the Yugüe platform's surface was raised, and two additional substructures were built. Substructure 2 (Figure 6.1) consisted of at least two construction episodes. The earlier of these was identifiable only by a stratigraphic break 80 cm below the modern ground surface. An adobe block and a shaped stone were both found set into or sitting on this stratigraphic break. The later occupation represented the remnants of a small, poorly preserved ceremonial structure. All that remained of the superstructure itself were a few shaped blocks, one still supporting a fragment of adobe, and a circular stain of calcareous sediment (Figure 6.3). However, two caches located in the fill stratigraphically beneath these features attested to the Chacahua phase use of the area.

The Yugüe platform and summit substructures were part of ongoing acts that created and recreated a socially meaningful place through architecture. The platform itself was a mixed-use platform, used to support both residences and ceremonial structures. The flanks of the platform are lined with single-coursed stone foundations; hearths, occupation surfaces, and middens

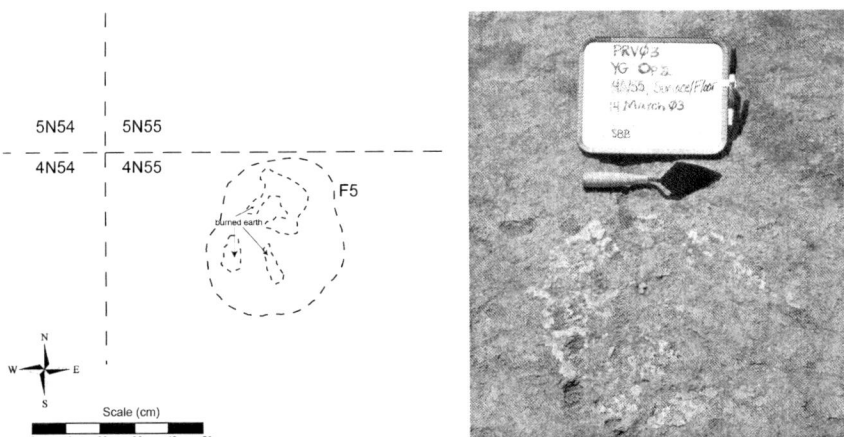

FIGURE 6.3. Calcareous feature, Substructure 2, Yugüe.

dating to the Late and Terminal Formative periods have been found in test pits near the platform's base (Barber 2009). Yugüe's platform was thus a profoundly inhabited location. Numerous scholars have noted that history and memory are often tied to physical locations on the landscape (e.g., Ashmore 2002; Barrett 1999; Basso 1996; Cattell and Climo 2002; Hirsch 1995; Pauketat and Alt 2003; Pred 1984; Van Dyke and Alcock 2003). In the case of Yugüe, the practices that produced collective history were permanently embodied in the physical site of their enactment. The shared history and practice characteristic of community identities were literally built into the site's architecture.

Embedding History in Place through Ritual

Although much of Yugüe's social significance would have emerged from the simple fact that people inhabited the site for many generations, they also used the site platform for a wide range of collective ritual acts. These acts, which included burial, caching, and feasting, were practices of affiliation that served to create and maintain a local community identity. Substructure 1 was used intensively as the site of all of these acts, beginning in the Miniyua phase.

Three burials, two caches, and a midden were associated with Substructure 1-sub2. The burials, like later interments in the substructure, represented the entire age spectrum of the site: a neonate, a juvenile (ca. 5 years), and an adult (Barber et al., Chapter 4). The juvenile and adult were interred in reference to the site-wide azimuth: the adult was oriented approximately 110°/290° while the juvenile was perpendicular at 15°/195°. The neonate was oriented east–west but was so small that it was not possible to determine an azimuth. The juvenile was interred with a small coarse brownware jar lidded with an upside-down fine brownware bowl and the adult was accompanied by four small coarse brownware jars. The same fill layer contained a cache of twenty whole vessels, mostly coarse brownware jars topped by upside-down fine brownware bowls. The placement of vessels in the offering suggests that they may have been interred as part of several events. The seven vessels to the north were laid out in a row and aligned with the north wall of Substructure 1-sub2 (Figure 6.2). The careful placement of these vessels in reference to architecture is distinct from the rest of the vessels, which show no obvious pattern. None of the vessels were damaged by a subsequent interment. For this reason, the possibility remains that the cache was deposited all at once or over a short enough time span that the exact locations of vessels were not forgotten.

Another cache was created as the result of food preparation and consumption. It consisted of three coarse brownware cooking jars that had been interred up to the neck in fill beneath an occupation surface outside the retaining wall of Substructure 1-sub2. The jars were covered with sherds from other vessels, rocks, perishable materials, and earth. The entire upper area was subsequently ignited, as demonstrated by ash and burned earth around the mouths of the vessels as well as by oxidation on the rims of the vessels themselves. The best-preserved of the vessels contained estuarine mussel shell and sat atop several grayware serving bowls. The events associated with the interment of these pots were repeated over some period of time since two of the three vessels had been damaged by the subsequent interment of the next. A second, nearly identical cache of three jars was found at the southeast base of the site platform. While none of the latter vessels held identifiable food remains, two contained ceramic potboilers. The sherd "lids" on the vessels in this second cache were intact, meaning that the contents of the vessels had not been removed after the jars were heated.

Further evidence for food preparation and consumption on Substructure 1-sub2 comes from a midden abutting the substructure's south wall. The lenses of the midden sloped down from the wall, indicating that the contents of the midden were discarded by people on the substructure's surface. The midden contained large sherds from food preparation and serving vessels, ash, bone, estuarine shell, and fragments of adobe. One sherd was probably from an imported Valley of Oaxaca grayware vessel.

Caching, burial, and food consumption all continued into the Chacahua phase on Substructure 1. A large cache containing fifty low-fired ceramic cylinders was placed above and around the earlier trio of cached cooking jars outside Substructure 1-sub2. The association between the cooking jars and the cylinders on Substructure 1 is confirmed by the presence of eighty-five ceramic cylinders in the fill above the three cooking jars cached at the base of the site platform. The vessels in both caches had clearly been interred over an extended period of time by different people, as they spanned multiple strata

Scale (cm)

FIGURE 6.4. Chacahua phase cylindrical offering vessels, Yugüe.

and were occasionally damaged by the subsequent interment of another cylinder. The cylinders were made with different pastes and were of different diameters; some were lidded, and some had narrow hollow centers (Figure 6.4). They look homemade, as if made by people with limited experience in pottery production. Their appearance is reminiscent of the ceramic cylinders used to elevate and separate vessels during the heating of seawater in salt production, although most of the Yugüe cylinders are larger (e.g., McKillop 1995, 224–225). However, the presence of lids on some vessels, the large size of many (several

175

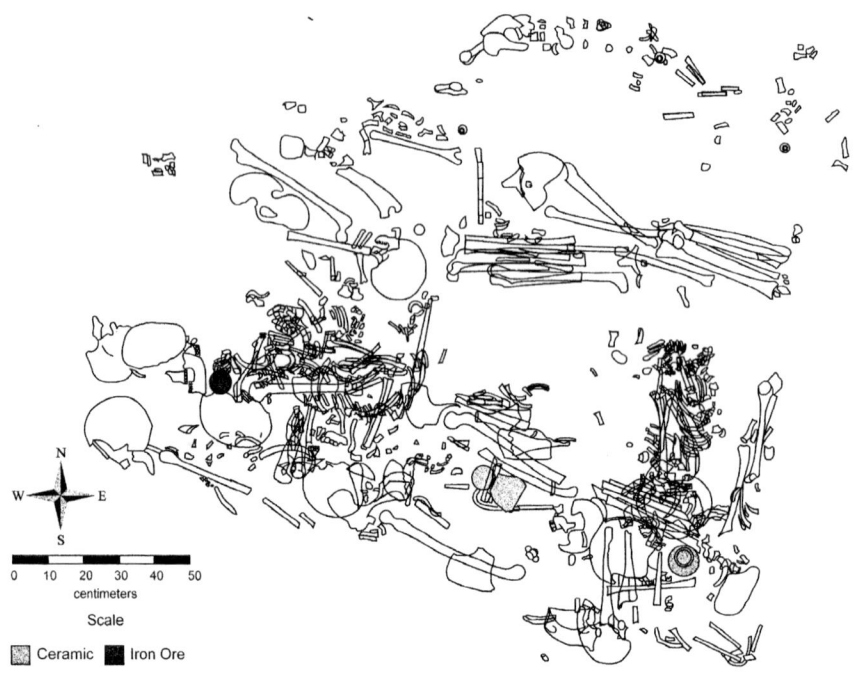

FIGURE 6.5. Chacahua phase cemetery, Substructure 1, Yugüe (from Barber and Joyce 2007: Figure 8.3; published with permission of the University Press of Colorado).

are 20 cm tall), the lack of brine or salt residue, and their placement in large groupings on the summit of a monumental structure indicate a different use for these vessels. Instead, their cylindrical shape likely refers to their ceremonial use since coarse brownware cylindrical vessels were widely used for caching valley-wide at this time (Barber et al. n.d.).

The intense and repetitive nature of offerings at Substructure 1 is reiterated in burial practices. The densely packed burials of at least forty-one individuals were recovered from an area of just over 7 m² (Figure 6.5). Most individuals had been disturbed by the placement of later burials, and some secondary burials may have been present. The cemetery contained individuals of all age ranges, from neonate to elderly adult (Barber et al., Chapter 4). While most individuals lacked funerary offerings, two had pyrite incrustations in their incisors, one juvenile was interred with a string of greenstone and white stone beads, and a subadult male was interred holding an elaborately incised bone flute in his left hand and wearing an iron ore and plaster mirror as a pectoral (Mayes and Barber 2008). Buried with two potent ritual objects, the latter individual was a local ritual practitioner capable of communicating between existential realms (Barber and Olvera 2012).

FIGURE 6.6. Cylindrical grayware serving vessels from Chacahua phase midden, Yugüe.

Substructure 1 was also used for ritual feasting in the Chacahua phase, as evidenced by a large midden located to the south of the cemetery (Area B, Figure 6.1). The midden was 12 m² in area and up to 30 cm deep. As with the caches and burials, the midden was notable for the density of materials it contained. Nearly 94 kg of sherds were removed from this context, of which 28.8 kg were rim sherds or decorated body sherds. A wide variety of other objects were also found within the midden, including lenses of ash and estuarine shell, carbonized organic materials, fragments of adobe, obsidian prismatic blades, ceramic figurines and earspools, greenstone, a ground stone axe, and fragments of mica.

Several characteristics of the midden indicate that it was deposited as the result of a large number of people eating together rather than as the result of many smaller food consumption events that took place over a long period of time. First, the deposit was undifferentiated both vertically and horizontally. Some of the largest sherds spanned the entire vertical extent of the deposit, indicating that the depth of the midden was the result of a single depositional event. There were horizontal cross-fits between sherds separated by over a meter, indicating that the areal extent of the midden was also a result of a single depositional event. In addition, the midden contained sherds from at least seventeen large cylindrical grayware bowls that would have been used to serve large quantities of food, possibly liquid (Figure 6.6). The characteristics of these vessels were quite consistent: everted or outleaning rims, scraped and/or smoothed exteriors, rim diameters from 25 to 35 cm, and no cracking or discoloration caused by exposure to cooking fires. The one partially reconstructable example of this vessel form had a capacity of approximately 9 L. Similar vessels are not found in the two known Chacahua phase domestic middens (Barber 2005; Joyce 1991a), and the cylindrical form is unusual in the Terminal Formative ceramic assemblage from the region (Joyce 1991a; Joyce et al. 1998;

Levine 2002, Chapter 8). The vessels appear to have been a special form used for serving at large gatherings.

Excavations on and around the Yugüe platform revealed at least 400 years of collective architectural and ritual activity. Building construction and renovation, burial, caching, and even food preparation and consumption were permanently fixed in Yugüe's site platform. These acts reveal the existence of a Terminal Formative local community: a supradomestic, place-based, and historically embedded social group. The density of materials on Substructure 1 emphasizes the ongoing significance of local communities as a social group in the Terminal Formative and the inclusiveness of this collectivity through time. People of all ages and of various social positions participated in ritual on Substructure 1. The strongly local character of this social group is also in evidence. The combined caches of cooking vessels and roughly made ceramic cylinders are unique to Yugüe—analogous deposits have not been found at other sites (cf. Barber 2005, 2009; Joyce 1991a; Levine and Joyce 2009; Workinger 2002; see also Barber et al. n.d.). Despite the growth of Río Viejo over the course of the Terminal Formative period, the idiosyncratic nature of the deposits on Substructure 1 offer little evidence for the influence of regional authorities in local ritual. Indeed, the significance of local community affiliation may have been so great at this time that community identity was integral to definitions of high status as well.

DEFINING STATUS AT OUTLYING SITES

High status also defined a social group in the Terminal Formative period, although its material expression was far more restrained than that of community identity. As discussed previously, elite identity was an outgrowth of heredity, exclusivity, and specialized knowledge. A wide body of archaeological literature on Mesoamerican elites has demonstrated the myriad ways that high-status social identities were defined in antiquity (e.g., Chase and Chase 1992; Houston et al. 2006; Inomata and Houston 2001). In the Terminal Formative lower Río Verde Valley, practices defining elite status identity generally occurred in restricted locations like residences and intimate public spaces, although elites also demonstrated their privileged access to resources and specialized knowledge in accessible public contexts like the community cemetery at Yugüe. The more public practices of affiliation, however, pertained to local community membership as much as they did high status.

Defining High Status in Domestic Spaces

Perhaps the most fundamental practices defining elite group membership were everyday, lived experiences shared by only a very small proportion of the regional population. Residences, and the activities undertaken there, thus played an important role in defining elite status. An elite residence excavated at Cerro de la Virgen (Residence 1) demonstrates that elites built and inhabited exclusive, elaborate domestic spaces. While there are no other fully excavated Chacahua phase residences from the lower Río Verde Valley, Residence 1 shares features such as large size and architectural embellishments with later Formative domestic structures from elsewhere in Oaxaca (e.g., Robles García 1988; Winter 1974, 1986). Residence 1 was built on a large terrace (Terrace 1) situated just below the summit of the hill on which the site was located. Three construction episodes were evident on Terrace 1, all dating to the Chacahua phase. Due to superposed architecture, it was not possible to confirm the function of earlier constructions. Given the presence of boulder metates, domestic refuse in fill, and grinding areas in bedrock outcrops on the terrace, all of the preserved structures likely were domestic.

While the earlier architecture was not as large and elaborate as the final residence on the terrace, the first and third construction episodes both provided evidence for labor-intensive construction techniques. The initial construction of Terrace 1 itself reveals considerable labor investment. Terrace 1 leveled off a shallow saddle between the summit of the hill to the northeast and an outcropping of bedrock to the southwest. Evidence from test pits across the terrace demonstrates that the soft grüs bedrock was intentionally smoothed prior to the placement of earthen fill. Over the entire 170 m² area of the terrace, bedrock levels differ by no more than about 30 cm—a phenomenon highly unlikely to occur under natural conditions given the softness of the stone (Raymond Mueller, personal communication, 2004). Leveling the bedrock probably was not necessary from an architectural or engineering standpoint since earthen fill 30 to 60 cm deep was subsequently placed above the leveled bedrock. While retention techniques for fill from the earliest construction episodes could not be determined, fill from the last occupation on the terrace was retained by sloping surfaces of uncut cobbles. The emplacement of fill and rubble would also have been a considerable undertaking due to the terrace's location near the summit of the hill. The earth used for fill would have been derived from the hill itself, given its sandy texture. Nonetheless, soils are as shallow as 10 cm in some areas of the hill below the terrace, meaning that procuring and transporting the fill would have been a labor-intensive task. At least part of the terrace's earliest surface was paved with granite flagstones, another uncommon and labor-intensive practice in the lower Río Verde Valley.

The remnants of two residences were recovered in excavation, but only the second was sufficiently preserved to allow a consideration of domestic architecture. The earlier structure, Residence 1-sub1, consisted of two single-course walls of faced cobbles set into earthen fill. The walls of two separate structures were present and were oriented to 131°/311° (NW–SE) or its perpendicular 38°/218°. Residence 1, the last construction on the terrace, consisted of a space 23 m long (N–S) and 20.7 m wide (E–W) defined by masonry walls oriented 114°/294°. Inhabited areas consisted of a 13 × 13 m open patio surrounded by elevated substructures on the northeast, southeast, and southwest sides (Figure 6.7). There was no evidence for sub- or superstructures on the northwest side of the patio. The substructures were fronted by an 80 cm wide paved bench—a second example of this unusual surfacing technique on Terrace 1. Access to the residence would have been limited to the northeastern side, where the terrace abuts an uphill slope. There, a low double-coursed foundation wall of lightly shaped boulders and cobbles (F9) separated residential space from the rest of the site. Given its width, F9 probably supported a fairly substantial barrier made of perishable materials. The residence was entered via an L-shaped passage leading to a four-step masonry stairway that descended to the patio. Masonry stairways are quite rare in the lower Río Verde Valley, with only two others currently documented for the entire pre-Columbian period: one elsewhere at Cerro de la Virgen (Barber 2005) and a second from nearby San Francisco de Arriba (Workinger 2002). All three are Terminal Formative in date. Masonry superstructure foundation walls were preserved on the northeastern and southwestern substructures. The two measurable rooms were about 3 × 5 m in size. There may have been superstructures on the southeastern substructure as well, but erosion into the arroyo below would have carried away foundation walls and surfaces. The location of wall abutments indicates that the residence was built in stages, with the northeastern substructure built first and others added on in a clockwise fashion.

In-situ contexts attest to both mundane and ceremonial activities at the residence. A small domestic midden associated with the earliest construction of the terrace contained ceramics; two bone fragments, sherds from two figurines; two rocks, one of them shaped; and half of a boulder metate. Vessel form proportions were comparable to those of early Terminal Formative domestic middens from Yugüe rather than the Chacahua phase midden from Substructure 1 (Barber 2005; Levine 2002). Coarse brownware vessels, used almost exclusively for food preparation and storage (and also caching, see below), predominated in the Cerro de la Virgen midden (60% of all vessels). There were fewer bowls and comals than in the Substructure 1 midden at Yugüe, and there were none of the large grayware cylindrical bowls. Indeed, there was nothing in the Cerro de la Virgen midden to indicate exclusivity or specialized domestic food preparation and consumption. Evidence for ceremonial activities undertaken on Terrace 1 took the form of cache deposits. Two were emplaced during the construction and occupation of Residence 1-sub1. The first, consisting of two small conical vessels, was set on the earliest terrace surface and covered by the fill into which the foundation walls of Residence 1-sub1 were set. The second, consisting of two large cylindrical vessels, was set just below the patio sur-

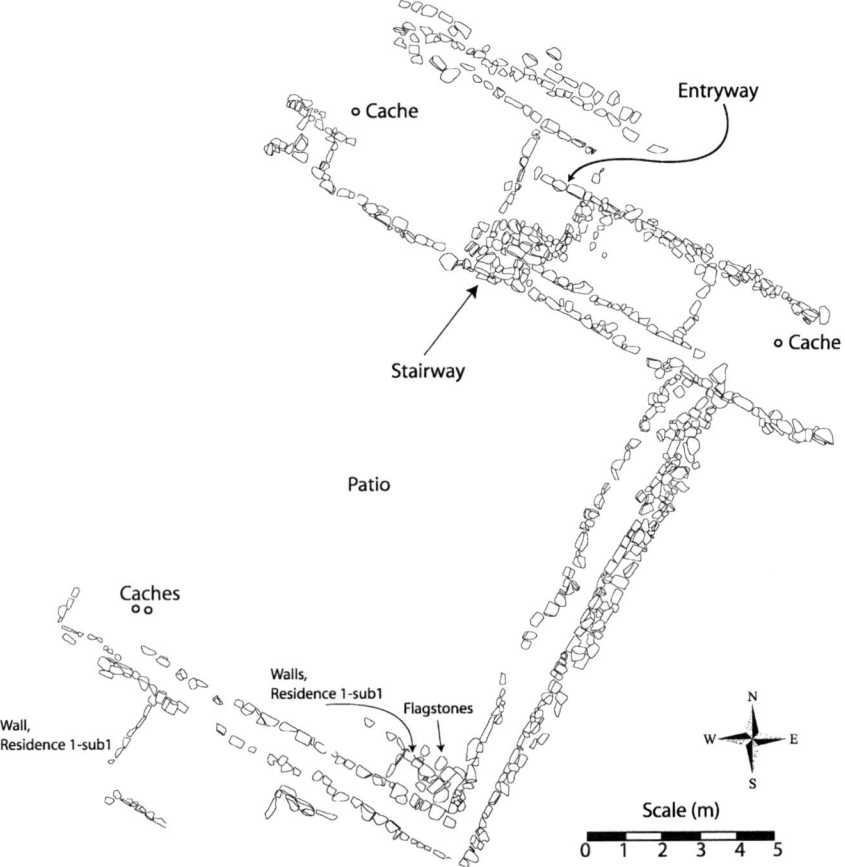

FIGURE 6.7. Plan view of Residence 1, Cerro de la Virgen.

face associated with Residence 1-sub1. Neither was associated with any structures. Two other caches were probably emplaced at the same time and were associated with Residence 1 itself. Both consisted of a single cylindrical vessel with a flat lid. One was located in the northern corner of the residence (Figure 6.8), the other in the eastern corner. The azimuth between the cached vessels (114°/294°) mirrored the alignment of the northeastern walls of the residence. No burials were recovered from Terrace 1, although two fragments of what may have been human long bone were found in fill.

Defining High Status in Restricted Public Contexts

While domestic architecture created exclusive residential spaces that defined a high-status lifestyle, elites in the lower Río Verde Valley also engaged

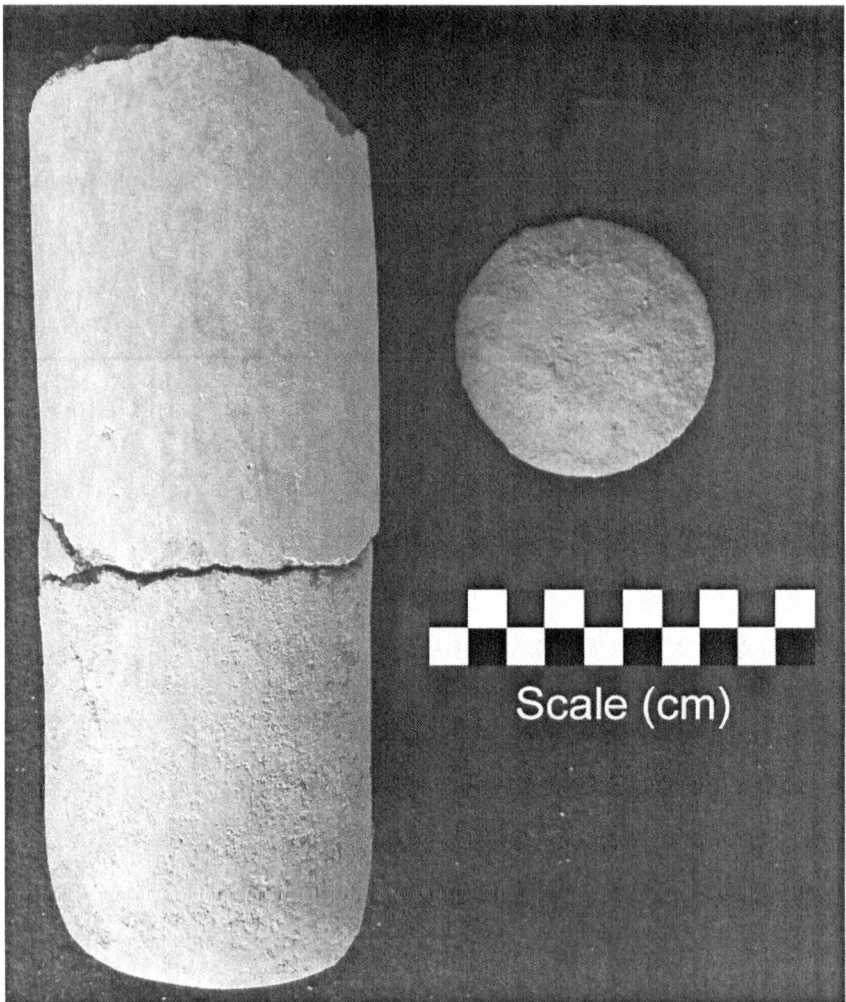

FIGURE 6.8. Cylindrical offering vessel, Cerro de la Virgen.

in extradomestic activities that reiterated specialized knowledge. At Yugüe, Substructure 2 on the eastern summit of the site platform supported a small Chacahua phase structure. As discussed previously, the superstructure itself was poorly preserved. However, a use surface was indicated by a stratigraphic break on and beneath which several features were recovered. The first was a cache consisting of four conical vessels surrounding a rectangular lidded ceramic box (Figure 6.9). The box was oriented approximately 98°/278°. Neither the cones nor the box contained anything. This offering bore a strong resemblance to a Chacahua phase cache uncovered by Andrew Workinger

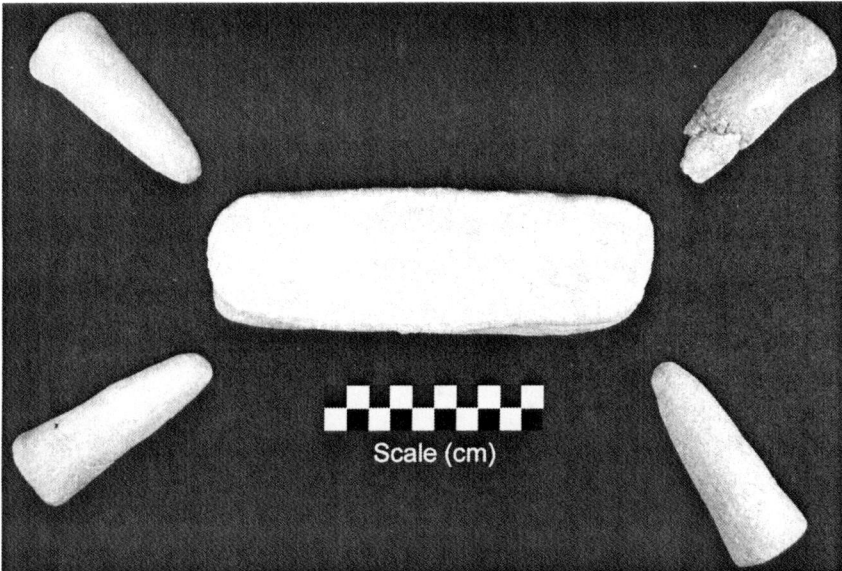

FIGURE 6.9. Cache of five vessels, Yugüe.

(2002, 204) at San Francisco de Arriba. He describes the offering as "four small copas . . . and a coarse brownware box" (2002, 204). The considerable similarity between the two caches could indicate regionally shared ceremonial practices.

The second cache was strongly reminiscent of the Miniyua phase interred cooking vessels recovered from Substructure 1 and the platform base. The Substructure 2 cache, which dated to the Chacahua phase, consisted of a coarse brownware cooking jar, grayware sherds, one sherd from a Valley of Oaxaca import, half of a local grayware bowl incised with the image of a man wearing a mask, ash, estuarine shell, fragments of sixteen different ceramic earspools, a ceramic figurine, and burned earth (Figure 6.10). The jar had broken apart in the centuries since its deposition, spilling its contents into the surrounding fill. The grayware bowl, other ceramic items, and burned earth were probably sitting atop the vessel mouth or around its rim at the time the offering was emplaced. The neck and rim of the vessel were oxidized.

Despite the general similarities to the earlier caches from Substructure 1 and the platform base, this cache had several significant differences, indicating that it may have been part of a high-status public ceremony. The earspools, the sherd from an imported vessel, and the bowl suggest that elites specifically were involved in the placement of this cache. Burial evidence from elsewhere in Mesoamerica suggests that earspools were associated with higher status during the Formative period (R. Joyce 1999). As a form of personal adornment, earspools were "intimately tied to the body" and would have

FIGURE 6.10. Contents of cached vessel, Substructure 2, Yugüe.

been an important statement of individuality (R. Joyce 1999, 19). Their presence in a cache may have served to identify an exclusive group of individuals who participated in the associated ceremony. The sherd from an imported vessel is significant because imported vessels are extremely rare in the lower Río Verde Valley during the Terminal Formative period (Barber 2005; Joyce 1991a, 1991b; Levine 2002, Chapter 8; Workinger 2002, Chapter 7). The local incised grayware was unusually elaborate and is one of only five known Chacahua phase vessels incised with an anthropomorph (Brzezinski 2011, Table 4.9). Javier Urcid (personal communication, 2009) has identified this individual as a regional variant of the Zapotec Xicani, a high-status sacrificial specialist who wears a mask with a long, upturned snout (Urcid 2005, 56).

Defining High Status in Accessible Contexts

The actions defining high-status identity discussed thus far were all undertaken in restricted contexts. Because elites were members of an exclusive and hereditary status group connected through specialized knowledge and privileges, it is no surprise that many of the acts that defined their status identity took place in locations where the general population could not participate. Yet some acts of affiliation occurred in more public locations. That is, such acts took place in contexts where the definition of high-status selves was directly contrasted to lower-status others. At outlying sites in the lower Verde during the Terminal Formative period, however, evidence for such public displays of status affiliation are uncommon.

Consumption of socially valuable items in mortuary offerings on Sub-structure 1 at Yugüe provided a means by which elites defined their difference from commoners (Barber et al., Chapter 4). A total of five burials on the substructure included grave goods or unusual personal adornment. The social status of the earliest buried individuals is unclear because there are no other Miniyua phase interments with which to compare. Their interment in a structure that was not residential may indicate that these individuals had exclusive privileges not enjoyed by the rest of the population. The much larger Chacahua phase burial sample provides evidence that valuable grave goods pertain to status rather than gender, age, or other social affiliations. Three individuals in the Chacahua phase cemetery were interred or adorned with greenstone and/or iron ore. B8-I8, an adult female, had circular pyrite incrustations in her upper incisors. While dental incrustations do not always indicate high status archaeologically (e.g., Krejci and Culbert 1995), they are rare in the lower Río Verde Valley. Pyrite, furthermore, was an imported raw material that occurred infrequently throughout the pre-Columbian era. B14-I16, an adolescent male, was wearing an iron ore and plaster mirror pectoral and holding an incised bone flute (Barber 2005; Barber and Olvera 2012; Barber et al. 2009, Chapter 4; Mayes and Barber 2008). B11-I12, a juvenile, was buried with a string of thirty-six greenstone and white stone or shell beads as well as a greenstone pendant carved in the shape of a human face.

Since the offerings are associated with individuals of both sexes and various ages and were made of socially valued raw materials, they probably defined the status of these individuals or the status of their respective kin groups. These offerings would have been a visible statement of status at the time of each individual's interment. More important, the reuse of the cemetery for subsequent burials would have made these offerings and adornments visible at later times (Barber et al., Chapter 4). The reexposure of valuable goods would have reiterated not just the privileges of certain people within the community of Yugüe; it would have emphasized the hereditary nature of those privileges by linking the descendants and kin of the dead to the valuables in the cemetery.

DEFINING LOCAL COMMUNITY
AND STATUS AT OUTLYING SITES

Local community and status were significant modalities of social identity during the Terminal Formative period. Archaeological evidence from sites predating the Terminal Formative indicates that local communities existed and persisted in the lower Río Verde Valley before and during political centralization

(Barber 2005; Barber and Joyce 2007; Barber et al. 2009; Joyce 1991a, 2010; Workinger 2002). By the end of the Terminal Formative period, Yugüe had a place-based history extending 500 years or more into the past. That history, and the place in which it had been enacted, was clearly relevant to the lived experiences of Yugüe's Terminal Formative residents. They engaged in a wide range of collective actions at the site that repeatedly referred to local spaces and histories. The site platform itself exemplified such actions by embedding collective labor in place. While mound construction in the Terminal Formative period was a regional phenomenon tied to political centralization (Barber and Joyce 2007; Joyce 2008; Joyce and Barber 2011), the use to which Yugüe's monumental architecture was put had a strongly local character. A single axis was employed to orient not just the site platform, but also substructures, caches, and burials for 400 years. Yugüe's azimuth was local, and it was historically significant to the people who lived there.

The acts undertaken atop the platform, and the memory of those acts, commemorated and reiterated a community identity that cross-cut status distinctions. Collective food preparation and consumption occurred in the Miniyua phase, as indicated by cached cooking vessels in two parts of the site and by the midden next to Substructure 1-sub2. Collective caching and burial were added to the repertoire of corporate social action by the Chacahua phase. The large cache of ceramic cylinders in the fill around the Miniyua phase ceramic cooking vessels demonstrates group participation in commemorating community history and ceremony. The cached cylinders were so diverse and poorly made that it seems likely these vessels produced by a number of people who knew very little about ceramic production or who lacked the resources to acquire finer vessels like those found at Cerro de la Virgen. Similarly, people of all ages, both sexes, and different statuses were represented in the cemetery. Collective public action at Yugüe was inclusive, encompassing the participation—even if only in death—of an extensive demographic.

The presence of clearly marked elites at the Yugüe cemetery demonstrates the increasing visibility of high-status individuals over the course of the Terminal Formative. B14-I16, the individual buried with a mirror and a flute, was interred in Yugüe's community cemetery and aligned to the site azimuth. Placement in a corporate burial site would have highlighted his membership in a local collectivity. The orientation of his body, mirroring that of others in the cemetery, would have referenced local history and emphasized his place in this collectivity. At the same time, the presence of the mirror and flute defined B14-I16 as an individual with the unique and potent capacity to communicate with inhabitants of the underworld and the celestial realm (Barber and Olvera 2012).

High-status affiliation was built into the landscape at Cerro de la Virgen. The highly restricted domestic spaces of Residence 1 created a multilayered boundary between elites and commoners. A physical distinction was created by the exterior wall and narrow entryway, which emphasized those who did and did not have access to the residence. The multigenerational ability to harness extra labor, a privilege of Mesoamerican elites, is evidenced by the examples of architectural elaboration present in two construction episodes on Terrace 1. The privileges enjoyed by the residence's inhabitants are also evident in the location of the terrace itself. Terrace 1 was built in an impractical location only a few meters below the summit of the hill. The nearest water supply was 300 m south of and 40 m downhill from the residence. Thus, there were considerable labor costs involved in bringing water, food, and other necessary goods up to the top of the hill. The impracticalities may have been outweighed, however, by the cosmological significance of the location. Residence 1 was situated only a few meters away from a public ceremonial structure. The right to live in such a potent location was probably a result of the specialized and hereditary knowledge of the residence's inhabitants (Clark 2004; Grove and Gillespie 1992; Hill and Clark 2001; Marcus 1989).

In addition to establishing exclusivity and specialized knowledge through architecture, elites defined their social status through ritual. The two caches from Residence 1 were located near the perimeter of the domestic space and may have delimited a physical and social boundary between the household and others. While not necessarily a practice confined to elites (e.g., Gonlin and Lohse 2007), the demarcation of a boundary between Residence 1 and the rest of the site was nonetheless a practice of definition. It entailed creating a conceptual distinction between those who lived within its perimeter and those who did not. Rituals defining high-status group membership were also extended to intimate public locations in the Chacahua phase. Substructure 2 at Yugüe was a nondomestic facility in which ceremonial acts were undertaken by a small number of people at any one time. The sixteen earspool fragments cached with the cooking vessel and the Xicani image on the incised bowl indicate that high-status individuals produced the deposit. The Chacahua phase construction of Substructure 2, like that of the elaborate Residence 1 at Cerro de la Virgen, suggests that elites were willing to define their status group membership in increasingly visible ways by the end of the Formative period. Access to the specialized knowledge so important to high status remained restricted in that pertinent ceremonial acts took place in intimate locations like small public buildings and residences. Yet the prominence of the architecture itself provided a highly visible and permanent marker of elite privileges within communities like Yugüe and Cerro de la Virgen.

CONCLUSION

Political centralization was an ongoing process, one that emerged from negotiations between the various social and political interests that constituted the lower Río Verde Valley's first regional polity. The inhabitants of outlying sites were active participants in these negotiations. In accessible public spaces, residents of outlying sites did not define themselves primarily as subjects of regional political authority but rather as active members of their local communities. Indeed, the symbolic presence of Río Viejo's rulers is difficult to ascertain in the extensive record of public ceremony at Yugüe. Local elites, in turn, were members of both their communities and their status group. At Yugüe they participated in acts such as caching and burial that reiterated their historic and place-based connection to members of other status groups. As the Terminal Formative progressed, however, elites may have become more willing to highlight their differences from other community members. Elites produced clearly bounded domestic spaces that distinguished them from members of other status groups. They built structures for exclusive ritual, and they employed items of social value in cemetery burial where such objects would have served as visible demonstrations of status inequality. The apparent contradictions in some of these actions, as well as the near invisibility of regional political authority, emphasize the multivalent nature of social relations in the lower Río Verde Valley during the Terminal Formative period.

ACKNOWLEDGMENTS

I would like to thank the Instituto Nacional de Antropología e Historia for sanctioning the excavations and artifact analysis on which this chapter is based. I am particularly indebted to the president and members of the Consejo de Arqueología as well as current and former directors of the Centro INAH-Oaxaca, including Enrique Fernandez Dávila and Eduardo López Calzada. Funding for archaeological field research in the lower Río Verde Valley was provided by grants from the following organizations: National Science Foundation (BCS–0202624), Foundation for the Advancement of Mesoamerican Studies (#02060), the Association of Women in Science, the Women's Forum Foundation of Colorado, Sigma Xi, Colorado Archaeological Society, and the University of Colorado at Boulder. I would like to thank Arthur Joyce for inviting me to participate in this volume and for his feedback on earlier drafts of this chapter. Valuable feedback was also provided by two anonymous reviewers. All problems and errors are my own.

NOTES

1. Because public spaces at the site have not been excavated, its construction date remains conjectural (Barber 2005).

2. 2200 $\pm$ 40 BP, or 250 BC (281 cal BC; Beta-195210).

3. The substructure's width could not be determined due to superposed modern architecture.

REFERENCES CITED

Anderson, Benedict R. 1991. *Imagined Communities: Reflections on the Origin and Spread of Nationalism*. London: Verso.

Ashmore, Wendy. 2002. "'Decisions and Dispositions': Socializing Spatial Archaeology." *American Anthropologist* 104 (4): 1172–83. http://dx.doi.org/10.1525/aa.2002.104.4.1172.

Barber, Sarah B. 2005. *Heterogeneity, Identity, and Complexity: Negotiating Status and Authority in Terminal Formative Coastal Oaxaca*. PhD dissertation, Department of Anthropology, University of Colorado, Boulder. Ann Arbor, MI: University Microfilms.

Barber, Sarah B. 2009. Excavaciones de prueba en el valle inferior del Río Verde. In "El proyecto Río Verde," ed. Arthur A. Joyce and Marc N. Levine, 228–321. Final report submitted to the Consejo de Arqueología, Instituto Nacional de Antropología e Historia, Mexico City.

Barber, Sarah B., and Arthur A. Joyce. 2003. "Landscapes of Power, Landscapes of Decline: The Practice of Place." Paper presented at the 103rd Annual Meeting of the American Anthropological Association, San Francisco.

Barber, Sarah B., and Arthur A. Joyce. 2007. "Polity Produced and Community Consumed: Negotiating Political Centralization in the Lower Río Verde Valley, Oaxaca." In *Mesoamerican Ritual Economy: Archaeological and Ethnological Perspectives*, ed. E. Christian Wells and Karla L. Davis-Salazar, 221–44. Boulder: University Press of Colorado.

Barber, Sarah B., and Mireya Olvera. 2012. "A Divine Wind: The Arts of Death and Music in Ancient Oaxaca." *Ancient Mesoamerica* 23(1): 9–24.

Barber, Sarah B., Gonzalo A. Sanchez Santiago, and Mireya Olvera. 2009. "Sounds of Death and Life in Mesoamerica: The Bone Flutes of Ancient Oaxaca." *Yearbook of Traditional Music* 41: 40–56.

Barber, Sarah B., Andrew Workinger, and Arthur Joyce. N.d. "Situational Inalienability and Social Change in Formative Period Coastal Oaxaca." In *Inalienable Possessions in the Archaeology of Mesoamerica*, ed. Brigitte Kovacevich and Michael G. Callaghan. Washington, DC: American Anthropological Association, under review.

Barrett, John C. 1999. "The Mythical Landscapes of the British Iron Age." In *Archaeologies of Landscape*, ed. Wendy Ashmore and A. Bernard Knapp, 253–65. Malden, MA: Blackwell.

Basso, Keith H. 1996. *Wisdom Sits in Places: Landscape and Language among the Western Apache*. Albuquerque: University of New Mexico Press.

Bell, Catherine M. 1992. *Ritual Theory, Ritual Practice*. New York: Oxford University Press.

Bourdieu, Pierre. 1977. *Outline of a Theory of Practice*. Cambridge: Cambridge University Press.

Brzezinski, Jeffrey S. 2011. "Worldview, Ideology, and Ceramic Iconography: A Study of Ideological Messaging on Late Terminal Formative Grayware Serving Vessels from the Lower Río Verde Valley of Pacific Coastal, Oaxaca, Mexico." MA thesis, Department of Anthropology, University of Central Florida, Orlando.

Casella, Eleanor Conlin, and Chris Fowler. 2004. "Beyond Identification: An Introduction." In *The Archaeology of Plural and Changing Identities: Beyond Identification*, ed. Eleanor C. Casella and Chris Fowler, 1–8. New York: Springer.

Cattell, Maria G., and Jacob Climo. 2002. "Meaning in Social Memory and History: Anthropological Perspectives." In *Social Memory and History: Anthropological Perspectives*, ed. Jacob Climo and Maria G. Cattell, 1–36. Walnut Creek, CA: AltaMira.

Chase, Diane Z., and Arlen F. Chase, eds. 1992. *Mesoamerican Elites*. Norman: University of Oklahoma Press.

Clark, John E. 2004. "Mesoamerica Goes Public: Early Ceremonial Centers, Leaders, and Communities." In *Mesoamerican Archaeology: Theory and Practice*, ed. Julia A. Hendon and Rosemary A. Joyce, 43–72. Malden, MA: Blackwell.

Cohen, Jeffrey H. 1999. *Cooperation and Community: Economy and Society in Oaxaca*. Austin: University of Texas Press.

Friedman, Jonathan. 1994. *Cultural Identity and Global Process*. London: Sage Publications.

Gonlin, Nancy, and Jon C. Lohse, eds. 2007. *Commoner Ritual and Ideology in Ancient Mesoamerica*. Boulder: University Press of Colorado.

Grove, David C., and Susan D. Gillespie. 1992. "Ideology and Evolution at the Pre-State Level." In *Ideology and Pre-Columbian Civilizations*, ed. Arthur A. Demarest and Geoffrey W. Conrad, 15–36. Santa Fe, NM: School of American Research Press.

Hill, Warren D., and John E. Clark. 2001. "Sports, Gambling, and Government: America's First Social Compact?" *American Anthropologist* 103 (2): 331–45. http://dx.doi.org/10.1525/aa.2001.103.2.331.

Hirsch, Eric. 1995. "Introduction." In *The Anthropology of Landscape: Perspectives on Place and Space*, ed. Eric Hirsch and Michael O'Hanlon, 1–30. New York: Clarendon Press.

Houston, Stephen D., David Stuart, and Karl A. Taube. 2006. *The Memory of Bones: Body, Being, and Experience among the Classic Maya*. Austin: University of Texas Press.

Inomata, Takeshi, and Stephen Houston, eds. 2001. *Royal Courts of the Ancient Maya*. Boulder, CO: Westview Press.

Insoll, Timothy. 2007. "Introduction: Configuring Identities in Archaeology." In *The Archaeology of Identities: A Reader*, ed. Timothy Insoll, 1–18. London: Routledge.

Janusek, John W. 2004. *Identity and Power in the Ancient Andes: Tiwanaku Cities through Time*. New York: Routledge. http://dx.doi.org/10.4324/9780203324615.

Jenkins, Richard. 1996. *Social Identity*. London: Routledge.

Jones, Sian. 1996. "Discourses of Identity in the Interpretation of the Past." In *Cultural Identity and Archaeology: The Construction of European Communities*, ed. Paul Graves-Brown, Sian Jones, and Clive Gamble, 62–80. London: Routledge.

Joyce, Arthur A. 1991a. *Formative Period Occupation in the Lower Río Verde Valley, Oaxaca, Mexico: Interregional Interaction and Social Change*. PhD dissertation, Department of Anthropology, Rutgers University, New Brunswick, NJ. Ann Arbor, MI: University Microfilms.

Joyce, Arthur A. 1991b. "Formative Period Social Change in the Lower Río Verde Valley, Oaxaca Mexico." *Latin American Antiquity* 2 (2): 126–50. http://dx.doi.org/10.2307/972274.

Joyce, Arthur A., ed. 1999. "El proyecto patrones de asentamiento del Río Verde." Final report submitted to the Consejo de Arqueología, Instituto Nacional de Antropología e Historia, Mexico City.

Joyce, Arthur A. 2000. "The Founding of Monte Albán: Sacred Propositions and Social Practices." In *Agency in Archaeology*, ed. Macia-Anne Dobres and John Robb, 71–91. London: Routledge.

Joyce, Arthur A. 2005. "La arqueologia del bajo Río Verde." *Acervos* 7 (29): 16–36.

Joyce, Arthur A. 2008. "Domination, Negotiation, and Collapse: A History of Centralized Authority on the Oaxaca Coast Before the Late Postclassic." In *After Monte Albán: Transformation and Negotiation in Oaxaca, Mexico*, ed. Jeffrey Blomster, 219–54. Boulder: University Press of Colorado.

Joyce, Arthur A. 2010. *Mixtecs, Zapotecs, and Chatinos: Ancient Peoples of Southern Mexico*. Malden, MA: Wiley-Blackwell.

Joyce, Arthur A., and Sarah B. Barber. 2011. "Excavating the Acropolis at Río Viejo, Oaxaca, Mexico." *Mexicon* 33 (1): 15–20.

Joyce, Arthur A., Marcus Winter, and Raymond G. Mueller. 1998. *Arqueología de la costa de Oaxaca: Asentamientos del periodo formativo en el valle del Río Verde inferior*. Estudios de Antropología e Historia 40. Oaxaca: Centro INAH–Oaxaca.

Joyce, Rosemary A. 1999. "Social Dimensions of Pre-Classic Burials." In *Social Patterns in Pre-Classic Mesoamerica*, ed. David C. Grove and Rosemary Joyce, 15–48. Washington, DC: Dumbarton Oaks Research Library.

Krejci, Estella, and T. Patrick Culbert. 1995. Preclassic and Classic Burials and Caches in the Maya Lowlands. In *The Emergence of Lowland Maya Civilization: The Transition from the Preclassic to the Early Classic*, ed. Nikolai Grube, 103–16. Acta Mesoamericana, vol. 8. Mèockmèuhl, Germany: A. Saurwein.

Levine, Marc. 2002. "Ceramic Change and Continuity in the Lower Río Verde Region of Oaxaca, Mexico: The Late Formative to Early Terminal Formative Transition." MA thesis, Department of Anthropology, University of Colorado, Boulder.

Levine, Marc N., and Arthur A. Joyce. 2009. Excavaciones profundas en la Estructura 2 del Montículo 1 de Río Viejo. In "El Proyecto Río Verde," ed. Arthur A. Joyce and Marc N. Levine, 81–140. Final report submitted to the Consejo de Arqueología, Instituto Nacional de Antropología e Historia, Mexico City.

Marcus, Joyce. 1989. "Zapotec Chiefdoms and the Nature of Formative Religions." In *Regional Perspectives on the Olmec*, ed. Robert J. Sharer and David C. Grove, 148–97. Cambridge: Cambridge University Press.

Mayes, Arion, and Sarah B. Barber. 2008. "Osteobiography of a High Status Burial from the Lower Río Verde Valley of Oaxaca, Mexico." *International Journal of Osteoarchaeology* 18 (6): 573–88. http://dx.doi.org/10.1002/oa.1011.

McKillop, Heather. 1995. "Underwater Archaeology, Salt Production, and Coastal Maya Trade at Stingray Lagoon, Belize." *Latin American Antiquity* 6 (3): 214–28. http://dx.doi.org/10.2307/971673.

Meskell, Lynn. 2001. "Archaeologies of Identity." In *Archaeological Theory: Breaking the Boundaries*, ed. Ian Hodder, 187–213. Cambridge: Polity Press.

Monaghan, John. 1995. *The Covenants with Earth and Rain: Exchange, Sacrifice and Revelation in Mixtec Society*. Norman: University of Oklahoma Press.

Pauketat, Timothy R., and Susan M. Alt. 2003. "Mounds, Memory, and Contested Mississippian History." In *Archaeologies of Memory*, ed. Ruth M. Van Dyke and Susan E. Alcock, 151–79. Malden, MA: Blackwell. http://dx.doi.org/10.1002/9780470774304.ch8.

Pred, Allan. 1984. "Place as Historically Contingent Process: Structuration and the Time-Geography of Becoming Places." *Annals of the Association of American Geographers* 74 (2): 279–97. http://dx.doi.org/10.1111/j.1467-8306.1984.tb01453.x.

Robles García, Nelly M. 1988. *Las unidades domésticas del Preclásico Superior en la Mixteca Alta.* BAR International Series 407. Oxford: British Archaeological Reports.

Schortman, Edward M., and Seiichi Nakamura. 1991. "A Crisis of Identity: Late Classic Competition and Interaction on the Southeast Maya Periphery." *Latin American Antiquity* 2 (4): 311–36. http://dx.doi.org/10.2307/971781.

Schortman, Edward M., Patricia A. Urban, and Marne Ausec. 2001. "Politics with Style: Identity Formation in Prehispanic Southeastern Mesoamerica." *American Anthropologist* 103 (2): 312–30. http://dx.doi.org/10.1525/aa.2001.103.2.312.

Urban, Patricia A., and Edward M. Schortman. 2004. "Opportunities for Advancement: Intra-Community Power Contests in the Midst of Political Decentralization in Terminal Classic Southeastern Mesoamerica." *Latin American Antiquity* 15 (3): 251–72. http://dx.doi.org/10.2307/4141574.

Urcid, Javier. 2005. *Zapotec Writing: Knowledge, Power, and Memory in Ancient Oaxaca.* Foundation for the Advancement of Mesoamerican Studies, Coral Gables, FL. http://www.famsi.org/zapotecwriting/.

Van Dyke, Ruth M., and Susan E. Alcock. 2003. "Archaeologies of Memory: An Introduction." In *Archaeologies of Memory*, ed. Ruth M. Van Dyke and Susan E. Alcock, 1–13. Malden, MA: Blackwell. http://dx.doi.org/10.1002/9780470774304.ch1.

Watanabe, John M. 1992. *Maya Saints and Souls in a Changing World.* Austin: University of Texas Press.

Weber, Max. 1968. *Economy and Society*, vol. 1. New York: Bedminster Press.

Winter, Marcus. 1974. "Residential Patterns at Monte Alban, Oaxaca, Mexico." *Science* 186, no. 4168 (Dec. 13): 981–87. http://dx.doi.org/10.1126/science.186.4168.981. Medline:17843045.

Winter, Marcus. 1986. "Unidades habitacionales prehispánicas en Oaxaca." In *Unidades habitacionales mesoaméricanas y sus areas de actividad*, ed. Linda Manzanilla, 325–74. Serie Antropológica 76. Mexico City: Instituto Nacional de Antropología e Historia.

Workinger, Andrew. 2002. *Coastal/Highland Interaction in Prehispanic Oaxaca, Mexico: The Perspective from San Francisco de Arriba.* PhD dissertation, Department of Anthropology, Vanderbilt University, Nashville, TN. Ann Arbor, MI: University Microfilms.

Yaeger, Jason. 2000. "The Social Construction of Communities in the Classic Maya Countryside." In *The Archaeology of Communities: A New World Perspective*, ed. Marcello A. Canuto and Jason Yaeger, 123–42. London: Routledge.

Yaeger, Jason, and Marcello A. Canuto. 2000. "Introducing an Archaeology of Communities." In *The Archaeology of Communities: A New World Perspective*, ed. Marcello A. Canuto and Jason Yaeger, 1–15. London: Routledge.

SEVEN

COASTAL/HIGHLAND INTERACTION IN OAXACA, MEXICO

The Perspective from San Francisco de Arriba

ANDREW WORKINGER

At first glance, interaction between ancient polities of unequal socio-political complexities suggests a situation of dominance. Yet, as archaeologists continue to broaden their focus from major centers to peripheral regions, such an assumption becomes less tenable (Stein 1999). It is increasingly apparent that there exists great variability in the archaeological record when it comes to the dynamics of inter-regional interaction, particularly when agency is taken into account.

Situated in a narrow secondary valley of the lower Río Verde region in Oaxaca, Mexico, San Francisco de Arriba was the focus of archaeological investigations geared toward understanding the site's role in a complex network of prehispanic exchange and interaction (Figure 7.1). The results of the San Francisco de Arriba Archaeological Project and those of other projects on the coast of Oaxaca (Joyce 2003, 2010; Levine, Chapter 8; Workinger 2002a; Workinger and Joyce 2009; Zeitlin 1990; Zeitlin and Joyce 1999) question the unidirectional view of interregional interaction held by some highland researchers (Balkansky 2002; Marcus 1976, 1983; Marcus and Flannery 1996; Redmond and Spencer 2006; Sherman et al. 2010; Spencer 2007; Spencer and Redmond 1997). Specifically, the project considered the claim that San Francisco de Arriba had

DOI: 10.5876/9781607322023.c07

FIGURE 7.1. Excavations at Operation 99B along Ridgeline 2 at San Francisco de Arriba.

been incorporated as the southernmost boundary of a Terminal Formative Zapotec empire, and it sought to clarify the site's ties with central Mexico, particularly the city of Teotihuacan during the Early Classic (Figure 1.3). These issues were addressed by various means, including surface collections and a test pitting program carried out in 1997 and broader excavations conducted in 1998 and 1999 (Figure 7.2). A systematic survey of the Río San Francisco Valley was undertaken to place the site of San Francisco de Arriba within a regional perspective and to gain an understanding of the area's settlement patterns. Neutron activation analysis of recovered ceramics aided in differentiating between local and imported pottery. Neutron activation was also used to identify the sources of imported obsidian recovered at San Francisco de Arriba and to propose potential trade networks and interregional relationships otherwise invisible in the archaeological record.

Home to Monte Albán, one of Mesoamerica's earliest states, Oaxaca provides an ideal location for studying the sociopolitical impact that emerging states had on their surrounding hinterlands. Contact between populations in the form of trade, warfare, or even indirect interaction is often credited with sparking major sociopolitical change. Using a modified world-systems perspective, Chase-Dunn and Hall (1991) define two specific classes of interaction based on the relationship between the interacting societies. Core/periphery differentiation applies to reciprocal relations between two or more societies organized at different levels of complexity and with different population densities. Such interaction is characterized by an economic system in which partners of unequal complexity are interdependent upon the exchange of prestige goods. Core/periphery hierarchy includes the political, economic, and/or ideo-

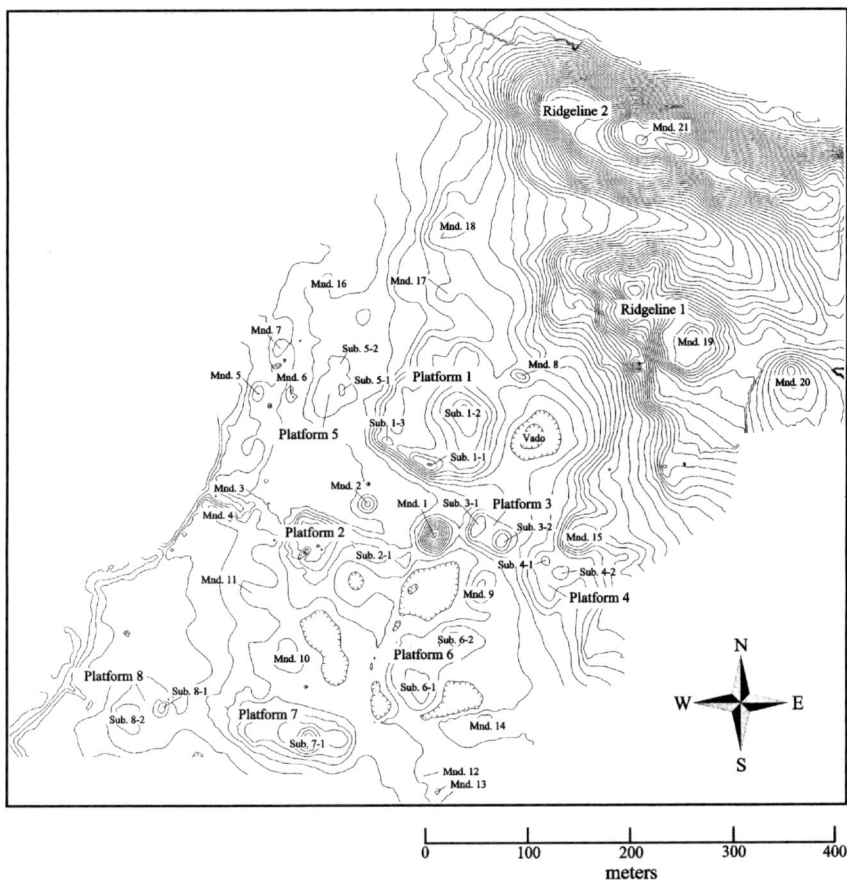

FIGURE 7.2. Topographic map of San Francisco de Arriba with mound, platform, and ridgeline identifications (contour interval = 1 m).

logical domination of one society by another within the same world-system (Chase-Dunn and Hall 1991, 19). This hierarchy implies an asymmetrical exchange of goods that is dominated in some fashion by the core. The resulting framework allows for a variety of types of interaction ranging from the exchange of ideas to outright military conquest, and it provides an alternative to the commonly held view that contact between groups of varying complexity necessarily involves exploitation (e.g., Wallerstein 1974).

The effects of interaction upon the political, economic, and social conditions of the periphery may also vary. The exchange of information, including belief systems, within a context of core/periphery differentiation can often lead to cultural change in both partners (Schortman and Urban 1994; Stein 1999) and is argued in some cases to provide the necessary impetus for state formation in the periphery (Price 1978). On the other hand, the domination of a world-system by the core may also result in the deliberate underdevelopment of the periphery in order to maintain a secure source of prestige-enhancing goods for the core elite (cf. Spencer 1982).

A modified form of Wallerstein's (1974) world-system has been applied to the Zapotec capital of Monte Albán and its hinterlands (Blanton and Feinman 1984; Blanton et al. 1999). First occupied around 500 BC, Monte Albán grew quickly, and some believe that by the Terminal Formative period (150 BC–AD 250), it was able to gain control of a small territorial empire, including some regions outside the Valley of Oaxaca (Balkansky 2002; Marcus and Flannery 1996; Redmond and Spencer 2006; Spencer and Redmond 1997). The basis for these imperial claims comes in two forms: the spread of grayware ceramics common to the Valley of Oaxaca as well as the interpretation of toponyms at Monte Albán possibly celebrating foreign conquests (Marcus and Flannery 1996; Marcus 1976, 1980, 1983, 1984, 1992a, 1992b). Terminal Formative grayware ceramics similar to those found in the Valley of Oaxaca were identified at San Francisco de Arriba when it was briefly visited as part of a broader reconnaissance of the Oaxaca coast (DeCicco and Brockington 1956). Later, a carved stone on Monte Albán's Building J was interpreted by Marcus (1976) as marking the conquest of Tututepec, a site only 3 km from San Francisco de Arriba. Other carved stones on Building J suggested additional conquests, and soon a territory covering a large portion of the modern state was claimed as a Zapotec empire with San Francisco de Arriba as the southernmost point (Marcus and Flannery 1996).

As archaeologists we are perhaps initially drawn to the idea of world-systems because of our reliance on material factors, which are more easily approachable in the archaeological record. Rather than focusing on unequal political and economic relations among polities as in world-systems theory, other theoretical approaches to interaction emphasize the variable interests and motivations of actors within the interacting regions, including social identities and the significance of such interaction (Schortman 1989; Schortman and Urban 1987; Stark 1990; Stein 1999, 2002). Societies are recognized as being composed of individuals and factions seeking to further their own short-term goals rather than as reified systems acting in concert (Brumfiel 1992; Brumfiel and Fox 1994). It is at the micro level that models of interregional interaction best explain the archaeological data.

One alternative to world-systems theory is Schortman's (1989) use of salient identities, which enables archaeologists to address not only who was involved in trade and other forms of interaction, but also their motives for doing so. Salient identities develop when people "recognize that their own interests are served best by repeatedly uniting with holders of the same identity in opposition to members of other social identities" (Schortman 1989, 55). The difference here is that holders of the same identity can cross-cut the traditional cultural boundaries that are emphasized in world-systems theory (Schortman and Urban 1987). Regardless of polity, members of the elite may share similar identities created in part through interaction with one another. Rather than between polities, peaceful interaction is best viewed as taking place between people who share salient social identities. Schortman's (1989) model of extensive salient-identity networks provides a compelling explanation of how dispersed elites came to share common assumptions, values, and standards through interregional interaction. Most visibly involving the exchange of high-status exotic goods, salient identity networks contributed to social inequalities which in turn necessitated further trade to preserve those inequalities (Clark and Blake 1994; Schortman 1989, 59).

A second alternative to the dominant core/underdeveloped periphery world-system approach is provided by Stein (1999, 2002), who believes that the power of the core is often exaggerated at the expense of periphery. As in the salient-identity model, Stein (1999) proposes a more flexible model based upon the often conflicting interests of institutions and individuals as they pertain to interregional interaction. What benefits the individual may not be in the best interest of the group. His trade-diaspora model also makes fewer assumptions about the role of the core in interregional trade, giving more consideration to endogenous peripheral processes (Stein 1999).

Interregional interaction can have a significant impact on both periphery and core and recent approaches convincingly illustrate that unidirectional models, involving the core's power and impact on the periphery, can no longer be taken for granted. The San Francisco de Arriba Archaeological Project examined core/periphery relations in Oaxaca by documenting interaction between the highlands and the coast. Particular attention was paid to developments in the lower Río Verde region that might have indicated domination by the highlands, including shifts in settlement patterns, construction of fortifications, and economic upheaval. This chapter considers whether San Francisco de Arriba was part of a Terminal Formative world-system centered at Monte Albán. I will also consider whether relations between Monte Albán and San Francisco de Arriba were asymmetrical or if San Francisco de Arriba could have participated in a Monte Albán world-system while remaining independent. With this in mind, we can turn to the archaeological site of San Francisco de Arriba and evaluate first the nature and then the impact of its interregional relationships.

THE MATERIAL CONSEQUENCES OF INTERREGIONAL INTERACTION

Once Tututepec and San Francisco de Arriba were singled out as sites of possible Zapotec aggression, the question of highland domination of the coast received a great deal of attention by Oaxacan archaeologists (Balkansky 1998, 2002; Joyce 1991, 1993, 2003; Marcus and Flannery 1996; Redmond and Spencer 2006; Sherman et al. 2010; Spencer 2007; Workinger 2002a; Workinger and Joyce 2009; Zeitlin 1990; Zeitlin and Joyce 1999). Further questions of domination were raised regarding the relationship between the powerful highland polity of Teotihuacan and the lower Río Verde region (Joyce 1993, 2003). Joyce (2003) suggests that the discovery of Teotihuacan-style ceramics and high frequencies of Teotihuacan-controlled obsidian, coupled with the decline of the regional capital of Río Viejo and a movement of settlement into the piedmont, might indicate a foreign incursion in the Early Classic Coyuche phase (AD 250–500).

Archaeologists on the coast of Oaxaca favor a more nuanced approach to interaction rather than one of simple unidirectional domination (e.g., Joyce 1991, 1993, 2003; Workinger 2002a; Workinger and Joyce 2009; Zeitlin and Joyce 1999). To achieve a better understanding of interregional interaction and what it entailed, I compiled a list of possible scenarios ranging from indirect contact to all-out imperial conquest. Each scenario is accompanied by a set of expected archaeological correlates, which could then be compared to the data generated from the investigations at San Francisco de Arriba (Table 7.1).

While preliminary investigations at San Francisco de Arriba readily documented evidence of interaction, the mechanisms and social contexts of exchange were not as apparent (Workinger and Joyce 1997). The lowest-intensity form of interaction with the highlands would be indirect, or down-the-line exchange (Renfrew et al. 1969), whereby any goods or ideas reaching the coast would have passed through many intermediate parties. A consequence of all of this "handling" might be that intervening populations as well as coastal inhabitants reinterpreted the meanings of the original item or idea. This type of contact would be difficult to detect archaeologically, but it might include the adoption of a few highland cultural traits such as pottery styles or the occasional trade item exchanged through intermediary regions.

A scenario of elite mutual interdependence allows for the exchange or emulation of prestige items, with neither polity dominating the other. The elite of both areas use the imported goods/ideas to bolster their own local prestige and authority (Grove and Gillespie 1992; Helms 1979; Stark 1990). Portable items such as Monte Albán serving vessels as well as examples of art and architecture steeped in Zapotec symbolism might be found concentrated in coastal elite contexts. During the Early Classic period, we might expect to see Teotihuacan-style ceramics and perhaps architectural elements associated with this polity. Other imports from the highlands would likely consist of technological innovations of use to coastal elite for maintaining their high-status positions. Importantly, the emulation of highland elite, either through the exchange of goods or through the adoption of prestige markers, should not be

TABLE 7.1. Interaction scenarios and their archaeological correlates

Type of Interaction	Archaeological Correlates
Indirect, or "down-the-line" trade	Occasional trade items or local reinterpretations
Elite interdependence	Exchange of items from both areas concentrated in hands of elites
Periodic raiding	Defensive constructions if severe; evidence of conflict (e.g., burning, traumatic injuries); shifts in settlement patterns
Foreign outpost or enclave	Concentrations of foreign goods; stockpiling of local goods for shipment to the core; preferential treatment of the local elite
Imperial colonization	Economic reorganization to tributary state; evidence of elite administrators plus colonists; military garrisons
Territorial conquest (Monte Albán)	Same as for colonization with addition of evidence of conflict
Hegemonic conquest (Teotihuacan)	Similar to evidence for territorial conquest but without administrative presence or reorganization of settlement patterns

taken as evidence of subordination (Demarest and Foias 1993; Schortman and Urban 1994; Stein 1999).

Coastal exports to the Valley of Oaxaca and central Mexico may be more difficult to isolate as they would likely have included such perishables as cotton, salt, dried fish, a marine shell dye called *púrpura*, cacao, exotic animal pelts, and feathers. More tangible coastal trade items would include shell and perhaps ceramics. No evidence of conflict (i.e., a shift in settlement patterns or defensive fortifications) or political control (i.e., Zapotec or Teotihuacan administrative facilities) should be encountered. Archaeologists working on the coast give the most consideration to this scenario of mutual elite interdependence during the Late Formative, perhaps giving way to occasional Zapotec raiding in the Terminal Formative (Brockington 1983; Joyce 1991; Workinger 1999; Workinger and Joyce 2009; Zeitlin 1993; Zeitlin and Joyce 1999).

Interregional relations are not always peaceful and sometimes involve occasional acts of military force to capture goods or even people. This type of raiding has been raised as a possibility of interaction between the lower Río Verde region and the Valley of Oaxaca (e.g., Joyce 1993, 74). Within such a relationship, San Francisco de Arriba would have been subjected to episodic raiding by Monte Albán, but never conquered and incorporated into the polity. Located on a possible trade route linking the highlands with the sea, San Francisco de Arriba would be expected to yield evidence of defensive constructions if the intensity of raiding was severe. Some evidence of military conflict may exist (e.g., defensive walls, burning, or possibly evidence of traumatic injuries in human remains), but highland pottery styles would not replace local ones nor would there be evidence of foreign administrative facilities. Friction would also be manifested by a change in settlement patterns, presumably a nucleation of settlement for defensive reasons or a shift to defensible piedmont locations. Such a prospect would not likely apply to Teotihuacan, as repeated raids on the distant lower Río Verde would have been prohibitively costly. Prehispanic warfare was limited by such factors as harvest schedules, poorly maintained roads, and a lack of beasts of burden (Hassig 1992).

A more intensive interaction scenario would involve an isolated core outpost or enclave. This form of interaction has several permutations, some of which include the domination of the host community, while others do not. In the case of the latter, the trading enclave or diaspora simply takes advantage of its ability to act as a cultural mediator to facilitate trade (Stein 1999). In the case of domination, however, an enclave can be an "instrument of expansion" lying somewhat closer to all-out colonization or conquest than to the scenario of elite relations described above. Trading enclaves are characterized by a small number of migrants from the core settling in a strategic, albeit sociopolitically less complex, area in the periphery as a "cost-efficient form of channeling exchange" back to the core (Algaze 1993, 304). Local elites benefit in the short run by opening trade relations with the more powerful polity and therefore condone the initial intrusion.

The material manifestations of such an outpost would be difficult to detect, as they would be quite localized. In the case of San Francisco de Arriba, we would expect to see high concentrations of Valley of Oaxaca or central Mexican artifacts and architecture in the area of the site inhabited by foreigners, and all but absent in other areas and at other sites in the region (Workinger 2002a). San Francisco de Arriba's dominance of the Río San Francisco Valley would have made it the clear choice for such an outpost. Included in the archaeological remains of an outpost would be domestic refuse characteristic of foreign domestic practices, belonging to what Burmeister (2000) calls the "internal domain." Evidence of stockpiling local goods for transshipment to the core would also be present. High-status residences of the local elite would indicate a preferential relationship with the core and its representatives.

In the more intrusive case of imperial colonization, the weaker site or polity capitulates in the face of violence and the more powerful polity settles en masse, assuming political and economic control. As has been proposed by Marcus and Flannery (1996), Monte Albán was in a few cases able to exert administrative control over various hinterland regions by means of coercive colonization and/or marital alliance, thus avoiding the costs associated with outright military conquest. Evidence of Zapotec colonization of the coast would likely be similar to that of conquest (considered below) including the mobilization of tribute items and the formation of a buffer zone between San Francisco de Arriba and the Río Viejo polity to the south, which is not argued to have been conquered. Colonization would involve the use of everyday Valley of Oaxaca items by Zapotec immigrants but would not be expected in conquest scenarios. Domination of the coastal periphery by Monte Albán either through colonization or by conquest would fit Chase-Dunn and Hall's (1991) definition of core/periphery hierarchy and would be accompanied by the deliberate underdevelopment of the periphery's political system.

Archaeologically, the colonization of the Río San Francisco Valley by Zapotecs would be manifested by the construction of military garrisons and a reduction in the settlement hierarchy as local labor was forcibly resettled to better suit an export-oriented economy (see Spencer 1982). If the elite of San Francisco de Arriba capitulated to Monte Albán's threats, excavations by the San Francisco de Arriba Archaeological Project should reveal few indications of actual military conflict, but would reveal the presence of Zapotec elite who had been sent to administer and guard the imperial frontier as well as their accompanying status and ethnic markers.

Colonization of the site by Teotihuacan would be similar, although without the fortifications expected from a Zapotec incursion. Given the distances involved, Teotihuacan's influence outside of the Basin of Mexico appears to have been hegemonic rather than territorial and would have been based upon local goodwill or threats of reprisal rather than the presence of soldiers (Smith and Montiel 2001). The idea of Teotihuacan colonists outside of the Basin of Mexico has been around for quite some time (Kidder et al. 1946), though the evidence used to weigh such considerations has not always been consistent. The foremost indicator of a Teotihuacan presence outside central Mexico has traditionally been *talud-tablero* architecture, the argument being that such architectural elements could only have been conveyed directly (Kidder et al. 1946; Sanders 1977; Santley 2004). Other possible markers of Teotihuacan colonization include concentrations of imported ceramics, green obsidian, and iconography.

In the final and most extreme form of interregional relations, the more powerful polity defeats another in armed conflict and assumes political and economic control through imperial conquest. A territorial type of empire such as the one posited for the Terminal Formative Zapotec involves the direct administration of the defeated polity by imperial functionaries and oftentimes involves the movement of colonists, including soldiers, to the newly conquered region (Hassig 1985, 1992; Luttwak 1976). In terms of coastal Oaxaca, the Río San Francisco Valley (but not the remainder of the lower Río Verde region) would have been incorporated into a Monte Albán empire by means of military force. If this were the case, we would expect to see evidence of conquest similar to what has been found in the Cañada de Cuicatlán (Figure 1.1), a region north of Monte Albán also purported to have fallen to Zapotec imperial conquest (Redmond 1983; Spencer 1982; Spencer and Redmond 1997). There, manifestations of conquest are argued to include the burning of a site, skeletons exhibiting traumatic wounds, the development of defensive fortifications, a disruption in settlement patterns, and the formation of a buffer zone free of settlement between the Cañada and the politically independent Tehuacán Valley to the north.

The full-scale conquest associated with a territorial empire is the most straightforward scenario to recognize as it has the greatest impact on the archaeological record (Hassig 1992; Sinopoli 1994; Smith and Montiel 2001). We know from ethnohistoric documents that some Postclassic Zapotec frontiers were governed by core elites, sometimes even members of the ruling lineage (Burgoa 1989 [1674]; Córdova 1942 [1574]; Redmond 1983). If Zapotec strategy did not change significantly between the Terminal Formative and the Postclassic periods, we would expect to find numerous examples of Valley of Oaxaca prestige items, architecture, and mortuary practices concentrated at the site of San Francisco de Arriba. The process of maintaining the allegiance of military leaders through rewards from the core, oftentimes to stave off possible insurrections, is archaeologically well documented (Berdan et al. 1996; Blanton and Feinman 1984; Morrison and Sinopoli 1992; Stein 1989).

A thorough economic reorganization of San Francisco de Arriba and the Río San Francisco Valley would also be apparent if the site were incorporated into a Zapotec empire. There can be important ideological and political reasons for conquest (cf. Demarest and Conrad 1984), but economic factors often predominate (e.g., Ekholm and Friedman 1979; Hirth 1978; Spencer 1982) and the subordinate polities are marked by realignment to a tributary state. A Zapotec administrative facility or other form of "imperial infrastructure" (Smith and Montiel 2001) to facilitate the transport of coastal goods to Monte Albán might be evidenced at the site by palaces, storehouses, or temples constructed in Valley of Oaxaca style. Pooling of high-value/low-bulk coastal resources such as shell, animal pelts, or feathers might also indicate economic domination by Monte Albán. Such items would have been easier to carry through the mountains to the highlands than heavy and bulky food. Economic and political domination by Monte Albán would also likely be reflected in the archaeological record by an increase in the items traded into the site via the Valley of Oaxaca (Smith 1987).

An imperialistic scenario should also result in the development of an uninhabited buffer zone (Hirth 1978, 1980, 93) separating San Francisco de Arriba from the presumably hostile floodplain of the lower Río Verde Valley to the south, much like that seen between the Cañada de Cuicatlán and the Tehuacán Valley (Redmond 1983). Although Marcus and Flannery (1996, 202) consider the southern lower Río Verde region to have been weak, survey and excavation show that it was dominated by Río Viejo, a site which reached 225 ha and commanded a five-tiered settlement hierarchy in the Terminal Formative (Joyce 2008, Chapter 1). When expanding polities meet powerful enemies along their frontiers, it is not unreasonable to expect an escalation of military activities, including the construction of fortifications (Gorenstein 1985; Elam 1989, 1993; Hyslop 1990; Whittaker 1994). Nor is imperial conquest usually a one-time event. Instead, the subordinate region often rebels and must be conquered repeatedly, increasing the chances that evidence of such conflict would be preserved (Sinopoli 1994). In addition to an unoccupied buffer, the survey of the Río San Francisco Valley should also locate a "cultural boundary" (Redmond 1983) separating Zapotec-controlled San Francisco de Arriba from the rest of the lower Río Verde.

Imperial conquest by Teotihuacan would not be as archaeologically visible. If the central Mexican capital had imperial ambitions outside central Mexico (Cowgill 2003), it would have taken a hegemonic approach in which administrative infrastructure like that outlined above would have been unnecessary (Hassig 1992; Smith and Montiel 2001; Stark 1990). Whereas territorial empires such as that argued for Monte Albán are generally small, contiguous, and directly administered, hegemonic empires can be larger in scale, rely upon local rulers to maintain tribute schedules, and will often bypass territories too difficult or costly to control (Hassig 1992). The hegemonic approach relies upon the co-option of the local elite, a strategy that on the coast of Oaxaca would be marked by the concentrated presence of Teotihuacan prestige items designed to ensure their continued support.

EVALUATING THE INTERACTION SCENARIOS

Indirect exchange, elite relations, occasional raiding, colonization, and territorial and hegemonic conquest represent the range of interaction scenarios between San Francisco de Arriba and the highland regions of the Valley of Oaxaca and central Mexico. The expected material consequences of such interaction will now be used to evaluate the data gathered at San Francisco de Arriba and the surrounding lower Río Verde Valley.

The Lower Río Verde Region and Monte Albán

The earliest concrete evidence for interaction between the lower Río Verde region and the Valley of Oaxaca comes in the form of Late Formative (400–150 BC) and the occasional Terminal Formative imported grayware vessel (Joyce 1991, 517–535; Joyce et al. 2006). At San Francisco de Arriba these ceramics were found clustered in a high-status area of the site overlooking the main plaza and are characterized by their relatively grainy paste and glossy burnish. Initial field identification of imports was corroborated by instrumental neutron activation analysis (Workinger 2002a). The importation of Valley of Oaxaca ceramics all but ends with the early Terminal Formative Miniyua phase (150 BC–AD

100), a time when the coast appears to have been cut off from the highlands, perhaps due to heightened conflicts there (Feinman and Nicholas 1990; Joyce 1991, 1993; Spencer 1982; Spores 1972; Winter 1989).

Valley of Oaxaca influence nevertheless continues in the lower Río Verde region during the Miniyua phase when some local ceramics are fashioned in highland styles. Foremost among these imitations is the G.12 type, a conical bowl with two lines incised on the rim and occasionally with a combed interior base. Vessels stylistically similar to highland G.12s were produced on the coast in both gray and fine brown pastes, although fine brownwares lacked the combed bases (Joyce 1991, 1993; Levine 2002, Chapter 8; Workinger 2002a). The technology required to manufacture graywares had reached the coast by the Miniyua phase, illustrating that coastal/highland interaction was not limited to the exchange of material goods. As other regions in Oaxaca were producing graywares at the same time (Gaxiola 1984; Spores 1972; Zeitlin 1979), it is not clear whether the technology and stylistic attributes arrived directly from the Valley of Oaxaca or indirectly from another region (Joyce 1991; Levine 2002, Chapter 8).

The imported ceramics recovered from Minizundo phase contexts at San Francisco de Arriba may have arrived from the Valley of Oaxaca via intervening regions, opening the possibility that direct exchange between the two regions never took place. From an archaeological perspective it is difficult to distinguish between an indirect trade scenario and the more direct, face-to-face form of interaction. In the latter case, actual contact would have taken place between the elite of the coast and their Valley of Oaxaca counterparts sharing aspects of a common salient identity. Both would have profited by supporting each other's social status through exchange, and the terms would therefore have been reciprocal. Valley of Oaxaca items should be concentrated in elite areas at coastal sites, such as the elite residence or public building that overlooked the main plaza of San Francisco de Arriba investigated in Operation 99E. Excavations there recovered sherds from imported vessels in conjunction with relatively high concentrations of both bone and obsidian (Figure 7.3).

Yet other possible examples of Late Formative Valley of Oaxaca imports were found in Operations 99A, 99B, 99F, and 99I, the first two from the seemingly lower-status Ridgeline 2 and the latter two from a large platform just off the main plaza (Figures 7.3 and 7.4). These findings could be construed as evidence of a relatively decentralized or corporate polity (Blanton and Peregrine 1997) in which not just the elite had access to down-the-line highland goods, though I find it more probable that the site's elite were redistributing these imports as political capital. Taking into account San Francisco de Arriba's size and internal complexity relative to other sites in the Río San Francisco Valley, we can assume that it was probably the seat of a chiefdom by the Minizundo phase. At 95 ha, San Francisco de Arriba was the largest site in the Río San

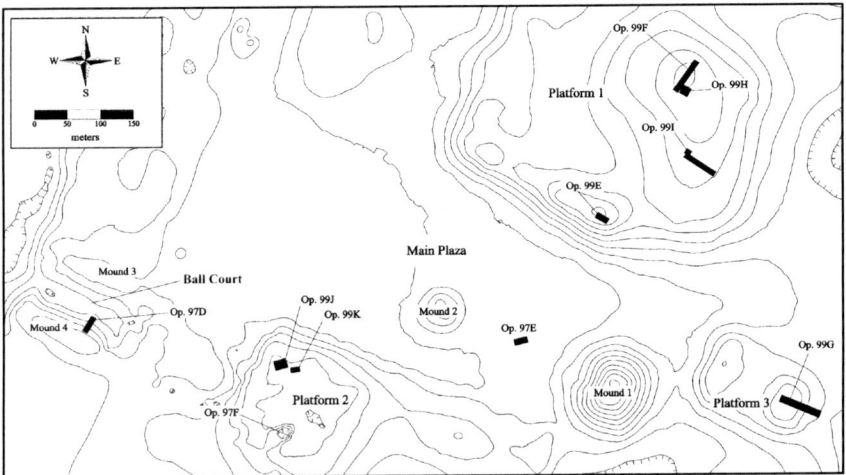

FIGURE 7.3. Excavations in the acropolis and adjacent structures (excavations not drawn to scale).

Francisco Valley by a magnitude of 10 and one of the largest in Oaxaca at the time.

A third interaction scenario involves imperial colonization, the large-scale movement of Zapotecs to the coast without actual violence. One of Marcus and Flannery's (1996, 199) criteria for Zapotec colonization is the "swamping" of local assemblages with Valley of Oaxaca grayware ceramics in the Terminal Formative period. During the Minizundo phase graywares accounted for 3.7 percent of the ceramic assemblage, most or all of which were imports. Neutron activation analysis of seven grayware sherds has identified the Valley of Oaxaca and Mixteca Alta as source regions. With the introduction of locally made graywares in the subsequent Miniyua phase, the proportion of graywares within the ceramic assemblage at San Francisco de Arriba rose to 27.3 percent. Because Minizundo phase sherds (with their lack of local graywares) were found redeposited in all Miniyua phase contexts, it is likely that the proportion of local graywares in the Miniyua phase was even higher. This ratio does not represent a swamping of local ceramic styles by highland ones and is substantially lower than the 61.6 percent reported from a sample of sites in the autonomous lower Río Verde floodplain to the south (Levine 2002, Chapter 8).

The territorial Zapotec empire proposed by Marcus and Flannery (1996; Marcus 1983, 1992a) would have entailed the replacement of local elites with imperial governors from the Valley of Oaxaca. Zapotec garrisons would have been maintained at San Francisco de Arriba to fortify and preserve the political boundary even if military force was not initially required for colonization. All of this should have left an unmistakable imprint at San Francisco de Arriba,

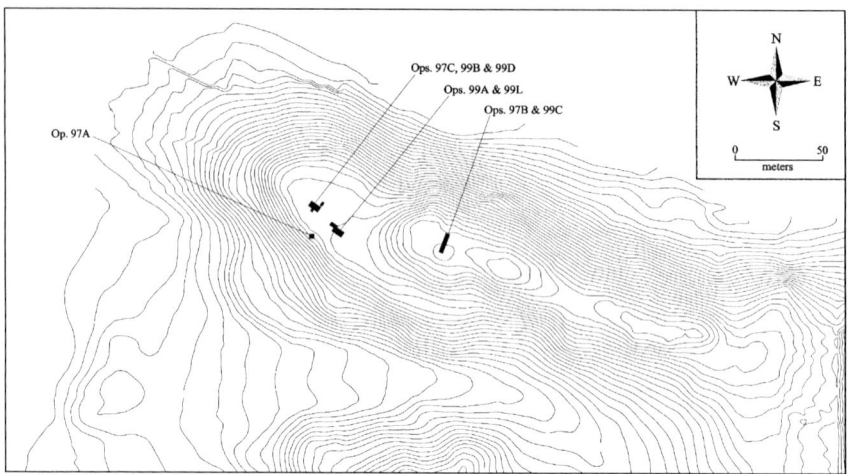

FIGURE 7.4. Excavations on Ridgeline 2 (excavations not drawn to scale).

including the importation of elaborate elite items to ensure the continued loyalty of imperial functionaries and soldiers. Zapotecs would also have most likely brought with them the architectural canons and mortuary traditions of the Valley of Oaxaca, much like what occurred at the Zapotec barrio in Teotihuacan (Spence 1992). The excavations of the San Francisco de Arriba Archaeological Project, however, did not uncover any such evidence.

A second criterion for Zapotec colonization is an unoccupied area south of San Francisco de Arriba, forming a buffer between it and the independent polity controlled by Río Viejo. During the survey of the area south of San Francisco de Arriba, six sites were found to have been occupied during the time of the proposed imperial expansion. These sites exhibited ceramic assemblages consistent with those from both San Francisco de Arriba and Río Viejo, failing to demonstrate a boundary marked by clear distinctions in ceramic styles like that found between the Cañada de Cuicatlán and the adjacent Tehuacán Valley (Redmond 1983). Survey in and around Río Viejo suggests its inhabitants never felt threatened by outsiders until the very end of the Formative at ca. AD 250 (Joyce 2003; Joyce et al. 1999). At 225 ha, it was a sprawling, unprotected site in the floodplain of the Río Verde. Thus the continuity in settlement and lack of a cultural boundary help to refute the claim of San Francisco de Arriba's colonization by the Zapotec. Considering the ceramic ties, architectural similarities, and geographical proximity (12 km), it is likely that the inhabitants of the Río San Francisco Valley shared a common ethnic identity with the people of Río Viejo and the other sites located on the floodplain of the Río Verde, and it is improbable that such a group would have willingly ceded the Río San Francisco Valley portion of its polity.

Territorial empires, such as that proposed for the Zapotec, also involve the economic reorganization of conquered regions (D'Altroy and Earle 1985; Hassig 1992; Schreiber 1987, 1999; Sinopoli 1994; Spencer 1982). If the economy of San Francisco de Arriba was similarly altered, we would expect to see strict control of trade into the site by imperial governors. It is not unreasonable to suppose that a colonized region would be forced to trade with the core at discriminatory terms (e.g., the British colonies in America). Such unidirectional trade would have taken place at the expense of exchange with other regions (Stark 1990; Stein 1999). If colonized, San Francisco de Arriba's Terminal Formative obsidian source utilization should therefore resemble Monte Albán's much more than Río Viejo's. Neutron activation analysis, however, shows that San Francisco de Arriba and other lower Río Verde floodplain sites were likely acquiring their obsidian via the Mixteca Alta and the Isthmus of Tehuantepec rather than through the Valley of Oaxaca. The lower Río Verde region, including San Francisco de Arriba, was using obsidian from six sources at the time, only two of which were used by Monte Albán (Joyce et al. 1995; Workinger 2001).

Economic reorganization would also be evident from the data collected during the systematic survey of the Río San Francisco Valley. If it was colonized, we would expect to see major disruptions in settlement patterns as people were forcibly moved to better exploit local resources to be channeled north to Monte Albán (Spencer 1982). The results of the survey documented no disruptions in settlement between the Late and Terminal Formative periods. In addition, sites located along the unprotected margin of the Río San Francisco demonstrate a lack of concern with defense (Workinger 2002b).

The final possible form of interaction between San Francisco de Arriba and the Valley of Oaxaca is territorial conquest. The criteria for Zapotec conquest would encompass all of the above correlates of colonization with a few additions. The inhabitants of San Francisco de Arriba would likely have fortified the site against attack, or if that failed, site-wide burning, human remains exhibiting traumatic wounds, and objects of oppression such as a skull rack could be expected. Excavations along Ridgeline 2 (Figure 7.4), the northern and most defensible area of the site, found no evidence of fortifications. Instead, structures uncovered there revealed the site's residential and ceremonial nature (Workinger 2002a, 97–147). No other signs of conflict were found at San Francisco de Arriba or at other sites located during the survey, and the possibility of a Zapotec conquest in the Terminal Formative appears less and less likely.

The Lower Río Verde Region and the Southern Isthmus of Tehuantepec

Although the exchange of goods with the Valley of Oaxaca essentially ceased with the Miniyua phase, the lower Río Verde region hardly continued in isolation. The recovery of white-rim blackwares from half of the excavation units in 1998–1999 at San Francisco de Arriba suggests that this was a widely distributed yet still rare trade item during the Terminal Formative period. The white-rim blackwares match those produced in the southern Isthmus of Tehuantepec (Wallrath 1967; Zeitlin 1979), although this is not yet confirmable by neutron activation analysis. The importation of these wares may have been spurred by the decline of Valley of Oaxaca imports to the lower Río Verde region. Casting about for high-status items to bolster their positions of authority, the elite of the area may have opened new trade connections or strengthened existing ones with the southern Isthmus of Tehuantepec in the Miniyua phase. For example, evidence suggests that the exchange of obsidian during the Late Formative may have set the stage for the subsequent trade of other items such as ceramics. Comparisons of Late Formative obsidian data from various regions of Oaxaca show similarities between the lower Río Verde and the southern Isthmus of Tehuantepec, an indication that obsidian was traded south across the isthmus from Gulf coastal sources such as Guadalupe Victoria and Zaragoza before making its way west along the Pacific coast (Workinger 2001), possibly using the coastal trade route described by Pye and Gutiérrez (2007).

The Lower Río Verde Region and Teotihuacan

During the Early Classic Coyuche phase the lower Río Verde region was able to reestablish ties with Teotihuacan, a powerful highland trading partner in central Mexico. This relationship is documented ceramically at San Francisco de Arriba by the occasional probable imitation thin orangeware sherd as well as a few local vessels following traditional Teotihuacan forms. In terms of other trade goods, the intensity of interaction is much more apparent.

A significant deposit of obsidian was discovered at San Francisco de Arriba within Operation 99A and the adjoining extension, Operation 99L (Figure 7.4). This deposit was found in conjunction with ceramics dating to the Coyuche phase, the time when the effects of Teotihuacan's trade were felt throughout much of Mexico. Of the 285 pieces of obsidian recovered from this deposit, 85 percent (n = 243) were green and presumably all from the Teotihuacancontrolled source at Pachuca, Hidalgo.[1] This frequency is only slightly higher than the site-wide average at San Francisco de Arriba during the Coyuche phase. The obsidian data from San Francisco de Arriba contradict observations made by Stark (1990, 255), who writes, "In regions well beyond Teotihuacan's immediate hinterland, Teotihuacan-controlled green obsidian was generally a minor element in importation patterns that drew predominantly from other sources." The unusually high frequency of Pachuca obsidian also questions the claim made by Clark (1986, 64), who argues that the total amount of green obsidian found outside central Mexico in the Classic period "would only fill a couple of shoe boxes." Such a high frequency of Pachuca obsidian at San Francisco de Arriba is indicative of a trade relationship that does not appear to have been paralleled outside of Teotihuacan's immediate hinterland, even at proposed enclaves like Kaminaljuyú (Braswell 2003) and Matacapan (Santley 1989). The strong presence of Pachuca obsidian, despite a lack of Teotihuacan ceramic imports, is interesting but only presages a similar separation of ceramic and obsidian trade networks that took place among the Aztecs in the Late Postclassic (Smith 1990). Certainly obsidian was easier to transport than ceramic vessels.

Like San Francisco de Arriba, the site of Río Viejo has high frequencies of Pachuca obsidian in the Coyuche phase but, in addition, has a relatively greater (although still rare) occurrence of central Mexican ceramic markers in high-status burials, including probable imitation thin orangeware vessels, cylindrical tripod vessels with slab feet, and coffee/cacao bean appliqués (Joyce 1991, 1993, 2003). Río Viejo abruptly declined from 200 ha in the late Terminal Formative Chacahua phase (AD 100–250) to 75 ha in the Coyuche phase (AD 250–500), and during that same period occupation in the piedmont rose from 38 to 63 percent (Joyce 2003, 64). Considering these data, Joyce (2003) raises the possibility that the changes seen in the lower Río Verde Valley could have been the result of conquest by Teotihuacan (however, for an alternative explanation, see Joyce 2008, 2010, Chapter 1; Joyce et al., Chapter 5). Given the archaeological footprint for interaction with Teotihuacan at other sites, such as Tikal, Kaminaljuyú, and perhaps Matacapan, Mirador, Montana, Los Horcones, and Copán, I am less willing to consider this as a likely possibility. The form of interaction documented at these sites is debated, although in many instances local architecture was shaped by central Mexican styles and elite ceramic assemblages incorporated many central Mexican traits, if not actual imported vessels (Agrinier 1975, 1991; Bove and Medrano Busto 2003; Brown 1977; Cowgill 2003; Kidder et al. 1946; Parsons 1991; Sanders 1977; Santley 1989). The same material consequences of interregional interaction that were used to assess the relationship between the coast and Monte Albán can be applied to the coast's relationship with Teotihuacan.

Down-the-line trade, with its expected drop-off the farther one travels from the source (Renfrew 1977), does not suit the San Francisco de Arriba data. It might explain the rare Teotihuacan-influenced ceramics at the site, yet fails altogether when confronted with the extraordinary frequency of Teotihuacan-controlled Pachuca obsidian. Because sites in intervening areas do not show similar frequencies, there instead seems to have been a direct supply mechanism between producers in central Mexico and the consumers in the lower Río Verde region.

When evaluating the possibility of a Teotihuacan core outpost/trade diaspora, we should expect no evidence of warfare or conflict. Rather, a small number of colonists from Teotihuacan would have been welcomed on the coast, as their presence would have significantly raised and reinforced the prestige of local rulers. Such a movement of Teotihuacanos to peripheral regions may have been spurred by a top-heavy social hierarchy in central Mexico where too many elite were competing for a limited amount of power and prestige. The solution, some argue, was either to leave voluntarily or be forced to live elsewhere (Clark 1986; Stark 1989, 1990). In this example, the colonists act as a "safety valve" to diffuse social conflict at home (Stein 1999, 70). Teotihuacan stood to gain either way; there would be less competition among the elite, new markets would be opened, and the prestige of the city would be enhanced as migrant families spread to different regions of Mesoamerica.

In the case of a Teotihuacan core outpost on the coast, prestige items from the highlands would have been given to coastal elites who shared a common ideological bond. This interaction would have forged and helped maintain a coastal-elite salient identity apart from their subordinates, who would not have been given direct access to these goods. In return, the colonists would have controlled an asymmetrical trade with Teotihuacan. Evidence of the stockpiling of lowland goods ready for shipment to the highlands might therefore be found at San Francisco de Arriba or other coastal sites. Ceramic styles and conservative central Mexican traditions such as burial practices and architecture would have been brought from Teotihuacan with the colonists and examples would be abundant within their enclave, as some have argued for Matacapan (Ortiz and Santley 1998; Santley 1989; Santley et al. 1986), Kaminaljuyú (Brown 1977; Kidder et al. 1946; Parsons 1991), and more recently Montana (Bove and Medrano Busto 2003).

At San Francisco de Arriba there are no signs of such a trading colony and no Teotihuacano households producing utilitarian wares in highland styles or practicing the domestic rituals that appear to be associated with *candeleros*. The ceramics from surface collections taken throughout the site, some of which were perhaps influenced by central Mexican conventions, do not suggest a concentration of foreign traders. Architecturally speaking, none of the structures at San Francisco de Arriba exhibit the *talud-tablero* architecture so associated with central Mexico, nor are there any Early Classic stone monuments at San Francisco de Arriba. Such monuments would have been ideal vehicles for exhibiting Teotihuacan-inspired imagery, as they were in other regions of Mesoamerica, especially in the Maya lowlands (Stuart 2000). Rivera (2011) has recently found a carved stone depicting a figure attired in central-Mexican-influenced dress at Cerro de la Tortuga, about 30 km northeast of San Francisco de Arriba; similar imagery has not been discovered in the lower Río Verde region.

When evaluating the possibility of Teotihuacan imperial control of San Francisco de Arriba and the lower Río Verde region in general, it is first necessary to address feasibility. It is notable that there were significantly fewer Teotihuacanos than their successors in central Mexico, the Aztec (Hassig 1992; Santley 1983). The limited number of warriors available for far-flung conquests casts doubt upon their presence on the coast of Oaxaca, particularly given their proposed presence elsewhere in Mesoamerica. The lower Río Verde region is approximately 650 km from Teotihuacan, a long and difficult march and probably without the cachet associated with the Maya centers of Tikal and Kaminaljuyú. It is reasonable to ask what might have drawn the central Mexicans so far from their homeland. The lower Río Verde region has no obsidian sources, but it does have other resources that might attract highland populations. Coastal products such as salted fish and shrimp, marine shell, cacao, cotton, *púrpura* dye, animal pelts, and feathers would have been sought after by the inhabitants of Teotihuacan; yet these same items would have been available from coastal areas much closer than the lower Río Verde.

Teotihuacan's most direct route to coastal and lowland resources was south to the coast of Guerrero. There, evidence of contact with Teotihuacan is easily recognizable (Ekholm 1948; Lister 1971; Paradis 2001; Weitlaner 1948; Weitlaner and Barlow 1944). Other signs of contact with central Mexico in the Classic period include *talud-tablero* architecture found at El Mexiquito (Armillas 1948) and the Mezcala-style objects and granular ware ceramics produced in Guerrero but found at Teotihuacan (Paradis 2001). The coastal environment around Acapulco and the mouth of the Río Balsas is similar to that found in the lower Río Verde region and it seems apparent that Teotihuacan would have chosen to exploit their much closer resources rather than expend the energy needed to reach the lower Río Verde.

In this scenario of hegemonic conquest by Teotihuacan, coastal defensive fortifications, skeletons with traumatic injuries, and the burning of structures could all be present. Hegemonic empires, because they generally maintain tributary compliance through the threat of reprisal rather than the physical presence of imperial functionaries and garrisons (Hassig 1992; Luttwak 1976), would not require the construction of elaborate administrative buildings. A small number of prestige goods from the core would be concentrated in the hands of the local rulers, given in efforts to co-opt their allegiance and to maintain tributary schedules (Smith and Montiel 2001).

Neither hegemonic conquest nor the core outpost/trade diaspora scenario would result in the reorganization of settlement patterns because the export of agricultural staples to central Mexico would have been uneconomical from this distance (Drennan 1984; Hassig 1985). I believe that the sudden increase in piedmont settlement witnessed outside of the Río San Francisco Valley during the Coyuche phase by Joyce (2003) was the result of regional fragmentation following the calamitous decline of the regional capital of Río Viejo (see Joyce 2008, 2010, Chapter 1). The lower Río Verde region was governed by a single primary center in the Chacahua phase, but by as many as eight competing centers in the Coyuche phase (Joyce 2003). My survey of the Río San Francisco Valley found no disruptions in settlement between the Chacahua and Coyuche phases when piedmont settlement instead declined slightly to 31.3 percent from 34.1 percent, suggesting that it was localized conflict which caused the disturbance in settlement witnessed to the south rather than the fallout from imperial conquest (also see Joyce 2008, 2010, Chapter 1).

In terms of ceramic ties between the coast and central Mexico, the occasional example of presumably locally manufactured thin orangeware indicates that the elite at Río Viejo, and to a lesser degree San Francisco de Arriba, were willing to emulate their more powerful neighbors to the north. Similar imitation of Teotihuacan-style ceramic wares is seen throughout much of Mesoamerica at the time (e.g., Agrinier 1975; Ball 1983; DuSolier 1945; Kidder et al. 1946; Laporte and Fialko 1987; Martínez López 1994; Paddock 1972; Stark 1989). Cylindrical tripod vases and other forms found at Río Viejo are almost certainly local interpretations, or even reinterpretations of Teotihuacan trade goods (Joyce 2003).

The anomalous frequencies of Teotihuacan-controlled Pachuca obsidian at both San Francisco de Arriba and Río Viejo can be explained either as the product of intensive exchange between elites (see also Joyce 2003) or non-elite trade by merchants. Michelle Butler (personal communication, 2011) has recently reported high percentages of Pachuca obsidian at Charco Redondo, which was also a primary center during the Early Classic period. The absence of green obsidian at two second-order sites that have been excavated in the region (Joyce 2003) supports the elite relations hypothesis, although the sample is quite small and requires further corroboration. One problem with the idea of elite control of green obsidian exchange is the fact that green blades are found in very mundane contexts at San Francisco de Arriba. This could be explained if the elites of the lower Río Verde region were monopolizing the trade in Pachuca obsidian and then redistributing it as a means of gaining/maintaining allegiance. Perhaps more problematic is the lack of elaborate obsidian artifact types such as sequins, humanoid eccentrics, laurel-leaf knives, and stemmed projectile points, which would be expected if the elite relations with central Mexico were close. An alternative explanation converts the green obsidian from gift, with its inalienable connection to the giver, to commodity, in which case the obsidian marks no special relationship between the producer and the consumer (Gregory 1982). This is contra Spence's (1996) view of Pachuca obsidian's role in the Maya region. There, green obsidian was found largely in caches and elite burials, more indicative of exchange based on elite relations than the data from the Oaxacan coast. If, indeed, the Pachuca obsidian was considered a commodity, then it may have arrived at San Francisco de Arriba and Río Viejo on the backs of merchants.

Although it was surprising that the ceramics of San Francisco de Arriba did not show the same degree of interaction with Teotihuacan as did its obsidian assemblage, the two were not necessarily traded via the same means. A more recent example of this phenomenon is seen in the Late Postclassic when the distribution of Aztec trade ceramics did not closely follow the distribution of Aztec-controlled obsidian (Smith 1990). This holds true in the Valley of Oaxaca where the frequency of Pachuca obsidian during the Postclassic ranges from 47 percent to 100 percent (Parry 1990). When these frequencies are compared with the total of ten Late Postclassic Aztec sherds found in the Valley of Oaxaca (Blanton 1983), the resulting incongruity mirrors that seen at San Francisco de Arriba six centuries earlier.

Importantly, there is precedent for the high frequencies of Pachuca obsidian seen at San Francisco de Arriba during the Coyuche phase. Trade with central Mexico for obsidian began with San Francisco de Arriba's earliest occupation in the late Middle Formative Charco phase (700–400 BC), and 86 percent of the subsequent Minizundo phase sample came from central Mexican sources. The importation of Pachuca obsidian also began as early as the Minizundo phase (Workinger 2001). This cumulative evidence points to a long-term relationship rather than a sudden influx of trade items on the heels of colonization or military conquest. The coastal rulers either controlled some product or products valuable enough to attract the attention of Teotihuacan traders, or were themselves exotic enough to lend prestige just through interaction and the exchange of ideas.

The Lower Río Verde Region and the Mixteca Alta

An unanticipated finding of the San Francisco de Arriba Archaeological Project was the early contact between the coast and the Mixteca Alta. Postclassic Mixtec *cacicazgos* of all sizes developed exchange networks that took advantage of the ecological complementarity between the highlands and the coast, sometimes cementing the ties with marriage alliances (Joyce et al. 2004; Monaghan 1994; Spores 1974, 1984, 1993). Holding lands in both lowland and highland areas enabled farmers to stagger crop harvests, particularly corn, to help reduce risk and ensure a steady food source. This symbiosis dates back as far as 400 years before the Spanish Conquest (Spores 1993) and quite likely further (Joyce 1993).

It was nevertheless a surprise when, in the neutron activation analysis of seven Minizundo phase coarse brownwares recovered from San Francisco de Arriba, one was found to be an import from the Mixteca Alta. Furthermore, the coast's dependence on central Mexican obsidian sources, beginning in the

Minizundo phase and continuing through the entire sequence, suggests that it was arriving via the Mixteca Alta and Baja (Workinger 2001). Investigations in intervening areas, including sourcing studies, would shed considerable light on the route and the mechanism by which this obsidian reached the lower Río Verde region.

INTERREGIONAL INTERACTION AND ITS EFFECTS ON SOCIOPOLITICAL COMPLEXITY

The expansion of early states is often credited for the growth of sociopolitical complexity in peripheral regions (Algaze 1993; Fried 1967; Joyce 1993; Price 1978; Stark 1990). Some scholars take the position that such interaction is one-sided, with the core necessarily dominating the periphery (e.g., Wallerstein 1974; Marcus and Flannery 1996). When confronted with the data available from the lower Río Verde region, however, arguments for a core/periphery hierarchy are not supported.

Survey and excavation data reveal that the Río San Francisco Valley was dominated by the site of San Francisco de Arriba as early as the Minizundo phase. Considering its size and architectural complexity, San Francisco de Arriba was the center of a chiefdom and one of the largest sites in Oaxaca at the time. With a population estimated between 1,364 and 3,410, the Río San Francisco Valley was a force for any potential invaders to reckon with, particularly when aided by Río Viejo and other sites in the region. San Francisco de Arriba would not have been an easy target for conquest considering Monte Albán's limited military resources, the rugged intervening topography, and the other regions claimed to have been under Zapotec control at the time (Joyce 2003; Workinger 2002a; Workinger and Joyce 2009; Zeitlin and Joyce 1999). When we consider the archaeological correlates of interaction outlined above, there is ample evidence from the San Francisco de Arriba Archaeological Project to question the claims of a Zapotec colonization or conquest of the Río San Francisco Valley. This means that any sociopolitical impact the Monte Albán state may have had on the coast was consciously adopted by coastal elites rather than imposed upon them from the outside, a scenario that fits well with the idea of salient identities.

Regarding the influence of interregional interaction on the early sociopolitical development of the lower Río Verde region, too little is known of the late Middle Formative Charco phase to draw definitive conclusions. Indications so far point to small settlements at the time, with the exception of Charco Redondo (Joyce 1994; Joyce et al. 1999). This all changed in the Minizundo phase, a time when sites such as Charco Redondo and San Francisco de Arriba clearly controlled their respective areas of the lower Río Verde. The rise in social complexity coincides with the first evidence of interaction between the lower Río Verde region and the Valley of Oaxaca. The Late Formative period also marked the beginning of a long-term interregional relationship between the coast and the Mixteca Alta.

Coastal interaction with the Valley of Oaxaca and the Mixteca Alta in the Minizundo phase took the form of trade between elites who shared a salient identity and who used prestige-laden foreign goods to support and increase their social status. Coastal elites imported grayware vessels from the Valley of Oaxaca that served as prestige goods. Items imported from the Mixteca Alta possibly included cochineal, maguey products such as fibers for clothing and pulque (a fermented beverage), as well as minerals (Spores 1984). These elite relations were self-serving, undertaken for self-aggrandizement and at the expense of the polity as a whole. By monopolizing these external contacts, the rulers of San Francisco de Arriba were able to control the importation of valued commodities, ideas, and manufactured goods. These could then be used to gain the allegiance of local populations in the form of gifts, which were anything but free (Clark and Blake 1994; Mauss 1990 [1950]; Orenstein 1980). There were probably also competing factions within the elite, each of which attempted to cultivate the most prestigious interaction partners and monopolize external resources. Elite networks involving the exchange of goods and ideas thus served as a means of not only maintaining but increasing social inequality.

The question becomes, what effect, if any, did interaction with the Valley of Oaxaca and the Mixteca Alta have on the rising complexity of the lower Río Verde region in the Late/Terminal Formative? There is no reason not to consider the possibility that the importation of ideas and prestige items helped certain individuals on the coast to rise socially and politically above the remaining population. The Valley of Oaxaca, after all, had demonstrated a three-tiered settlement hierarchy between 1150 and 700 BC, as well as status differences suggestive of a chiefdom by 700–500 BC (Blanton et al. 1999), if not earlier (Flannery and Marcus 1983; Marcus and Flannery 1996). Joyce (1991, 2003) has long held open the possibility that the Valley of Oaxaca affected social developments in the lower Río Verde region. He argues that conflicts in the highlands of Oaxaca during the Terminal Formative period cut off important trade contacts, forcing coastal elites to turn to local craftsmen for the production of prestige items (Joyce 1993, 73). It was at this time that the technology needed to manufacture graywares reached the coast and production may have been initially financed or otherwise controlled by the elite, further enhancing their high status (Joyce 1993). Shortly thereafter, non-elite potters could have easily adopted the kiln technologies needed to produce graywares, leading to the high frequencies of this paste type later in the Miniyua phase (cf. Levine 2002, Chapter 8). This interpretation fits well with the data collected during the San Francisco de Arriba Archaeological Project.

At the same time, the site of Río Viejo on the western side of the Río Verde grew to 225 ha from only 25 ha in the Late Formative period, becoming the regional capital. In the lower Río Verde Valley, survey has documented a five-tiered settlement hierarchy in the Terminal Formative period (Joyce 2003), a complexity suggestive of state organization. Did the Zapotecs contribute to the rise of the state in the lower Río Verde region? If so, it was only indirectly. As survey and excavation in the region have convincingly demonstrated, the lower Río Verde region never reacted to a threat from the Valley of Oaxaca. Continuities in settlement patterns between the Late Formative and the Terminal Formative periods, as well as excavation data, indicate that a state-level sociopolitical organization seen at Río Viejo in the Miniyua phase was neither imposed directly by Zapotec imperial administrators nor indirectly by a garrisoned imperial boundary at San Francisco de Arriba.

Did the cessation of exchange between the Valley of Oaxaca and the lower Río Verde region prompt coastal elites to expand trade with the southern Isthmus of Tehuantepec? Comparisons of obsidian sourcing data suggest that obsidian from Gulf coastal sources was traded across the isthmus and then west along the coast to the lower Río Verde region beginning in the Minizundo phase. This early trade connection may have been expanded in the Miniyua phase when highland conflicts cut off the supply of Valley of Oaxaca imports to the lower Río Verde region. The distribution of Terminal Formative isthmian white-rim blackwares at San Francisco de Arriba resembles that of the Late Formative highland graywares, which were concentrated in elite contexts but also present in low numbers throughout the site. I believe this pattern is the result of chiefly redistribution, a means of co-opting the allegiance of the non-elite.

It is not clear if direct contact continued with the Valley of Oaxaca into the Miniyua phase. The obsidian data, heavily weighted toward central Mexican sources, suggest that contact with the Mixteca Alta continued. Valley of Oaxaca imports ended, but grayware ceramics are produced locally for the first time in the lower Río Verde, some of which are decorated in Valley of Oaxaca styles. It is possible, even likely, that the ceramic technology and styles could have been adopted from intervening regions such as the southern Isthmus of Tehuantepec, the Mixteca Alta, or the Mixteca Baja, all three of which were producing gray-ware ceramics at the time (see Levine 2002, Chapter 8). However these styles reached the lower Río Verde, coastal elites continued to use some Valley of Oaxaca diacritics in the Terminal Formative period.

CONCLUSIONS

The material correlates of interregional interaction considered by the San Francisco de Arriba Archaeological Project, plus the multiple avenues by which they were addressed, sharply question the criteria and claims of colonization and conquest set forth by highland researchers. Instead, it is apparent that local elite were taking advantage of a shared salient identity as a conduit for the trade of prestige goods with the Valley of Oaxaca during the Late Formative. Prestige items from the highlands, particularly grayware ceramics, were used to support an ideology that legitimized growing status inequalities. Accordingly, these ceramics were found concentrated in high-status areas of San Francisco de Arriba. In return for highland imports and ideologies, the lower Río Verde region was likely trading coastal resources such as marine shell, cotton, and cacao. The scenario of reciprocal elite relations also best explains the extraordinary frequencies of Teotihuacan-controlled Pachuca obsidian at San Francisco de Arriba in the Early Classic period, although it is more difficult to pinpoint the goods or ideas traded to central Mexico in return. Teotihuacan's population—both elite and commoner—could very well have created a demand for coastal resources that could not be met by nearby sites on the coast of Guerrero. The fact that the goods were largely perishable would also have required their constant replenishment (Spence 1996).

My interpretation of the data collected from San Francisco de Arriba and the surrounding valley fails to support a world-systems approach, which assumes domination of the periphery by the core. The world-systems model is inadequate in this situation because of its conflation of ideology, politics, and economics; if evidence of one is found in the periphery, it is assumed all are present (Stein 1999). Valley of Oaxaca graywares in the Late Formative and central Mexican obsidian in the Early Classic cannot be equated with conquest. The presence of highland-inspired ceramic styles on the coast in no way suggests economic or political domination, but rather a deliberate adoption by local elites as a means of justifying and growing their positions of authority. Instead, my analysis underscores the views of other coastal researchers who argue that the strategies of interregional interaction adopted by highland polities must have varied from region to region (Joyce 1993; Levine 2002; Zeitlin and Joyce 1999).

ACKNOWLEDGMENTS

Financial support for the 1997 season of the San Francisco de Arriba Archaeological Project was provided by Sigma Xi, the Explorers Club, and an anonymous foundation. Additional funding for the 1998–1999 field season was provided by the Wenner-Gren Foundation. Neutron activation analysis of obsidian was performed by Michael Glascock of the University of Missouri Research Reactor and was supported in part by grant SBR–9802366 from the National Science Foundation in addition to a dissertation enhancement grant from Vanderbilt University. Neutron activation analysis of ceramics was funded by the Vanderbilt University Research Fund of Arthur Joyce as part of the greater Oaxacan Ceramic Database Project. The San Francisco de Arriba Archaeological Project was carried out under the auspices of the Instituto Nacional de Antropología e Historia in Mexico. Therefore, I would like to thank Joaquín García-Bárcena, president of the Consejo de Arqueología in Mexico City, and Eduardo López Calzada, director of the Centro INAH-Oaxaca. A debt of gratitude is owed to the people of San Francisco de Arriba, who worked hard gathering the data used in this article. I would like to thank Arthur Joyce and Nick Honerkamp for their comments on an earlier draft of this chapter.

NOTE

1. A single artifact from San Francisco de Arriba was found to have come from Tulancingo, the only other Mesoamerican source that produces green obsidian. This particular example, a fragmentary biface, happened to be a streaked black and gray.

REFERENCES CITED

Agrinier, Pierre. 1975. *Mounds 9 and 10 at Mirador, Chiapas.* Papers of the New World Archaeological Foundation No. 28. Provo, UT: Brigham Young University.

Agrinier, Pierre. 1991. "The Ballcourts of Southern Chiapas, Mexico." In *The Mesoamerican Ballgame,* ed. Vernon L. Scarborough and David R. Wilcox, 175–94. Tucson: University of Arizona Press.

Algaze, Guillermo. 1993. "Expansionary Dynamics of Some Early Pristine States." *American Anthropologist* 95 (2): 304–33. http://dx.doi.org/10.1525/aa.1993.95.2.02a00030.

Armillas, Pedro. 1948. "Arqueología del occidente de Guerrero." In *El occidente de México,* 74–76. Mexico City: IV Mesa Redonda de la Sociedad de Antropología Mexicana.

Balkansky, Andrew. 1998. "Origin and Collapse of Complex Societies in Oaxaca (Mexico): Evaluating the Era from 1965 to the Present." *Journal of World Prehistory* 12 (4): 451–93. http://dx.doi.org/10.1023/A:1022870516264.

Balkansky, Andrew. 2002. *The Sola Valley and the Monte Albán State: A Study of Zapotec Imperial Expansion.* Museum of Anthropology, University of Michigan Memoir No. 36. Ann Arbor: University of Michigan.

Ball, Joseph W. 1983. "Teotihuacan, the Maya, and Ceramic Interchange: A Contextual Perspective." In *Highland-Lowland Interaction in Mesoamerica: Interdisciplinary Approaches,* ed. Arthur G. Miller, 125–45. Washington, DC: Dumbarton Oaks.

Berdan, Frances F., Richard E. Blanton, Elizabeth H. Boone, Mary G. Hodge, Michael E. Smith, and Emily Umberger. 1996. *Aztec Imperial Strategies.* Washington, DC: Dumbarton Oaks.

Blanton, Richard E. 1983. "The Aztec Garrison of 'Acatepec.'" In *The Cloud People: Divergent Evolution of the Zapotec and Mixtec Civilizations,* ed. Kent V. Flannery and Joyce Marcus, 318. New York: Academic Press.

Blanton, Richard E., and Gary M. Feinman. 1984. "The Mesoamerican World System." *American Anthropologist* 86 (3): 673–82. http://dx.doi.org/10.1525/aa.1984.86.3.02a 00100.

Blanton, Richard E., Gary M. Feinman, Stephen Kowalewski, and Linda Nicholas. 1999. *Ancient Oaxaca*. Cambridge: Cambridge University Press. http://dx.doi. org/10.1017/CBO9780511607844

Blanton, Richard E., and Peter N. Peregrine. 1997. "Main Assumptions and Variables for Economic Analysis beyond the Local System." In *Economic Analysis beyond the Local System*, ed. Richard Blanton, Peter Peregrine, Deborah Winslow, and Thomas Hall, 3–12. Lanham, MD: University Press of America.

Bove, Frederick J., and Sonia Medrano Busto. 2003. "Teotihuacan, Militarism, and Pacific Guatemala." In *The Maya and Teotihuacan: Reinterpreting Early Classic Interaction*, ed. Geoffrey E. Braswell, 45–79. Austin: University of Texas Press.

Braswell, Geoffrey E. 2003. "Understanding Early Classic Interaction between Kaminaljuyú and Central Mexico." In *The Maya and Teotihuacan: Reinterpreting Early Classic Interaction*, ed. Geoffrey E. Braswell, 105–42. Austin: University of Texas Press.

Brockington, Donald L. 1983. "The View from the Coast: Relationships between the Coast and the Valley of Oaxaca." *Notas Mesoamericanas* 9: 25–31.

Brown, Kenneth L. 1977. "The Valley of Guatemala: A Highland Port of Trade." In *Teotihuacan and Kaminaljuyú: A Study in Prehistoric Culture Contact*, ed. William T. Sanders and Joseph W. Michels, 205–395. University Park: Pennsylvania State University Press.

Brumfiel, Elizabeth M. 1992. "Distinguished Lecture in Archaeology: Breaking and Entering the Ecosystem; Gender, Class and Faction Steal the Show." *American Anthropologist* 94: 551–67. http://dx.doi.org/10.1525/aa.1992.94.3.02a00020.

Brumfiel, Elizabeth M., and Richard A. Fox, eds. 1994. *Factional Competition and Political Development in the New World*. Cambridge: Cambridge University Press. http:// dx.doi.org/10.1017/CBO9780511598401.

Burgoa, Fr. Francisco de. 1989 [1674]. Geográfica descripción. Mexico City: Editorial Porrua.

Burmeister, Stefan. 2000. "Archaeology and Migration: Approaches to an Archaeological Proof of Migration." *Current Anthropology* 41 (4): 539–67. http://dx.doi.org /10.1086/317383.

Chase-Dunn, Christopher K., and Thomas D. Hall. 1991. "Conceptualizing Core/ Periphery Hierarchies." In *Core/Periphery Relations in Precapitalist Worlds*, ed. Christopher K. Chase-Dunn and Thomas D. Hall, 5–44. Boulder, CO: Westview Press.

Clark, John E. 1986. "From Mountains to Molehills: A Critical Review of Teotihuacan's Obsidian Industry." In *Research in Economic Anthropology* Supplement 2, ed. Barry L. Isaac, 23–74. Greenwich, CT: JAI Press.

Clark, John E., and Michael Blake. 1994. "The Power of Prestige: Competitive Generosity and the Emergence of Rank Societies in Lowland Mesoamerica." In *Factional Competition and Political Development in the New World*, ed. Elizabeth M. Brumfiel and Richard A. Fox, 17–30. Cambridge: Cambridge University Press. http://dx.doi. org/10.1017/CBO9780511598401.003.

Córdova, Fr. Juan de. 1942 [1574]. *Vocabulario en lengua Zapoteca*. Mexico City: Biblioteca Linguística Mexicana I.

Cowgill, George L. 2003. "Teotihuacan and the Maya in Mesoamerican Perspective." In *The Maya and Teotihuacan: Reinterpreting Early Classic Interaction*, ed. Geoffrey E. Braswell, 315–35. Austin: University of Texas Press.

D'Altroy, Terrence N., and Timothy K. Earle. 1985. "Staple Finance, Wealth Finance, and Storage in the Inka Political Economy." *Current Anthropology* 26 (2): 187–206. http://dx.doi.org/10.1086/203249.

DeCicco, Gabriel, and Donald L. Brockington. 1956. *Reconocimiento arqueológico en el suroeste de Oaxaca*. Direccíon de Monumentos Prehispánicos Informe No. 6. Mexico City: Instituto Nacional de Antropología e Historia.

Demarest, Arthur A., and Geoffrey W. Conrad. 1984. *Religion and Empire*. Cambridge: Cambridge University Press.

Demarest, Arthur A., and Antonia E. Foias. 1993. "Mesoamerican Horizons and the Cultural Transformations of Maya Civilization." In *Latin American Horizons*, ed. Don S. Rice, 147–91. Washington, DC: Dumbarton Oaks.

Drennan, Robert D. 1984. "Long-Distance Transport Costs in Pre-Hispanic Mesoamerica." *American Anthropologist* 86 (1): 105–12. http://dx.doi.org/10.1525/aa.1984.86.1.02a00100.

DuSolier, Wilifrido. 1945. "La cerámica arqueológica de El Tajín." *Anales del Museo Nacional de Arqueología Historia y Etnografía* 3: 147–92.

Ekholm, Gordon F. 1948. "Ceramic Stratigraphy at Acapulco, Guerrero." In *El occidente de México*, 95–104. Mexico: IV Mesa Redonda de la Sociedad de Antropología Mexicana.

Ekholm, Kasja, and Jonathon Friedman. 1979. "'Capital' Imperialism and Exploitation in Ancient World-Systems." In *Power and Propaganda: A Symposium on Ancient Empires*, ed. Mogens T. Larsen, 41–58. Copenhagen: Akademisk Forlag.

Elam, J. Michael. 1989. "Defensible and Fortified Sites." In *Monte Albán's Hinterlands*, Part 2, ed. Stephen Kowalewski, Gary Feinman, Linda Finsten, Richard Blanton, and Linda Nicholas, 385–407. University of Michigan Museum of Anthropology Memoirs No. 23. Ann Arbor: University of Michigan.

Elam, J. Michael. 1993. *Obsidian Exchange in the Valley of Oaxaca, Mexico, 2500–500 BP*. PhD dissertation, Department of Anthropology, University of Missouri–Colombia. Ann Arbor, MI: University Microfilms.

Feinman, Gary M., and Linda Nicholas. 1990. "At the Margins of the Monte Albán State: Settlement Patterns in the Ejutla Valley, Oaxaca, Mexico." *Latin American Antiquity* 1 (3): 216–46. http://dx.doi.org/10.2307/972162.

Flannery, Kent V., and Joyce Marcus. 1983. "The Growth of Site Hierarchies in the Valley of Oaxaca: Part I." In *The Cloud People: Divergent Evolution of the Zapotec and Mixtec Civilizations*, ed. Kent V. Flannery and Joyce Marcus, 54–64. New York: Academic Press.

Fried, Morton H. 1967. *The Evolution of Political Society: An Essay in Political Anthropology*. New York: Random House.

Gaxiola, Margarita. 1984. *Huamelulpan: Un centro urbano de la Mixteca Alta*. Colección Científica No. 14. Mexico City: Instituto Nacional de Antropología e Historia.

Gorenstein, Shirley. 1985. *Acámbaro: Frontier Settlement on the Tarascan-Aztec Border.* Vanderbilt University Publications in Anthropology No. 32. Nashville, TN: Vanderbilt University.

Gregory, Christopher A. 1982. *Gifts and Commodities.* New York: Academic Press.

Grove, David C., and Susan D. Gillespie. 1992. "Ideology and Evolution at the Pre-State Level." In *Ideology and Pre-Colombian Civilizations,* ed. Arthur A. Demarest and Geoffrey W. Conrad, 15–36. Santa Fe, NM: School of American Research Press.

Hassig, Ross. 1985. *Trade, Tribute and Transportation.* Norman: University of Oklahoma Press.

Hassig, Ross. 1992. *War and Society in Ancient Mesoamerica.* Berkeley: University of California Press. http://dx.doi.org/10.1525/california/9780520077348.001.0001.

Helms, Mary W. 1979. *Ancient Panama: Chiefs in Search of Power.* Austin: University of Texas Press.

Hirth, Kenneth G. 1978. "Teotihuacan Regional Population Administration in Eastern Morelos." *World Archaeology* 9(3): 320–33. http://dx.doi.org/10.1080/00438243.1973.9979706. Medline:16470976.

Hirth, Kenneth G. 1980. *Eastern Morelos and Teotihuacan.* Vanderbilt University Publications in Anthropology No. 25. Nashville, TN: Vanderbilt University.

Hyslop, John. 1990. *Inka Settlement Planning.* Austin: University of Texas Press.

Joyce, Arthur A. 1991. *Formative Period Occupation in the Lower Río Verde Valley, Oaxaca, Mexico: Interregional Interaction and Social Change.* PhD dissertation, Department of Anthropology, Rutgers University, New Brunswick, NJ. Ann Arbor, MI: University Microfilms.

Joyce, Arthur A. 1993. "Interregional Interaction and Social Development on the Oaxaca Coast." *Ancient Mesoamerica* 4 (1): 67–84. http://dx.doi.org/10.1017/S0956536100000791.

Joyce, Arthur A. 1994. "Late Formative Community Organization and Social Complexity on the Oaxaca Coast." *Journal of Field Archaeology* 21:147–68.

Joyce, Arthur A. 2003. "Imperialism in Pre-Aztec Mesoamerica: Monte Albán, Teotihuacan, and the Lower Río Verde Valley." In *Ancient Mesoamerica Warfare,* ed. Kathryn Brown and Travis M. Stanton, 49–72. Walnut Creek, CA: AltaMira Press.

Joyce, Arthur A. 2008. "Domination, Negotiation, and Collapse: A History of Centralized Authority on the Oaxaca Coast Before the Late Postclassic." In *After Monte Albán: Transformation and Negotiation in Oaxaca, Mexico,* ed. Jeffrey Blomster, 219–54. Boulder: University Press of Colorado.

Joyce, Arthur A. 2010. *Mixtecs, Zapotecs, and Chatinos: Ancient Peoples of Southern Mexico.* Malden, MA: Wiley-Blackwell.

Joyce, Arthur A., J. Michael Elam, Michael Glascock, Hector Neff, and Marcus Winter. 1995. "Exchange Implications of Obsidian Source Analysis from the Lower Río Verde Valley, Oaxaca, Mexico." *Latin American Antiquity* 6 (1): 3–15. http://dx.doi.org/10.2307/971597.

Joyce, Arthur A., Hector Neff, Mary S. Thieme, Marcus Winter, J. Michael Elam, and Andrew Workinger. 2006. "Ceramic Production and Exchange in Late/Terminal Formative Period Oaxaca." *Latin American Antiquity* 17 (4): 579–94. http://dx.doi.org/10.2307/25063073.

Joyce, Arthur A., Andrew Workinger, Byron Hamann, Peter Kroefges, Maxine Oland, and Stacie M. King. 2004. "Lord 8 Deer 'Jaguar Claw' and the Land of the Sky: The Archaeology and History of Tututepec." *Latin American Antiquity* 15 (3): 273–97. http://dx.doi.org/10.2307/4141575.

Joyce, Arthur A., Andrew Workinger, Scott Hutson, Stacie King, Neil Ross, Michael Swanton, Karolo Aparicio, Brant Schwartz, Brigham Golden, Billiana Miteva, Matthew Dudgeon, and Nicole Falgoust. 1999. Recorrido regional de superficie. In "El proyecto patrones de asentamiento del Río Verde," ed. Arthur A. Joyce, 5–36. Final report submitted to the Consejo de Arqueología, Instituto Nacional de Antropología e Historia, Mexico City.

Kidder, Alfred V., Jesse D. Jennings, and Edwin M. Shook. 1946. *Excavations at Kaminaljuyú, Guatemala*. Washington, DC: Carnegie Institution of Washington.

Laporte, Juan Pedro, and Vilma Fialko C. 1987. "La cerámica del Clásico Temprano desde mundo perdido, Tikal." In *Maya Ceramics*, ed. Prudence Rice and Robert Sharer, 123–82. BAR International Series 345. Oxford: British Archaeological Reports.

Levine, Marc N. 2002. "Ceramic Change and Continuity in the Lower Río Verde Region of Oaxaca Mexico: The Late Formative to Early Terminal Formative Transition." MA thesis, Department of Anthropology, University of Colorado, Boulder.

Lister, Robert H. 1971. "Archaeological Synthesis of Guerrero." In *The Handbook of Middle American Indians*, vol. 11, ed. Gordon Ekholm and Ignacio Bernal, 619–31. Austin: University of Texas Press.

Luttwak, Edward. 1976. *The Grand Strategy of the Roman Empire: From the First Century BC to the Third*. Baltimore: Johns Hopkins University Press.

Marcus, Joyce. 1976. "The Iconography of Militarism at Monte Albán and Neighboring Sites in the Valley of Oaxaca." In *Origins of Religious Art and Iconography in Preclassic Mesoamerica*, ed. Henry B. Nicholson, 125–39. Los Angeles: UCLA Latin American Center Publications.

Marcus, Joyce. 1980. "Zapotec Writing." *Scientific American* 242 (2): 50–64. http://dx.doi.org/10.1038/scientificamerican0280-50.

Marcus, Joyce. 1983. "The Conquest Slabs of Building J, Monte Albán." In *The Cloud People: Divergent Evolution of the Zapotec and Mixtec Civilizations*, ed. Kent V. Flannery and Joyce Marcus, 106–8. New York: Academic Press.

Marcus, Joyce. 1984. "Mesoamerican Territorial Boundaries: Reconstructions from Archaeology and Hieroglyphic Writing." *Archaeological Review from Cambridge* 3: 48–62.

Marcus, Joyce. 1992a. *Mesoamerican Writing Systems*. Princeton, NJ: Princeton University Press.

Marcus, Joyce. 1992b. "Political Fluctuations in Mesoamerica." *National Geographic Research and Exploration* 8: 392–411.

Marcus, Joyce, and Kent V. Flannery. 1996. *Zapotec Civilization*. New York: Thames and Hudson.

Martínez López, Cira. 1994. "La cerámica de estilo teotihuacano en Monte Albán." In *Monte Albán Estudios Recientes*, ed. Marcus Winter, 25–53. Contribución No. 2 del Proyecto Especial Monte Albán 1992–1994. Oaxaca: INAH.

Mauss, Marcel. 1990. *The Gift*. Trans. W. D. Halls. New York: W. W. Norton. First published 1950 as *Essai sur le don* by Presses Universitaires de France.

Monaghan, John. 1994. "Irrigation and Ecological Complementarity in Mixtec Cacicazgos." In *Caciques and Their People*, ed. Joyce Marcus and Judith F. Zeitlin, 143–61. University of Michigan Museum of Anthropology Anthropological Papers No. 89. Ann Arbor: University of Michigan.

Morrison, Kathleen D., and Carla M. Sinopoli. 1992. "Economic Diversity and Integration in a Pre-Colonial Indian Empire." *World Archaeology* 23 (3): 335–52. http://dx.doi.org/10.1080/00438243.1992.9980184.

Orenstein, Henry. 1980. "Asymmetrical Reciprocity: A Contribution to the Theory of Political Legitimacy." *Current Anthropology* 21 (1): 69–91. http://dx.doi.org/10.1086/202402.

Ortiz, Ponciano, and Robert Santley. 1998. "Matacapan: Un ejemplo de enclave teotihuacano en la costa del Golfo." In *Los ritmos de cambio en Teotihuacan: Refelxiones y discusiones de su cronología*, ed. Rosa Brambila and Rubén Cabrera, 377–460. Mexico City: Instituto Nacional de Antropología e Historia.

Paddock, John. 1972. "Distribución de rasgos teotihuacanos en Mesoamerica." In *Teotihuacan: XI Mesa Redonda*, 223–39. Mexico City: Sociedad Mexicana de Antropología.

Paradis, Louise I. 2001. "Guerrero Region." In *Archaeology of Ancient Mexico and Central Mexico*, ed. Susan Toby Evans and David L. Webster, 313–22. New York: Garland.

Parry, William J. 1990. "Postclassic Chipped Stone Tools from the Valley of Oaxaca, Mexico: Indications of Differential Access to Obsidian." In *Nuevos enfoques en el estudio de la lítica*, ed. Maria de los Dolores Soto de Arechavaleta, 331–45. Mexico City: Universidad Autonoma de Mexico.

Parsons, Lee A. 1991. "The Ballgame in the Southern Pacific Cotzumalhuapa Region and Its Impact on Kaminaljuyú during the Middle Classic." In *The Mesoamerican Ballgame*, ed. Vernon L. Scarborough and David R. Wilcox, 190–212. Tucson: University of Arizona Press.

Price, Barbara J. 1978. "Secondary State Formation: An Explanatory Model." In *Origins of the State*, ed. Ronald Cohen and Elman R. Service, 161–86. Philadelphia: Institute for the Study of Human Issues.

Pye, Mary, and Gerardo Gutiérrez. 2007. "The Pacific Coast Trade Route of Mesoamerica: Iconographic Connections between Guatemala and Guerrero." In *Archaeology, Art, and Ethnogenesis in Mesoamerican Prehistory: Papers in Honor of Gareth W. Lowe*, ed. Lynneth Lowe and Mary Pye, 229–46. Papers of the New World Archaeological Foundation 68. Provo, UT: Brigham Young University.

Redmond, Elsa M. 1983. *A Fuego y Sangre: Early Zapotec Imperialism in the Cuicatlán Cañada, Oaxaca*. University of Michigan Museum of Anthropology Memoirs No. 16. Ann Arbor: University of Michigan.

Redmond, Elsa M., and Charles S. Spencer. 2006. "From Raiding to Conquest: Warfare Strategies and Early State Development in Oaxaca, Mexico." In *The Archaeology of Warfare: Prehistories of Raiding and Conquest*, ed. Elizabeth N. Arkush and Mark W. Allen, 336–93. Gainesville: University Press of Florida.

Renfrew, Colin. 1977. "Alternate Models for Exchange and Spatial Distribution." In *Exchange Systems in Prehistory*, ed. Timothy K. Earle and Jonathon E. Ericson, 71–91. New York: Academic Press.

Renfrew, Colin, J. E. Dixon, and J. R. Cann. 1969. "Further Analysis of Near Eastern Obsidian." *Proceedings of the Prehistoric Society* 34: 319–31.

Rivera Guzmán, Ángel Iván. 2011. "Cerro de la Tortuga: Un sitio arqueológico con iconografía teotihuacana en la región Chatina, Costa de Oaxaca." In *Monte Albán en la encrucijada regional y disciplinaria: Memoria de la quinta Mesa Redonda de Monte Albán*, ed. Nelly M. Robles García and Ángel Rivera Guzmán, 429–44. Mexico City: Instituto Nacional de Antropología e Historia.

Sanders, William T. 1977. "Ethnographic Analogy and the Teotihuacan Horizon Style." In *Teotihuacan and Kaminaljuyú: A Study in Prehistoric Culture Contact*, ed. William T. Sanders and Joseph W. Michels, 397–408. University Park: Pennsylvania State University Press.

Santley, Robert S. 1983. "Obsidian Trade and Teotihuacan Influence in Mesoamerica." In *Highland-Lowland Interaction in Mesoamerica: Interdisciplinary Approaches*, ed. Arthur G. Miller, 69–124. Washington, DC: Dumbarton Oaks.

Santley, Robert S. 1989. "Economic Imperialism, Obsidian Exchange, and Teotihuacan Influence in Mesoamerica." In *La obsidiana en Mesoamerica*, ed. Margarita Gaxiola and John E. Clark, 321–29. Colección Científica No. 176. Mexico City: INAH.

Santley, Robert S. 2004. "What Was Teotihuacan Doing in the Maya Region?" *Journal of Anthropological Research* 60: 379–96.

Santley, Robert S., Janet Kerley, and Ronald R. Kneebone. 1986. "Obsidian Working, Long-Distance Exchange, and the Politico-Economic Organization of Early States in Central Mexico." In *Research in Economic Anthropology* Supplement 2, ed. Barry L. Isaac, 101–32. Greenwich, CT: JAI Press.

Schortman, Edward M. 1989. "Interregional Interaction in Prehistory: The Need for a New Perspective." *American Antiquity* 54 (1): 52–65. http://dx.doi.org/10.2307/281331.

Schortman, Edward M., and Patricia A. Urban. 1987. "Modeling Interregional Interaction in Prehistory." In *Advances in Archaeological Method and Theory*, ed. Michael B. Schiffer, 37–95. New York: Academic Press.

Schortman, Edward M., and Patricia A. Urban. 1994. "Living on the Edge: Core/Periphery Relations in Ancient Southeastern Mesoamerica." *Current Anthropology* 35 (4): 401–30. http://dx.doi.org/10.1086/204293.

Schreiber, Katharina J. 1987. "Conquest and Consolidation: A Comparison of the Wari and Inka Occupations of a Highland Peruvian Valley." *American Antiquity* 52 (2): 266–84. http://dx.doi.org/10.2307/281780.

Schreiber, Katharina J. 1999. "Regional Approaches to the Study of Prehistoric Empires." In *Settlement Pattern Studies in the Americas: Fifty Years since Virú*, ed. Brian R. Billman and Gary M. Feinman, 160–71. Washington, DC: Smithsonian Institution.

Sherman, R. Jason, Andrew K. Balkansky, Charles S. Spencer, and Brian D. Nicholls. 2010. "The Expansionary Dynamics of the Nascent Monte Albán State." *Journal of Anthropological Archaeology* 29 (3): 278–301. http://dx.doi.org/10.1016/j.jaa.2010.04.001.

Sinopoli, Carla M. 1994. "The Archaeology of Empires." *Annual Review of Anthropology* 23 (1): 159–80. http://dx.doi.org/10.1146/annurev.an.23.100194.001111.

Smith, Michael. 1987. "The Expansion of the Aztec Empire." *American Anthropologist* 88: 70–91. http://dx.doi.org/10.1525/aa.1986.88.1.02a00050.

Smith, Michael. 1990. "Long-Distance Trade under the Aztec Empire: The Archaeological Evidence." *Ancient Mesoamerica* 1 (2): 153–69. http://dx.doi.org/10.1017/S0956536100000183.

Smith, Michael, and Lisa Montiel. 2001. "The Archaeological Study of Empires and Imperialism in Prehispanic Central Mexico." *Journal of Anthropological Archaeology* 19: 1–40.

Spence, Michael W. 1992. "Tlailotlacan, a Zapotec Enclave in Teotihuacan." In *Art, Ideology, and the City of Teotihuacan*, ed. Janet C. Berlo, 59–88. Washington, DC: Dumbarton Oaks.

Spence, Michael W. 1996. "Commodity or Gift: Teotihuacan Obsidian in the Maya Region." *Latin American Antiquity* 7 (1): 21–39. http://dx.doi.org/10.2307/3537012.

Spencer, Charles S. 1982. *The Cuicatlán Cañada and Monte Albán*. New York: Academic Press.

Spencer, Charles S. 2007. "Territorial Expansion and Primary State Formation in Oaxaca, Mexico." In *Latin American Indigenous Warfare and Ritual Violence*, ed. Richard J. Chacon and Rubén G. Mendoza, 55–72. Tucson: University of Arizona Press.

Spencer, Charles S., and Elsa M. Redmond. 1997. *Archaeology of the Cañada de Cuicatlán, Oaxaca*. New York: American Museum of Natural History.

Spores, Ronald. 1972. *An Archaeological Settlement Survey of the Nochixtlan Valley, Oaxaca*. Vanderbilt University Publications in Anthropology No. 1. Nashville, TN: Vanderbilt University.

Spores, Ronald. 1974. "Marital Alliance in the Political Integration of Mixtec Kingdoms." *American Anthropologist* 76 (2): 297–311. http://dx.doi.org/10.1525/aa.1974.76.2.02a00030.

Spores, Ronald. 1984. *The Mixtecs in Ancient and Colonial Times*. Norman: University of Oklahoma Press.

Spores, Ronald. 1993. "Tututepec: A Postclassic-Period Mixtec Conquest State." *Ancient Mesoamerica* 4 (1): 167–74. http://dx.doi.org/10.1017/S0956536100000845.

Stark, Barbara L. 1989. *Patrata Pottery: Classic Period Ceramics of the South-central Gulf Coast, Veracruz, Mexico*. Anthropological Papers of the University of Arizona Press No. 51. Tucson: University of Arizona Press.

Stark, Barbara L. 1990. "The Gulf Coast and the Central Highlands of Mexico: Alternative Models for Interaction." In *Research in Economic Anthropology*, vol. 12, ed. Barry L. Isaac, 243–85. Greenwich, CT: JAI Press.

Stein, Burton. 1989. *Vijayanagra*. Cambridge: Cambridge University Press. http://dx.doi.org/10.1017/CHOL9780521266932.

Stein, Gil J. 1999. *Rethinking World Systems*. Tucson: University of Arizona Press.

Stein, Gil J. 2002. "From Passive Periphery to Active Agents: Emerging Perspectives in the Archaeology of Interregional Interaction." *American Anthropologist* 104 (3): 903–16. http://dx.doi.org/10.1525/aa.2002.104.3.903.

Stuart, David. 2000. "'The Arrival of Strangers': Teotihuacan and Tollan in Classic Maya History." In *Mesoamerica's Classic Heritage: From Teotihuacan to the Aztecs*, ed. Davíd Carrasco, Lindsay Jones, and Scott Sessions, 465–513. Boulder: University Press of Colorado.

Wallerstein, Immanuel M. 1974. *The Modern World-System*. New York: Academic Press.

Wallrath, Matthew. 1967. *Excavations in the Tehuantepec Region, Mexico*. Transactions of the American Philosophical Society No. 57, Part 2. Philadelphia: American Philosophical Society.

Weitlaner, Roberto J. 1948. "Exploración arqueológica en Guerrero." In *El occidente de Mexico*, 77–85. IV Mesa Redonda de la Sociedad de Antropología Mexicana, Mexico City.

Weitlaner, Roberto J., and Robert H. Barlow. 1944. "Expeditions in Western Guerrero." *Tlalocan* 1: 364–75.

Whittaker, C. R. 1994. *Frontiers of the Roman Empire*. Baltimore: Johns Hopkins University Press.

Winter, Marcus. 1989. *Oaxaca: The Archaeological Record*. Mexico City: Minutiae Mexicana.

Workinger, Andrew. 1999. "Highland/Lowland Interaction in Oaxaca: Preliminary Findings from San Francisco de Arriba." Paper presented at the 64th Annual Meeting of the Society for American Archaeology, Chicago.

Workinger, Andrew. 2001. "Obsidian and Trade at San Francisco de Arriba, Oaxaca, Mexico." Paper presented at the 66th Annual Meeting of the Society for American Archaeology, New Orleans.

Workinger, Andrew. 2002a. *Coastal/Highland Interaction in Prehispanic Oaxaca: The Perspective from San Francisco de Arriba*. PhD dissertation, Department of Anthropology, Vanderbilt University, Nashville, TN. Ann Arbor, MI: University Microfilms.

Workinger, Andrew. 2002b. "Surface Survey in the Río San Francisco Valley." Paper presented at the 67th Annual Meeting of the Society for American Archaeology, Denver.

Workinger, Andrew, and Arthur A. Joyce. 1997. "The Boundary Implications of San Francisco de Arriba: Preliminary Observations." Paper presented at the 62nd Annual Meeting of the Society for American Archaeology, Nashville, TN.

Workinger, Andrew, and Arthur A. Joyce. 2009. "Reconsidering Warfare in Formative Period Oaxaca." In *Blood and Beauty: Organized Violence in the Art and Archaeology of Mesoamerica and Central America*, ed. Heather Orr and Rex Koontz, 3–38. Los Angeles: Cotsen Institute of Archaeology at UCLA.

Zeitlin, Robert N. 1979. *Prehistoric Long-Distance Exchange on the Southern Isthmus of Tehuantepec, Mexico*. PhD dissertation, Department of Anthropology, Yale University, New Haven, CT. Ann Arbor, MI: University Microfilms.

Zeitlin, Robert N. 1990. "The Isthmus and the Valley of Oaxaca: Questions about Zapotec Imperialism in Formative Period Mesoamerica." *American Antiquity* 55 (2): 250–61. http://dx.doi.org/10.2307/281646.

Zeitlin, Robert N. 1993. "Pacific Coastal Laguna Zope: A Regional Center in the Terminal Formative Hinterlands of Monte Albán." *Ancient Mesoamerica* 4: 85–101. http://dx.doi.org/10.1017/S0956536100000808.

Zeitlin, Robert N., and Arthur A. Joyce. 1999. "The Zapotec-Imperialism Argument: Insights from the Oaxaca Coast." *Current Anthropology* 40 (3): 383–92. http://dx.doi.org/10.1086/200029.

EXAMINING CERAMIC EVIDENCE FOR THE ZAPOTEC IMPERIALISM HYPOTHESIS IN THE LOWER RÍO VERDE REGION OF OAXACA, MEXICO

MARC N. LEVINE

Monte Albán emerged as one of Mesoamerica's first urban societies and a regional center in Oaxaca during the Late/Terminal Formative periods (Blanton 1978; Blanton et al. 1999; Flannery and Marcus 1983; Joyce 2000; Joyce and Winter 1996; Marcus and Flannery 1996; Winter 1989). Scholars have proposed that at this time, during the Pe (300–100 BC) and Nisa (100 BC–AD 200) phases, the Zapotecs undertook an imperial program of expansion to bring hinterland communities under their power (Marcus and Flannery 1996). Whether by colonization, negotiated takeover, or outright conquest, the goal was the same: to increase the frequency and variety of tribute goods flowing to Monte Albán. This argument, referred to as the Zapotec Imperialism Hypothesis (ZIH), has broad ramifications for the interpretation of the early development of Monte Albán and, by extension, Formative period contexts throughout Oaxaca (Zeitlin and Joyce 1999). Among the regions claimed to have been conquered by the Zapotecs, the lower Río Verde region of coastal Oaxaca is of primary interest here (Figure 1.1).

Proponents of the ZIH draw heavily on ceramic evidence to make their case. Marcus and Flannery (1996, 199) write that "the spread of Monte Albán II pottery . . . is one of our best lines of

DOI: 10.5876/9781607322023.c08

circumstantial evidence for the expansion of the Zapotec . . . what we are talk-ing about are those regions whose previously autonomous ceramics are liter-ally swamped or replaced by Monte Albán gray wares." The lower Río Verde region is listed as one of these areas where changes in local pottery indicate conquest by Monte Albán. To evaluate this claim, I carried out a detailed analy-sis of stylistic change and continuity in lower Río Verde ceramics dating to the periods just before and following the hypothesized Zapotec conquest. I pres-ent the results of the ceramic analysis below and argue that lower Río Verde graywares cannot be directly linked to Monte Albán, but instead represent a regionally distinct variety of a grayware style found throughout Oaxaca. In addition to a critical analysis of lower Río Verde graywares, I consider other characteristics of the ceramic assemblage, such as patterns of exchange, which might bear on the question of a possible Zapotec takeover. This chapter seeks to address only the ceramic evidence offered in support of the ZIH, whereas critical discussions of other archaeological evidence from the lower Río Verde region appear elsewhere (e.g., Joyce 1991a, 1991b, 1993a, 2003; Workinger 2002, Chapter 7; Workinger and Joyce 2009; Zeitlin and Joyce 1999). Having found little ceramic evidence in support of the ZIH, I provide an alternative explana-tion for the adoption of grayware pottery in the lower Verde region. In contrast to the more passive view of graywares representing mere signifiers of conquest, I consider these vessels in a more active sense, as having important roles within larger practices affirming conceptions of local identity and broader social affiliations.

Most researchers agree that multiple lines of archaeological evidence, rather than ceramic data alone, are necessary to build strong cases for con-quest in the ancient world (Schreiber 1987; Smith and Montiel 2001; Stark 1990). Nonetheless, ceramics remain an important data set that provide clues regard-ing the nature of interpolity relationships, including evidence for conquest and colonization (e.g., Ball 1983; Foias and Bishop 1997; Hegmon 1994; Smyth 2009; Stark 1990). This chapter demonstrates, however, that casual appraisals of ceramic data will not do; only detailed studies of ceramics provide the ana-lytical rigor and resolution needed to adequately consider implications for con-quest in the archaeological record.

THE ZAPOTEC IMPERIALISM HYPOTHESIS (ZIH)

The most complete articulation of the ZIH appears in Marcus and Flannery's (1996) *Zapotec Civilization: How Urban Society Evolved in Mexico's Oaxaca Valley* (also see earlier iterations and references to the ZIH in Blanton et al. [1982]; Flannery and Marcus [1983]; Marcus [1976, 1983, 1992]; Kowalewski et al. [1989]; Redmond and Spencer [1983]; Redmond [1983]; and Spencer [1982]). In *Zapotec Civilization* Marcus and Flannery argue that Monte Albán's development as a regional power was intertwined with a strategy of territorial expansion. Iconographic support for the ZIH comes from the interpretation of more than forty carved stones or "conquest slabs" embedded in the exterior of Building J, located at the southern end of Monte Albán's Main Plaza. Following Alfonso Caso (1938), Marcus (1976, 130; 1983, 108; Marcus and Flannery 1996, 195–207) argues that the Building J inscriptions include the place-name glyphs of Monte Albán's vanquished rivals. Based on comparisons with place-names appearing on Aztec tribute lists from more than a millennium later, Marcus links the glyphs with specific areas of Formative Oaxaca that were either conquered or colonized by Monte Albán. Justification for the ZIH also relies heavily on interpretations of ceramic data; particularly the diffusion of grayware pottery during the Late/Terminal Formative, viewed as largely coeval with the march of Zapotec imperial expansion (Marcus and Flannery 1996, 199). Why grayware pottery, as opposed to other types, should serve as a barometer for Monte Albán's influence is not fully explained. Furthermore, grayware production dates back to the San José phase (1150–850 BC) in the Valley of Oaxaca, centuries prior to the establishment of Monte Albán (Flannery and Marcus 1994).

Marcus and Flannery (1996, 199–205) argue that Monte Albán, having consolidated power in the Valley of Oaxaca, conquered or colonized several areas of Oaxaca, including the "Tututepec region" (located in the lower Río Verde region), Ocelotepec, Peñoles, Sosola, Cañada de Cuicatlán, and the valleys of Miahuatlán, Nejapa, and Ejutla (Figure 1.1). Interregional expansion is presented as key to understanding Monte Albán's transformation from a chiefdom to a state-level society and similar to analogous processes among emergent states in Mesoamerica and throughout the world (Marcus and Flannery 1996, 195; Redmond and Spencer 2006; Spencer 2010).

Archaeological research in the Cañada de Cuicatlán (Redmond 1983; Spencer and Redmond 1997, 2001), Sola Valley (Balkansky 2002), and Ejutla Valley (Feinman and Nicholas 1990) has generated some evidence for Zapotec expansion, conquest, and/or colonization.[1] Perhaps the best archaeological evidence for conquest comes from the Cañada de Cuicatlán, located north of the Valley of Oaxaca. Concurrent with the purported Zapotec incursion is evidence for a shift in settlement to more defensible piedmont areas, a proliferation of local ceramic types mirroring those of Monte Albán, evidence of warfare at a handful of sites (e.g., Llano Perdido), and a possible Zapotec garrison at Quiotepec (but see Workinger 2002, 381–383; Workinger and Joyce 2009, 17–18; Urcid 1994).

Monte Albán's hypothetical conquest of the lower Río Verde region hinges on Marcus's (1983, 108) identification of the place-name appearing on Lápida 57, one of the Building J conquest slabs. Based on its resemblance to an Aztec place-name from the Codex Mendoza, Marcus argues that Lápida 57 should be read as "hill of the bird." She then links this stone with a hill located in the lower Río Verde region and within the Late Postclassic settlement of Tututepec, also known as "hill of the bird." In a later publication Marcus and Flannery (1996, 201) amend their argument, claiming that Lápida 57 actually refers to the neighboring and earlier site of San Francisco de Arriba, where De Cicco and Brockington (1956) noted the presence of supposed Monte Albán–style pottery. Marcus's methodological approach for deciphering Zapotec place-names, her identification of the "hill of the bird" toponym, and its tenuous link to the lower Río Verde region and San Francisco de Arriba have been critiqued at length elsewhere (see de la Cruz 2011; Workinger 2002, 378–387; Workinger and Joyce 2009, 13–16).

Researchers have devoted much effort to examining Late and Terminal Formative interregional interaction linking the lower Verde with other regions of Oaxaca, particularly the Valley of Oaxaca and Monte Albán (Joyce 1991a, 1991b, 1993a, 2003, Joyce et al. 1998; Workinger 2002; Workinger and Joyce 2009). There is evidence for contact with the Valley of Oaxaca in Late Formative times, but this tapers off in the early Terminal Formative, and there are no clear signs of a Zapotec conquest for either period. Andrew Workinger's (2002, Chapter 7) survey and excavation work at San Francisco de Arriba actively sought evidence for a Zapotec incursion—but found none. In spite of the growing body of archaeological data to the contrary, the contention that Monte Albán conquered part or all of the lower Verde region is common in the extant literature, and ceramic evidence remains at the crux of the argument (e.g., Balkansky 1998, 469–472; 2001, 2002, 95; Redmond and Spencer 2006; Sherman et al. 2010; Spencer 2007; Spencer et al. 2008).

BACKGROUND

Rather than focusing on external influences alone, a thorough examination of how or why graywares were adopted in the lower Verde region requires an engagement with the local archaeological context. In the ceramic chronology of the lower Río Verde region, the Late Formative period correlates with the Minizundo phase (400–150 BC), and the early Terminal Formative is associated with the Miniyua phase (150 BC–AD 100), when graywares were produced locally for the first time (Figure 1.5). Local grayware production implies the adoption of the reduced firing technique, whereby pots were fired in an oxygen-deprived environment to achieve a distinctive gray color. Joyce's (1991a) typology of lower Verde ceramics, including petrographic (Banker and Joyce 1991) and neutron activation analyses (Joyce et al. 2006), created the foundation for more detailed studies of local and imported pottery (also see Workinger 2002). These studies also helped identify foreign ceramic imports and established that Miniyua graywares were local products.

More than two decades of continuous archaeological research in the lower Verde region indicate that the Minizundo to Miniyua phase transition was a time of increasing population growth and sociopolitical development (Joyce 2005, 2010; Chapter 1). During the Minizundo phase, complex polities emerged at Charco Redondo and San Francisco de Arriba (Joyce 1993a, 71–72; 1994, 163; Workinger 2002, 405–406). Both were primary centers atop a three-tiered regional settlement hierarchy (Figure 1.2) and were by far the largest settlements in the region: Charco Redondo measured approximately 70 ha, and San Francisco de Arriba 95 ha (Joyce 1999, 16; Workinger 2002, 248). But by the beginning of the Miniyua phase, there were clear signs of sociopolitical reorganization. The regional settlement hierarchy increased from three to five tiers, and instead of having two regional centers, as was the case earlier, Río Viejo became the singular capital (Joyce 2003). The capital flourished: it grew to 225 ha in the Miniyua phase and by the Chacahua phase a mounded acropolis had been constructed at the site's core (Joyce 2006; Joyce and Barber 2011; Joyce et al., Chapter 5; Levine et al. 2004). The Miniyua phase was also a time of significant demographic growth. Compared with the earlier Minizundo phase, the total number of sites doubled, and the occupational area covered by settlements increased by one third (Joyce 1999, 2003). While Río Viejo participated in networks of exchange with other regions of Oaxaca and beyond, no archaeological evidence suggests that its rise to regional prominence was a direct result of foreign influences. It is within this local context of development and sociopolitical reorganization that we must seek to understand the adoption of graywares in ca. 150 BC.

CERAMIC SAMPLE AND ANALYSIS METHODOLOGY

The ceramic study included three Minizundo and three Miniyua phase samples from excavations at five sites in the lower Verde region (Figures 1.2 and 1.5). The samples were selected from unmixed deposits associated with diagnostic Minizundo or Miniyua sherds. Only rim sherds were included in the study, as undecorated body sherds were previously quantified and discarded (no complete vessels were present). The samples were selected from sites representing different ranks within the lower Verde regional settlement hierarchy to lessen the possibility of bias due to variation in site size or function (Table 8.1). All but one of the samples was drawn from primary midden contexts associated with commoner residences. The exception was a Minizundo phase sample from San Francisco de Arriba consisting of redeposited sherds from house-mound fill, possibly associated with an elite residence (see Levine 2002, 92–106, for a detailed discussion of sample contexts).

I began the analysis by sorting sherds into established paste categories (coarse brownware, fine brownware, and grayware) for the lower Verde region,

TABLE 8.1. Ceramic samples analyzed from the lower Río Verde region

Sample	Site Name	Phase	Rim Sherd Count	Sherd Weight (g)	Site Size[a] (ha)	Site Rank[c]	Source
CR86P2-15	Charco Redondo	Minizundo	241	7358	70	1	Gillespie 1987
SFA99E-13 to 21	San Francisco de Arriba	Minizundo	324	5597	95[b]	1	Workinger 2002, 171
YG0C-13, 14, 16, 17	Yugüe	Minizundo	85	2575	10	2	Barber 2009
YG0B-10 to 12	Yugüe	Miniyua	553	14,467	10	3	Barber 2009
RA0B-14 to 19	Río Antiguo	Miniyua	271	5556	2	4	Barber 2009
RV94B-6 to 14	Río Viejo	Miniyua	628	13,604	225	1	Workinger and Joyce 1999

[a] Data from Joyce (1999), except where noted.
[b] Workinger (2002, 248).
[c] Refers to site ranking within lower Río Verde region settlement hierarchy; information provided by Joyce (personal communication, 2002).

based on the pottery's constituent elements of clay and temper, as well as their alteration during firing (Joyce 1991a, 129–160). Ceramic studies in Oaxaca, following Caso and colleagues (1967), have traditionally used a modal classification system based on paste color, composition, form, and decoration—as opposed to the type/variety system used in other regions of Mesoamerica (see Culbert and Rands 2007). I then sorted the sherds into seven discrete categories based on ceramic paste and vessel form that later served as analogous units for making comparisons. The seven categories included coarse brownware bowls, fine brownware bowls, grayware bowls, grayware composite-silhouette bowls, coarse brownware jars, fine brownware jars, and grayware jars (Figures 8.1–8.11).

I recorded nearly two dozen attributes for each sherd, including metric dimensions, formal characteristics, details of surface treatment, and decoration (Levine 2002, 219–222). These data allowed for synchronic and diachronic comparisons of pottery attributes within and between general vessel categories. These comparisons included a fine-grained assessment of style and production methods, especially taking note of the *chaîne opératoire*, or operational sequence of production steps (Lemmonier 1992, 25–50). This was especially helpful in evaluating how closely lower Verde graywares resembled those from Monte Albán in terms of particular attributes and production techniques. Attention to discrete production steps brought to light a host of relatively unintentional attributes, such as vessel-forming techniques that reflect ingrained "ways of potting" (Costin and Hagstrum 1995, 622; Dietler and Herbich 1998). These attributes are more resistant to change and thus useful in distinguishing distinct potting traditions. The stylistic analysis also included an evaluation of vessel function and context of use.

Based on the ceramic attribute analysis, I also calculated the average production step measure (Feinman 1980; Feinman et al. 1981) for all seven vessel categories, providing an ordinal index of labor investment for each category (see also Levine 2002, 87–92). The labor investment estimates thus facilitated diachronic and synchronic comparisons within and between vessel categories and contributed to broader interpretations of the ceramic data. The following section presents the results of the comparative analysis of Minizundo and Miniyua phase pottery from the lower Río Verde region.

EVALUATING CERAMIC EVIDENCE FOR THE ZIH

Does ceramic data from the lower Verde region support the claim that pottery from this area was "swamped or replaced by Monte Albán graywares," considered a key correlate of Zapotec conquest (Marcus and Flannery 1996, 199)? I address the two constituent parts of this question in turn: (1) did graywares dominate the lower Verde assemblage and (2) were they stylistically linked to Monte Albán?

During the Late Formative Minizundo phase, only imported graywares were available in the lower Verde region, primarily from the Valley of Oaxaca (e.g., types G.12, G.13, G.16, and G.17; Joyce 1991a, 144; Joyce et al. 2006; Workinger 2002, 347–349).[2] But beginning in the early Terminal Formative Miniyua phase, graywares were made locally for the first time and came to represent more than half (61.6%) of the lower Verde ceramic assemblage (Table 8.2). With the commencement of grayware production in the Miniyua phase, there was a sharp drop in the production of coarse brownware pottery (from 63.5% to 18.2%) and a more modest decline in fine brownwares (from 33.8% to 19.8%). Chi-square tests confirm that these were significant changes, as was the decline in the percentage of imported pottery from the Minizundo (2.6%) to Miniyua (0.5%) phases. Thus, graywares indeed became the most popular pottery class in the Miniyua phase, but changes in specific vessel forms and frequencies help to more fully explain this phenomenon.

Miniyua phase graywares were largely comprised of unrestricted bowls, composite-silhouettes, and jars used for serving food or drink (Figures 8.8–8.11). The graywares were not slipped, but nearly all were decorated, most often with incised lines and other designs. Grayware bowls usually had outleaning or outcurving walls as well as rims that also ranged from outleaning to outcurving. Among the bowls, most prevalent was a type similar to the

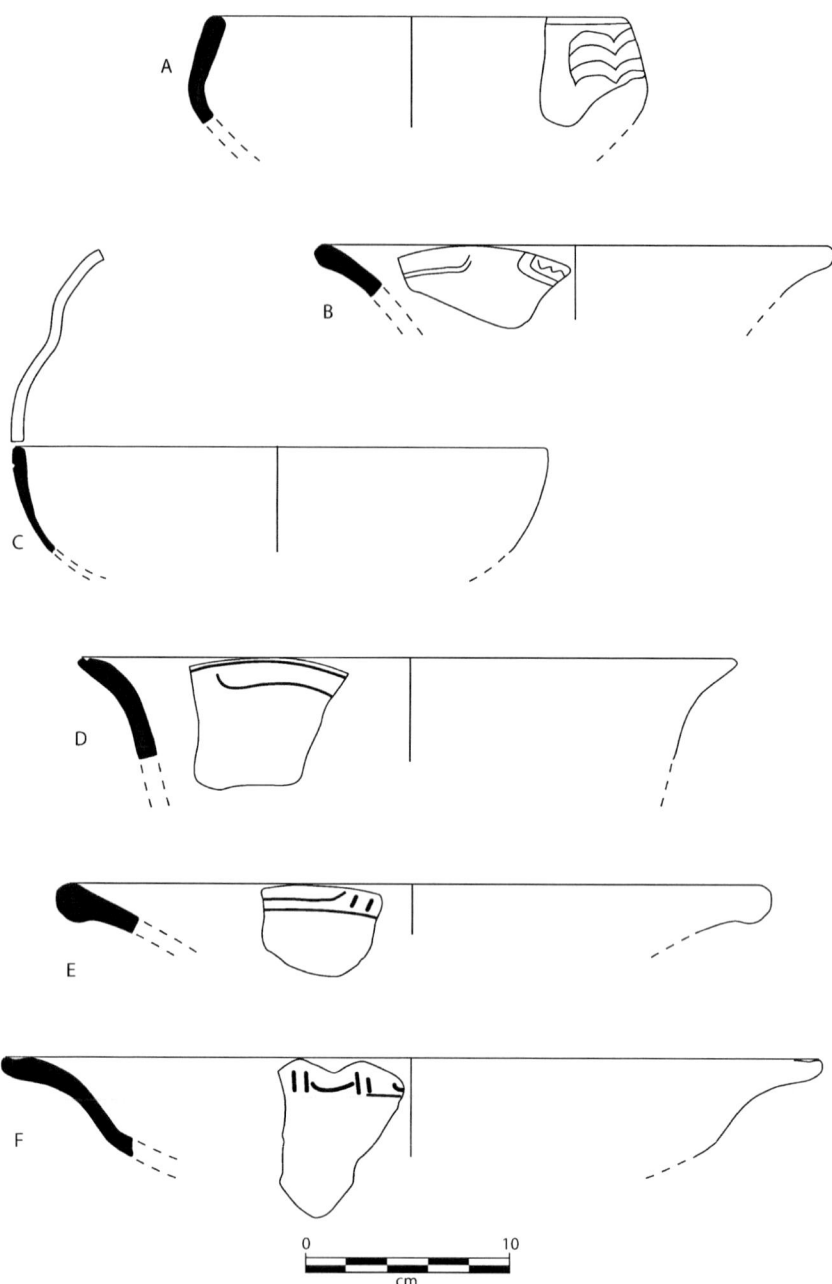

FIGURE 8.1. Minizundo phase fine brownware bowls. *A* and *C* have red slip on rims and exteriors; *B, D,* and *E* have red slip on rims and interiors; *F* is unslipped.

TABLE 8.2. Frequency of ceramic paste types through time in the lower Río Verde region

Paste Type	Minizundo Phase		Miniyua Phase	
	Rim Sherd Count	%	Rim Sherd Count	%
Coarse Brownware	413	63.5	264	18.2
Fine Brownware	220	33.8	287	19.8
Grayware	NA	NA	894	61.6
Other/Imports	17	2.6	7	0.5
Totals	650	99.9	1,452	100.1

highland G.12, a conical bowl with two lines incised on the interior rim and sometimes including a combed base (Caso et al. 1967; see also Feinman et al. 1989; Spencer et al. 2008).

The initial production of grayware bowls in the lower Verde region is associated with a drop (from 62.5% to 2.8%) in the overall proportion of coarse brownware bowls relative to total bowls from the Minizundo to Miniyua phase (Table 8.3). Minizundo coarse brownware bowls represented a diverse group of cooking, food preparation, and decorated serving wares (Figure 8.4). Bowl wall forms were typically outleaning, outcurving, or incurving-divergent, while rims were most often direct and, less often, outcurving or outleaning. The majority of bowls were slipped, red being the most popular color, and exhibited a variety of incised designs. In contrast, the Miniyua phase coarse brownware bowls were mostly utilitarian types with less formal variability and, although they remained slipped, few displayed any incised decoration (Figure 8.5). Thus, Miniyua phase potters continued making the more plain utilitarian types of coarse brownware bowls, but decorated varieties fell out of favor and were supplanted by grayware bowls.

Although the frequency of fine brownware bowls was similar during the Minizundo and Miniyua phases, they underwent significant stylistic changes through time. Minizundo fine brownware bowls were almost always slipped and decorated with incised designs (Figure 8.1). Among the great diversity of vessel forms were unrestricted bowls with outleaning or outcurving walls as well as restricted varieties with incurving walls. Rims were usually direct, outleaning, or outcurving. The Miniyua fine brownware bowls had thinner walls that were usually outleaning and displayed a narrower variety of surface decoration (Figure 8.2). Miniyua bowls typically had one or two lines lightly incised along their interior, akin to the G.12, and often with black and/or red painted rims, although there were no fine brownware examples with combed bases (cf. Figure 8.8b). In Minizundo times, fine brownware bowls were used for light, everyday serving duties and appear to have retained this role in the Miniyua phase, existing alongside more popular grayware bowls. Apart from differences

TABLE 8.3. Frequency of ceramic vessel categories through time in the lower Río Verde region

Bowl Categories	Minizundo Phase		Miniyua Phase	
	Count	%	Count	%
Coarse Brownware Bowls	217	62.5	31	2.8
Fine Brownware Bowls	121	34.9	258	23.7
Fine Brownware Composite Silhouette Bowls	1	0.3	0	0.0
Other Grayware Bowls	0	0.0	596	54.7
Grayware Composite Silhouette Bowls	0	0.0	200	18.3
Other Bowls	8	2.3	5	0.5
Bowl Totals	347	100	1,090	100
Jar Categories				
Coarse Brownware Jars	78	75.7	133	73.9
Fine Brownware Jars	23	22.3	5	2.8
Grayware Jars	0	0.0	41	22.8
Other Jars	2	1.9	1	0.5
Jar Totals	103	99.9	180	100

Note: Frequencies are calculated as a proportion of all rim sherds within the assemblage identified as either a bowl or jar. Comals and other less frequent vessel types were omitted. Sherd weight proportions are presented in Levine (2002).

in decoration and firing, Miniyua fine brownware and grayware bowls were quite similar in other respects (cf. Figures 8.2e and 8.8d). The most common bowls had outleaning walls with exterior thickened, incised rims, scraped and wiped exteriors, and moderately burnished interiors.

Fine brownware composite silhouette bowls were only a small fraction (0.2%) of the overall Minizundo assemblage and disappeared altogether in the Miniyua phase when grayware composite silhouettes became prevalent (13.8% of all rim sherds from bowls). The Miniyua grayware composite silhouettes were highly distinctive, with thin walls (averaging 5 mm thick) including one or two angle breaks and representing a variety of unrestricted and restricted bowl forms (Figures 8.9 and 8.10). Between the vessels' subtle exterior rim and basal flanges, nearly all (98%) displayed complex incised and excised abstract designs. Though decoration was quite variable, a number of motifs appeared repeatedly (e.g., Figure 8.9a–d). Most of the composite silhouettes were quite small; a histogram plot revealed a bimodal distribution with 88 percent of the vessels clustering around 16 cm in diameter, with the remaining minority around 31 cm (see Levine 2002, 148–149). The analysis of production steps

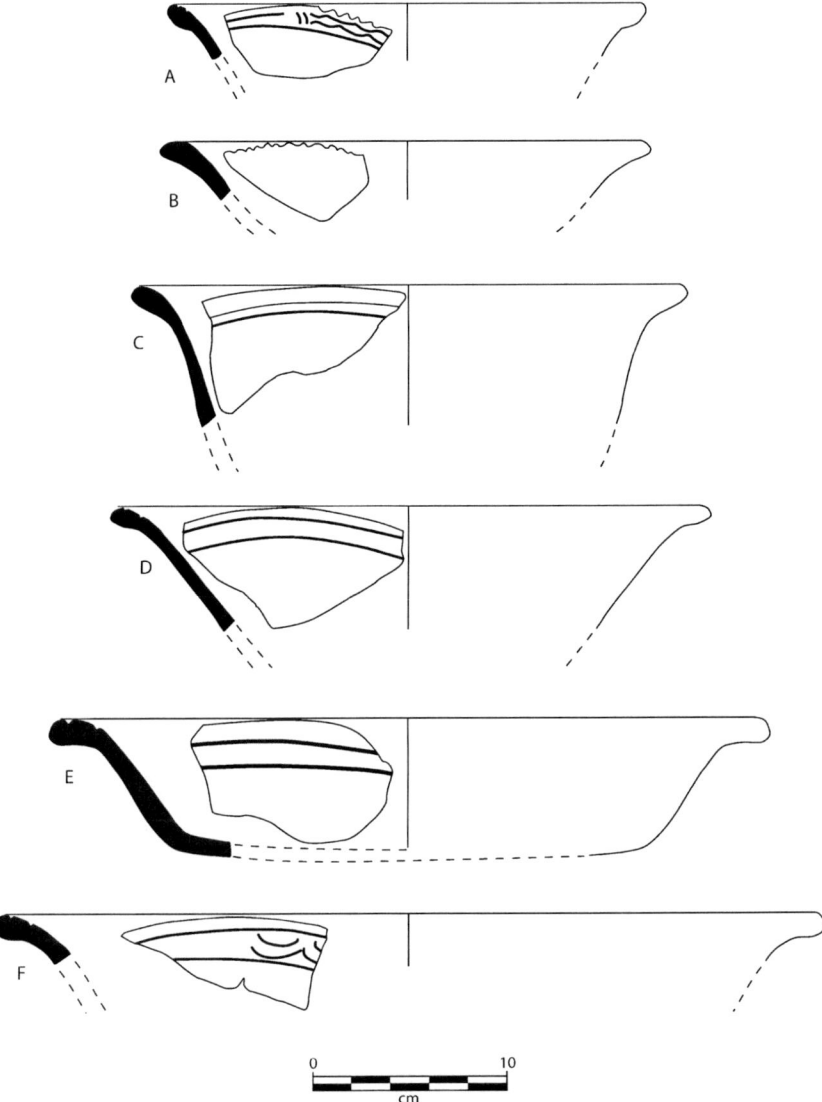

FIGURE 8.2. Miniyua phase fine brownware bowls. *A* has alternating red and black slip on interior rim; *B* has red slip on rim and black slip on interior; *C* and *F* have red slip on rim; *D* is unslipped; and *E* has gray slip on interior.

indicates that composite silhouettes were the most labor intensive of all Miniyua ceramic types (Table 8.4). The size, form, fragility, and decoration of the small composite silhouettes suggest that they served as specialized drinking vessels, likely used in ritual contexts. Furthermore, the fact that

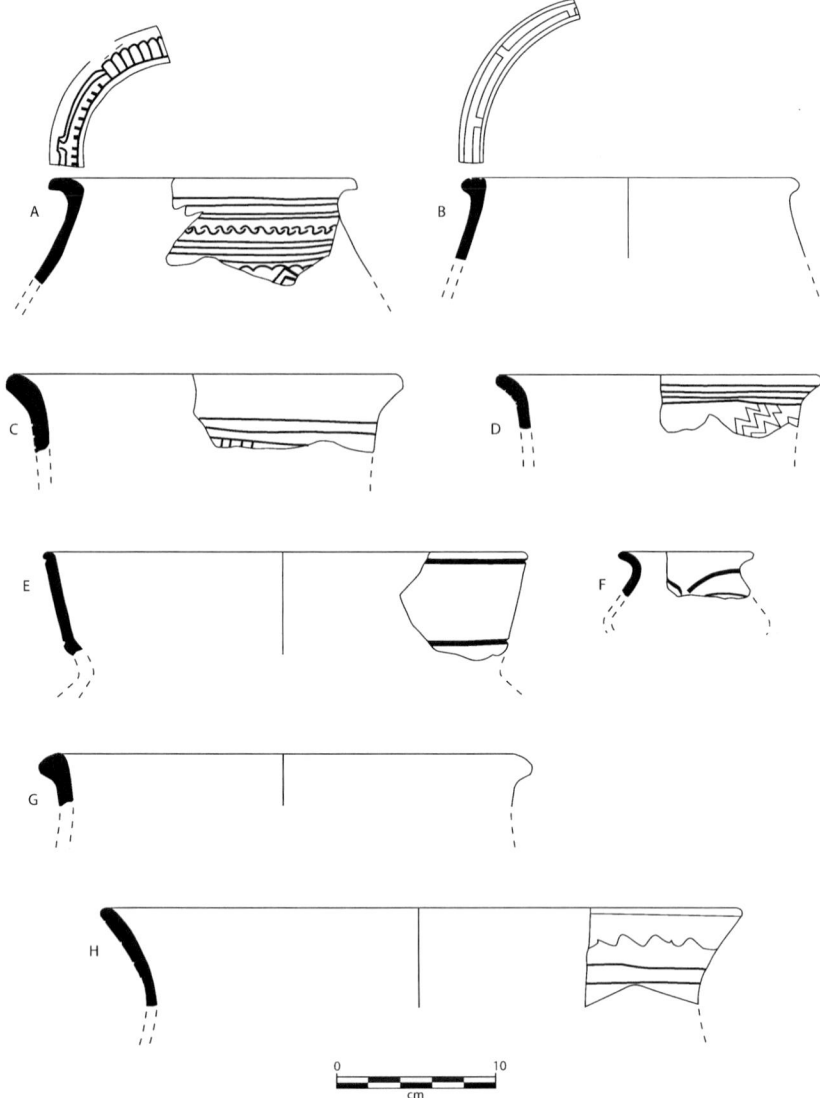

FIGURE 8.3. Minizundo phase fine brownware jars. *A* has black slip on rim and exterior; *B* has red slip on rim and exterior; *C* and *D* have red slip on interior and exterior; *E* has gray slip on rim and exterior; *F*, *G*, and *H* are unslipped.

lower Verde composite silhouettes are much more numerous than similar vessel types from other regions of Terminal Formative Oaxaca (Joyce 1993b, 21) suggests that they played a more active role in social life, perhaps in conjunction with new sets of practices.

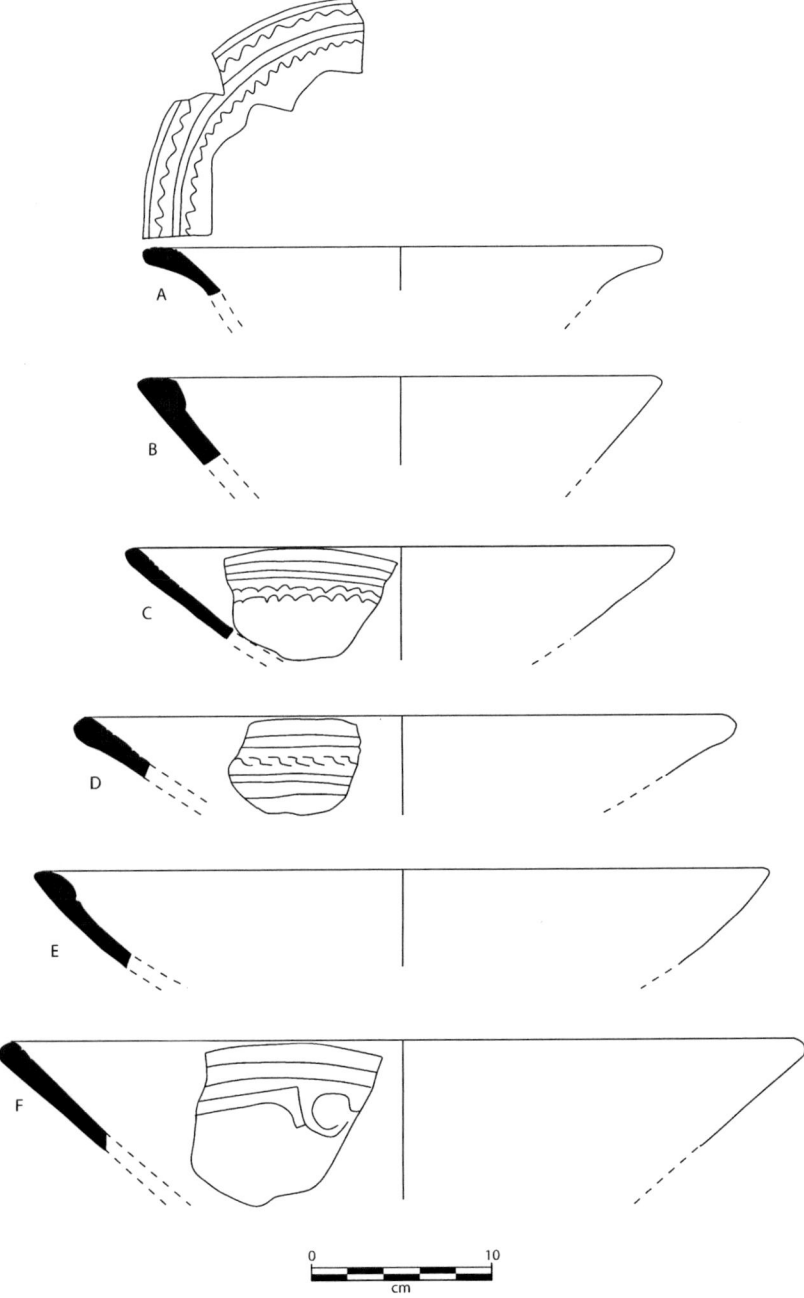

FIGURE 8.4. Minizundo phase coarse brownware bowls. *A* has black slip on rim; *B* has red slip on rim with brown slip on interior and exterior; *C* and *D* are unslipped; *E* has red slip on interior and exterior; *F* has black slip on rim and interior.

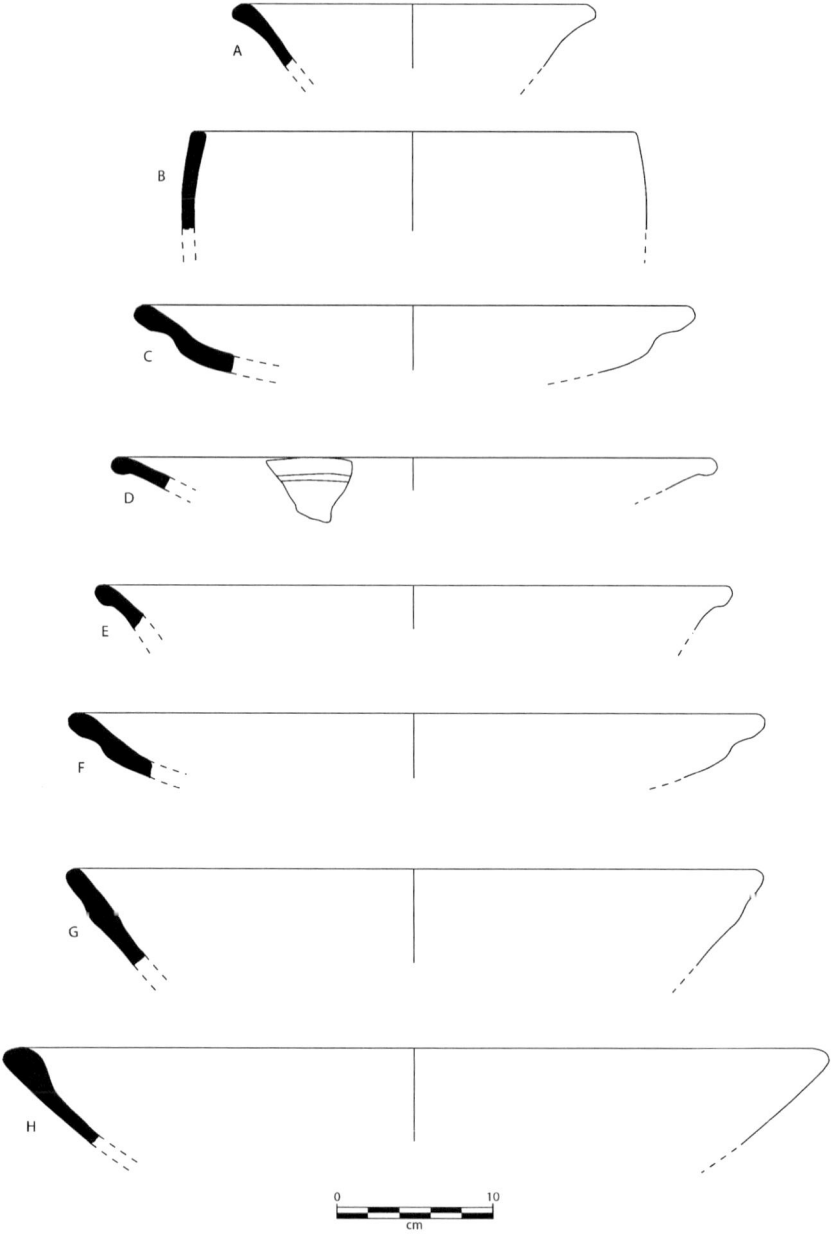

FIGURE 8.5. Miniyua phase coarse brownware bowls. *A* and *H* have red slip on interiors and exteriors; *B*, *D*, and *E* are unslipped; *C* and *F* have black slip on rims; *G* has black slip on rim and interior.

TABLE 8.4. Production step measures for lower Río Verde region ceramics through time

Vessel Category	Minizundo Phase	Miniyua Phase
Coarse Brownware Bowl	3.18	2.9
Fine Brownware Bowl	4.78	5.32
Grayware Composite Silhouette Bowl	NA	5.82
Other Grayware Bowl	NA	5.57
Coarse Brownware Jar	2.68	3.5
Fine Brownware Jar	4.09	4.63
	($n = 16$)	($n = 4$)
Grayware Jar	NA	4.97

Note: PSM for each vessel category is based on a sample of 30 randomly selected rim sherds unless otherwise indicated; adapted from Feinman (1980) and Feinman et al. (1981).

The increase in frequency of grayware jars (from 0% to 22.8%) in the lower Verde ceramic assemblage through time coincided with a decrease in the proportion of fine brownware jars (from 22.3% to 2.8%), suggesting that the former replaced the latter in the Miniyua phase (Table 8.3, Figures 8.3 and 8.11). More than half of the grayware jars displayed incised or excised decorations, and virtually all were burnished. In addition, roughly a quarter of the grayware jars featured small nubbin appliqués, probably both decorative and useful as handles or grips. Overall, the jars represent a relatively high labor investment (Table 8.4) and constitute a regionally distinct type.

The frequency of utilitarian coarse brownware jars remained stable through time, representing roughly three-quarters of all jars in both the Minizundo and Miniyua phases (Table 8.3, Figures 8.6 and 8.7). These thick-walled jars of various sizes would have been ideal for cooking and storage. The coarse brownware jars remained largely consistent stylistically through time. Virtually all of the jars were slipped either red or black on their exteriors during both phases, although slips were applied to the rim in a minority (20%) of the Miniyua phase jars. Less subtle was the shift from exterior thickened rims in the Minizundo phase to hyper-thickened or "bolstered" rims in the Miniyua phase (Figure 8.7h–i). The Miniyua phase coarse brownware jars thus retained traditional characteristics, while adding novel attributes that resulted in a distinctive, if not unique, lower Verde region style.

To summarize, when grayware production began, decorated coarse brownware serving bowl varieties and fine brownware jars were phased out, while fine brownware bowls underwent stylistic changes. In addition, Minizundo fine brownware composite silhouettes were supplanted by grayware varieties, which became increasingly prominent in the Miniyua phase. This analysis indicates that Miniyua phase potters were amenable to change and innovation; they adopted a new paste type (graywares) with its associated

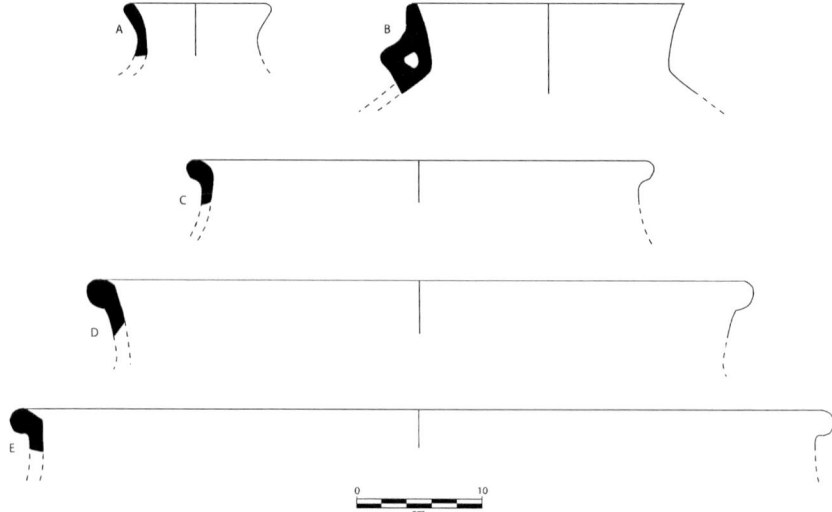

FIGURE 8.6. Minizundo phase coarse brownware jars. *A* has brown slip on interior and exterior; *B, C,* and *E* are unslipped; *D* has brown slip on exterior.

reduce-firing technique, added a limited number of new vessel forms, used new decorative motifs, and modified modes of vessel surface treatment. Even still, these modifications do not represent a clear shift toward greater stylistic affinities with Monte Albán pottery. The ceramic changes from the Minizundo to Miniyua phase is balanced out by a measure of conservatism, with continuity in traditional paste types, vessel forms, surface finishing, and decoration or lack thereof. Thus, the Miniyua phase assemblage is better described as transformed and modified rather than "swamped" by Monte Albán pottery, which would imply wholesale replacement.

Among the Miniyua ceramics, locally made grayware G.12-style bowls and composite silhouettes bear the strongest resemblance to pottery from the Valley of Oaxaca and other regions (Joyce 1993b). For this reason, I discuss these two vessel types in greater detail to determine how similar they really are to Monte Albán pottery types. The distinctive conical G.12 bowls, dubbed by Caso and colleagues (1967, 25–26), appear to have been first developed in the Valley of Oaxaca during the Pe phase (300–100 BC). Richard Blanton and colleagues (1981, 81; 1999, 97–88) contend that G.12s represented an innovation in ceramic production technology—a highly standardized utilitarian bowl manufactured for stackability and easy transport. Shortly after G.12s made their debut at Monte Albán, communities outside the Valley of Oaxaca began to emulate G.12s. Early examples from the Mixteca Alta come from Ramos phase (300 BC–AD 300) deposits at Monte Negro (Caso et al. 1967, 29; Acosta

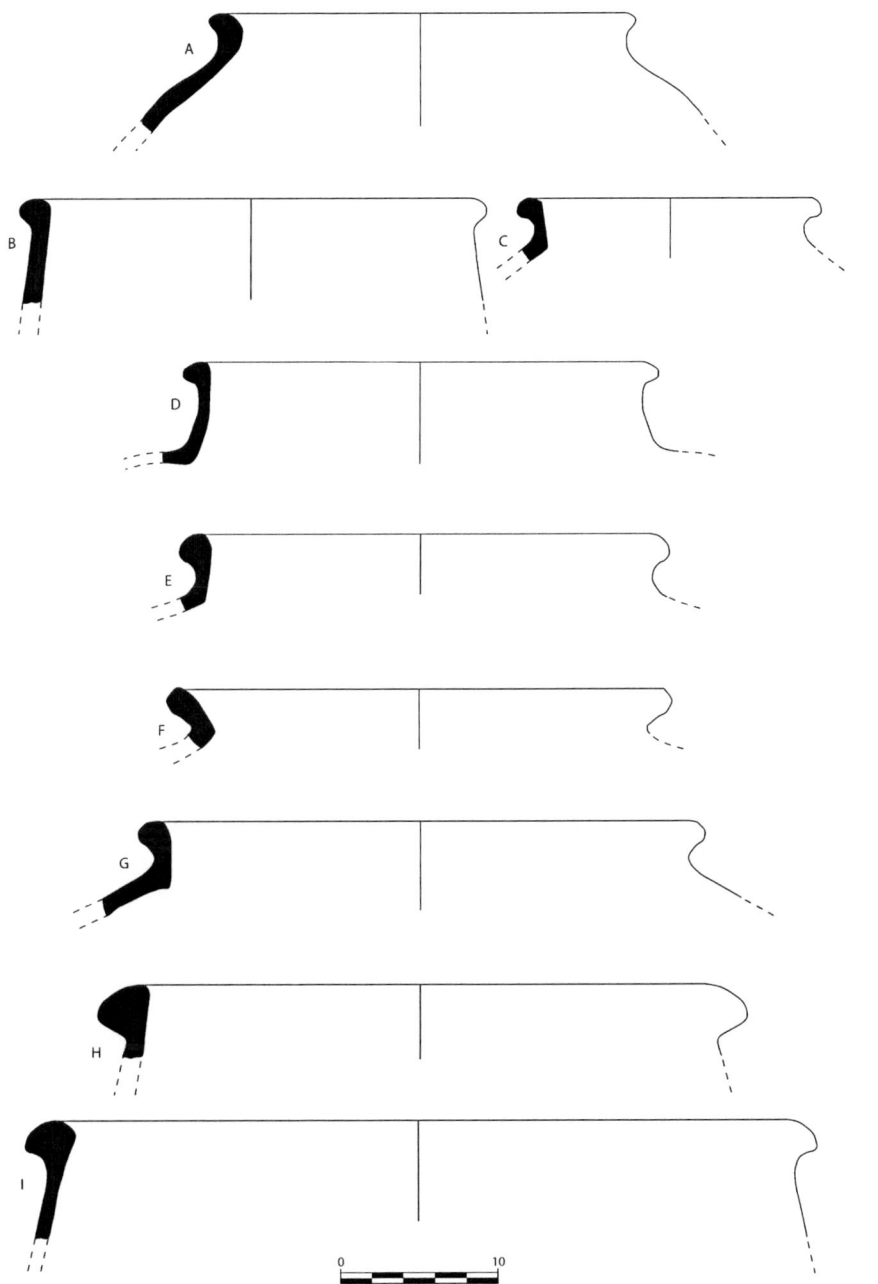

FIGURE 8.7. Miniyua phase coarse brownware jars. *A, E,* and *H* have red slip on rims and exteriors; *B* and *G* have black slip on rims and exteriors; *C* is unslipped; *D* has black slip on rim; *F* has black slip on interior; *I* has brown slip on interior and exterior.

and Romero 1992, 51) and Yucuita (Spores 1983, 121),[3] while others are reported from Huamelulpan period I (400–100 BC) contexts at Huamelulpan (Gaxiola 1984: Figure 18a–c, e). G.12 variants from the Cañada de Cuicatlán area, dating to the Lomas phase (300 BC–AD 200), are nearly identical to those from Monte Albán (Spencer and Redmond 1997, 288–289; 2001, 224). Even farther afield, G.12-style vessels dating to the Ñudee phase (300 BC–AD 300) have been found at Cerro de las Minas in the Mixteca Baja (Winter et al. 1991, 142; Winter 1996, 33). In southern Oaxaca researchers report small numbers of G.12-like bowls from the Isthmus of Tehuantepec dating to ca. 200 BC (Zeitlin 1993: Figure 6, c–d) and much higher quantities from Miniyua phase contexts in the lower Río Verde region (Joyce 1991a).

Joyce's (1993b) comparative study of Late/Terminal Formative ceramics from throughout Oaxaca demonstrates that G.12-style bowls from Monte Albán and the Cañada de Cuicatlán were very similar, but those from the Mixteca Baja, Mixteca Alta, Isthmus of Tehuantepec, and lower Verde regions retained regional distinctions. The study also reveals that graywares had diffused throughout much of Oaxaca prior to their adoption in the lower Verde region. Thus, it is not a foregone conclusion that graywares reached the coast directly from Monte Albán, as opposed to other areas. Ceramic sourcing studies by Joyce and colleagues (2006) provide additional confirmation that graywares were made locally in the lower Verde region, Valley of Oaxaca, and Mixteca Alta. By the Miniyua phase, virtually all of the graywares in the lower Río Verde region were made locally.

Compared with G.12s from the Valley of Oaxaca, the lower Verde varieties are distinct in form, decoration, and surface treatment. The lower Verde G.12s have thinner walls that are outleaning or outcurving, rims that are thickened and outcurving (versus direct rims in the Valley of Oaxaca), and bases that are more rounded, as opposed to flat (Figure 8.12). The incised lines below the interior rim are also finer and shallower in comparison with the lines on the Monte Albán G.12s. In addition, lower Verde G.12 interior surfaces are only moderately burnished, and exteriors are typically wiped and unburnished. This contrasts with Monte Albán G.12s, which are well burnished, resulting in a waxy appearance. The lower Verde G.12s were also less dense and lighter in weight, probably due to differences in paste composition and lower firing temperatures.

Elements of the form, decoration, paste, and surface treatment of lower Verde G.12s reflect local "ways of potting," with attributes paralleling earlier Minizundo phase vessels and contemporaneous Miniyua phase types (Levine 2002, 166–167). For instance, lower Verde G.12s exhibit outleaning walls and exterior thickened rims, common among earlier Minizundo fine brownware bowls. Lower Verde G.12s and Miniyua fine brownware bowls both have exteriors that were scraped, wiped, occasionally smoothed, and less commonly

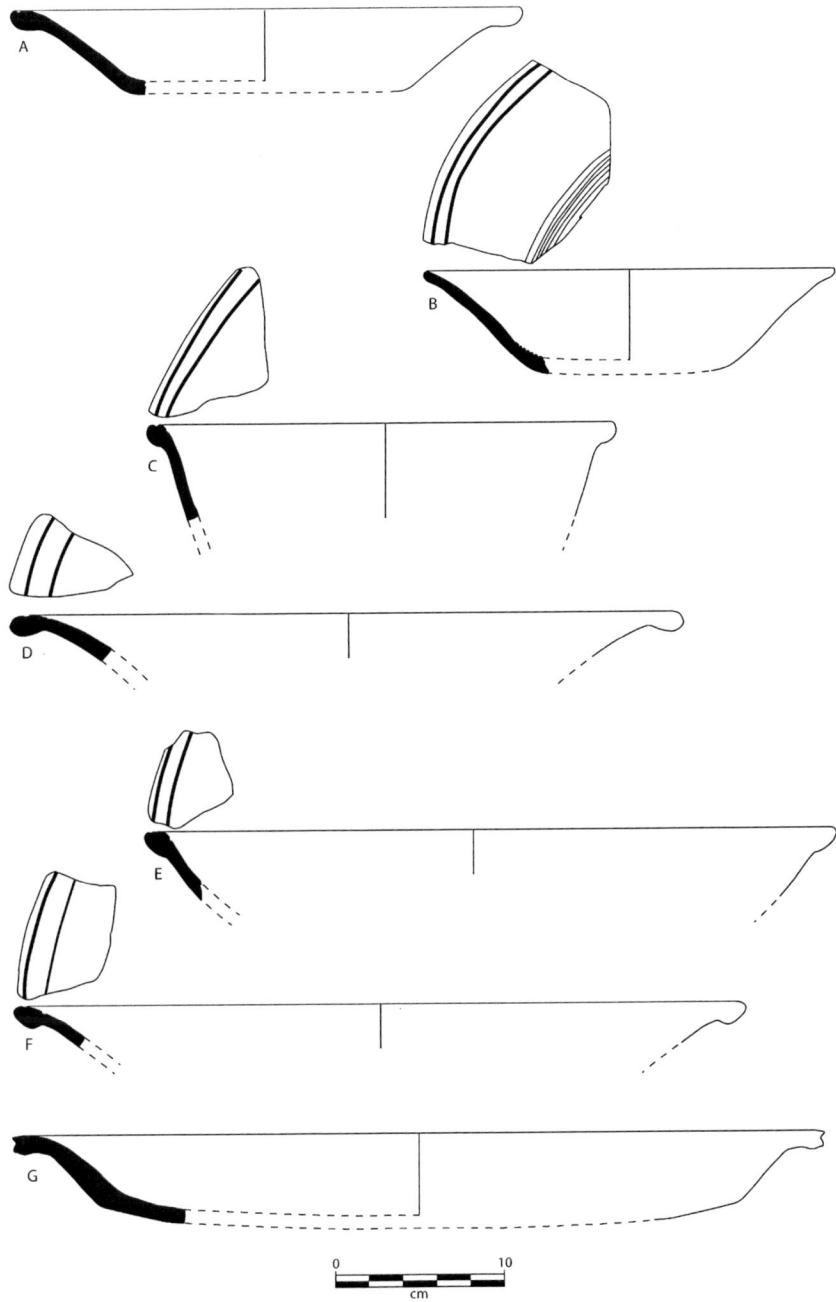

FIGURE 8.8. Miniyua phase G.12-style grayware bowls. *A* has one incised line on interior; *B* has two incised lines on interior and a combed base; *C–F* have two incised lines on interior; *G* has no incised lines, but a grooved rim.

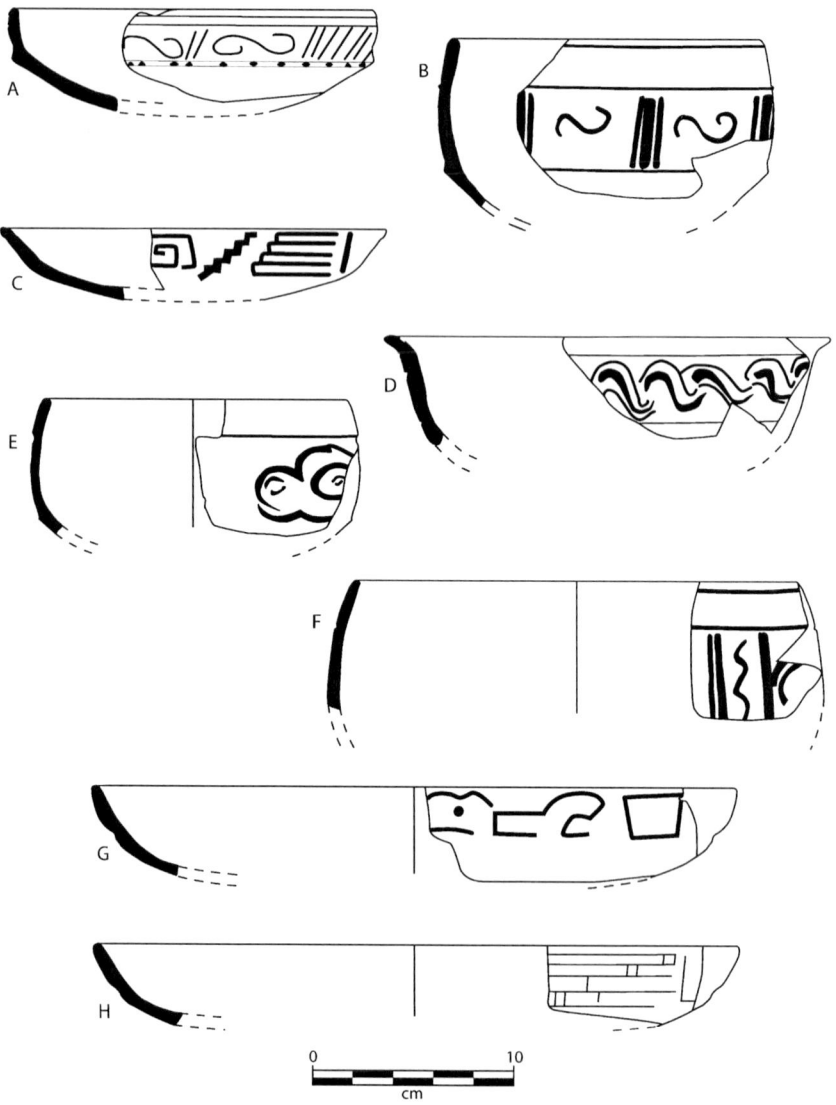

FIGURE 8.9. Miniyua phase grayware composite silhouette bowls. The vessel diameters are as follows: *A*, 18 cm; *B* and *E*, 15 cm; *C*, 19 cm; *D* and *F*, 22 cm; *G* and *H*, 32 cm.

burnished. If the Zapotecs had conquered or colonized the lower Verde region and brought grayware ceramics, Miniyua phase G.12s should more closely resemble those from Monte Albán. Instead, lower Verde G.12s represent the melding of a foreign style with local traditions. But to be clear, this foreign style cannot be attributed to Zapotec influence, as lower Verde region G.12s bear no

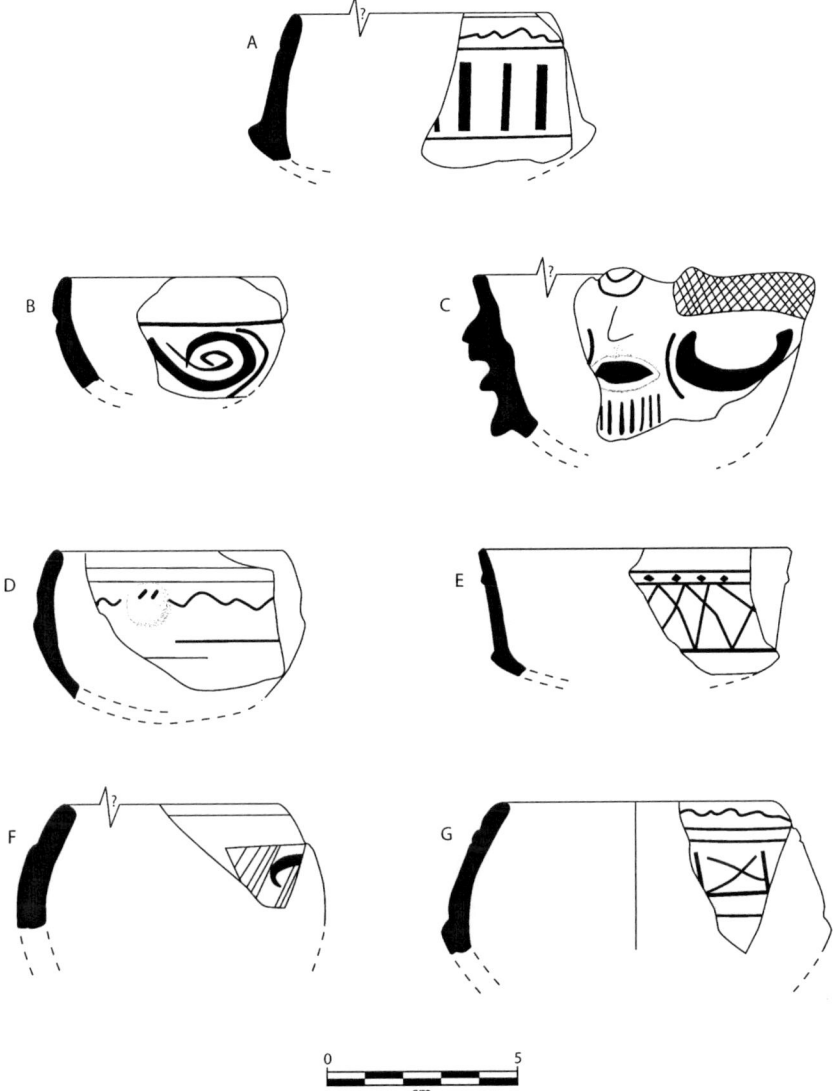

FIGURE 8.10. Miniyua phase grayware composite silhouette bowls.

stronger resemblance to those from Monte Albán than they do to G.12s from other regions of Oaxaca, including the Mixteca Alta, Mixteca Baja, Isthmus of Tehuantepec, and Cañada de Cuicatlán (Joyce 1993b).

Lower Verde grayware composite silhouettes also exhibit a modicum of stylistic crossties with pottery from other regions of Oaxaca, but the strongest connections are with the Mixteca Alta and Baja, not Monte Albán (Joyce

247

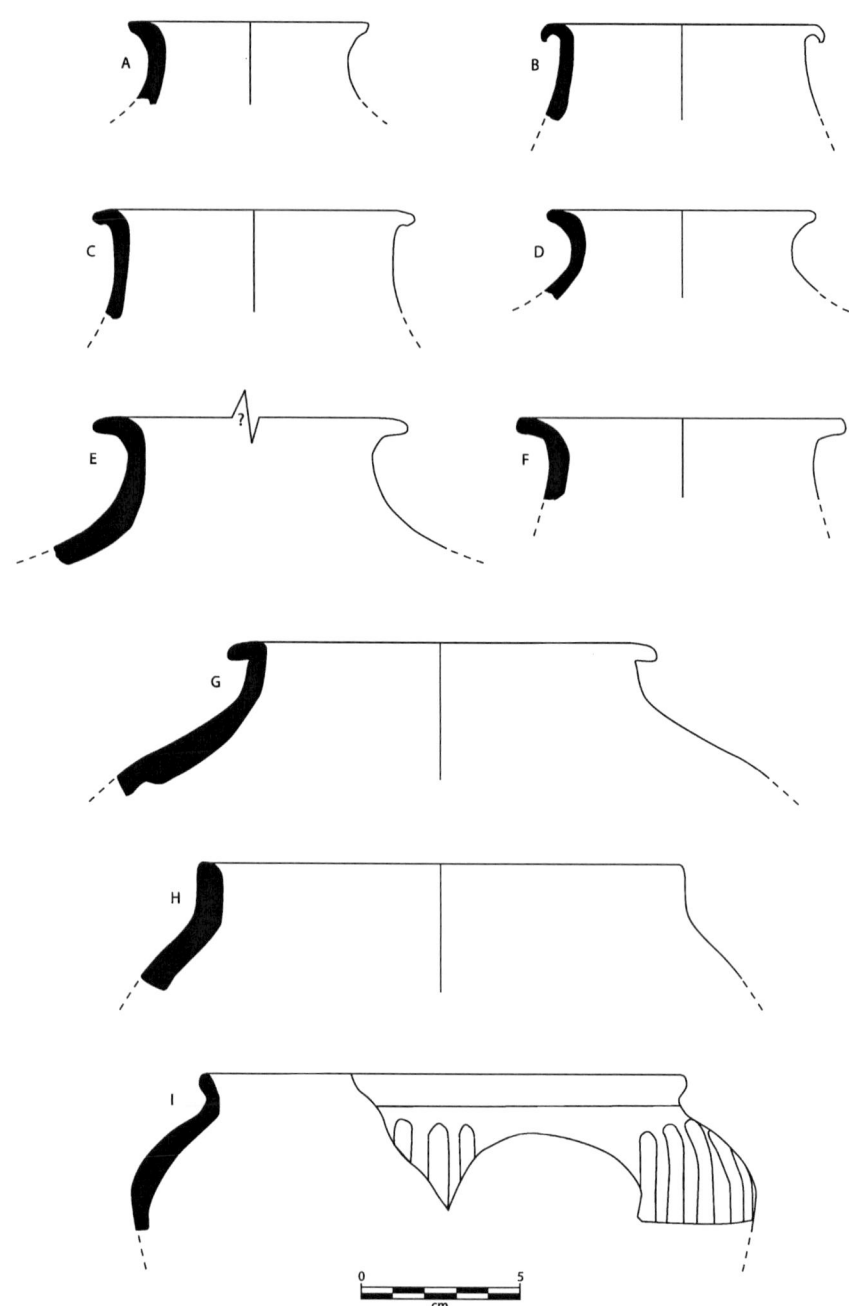

FIGURE 8.11. Miniyua phase grayware jars.

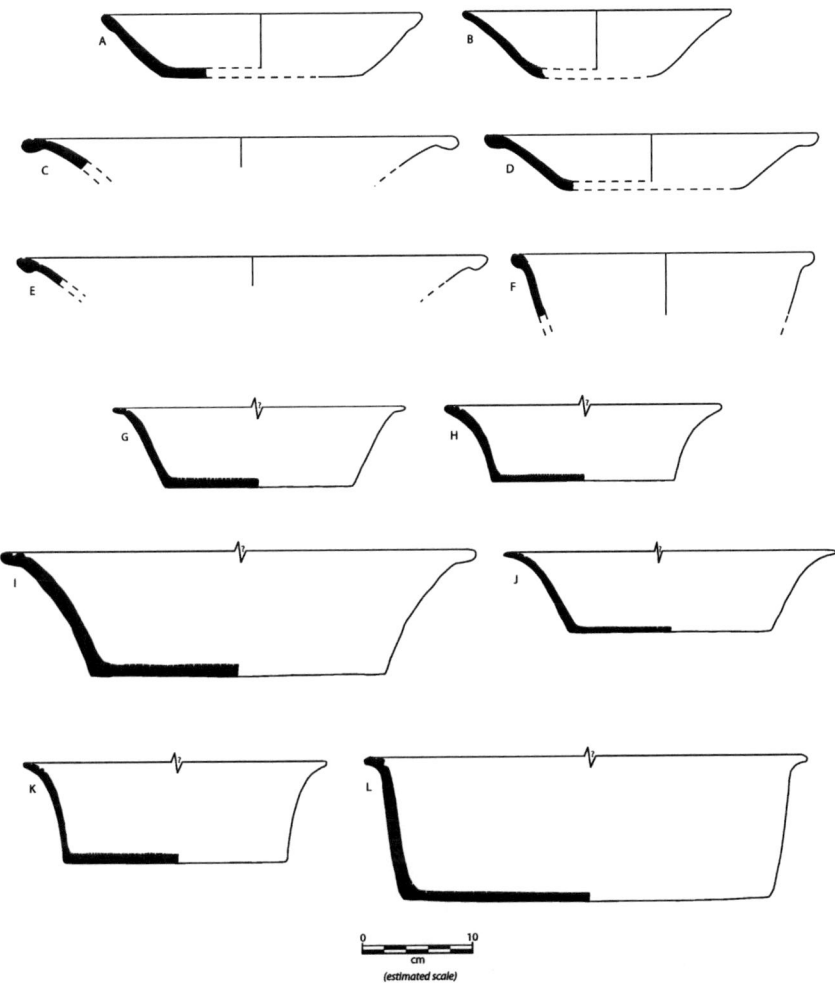

FIGURE 8.12. G.12-style grayware bowls from the lower Río Verde region (*A–F*) and Monte Albán (*G–L*). Monte Albán G.12s redrawn and modified from Caso et al. (1967: Figuras 130 and 131).

1993b). The lower Verde region and highland Mixtec area composite silhouettes overlap most clearly in terms of wall thickness, wall form, and incised decoration (cf. Gaxiola 1984, 32, Figura 20e–g; also see Joyce 1993b, 21–22). Stylistic similarities notwithstanding, the lower Verde composite silhouettes remain highly distinct, most clearly visible in their variety of incised and excised decoration. In comparison with the more sparingly decorated composite silhouettes from Monte Albán (Caso et al. 1967: Figura 128), nearly all of the lower Verde varieties are decorated and include more complex designs.

Furthermore, the higher frequency of composite silhouette bowls in the lower Verde region indicates that these vessels were used to a far greater degree than in other regions.

The ceramic analysis demonstrates that locally made graywares were very common in the lower Verde region during the Miniyua phase, but were not identical to those of Monte Albán and thus cannot be linked directly to the Zapotec capital. Having discredited the grayware ceramic evidence offered in support of the ZIH, I evaluate other ceramic evidence that may bear on the question of a Zapotec conquest of the lower Verde region. First, if Monte Albán had conquered or colonized the lower Verde region, it would have presumably led to an increase in the intensity of social, political, and economic interaction between the two areas. Although we cannot assume that conquest inevitably leaves its mark on local ceramic traditions, in cases where it does, there is little reason to believe that stylistic similarities would be limited to one particular paste type (i.e., graywares). In their detailed description of Lomas phase pottery from the Cañada de Cuicatlán, for instance, Spencer and Redmond (1997, 153–191) discuss a number of local grayware and plainware vessels that imitate Nisa phase types (e.g., G.12, G.15, G.17, G.21, G25, G.26, C.6, C.7, and C.11; see Caso et al. 1967). In contrast, only lower Verde G.12s and composite silhouettes exhibit a general resemblance to varieties from other areas of Oaxaca, while the remaining Miniyua phase pottery maintains a distinctive local character. During the Minizundo and Miniyua phases, the use of slip and fine incised decoration on coarse and fine brownware jars and bowls sets this pottery apart from that of other regions. If the Zapotecs had conquered the lower Verde region, why is the ceramic pattern not more like that of the Cañada de Cuicatlán, where a range of local pottery types mimicked those of Monte Albán?

Spencer and colleagues (Sherman et al. 2010; Spencer 2007; Spencer et al. 2008) have more recently argued that the presence of imported Monte Albán creamwares at sites throughout Oaxaca, including the lower Verde region, may reflect the influence of the Zapotec state. They focus on De Cicco and Brockington's (1956) report from a brief surface survey at San Francisco de Arriba alleging strong parallels between a lower Verde pottery paste type and Monte Albán creamwares; but these observations are now recognized as incorrect. Spencer and colleagues overlook more comprehensive studies of lower Río Verde region ceramics that report few if any parallels between local wares and Monte Albán creamwares, whether in paste, form, or decoration (e.g., Joyce 1991a; Banker and Joyce 1991; Joyce et al. 2006; Levine 2002; Workinger 2002). Furthermore, only three Valley of Oaxaca creamware imports have thus far been reported from unmixed deposits excavated in the lower Verde region, far below the quantity reported from the Cañada de Cuicatlán (cf. Spencer et al. 2008, 335; see also Workinger and Joyce 2009, 21).

A comparison of the proportion of Monte Albán imports with that of the lower Verde region before and after the proposed Zapotec conquest is also informative, as ceramic exchange patterns provide an important line of evidence for studying the nature of interregional relations among polities (Stark 1990). Ceramic data must, however, be interpreted with great care, as studies demonstrate that neither the distribution of imports nor copies of imperial pottery can be expected to neatly mark the territory of ancient empires (Schreiber 1992; Smith and Montiel 2001). Nonetheless, in cases where ceramic exchange relationships are documented between two polities prior to conquest, military intervention is expected to engender closer relations, which should lead to a greater frequency of ceramic exchange. Spencer and Redmond's (1997, 140–152) analysis of ceramic material from La Coyotera, located in the Cañada de Cuicatlán, reveals that Monte Albán imports jumped from 2.6 percent of the Perdido phase (750–300 BC) assemblage to 6.8 percent in the subsequent Lomas phase (300 BC–AD 200), when the area was allegedly invaded and subjugated by the Zapotecs (see also Spencer and Redmond 2001, 224). If the lower Río Verde region was conquered, we would expect a similar pattern; yet we see the opposite: Monte Albán imports drop from 1.2 percent of all Minizundo phase rim sherds to only 0.2 percent in the Miniyua phase (Levine 2002, 224). Furthermore, none of the pottery imported to the lower Verde region include types that were arguably most iconic or emblematic of the Zapotec state during the Nisa phase, such as bridge-spout jars or elaborate effigy urns.[4] Joyce (1993a, 2003) argues that Minizundo phase import patterns in the lower Verde region most likely reflect prestige-goods trade among regional elites, while the falloff in exchange with the Valley of Oaxaca during the Miniyua phase could be due to a disruption in trade routes associated with interpolity conflict in highland Oaxaca.

Although the circumstances of Teotihuacan's imperial pursuits differ from those of Monte Albán, Michael Smyth's (2009) study of the "Teotihuacan factor" at sites in northern Yucatan, which examines archaeological evidence for different modes of interaction, provides an instructive framework for assessing ceramic evidence for the ZIH (see also Pool, Chapter 10). Smyth gauges the intensity of Teotihuacan's impact on Acanceh, Chac II, Dzibilchaltun, Oxkintok, and Yaxuna in terms of "influence, interaction, or intrusion." To Smyth (2009, 396–397), evidence for "influence" would indicate a relationship in which one polity has sway over another, but only through indirect means and without force. Mechanisms of influence include down-the-line trade or the diffusion of ideas or styles that are reproduced or emulated by others. "Interaction" connotes more proximal relationships among polities that are mediated through direct contact and often bidirectional. Here traders, emissaries, or pilgrims bearing goods, ideas, and knowledge of specialized foreign technologies facilitate exchange. Smyth's most intensive mode of foreign impact is "intrusion," including all forms of interloping—such as migration, conquest, and colonization. Instances of intrusion may be identifiable in the local context where there are "significant quantities of *all* defined categories of artifacts, architecture, and iconography" from the foreign polity (Smyth 2009, 397). Furthermore, foreign imports and locally made imitations, as well as local adaptations of foreign symbols or iconography, should be found in local elite and commoner contexts. Using Smyth's classification scheme to consider Monte Albán's impact on the lower Verde region in the Miniyua phase, at most the ceramic evidence could be viewed as supporting a relationship of "influence," while there is little to recommend a case for "interaction," and no signs whatsoever for "intrusion." The meager ceramic evidence for Smyth's conception of "influence" includes the small proportion of Valley of Oaxaca imports (0.2%) in the lower Verde region in the Miniyua phase and the limited number of stylistic crossties (G.12s and composite silhouettes) with the Valley of Oaxaca.

The comparative study of Minizundo and Miniyua phase pottery reveals change through time, most notably the adoption of graywares, but also demonstrates overarching continuity in vessel attributes and production techniques. While the lower Río Verde G.12s and composite silhouettes exhibit stylistic crossties with other regions, they retain distinctly local attributes. Miniyua phase G.12s and composite silhouettes appear to be closest stylistically to examples from the Mixteca Alta, not Monte Albán. Supporters of the ZIH continue to stress ceramic evidence for conquest, recently arguing that there are high numbers of Monte Albán creamware imports in the lower Verde region or that local imitations of creamwares were made on the coast. In fact, only a small number of imported creamwares have been recovered, and no Minizundo or Miniyua phase ceramics bear any resemblance to Valley of Oaxaca creamwares. Finally, Monte Albán imports to the lower Río Verde region fell in the Miniyua phase, in contrast to an expected increase in imports if Zapotecs had subjugated the area. This study rejects the ceramic evidence put forth in support of the application of the ZIH to the lower Río Verde region. Below I provide an alternative explanation for the appearance of grayware pottery at the onset of the Miniyua phase ca. 150 BC.

BEYOND ZAPOTEC IMPERIALISM

The ZIH fails to consider how local dynamics may have figured in the adoption of grayware pottery in the lower Verde region. For instance, how does this shift in pottery production articulate with archaeological evidence for sociopolitical or economic changes during the Minizundo to Miniyua phase transition? While the ZIH treats graywares as passive correlates for the inexorable march of Zapotec expansion, here they are considered as playing an active role in household practices that were implicated in larger processes of identity formation at the local and interregional scales and whose initial production coincided with the establishment of a new regional capital at Río Viejo in the Miniyua phase.

The assumption that grayware pottery was imposed upon the people of the lower Verde region is highly suspect. Lacking evidence for Zapotec conquest, another scenario is more likely—that lower Verde potters freely adopted graywares. This reasoning resonates with the fact that graywares diffused in advance of the supposed Zapotec conquerors in some areas, and extended far beyond their reach in many other areas. Most Oaxacan populations probably chose to produce graywares willingly because of real or perceived advantages, not because of Zapotec coercion. In terms of graywares' advantages, there is no indication that they had superior performance characteristics, but rather that they provided rewards in some other sociocultural or political realm. These benefits are considered in light of local evidence from the lower Verde region.

The high frequency of graywares found in commoner household contexts demonstrates that they were used with great regularity and that they were available to all (Table 8.1). People continued to use both grayware and fine brownware serving bowls in the Miniyua phase, though their size and form overlapped considerably. This suggests that grayware bowls may have been used in somewhat differentiated serving contexts where distinctive bowls were preferred. Grayware bowls had a smoky gray surface, often with simple incised lines, while fine brownwares had a medium buff color, incised decoration, and often black and/or red slipped rims. Given that only a small number of imported graywares were available in the Minizundo phase, the fact that they became exceedingly common in the Miniyua phase—when they were first produced locally—indicates that they were highly sought after and probably held in higher esteem than more traditional wares. Grayware bowls and composite silhouettes had the highest production step measures among all Miniyua phase vessel categories (Table 8.4), demonstrating that they were indeed labor intensive and further supporting the notion that they were highly valued.

Graywares were probably not initially adopted for their novel appearance, but more likely for their strong links to practices with broad social and political ramifications. Barber and Joyce (2007; Joyce 2008, 2010) argue that the Terminal Formative period in the lower Verde region was a time of increasing social differentiation and political centralization, where elites struggled to negotiate the terms of their relationships with a burgeoning commoner populace. These negotiations crosscut social factions and statuses and were vital components in the construction of a regional political identity (Barber 2005, 304). What is meant by "negotiation" here is the manner in which social groups interact to define their identity, roles, and positions in relation to one another (Joyce 2010, 27–32; Levine 2011). Social negotiation can take place in a literal sense, but archaeological methods are more attuned to identifying discursive contexts of negotiation, such as ritualized practices (e.g., feasts) that served to symbolize, reinforce, and challenge social relations (Dietler 2001). Based on her research at the lower Verde site of Yugüe, Barber (2005, Chapter 6) argues that during the Terminal Formative period, elites and commoners came together during mortuary rituals, feasts, and monument construction projects to express notions of corporate solidarity and common history (see also Barber and Joyce 2007). Used as elements within these larger practices, graywares may have materialized an emergent, shared political identity. A Miniyua phase midden (F46) associated with ritual feasting at Yugüe Substructure 1 included a significant proportion of graywares, although paste and vessel form frequencies are not yet available (Barber 2005, 163). Interestingly, archaeological excavations at several lower Verde sites, including San Francisco de Arriba (Workinger 2002, 191–230), Yugüe (Barber 2005, 162), and Cerro de la Cruz (Joyce 1991a) indicate that grayware vessels were rarely deposited in Miniyua phase caches or burials, although they became more common in the later Chacahua phase (AD 100–250). These patterns suggest that during the Miniyua phase, grayware pottery was most appropriate for integrative practices among the living, as opposed to ritual contexts where communication with supernaturals or ancestors was paramount.

While graywares were used in public contexts that were loci of negotiation among disparate lower Verde social collectivities, they were also found in household contexts, indicating frequent and regular use. In the domestic setting commoners and elites may have "lived" their political identities through regularized practices of eating and food sharing within and perhaps between households (see Hepp and Joyce, Chapter 9), using grayware vessels that cited their social affiliations. Citing a polity-wide social affiliation that crosscut the social spectrum may have promoted a feeling of belonging or sameness during a time of change and uncertainty. As the regional population became more concentrated at Río Viejo in the Miniyua phase, social mechanisms may have emerged to mediate and integrate social factions with alternatively competing and coinciding interests. Barber (2005, 70) notes that regional political identities should be manifest in the archaeological record in symbolically charged materials distributed at the regional scale. Miniyua phase graywares are indeed found across the lower Verde region, and although generally lacking in elaborate iconography, their appearance contrasts sharply with traditional coastal wares and could have provided a clear expression of political identity.

Grayware composite silhouettes may have held a privileged role in practices of social negotiation. Most were relatively small containers, suitable for a single serving of food or drink, most probably the latter. The vessels' exteriors displayed incised and excised decorations, probably having symbolic connotations, although these remain obscure. The decorations include geometric, linear, and curvilinear patterns, while at least one example included the modeled portrait of an adult male or ancestor (Figure 8.10c). Many of the decorative motifs repeat at various sites in the lower Verde region and in contexts spanning much of the Miniyua phase (Levine 2002, 190). This suggests that in most cases the composite silhouette decorations transcended personal expression and more likely referred to larger social affiliations. The composite silhouettes may have been featured prominently in social practices where sharing food and drink served to lubricate interactions characterized by negotiation. Perhaps the composite silhouette was even recognized as part of the necessary "equipment" for such practices. This assessment of the role of composite silhouettes in lower Verde society, however, remains tentative in the absence of more directly supporting archaeological evidence.

The adoption of grayware ceramics may have also played an active role in expressing interregional connections. The sociopolitical reorganization that occurred during the Minizundo to Miniyua phase transition may have spurred lower Verde people to seek new exchange partners or intensify relationships with already established peers. For instance, evidence for decreasing interaction with the Valley of Oaxaca in the Miniyua phase may have encouraged the pursuit of new exchange relationships with regions including the Mixteca Alta, the southern Isthmus of Tehuantepec, and the Basin of Mexico (Joyce et al. 1995, 2006; Workinger 2002). Joyce and Barber (Barber and Joyce 2007; Joyce 2005, 2006, 2008, 2010; Joyce et al., Chapter 5; Joyce and Barber 2011) view the construction of the Mound 1 acropolis at Río Viejo in the Terminal Formative, in part, as an elite strategy to broadcast their clout and expand their influence beyond Río Viejo. The initiation of local grayware production may be seen in a somewhat similar light, as a new expression of lower Verde social identity underscoring connections with exchange partners, but in contrast to the acropolis construction at Río Viejo, the impetus for the adoption of graywares likely came from commoners. Grayware pottery is found in both elite and commoner contexts, and the absence of ceramic workshops in elite residential areas of Río Viejo, along with ethnographic data demonstrating that potters are often low-status individuals, reinforces the assertion that adopting graywares was not a top-down directive from elites. By becoming people who "ate and drank from gray bowls," like many of their peers throughout Oaxaca, lower Verde people could express or perhaps claim a shared heritage that affirmed enduring relations with other groups. Schortman (1989, 56) writes that "changed conditions require novel strategies of interaction and a concomitant reshuffling of identities and their priorities to promote new interaction patterns." In a sense, eating from gray bowls could have been one way for lower Verde people to signal or enact their affiliation with potential exchange partners in other areas of Oaxaca who also ate from gray bowls.

CONCLUSION

This chapter rejects the claim that lower Río Verde graywares are clear imitations of Monte Albán graywares, which has long been cited as a crucial piece of evidence in support of the ZIH. The lower Verde graywares do not replicate those of Monte Albán, but instead incorporate attributes of a nearly pan-Oaxacan Formative period grayware tradition that was then executed in a local style. If anything, the most "international" of the lower Verde graywares, the G.12 style bowls, appear to have the closest stylistic affinities to the Mixteca Alta and Baja rather than the Valley of Oaxaca.

I propose that lower Verde people actively sought out graywares as part of a broader effort to articulate and materialize—in form and practice—a new regional political identity that simultaneously expressed in-group belongingness among lower Verde people and strong connections to other Oaxacan groups who ate and drank from gray bowls. Writ large, the initial diffusion of grayware pottery throughout Oaxaca may be better understood as having been inextricable from the adoption of practices in which they were used. In other words, the spread of grayware pottery had more to do with the acquisition of distinctive ceramics marking particular social practices and signifying social and political affiliations than any simple desire to possess gray-colored pottery. The sweeping distribution of graywares across greater Oaxaca by the end of the Formative period demonstrates that in most cases people actively sought out this type of pottery rather than having it imposed upon them by Monte Albán.

ACKNOWLEDGMENTS

This chapter is an outgrowth of my MA thesis, so I would like to thank my thesis advisor, Art Joyce, and committee members Cathy Cameron and Payson Sheets for their guidance and critical feedback on my earlier work. Financial support for my MA research was provided by a Walker Van Riper Grant (University of Colorado Museum of Natural History), a Beverly Sears Dean's Small Grant (University of Colorado Graduate School), and a grant from the University of Colorado Anthropology Department. I also wrote my MA thesis with support from a National Science Foundation Graduate Research Fellowship. I thank Art Joyce for access to ceramic material from Yugüe, Río Antiguo, and Río Viejo. I also thank Andy Workinger and Susan Gillespie for permission to analyze their pottery samples from San Francisco de Arriba and Charco Redondo, respectively. In Oaxaca, I thank Marcus Winter and the INAH staff at Cuilapan for helping with access to ceramic collections and work space. I also thank Robert Markens and Cira Martínez López for sharing their voluminous knowledge of Oaxacan pottery. A host of people provided helpful comments on earlier drafts of this chapter, including Art Joyce, Stacy Barber, Chip Colwell Chanthaponh, Jamie Forde, Craig Lee, Maxine McBrinn, and two anonymous reviewers.

NOTES

1. While researchers have more recently turned their attention to investigating the nature and timing of Zapotec expansion (cf. Balkansky 2002; Redmond and Spencer 2006; Sherman et al. 2010; Spencer 2007; Spencer et al. 2008), the central tenets of the ZIH remain unchanged.

2. Probable Late Formative grayware imports from the Cañada de Cuicatlán are also reported by Joyce (1991a, 144).

3. Caso and colleagues (1967) refer to these as "G.14s," though they are nearly identical to Valley of Oaxaca G.12s.

4. Within the territory of Teotihuacan, argued by some to have constituted an empire, researchers report the presence of highly distinctive and elaborately crafted ceramic censers that perfectly imitated those of the capital (e.g., Smith and Montiel 2001, 258).

REFERENCES CITED

Acosta, Jorge R., and Javier Romero. 1992. *Exploraciones en Monte Negro, Oaxaca: 1937–1938, 1938–39 y 1939–40*. Mexico City: Instituto Nacional de Antropología e Historia.

Balkansky, Andrew K. 1998. "Origin and Collapse of Complex Societies in Oaxaca (Mexico): Evaluating the Era from 1965 to the Present." *Journal of World Prehistory* 12 (4): 451–93. http://dx.doi.org/10.1023/A:1022870516264.

Balkansky, Andrew K. 2001. "On Emerging Patterns in Oaxaca Archaeology." *Current Anthropology* 42 (4): 559–61. http://dx.doi.org/10.1086/322545.

Balkansky, Andrew K. 2002. *The Sola Valley and the Monte Albán State: A Study of Zapotec Imperial Expansion*. Memoirs of the University of Michigan Museum of Anthropology No. 36. Ann Arbor: University of Michigan.

Ball, Joseph. 1983. Teotihuacan, the Maya, and Ceramic Interchange: A Contextual Perspective. In *Highland-Lowland Interaction in Mesoamerica: Interdisciplinary Approaches*, ed. Arthur G. Miller, 125–43. Washington, DC: Dumbarton Oaks.

Banker, Sherman, and Arthur A. Joyce. 1991. "Petrographic Analysis of Ceramics." In *Formative Period Occupation in the Lower Río Verde Valley, Oaxaca, Mexico: Interregional Interaction and Social Change*, by Arthur A. Joyce, 883–915. PhD dissertation, Department of Anthropology, Rutgers University, New Brunswick, NJ. Ann Arbor, MI: University Microfilms.

Barber, Sarah B. 2005. *Heterogeneity, Identity, and Complexity: Negotiating Status and Authority in Terminal Formative Coastal Oaxaca*. PhD dissertation, Department of Anthropology, University of Colorado, Boulder. Ann Arbor, MI: University Microfilms.

Barber, Sarah B. 2009. Excavaciones de prueba en el valle inferior del Río Verde. In "El Proyecto Río Verde," ed. Arthur A. Joyce and Marc N. Levine, 228–321. Final report submitted to the Consejo de Arqueología, Instituto Nacional de Antropología e Historia, Mexico City.

Barber, Sarah B., and Arthur A. Joyce. 2007. "Polity Produced and Community Consumed: Negotiating Political Centralization through Ritual in the Lower Río Verde Valley Oaxaca." In *Mesoamerican Ritual Economy: Archaeological and Ethnological Perspectives*, ed. E. Christian Wells and Karla L. Davis-Salazar, 221–44. Boulder: University Press of Colorado.

Blanton, Richard E. 1978. *Monte Albán: Settlement Patterns at the Ancient Zapotec Capital*. New York: Academic Press.

Blanton, Richard E., Gary M. Feinman, Stephen A. Kowalewski, and Linda Nicholas. 1999. *Ancient Oaxaca*. Cambridge: Cambridge University Press. http://dx.doi.org/10.1017/CBO9780511607844.

Blanton, Richard E., Stephen A. Kowalewski, Gary Feinman, and Jill Appel. 1982. *Monte Albán's Hinterland Part I: Prehispanic Settlement Patterns of the Central and Southern Parts of the Valley of Oaxaca, Mexico*. Prehistory and Human Ecology of the Valley of Oaxaca, Memoirs of the University of Michigan Museum of Anthropology No. 15. Ann Arbor: University of Michigan.

Blanton, Richard E., Stephen A. Kowalewski, Gary M. Feinman, and Laura M. Finsten. 1981. *Ancient Mesoamerica: A Comparison of Change in Three Regions*. Cambridge: Cambridge University Press.

Caso, Alfonso. 1938. *Exploraciones en Oaxaca, quinta y sexta temporadas 1936–1937*. Publicación 34. Mexico City: Instituto Panamericano de Geografía e Historia.

Caso, Alfonso, Ignacio Bernal, and Jorge R. Acosta. 1967. *La cerámica de Monte Albán*. Memorias del Instituto Nacional de Antropología e Historia 13. Mexico City: INAH.

Costin, Cathy L., and Melissa B. Hagstrum. 1995. "Standardization, Labor Investment, Skill, and the Organization of Ceramic Production in Late Prehispanic Highland Peru." *American Antiquity* 60 (4): 619–39. http://dx.doi.org/10.2307/282046.

Culbert, T. Patrick, and Robert L. Rands. 2007. "Multiple Classifications: An Alternative Approach to the Investigation of Maya Ceramics." *Latin American Antiquity* 18 (2): 181–90. http://dx.doi.org/10.2307/25063103.

De Cicco, Gabriel, and Donald Brockington. 1956. *Reconocimiento arqueológico en el sureste de Oaxaca*. Dirección de Monumentos Prehispánicos Informe No. 6. Mexico City: Instituto Nacional de Antropología e Historia.

De la Cruz, Victor. 2011. "El topónimo de Sola (de Vega) en el edificio J de Monte Albán." Paper presented at the 6th Mesa Redonda de Monte Albán, Oaxaca, Mexico.

Dietler, Michael. 2001. "Theorizing the Feast: Rituals of Consumption, Commensal Politics and Power in African Contexts." In *Feasts: Archaeological and Ethnographic Perspectives on Food, Politics, and Power*, ed. Michael Dietler and Brian Hayden, 65–114. Washington, DC: Smithsonian Institution Press.

Dietler, Michael, and Ingrid Herbich. 1998. "*Habitus*, Techniques, Style: An Integrated Approach to the Social Understanding of Material Culture and Boundaries." In *The Archaeology of Social Boundaries*, ed. Miriam T. Stark, 232–63. Washington: Smithsonian Institution Press.

Feinman, Gary. 1980. *The Relationship between Administrative Organization and Ceramic Production in the Valley of Oaxaca, Mexico*. PhD dissertation, Department of Anthropology, City University of New York, New York. Ann Arbor, MI: University Microfilms.

Feinman, Gary M., Sherman Banker, Reid Cooper, Glen Cook, and Linda Nicholas. 1989. "A Technological Perspective on Changes in the Ancient Oaxacan Grayware Ceramic Tradition: Preliminary Results." *Journal of Field Archaeology* 16 (3): 331–44. http://dx.doi.org/10.2307/529837.

Feinman, Gary M., and Linda M. Nicholas. 1990. "The Margins of the Monte Albán State: Settlement Patterns in the Ejutla Valley, Oaxaca, Mexico." *Latin American Antiquity* 1 (3): 216–46. http://dx.doi.org/10.2307/972162.

Feinman, Gary M., Steadman Upham, and Kent Lightfoot. 1981. "The Production Step Measure: An Ordinal Index of Labor Input in Ceramic Manufacture." *American Antiquity* 46 (4): 871–84. http://dx.doi.org/10.2307/280113.

Flannery, Kent V., and Joyce Marcus, eds. 1983. *The Cloud People: Divergent Evolution of the Zapotec and Mixtec Civilizations.* New York: Academic Press.

Flannery, Kent V., and Joyce Marcus, eds. 1994. *Early Formative Pottery of the Valley of Oaxaca, Mexico.* Prehistory and Human Ecology of the Valley of Oaxaca, Vol. 10. Memoirs of the Museum of Anthropology, University of Michigan No. 27. Ann Arbor: University of Michigan.

Foias, Antonia, and Ronald L. Bishop. 1997. "Changing Ceramic Production and Exchange in the Petexbatun Region, Guatemala: Reconsidering the Classic Maya Collapse." *Ancient Mesoamerica* 8 (2): 275–91. http://dx.doi.org/10.1017/S09565361 00001735.

Gaxiola, Margarita. 1984. *Huamelulpan: Un centro urbano de la Mixteca Alta.* Colección Científica. Mexico City: Instituto Nacional de Antropología e Historia.

Gillespie, Susan. 1987. "Excavaciones en Charco Redondo 1986." Report submitted to the Centro INAH Oaxaca, Instituto Nacional de Antropología e Historia, Oaxaca.

Hegmon, Michelle. 1994. "Boundary Making Strategies in Early Pueblo Societies: Style and Architecture in the Kayenta and Mesa Verde Regions." In *The Ancient Southwestern Community: Models and Methods for the Study of Prehistoric Social Organization,* ed. Wirt H. Wells and Robert D. Leonard, 171–90. Albuquerque: University of New Mexico Press.

Joyce, Arthur A. 1991a. *Formative Period Occupation in the Lower Río Verde Valley, Oaxaca, Mexico: Interregional Interaction and Social Change.* PhD dissertation, Department of Anthropology, Rutgers University, New Brunswick, NJ. Ann Arbor, MI: University Microfilms.

Joyce, Arthur A. 1991b. "Formative Period Social Change in the Lower Río Verde Valley, Oaxaca, Mexico." *Latin American Antiquity* 2 (2): 126–50. http://dx.doi.org/10.23 07/972274.

Joyce, Arthur A. 1993a. "Interregional Interaction and Social Development on the Oaxaca Coast." *Ancient Mesoamerica* 4 (1): 67–84. http://dx.doi.org/10.1017/S09565 36100000791.

Joyce, Arthur A. 1993b. "The Interregional Impact of State Formation in Oaxaca." Report submitted to the American Museum of Natural History on research activities performed as a Kalbfleisch Fellow, American Museum of Natural History, New York.

Joyce, Arthur A. 1994. "Late Formative Community Organization and Social Complexity on the Oaxaca Coast." *Journal of Field Archaeology* 21: 147–68.

Joyce, Arthur A., ed. 1999. "El proyecto patrones de asentamiento del Río Verde." Final report submitted to the Consejo de Arqueología, Instituto Nacional de Antropología e Historia, Mexico City.

Joyce, Arthur A. 2000. "The Founding of Monte Albán: Sacred Propositions and Social Practices." In *Agency in Archaeology*, ed. Marcia-Anne Dobres and John E. Robb, 71–91. London: Routledge.

Joyce, Arthur A. 2003. "Imperialism in Pre-Aztec Mesoamerica: Monte Albán, Teotihuacan, and the Lower Río Verde Valley." In *Ancient Mesoamerica Warfare*, ed. M. Kathryn Brown and Travis M. Stanton, 49–72. Walnut Creek, CA: AltaMira Press.

Joyce, Arthur A. 2005. "La arqueología del bajo Río Verde." *Acervos* 7 (29): 16–36.

Joyce, Arthur A. 2006. "The Inhabitation of Río Viejo's Acropolis." In *Space and Spatial Analysis in Archaeology*, ed. Elizabeth C. Robertson, Jeffrey D. Seibert, Deepika C. Fernández, and Marc U. Zender, 83–96. Albuquerque: University of New Mexico Press; Calgary: University of Calgary Press.

Joyce, Arthur A. 2008. "Domination, Negotiation, and Collapse: A History of Centralized Authority on the Oaxaca Coast Before the Late Postclassic." In *After Monte Albán: Transformation and Negotiation in Oaxaca, Mexico*, ed. Jeffrey Blomster, 219–54. Boulder: University Press of Colorado.

Joyce, Arthur A. 2010. *Mixtecs, Zapotecs, and Chatinos: Ancient Peoples of Southern Mexico*. Malden, MA: Wiley-Blackwell Press.

Joyce, Arthur A., and Sarah B. Barber. 2011. "Excavating the Acropolis at Río Viejo, Oaxaca, Mexico." *Mexicon* 33 (1): 15–20.

Joyce, Arthur A., J. Michael Elam, Michael D. Glascock, Hector Neff, and Marcus Winter. 1995. "Exchange Implications of Obsidian Source Analysis from the Lower Río Verde Valley, Oaxaca, Mexico." *Latin American Antiquity* 6 (1): 3–15. http://dx.doi.org/10.2307/971597.

Joyce, Arthur A., Hector Neff, Mary S Thieme, Marcus Winter, J. Michael Elam, and Andrew Workinger. 2006. "Ceramic Production and Exchange in Late/Terminal Formative Period Oaxaca." *Latin American Antiquity* 17 (4): 579–94. http://dx.doi.org/10.2307/25063073.

Joyce, Arthur A., and Marcus Winter. 1996. "Ideology, Power, and Urban Society in Pre-Hispanic Oaxaca." *Current Anthropology* 37 (1): 33–47. http://dx.doi.org/10.1086/204473.

Joyce, Arthur A., Marcus Winter, and Raymond G. Mueller. 1998. *Arqueología de la costa de Oaxaca: Asentamientos del periodo formativo en el valle del Río Verde inferior*. Estudios de Antropología e Historia No. 40. Oaxaca: Centro INAH Oaxaca.

Kowalewski, Stephen A., Gary M. Feinman, Laura Finsten, Richard E. Blanton, and Linda M. Nicholas. 1989. *Monte Albán's Hinterland, Part II: The Prehispanic Settlement Patterns of Tlacolula, Etla, and Ocotlán, the Valley of Oaxaca, Mexico*. Memoirs of the University of Michigan Museum of Anthropology No. 23. Ann Arbor: University of Michigan.

Lemmonier, Pierre. 1992. *Elements for an Anthropology of Technology*. Anthropological Papers, Museum of Anthropology, University of Michigan No. 88. Ann Arbor: University of Michigan.

Levine, Marc N. 2002. "Ceramic Change and Continuity in the Lower Río Verde Region of Oaxaca, Mexico: The Late Formative to Early Terminal Formative Transition." MA thesis, University of Colorado, Boulder.

Levine, Marc N. 2011. "Negotiating Political Economy at Late Postclassic Tututepec (Yucu Dzaa), Oaxaca, Mexico." *American Anthropologist* 113 (1): 22–39. http://dx.doi.org/10.1111/j.1548-1433.2010.01304.x.

Levine, Marc, Arthur A. Joyce, and Paul Goldberg. 2004. "Earthen Mound Construction at Río Viejo on the Pacific Coast of Oaxaca, Mexico." Paper presented at the 69th Annual Meeting of the Society for American Archaeology, Montreal.

Marcus, Joyce. 1976. "The Iconography of Militarism at Monte Albán and Neighboring Sites in the Valley of Oaxaca." In *Origins of Religious Art and Iconography in Preclassic Mesoamerica*, ed. Henry B. Nicholson, 125–39. Los Angeles: UCLA Latin American Center Publications.

Marcus, Joyce. 1983. "The Conquest Slabs of Building J, Monte Albán." In *The Cloud People: Divergent Evolution of the Zapotec and Mixtec Civilizations*, ed. Kent V. Flannery and Joyce Marcus, 106–8. New York: Academic Press.

Marcus, Joyce. 1992. *Mesoamerican Writing Systems*. Princeton, NJ: Princeton University Press.

Marcus, Joyce, and Kent Flannery. 1996. *Zapotec Civilization*. London: Thames and Hudson.

Redmond, Elsa M. 1983. *A Fuego y Sangre: Early Zapotec Imperialism in the Cuicatlán Cañada, Oaxaca*. Museum of Anthropology, University of Michigan Memoirs 16. Ann Arbor: University of Michigan.

Redmond, Elsa M., and Charles S. Spencer. 1983. "The Cuicatlán Cañada and the Period II Frontier of the Zapotec State." In *The Cloud People: Divergent Evolution of the Zapotec and Mixtec Civilizations*, ed. Kent V. Flannery and Joyce Marcus, 117–20. New York: Academic Press.

Redmond, Elsa M., and Charles S. Spencer. 2006. "From Raiding to Conquest: Warfare Strategies and Early State Development in Oaxaca, Mexico." In *The Archaeology of Warfare: Prehistories of Raiding and Conquest*, ed. Elizabeth N. Arkush and Mark W. Allen, 336–93. Gainesville: University Press of Florida.

Schortman, Edward M. 1989. "Interregional Interaction in Prehistory: The Need for a New Perspective." *American Antiquity* 54 (1): 52–65. http://dx.doi.org/10.2307/281331.

Schreiber, Katharina J. 1987. "Conquest and Consolidation: A Comparison of the Wari and Inka Occupations of a Highland Peruvian Valley." *American Antiquity* 52 (2): 266–84. http://dx.doi.org/10.2307/281780.

Schreiber, Katharina J. 1992. *Wari Imperialism in Middle Horizon Peru*. Anthropological Paper No. 87. Ann Arbor: University of Michigan Museum of Anthropology.

Sherman, R. Jason, Andrew Balkansky, Charles S. Spencer, and Brian Nicholls. 2010. "Expansionary Dynamics of the Nascent Monte Albán State." *Journal of Anthropological Archaeology* 29 (3): 278–301. http://dx.doi.org/10.1016/j.jaa.2010.04.001.

Smith, Michael E., and Lisa Montiel. 2001. "The Archaeological Study of Empires and Imperialism in Prehispanic Central Mexico." *Journal of Anthropological Archaeology* 19: 1–40.

Smyth, Michael P. 2009. "Beyond Economic Imperialism: The Teotihuacan Factor in Northern Yucatan." *Journal of Anthropological Research* 64 (3): 395–409.

Spencer, Charles S. 1982. *The Cuicatlán Cañada and Monte Albán*. New York: Academic Press.

Spencer, Charles S. 2007. "Territorial Expansion and Primary State Formation in Oaxaca, Mexico." In *Latin American Indigenous Warfare and Ritual Violence*, ed. Richard J. Chacon and Rubén G. Mendoza, 55–72. Tucson: University of Arizona Press.

Spencer, Charles S. 2010. "Territorial Expansion and Primary State Formation." *Proceedings of the National Academy of Sciences of the United States of America* 107, no. 16 (Apr. 20): 7119–26. http://dx.doi.org/10.1073/pnas.1002470107. Medline:20385804.

Spencer, Charles S., and Elsa M. Redmond. 1997. *Archaeology of the Cañada de Cuicatlán, Oaxaca*. Anthropological Papers No. 80. New York: American Museum of Natural History.

Spencer, Charles S., and Elsa M. Redmond. 2001. "Multilevel Selection and Political Evolution in the Valley of Oaxaca, 500–100 BC." *Journal of Anthropological Archaeology* 20 (2): 195–229. http://dx.doi.org/10.1006/jaar.2000.0371.

Spencer, Charles S., Elsa M. Redmond, and Christina Elson. 2008. "Ceramic Microtypology and the Territorial Expansion of the Early Monte Albán State in Oaxaca, Mexico." *Journal of Field Archaeology* 33 (3): 321–41. http://dx.doi.org/10.1179/009346908791071222.

Spores, Ronald. 1983. "Ramos Phase Urbanization in the Mixteca Alta." In *The Cloud People: Divergent Evolution of the Zapotec and Mixtec Civilizations*, ed. Kent V Flannery and Joyce Marcus, 120–23. New York: Academic Press.

Stark, Barbara. 1990. "The Gulf Coast and the Central Highlands of Mexico: Alternative Models for Interaction." *Research in Economic Anthropology* 21: 243–85.

Urcid, Javier. 1994. "Mound J at Monte Albán and Zapotec Political Geography during Period II (200 BC–AD 200)." Paper presented at the 59th Annual Meeting of the Society for American Archaeology, Anaheim, CA.

Winter, Marcus. 1989. *Oaxaca: The Archaeological Record*. Mexico City: Minutiae Mexicana.

Winter, Marcus. 1996. *Cerro de las Minas: Arqueología de la Mixteca Baja*. Oaxaca: Casa de la Cultura de Huajapan de León.

Winter, Marcus, Antonia Montague, and Geraldina Tercero. 1991. "Cerámica de Cerro de las Minas." In *Exploraciones arqueológicas en Cerro de las Minas, Mixteca Baja, Oaxaca: Temporadas 1987–1990*, ed. Marcus Winter, 140–72. Informe Preliminar, Centro Regional Oaxaca. Oaxaca: Instituto Nacional de Antropología e Historia.

Workinger, Andrew. 2002. *Coastal/Highland Interaction in Prehispanic Oaxaca, Mexico: The Perspective from San Francisco de Arriba*. PhD dissertation, Department of Anthropology, Vanderbilt University, Nashville, TN. Ann Arbor, MI: University Microfilms.

Workinger, Andrew G., and Arthur A. Joyce. 1999. Excavaciones arqueológicas en Río Viejo. In "El proyecto patrones de asentamiento del Río Verde," ed. Arthur A. Joyce, 51–119. Final report submitted to the Consejo de Arqueología, Instituto Nacional de Antropología e Historia, Mexico City.

Workinger, Andrew G., and Arthur A. Joyce. 2009. "Reconsidering Warfare in Formative Period Oaxaca." In *Blood and Beauty: Organized Violence in the Art and Archaeol-*

ogy of Mesoamerica and Central America, ed. Heather Orr and Rex Koontz, 3–38. Los Angeles: Cotsen Institute Press.

Zeitlin, Robert. 1993. "Pacific Coastal Laguna Zope: A Regional Center in the Terminal Formative Hinterlands of Monte Albán." *Ancient Mesoamerica* 4 (1): 85–101. http://dx.doi.org/10.1017/S0956536100000808.

Zeitlin, Robert, and Arthur Joyce. 1999. "The Zapotec-Imperialism Argument: Insights from the Oaxaca Coast." *Current Anthropology* 40 (3): 383–92. http://dx.doi.org/10.1086/200029.

NINE

FROM FLESH TO CLAY

*Formative Period Iconography from
Oaxaca's Lower Río Verde Valley*

GUY DAVID HEPP AND ARTHUR A. JOYCE

This chapter presents our analysis of 256 Formative period (1600 BC–
AD 250) ceramic figurines, musical instruments, and iconographic
vessel appliqués from the lower Río Verde Valley of coastal Oaxaca,
Mexico (Barber 2005; Barber and Hepp 2012; Fernández Pardo 1993;
Hepp 2007, 2009; Hepp and Hepp n.d.; Joyce 1991, 2005). The collection includes anthropomorphic, zoomorphic, and transformational
figures that combine human and nonhuman traits. The purpose of
our analysis is twofold. First, the study allows us to describe physical attributes of the collection, including dimensions and patterns of
diagnostic accoutrements such as clothing, jewelry, hairstyles, and
anatomical features. We consider these characteristics representative of Formative period figurines from the lower Río Verde Valley,
as the sample spans two millennia and comes from eight sites in the
region. Second, contextual, temporal, and iconographic patterns in
the collection inform our arguments about the social significance
of the artifacts. Specifically, we interpret ceramic iconographic
artifacts as focal points for public and domestic ritual behavior. We
argue that figurine use operated in both private and public contexts
and that public activities were carried out in domestic spaces as well
as in nondomestic, communal settings (e.g., ceremonial spaces). We

DOI: 10.5876/9781607322023.c09

TABLE 9.1. Frequency of figurine elements

Figurine Element	Count	Percentage of Collection
Head	72	28.1
Head and Torso	9	3.5
Head, Torso, and Limb(s)	19	7.4
Torso and Limb(s)	51	19.9
Torso	9	3.5
Limb	70	27.3
Unknown	26	10.2
Total	256	100

define "domestic" as those contexts associated with both physical houses and the house as a unit of social interaction (Gillespie 2000, 23, 51; Lévi-Strauss 1963; Monaghan 1995, 15, 244–246). We propose a set of overlapping figurine-related practices including ancestor remembrance, performative ritual, mimetic co-option of symbolic power, religious symbolism, life history commemoration, and perhaps children's games. Figurines were likely also material symbols forming a commentary on social constructions of gender, age, and kinship (Blomster 2009; Cyphers Guillén 1993, 129; Joyce 2000, 2002, 2003; Nelson 1997, 126; Taussig 1993; Tedlock 2005, 32; Tilley 1999; Winter 1992, 26; 2005).

The lower Río Verde Valley figurines were excavated from Early Formative through Terminal Formative period contexts at the sites of Barra Quebrada, Cerro de la Cruz, Cerro de la Virgen, Corozo, La Consentida, Loma Reyes, Río Viejo, and Yugüe (Figure 1.2; Barber 2005, Chapter 6; Hepp 2011a, 2011b; Joyce 1991, 2010; Joyce and Levine 2009; Joyce and Winter 1989). A few figurines were excavated from Terminal Formative/Classic period transitional deposits. The largest single category of artifact element was heads, though torsos and limbs were also common. Table 9.1 summarizes the figurine elements comprised by the collection. We evaluate the iconography of each item according to varying levels of analytical confidence and differentiate figurines that can definitely be assigned to a particular category from those whose identity is less certain. In the latter instance, we assign figurines to "possible" categories. In some cases a figurine might be assigned to more than one category if its imagery is ambiguous due to breakage, erosion, or artistic style (Table 9.2).[1] Like other Formative period collections, these figurines include more identifiable females than males among anthropomorphs, and more anthropomorphs than zoomorphs, although sex and gender are not clearly portrayed in the majority of figurines. We consider some figurines with apparently fantastical forms to represent transformational entities. Those combining human and animal elements, for example, may relate to nagualistic and tonalistic beliefs or depict characters

TABLE 9.2. Frequency of artifact forms

Artifact Type	Possible	Definite	Total
Anthropomorphs	85	94	179
Zoomorphs	59	43	102
Transformationals	23	5	28

TABLE 9.3. Artifact dimensions

	Height (mm)	Maximum width (mm)	Maximum thickness (mm)	Weight (g)
Number of Cases	256	256	256	256
Minimum	11	9	4	1
Maximum	150	86	68	198
Average	42.0	29.8	18.2	21.6
Standard Deviation	18.7	13.4	8.1	24.9

from a divine or ancestral pantheon. We examine ceramic whistles, ocarinas (whistle-like instruments with finger stops for playing multiple notes), flutes, and vessel appliqués in order to describe artifacts overlooked by previous studies and to demonstrate similarities they share with figurines as small-scale representations of people and beings of interest to ancient coastal Oaxacans. We frequently refer to these artifacts simply as figurines.

The figurines in the collection are mostly hand-formed, with a few potentially mold-made facial elements. Firing techniques changed through time, beginning with oxidized medium and coarse brownwares in the Early Formative. By the Terminal Formative, some figurines were fine graywares fired in a reducing environment. Grit, sand, and organics were common tempering materials. We analyzed all figurines with a Munsell soil color chart. They range from reddish yellow (7.5YR 7/8) to nearly black (10YR 3/1) in color. Several figurines are painted, slipped, or washed, often in white, red, or yellow. Fingerprint samples have been collected from seventy-one artifacts, though these await analysis. The context, construction, and iconographic interpretation of all but the recently excavated La Consentida artifacts are discussed by Hepp (2007, 169–244, 2009), although we have reinterpreted some data for this chapter. Table 9.3 summarizes basic dimensions of the artifacts.

THEORETICAL CONCERNS

Previous approaches to symbolism and iconography, which we feel are applicable to figurine studies, include personhood theory (Conklin and Morgan 1996; Fortes 1987; Gillespie 2001; La Fontaine 1978; Mauss 1985 [1938]; Muratorio

1998; Vilaça 2002), gender theory (Conkey and Gero 1997; Cyphers Guillén 1993; Joyce 1998, 2000, 2002, 2003; Marcus 1998; Munson 2000; Nanda 1999; Stephen 1991, 2002; Tedlock 2005; Whitehead 1981), ritual in house societies (Gillespie 2000), materiality (Miller 2005; Tilley 1999), agency and structuration (Faust and Halperin 2009, 11; Giddens 1979; Pauketat 2001; Sewell 1992), and mimesis (Benjamin and Tarnowski 1979 [1933]; Taussig 1993). Following Michael Taussig (1993), we take the "mimetic faculty" to be the predilection humans carry to co-opt the sources of symbolic power they perceive around them. People emulate selected entities in natural, social, and spiritual realms. The copy will then draw "on the character and power of the original," as in the axiomatic ethnographic constructs of sympathetic and contagious magic (Taussig 1993, xiii, 7, 105). Mimesis and the related concept of alterity, or the conceptualizing of the Other, can be theorized from multiple perspectives. Symbolic emulation can take place on a grand scale, such as the sacred mountain, cave, and water source motif recreated in the architecture of Dos Pilas in the Petexbatún (Brady 1991, 1997). On the Oaxacan coast, the sacred hill and spring theme has been identified by Barber (2005, 273) as potentially related to the founding of Cerro de la Virgen. Mimesis can also occur at a small scale, such as the seemingly simple act of depicting an animal, divine character, or ancestor in miniaturized form.

In discussing figurines, we both build upon and diverge somewhat from previous studies in Mesoamerica and elsewhere (Arroyo 2002; Blomster 2002, 2009; Brockington 2001; Cyphers Guillén 1993; Faust and Halperin 2009; Fernández Pardo 1993; Joyce 2000, 2002, 2003, 2009; Lesure 1997, 1999, 2011; Marcus 1998, 2009; Verhoeven 2002). Figurines are often considered artifacts specific to domestic material culture in the Mesoamerican archaeological record (Drennan 1976, 352; Marcus 1998). Authors such as Clark (1994, 264) and Lesure (1995, 244–245; 1999, 214–216) have studied stylistic variation between figurines found in public mounds and those from domestic areas in the hopes of understanding their different uses in those contexts. In our own case, we note that figurines deposited in public spaces in coastal Oaxaca indicate a complicated set of uses beyond the household. It is probable that figurines, to the extent they were involved in household ritual, were part of domestic traditions that tied people together on a *public* scale of interaction (Barber 2005, 56, 60–61, 271; Barber and Hepp 2012; Drennan 1976, 352; Hepp 2007, 81–93, 2009; Joyce 2000, 28; Lesure 2011, 126; Lesure and Blake 2002, 7). On the basis of our figurine data, we thus propose that there was a dynamic interplay between domestic and public life in ancient coastal Oaxaca. We refer to this blurred line between public and household contexts as "communal domesticity," by which we mean a network of public social interactions linking individuals, households, and corporate groups. This overlap between the "public" and "private" realms of social life recalls practice theory, in that daily interaction promotes the construction of communal identity, while differential participation in that community ethic contributes to social distinctions according to status, gender, age, and affiliations of lineage, kinship, or corporate group (Giddens 1979; A. Joyce 2004, 212; Monaghan 1995, 15, 244–246; Robin 2002).

Identities involving gender and sex have also figured prominently in studies of Formative period figurines (e.g., Cyphers Guillén 1993; Joyce 2002, 2003, 2009; Lesure 1997). Joyce Marcus's (1998) study of women's rituals in the Valley of Oaxaca inferred sex and gender based on anatomical characteristics, hairstyles, ornamentation, and clothing depicted on Formative period figurines. Marcus (1998, 4, 158) identified head fragments with the most elaborate hairstyles, for example, as likely gendered feminine. Early and Middle Formative figurines in highland Oaxaca, argued Marcus (1998, 3), were mostly intended for use by women in household ritual, likely to call upon the spirits of ancestors to aid in daily life. One must remain cautious, however, not to conflate household occupational roles with gender, or gender roles with biological sex. Through a feminist analysis of bioarchaeology, Geller (2008) argued that the material realities of biological sex and corporeality are given culturally defined meanings in much the same way as gender. Geller (2008, 129) cautioned archaeologists against ignoring the materiality of the body and argued that we must consider the complex intersection of biological sex, corporeality, and cultural meanings. Biological anthropology, for its part, has tended to conflate gender with biological sex, thus reifying a Western two-gendered and two-sexed set of dichotomies. Researchers hoping to move beyond the polemics of these approaches must acknowledge the social realities of non-Western sex and gender systems. In addition, current scholarship underscores the importance of both the biological and culturally ascribed nature of sex, which may in some societies be divided differently than into a male/female binary (Geller 2008).

Ethnographic and ethnohistoric observations suggest that gender categories in prehispanic Oaxaca differed from Western male/female binaries. For example, Lynn Stephen (1991, 76–77) has discussed divisions and significant overlap in gendered labor activities in the highland Zapotec town of Teotitlán del Valle. Stephen (2002) also described the *muxe* as a category for berdache or hijra-like individuals in Isthmian Zapotec communities who constitute a "third gender" by participating in feminine activities despite being sexed male. The category of *muxe* exists as a third gender rather than as a third sex precisely because the individuals are seen as phenotypically normal males who perform social roles not traditionally fulfilled by men. Being *muxe* is thus based on gendered performance as well as beliefs about the nature of the body. Isthmian Zapotecs therefore appear to conceptualize three genders divided across two biological categories. These lines of evidence remind researchers to question adherence to a simple two-gendered system (Nanda 1999; Stephen 2002, 43; Whitehead 1981).

Likewise, Kevin Terraciano (1994, 393; 2000, 2001) used archival data and linguistic philology to describe the Mixtec gender system as based on complementarity and reciprocity. Even the Mixtec worldview depends upon balanced interaction of the sexes, as when the male sky impregnates the female earth at the beginning of each growing season (Terraciano 1994, 394). Lisa Sousa (1997, 1998) reached conclusions consistent with Terraciano's through her use of colonial legal documents illustrating the autonomy of indigenous Oaxacan women. Similarly, Taylor (1979, 155) found evidence of village uprisings in colonial Oaxaca in which Mixtec women were "vanguards" of resistance, due in part to their integral role in village social networks. Such resistance, sometimes considered criminally rebellious, was possible because of prehispanic traditions of gender complementarity that contrasted with the androcentric hierarchy of the Spanish. The ethnographic and ethnohistorical data show that we must avoid imposing Western categories of sex and gender on the prehispanic past. In the next section we consider the iconography of the lower Río Verde Valley figurines as representations of aspects of identity related to sex, gender, and age.

ANTHROPOMORPHIC FIGURINES: SEX, GENDER, AND AGE

Ninety-four positively identified anthropomorphs constitute one of the largest categories of artifacts considered here. Table 9.4 presents the sexed and gendered demographics of the figurine collection. Artifacts designated feminine and masculine are those for which we have reason to interpret *gender* as suggested by accoutrements such as clothing, jewelry, and hairstyles. These examples bear no anatomical traits specifically indicative of male or female sex. Those which we designate as male or female show physical features indicative of such interpretations. As Table 9.4 demonstrates, the figurines fit the common Formative period pattern of including a higher proportion of female/feminine representations than male/masculine ones, although the majority of figurines lack obvious depictions of sex or gender (Joyce 2000, 2002, 2003; Marcus 1998; Wolf 1959, 57). Interpreting the meaning of the figurines was complicated by the fact that many were fragmentary. That the majority of figurines were broken may represent more than the abuses of deposition and preservation and may relate to practices of "retiring" figurines via intentional breakage after their use life was deemed over. Similar processes have been suggested by Shafer and Taylor (1986, 51) to explain "kill holes" in the Classic Mimbres pottery of the American Southwest, and the practice of ritually retiring objects has been long recognized in Mesoamerican assemblages (Joyce 2009, 416; Smith 2005 [1932]) and among Formative period Oaxacan figurines specifically (Blomster 2009, 141–142).

We conceptualize sex and gender as separate but related variables through which aspects of identity are performed and negotiated. Wherever visible,

TABLE 9.4. Sex and gender in the lower Río Verde collection, organized by figurine type

Sex and Gender	Anthropomorphs	Zoomorphs	Transformationals	Unknown	Total
Female	14	0	1	0	15
Feminine	22	0	1	0	23
Male	0	1	1	0	2
Masculine	15	0	0	0	15
Neutral or Unknown	43	42	2	114	201
Total	94	43	5	114	256

primary or secondary sexual characteristics, such as breasts for women and beards for men, serve as evidence for the classification of a figurine's intended "sex." For example, the artifact in Figure 9.1a is sexed female, as indicated by a pregnant belly. This body shape differs from an overweight male in the high angle of the stomach and in the shape of the hips and buttocks. We classify the artifact in Figure 9.1b as sexed female based on the presence of breasts. This figurine's exaggerated belly button fits with an artistic convention for feminine representation elsewhere in Formative Mesoamerica (Joyce 2000, 29–34; Marcus 1998). In many cases determination of sex is not possible. Ancient Oaxacans may have conceived of more than two biological sexes, and sex may have been downplayed or not signified in sexually neutral human representations (Blomster 2009, 121; Joyce 2003).

We utilize documented Mesoamerican artistic conventions as indications of gender. The depiction of exaggerated belly buttons, certain hairstyles, traditions of body position, clothing, and certain forms of ornamentation, for example, have all been linked to feminine representation (Joyce 2000, 29–34; 2002, 81–83; Marcus 1998, 4; Nelson 1997). While imperfect (see Lesure 2011, 29–32), this method allows the fullest interpretation of demographic patterns among the figurines. We interpret the artifacts in Figures 9.1c and 9.1d as gendered feminine based on an apparent skirt and an elaborately ornamented hairstyle, respectively. We support this interpretation with ethnohistoric evidence regarding indigenous Oaxacan bodily adornment, as well as conventions noted in other figurine studies (Joyce 2000, 28–33; Marcus 1998, 31–38, 58, 59). Rosemary Joyce (2000, 30; 2002, 82–83) has identified certain forms of loincloths and lip plugs as possible indicators of masculinity. Some figurines from our own study (e.g., Figure 9.2) may fit this pattern and depict what we interpret as masculine characters with lip plugs or labrets.

Some figurines may have been anthropomorphic "templates," upon which various identities could be mapped by use of different accoutrements (Joyce 2000: Figure 9.3). Such artifacts have an androgynous form when preserved in the archaeological record, but could have been dressed, painted, or decorated

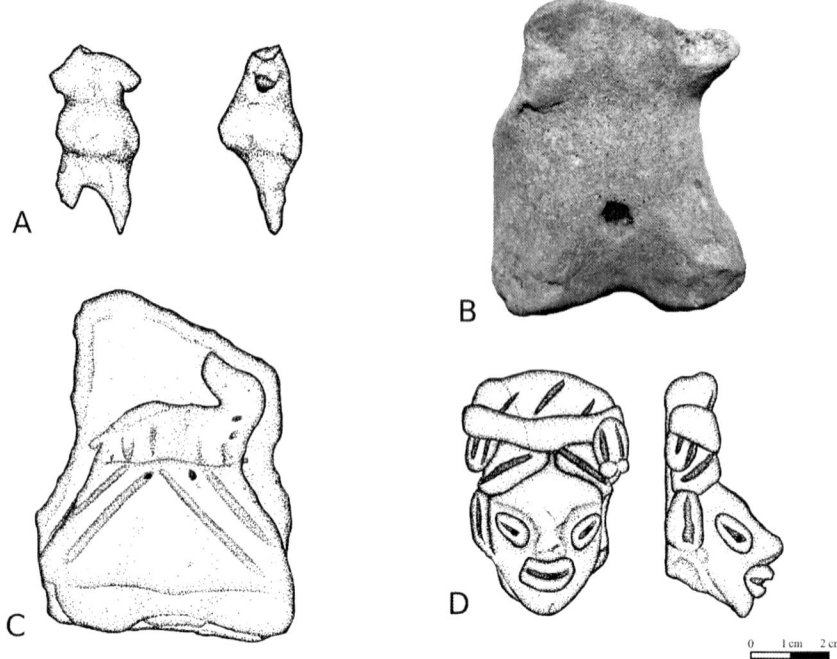

FIGURE 9.1. Female and feminine figurines. *A*, Miniyua phase figurine from Yugüe (after Hepp 2009: Figure 6.2). *B, C*, Chacahua phase figurines from elite residence at Cerro de la Virgen (after Hepp 2009: Illustration 1, Photo 1148). *D*, Chacahua phase figurine at Corozo (after Hepp 2009: Figure 6.1).

in antiquity to take on specific but modifiable identities. Figure 9.3a depicts a unique anthropomorph from Yugüe. Note the unusual head, neck, and shoulder pattern that may be hair, clothing, or even tattoos. Holes through the ears and a gap in the lower lip permit this figurine to wear detachable earrings and a lip plug or labret. The item may also have been clothed with perishable garments when in use (see Coe and Diehl 1980, 260). The addition of clothing and ornaments may have allowed the figurine to take on a variety of identities related to gender, status, and age.

In our sample, we recognize an unusual head fragment as a possible import from the Valley of Oaxaca (Figure 9.4a; the figurine in Figure 9.4b may be similar, though the head is unfortunately broken). This artifact resembles a Late Formative period figurine from the Valley of Oaxaca (Figure 9.4c) that was previously discussed by Marcus (1998, 305; see also Whalen 1981). Marcus (1998, 2) interpreted the highland artifact as indicative of tabular cranial deformation. A similar figurine depicted in Figure 9.4d is from a Terminal Formative context in the Valley of Oaxaca (Bernal 1946, 125). The Valley of Oaxaca figurines

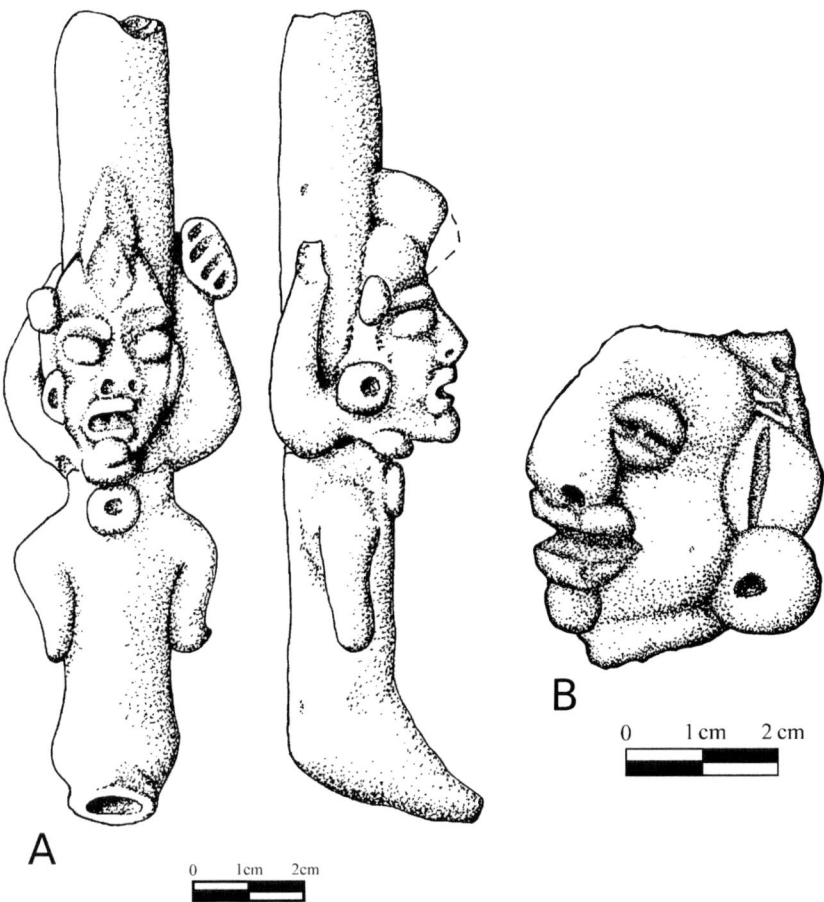

FIGURE 9.2. Anthropomorphic musical instruments interpreted as masculine based on presence of lip jewelry. *A*, Flute from Chacahua phase elite residence at Cerro de la Virgen (after Hepp 2009: Illustration 16). *B*, Flute fragment from Miniyua phase domestic midden at Yugüe (after Hepp 2009: Figure 13).

share with the lower Río Verde Valley artifact (Figure 9.4a) an exaggerated head shape that, assuming some degree of realism in representation, seems to surpass the possibilities that cranial deformation, hairstyle, or headgear alone could afford. One possible interpretation of these figurines is that they represent the Mesoamerican maize god (Taube 1993). Taube has argued (1993, 66–67; 2000, 297) that in various iconographic traditions, the maize god has been depicted with an elongated head topped with a small tuft reminiscent of the silky top of a maize cob and sometimes with maize ears in his headdress. Because of this god's role as progenitor to humanity in Aztec and Maya

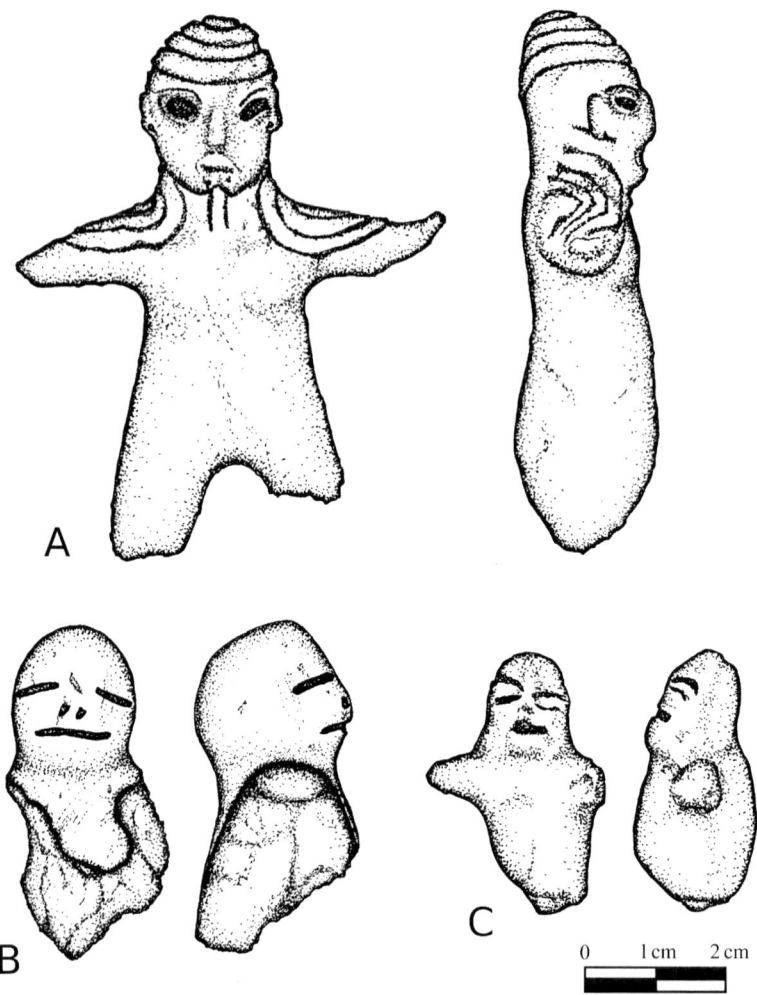

FIGURE 9.3. Figurines that may have acted as anthropomorphic "templates." *A,* Miniyua phase at Yugüe (after Hepp 2009: Figure 2.1). *B,* Chacahua phase at Río Viejo (after Hepp 2009: Illustration 7). *C,* Miniyua phase domestic midden at Río Viejo (after Hepp 2009: Illustration 5).

tradition, the very flesh of humankind was believed to be composed of maize (Taube 1993, 67, 75).

The figurines in Figure 9.4 may also allegorically reference both the maize god and human fertility, since ethnohistorically recorded Oaxacan notions of human reproduction contain allegories to rain, earth, and the sprouting of plants (e.g., Sousa 1998, 108; Terraciano 1994, 394). Symbolic references to maize and to human reproductive anatomy may not be mutually exclusive. Three interpretations of these figurines thus include exaggerated cranial defor-

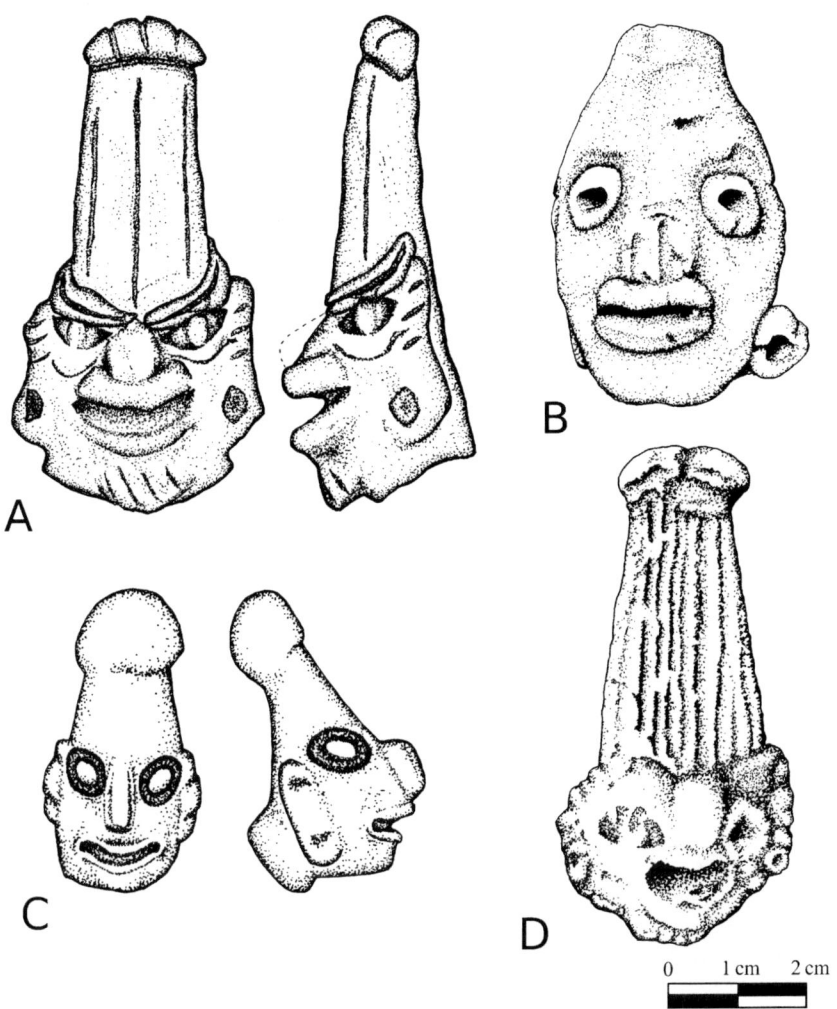

FIGURE 9.4. Stylistically similar figurines from the lower Río Verde Valley and the Valley of Oaxaca. *A*, Miniyua phase figurine from domestic context at Río Viejo (after Hepp 2009: Figure 6.10). *B*, Minizundo phase figurine from the patio at Cerro de la Cruz. *C*, Late Formative figurine from Feature 51, Household Unit 1c–1, Tomaltepec (redrawn from Whalen 1981: Plate 52, no. 64). *D*, Terminal Formative figurine from the Valley of Oaxaca (redrawn from Bernal 1946, 125).

mation, maize symbolism, and an additional tentative possibility, that of male sexual anatomy. If figurines existed within a system of gender complementarity and reciprocity, as inferred from historical analyses of early colonial Mixtec gender concepts (Sousa 1997, 1998, 108; Spores 1997, 186; Stern 1995, 242, 248; Taylor 1979, 108; Terraciano 1994, 393; 2000, 16; 2001), linguistic study

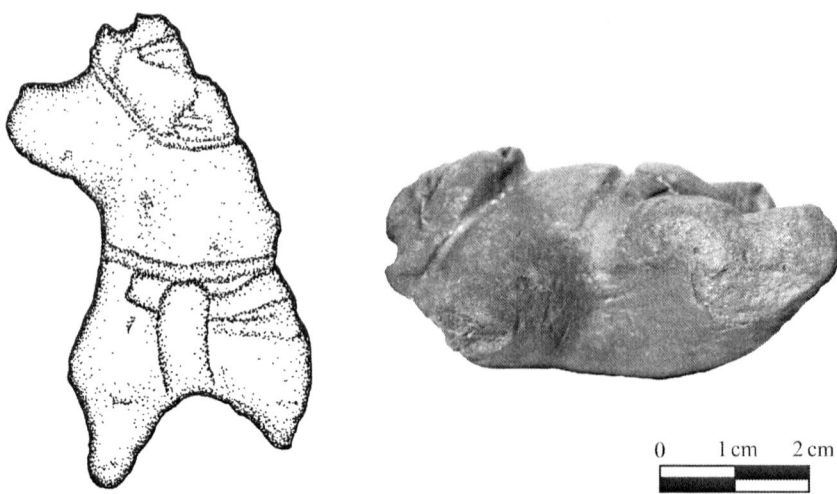

0   1 cm   2 cm

FIGURE 9.5. Two views of a possible infant figurine from a domestic midden at Minizundo/ Miniyua phase Río Viejo (after Hepp 2009: Illustration 15, Photo 463).

(Terraciano 1994, 176–177), and Zapotec ethnography (Stephen 2002, 41–59), we might expect to find items depicting amplified "maleness" as complementary to "femaleness" (though see Stephen's [2002] warning against facile sex and gender dichotomies). Depictions of male reproductive anatomy are not unknown in Mesoamerica, as stone sculptures from the Banderas Valley of Jalisco and Nayarit have shown. These sculptures also demonstrate, however, that depictions of both male and female anatomy may occur on a single artifact (Mountjoy and Beltrán 2005; see also Lesure 2011, 29–32). The classification of the figurine from our study as male is supported by the depiction of a beard. The striking similarities between the Valley of Oaxaca figurines and the coastal examples suggest contact between the two regions.

As Rosemary Joyce (2000, 35–37) has argued, age in ancient Mesoamerica was often a more important social variable than gender, and these two aspects of identity were closely interrelated. Some coastal figurines, such as the one represented in Figure 9.5, may depict human infants. Note that this figurine was constructed so it could not stand. The back has been flattened (perhaps indicating that the artifact was intended to lie on its back), and all four limbs are lifted off the ground when the figure is supine. In addition, the disproportionate size of the head is consistent with those of human infants. The object might have represented a child during events focused on motherhood, female maturity, or the early stages of the human life cycle (Mary Pohl, personal conversation, 2007; Tedlock 2005; Winter 1992). Joyce (2000, 30) has suggested, however, that loincloths often depict adult males. Marcus (1998, 158) interpreted a figurine with a loincloth similar to the one shown in Figure 9.5

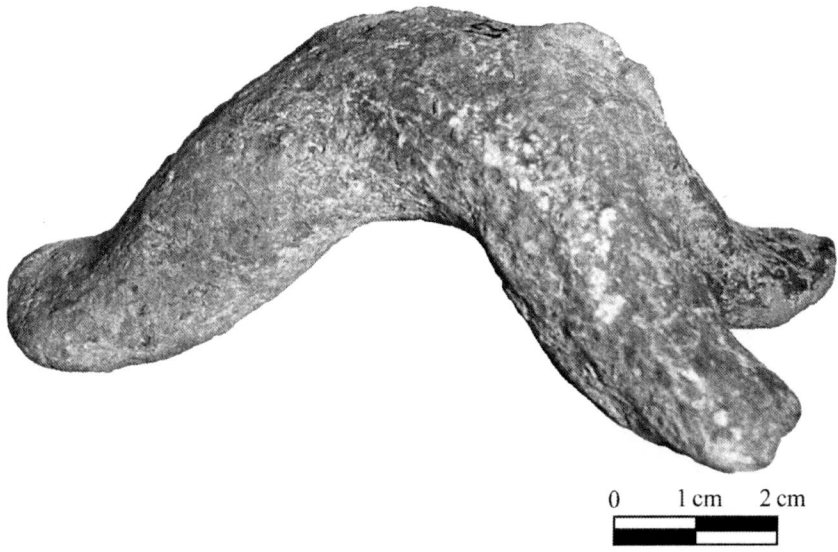

0   1 cm   2 cm

FIGURE 9.6. A possible Miniyua/Chacahua phase acrobat figurine from a public building at Yugüe (after Hepp 2009: Figure 4.2).

as a possible acrobat, a conclusion that fits with evidence of acrobat depiction at Tlatilco (Coe 1965: Figure 75). Given these various conclusions, the figurine in Figure 9.5 may represent an infant, an adult male, or perhaps an acrobat. Another figurine from the lower Río Verde collection (Figure 9.6) appears to bend backward in an "acrobatic" posture, although it lacks a loincloth. Acrobat figurines seem to imply public ritual performances that may have incorporated members of the community as spectators or participants.

ANTHROPOMORPHIC VESSEL APPLIQUÉS

One notable artifact type in our study consists of vessel appliqués bearing depictions of human faces (Figure 9.7). The anthropomorphic appliqués occurred in domestic middens, a possible feasting deposit, public ceremonial structures, an elite residence, and construction fill (Barber 2005; Hepp 2007, 180–224; 2009; Joyce 1991, 2006). Chipping at the facial margins supports the interpretation that the appliqués were intentionally removed from the vessels on which they were originally located. The exaggerated size of the closed eyes and open mouths draws attention to these features and suggests that the appliqués were images of the deceased, serving as "death masks" of revered ancestors, either specific or generalized. Accoutrements depicted on several of their foreheads are similar to both actual and iconographic mirrors found throughout much of Formative Mesoamerica, which have been interpreted as symbolic of elite

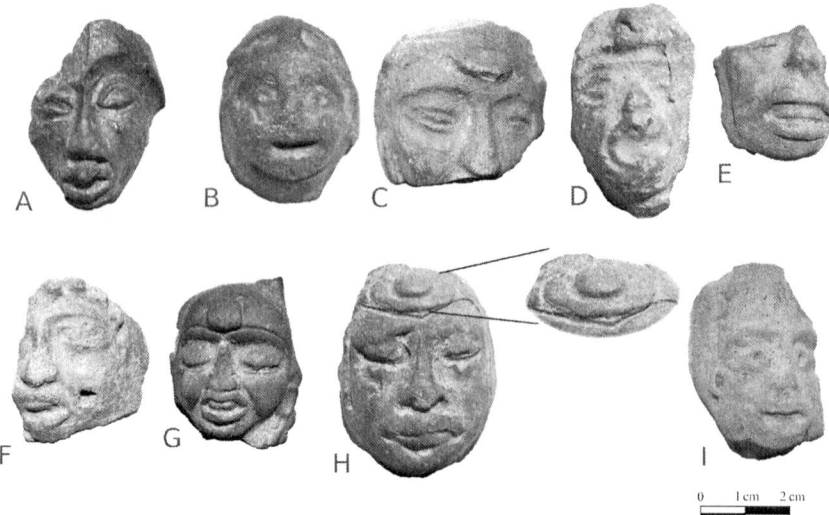

FIGURE 9.7. Anthropomorphic vessel appliqués from the lower Río Verde Valley. Note the closed or drooping eyes and open mouths. *A*, Minizundo phase feasting or high-status midden at Cerro de la Cruz (after Hepp 2009: Photo 548). *B*, Miniyua or Chacahua phase public building at Yugüe (after Hepp 2009: Photo 938). *C*, Miniyua phase at Yugüe (after Hepp 2009: Photo 772). *D*, Miniyua phase domestic midden at Yugüe (after Hepp 2009: Photo 782). *E*, Chacahua phase public building at Yugüe (after Hepp 2009: Photo 992). *F, G*, Possible Coyuche phase domestic midden at Río Viejo (after Hepp 2009: Figure I, Photo 262). *H*, Minizundo phase at Río Viejo; inset indicates possible mirror accoutrement (after Hepp 2009: Figure J). *I*, Chacahua phase elite residence at Cerro de la Virgen (after Hepp 2009: Photo 979).

status (e.g., Ashmore 2004, 184–185; Blomster 2004, 85, 186; Heyden 1991, 195; Saunders 2001; Winter 1992, 30). Mirrors may have been used in divination, likely as symbolic of water, caves, and a connection between planes of existence (Ashmore 2004, 184–185; Taube 1992). On the Oaxaca coast, Barber (2005, 107, 226–227; Barber et al., Chapter 4) discovered an iron ore mirror in a high-status Chacahua phase burial that also contained an elaborate bone flute (Figure 1.10). If mirrors were the headgear of elites, then perhaps figures wearing mirrors represent elite ancestors remembered on curated ceramic appliqués. Human faces on ceramic vessels from the Oaxaca coast also somewhat resemble the imagery on Preclassic Maya anthropomorphic spouted cacao vessels, which are often found in burial contexts (Culbert 1993; Powis et al. 2002).

Most of the anthropomorphic appliqués in the lower Río Verde Valley were discovered in Late or Terminal Formative contexts. The observation that many appliqués were curated indicates that they may have been manufactured long before their time of deposition. Because lower Río Verde Valley populations produced no local graywares before the Miniyua phase, we infer that several appliqués from Minizundo deposits may have been imported (Joyce 1991, 147). The appliqué in Figure 9.7a, for example, is a grayware from a Minizundo phase midden at Cerro de la Cruz, which also contained ceramics imported from the Valley of Oaxaca (Joyce 1991, 264–265).

ZOOMORPHIC FIGURINES

The collection considered here includes forty-three definite and an additional fifty-nine possible zoomorphs (Hepp 2007, 67; 2011a, 2011b.). The zoomorphs include birds, dogs, bats, lizards, and a turtle or armadillo (Figure 9.8). Other examples include possible deer, fish, and monkeys. Of the forty-three definite zoomorphs in the collection, eighteen appear to be dogs (Figure 9.9). The prevalence of dog depictions likely represents both the pragmatic status of dogs as closely tied to humans and also their symbolic status in the ideology of native America (Schwartz 1997, 8, 16). Dog depiction by ancient Oaxacans reflected their complex identities in the Mesoamerican worldview, including as domestic animals, as a source of protein, as intermediaries between the worlds of the living and the dead, and even as death omens (Coe and Diehl 1980, 282; Marcus 1998, 22; Marcus and Flannery 1996, 115–116; Schwartz 1997, 23, 66). According to Dyk (1959), Mixtecs tell a story about dogs and the first time the sun shone upon the earth. Separated from their human companions due to fear of the new sun, some of the dogs were forced to become coyotes, distancing themselves from human culture and reversing the domestication process. Urcid (2005) has discussed iconographic evidence for dog sacrifice, especially of puppies, in Zapotec ritual contexts. The symbolic importance of dogs, according to Urcid (2005, 41–42), related to their role as guides during liminal periods in which the dead journeyed through the underworld. The remains of dogs have been recovered from both high-status and low-status burials in the Valley of Oaxaca (Urcid 2005, 36–37). A dog burial was also recovered from an Early Postclassic period context at Río Viejo.

Dog figurines in the lower Río Verde collection were found in various domestic middens, a public building, and an elite residence. The sites of Yugüe and Río Viejo produced the highest frequency of dog figurines. Many of the dog figurines are burnished, and almost all share a specific, caricatured body form. Whereas 9.8 percent of the 256 figurines in the overall collection showed recognizable burnishing, we find a much higher incidence of burnishing among the dog figurines—38.9 percent. The standardized style of dog depiction indicates a social convention for figurine production and likely use. The ceramic dog form itself is one of recognizable, exaggerated features. In addition, the slender grayware dogs of the lower Río Verde Valley are similar to figurines found in highland Oaxaca. As Martínez López and Winter discussed (1994, 7, 110–143), dog figurines with caricatured, slender bodies are known from

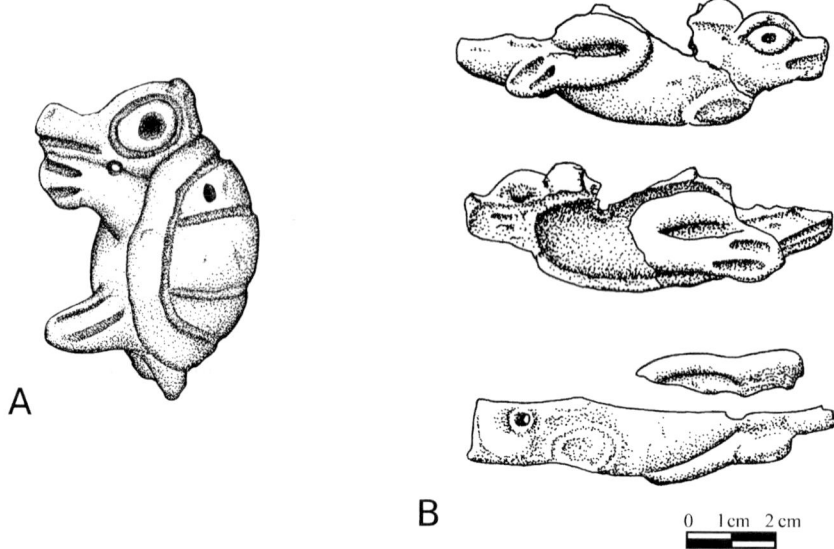

FIGURE 9.8. Zoomorphic figurines from the lower Río Verde Valley. *A,* Turtle or armadillo ocarina from Chacahua phase ceramic dump (after Hepp 2009: Figure F). *B,* Lizard ocarina from Miniyua or Chacahua phase public ceremonial structure at Yugüe.

Terminal Formative deposits in highland Oaxaca (see also Marcus 1998, 275). One Minizundo phase grayware dog from Río Viejo was probably imported, as local graywares were not produced at this time (Joyce 1991, 147).

Bird figurines in the collection are another example of images inspired by the natural world (Figure 9.10). Birds in the lower Río Verde collection are found in the form of figurines, whistles, and ocarinas, with some likely representing birds of prey. It is notable that 42.9 percent of the birds were musical instruments, while only 9.8 percent of the artifacts in the total collection were confidently identified as such. We argue that bird whistles and ocarinas in particular were an attempt to mimetically capture the essence of an animal, as they look and also *sound* like the creatures they represented (Barber and Hepp 2012; Taussig 1993). The act of bird imitation with musical instruments caused others in the community to hear the user as a bird, thus imbuing the individual with a birdlike identity recognizable to an audience. In addition, bird of prey iconography may have served to capture the animals' hunting prowess or spiritual essence. Use of such imagery may have allowed ritual practitioners to acquire those traits in some way. There are ethnohistoric and archaeological data indicating that birds and bird imagery played an important role in prehispanic ceremony. For example, Marcus (1998, 12) has described Zapotec divination events in which ritual specialists might question the fate of the community

FIGURE 9.9. Dog figurines from Formative coastal Oaxaca. *A,* Miniyua phase domestic midden at Yugüe (after Hepp 2009: Photo 765). *B,* Public ritual midden at Chacahua phase Yugüe (after Hepp 2009: Figure H).

by reference to birds, which were believed to foretell the future. According to Marcus (1998), highland Zapotecs sacrificed quails and doves during funeral ceremonies, and their ceramic depictions may have accompanied those of ancestors in household rituals. Like dogs, birds were intermediaries between the living and the dead, as they were capable of flying between worlds (Marcus 1998, 22).

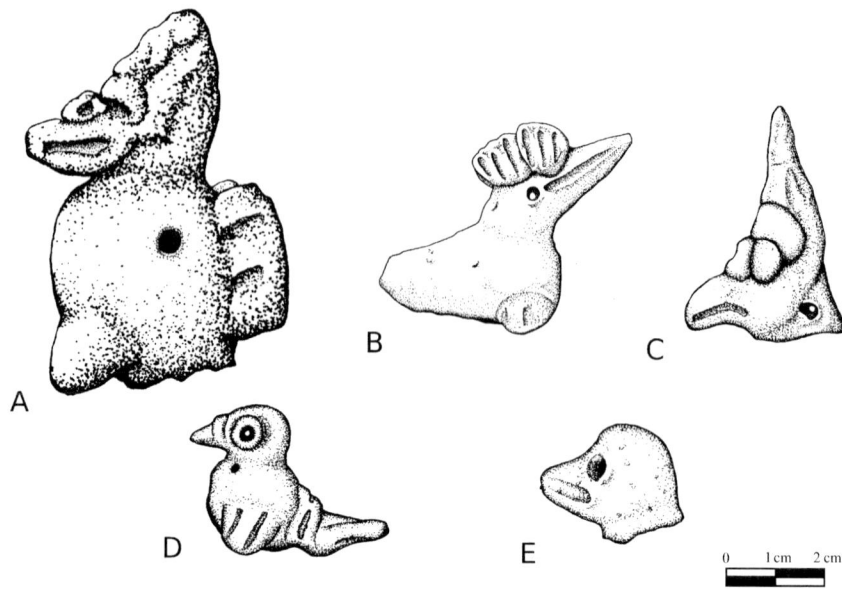

FIGURE 9.10. Bird figurines and musical instruments. *A*, Miniyua phase domestic midden at Yugüe (after Hepp 2009: Illustration 9). *B*, Miniyua phase public ritual midden at Yugüe. *C, D,* Terminal Formative/early Classic transitional elite residence at Cerro de la Virgen (after Hepp 2009: Figure G; Illustration 22). *E,* Early Formative platform fill at La Consentida.

Urcid (2005, 62–63) suggested that birds may have been sacrificed during tomb reopening ceremonies. Urcid's (2005, 42, 103–104) analysis of carved stelae at Monte Albán indicated that bird sacrifice was a rite often performed specifically to honor one's ancestors and that such practices may have symbolized resurrection of the soul. Urcid (2005, 54) has shown that Glyph U is representative of the broad-billed bird deity (perhaps a macaw) who supercilliously ruled the earth before the coming of humanity. The glyph, according to Marcus (1983, 191), may have come to signify royal descent. This may explain why bird symbolism among ancient Zapotecs differed from dog symbolism in that it was restricted to elite tombs rather than burials of all social status groups (Urcid 2005, 41–42).

Other research in Formative Mesoamerica has demonstrated ideological connections between bird imagery and cosmology. Bird symbolism may often have been associated with the sun, and owls in particular may have represented the night sky (Urcid 2005, 77). The significance of bird sounds may also be represented on Formative imagery elsewhere in Mesoamerica. For example, an Olmec roller stamp discussed by Pohl and associates (2002) contains an image of a bird that appears to be "speaking" by virtue of possible calendrical glyphs carved near its mouth.

FIGURE 9.11. Terminal Formative transformational figurines. *A,* Chacahua phase public building at Yugüe. *B,* Chacahua phase elite residence at Cerro de la Virgen (after Hepp 2009: Figure D). *C,* Miniyua phase domestic midden at Río Viejo (after Hepp 2009: Illustration 8).

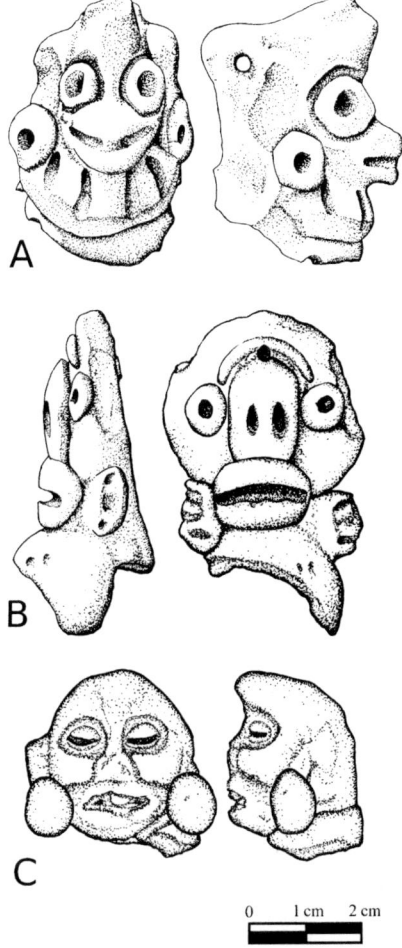

TRANSFORMATIONAL FORMS

Transformational artifacts, which we define as those combining human, animal, or possibly divine characteristics, are one of the rarer types in the collection (Figures 9.11 and 9.12). For example, the figurines in Figure 9.11 appear to combine anthropomorphic traits (jewelry) and zoomorphic traits (e.g., monkey-like faces), much like were-jaguars from the Gulf coast and Chalcatzingo in Morelos (Saunders 1994). Formative period figurines from elsewhere in Oaxaca have previously been interpreted as indicative of naguals or transformational creatures (Blomster 1998, 2002, 2009).

The transformational figurines suggest that ancient coastal Oaxacans valued shamanic beings who could cross the boundaries between the human and animal realms (Foster 1944; Gutiérrez and Pye 2010; Kaplan 1956; Rojas 1947). We argue that such ceramic depictions represent a cultural belief held by ancient Oaxacans regarding the nature of human, animal, and divine identity, namely that the boundaries between them could be crossed or blurred, provided one held the appropriate skills, beliefs, or associations. Characters capable of crossing a porous boundary between human and nonhuman identities were regarded elsewhere in ancient Mesoamerica as possessing great power, as demonstrated by Nicholas Saunders's (1994) analysis of Olmec were-jaguars. Foster (1944) differentiated nagualism, or the ability for an individual to transform into an animal, from the related concept of the tonal, or animal spirit guide. Despite its subtle differences from nagualism, one can identify in tonalism an interest in associating

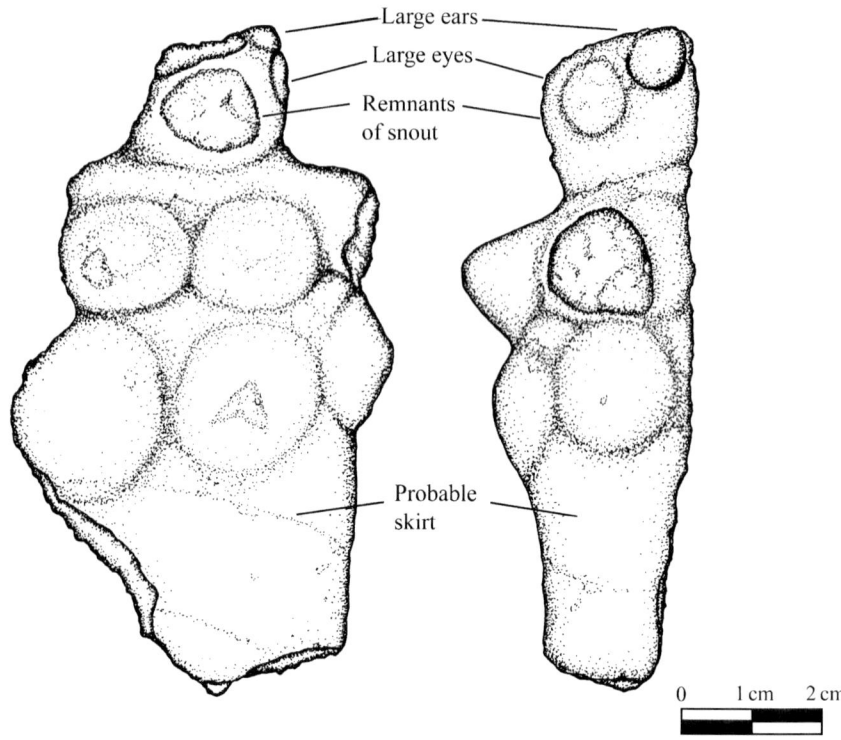

FIGURE 9.12. Transformational figurine incorporating human female and animal characteristics from a Minizundo phase domestic midden at Río Viejo (after Hepp 2009: Figure A).

the identity of animal and human in such a way as to blur sharp dichotomies regarding the cultural and the natural world. Gutiérrez and Pye (2010) have suggested that there may not be a strict division in Mesoamerican belief systems between the tonal and the nagual and that the two are really academic categories imposed upon a wide variety of beliefs.

Transformational figurines elsewhere in Mesoamerica have been described as representing community elders or dancers wearing animal costumes. Lesure (1997, 240, 247) has interpreted Formative figurines from the Soconusco region of Chiapas as costumed dancers. Similarly, Winter (1992, 26) described Formative figurines from highland Oaxaca as costume wearers. While we recognize these interpretations as valid in certain cases, we interpret examples from the coastal Oaxacan collection as depicting actual nagualistic creatures because their fantastical characteristics go beyond the face or costume to include the individual's body. Figure 9.12, for example, illustrates an artifact from Río Viejo, which is the most easily recognizable transformational form in the collection. The feminine and female human traits visible in this example include a patterned skirt and exaggerated breasts, respectively. Apparent animal traits include large ears, a snout, and side-oriented eyes. The swollen abdomen may indicate pregnancy. Note also the unusual conical shapes on the stomach, which suggest that this creature is not merely a human wearing a mask. The transformational nature of this female figurine may indicate that some women in coastal Oaxacan society were shamans performing ceremonies involving converging identities (Tedlock 2005).

If Formative period Oaxacan beliefs included a tonalistic or nagualistic relationship between humans and animals (Barber and Hepp 2012; Bartolomé and Barabas 1996; Foster 1944; Gutiérrez and Pye 2010; Hepp 2007, 2009; Kaplan 1956; Rojas 1947; Saunders 1994), then the wearing of costumes during performative ritual was likely tantamount to embodying animal characteristics. Figurines representing such creatures may indicate the perceived outcome of a ceremony in which actual participants wore fantastic costumes. One could depict this act by showing either costumed humans or the nagual creatures themselves, because there would have been no difference for participants. For example, Monaghan (1995, 151) has discussed contemporary Mixtec festivals in which masked dancers take on numerous and malleable identities (including those of other genders or of animals) depending on their masks, costumes, and enacted roles in the ceremony. For these dancers, to wear a mask is literally to *become* the character the mask represents.

TEMPORAL PATTERNS IN FORMATIVE PERIOD FIGURINE STYLES

Changes through time in figurine styles indicate a diversification of iconographic depiction from predominantly human representation to that of animals, transformationals, and other possibly divine forms. This pattern is consistent with data from Formative highland Oaxaca, where zoomorphs were introduced long after the first anthropomorphic figurines (Blomster 2009, 131; Winter 2005, 52). To explore changes in figurine style through time, we sorted according to time period all figurines from the collection that are securely dated and confidently identified according to anthropomorphic, zoomorphic, and transformational categories (Table 9.5). Initial steps in developing a regional figurine chronology are daunting, but we propose a provisional one for the lower Río Verde Valley in which styles of representation diversified through time during the Formative period. The regional collection was dominated during early periods by solid-bodied female and feminine anthropomorphs. Over time the iconographic set expanded to include small but important categories such as masculine forms, zoomorphs, transformationals, possible imports, and other iconographic artifacts such as human face appliqués and musical instruments.

TABLE 9.5. Figurine types through time

	Anthropo-morphs	Zoomorphs	Transfor-mationals	Unidentified	Subtotal by Time Period
Early and Middle Formative	15 (44.1%)	1 (2.9%)	0 (0.0%)	18 (52.9%)	34
Late Formative	15 (22.1%)	5 (7.4%)	1 (1.5%)	47 (69.1%)	68
Terminal Formative	52 (42.6%)	32 (26.2%)	2 (1.6%)	36 (29.5%)	122
Terminal Formative / Early Classic Transitional	10 (41.7%)	4 (16.7%)	2 (8.3%)	8 (33.3%)	24
Subtotals by Type	92	42	5	109	248

Note: Includes only securely dated artifacts. Percentages reflect proportion of a given type in each time period.

Early/Middle Formative period artifacts were all anthropomorphs with the exception of a single bird figurine fragment from the site of La Consentida (Figure 9.10e). Preliminary excavations at La Consentida near the coastal estuaries to the east of the Río Verde have produced twenty-eight solid-bodied, mostly anthropomorphic ceramic figurines. Three AMS radiocarbon dates from secure contexts at La Consentida firmly establish the site's initial Early Formative period occupation (Table 9.6). The sample of diagnostic ceramics that has been recovered at the site also supports an Early Formative date (Hepp 2011a). Twenty-five (89.3%) of the La Consentida figurine fragments are portions of definite or probable anthropomorphs (Figure 9.13). Of the six human figurines from La Consentida with identifiable indications of biological sex or gender, all are female or feminine. This pattern fits with Formative figurines elsewhere in Mesoamerica (see Cyphers Guillén 1993; Joyce 2000; Lesure 1997; Marcus 1998) and indicates inhabitants' strong interest in the female body and likely in the construction of feminine gender roles and sociality. Most of the figurines at La Consentida were recovered from a platform fill, but two were associated with a burial. Six anthropomorphic figurines from securely dated late Middle Formative Charco phase (700–400 BC) deposits were recovered from a domestic midden at the site of Corozo (Figure 9.14). Both the La Consentida and Corozo figurines seem to depict the human form in a more naturalized, simplified style than do later examples, though the head fragment in Figure 9.14b bears headgear as well as possibly gauged ear and cheek jewelry.

Several figurines stylistically similar to Early Formative period examples from other areas of Mesoamerica were discovered in Terminal Formative deposits at Río Viejo, Loma Reyes, and Cerro de la Cruz. We suggest that these may have been curated, redeposited, or heirloomed from earlier time periods. The cocked hat or side-oriented topknot appliqué present on the artifact shown in Figure 9.15 suggests an Early Formative date, as does the presence of large

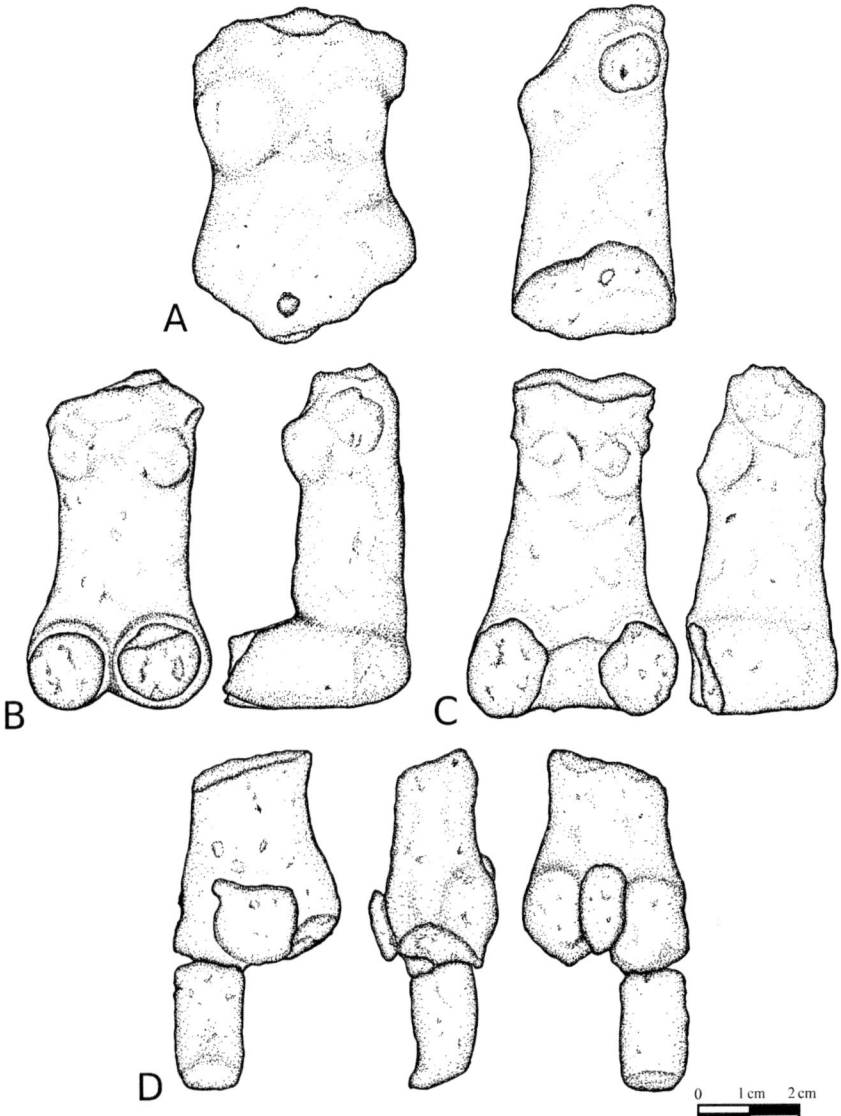

FIGURE 9.13. Female anthropomorphic figurines from La Consentida (from mound fill and burial contexts).

cheeks, a frowning mouth, and raised and incised "coffee bean" shaped eyes (Blomster 1998, 2002). The topknot appliqués shown in Figures 9.15 and 9.16 are similar in style to "Type 8" figurines described at La Blanca in the Río Naranjo area by Arroyo (2002, 213–215, 219), which are also similar to some artifacts

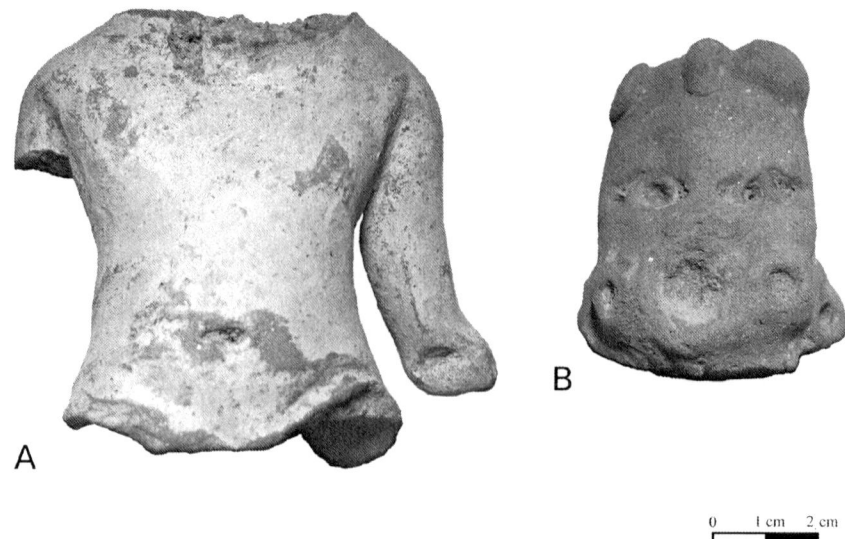

FIGURE 9.14. Middle Formative Charco phase anthropomorphs from domestic midden at Corozo. *A,* Torso fragment with white paint or slip (after Hepp 2009: Photo 834). *B,* Head fragment with headgear, earspools, and possible cheek jewelry (after Hepp 2009: Photo 840).

FIGURE 9.15. Small head fragment bearing Early Formative iconographic style. Miniyua phase public ritual midden at Yugüe (after Hepp 2009: Figure 5.3).

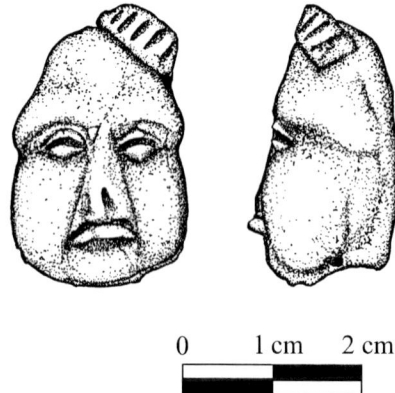

at La Victoria, Chiapa de Corzo, and San Lorenzo. Blomster (personal communication, 2011) has suggested that the figurines in Figures 9.15 and 9.16 bear resemblance to Early Formative examples from the Mixteca Alta.

Zoomorphic and transformational forms became much more common during the Late and Terminal Formative periods, when status distinctions were also increasing in the region (Barber and Joyce 2007; Barber et al., Chapter 4; Barber, Chapter 6; Joyce 2005, 2010, Chapter 1). Zoomorphs increased from

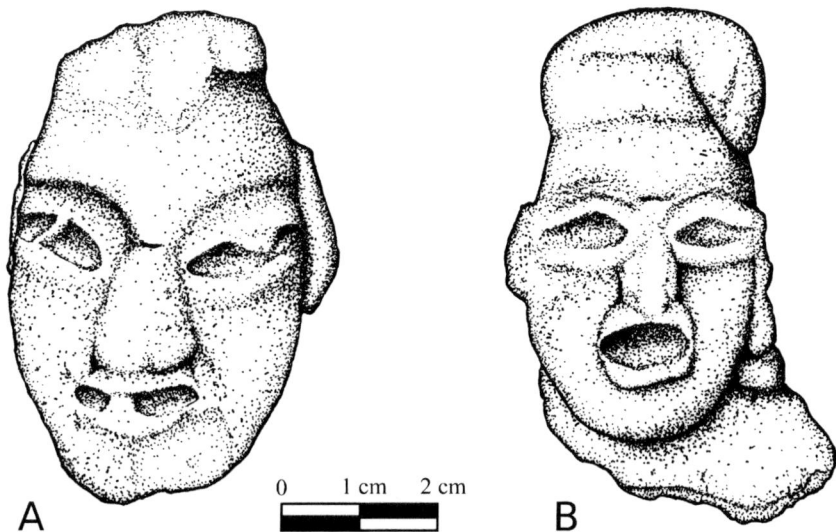

0   1 cm   2 cm

A   B

FIGURE 9.16. Figurine heads bearing Early Formative stylistic elements such as head appliqué and cheek style. *A*, Miniyua or Chacahua phase Loma Reyes (after Hepp 2009: Figure 6.8). *B*, Miniyua phase domestic midden at Rio Viejo (after Hepp 2009: Figure 6.5).

TABLE 9.6. AMS radiocarbon dates from La Consentida

AMS Carbon Date	Calibrated Date[a]	Material	Context
3480 ± 60	1951–1638 cal BC	wood charcoal	Earthen floor or surface
3482 ± 40	1908–1692 cal BC	carbon-rich sediment	Hearth
3358 ± 43	1744–1529 cal BC	carbon-rich sediment	Hearth

[a] Calibrated using IntCal 09 curve provided by OxCal 4.1 and reported with 95.4 percent confidence.

7.4 percent to 26.2 percent between the Late and Terminal Formative periods. Four of the five transformational forms also date to the Terminal Formative, and the other example comes from the Late Formative period. This diversification of imagery through time may indicate that the Terminal Formative was marked by a greater attention to animal representation or the importance of identities blended through nagualism and/or tonalism. Perhaps the increase in transformational forms relates to rising social distinctions justified through religious ritual.

CONCLUDING REMARKS

The iconographic artifacts discussed here depict people, animals, and divine or transformational characters. They serve as evidence of the social and ritual concerns of the people who made them. Ancient Oaxacans were interested in the human body and in the social roles ascribed to and inscribed upon bodies. They demonstrated an interest in sex and gender by forming ceramic images of women and feminine characters, as well as fewer masculine examples. This pattern fits with those of other contemporaneous figurine assemblages in Formative Mesoamerica (Joyce 2000, 2003; Marcus 1998). The majority of figurines did not permit interpretations of sex or gender, however. Another variable of social differentiation may have been age, which interacted with gender to obviate simple masculine/feminine dichotomies (Joyce 2000). Examples of age as a social variable include figurines depicting life-cycle stages such as infancy, pregnancy, and perhaps death. Elaborate accoutrements on some figurines (e.g., Figures 9.1d and 9.2) may have stressed identities of individual people, while other nonindividualized examples (e.g., Figures 9.1a, 9.1b, 9.3b, 9.3c, and 9.14) may have represented generalized ancestors or the proscription of social statuses. Worship or remembrance of deceased ancestors is suggested by the apparently curated anthropomorphic face appliqués (Figure 9.7). Figurine makers and users were also interested in the animals they felt held spiritual power and in shamanic beings who could cross the boundaries between the human and animal realms and between the physical world and the spiritual one. Ethnohistoric and ethnographic evidence on the nature of nagualism and tonalism may be appropriate analogs for ritual practices involving transformational figurines (Bartolomé and Barabas 1996; Gutiérrez and Pye 2010; Sousa 1998, 108–130). Such beliefs may also be demonstrated by the recurring, stylized zoomorphs in the collection, some of which (birds and dogs) are related to documented Mesoamerican beliefs regarding journeys through the underworld and contact with the ancestors (Córdova 1886 [1578], 1942 [1578]; Marcus 1998; Urcid 2005).

Figurine provenience on the Oaxacan coast is diverse, ranging from public buildings, feasting middens, and a ceremonial cache to domestic middens and a high-status residence (Barber 2005, Chapter 6; Hepp 2007, 2009, 2011a, 2011b; Joyce 1991, 1999; Joyce and Levine 2009). Taking the sample as a whole, the contextual associations of the collection support our argument that figurines and iconographic ceramic artifacts were both *domestic* and *public* (as opposed to strictly private) in their use in the lower Río Verde Valley (Barber 2005; Joyce 1991). We suggest that figurines and other small-scale iconographic artifacts were focal points in social activities that *merged* the domestic and public spheres of Formative era life in Mesoamerica.

Figurine production and use may have served not just for enacting religious ritual and contacting ancestors, but also for commenting on aspects of social identity. Such practices may explain the preponderance of depictions of human and especially *female* and *feminine* human bodies in comparison to other types. If figurines were not a commentary on the nature of specific social identities, one would expect them to depict members of all ages and genders equally. The fact that anthropomorphic figurines are found in diverse contexts in coastal Oaxaca suggests that negotiation of social roles was not restricted to a specific spatial setting. Rosemary Joyce (2000, 28; 2004) reached a similar conclusion when she stated that public and domestic spaces were not mutually exclusive and that communal spaces in general underwent a change during the Formative period, as they became venues for performances through which community members expressed and negotiated their social roles. The notion of a communal domesticity perhaps explains how households were increasingly affiliated with broader social networks as the scale of community organization expanded through the Formative period (see Barber 2005, Chapter 6; Barber and Joyce 2007; Joyce 2005, 2010, 180–195; Chapter 1; Joyce et al., Chapter 5).

Ritual behavior in ancient Mesoamerican villages was dynamic in that people of diverse identities participated in it differentially (Barber and Joyce 2007; Blomster 1998; Cyphers Guillén 1993; Gillespie 2001; Lesure and Blake 2002; Marcus 1998; Urcid 2005). It has often been assumed that rituals involving figurines were performed by women because of the preponderance of female imagery on Formative figurines coupled with their use in domestic settings. To assume that females were always the primary actors in domestic spaces and that males were always primary actors in public settings, however, forges false dichotomies about both identity and communal spaces. At Paso de la Amada, for example, Lesure and Blake (2002, 9) found a pattern of figurine deposition precluding a simple gender dichotomy. Female figurines deposited adjacent to public platforms and burial patterns indicating a lack of division by gender and age categories are "incompatible with the notions of gender exclusivity (Lesure and Blake 2002, 9)." The relative ubiquity of figurine deposition at coastal Oaxacan sites casts similar doubt on simple behavioral divisions along gender lines (*contra* Marcus 1998, 9), suggesting a significant degree of gender complementarity as documented ethnohistorically. While the presence of figurines in public contexts may indicate the active role of women in public ritual discourse, it may also indicate the active role of men in figurine-related behavior. In addition, a modern Western gender dichotomy may be wholly inappropriate for application to Formative period Mesoamerica (Blomster 2009; Nanda 1999; Nelson 1997; Sousa 1997, 1998; Stephen 1991, 2002; Terraciano 1994; Whitehead 1981). Finally, children's play is all too often overlooked in archaeological interpretation. As Winter (2005, 49–51) has argued, children may have used figurines as playthings, and archaeologists must remain open to such activities as explaining aspects of the material record (also see Kamp 2001, 427).

A major purpose for studying figurines is to understand what their attributes, artistic style, and circumstances of deposition can tell us about their meanings and the social contexts in which they were used. We find that figurine-related practices in the lower Río Verde Valley included those involving the development of social identities, rituals marking life-cycle events (including infancy, pregnancy, and death), and shamanic efforts to harness the power of the spiritual realm through the mimetic figurine. As implied by our model of communal domesticity, public and private spheres of interaction likely lacked a definitive separation during the Formative period, and ritual behaviors associated with different zones of community space probably overlapped. To the extent that increasing social differentiation during the Terminal Formative altered this paradigm, it did so based on negotiation between members of differing status groups and on manipulation of the same sorts of social categories and local identities understood during earlier periods (Barber and Joyce 2007; Barber, Chapter 6). We argue that issues such as personhood construction, ancestor worship, sex and gender roles, age, spiritual power, and human/animal identity relations as represented through small-scale iconography were all at the forefront of ancient Oaxacan worldviews. Figurines served not just as mimetic representations of their intended subjects, but also as physical expressions of a general Mesoamerican philosophy regarding identity and the nature of worldly and divine realms, one in which the spirits of animals or people could be called upon to join the corporeal world by residing in the temporary vessel of the ceramic figurine.

ACKNOWLEDGMENTS

We would like to thank Mary Pohl, Jeffrey Blomster, John Clark, Christopher Pool, Sarah Barber, Ivy Hepp, Josephine Knight, and others who read and responded to various iterations of this study over the years. A University of Colorado Anthropology Graduate Student Research Award and a Colorado Archaeological Society Alice Hamilton Scholarship Award generously provided partial funding for this project.

NOTE

1. A single figurine may simultaneously be categorized as a "possible anthropomorph" and a "possible zoomorph," so the combined count of figurines in Table 9.2 exceeds the number of figurines in the study.

REFERENCES CITED

Arroyo, Barbara. 2002. Appendix I: Classification of La Blanca Figurines. In *Early Complex Society in Pacific Guatemala: Settlements and Chronology of the Río Naranjo, Guatemala*, ed. Michael W. Love, 205–35. Papers of the New World Archaeological Foundation 66. Provo, UT: New World Archaeological Foundation.

Ashmore, Wendy. 2004. "Classic Maya Landscapes and Settlement." In *Mesoamerican Archaeology*, ed. Julia A. Hendon and Rosemary A. Joyce, 169–91. Malden, MA: Blackwell.

Barber, Sarah B. 2005. *Heterogeneity, Identity, and Complexity: Negotiating Status and Authority in Terminal Formative Coastal Oaxaca*. PhD dissertation, Department of Anthropology, University of Colorado, Boulder. Ann Arbor, MI: University Microfilms.

Barber, Sarah B., and Guy David Hepp. 2012. "Ancient Aerophones of Coastal Oaxaca, Mexico: The Archaeological and Social Context of Music." In *Sound from the Past: The Interpretation of Musical Artifacts in an Archaeological Context*, ed. Ricardo Eichmann, Fang Jianjun, and Lars-Christian Koch. Studien zur Musikarchäologie VIII, Orient-Archäologie 27. Berlin: German Institute of Archaeology, 259–70.

Barber, Sarah B., and Arthur A. Joyce. 2007. "Polity Produced and Community Consumed: Negotiating Political Centralization through Ritual in the Lower Río Verde Valley, Oaxaca." In *Ritual Economy: Archaeological and Ethnological Perspectives*, ed. E. Christian Wells and Karla L. Davis-Salazar, 221–44. Boulder: University Press of Colorado.

Bartolomé, Miguel A., and Alicia M. Barabas. 1996. *Tierra de la palabra: Historia y etnografía de los Chatinos de Oaxaca*. 2nd ed. Oaxaca City: Instituto Oaxaqueño de las Culturas; Mexico City: Instituto Nacional de Antropología e Historia.

Benjamin, Walter, and Knut Tarnowski. 1979. "Doctrine of the Similar." *New German Critique, NGC* 17 (17): 65–69. http://dx.doi.org/10.2307/488010.

Bernal, Ignacio. 1946. "La Cerámica preclasica de Monte Albán." MA thesis, Escuela Nacional de Antropología e Historia, Mexico City.

Blomster, Jeffrey P. 1998. "Context, Cult, and Early Formative Period Public Ritual in the Mixteca Alta: Analysis of a Hollow-Baby Figurine from Etlatongo, Oaxaca." *Ancient Mesoamerica* 9 (2): 309–26. http://dx.doi.org/10.1017/S0956536100002017.

Blomster, Jeffrey P. 2002. "What and Where Is Olmec Style? Regional Perspectives on Hollow Figurines in Early Formative Mesoamerica." *Ancient Mesoamerica* 13 (2): 171–95. http://dx.doi.org/10.1017/S0956536102132196.

Blomster, Jeffrey P. 2004. *Etlatongo: Social Complexity, Interaction, and Village Life in the Mixteca Alta of Oaxaca, Mexico*. Belmont, CA: Wadsworth/Thomson Learning.

Blomster, Jeffrey P. 2009. "Identity, Gender, and Power: Representational Juxtapositions in Early Formative Figurines from Oaxaca, Mexico." In *Mesoamerican Figurines: Small-Scale Indices of Large-Scale Social Phenomena*, ed. Christina T. Halperin, Katherine A. Faust, Rhonda Taube, and Aurore Giguet, 119–48. Gainesville: University Press of Florida.

Brady, James E. 1991. "Caves and Cosmovision at Utatlan." *California Anthropologist* 18 (1): 1–10.

Brady, James E. 1997. "Settlement Configuration and Cosmology: The Role of Caves at Dos Pilas." *American Anthropologist* 99 (3): 602–18. http://dx.doi.org/10.1525/aa .1997.99.3.602.

Brockington, Donald L. 2001. "Anthropomorphic Figurines from the Oaxaca Coast." In *The New World Figurine Project*, vol. 2, ed. Terry Stocker and Cynthia L. Otis Charlton, 1–24. Provo, UT: Research Press at Brigham Young University.

Clark, John E. 1994. *The Development of Early Formative Rank Societies in the Soconusco, Chiapas, Mexico.* PhD dissertation, Department of Anthropology, University of Michigan, Ann Arbor. Ann Arbor, MI: University Microfilms.

Coe, Michael D. 1965. *The Jaguar's Children: Pre-Classic Central Mexico.* New York: Museum of Primitive Art.

Coe, Michael D., and Richard A. Diehl. 1980. *In the Land of the Olmec*, Volume 1: *The Archaeology of San Lorenzo Tenochtitlán.* Austin: University of Texas Press.

Conkey, Margaret W., and Joan M. Gero. 1997. "Programme to Practice: Gender and Feminism in Archaeology." *Annual Review of Anthropology* 26 (1): 411–37. http://dx.doi.org/10.1146/annurev.anthro.26.1.411.

Conklin, Beth A., and Lynn M. Morgan. 1996. "Babies, Bodies, and the Production of Personhood in North America and a Native Amazonian Society." *Ethos (Berkeley, Calif.)* 24 (4): 657–94. http://dx.doi.org/10.1525/eth.1996.24.4.02a00040.

Córdova, Fray Juan de. 1886 [1578]. *Arte del idioma zapoteca.* Mexico City: Pedro Balli.

Córdova, Fray Juan de. 1942 [1578]. *Vocabulario en lengua zapoteca.* Mexico City: Pedro Charte and Antonio Ricardo.

Culbert, T. Patrick. 1993. *The Ceramics of Tikal: Vessels from the Burials, Caches and Problematical Deposits.* Tikal Report No. 25, University Museum Monograph 81. Philadelphia: University Museum, University of Pennsylvania.

Cyphers Guillén, Ann. 1993. "Women, Rituals, and Social Dynamics at Ancient Chalcatzingo." *Latin American Antiquity* 4 (3): 209–24. http://dx.doi.org/10.2307/971789.

Drennan, Robert D. 1976. "Interregional Religious Networks: Religion and Social Evolution in Formative Mesoamerica." In *The Early Mesoamerican Village*, ed. Kent V. Flannery, 345–68. San Diego: Academic Press.

Dyk, Anne. 1959. "Mixteco Texts." In *Publication of the Summer Institute of Linguistics of the University of Oklahoma*, ed. Benjamin Elson. Norman: University of Oklahoma Press.

Faust, Katherine A., and Christina T. Halperin. 2009. "Approaching Mesoamerican Figurines." In *Mesoamerican Figurines: Small-Scale Indices of Large-Scale Social Phenomena*, ed. Christina T. Halperin, Katherine A. Faust, Rhonda Taube, and Aurore Giguet, 1–22. Gainesville: University Press of Florida.

Fernández Pardo, Ligia A. 1993. "Figurillas de cerámica del valle del Río Verde Inferior, Oaxaca." Licenciatura thesis, Universidad Autónoma de Guadalajara, Zapopan.

Fortes, Meyer. 1987. "The Concept of the Person." In *Religion, Morality, and the Person: Essays on Tallensi Religion*, ed. Jack Goody, 247–86. New York: Cambridge University Press. http://dx.doi.org/10.1017/CBO9780511557996.011.

Foster, George M. 1944. "Nagualism in Mexico and Guatemala." *Acta Americana* 2: 85–103.

Geller, Pamela A. 2008. "Conceiving Sex: Fomenting a Feminist Bioarchaeology." *Journal of Social Archaeology* 8 (1): 113–38. http://dx.doi.org/10.1177/1469605307086080.

Giddens, Anthony. 1979. *Central Problems in Social Theory.* Berkeley: University of California Press.

Gillespie, Susan D. 2000. "Lévi-Strauss: Maison and Société à Maisons." In *Beyond Kinship: Social and Material Reproduction in House Societies*, ed. Rosemary A. Joyce and Susan D. Gillespie, 22–52. Philadelphia: University of Pennsylvania Press.

Gillespie, Susan D. 2001. "Personhood, Agency, and Mortuary Ritual: A Case Study from the Ancient Maya." *Journal of Anthropological Archaeology* 20 (1): 73–112. http://dx.doi.org/10.1006/jaar.2000.0369.

Gutiérrez, Gerardo, and Mary E. Pye. 2010. "Iconography of the Nahual: Human-Animal Transformations in Preclassic Guerrero and Morelos." In *The Place of Stone Monuments: Context, Use, and Meaning in Mesoamerica's Preclassic Transition*, ed. Julia Guernsey, John E. Clark, and Barbara Arroyo, 27–95. Washington, DC: Dumbarton Oaks.

Hepp, Guy David. 2007. "Formative Period Ceramic Figurines from the Lower Río Verde Valley, Coastal Oaxaca, Mexico." MA thesis, Florida State University, Tallahassee.

Hepp, Guy David. 2009. *Formative Period Figurines of Coastal Oaxaca, Mexico: Ancient Mesoamerican Ceramic Iconography from the Lower Río Verde Valley*. Saarbrücken, Germany: VDM Verlag Dr. Müller.

Hepp, Guy David. 2011a. "The Material Culture of Incipient Social Complexity in Coastal Oaxaca: The Ceramics of La Consentida." Paper presented at the 76th Annual Meeting of the Society for American Archaeology, Sacramento, CA.

Hepp, Guy David. 2011b. Proyecto La Consentida 2009. In "El proyecto Río Verde: Informe técnico de la temporada de 2009," ed. Sarah B. Barber and Arthur A. Joyce, 146–184. Final report submitted to the Consejo de Arqueología, Instituto Nacional de Antropología e Historia, Mexico City.

Hepp, Guy David, and Ivy A. Hepp. N.d. "Aspects of Dress and Ornamentation in Coastal Oaxaca's Formative Period." In *Transcendent Treasures: Dress, Regalia, and Adornment in Early Mesoamerica and Central America*, ed. Hearther Orr and Mathew Looper. Boulder: University Press of Colorado, in press.

Heyden, Doris. 1991. "Dryness before the Rains: Toxcatl and Tezcatlipoca." In *To Change Place: Aztec Ceremonial Landscapes*, ed. Davíd Carrasco, 188–204. Niwot: University Press of Colorado.

Joyce, Arthur A. 1991. *Formative Period Occupation in the Lower Río Verde Valley, Oaxaca, Mexico: Interregional Interaction and Social Change*. PhD Dissertation, Department of Anthropology, Rutgers University, New Brunswick, NJ. Ann Arbor, MI: University Microfilms.

Joyce, Arthur A., ed. 1999. "El proyecto patrones de asentamiento del Río Verde." Final report submitted to the Consejo de Arqueología, Instituto Nacional de Antropología e Historia, Mexico City.

Joyce, Arthur A. 2004. "Sacred Space and Social Relations in Oaxaca." In *Mesoamerican Archaeology: Theory and Practice*, ed. Julia A. Hendon and Rosemary A. Joyce, 192–216. Malden, MA: Blackwell.

Joyce, Arthur A. 2005. "La arqueología del bajo Río Verde." *Acervos: Boletín de los Archivos y Bibliotecas de Oaxaca* 7 (29): 16–36.

Joyce, Arthur A. 2006. "The Inhabitation of Río Viejo's Acropolis." In *Space and Spatial Analysis in Archaeology*, ed. Elizabeth C. Robertson, Jeffrey D. Seibert, Deepika C. Fernández, and Marc U. Zender, 83–96. Albuquerque: University of New Mexico Press; Calgary: University of Calgary Press.

Joyce, Arthur A. 2010. *Mixtecs, Zapotecs, and Chatinos: Ancient Peoples of Southern Mexico*. Malden, MA: Wiley-Blackwell.

Joyce, Arthur A., and Marc N. Levine, eds. 2009. "El proyecto Río Verde." Final report submitted to the Consejo de Arqueología, Instituto Nacional de Antropología e Historia, Mexico City.

Joyce, Arthur A., and Marcus Winter. 1989. "Investigaciones arqueológicas en la cuenca del Río Verde inferior, 1988." *Notas Mesoamericanas* 11: 249–62.

Joyce, Rosemary A. 1998. "Performing the Body in Pre-Hispanic Central America." *Res: Anthropology and Aesthetics* 33: 147–65.

Joyce, Rosemary A. 2000. *Gender and Power in Prehispanic Mesoamerica.* Austin: University of Texas Press.

Joyce, Rosemary A. 2002. "Beauty, Sexuality, Body Ornamentation, and Gender in Ancient Mesoamerica." In *In Pursuit of Gender: Worldwide Archaeological Approaches,* ed. Sarah Milledge Nelson and Myriam Rosen-Ayalon, 81–92. New York: AltaMira Press.

Joyce, Rosemary A. 2003. "Making Something of Herself: Embodiment in Life and Death at Playa de los Muertos, Honduras." *Cambridge Archaeological Journal* 13 (2): 248–61. http://dx.doi.org/10.1017/S0959774303240142.

Joyce, Rosemary A. 2004. "Unintended Consequences? Monumentality as a Novel Experience in Formative Mesoamerica." *Journal of Archaeological Method and Theory* 11 (1): 5–29. http://dx.doi.org/10.1023/B:JARM.0000014346.87569.4a.

Joyce, Rosemary A. 2009. "Making a World of Their Own: Mesoamerican Figurines and Mesoamerican Figurine Analysis." In *Mesoamerican Figurines: Small-Scale Indices of Large-Scale Social Phenomena,* ed. Christina T. Halperin, Katherine A. Faust, Rhonda Taube, and Aurore Giguet, 407–25. Gainesville: University Press of Florida.

Kamp, Kathryn A. 2001. "Prehistoric Children Working and Playing: A Southwestern Case Study in Learning." *Journal of Anthropological Research* 57 (4): 427–50.

Kaplan, Lucille N. 1956. "Tonal and Nagual in Coastal Oaxaca, Mexico." *Journal of American Folklore* 69 (274): 363–68. http://dx.doi.org/10.2307/536346.

La Fontaine, Jean S. 1978. "Introduction." In *Sex and Age as Principles of Social Differentiation,* ed. Jeam S. La Fontaine, 1–20. New York: Academic Press.

Lesure, Richard G. 1995. *Paso de la Amada: Sociopolitical Dynamics in an Early Formative Community.* PhD dissertation, Department of Anthropology, University of Michigan, Ann Arbor. Ann Arbor, MI: University Microfilms.

Lesure, Richard G. 1997. "Figurines and Social Identities in Early Sedentary Societies of Coastal Chiapas, Mexico, 1550–800 BC." In *Women in Prehistory: North America and Mesoamerica,* ed. Cheryl Claassen and Rosemary A. Joyce, 227–48. Philadelphia: University of Pennsylvania Press.

Lesure, Richard G. 1999. "Figurines as Representations and Products at Paso de la Amada, Mexico." *Cambridge Archaeological Journal* 9 (2): 209–20. http://dx.doi.org/10.1017/S0959774300015389.

Lesure, Richard G. 2011. *Interpreting Ancient Figurines: Context, Comparison, and Prehistoric Art.* New York: Cambridge University Press. http://dx.doi.org/10.1017/CBO9780511973376.

Lesure, Richard G., and Michael Blake. 2002. "Interpretive Challenges in the Study of Early Complexity: Economy, Ritual, and Architecture at Paso de la Amada, Mexico." *Journal of Anthropological Archaeology* 21 (1): 1–24. http://dx.doi.org/10.1006/jaar.2001.0388.

Lévi-Strauss, Claude. 1963. "Structural Analysis in Linguistics and in Anthropology." In *Structural Anthropology*, trans. Claire Jacobson and Brooke Schoepf, 31–54. New York: Basic Books.

Marcus, Joyce. 1983. "Changing Patterns of Stone Monuments after the Fall of Monte Alban, A.D. 600–900." In *The Cloud People: Divergent Evolution of the Zapotec and Mixtec Civilizations*, ed. Kent V. Flannery and Joyce Marcus, 191–97. New York: Academic Press.

Marcus, Joyce. 1998. *Women's Ritual in Formative Oaxaca: Figurine Making, Divination, Death and the Ancestors*. Prehistory and Human Ecology of the Valley of Oaxaca 11. Ann Arbor: University of Michigan Press.

Marcus, Joyce. 2009. "Rethinking Figurines." In *Mesoamerican Figurines: Small-Scale Indices of Large-Scale Social Phenomena*, ed. Christina T. Halperin, Katherine A. Faust, Rhonda Taube, and Aurore Giguet, 25–50. Gainesville: University Press of Florida.

Marcus, Joyce, and Kent V. Flannery. 1996. *Zapotec Civilization: How Urban Society Evolved in Mexico's Oaxaca Valley*. London: Thames and Hudson.

Martínez López, Cira, and Marcus Winter. 1994. *Figurillas y silbatos de cerámica de Monte Albán*. Contribución No. 5 del Proyecto Especial Monte Albán 1992–1994. Oaxaca: Centro INAH–Oaxaca.

Mauss, Marcel. 1985 [1938]. "Une Catégorie de L'Esprit Humain: La Notion de Personne Celle de "Moi." In *The Category of the Person: Anthropology, Philosophy, History*, ed. Michael Carrithers, Steven Collins, and Steven Lukes, 1–25. New York: Cambridge University Press.

Miller, Daniel, ed. 2005. *Materiality*. Durham, NC: Duke University Press.

Monaghan, John. 1995. *The Covenants with Earth and Rain: Exchange, Sacrifice, and Revelation in Mixtec Sociality*. Norman: University of Oklahoma Press.

Mountjoy, Joseph B., and José C. Beltrán. 2005. "Anthropomorphic Peg-Based Sculptures from the Banderas Valley of Coastal West Mexico." *Ancient Mesoamerica* 16 (2): 155–68. http://dx.doi.org/10.1017/S0956536105050157.

Munson, Marit K. 2000. "Sex, Gender, and Status: Human Images from the Classic Mimbres." *American Antiquity* 65 (1): 127–43. http://dx.doi.org/10.2307/2694811.

Muratorio, Blanca. 1998. "Indigenous Women's Identities and the Politics of Cultural Reproduction in the Ecuadorian Amazon." *American Anthropologist* 100 (2): 409–20. http://dx.doi.org/10.1525/aa.1998.100.2.409.

Nanda, Serena. 1999. *The Hijras of India: Neither Man nor Woman*. 2nd ed. Belmont, CA: Wadsworth.

Nelson, Sarah M. 1997. *Gender in Archaeology: Analyzing Power and Prestige*. Walnut Creek, CA: Altamira Press.

Pauketat, Timothy R. 2001. "Practice and History in Archaeology." *Anthropological Theory* 1 (1): 73–98.

Pohl, Mary, Kevin O. Pope, and Christopher von Nagy. 2002. "Olmec Origins of Mesoamerican Writing." *Science* 298, no. 5600 (Dec. 6): 1984–87. http://dx.doi.org/10.1126/science.1078474. Medline:12471256.

Powis, Terry G., Fred Valdez Jr., Thomas R. Hester, W. Jeffrey Hurst, and Stanley M. Tarka Jr. 2002. "Spouted Vessels and Cacao Use among the Preclassic Maya." *Latin American Antiquity* 13 (1): 85–106. http://dx.doi.org/10.2307/971742.

Robin, Cynthia. 2002. "Outside of Houses: The Practices of Everyday Life at Chan Nòohol, Belize." *Journal of Social Archaeology* 2 (2): 245–68. http://dx.doi.org/10.11 77/1469605302002002397.

Rojas, Alfonso V. 1947. "Kinship and Nagualism in a Tzeltal Community, Southeastern Mexico." *American Anthropologist* 49 (4): 578–87. http://dx.doi.org/10.1525/aa.19 47.49.4.02a00050.

Saunders, Nicholas J. 1994. "Predators of Culture: Jaguar Symbolism and Mesoamerican Elites." *World Archaeology* 26 (1): 104–17. http://dx.doi.org/10.1080/00438243.1 994.9980264.

Saunders, Nicholas J. 2001. "A Dark Light: Reflections on Obsidian in Mesoamerica." *World Archaeology* 33 (2): 220–36. http://dx.doi.org/10.1080/00438240120079262.

Schwartz, Marion. 1997. *A History of Dogs in the Early Americas.* New Haven, CT: Yale University Press.

Sewell, William H., Jr. 1992. "A Theory of Structure: Duality, Agency, and Transformation." *American Journal of Sociology* 98 (1): 1–29. http://dx.doi.org/10.1086/229967.

Shafer, Harry J., and Anna J. Taylor. 1986. "Mimbres Mogollon Pueblo Dynamics and Ceramic Style Change." *Journal of Field Archaeology* 13 (1): 43–68. http://dx.doi.org /10.2307/529911.

Smith, Ledyard. 2005 [1932]. "Two Recent Ceramic Finds at Uaxactun." *Contributions to American Archaeology* 2 (5): 1–25. Publication No. 43, Carnegie Institution of Washington. Electronic version of original 1932 publication: http://www.mesoweb. com/publications/CAA/05.html.

Sousa, Lisa. 1997. "Women and Crime in Colonial Oaxaca: Evidence of Complementary Gender Roles in Mixtec and Zapotec Societies." In *Indian Women of Early Mexico*, ed. Susan Schroeder, Stephanie Wood, and Robert Haskett, 199–214. Norman: University of Oklahoma Press.

Sousa, Lisa. 1998. *Women in Native Societies and Cultures of Colonial Mexico.* PhD dissertation, Department of History, University of California, Los Angeles. Ann Arbor, MI: University Microfilms.

Spores, Ronald. 1997. "Mixteca Cacicas: Status, Wealth, and the Political Accommodation of Native Elite Women in Early Colonial Oaxaca." In *Indian Women of Early Mexico*, ed. Susan Schroeder, Stephanie Wood, and Robert Haskett, 185–198. Norman: University of Oklahoma Press.

Stephen, Lynn. 1991. *Zapotec Women.* Austin: University of Texas Press.

Stephen, Lynn. 2002. "Sexualities and Genders in Zapotec Oaxaca." *Latin American Perspectives* 29 (2): 41–59. http://dx.doi.org/10.1177/0094582X0202900203.

Stern, Stephen J. 1995. *The Secret History of Gender: Women, Men, and Power in Late Colonial Mexico.* Chapel Hill: University of North Carolina Press.

Taube, Karl A. 1992. "The Iconography of Mirrors at Teotihuacan." In *Art, Ideology, and the City of Teotihuacan*, ed. Janet C. Berlo, 169–204. Washington, DC: Dumbarton Oaks.

Taube, Karl A. 1993. *Aztec and Maya Myths: The Legendary Past.* Austin: University of Texas Press.

Taube, Karl A. 2000. "Lightning Celts and Corn Fetishes: The Formative Olmec and the Development of Maize Symbolism in Mesoamerica and the American Southwest." In *Olmec Art and Archaeology in Mesoamerica*, ed. John E. Clark and Mary

E. Pye, 296–337. Studies in the History of Art no. 58. Washington, DC: National Gallery of Art.

Taussig, Michael. 1993. *Mimesis and Alterity: A Particular History of the Senses*. New York: Routledge.

Taylor, William B. 1979. *Drinking, Homicide, and Rebellion in Colonial Mexican Villages*. Stanford, CA: Stanford University Press.

Tedlock, Barbara. 2005. *The Woman in the Shaman's Body*. New York: Bantam Books.

Terraciano, Kevin. 1994. *Ñudzahui History: Mixtec Writing and Culture in Colonial Oaxaca*. PhD dissertation, Department of History, University of California, Los Angeles. Ann Arbor, MI: University Microfilms.

Terraciano, Kevin. 2000. "The Colonial Mixtec Community." *Hispanic American Historical Review* 80 (1): 1–42. http://dx.doi.org/10.1215/00182168-80-1-1.

Terraciano, Kevin. 2001. *The Mixtecs of Colonial Oaxaca: Nudzahui History, Sixteenth through Eighteenth Centuries*. Stanford, CA: Stanford University Press.

Tilley, Christopher. 1999. *Metaphor and Material Culture*. Malden, MA: Blackwell Publishers.

Urcid, Javier. 2005. *Zapotec Writing: Knowledge, Power, and Memory in Ancient Oaxaca*. Coral Gables, FL: Foundation for the Advancement of Mesoamerican Studies. http://www.famsi.org/zapotecwriting/.

Verhoeven, Marc. 2002. "Ritual and Ideology in the Pre-Pottery Neolithic B of the Levant and Southeast Anatolia." *Cambridge Archaeological Journal* 12 (2): 233–58. http://dx.doi.org/10.1017/S0959774302000124.

Vilaça, Aparecida. 2002. "Making Kin out of Others in Amazonia." *Journal of the Royal Anthropological Institute* 8 (2): 347–65. http://dx.doi.org/10.1111/1467-9655.00007.

Whalen, Michael E. 1981. *Excavations at Santo Domingo Tomaltepec: Evolution of a Formative Community in the Valley of Oaxaca, Mexico*. Prehistory and Human Ecology of the Valley of Oaxaca 12. Memoirs of the Museum of Anthropology, vol. 4. Ann Arbor: University of Michigan Press.

Whitehead, Harriet. 1981. "The Bow and the Burden Strap: A New Look at Institutionalized Homosexuality." In *Sexual Meanings: The Cultural Construction of Gender and Sexuality*, ed. Sherry B. Ortner and Harriet Whitehead, 113–28. Cambridge: Cambridge University Press.

Winter, Marcus. 1992. *Oaxaca: The Archaeological Record*. 2nd ed. Mexico City: Minutiae Mexicana.

Winter, Marcus. 2005. "Producción y uso de figurillas tempranas en el valle de Oaxaca." *Acervos: Boletín de los Archivos y Bibliotecas de Oaxaca* 7 (29): 37–54.

Wolf, Eric R. 1959. *Sons of the Shaking Earth: The People of Mexico and Guatemala—Their Land, History, and Culture*. Chicago: University of Chicago Press.

TEN

COASTAL OAXACA AND FORMATIVE DEVELOPMENTS IN MESOAMERICA

CHRISTOPHER A. POOL

Over the past two decades, archaeologists have focused increasingly on how individuals and groups use material, social, and ideological resources to acquire and maintain power (e.g., Baines and Yoffee 1998; Blanton et al. 1996; Clark and Blake 1994; Demarest and Conrad 1992; Demarrais et al. 1996; Earle 1997). Arthur Joyce has been a particularly thoughtful proponent of archaeological approaches that, drawing on Giddens (e.g., 1984), view "people as dynamic actors in a social process" and "population-level phenomena . . . as the outcome of behavioral strategies which are both enabled and constrained by the biophysical and social environment" (Joyce and Winter 1996, 35). In this volume Joyce and his collaborators demonstrate the value of an actor-based framework for multidisciplinary research that combines environmental, sociopolitical, and ideological investigation.

The Formative period focus of their research in the lower Río Verde Valley of coastal Oaxaca offers rich opportunities for comparison with the development of sociopolitical complexity in other regions of Mesoamerica. While Mesoamerica in general exhibits a shared pattern of increasing population and complexity through the Formative period, social change was not uniform through time or

DOI: 10.5876/9781607322023.c10

across space. Instead, the timing of critical events and the implementation of particular political strategies varied between and within regions as environmental change, distant wars, shifting alliances, internal social processes, and the competing interests of local actors conspired to promote the growth and dissolution of communities and polities across Mesoamerica. The multidisciplinary research conducted in the lower Río Verde Valley illuminates the interplay of these processes.

In the pages that follow I will situate the lower Río Verde Valley within the broader context of Formative period developments elsewhere in Mesoamerica. After a general overview of developments in the Archaic and Early to Middle Formative periods, I will focus on a comparison of the lower Río Verde Valley with trajectories of sociopolitical organization and practice at Monte Albán in the Valley of Oaxaca (Figure 1.1) and Tres Zapotes in the Papaloapan basin of southern Veracruz (Figure 1.3). Both of these sites were the capitals of powerful polities in the Late and Terminal Formative periods, contemporaneous with the florescence of Charco Redondo, San Francisco de Arriba, and Río Viejo in the lower Río Verde Valley. In the course of their history they faced similar challenges to those of the Río Verde, importing materials necessary to meet daily needs and reinforce differential status, contending with powerful neighbors, striving to resolve tensions between emerging hierarchies and communal interests, and staving off collapse. Representing both highland and lowland environments as well as three different ethnolinguistic groups (Chatino, Zapotec, and Zoquean) with very different regional political histories, the commonalities and contrasts in their solutions to social challenges underscore the complex interplay of behavioral strategies that have been broadly categorized as corporate and exclusionary or network (Blanton 1998; Blanton et al. 1996; Feinman 2001).

ANTECEDENTS: THE ARCHAIC THROUGH MIDDLE FORMATIVE PERIODS

The roots of indigenous Mesoamerican subsistence and settled life lie in the domestication of a variety of plants in the Archaic period (ca. 8000–1600 BC). Consequently, subsistence practices and their effects on settlement and mobility patterns have dominated research on the Archaic period since Richard S. MacNeish began his search for the origins of domesticated maize in the 1950s. In very broad terms, the story of the Archaic is one of initially mobile hunter-gatherers gradually increasing their reliance on plant foods, domesticating several of them, as their movements became more restricted and their settlements more permanent (Flannery 1986; Smith 1997, 2000) In some environments with abundant and intensifiable resources, such as coastal estuaries and the shores of highland lakes, sedentism may have been less dependent on the adoption of cultivars (e.g., Clark 1994, 194; Niederberger 1976; Stark 1981; Voorhies 1996). Nevertheless, pollen and phytolith data collected from sediment cores over the last twenty years has turned up surprising evidence for very early land clearance and maize cultivation in the coastal lowlands—as early as 5100 cal BC at San Andrés, Tabasco (Pohl et al. 2007; Pope et al. 2001), by 4500 BC in the Gulf lowlands of central Veracruz (Goman et al., Chapter 2; Sluyter and Domínguez 2006), and by about 2880 cal BC at slightly higher elevations in the Tuxtla Mountains of southern Veracruz (Goman and Byrne 1998). As Goman and her colleagues (Chapter 2) point out, such early dates in the coastal lowlands favor the hypothesis that maize was domesticated from teosinte in a lowland setting such as the Río Balsas (Holst et al. 2007; Piperno et al. 2007; Ranere et al. 2009).

Although the current evidence relating to Archaic and very early Formative occupations in the lower Río Verde Valley is scarce, indications of maize cultivation and forest clearance by 2750 cal BC fit a broader pattern of late Archaic maize cultivation on both coasts of Mesoamerica. Unlike most areas, however, there appears to have been a retraction of maize cultivation in the Early Formative period. In this regard, the geomorphological research reported by Mueller and his colleagues (Chapter 3) suggests that the initiation of changes in depositional regimes near the beginning of the Early Formative period contributed to the retraction of maize cultivation and perhaps delayed substantial occupation until after about 700 cal BC during the local late Middle Formative period.[1] There also is little evidence from pollen, phytoliths (Goman et al., Chapter 2), or stable isotopes in human bone (Taylor et al. 2009) for a linkage between maize agriculture, population increase, and the initial emergence of a two-tiered settlement hierarchy in the Middle Formative period. This is not quite so surprising as it may seem. Paleoethnobotanical and isotopic studies in the Gulf coast (Arnold 2000, 2009; VanDerwarker 2003; see also Borstein 2001) and the Soconusco (Blake et al. 1992; Chisholm et al. 1993; cf. Ambrose and Norr 1992) suggest that maize was a minor component of diets in some of the most populous and complexly organized societies of the Early Formative period.

I suspect that reliance on this resource was not as great as the term "maize agriculture" might imply, however. On the Gulf coast faunal evidence suggests that maize was a relatively minor component of a mixed fishing-hunting-gathering-cultivating economy in the Archaic period, despite its association with increased burning (Pope et al. 2001), and recent opinion favors the idea that Early Formative reliance on maize in the lowlands was variable and considerably less than during the Middle Formative period (e.g., Arnold 1996, 2000, 2009; Borstein 2001; Rust and Leyden 1994; see also VanDerwarker 2006).

The Middle Formative period was a time of increasing population and sociopolitical complexity across most of Mesoamerica. Regional-scale surveys document increases in the number and average size of sites, as well as the size of the largest sites, in much of central Mexico, Oaxaca, the southern and south-central Gulf coast, and the Guatemala highlands (e.g., Arnold and Stark 1997; Daneels 1997; Grove 1987; Kowalewski et al. 1989; Sanders et al. 1979; Santley and Arnold 1996; von Nagy 2003). Systematic regional-scale survey data are more scarce in the Maya lowlands, but large-site surveys and excavations indicate a proliferation of villages, with substantial public architecture emerging in northern Yucatán and the Petén before 400 BC (Andrews 1981; Clark and Hansen 2001; Ringle 1999, 189).

There are significant exceptions to the macroregional pattern of increasing population and complexity, however. An important one is the dramatic demographic and political collapse in the middle Coatzacoalcos River basin following the fall of San Lorenzo at the close of the Early Formative period (Symonds et al. 2002). In fact, recent surveys have shown the southern Gulf lowlands to be a remarkably dynamic region, with complex polities and their supporting populations waxing and waning at different times in the areas of San Lorenzo, Laguna de los Cerros, La Venta, Tres Zapotes, and the Tuxtla Mountains (Borstein 2001; Killion and Urcid 2001; Loughlin and Pool 2007; Rust and Sharer 1988; Santley et al. 1997; Stoner 2008; Symonds et al. 2002; von Nagy 1997, 2003). The Pacific coast of Chiapas and Guatemala is another area where precocious development of complex polities was followed by decline and a sequence of shifting subregional political and demographic apogees (Clark 1997, 2007; Clark and Pye 2000; Love 1999; 2002). Within these lowland sequences, the timing of developments around Izapa in the Chiapas piedmont and on the western margin of the Tuxtla Mountains near Tres Zapotes are more similar to the Late to Terminal Formative apogee in the lower Río Verde Valley.

Much of the discussion of the development of sociopolitical complexity in the Early and Middle Formative periods of Mesoamerica revolves around the significance of interaction with the Olmec culture of the southern Gulf coast. Whereas some scholars view interaction with and dominance by the Olmecs as key to the development of sociopolitical hierarchies in Mesoamerica and their supporting ideology (e.g., Clark 1997, 2005; Diehl and Coe 1995), others emphasize local processes and the mutually reinforcing effects of interregional interaction (e.g., Flannery and Marcus 1994, 2000; Grove 1989, 1993). In either case, the inhabitants of the lower Río Verde Valley seem to have participated little in the networks that spread "Olmec-style" pottery, figurines, and sculptures through much of Mesoamerica, despite a handful of figurines that exhibit some elements in common with Early Formative figurines from San Lorenzo, La Blanca, and other sites in the Gulf coast, Chiapas, and coastal Guatemala (Hepp and Joyce, Chapter 9). The sparse occupation and apparent lack of sociopolitical hierarchy in the Early Formative period would appear to have left the lower Río Verde inhabitants with little need or opportunity for the adoption of the symbol set that signaled participation in Early Horizon interaction networks, in contrast to their contemporaries in the Oaxaca highlands (Blomster 2004; Flannery and Marcus 1994) or the southern Isthmus of Tehuantepec (Winter and Blomster 2008).

During the Middle Formative period, Olmec interaction became more focused on regional centers located on routes to sources of valued materials, especially greenstone and obsidian (Grove 1993). Outside of a corridor running from central Veracruz through Morelos and the Balsas River Valley, developments in western Mesoamerica owed little to direct interaction with Olmecs, and the same appears to be true of the lower Río Verde Valley. Chemical analysis of obsidian from Charco phase deposits (Joyce et al. 1995) include Mexican sources (Pico de Orizaba, Guadalupe Victoria, and Zaragoza) that are also prevalent in Tres Zapotes and other western Gulf Olmec sites (Hester et al. 1971; Knight and Glascock 2009; Pool et al. n.d.; Santley et al. 2001) but lack the Paredón source present in Middle Formative contexts at Tres Zapotes (Pool et al., n.d.) and San Andrés, Tabasco (Doering 2002), as well as the Guatemalan sources found in eastern Early and Middle Formative Gulf Olmec sites (Cobean et al. 1971, 1991). Gulf Olmec-style monuments, greenstone figurines, carved celts, and other elements of the "Middle Formative Ceremonial Complex" (Reilly 1995) are apparently absent from the lower Río Verde. The out-of-the-way location and the lack of sources of greenstone, obsidian, iron ore, or other hard-to-come-by materials apparently kept the lower Río Verde apart from the major corridors of Olmec interaction, although their exchange networks intersected at specific source localities.

By the end of the Middle Formative period, the lower Río Verde Valley shared with much of Mesoamerica a more strongly maize-based agricultural economy and a settlement hierarchy of at least two tiers. The settlement system was highly primate, with the largest settlement at Charco Redondo containing 97 percent of the occupied area in the lower valley. In terms of the spatial distribution of population and presumably economic and political institutions, the emerging lower Río Verde polity appears highly centralized. Nevertheless, inequalities in social status and political authority, insofar as they can be judged from the nonperishable remains of architectural investment and artifact inventories, appear muted (Joyce, Chapter 1). In this respect the lower Río Verde contrasts with the trans-Isthmian lowlands and the Chiapas and Guatemala highlands where complex polities had long emphasized the power and authority of individual elite rulers, but also with the Valley of Oaxaca and central Mexico where social inequality seems more pronounced in the late Middle Formative period.

COMPLEX TRANSFORMATIONS: THE LATE
AND TERMINAL FORMATIVE PERIODS

In terms of the scale, pace, and ubiquity of social and political transformations, the four centuries or so of the Late Formative period were unprecedented in Mesoamerica. Monumental architecture, urban centers, and complex polities proliferated as many areas experienced exponential population growth and interaction networks generally became more regionalized. In central Mexico, Cuicuilco and Teotihuacan developed into urban centers and vied with one another for supremacy in the Valley of Mexico (Sanders 1981). In the Valley of Oaxaca the newly founded city of Monte Albán grew, and its rulers began to proclaim their conquests (Marcus and Flannery 1996, 139–172), while Chiapa de Corzo flourished in the Grijalva depression, Izapa became a major cultural and political center in the Pacific piedmont, and Kaminaljuyú dominated the Valley of Guatemala. In emerging cities from Komchén in Yucatan to Cerros and Uaxactún in the south, the lowland Maya built temples and palaces, and at El Mirador they raised some of the most massive Maya constructions ever built. Mesoamerica's most sophisticated writing systems, the Maya, epi-Olmec (or Isthmian), and Zapotec, were developed and refined during the Late and Terminal Formative periods, and regional iconographic conventions for expressing religious and political ideology were established that would continue through the Classic and Postclassic periods. In these material expressions of inequality and political hierarchy we see the efforts of emerging and established elites to legitimate their positions of privilege, power, and authority using a variety of tactics and with varying degrees of complicity on the part of their followers.

Exclusive and Collective Interests in the Formative Period

In their 1996 article Blanton and colleagues called attention to the two kinds of power strategies they characterized as corporate and exclusionary and what they perceived as a historical alternation between the two as dominant strategies in the political economies of Mesoamerican regions. With reference to the Early and Middle Formative periods, they emphasize the exclusionary character of political economies, focusing on the personalized representations of rulers in Olmec sites and the interregional networks by which Olmecs engaged with their contemporaries. In contrast, they describe Late Formative political economies broadly as adhering to corporate strategies that de-emphasize the power of individual rulers and their families and focus on integrative social mechanisms and broadly shared ideological themes of fertility, renewal, and the cosmos. Societies in which corporate strategies dominated are exemplified by the Late Formative (Late Preclassic) Maya polities centered at El Mirador, Uaxactún, and Cerros (Blanton et al. 1996, 9, 12) as well as Monte Albán in the Danibaan and Pe phases (Monte Albán I, Blanton et al. 1999, 129). For the Classic period, Teotihuacan and Maya polities serve as paragons of opposed corporate and exclusionary strategies, respectively (Blanton et al. 1996, 9–12). It should be noted, however, that the Late Formative political economy of Teotihuacan appears to have placed relatively more emphasis on the power of individual rulers, as suggested by excavations of offerings in the Feathered Serpent Pyramid and the Pyramid of the Moon (Cowgill 1997, 2003 Sugiyama 2005).

The "Dual-Processual Model" of Blanton and colleagues, especially as presented in the 1996 article and elsewhere (e.g., Feinman 2001), has received just criticism for characterizing societies as either corporate or exclusionary (e.g., Drennan and Peterson 2006). The recognition that there is a logical coherence in the ways material ("objective") and social or ideological ("symbolic") sources of power may be employed is useful, however, even if real actors sometimes violate that logic. The corporate-network distinction is particularly useful if we accept seriously the proposition that both broad types of power strategy "coexist to some degree in the political dynamics of all social formations" (Blanton et al. 1996, 2), that "elements of both approaches may . . . be employed in certain complex cases," and that the terms " 'corporate' and 'network' delimit political-economic strategies, not necessarily types of societies" (Blanton et al. 1996, 7). It is in this sense that I have found the corporate-exclusionary distinction useful in analyzing the political-economic strategies of actors who may use either set of tactics depending on specific circumstances and the level of political interaction at which they are employed (as within factions, between factions, or between polities and their representatives [Pool 2007, 2008]).

The "corporate" and exclusionary strategies conceived by Blanton and his collaborators are one manifestation of the fundamental struggle between individual and collective interests that has inspired philosophers and social theorists from Plato and Aristotle to Foucault, Bourdieu, and Giddens. The resolution of individual needs and desires with those of other individuals and of society as a whole is not just a preoccupation of Western republics and monarchies. It is a problem for all societies, whatever their specific form, and the resulting tension constitutes a dialectic that can be both a creative and destructive force in social evolution. How societies in different circumstances and with different histories have resolved that tension—or not—is a fascinating and necessary subject of anthropological archaeology.

Thus I turn to a brief comparison of the trajectories of three cases in which elites appear to have downplayed their individual status and power relative to communal interests at the level of polity governance: Monte Albán, Tres Zapotes, and the lower Río Verde Valley. I do not mean to imply that elites were absent in these cases or that they did not enjoy greater privilege, power, or authority than others. Neither do I hold that they employed only "corporate strategies" to acquire the same. Rather, I am interested in how differing strategies were directed toward different audiences and employed in varying social, political, and economic circumstances.

Monte Albán and the Valley of Oaxaca

As compared with that in the Río Verde Valley, variation in wealth and social status appear earlier in the Valley of Oaxaca. By 1000 cal BC some households were living in better-constructed residences, consuming more deer meat, and obtaining more exotic goods than their neighbors (Marcus and Flannery 1996, 96–106). In a San José phase cemetery at Tomaltepec six adult males were accorded special treatment, being interred in a flexed position, accompanied by several secondary burials and numerous ceramic vessels decorated with "fire serpent" motifs, and covered with stone slabs (Marcus and Flannery 1996, 96–97; Whalen 1981).[2] For the most part, however, wealth distinctions appear to have been gradational (Rosenswig 2000, 436–442), with magnetite being the only prestige good exclusively associated with higher-status burials and residences (Marcus and Flannery 1996, 102).

Scholars working in the Valley of Oaxaca disagree about the degree to which social distinctions also involved the ranking of descent groups (e.g., Marcus and Flannery 1996, 93–110) or a more egalitarian "dual barrio" moiety organization represented by the "fire serpent" and "were-jaguar" (possibly symbols of sky and earth) tied to residence and involvement in interregional exchange networks (Blanton et al. 1999, 35–36, 38; see also Rosenswig 2000, 436, 442). Others doubt the empirical evidence for moieties, questioning, among other things, the referents of the designs and the contemporaneity of their associated styles (Winter and Blomster 2008, 216–218). Most agree, however, that communal labor was engaged in the construction of public ritual buildings as opposed to large elite residences or elaborate burial monuments (Marcus and Flannery 1996, 109–110). Those researchers who argue for a moiety system also view it as consistent with corporate governance (Blanton et al. 1999, 41–42).

The focus on the construction of public ritual buildings continued into the Middle Formative period and became increasingly elaborated at San José Mogote and other head towns in the Valley of Oaxaca (Blanton et al. 1999, 44; Marcus and Flannery 1996, 126–131). One of those public buildings was a temple placed atop the massive, 15 m tall Mound 1 at San José Mogote. The temple was burned at some point in the Rosario phase (ca. 700–500 BC) during a time when raiding was becoming increasingly prevalent in the Valley of Oaxaca (Flannery and Marcus 2003). An elite residence subsequently built over the remains of the temple contained a double-chambered tomb built of stone masonry plastered with a smooth coating of mud. Social inequality, then, appears to have become pronounced and strongly emphasized in the construction and placement of elite residences and burial monuments. A three-tiered settlement hierarchy had emerged within the Etla subvalley, with San José Mogote at its head. Consequently, most authorities agree in classifying the San José Mogote polity at this time as a chiefdom, and many would classify it as a complex chiefdom (e.g., Marcus and Flannery 1996, 121). Nevertheless, some question whether hereditary descent groups structured hierarchical social relations in the Rosario phase (Blanton et al. 1999, 46), despite evidence for a heightened use of "descent rhetoric" expressed in tomb construction and offerings. Furthermore, increased social inequality, settlement hierarchies, and the concentration of power in the hands of elites within large centers appear to have developed in a context of heightened competition and raiding among groups of allied communities, as evidenced in the burning of public structures and the initiation of a tradition of carving monuments that linked themes of militarism, sacrifice, and public ritual (Joyce 2010, 123; Marcus and Flannery 1996, 128–130; Urcid 2005, 5–6, 154–155; 2008, 2011).

The founding of Monte Albán at about 500 BC was, of course, a transformative event in the history of the Valley of Oaxaca. By the end of the Danibaan phase at about 300 BC, Monte Albán was the largest settlement in the Valley of Oaxaca, having grown to 324 ha with an estimated population of around 5,000 people. By the end of the Pe phase at about 100 BC, the site covered 442 ha and is estimated to have had more than 17,000 inhabitants (Blanton et al. 1999, 53; Marcus and Flannery 1996, 139; Kowalewski et al. 1989: Appendix I; Spencer and Redmond 2004, 179). The rapid pace of population growth at Monte Albán strongly supports migration as the main factor in its expansion (Blanton et al. 1993, 73). Meanwhile, Danibaan phase populations declined dramatically at San José Mogote and other sites in the Etla arm of the Valley of Oaxaca, apparently providing part of the founding population of Monte Albán (Marcus and Flannery 1996, 139), as supported by similarities in architecture, iconography, and mortuary practices (Joyce 2004, 196). The net population decrease in the Etla arm, however, appears not to have been sufficient to account for all of the growth of Monte Albán. Therefore, pointing to growing populations elsewhere in the Valley of Oaxaca, Blanton and colleagues (1999, 53–54) argue that Monte Albán expanded as a consequence of regional population growth and ongoing rural-urban migration, with some inhabitants possibly coming from outside the valley.

The presence of three clusters of occupation surrounding the ceremonial space of the Main Plaza near the top of the main hill originally suggested to Blanton (1978, 37–39, 44–46) a possible association of barrios with three formerly independent polities in their respective arms of the valley, and led him to propose that Monte Albán was founded as a neutral, disembedded capital integrating the entire valley. Marcus and Flannery (1996, 139–154) subsequently argued, by analogy with ancient Greece, that the founding of Monte Albán constituted a synoikism (also spelled synoecism or synœcism), in which whole groups of villages relocated to form a new city, often for mutual defense. Citing Demand (1990), Blanton and his colleagues (1999, 63) point out that the process of political consolidation to which synoikism refers could involve the foundation, movement, or expansion of a capital; it could occur through physical movement (voluntary or coerced), as in the case of Megalopolis, or through the acceptance of political domination by previously autonomous villages or ethnic groups, as appears to initially have been the case for eighth-century Athens. Therefore, although Blanton et al. (1999, 64–65) acknowledge that defense from raiding may have played a part in the foundation of Monte Albán, they find a political synoikism involving a federation or coalition of polities more compatible with their model of a disembedded capital.

While acknowledging the site's defensive advantages, Joyce (2004, 2010, 128–141; Joyce and Winter 1996) underscores the role of ideology and the participation of commoners in the construction of sacred space as critical elements in the creation of Monte Albán as the capital of an emerging state. In Joyce's (2004) view the creation of Monte Albán and its ceremonial center was not just a response to military threat and an arrangement negotiated among elites, but also the expression of an ideology created to address the social disruptions of the late Middle Formative period, halt the defection of followers, and improve the fortunes of both nobility and commoner through new, more powerful ways of communicating with the sacred realm. Early construction that surrounded and defined the Main Plaza identified it as an *axis mundi*, set at the top of a "mountain of creation" (Figure 10.1). At the southwest corner of the plaza, on the same side as the setting sun, rows of *danzante* carvings on Building L-sub displayed the images of sacrificed victims (Coe 1962; Flannery and Marcus 1983, 89–90; Joyce 2004, 199) or individuals engaged in autosacrifice (Figure 10.2; Urcid 2011; see Joyce 2010, 136–137); at the opposite corner iconographic references to sky, rain, and lightning decorated a large architectural complex on the eastern portion of what became the North Platform (Joyce 2004, 199–201). High-status residences were concentrated nearby in Area A3, reinforcing the connection of elites with the celestial realm, and the burial of nobles in formal tombs expressed their elevated status while allowing contact with noble ancestors through tomb reentry ceremonies (Joyce 2004, 201).

Since they were first reported, many interpretations have been offered for the nearly 300 *danzantes* that originally covered the façade of Building L-sub (for a review, see Urcid 2011, 163). The one that gained the widest acceptance was Michael Coe's (1962) suggestion that the naked individuals in contorted poses, many with their eyes closed and blood flowing from their genitals, represented sacrificed captives (Flannery and Marcus 1983, 89–90; Marcus 1976,

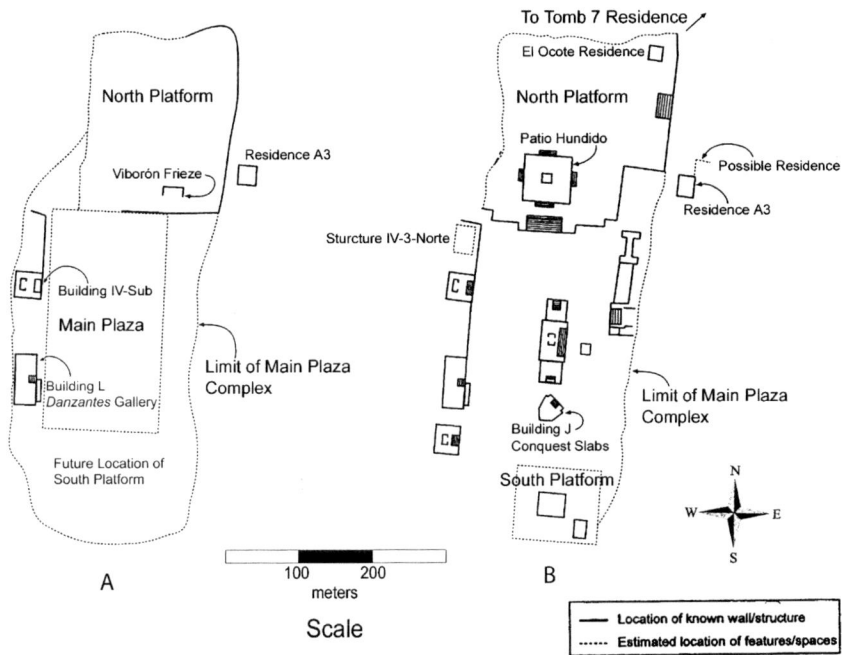

FIGURE 10.1. The Main Plaza at Monte Albán. *A*, Danibaan and Pe phases (500–100 BC); *B*, Nisa phase (100 BC–AD 200) (after Barber and Joyce 2006: Figures 8.2 and 8.3).

1992, 391–394; see also Joyce 2004, 200; Orr 1997; Scott 1978). The similarly carved Monument 3 of San José Mogote, which shows a named individual with blood flowing from his heart, marked as "precious," probably does represent a sacrificed captive (Urcid 2008, 2011, 223).

Javier Urcid (2011), however, has presented a strong argument that the *danzantes* on the façade of Building L-sub represent young men engaged in letting blood from their genitals in acts of autosacrifice and the ancestors whom they invoke through that act. They were apparently set on the façade in alternating rows of right- and left-facing young men on vertical slabs, with the ancestors lying horizontally over each row. Glyphic texts set at one end of the rows refer to the successive enthronement of three governors and accompanying sacrifices of other individuals (Urcid 2011, 183–186, 224). Urcid further hypothesizes that different sets of individuals (young men with tightly fitted caps, young men with oval pendants, rain-god impersonators, and old men) represent age grades within a warrior sodality, with the last three groups depicted on buildings that surmounted the L-sub platform. Other sets of images in the same technical style of *danzantes* exist at Monte Albán, but only four unequivocally represent the sacrifice of named captives, indicated by decapitated heads.

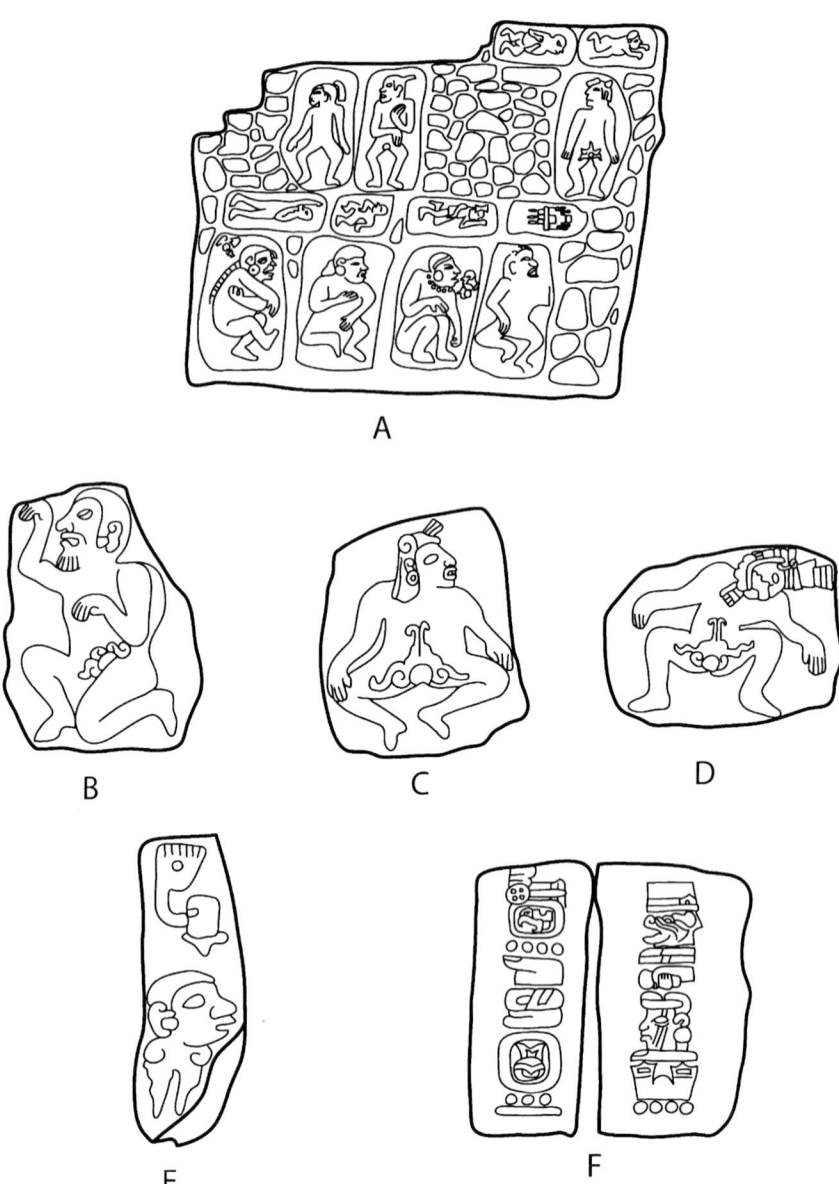

FIGURE 10.2. Carved stone monuments from Building L-sub at Monte Albán. A, In-situ monuments (after Winter 1989, 53). B, Elder from the upper rank (redrawn with permission from Javier Urcid). C, Young adult from the first rank in the lower row of Building L-sub (redrawn with permission from Javier Urcid). D, Rain-god impersonator (redrawn with permission from Javier Urcid). E, Decapitation (redrawn with permission from Javier Urcid). F, Monuments D-139 and D-140 with hieroglyphic inscriptions (redrawn with permission from Javier Urcid; after Joyce 2010: Figure 5.5; reproduced with permission of Wiley-Blackwell).

A fifth may represent the rain god accepting the sacrifice of a "jaguar lord" (Urcid 2011, 201–201).

If correct, Urcid's reconstruction has some important implications. First, it continues to support the idea that warfare was important to the formation of the early Zapotec state, but emphasizes its conceptual and ritual importance while suggesting less frequent battles and a reduced scale of captive sacrifice. Second, it frames warfare and autosacrifice by warriors as acts carried out for the well-being of the community. Third, it underscores the tension between corporate principals of governance, represented by a hierarchy of broadly achievable age grades and an elder council, and the more typically exclusionary mention of individual rulers and their victories (Urcid 2011, 225).

As important as Monte Alban's physical structures and iconography were the practices they framed. The relatively open setting of the early Main Plaza could have accommodated thousands of participants, noble and commoner, in public rituals and feasts. As Joyce (2004, 202–203, see also 2010, 139–146) argues, autosacrifice and the sacrifice of elite captives, by elites, placed nobles at the nexus of a sacred covenant between supernaturals and humans while linking that covenant to warfare. Participation of commoners, not only in rituals but in the construction of the edifices upon and before which they were performed, involved them in acts that benefited the common good while binding them to the rulers of Monte Albán. The (more or less) willing participation of commoners, however, also made them architects of their own subjugation, as the materialization of an ideology that privileged elites as ritual specialists extended the authority of elites to invoke supernatural forces and their power to rule over earthly inhabitants (see also Pauketat 2000). Through the Pe and Nisa phases, as they consolidated their control over the Valley of Oaxaca and expanded their rule beyond the valley, elites heightened their emphasis on the exclusive inheritance of authority from ancestors with increasingly elaborate tombs while decreasing access of non-elites to the ceremonial center of Monte Albán (Joyce 2004, 203). Thus, while the founders of Monte Albán were able to draw on a deep-rooted tradition of communal practice and ideology to consolidate their authority and to quell violent conflict, which had become increasingly frequent in the Valley of Oaxaca, the persistence and elaboration of mortuary practices and architectural conventions that distinguished elite households provided an avenue for implementing more exclusionary strategies after unification of the valley was achieved.

Tres Zapotes and the Eastern Lower Papaloapan Basin

The archaeological site of Tres Zapotes began its existence as an Early Formative Olmec village. It shared with its contemporaries, San Lorenzo, Laguna de los Cerros, and dozens of other Olmec villages ceramics carved with abstract representations of supernatural beings, forces, and concepts, as well as a handful of exotic imported items such as multiperforate ilmenite cubes and pieces of greenstone. The exchange networks by which they acquired obsidian overlapped with their neighbors to the east, but lacked the Guatemalan sources represented at San Lorenzo (Pool et al. 2010; n.d.), and in general, there is little evidence to support the idea that Tres Zapotes was the subject of a larger Early Formative center (Pool et al. 2010). To what degree social inequality existed within the Early Formative village is unknown.

During the Middle Formative period, exclusionary practices were a prominent feature of the relation between Olmec rulers and their subjects at Tres Zapotes and elsewhere as elites sought to monopolize economic and ideological sources of power (Pool 2007, 287–289). As Tres Zapotes grew into a regional center in its own right in the Middle Formative period, its leaders employed Olmec symbols to reinforce their power, authority, and elevated social status. Tres Zapotes had grown large enough early in the period to support chiefs with control over a labor force sufficient to haul basalt boulders from the slopes of a volcano over 5 km away and have two of them carved into colossal heads in their image. At least nine other sculptures representing humans and composite supernatural beings with human and animal features were carved over the course of the Middle Formative, including two stelae that bore representations of rulers (Pool 2010). In the most complete example, Stela A, the ruler and two flanking attendants stand between supernatural masks representing the earth or underworld below and the sky above, an explicit reference to the ruler as conduit between the layers of the cosmos (Figure 10.3).

At the center of the site was erected a low platform with natural basalt columns, in the center of which a short serpentinite column with a mat design on the side and a cleft at the upper end was buried upright through a hole carved in a basalt slab (Pool 2010: Figure 5.23). The three Middle Formative burials we have excavated include one adult and one child accompanied by greenstone beads (a jade necklace for the adult, a serpentine bracelet for the child), decorated pottery vessels, rounded pebbles, and, with the adult, obsidian blades. Another child burial had no accompanying grave goods. Whether variation in grave goods reflects gender, rank, or other social identity cannot be determined with this burial sample, but the monuments leave no doubt that substantial differences in power and status existed.

By 400 BC, then, Tres Zapotes was already more than 600 years old and had long been governed by rulers who used massive carved monuments to emphasize their personal qualities and their role as mediators between their subjects and the forces of the cosmos. Greenstone was used in public ritual as well as for personal adornment. Some, but not all, individuals were buried with greenstone jewelry and fancy pottery, suggesting that such items expressed certain aspects of social identity. Small quantities of jade likely came from Guatemala,

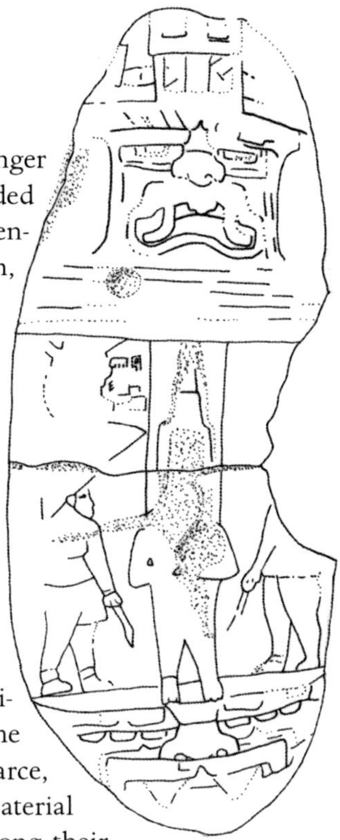

FIGURE 10.3. Stela A, Tres Zapotes (after Pool 2007:
Figure 7.4; reproduced with permission of Cambridge
University Press).

but exchange networks seem to have been stronger
with central and southern Mexico, which provided
virtually all the obsidian and much of the serpentine used at Tres Zapotes (Olaf Jaime-Riverón,
personal communication, 2009; Pool et al. n.d.).

The Late Formative period saw profound
changes in society and governance at Tres
Zapotes. The rate of regional population
growth increased markedly, and Tres Zapotes
grew three- to fivefold to achieve its maximum
extent of 500 ha (Pool and Loughlin 2006; Pool
and Ohnersorgen 2003). Exchange networks
shifted as obsidian from Guatemala (the San
Martín Jilotepeque source) appeared for the first
time and the obsidian from Zaragoza rose from
6 percent to 18 percent, foreshadowing its dominance in Classic period assemblages. At the same
time, greenstone of all sorts became very scarce,
depriving epi-Olmec leaders of an important material
for the expression of authority and power among their
Olmec predecessors.

Although low platforms had been built in the Middle Formative period,
the epi-Olmec rulers of Tres Zapotes embarked on major mound construction
programs for the first time in the Late Formative period. Four large mound-
plaza groups were built over the course of the Late and Terminal Formative
periods (Figure 10.4). Excavations in three of these groups produced radiocarbon dates that overlap in the Late Formative period (Pool 2008: Table 2). No
datable material was recovered from the fourth group, but ceramics suggest it
too was at least partly contemporaneous with the others. All four of the plaza
groups share the basic elements of a common plan consisting of a rectangular
plaza oriented approximately east–west, which is bounded to the north by a
long, loaf-shaped mound, at the west end by a tall pyramidal mound, and with
a low *adoratorio* on the central east–west axis of the plaza (Pool 2008). Three
of the plaza groups also have pyramidal mounds on the east end and other
low mounds around the plaza, but access to the plaza remains very open. The
areas of individual plazas range from 1.1 to 4.2 ha in the case of Group 2, which
is the most centrally located. On the north edge of the site, however, Group
3 contains three plazas whose areas sum to 4.0 ha, and the total volume of its

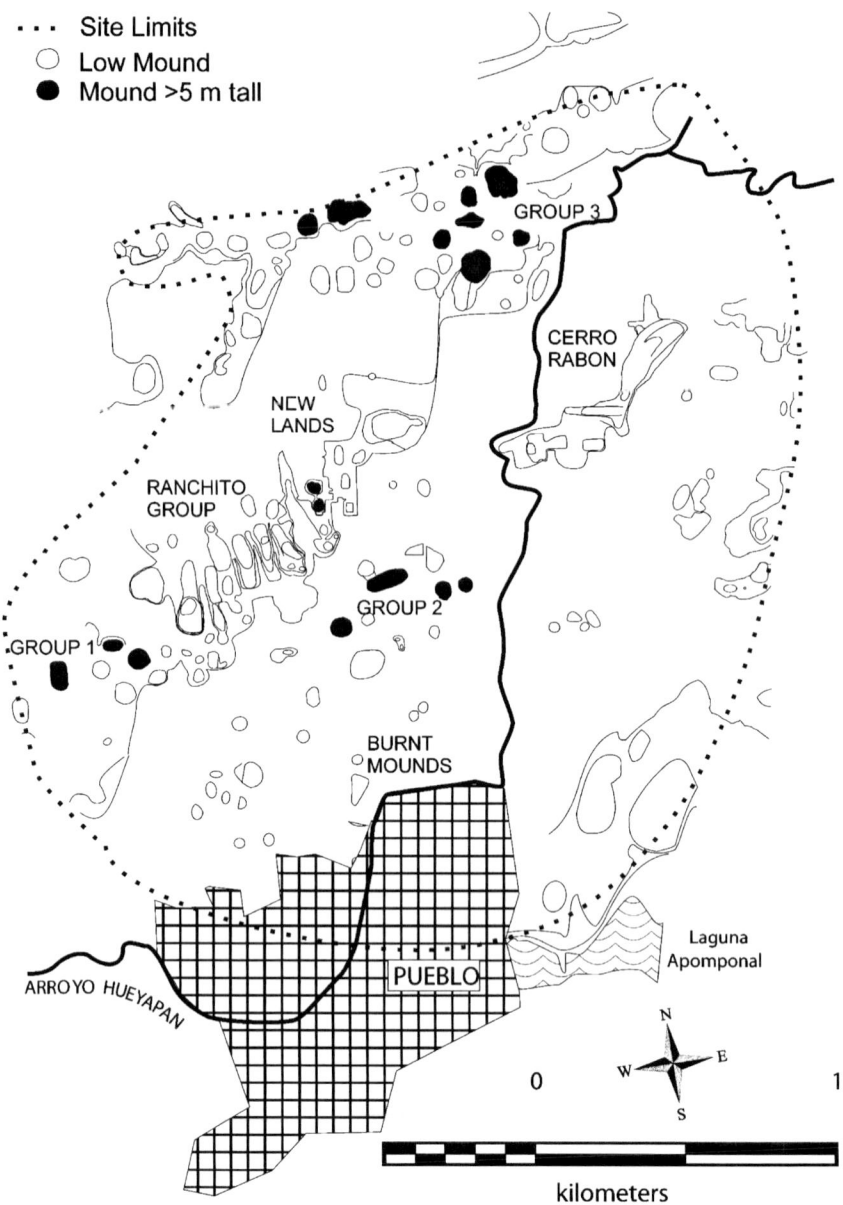

FIGURE 10.4. Plan of Tres Zapotes, Late Formative Hueyapan phase (400–1 BC).

construction, at 151,185 m³, is half again that of Group 2 (Sullivan 2002). Thus, there is no single plaza group that clearly dominates all others at Tres Zapotes. Furthermore, the plaza groups are regularly spaced at between 945 and 985 m,

316

 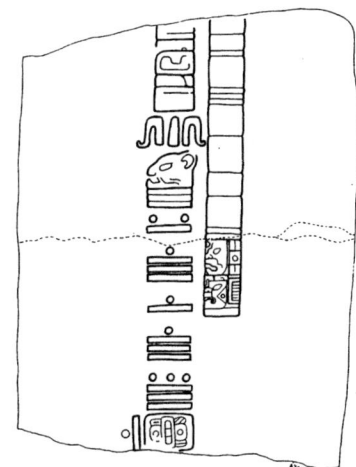

FIGURE 10.5. Stela C, Tres Zapotes (adapted from Clark and Pye 2000, 136, chapter frontispiece; drawing by Ayax Moreno, courtesy of John E. Clark, New World Archaeological Foundation).

and each is mutually visible with at least one other mound group (Pool 2008; Sullivan 2002). Excavations in middens associated with the long mounds reveal little difference in artifact inventories among these plaza groups, except for mica fragments recovered from a probable craft production context attached to Group 2. Obsidian working and ceramic manufacture within the mound groups produced implements and pottery types common to craft production contexts in non-elite residential settings (Pool 2003, 2005, 2010).

The replication of formal plans and mound functions among these plaza groups, the lack of a single group unambiguously larger than the others, the proximity of the groups, their intervisibility and their substantial contemporaneity lead me to conclude that governance was shared among multiple factions in Late Formative Tres Zapotes (Pool 2008). That conclusion is reinforced by an examination of Late and Terminal Formative monuments from Tres Zapotes (Pool 2010), which lack the emphasis on the individual person of the ruler seen in the Middle Formative stelae and colossal heads. With the possible exception of Monument F (Pool 2010: Figure 5.18), a human bust with a large rearward-projecting tenon, Late and Terminal Formative rulers are not depicted as individuals within the site of Tres Zapotes. For example, the most famous monument from Tres Zapotes, Stela C, shows a profile head and quadripartite symbol that seem to emerge, along with branching elements suggestive of vegetation, from the cleft brow of an earth monster mask (Figure 10.5), clearly derived from Olmec-style representations. The profile head, however, is highly conventionalized, and the overall design appears to focus on the role of the ruler as the conduit between the underworld and the sky, but not the ruler's individual qualities. The Long Count date carved in 32 BC on the reverse of the stela probably postdates this *axis mundi* image (Pool 2010) and may refer to an astronomical event (John Justeson, personal communication, 2003; Malmström 1997, 141–44); the accompanying epi-Olmec text is too eroded to be read. Stela D, which shows a person kneeling before two standing human figures, may depict an act of obeisance to a ruler and a warrior (Stirling 1943: Plate 14), but was recovered from a separate secondary center that Matthew Stirling (1943, 14) mislabeled Group 4 of Tres Zapotes. Other monuments attributable to the Late and Terminal Formative periods at Tres Zapotes either depict supernaturals or masked humans, refer to cosmological themes, or lack carving altogether.

Olmec monuments, however, were reused in Late Formative Tres Zapotes and located in contexts that adapted their meanings to new political practice and ideology (Pool 2010). The two colossal heads were set on the southern edges of the plazas in Group 1 and Group 2, directly opposite and facing the long mounds that appear to have supported the seats of elite administration and residence. Considering that these monuments were by then the images of ancient rulers, they would have reinforced the political authority of the leaders ensconced in these groups and perhaps their lineal claims to rulership as well. Similarly, the long mound of Group 2 was built opposite the basalt column altar with its serpentinite *axis mundi,* incorporating ancient claims to authority in the formal design of the group. The harsh treatment of later Middle Formative Olmec stelae, however, suggests that the political changes of the Late Formative may have been literally as well as figuratively revolutionary. The face of the ruler on Stela A was destroyed, and the recently recovered fragment of Stela F shows it was broken vertically through the head and torso of the ruler, whose facial features are missing from the recovered fragment (Pool 2010: Figure 5.22).

The replication of Tres Zapotes–style plaza groups at Late Formative secondary centers that included El Mesón may have symbolized the unity of the polity beyond its capital. Elements of exclusionary strategy were more evident in sculptural programs outside of Tres Zapotes, however. Stela D has been mentioned as one example; the two stelae recovered from El Mesón provide another (Loughlin 2004, 2009). Monument 1 is a natural basalt column carved with an elite individual wearing an elaborate headdress and standing between earth and sky bands. Monument 2 shows an elaborately costumed ruler standing on an altar with a double-headed serpent motif and faced by a smaller seated figure. Both continue the Olmec emphasis on the person of the ruler, but in a style that combines epi-Olmec and Izapan elements. Though muted at Tres Zapotes proper, exclusionary political strategies seem to have continued to be prominent outside Tres Zapotes. This trend culminates in the mid-second-century AD La Mojarra stela, which bears the image of ruler in impressive costume and accompanied by a long epi-Olmec text that has been interpreted as an account of the person's accomplishments leading up to his accession (Kaufman and Justeson 2001).

Meanwhile, at Tres Zapotes, the Terminal Formative period saw a diversification of spatial orders and a weakening of the corporate code that they materialized as the factional competition and exclusionary strategies that had been subordinated to the communal interests began to reassert themselves. Modifications to Group 2 maintained the old spatial order and enlarged the residential/administrative structure, but construction reconfigured Group 3 to restrict access to its principal plaza and place it on a north–south axis while the function of platforms in Group 1 shifted, placing the residential/administrative structure on the west end of the plaza (Pool 2008, 134–139). Preexisting plazas, however, continued to be preserved and presumably used (Sullivan 2002). This persistent respect of the ancient places of ritual and the common vision they expressed may have helped prevent the dissolution of Tres Zapotes into antagonistic segments (Pool 2008, 146).

The Lower Río Verde Valley

I refer the reader to Joyce's introduction for a detailed summary of the sequence of developments in the lower Río Verde Valley, here highlighting points most germane to this comparative discussion. After a period of experimentation with the cultivation of domesticated crops in the late Archaic period, the Early Formative period in the lower Río Verde Valley saw only sparse habitation by communities that apparently relied little on cultivation. Significant population increase was delayed until the Middle Formative period in tandem with a reliance on riverine resources, in part related to changes in the depositional regime of the Río Verde that increased alluvial deposition. A two-tiered settlement hierarchy with regional centers like Charco Redondo appeared, suggesting that political organization was also becoming more hierarchically structured. While it is possible, and even likely, that social inequalities were emerging as well, there are currently few archaeological data to assess that proposition for the Middle Formative Charco phase.

As in the Valley of Oaxaca and the lower Papaloapan Basin, the lower Río Verde Valley saw sociopolitical changes of unprecedented scale and import in the Late Formative period. A fivefold increase in occupied area in a span of less than 300 years bespeaks impressive increases in population as well as the expanding footprints of elite structures and public spaces. The establishment of a second (but not secondary) large center at San Francisco de Arriba apparently divided the valley into two polities. While evidence of warfare is lacking, it seems inevitable that the elites of the two centers should have found themselves in competition for followers, even if regional population increases provided ample numbers of supporters for both. The construction of a massive acropolis demonstrates the great success of San Francisco de Arriba's elites in mobilizing the labor of their subjects.

Elevated status and greater wealth found their expression in variations in the size of residences and quality of their construction materials as well as in the grave offerings interred with certain individuals, adults and children, associated with residential structures. Mortuary practices, however, also expressed affiliation with the community in public cemeteries where mainly adults were interred over several generations, along with a few children reinterred as secondary burials (Barber et al., Chapter 4).

Feasting involving multiple households also appears to have been widespread, judging from the presence of large cooking features in several Minizundo phase sites, including a feature in the flagstone patio of a complex on the upper terrace at Cerro de la Cruz that also contained a set of storerooms. Not only can one identify ethnographically many kinds of feasts held for a wide variety of economic, social, political, and religious purposes (Dietler 2001; Hayden 2001), but they are also potentially, even usually, polysemic events that may express simultaneously the mutual affiliation of the participants in a broad community, as well as distinctions—between host(s) and guests, patron(s) and clients, leader(s) and followers, men and women, elders and youths (e.g., Dietler 2001, 88–93). Feasting thereby may have served as one of the essential mechanisms of working through the contradictions between a traditional (in the lower Río Verde Valley) emphasis on community identity and emerging hierarchies of status and power. Similarly, a longstanding commitment to communal ritual and cooperative labor found heightened expression in public construction projects that included the acropolis at San Francisco de Arriba.

Populations continued to increase over the next 400 years of the Terminal Formative period (150 BC–AD 250), although the rate of increase slowed, with occupied area growing by 234 percent (Joyce, Chapter 1). Río Viejo became the largest center in the region, at 225 ha, while Charco Redondo and San Francisco de Arriba were reduced to secondary-center status, along with comparably large centers with monumental architecture at Cerro de la Virgen and Tututepec. In other words, Río Viejo, which Joyce argues achieved urban status during the Terminal Formative period, stood at the head of a five-tiered settlement hierarchy integrating most, if not all, of the lower Río Verde Valley.

As the population became larger and more urban, it also became more heterogeneous, with more specialized social roles and greater inequalities in status and wealth being reflected in burials. The tension that was already evident in the Late Formative between traditional communal values and inherited inequalities were heightened with an expanding hierarchy of status and increasing diversity of roles. At the apex of this system the rulers of Río Viejo enlisted the collective labor of commoners in the construction of that site's massive acropolis, while elites throughout the region attracted local followers through larger and more elaborate communal feasts (Joyce et al., Chapter 5).

The challenge of maintaining traditional community integration amid growing social inequality is nowhere more evident than in the mortuary practices discussed by Barber and her colleagues (Chapter 4). In the Late Formative, some individuals, both children and adults, had been interred with grave goods in residential contexts, and burial in communal cemeteries was largely restricted to adults who were interred without grave goods. By the late Terminal Formative period, burial in communal cemeteries had been extended to all ages, but exotic offerings and items of personal adornment expressed the different social station of some individuals. The Late Formative burial practices are subject to multiple interpretations, including the possibility, advanced by Barber et al. (Chapter 4), that individuals became full members of the community only in adulthood (and in some cases posthumously) and that the expression of social inequality in death was confined to fellow members of a more restricted social group. Note that it is not necessarily the case that elites were previously excluded from burial in community cemeteries; it may be that it was simply inappropriate to display their wealth there. While we have no way of knowing who was included among the attendees at Terminal Formative burials, the interment in communal cemeteries of individuals adorned with and accompanied by exotic goods suggests that expressions of inequality were potentially displayed to a larger crowd in public mortuary ceremonies. An intriguing possibility, suggested by the burial of children in late Terminal Formative cemeteries, is that public expression of social inequality was made possible by an ideological shift that extended community membership to all inhabitants and that accepted variation in social status as a natural condition.

The Question of Conquest

One of the intriguing questions addressed in this volume is whether Zapotec conquest contributed to Terminal Formative developments in the lower Río Verde Valley. The identification of conquest assumes general importance, not only because it has been proposed as a primary cause for the origin of states (e.g., Carneiro 1970), but also because hegemony over distant places has been used more recently as prima facie evidence for the existence of states headed by Monte Albán (e.g., Marcus and Flannery 1996; Spencer 1998; Spencer and Redmond 2004) and San Lorenzo (e.g., Clark 2007; Clark and Pye 2000). Arguments for Monte Albán's conquest of polities in the Valley of Oaxaca and beyond have relied, in large part, on the identification of Late and Terminal Formative *danzante* monuments and toponymic "conquest slabs" as depictions of named and slain captives and overthrown places, respectively (Marcus 1976, 1983; Marcus and Flannery 1996, 198–207). Those interpretations have been challenged, both with respect to the specific places identified on the conquest slabs (Urcid 1994; Workinger and Joyce 2009) and whether conquest was the intended message (Urcid 2011; Urcid and Joyce 2011). The strongest archaeological evidence for conquest comes from the Cañada de Cuicatlán, where an episode of Late Formative warfare is indicated by the burning and abandonment of the site of Llano Perdido, a shift of settlement to defensible positions and walled sites, and a possible skull rack at La Coyotera that may have served as an emblem of state authority (Redmond 1983; Redmond and Spencer 2006, 365–375). Redmond and Spencer use the appearance of ceramic styles allied to the Valley of Oaxaca to identify Monte Albán as the aggressor.

In the absence of other evidence, researchers in the Valley of Oaxaca have relied heavily on ceramic styles regarded as being of central Oaxacan origin to support the conquest of San Francisco de Arriba by the Zapotec state controlled by Monte Albán. Levine's (Chapter 8) argument for a local tradition of lower Verde graywares is therefore an important challenge to the hypothesis of Zapotec expansion into the region. As Levine recognizes, however, the premise that conquest should increase the import and emulation of ceramics from the conquering polity is itself problematic (see also Zeitlin and Joyce 1999) and depends upon the enactment of specific practices of domination, resistance, and negotiation between imperial and local actors (e.g., Venter 2008). Critical issues include (1) which forms of pottery were imported and which were copied, (2) how, in what contexts, and by whom the imported and emulated vessels were used, and (3) by inference from context and form, what meanings were associated with such vessels in their home and host settings. Such considerations help to distinguish among different circumstances in which vessels may be imported, reproduced by knowledgeable immigrants, or emulated by local populations; such circumstances may include colonial enclaves, trade diaspora communities, refugee populations, occupying forces, imperial administrators, co-opted elites, political allies, itinerant merchants, and religious pilgrims, among others (e.g., Arnold and Santley 2008; Cohen 1971; Curtin 1984; Santley et al. 1987; Stein 1999).

The rich ethnohistorical record of the Aztec Triple Alliance provides the best documentation of an empire in Mesoamerica. Archaeological investigations in subject regions demonstrate that the material expression of Aztec hegemony was highly variable, particularly in the more distant provinces (e.g., Berdan et al. 1996). On the Gulf coast, for example, Aztec governors administered several provinces directly, the Aztecs established garrisons at Tochtepec, Coatzacoalcos, and Raya de Pánuco, colonies of Aztec families were placed in several undisclosed locations, and Tochtepec boasted an enclave of Aztec merchants (Umberger 1996). The material manifestations of these encroachments vary from place to place, however. Aztec-style sculptures were erected sporadically and Aztec-style temples are rare, though the latter were constructed at Castillo de Teayo and Santiago Huatusco (Umberger 1996). Aztec-style pottery is common in some areas, such as the Río Blanco/Mixtequilla region of central Veracruz between the Tochtepec and Cuetlaxtlan (Cotaxtla) provinces, where Garraty and Stark (2002) hypothesize that imperial control was exercised indirectly through the co-option of local elites (see also Curet et al. 1994; Ohnersorgen 2001; Stark 1990). In contrast, Aztec imports and local copies are rare in the Tuxtla region of the Tochtepec province and are confined mainly to locally made versions of Texcoco impressed censers (Venter 2008).

With such variation in material expression of ethnohistorically documented conquests, the demonstration of earlier conquests is a difficult task, as is reflected in debates over the significance of Teotihuacan influence in the Gulf coast and Maya regions (e.g., Arnold and Santley 2008; Braswell 2003; Cowgill 1997; Pool 1992; Santley 2007; Santley and Arnold 2004; Santley et al. 1987; Spence 1996; Stark 1990) as well as the interpretation of a probable Olmec enclave at Cantón Corralito, Chiapas (e.g., Cheetham 2010; Clark 2007). Smith and Montiel (2001, 249), considering the cases for Aztec, Toltec, and Teotihuacan empires, note that the act of conquest typically leaves few material remains because destruction is seldom total and damages to buildings and settlements may be soon repaired. Marcus and Flannery (1996, 128; Flannery and Marcus 2003), have used evidence for intense burning of a temple at San José Mogote (in combination with the iconographic evidence of the slain *danzante* figure on San José Mogote Monument 3) to support their argument for increased raiding at the end of the Rosario phase, citing Shaffer's (1993) conclusion that such large quantities of sintered daub could be produced only by intentional burning. Although I doubt that the intensity of a fire necessarily depends on its intent, in this case the burning of a temple coincides with practice and imagery in later central Mexican conquests; in other cases, widespread destruction of one or more settlements may offer additional support for an interpretation of violent conquest.

Destruction, however, is neither sufficient nor necessary evidence of external conquest. Smith and Montiel (2001, 249) therefore rely more heavily on evidence for continuing military and political control of provincial areas. Such evidence may include the construction of political infrastructure, indications of increased tribute demands in the form of intensified agricultural or craft production or a decline in the standard of living, reorganization of settlement to support economic and strategic ends, and the co-option of local elites as represented by high-value imperial imports in elite contexts or the emulation of imperial styles. On the other hand, Smith and Montiel (2001, 249) also note that hegemonic empires do not require the same degree of investment in infrastructure as do territorial empires. Smith and Montiel (2001, 249) argue that economic intensification and lowered standards of living can result from causes other than conquest, and, they imply, empires do not always engage in large-scale or systematic settlement changes. Furthermore, empires may engage in exchange with polities outside their control, and elites may copy the styles of other rulers without being subject to them.

In summary, multiple lines of evidence are required to demonstrate imperial conquest, as Levine underscores in this volume (Chapter 8). While evidence exists to suggest that Monte Albán extended its control to other areas (Spencer and Redmond 2003, 2004), Zapotec expansion into the lower Río Verde Valley has not yet been demonstrated.

DISCUSSION

In each of the preceding cases Late and Terminal Formative rulers sought to resolve the tension between hierarchical inequality and communal interests. The histories of the lower Río Verde Valley, the Valley of Oaxaca, and the southern Gulf coast, however, presented the ruling elites of these regions with different challenges. As described in this volume, the fundamental problem in the lower Río Verde Valley was how to accommodate increasing hierarchy within a tradition of communal cooperation. Part of the solution was the promotion of practices of affiliation that included non-elites as participants in the construction of massive platforms and the rituals conducted there. In addition, the shift to permitting individuals interred in public cemeteries to be accompanied by grave goods may be seen as a way of naturalizing inequalities in wealth—in effect, materializing Orwell's (1945) dictum that we are all equal (and so all welcome in the public cemetery), but some of us are more equal than others (and our burial wealth proves it). Feasts likewise marked occasions of communal celebration with practices of affiliation while simultaneously distinguishing some individuals and groups as hosts and providers.

The inhabitants of the Valley of Oaxaca had faced similar contradictions early in the Formative period and had responded with a similar suite of socially integrative practices. Differential access to iron ore, variation in the kind and quantity of grave goods, and differences in the quality of house construction suggest that some Early Formative individuals and households enjoyed higher status than others (Marcus and Flannery 1996, 103–104), even if ranking of Early Formative descent groups is debatable (Blanton et al. 1999, 39–43). Differential distributions of ceramic motifs interpreted as symbolic of sky and earth (Pyne 1976; Marcus 1989) between sites and between wards within San José Mogote suggest to some researchers the existence of a form of moiety organization in which political power was shared between the constituent groups (Blanton et al. 1999, 41; cf. Blomster 2004). By the early Middle Formative period, feasts and ceremonies conducted at public buildings constructed with the labor of multiple households and communities provided venues in which elites could legitimate their higher status as a general social good (Marcus and Flannery 1996, 108–109, 116).

The circumstances antecedent to the founding of Monte Albán were evidently more contentious than those that resulted in the establishment of Late Formative centers and the Terminal Formative ascendancy of Río Viejo in the Río Verde Valley. Raiding was increasingly prevalent in a more populous valley, where settlements clustered in the three valley arms with a more sparsely occupied buffer zone where the valley arms intersect (Kowalewski et al. 1989, 70–75; cf. Winter 2001, 282). The social distance between elites and commoners had also increased, judging from greater variation in the size and quality of residences, more pronounced differences in access to "fancy" graywares with negative-resist designs, and the interment of some individuals in stone masonry tombs in residential compounds (Marcus and Flannery 1996, 121–134), the last suggesting an increasing emphasis on descent for claims to property, power, and status (Blanton et al. 1999, 46). Still, elements of the old communal emphasis persisted. In general, collective labor was invested with greater intensity in public ceremonial structures than elite residences (the late construction of elite residences over a burned temple at San José Mogote notwithstanding). Although a handful of political and/or military leaders taken as captives were identified by name on "*danzante*" monuments in the Rosario phase and images of decapitated heads in the Danibaan phase, the names of captors and rulers were rarely displayed (an exception may be the texts set at the southeast corner of the *danzantes* gallery on Building L-sub at Monte Albán [Marcus and Flannery 1996, 161; Urcid 2011, 183–186]; see Figure 10.2f).

The founders of Monte Albán, then, had a long-established repertoire of "corporate" strategies to draw upon as they founded the capital and unified the valley: a cosmology that expressed the complementarity of opposites symbolized by earth and sky, east and west, life and death, which they expressed at the top of a symbolically charged hill in a neutral buffer zone in the center of the Valley of Oaxaca and the emerging Zapotec state. The public glorification of rulers, in permanent media, at least, seems to have been downplayed well into the Classic period. The Zapotec elites inserted themselves into this "corporate" ideology in a way that legitimated, preserved, and expanded their political authority. They rarely represented themselves in permanent media, except possibly as members of larger sodalities, but they sometimes personalized their defeated rivals. They made themselves the mediators with the cosmos as the performers of sacrifice and leaders of ritual for the public good, but buried their dead in tombs that afforded opportunities for the veneration of elite ancestors. And as they expanded their regional control in the Nisa phase, they imposed greater restrictions on entrance into the places of public ceremony. In short, the early political history of Monte Albán can be seen as one of carefully balancing collective and exclusive strategies to the benefit of the emerging state and its ruling elite (see also Urcid 2011, 225).

In contrast to the Oaxacan cases in which collective interests had figured prominently in polity governance in the centuries before the Late Formative period, the leaders of Tres Zapotes faced the challenge of fashioning community among disparate factions that were heirs to a long history of hierarchy controlled by rulers who celebrated their individual power and hereditary authority. Elites at Tres Zapotes continued to express their exclusive claims to status and power within the factions they led by placing their residences/administrative buildings on large elevated platforms and by incorporating ancient symbols of patrimonial authority in the plans of their formal plaza groups. In contrast, interfactional unity was expressed through the use of a common spatial order that associated political authority with cosmological precepts of directionality and centrality. Within the capital, the elites of the various factions refrained from glorifying themselves on stone monuments in sharp contrast to their Olmec predecessors. Late Formative monuments from the outlying Group 4, El Mesón, and Alvarado sites, however, show rulers in elaborate costume accompanied by kneeling or sitting subjects. Thus exclusionary claims to power were evidently an important component of political discourse among (and perhaps toward) rivals in the region.

BEYOND THE FORMATIVE PERIOD

In each of the cases I have considered in this essay, Late Formative consolidation accompanied by practices that emphasized collectivist themes in political ideology was followed by a growing tendency toward expressing the exclusivity of elite status or factional interests. The Classic period trajectories of these three polities differed substantially, though. In the Valley of Oaxaca, Monte Albán flourished, entering a Classic period "Golden Age" even as the territorial extent of its control contracted. Zapotec elites built larger palaces and were buried in increasingly elaborately appointed tombs, and on occasion Zapotec rulers claimed personal credit for their deeds, as in the case of the Early Classic ruler 12 Jaguar (Marcus and Flannery 1996, 216–221).

In the Terminal Formative period (AD 1–300) some elites at Tres Zapotes and at El Mesón modified the layouts of their plaza groups, diverging from the strongly replicated plan of the Late Formative (Pool 2007). Contemporaneous with the divergence of formal layouts at Tres Zapotes, the La Mojarra stela and the Tuxtla Statuette were carved, evidently proclaiming the ritual acts and military exploits of individual elites in the region (Justeson and Kaufman 1993, 2008). By the Early Classic period, civic-ceremonial centers were proliferating in the lower Papaloapan Basin and the Tuxtlas mountains, Cerro de las Mesas had become a major power west of the Papaloapan, and Tres Zapotes had begun a prolonged decline, which continued until its abandonment in the Late Classic period (AD 600–900).

Increased conflict and political fragmentation also characterized the Early Classic period in the lower Río Verde Valley (Joyce, Chapter 1). The polity centered at Río Viejo collapsed around AD 250, as the acropolis was destroyed and the site lost more than half of its areal extent, and settlement in the valley shifted to piedmont locations. Meanwhile, the communal emphasis in burial declined, as burial in residential contexts became the Early Classic norm and high-status burials became more elaborate, with imported goods from central Mexico reflecting shifts in socially and economically important external interactions.

CONCLUSIONS

In the last centuries of the Formative period, urban centers and complex polities proliferated across Mesoamerica. In some areas, such as the Maya highlands and at Teotihuacan, Late Formative elites effectively monopolized material, ideological, and social sources of power and expressed their exclusive rights to the same in the display of sumptuary goods, elaborate palaces and mortuary temples, restricted access to ritual spaces, and/or sculpture that emphasized the legitimacy and individuality of rulers. In many other regions, public expressions of elite exclusionary power were muted in favor more collective themes.

Such broad-scale comparisons emphasize the exclusionary and corporate extremes of political-economic behavior to useful effect. In this essay a more fine-grained examination of three cases in which corporate strategies have been argued to have predominated at the scale of polity governance emphasizes the historically situated and contextual nature of political practice. To be sure, Late Formative political actors in the lower Río Verde Valley, the Valley of Oaxaca, and the lower Papaloapan Basin faced the problem of resolving the interests of individuals and of society as a whole, as do members of all societies. They also faced the corollary problem, common to complex polities, of resolving the tensions between hierarchical power structures and the collective welfare. The cross-culturally common practices of feasting, participation in collective work projects, and a de-emphasis of personal glorification and wealth offered avenues for aligning elite and commoner interests. Shared elements of Mesoamerican religion and cosmology, such as dualism, the *axis mundi,* and the "mountain of creation," offered a common vocabulary through which hierarchy and complementarity could be engaged.

Political practice in each of these cases, however, also responded to a different history of governance within a different political landscape. In the lower Río Verde Valley those conditions included still-emerging social inequality within a relatively open social and demographic setting; in the Valley of Oaxaca an ancient legacy of communal practice was challenged by increasing hierarchy and endemic conflict. At Tres Zapotes a long history of Olmec rulership based on exclusionary principles inhibited cooperation among proliferating factions. Political success and social integration in these cases was realized not by a rejection of exclusionary strategies, but by effective implementation of a mix of strategies that supported elite claims to the legitimate use of power while accommodating them to changed political and economic circumstances. In the reuse of Olmec ruler portraits at Tres Zapotes, the increasing elaborateness of tombs in residential contexts at Monte Albán, and the inclusion of exotic prestige and wealth items with burials in lower Río Verde cemeteries, we can see the reinterpretation of exclusionary practices bounded with respect to when and where they were enacted and toward what audience they were directed. Such situationally bounded acts also provided a reservoir of practice from which later elites could draw in more explicit assertions of individual, familial, and class power.

ACKNOWLEDGMENTS

I thank John Clark and Jeffrey Blomster for improving this chapter with their helpful comments, Javier Urcid for helping me see the *danzantes* of Monte Albán in a new light, and Arthur Joyce for the opportunity to contribute to this volume. Any errors of fact or interpretation are my own.

NOTES

1. In most areas of Mesoamerica the Middle Formative period is considered to begin about 900 BC (1000 cal BC). In large part, this convention refers to changes in ceramic decoration and technology, including a decline in Early Horizon ("Olmec-style") ceramic motifs. The lack of Early Horizon motifs in the lower Río Verde Valley makes the 1000 cal BC watershed less relevant there.

2. Flexed position alone does not indicate higher status in Formative Oaxaca, but it is unusual in this cemetery (Whalen 1981), where it is also associated with more elaborate grave construction than most burials, a greater prevalence of secondary burials, and greater frequencies of ceramics with these motifs.

REFERENCES CITED

Ambrose, Stanley H., and Lynette Norr. 1992. "On Stable Isotopic Data and Prehistoric Subsistence in the Soconusco Region." *Current Anthropology* 33 (4): 401–4. http://dx.doi.org/10.1086/204088.

Andrews, E. Wyllys, V. 1981 "Dzibilchaltun." In *Supplement to the Handbook of Middle American Indians*, Volume 1: *Archaeology*, ed. Victoria Reifler Bricker, 313–41. Austin: University of Texas Press.

Arnold, Philip J., III. 1996. "Craft Specialization and Social Change along the Southern Gulf Coast of Mexico." In *Craft Specialization and Social Evolution: In Memory of V. Gordon Childe*, ed. Bernard Wailes, 201–7. Philadelphia: University of Pennsylvania Museum of Archaeology and Anthropology.

Arnold, Philip J., III. 2000. "Sociopolitical Complexity and the Gulf Olmecs: A View from the Tuxtla Mountains, Veracruz, Mexico." In *Olmec Art and Archaeology in Mesoamerica*, ed. John E. Clark and Mary E. Pye, 117–35. Washington, DC: National Gallery of Art.

Arnold, Philip J., III. 2009. "Settlement and Subsistence among the Early Formative Gulf Olmec." *Journal of Anthropological Archaeology* 28 (4): 397–411. http://dx.doi .org/10.1016/j.jaa.2009.08.001.

Arnold, Philip J., III, and Robert S. Santley. 2008. "Classic Currents in the West-Central Tuxtlas." In *Classic Period Cultural Currents in Southern and Central Veracruz*, ed. Philip J. Arnold and Christopher A. Pool, 293–321. Cambridge, MA: Harvard University Press; Washington, DC: Dumbarton Oaks.

Arnold, Philip J., III, and Barbara L. Stark. 1997. "Gulf Lowland Settlement in Perspective." In *Olmec to Aztec: Settlement Patterns in the Ancient Gulf Lowlands*, ed. Barbara L. Stark and Philip J. Arnold, III, 310–29. Tucson: University of Arizona Press.

Baines, John, and Norman Yoffee. 1998. "Order, Legitimacy, and Wealth in Ancient Egypt and Mesopotamia." In *Archaic States*, ed. Gary M. Feinman and Joyce Marcus, 199–260. Santa Fe, NM: School of American Research Press.

Barber, Sarah B., and Arthur A. Joyce. 2006. "When Is a House a Palace? Elite Residences in the Valley of Oaxaca." In *Palaces and Power in the Americas*, ed. Jessica J. Christie and Patricia J. Sarro, 211–55. Austin: University of Texas Press.

Berdan, Frances, Richard Blanton, Elizabeth Boone, Mary G. Hodge, Michael Smith, and Emily Umberger. 1996. *Aztec Imperial Strategies*. Washington, DC: Dumbarton Oaks Research Library and Collection.

Blake, Michael, Brian S. Chisholm, John E. Clark, Barbara Voorhies, and Michael W. Love. 1992. "Prehistoric Subsistence in the Soconusco Region." *Current Anthropology* 33 (1): 83–94. http://dx.doi.org/10.1086/204038.

Blanton, Richard. 1978. *Monte Albán: Settlement Patterns in the Ancient Zapotec Capital*. New York: Academic Press.

Blanton, Richard. 1998. "Beyond Centralization: Steps toward a Theory of Egalitarian Behavior in Archaic States." In *Archaic States*, ed. Gary M. Feinman and Joyce Marcus, 135–72. Santa Fe, NM: School of American Research.

Blanton, Richard, Gary M. Feinman, Stephen A. Kowalewski, and Laura M. Finsten. 1993. *Ancient Mesoamerica: A Comparison of Change in Three Regions*. Cambridge: Cambridge University Press.

Blanton, Richard, Gary M. Feinman, Stephen A. Kowalewski, and Linda M. Nicholas. 1999. *Ancient Oaxaca*. Cambridge: Cambridge University Press. http://dx.doi .org/10.1017/CBO9780511607844.

Blanton, Richard, Gary M. Feinman, Stephen A. Kowalewski, and Peter N. Peregrine. 1996. "A Dual-Processual Theory for the Evolution of Mesoamerican Civilization." *Current Anthropology* 37 (1): 1–14. http://dx.doi.org/10.1086/204471.

Blomster, Jeffrey P. 2004. *Etlatongo: Social Complexity, Interaction, and Village Life in the Mixteca Alta of Oaxaca, Mexico*. Case Studies in Archaeology. Belmont, CA: Thomson Wadsworth.

Borstein, Joshua P. 2001. *Tripping over Colossal Heads: Settlement Patterns and Population Development in the Upland Olmec Heartland*. PhD dissertation, Department of Anthropology, Pennsylvania State University, University Park. Ann Arbor, MI: University Microfilms.

Braswell, Geoffrey E., ed. 2003. *The Maya and Teotihuacan Reinterpreting Early Classic Interaction*. Austin: University of Texas Press.

Carneiro, Robert L. 1970. "A Theory of the Origin of the State: Traditional Theories of State Origins Are Considered and Rejected in Favor of a New Ecological Hypothesis." *Science* 169, no. 3947 (Aug. 21): 733–38. http://dx.doi.org/10.1126/science .169.3947.733. Medline:17820299.

Cheetham, David. 2010. "Cultural Imperatives in Clay: Early Olmec Carved Pottery from San Lorenzo and Cantón Corralito." *Ancient Mesoamerica* 21 (1): 165–85. http://dx.doi.org/10.1017/S0956536110000040.

Chisholm, Brian S., Michael Blake, and Michael W. Love. 1993. "More on Prehistoric Subsistence in the Soconusco Region: Response to Ambrose and Norr." *Current Anthropology* 34 (4): 432–34. http://dx.doi.org/10.1086/204187.

Clark, John E. 1994. "El sistema económico de los primeros olmecas." In *Los olmecas en Mesoamérica*, ed. John E. Clark, 189–201. Mexico City: Citibank.

Clark, John E. 1997. "The Arts of Government in Early Mesoamerica." *Annual Review of Anthropology* 26: 211–34. http://dx.doi.org/10.1146/annurev.anthro.26.1.211.

Clark, John E. 2005. "The Birth of Mesoamerican Metaphysics: Sedentism, Engagement, and Moral Superiority." In *Rethinking Materiality: The Engagement of Mind with the Material World*, ed. Elizabeth DeMarrais, Chris Gosden, and Colin Renfrew, 205–24. Cambridge: McDonald Institute for Archaeological Research.

Clark, John E. 2007. "Mesoamerica's First State." In *The Political Economy of Ancient Mesoamerica*, ed. John E. Clark and Vernon L. Scarborough, 11–46. Albuquerque: University of New Mexico Press.

Clark, John E., and Michael Blake. 1994. "The Power of Prestige: Competitive Generosity and the Emergence of Rank in Lowland Mesoamerica." In *Factional Competition and Political Development in the New World*, ed. Elizabeth M. Brumfiel and John W. Fox, 17–30. Cambridge: Cambridge University Press. http://dx.doi.org/10.1017 /CBO9780511598401.003.

Clark, John E., and Richard D. Hansen. 2001. "The Architecture of Early Kingship: Comparative Perspectives on the Origins of the Maya Royal Court." In *Royal Courts of the Ancient Maya*, Volume 2: *Data and Case Studies*, ed. Stephen D. Houston and Takeshi Inomata, 1–45. Boulder, CO: Westview.

Clark, John E., and Mary E. Pye. 2000. "The Pacific Coast and the Olmec Question." In *Olmec Art and Archaeology in Mesoamerica*, ed. John E. Clark and Mary E. Pye, 217–51. Washington, DC: National Gallery of Art.

Cobean, Robert H., Michael D. Coe, Edward A. Perry Jr., Karl K. Turekian, and Dinkar P. Kharkar. 1971. "Obsidian Trade at San Lorenzo Tenochtitlan, Mexico." *Science* 174, no. 4010 (Nov. 12): 666–71. http://dx.doi.org/10.1126/science.174.4010.666. Medline:17777326.

Cobean, Robert H., James R. Vogt, Michael D. Glascock, and Terrance L. Stocker. 1991. "High-Precision Trace-Element Characterization of Major Mesoamerican Obsidian Sources and Further Analyses of Artifacts from San Lorenzo Tenochtitlan, Mexico." *Latin American Antiquity* 2 (1): 69–91. http://dx.doi.org/10.2307/971896.

Coe, Michael D. 1962. *Mexico*. New York: Praeger.

Cohen, Abner. 1971. "Cultural Strategies in the Organization of Trading Diaspora." In *L'Evolution du Commerce en Afrique de L'Ouest*, ed. Claude Mesailloux, 266–81. Oxford: Oxford University Press.

Cowgill, George L. 1997. "State and Society at Teotihuacan, Mexico." *Annual Review of Anthropology* 26 (1): 129–61. http://dx.doi.org/10.1146/annurev.anthro.26.1.129.

Cowgill, George L. 2003. "Teotihuacán and Early Classic Interaction: A Perspective from Outside the Maya Region." In *The Maya and Teotihuacán: Reinterpreting Early Classic Interaction*, ed. Geoffrey Braswell, 315–35. Austin: University of Texas Press.

Curet, L. Antonio, Barbara L. Stark, and Vásquez Z. Sergio. 1994. "Postclassic Changes in Veracruz, Mexico." *Ancient Mesoamerica* 5 (1): 13–32. http://dx.doi.org/10.1017/S0956536100001000.

Curtin, Philip. 1984. *Cross Cultural Trade in World History*. Cambridge: Cambridge University Press. http://dx.doi.org/10.1017/CBO9780511661198.

Daneels, Annick. 1997. "El proyecto exploraciones en el centro de Veracruz 1981–1995." In *Memoria del coloquio arqueología del centro y sur de Veracruz*, ed. Sara Ladrón de Guevara and Vásquez Z. Sergio, 59–74. Xalapa: Universidad Veracruzana.

Demand, Nancy H. 1990. *Urban Relocation in Archaic and Classical Greece: Flight and Consolidation*. Norman: University of Oklahoma Press.

Demarest, Arthur A., and Geoffrey W. Conrad. 1992. *Ideology and the Evolution of Precolumbian Civilizations*. Cambridge: Cambridge University Press.

DeMarrais, Elizabeth, Luis Jaime Castillo, and Timothy K. Earle. 1996. "Ideology, Materialization, and Power Strategies." *Current Anthropology* 37 (1): 15–31. http://dx.doi.org/10.1086/204472.

Diehl, Richard A., and Michael D. Coe. 1995. "Olmec Archaeology." In *The Olmec World: Ritual and Rulership*, ed. Jill Guthrie and Elizabeth P. Benson, 11–25. Princeton, NJ: Art Museum, Princeton University.

Dietler, Michael. 2001. "Theorizing the Feast: Rituals of Consumption, Commensal Politics, and Power in African Contexts." In *Feasts: Archaeological and Ethnographic Perspectives on Food, Politics, and Power*, ed. Michael Dietler and Brian Hayden, 65–114. Washington, DC: Smithsonian Institution Press.

Doering, Travis. 2002. Obsidian Artifacts from San Andrés, La Venta, Tabasco, Mexico. MS thesis, Florida State University, Tallahassee.

Drennan, Robert D., and Christian E. Peterson. 2006. "Patterned Variation in Prehistoric Chiefdoms." *Proceedings of the National Academy of Sciences of the United States of America* 103, no. 11 (Mar. 14): 3960–67. http://dx.doi.org/10.1073/pnas.0510862103. Medline:16473941.

Earle, Timothy K. 1997. *How Chiefs Come to Power: The Political Economy in Prehistory*. Stanford, CA: Stanford University Press.

Feinman, Gary M. 2001. "Mesoamerican Political Complexity." In *From Leaders to Rulers*, ed. Jonathan Haas, 151–75. New York: Kluwer/Plenum Publishers. http://dx.doi.org/10.1007/978-1-4615-1297-4_8.

Flannery, Kent V., ed. 1986. *Guilá Naquitz*. New York: Academic Press.

Flannery, Kent V., and Joyce Marcus. 1983. "The Earliest Public Buildings, Tombs, and Monuments of Monte Albán." In *The Cloud People: Divergent Evolution of the Mixtec and Zapotec Civilizations*, ed. Kent V. Flannery and Joyce Marcus, 87–91. New York: Academic Press.

Flannery, Kent V., and Joyce Marcus. 1994. *Early Formative Pottery of the Valley of Oaxaca, Mexico*. Memoirs of the University of Michigan Museum of Anthropology No. 27. Ann Arbor: University of Michigan.

Flannery, Kent V., and Joyce Marcus. 2000. "Formative Mexican Chiefdoms and the Myth of the 'Mother Culture.'" *Journal of Anthropological Archaeology* 19 (1): 1–37. http://dx.doi.org/10.1006/jaar.1999.0359.

Flannery, Kent V., and Joyce Marcus. 2003. "The Origin of War: New ^{14}C Dates from Ancient Mexico." *Proceedings of the National Academy of Sciences of the United States of America* 100, no. 20 (Sep. 30): 11801–5. http://dx.doi.org/10.1073/pnas.1934526100. Medline:14500785.

Garraty, Christopher P., and Barbara L. Stark. 2002. "Imperial and Social Relations in Postclassic South-Central Veracruz, Mexico." *Latin American Antiquity* 13 (1): 3–33. http://dx.doi.org/10.2307/971739.

Giddens, A. 1984. *The Constitution of Society: Outline of the Theory of Structuration*. Berkeley: University of California Press.

Goman, Michelle, and Roger Byrne. 1998. "A 5000-Year Record of Agriculture and Tropical Forest Clearance in the Tuxtlas, Veracruz, Mexico." *Holocene* 8 (1): 83–89. http://dx.doi.org/10.1191/095968398670396093.

Grove, David C., ed. 1987. *Ancient Chalcatzingo*. Austin: University of Texas Press.

Grove, David C. 1989. "Olmec: What's in a Name?" In *Regional Perspectives on the Olmec*, ed. Robert J. Sharer and David C. Grove, 8–14. Cambridge: Cambridge University Press.

Grove, David C. 1993. "'Olmec' Horizons in Formative Period Mesoamerica: Diffusion or Social Evolution?" In *Latin American Horizons*, ed. D. S. Rice, 83–111. Washington, DC: Dumbarton Oaks Research Library and Collection.

Hayden, Brian. 2001. "Fabulous Feasts: A Prolegomenon to the Importance of Feasting." In *Feasts: Archaeological and Ethnographic Perspectives on Food, Politics, and Power*, ed. Michael Dietler and Brian Hayden, 23–64. Washington, DC: Smithsonian Institution Press.

Hester, Thomas Roy, Robert N. Jack, and Robert Fleming Heizer. 1971. "The Obsidian of Tres Zapotes, Veracruz, Mexico." *Contributions of the University of California Archaeological Research Facility* 13: 65–131.

Holst, Irene, J. Enrique Moreno, and Dolores R. Piperno. 2007. "Identification of Teosinte, Maize, and Tripsacum in Mesoamerica by Using Pollen, Starch Grains, and Phytoliths." *Proceedings of the National Academy of Sciences of the United States of America* 104, no. 45 (Nov. 6): 17608–13. http://dx.doi.org/10.1073/pnas.0708736104. Medline:17978176.

Joyce, Arthur A. 2004. "Sacred Space and Social Relations in the Valley of Oaxaca." In *Mesoamerican Archaeology*, ed. Julia A. Hendon and Rosemary A. Joyce, 192–216. Oxford: Blackwell.

Joyce, Arthur A. 2010. *Mixtecs, Zapotecs, and Chatinos: Ancient Peoples of Southern Mexico.* Malden, MA: Wiley-Blackwell.

Joyce, Arthur A., J. Michael Elam, Michael D. Glascock, Hector Neff, and Marcus Winter. 1995. "Exchange Implications of Obsidian Source Analysis from the Lower Río Verde Valley, Oaxaca, Mexico." *Latin American Antiquity* 6 (1): 3–15. http://dx.doi.org/10.2307/971597.

Joyce, Arthur A., and Marcus Winter. 1996. "Ideology, Power, and Urban Society in Prehispanic Oaxaca." *Current Anthropology* 37 (1): 33–86. http://dx.doi.org/10.10 86/204473.

Justeson, John S., and Terrence Kaufman. 1993. "A Decipherment of Epi-Olmec Hieroglyphic Writing." *Science* 259, no. 5102 (Mar. 19): 1703–11. http://dx.doi.org/10.1126/science.259.5102.1703. Medline:17816888.

Justeson, John S., and Terrence Kaufman. 2008. "The Epi-Olmec Tradition at Cerro de las Mesas in the Classic Period." In *Classic-Period Cultural Currents in Southern and Central Veracruz,* ed. Philip J. Arnold, III, and Christopher A. Pool, 159–96. Cambridge, MA: Harvard University Press; Washington, DC: Dumbarton Oaks.

Kaufman, Terrence, and John S. Justeson. 2001. *Epi-Olmec Writing and Texts.* Austin: Texas Workshop Foundation.

Killion, Thomas W., and Javier Urcid. 2001. "The Olmec Legacy: Cultural Continuity and Change in Mexico's Southern Gulf Coast Lowlands." *Journal of Field Archaeology* 28 (1/2): 3–25. http://dx.doi.org/10.2307/3181457.

Knight, Charles L.F., and Michael D. Glascock. 2009. "The Terminal Formative to Classic Period Obsidian Assemblage at Palo Errado, Veracruz, Mexico." *Latin American Antiquity* 20 (4): 507–24.

Kowalewski, Stephen A., Gary M. Feinman, Laura Finsten, Richard Blanton, and Linda Nicholas. 1989. *Monte Albán's Hinterland, Part II: The Prehispanic Settlement Patterns in Tlacolula, Etla, and Ocotlán, the Valley of Oaxaca, Mexico.* Museum of Anthropology Memoir 23. Ann Arbor: University of Michigan.

Loughlin, Michael. 2004. "Recorrido arqueológico El Mesón." Report submitted to Foundation for the Advancement of Mesoamerican Studies, Coral Gables, FL. http://www.famsi.org/reports/02058/index.html.

Loughlin, Michael. 2009. "The Tres Zapotes Regional Polity: A View from the Hinterland." Paper presented at the 74th Annual Meeting of the Society for American Archaeology, Atlanta.

Loughlin, Michael, and Christopher A. Pool. 2007. "The End of the Formative in Western Olman." Paper presented at the 72nd Annual Meeting of the Society for American Archaeology, Austin, TX.

Love, Michael W. 1999. "Ideology, Material Culture, and Daily Practice in Pre-Classic Mesoamerica: A Pacific Coast Perspective." In *Social Patterns in Pre-Classic Mesoamerica,* ed. David C. Grove and Rosemary A. Joyce, 127–53. Washington, DC: Dumbarton Oaks.

Love, Michael W. 2002. *Early Complex Society in Pacific Guatemala: Settlements and Chronology of the Río Naranjo, Guatemala.* Papers of the New World Archaeological Foundation 66. Provo, UT: New World Archaeological Foundation.

Malmström, Vincent Herschel. 1997. *Cycles of the Sun, Mysteries of the Moon: The Calendar in Mesoamerican Civilization.* Austin: University of Texas Press.

Marcus, Joyce. 1976. "The Iconography of Militarism at Monte Albán and Neighboring Sites in the Valley of Oaxaca." In *Origins of Religious Art and Iconography in Preclassic Mesoamerica*, ed. Henry Nicholson, 125–39. Los Angeles: UCLA Latin American Center Publications.

Marcus, Joyce. 1983. "The Conquest Slabs of Building J, Monte Albán." In *The Cloud People: Divergent Evolution of the Zapotec and Mixtec Civilizations*, ed. Kent V. Flannery and Joyce Marcus, 106–8. New York: Academic Press.

Marcus, Joyce. 1989. "Zapotec Chiefdoms and the Nature of Formative Religions." In *Regional Perspectives on the Olmec*, ed. Robert J. Sharer and David C. Grove, 148–97. Cambridge: Cambridge University Press.

Marcus, Joyce. 1992. *Mesoamerican Writing Systems*. Princeton, NJ: Princeton University Press.

Marcus, Joyce, and Kent Flannery. 1996. *Zapotec Civilization: How Urban Society Evolved in Mexico's Oaxaca Valley*. London: Thames & Hudson.

Niederberger, Christine. 1976. *Zohapilco: Cinco milenios de ocupación humana en un sitio lacustre de la Cuenca de México*. Mexico City: Instituto Nacional de Antropología e Historia.

Ohnersorgen, Michael Anthony. 2001. *Social and Economic Organization of Cotaxtla in the Postclassic Gulf Lowlands*. PhD dissertation, Department of Anthropology, Arizona State University, Phoenix. Ann Arbor, MI: University Microfilms.

Orr, Heather. 1997. *Power Games in the Late Formative Valley of Oaxaca: The Ballplayer Sculptures of Dainzú*. PhD dissertation, Department of Art History, University of Texas, Austin. Ann Arbor, MI: University Microfilms.

Orwell, George. 1945. *Animal Farm*. London: Martin Secker & Warburg.

Pauketat, Timothy R. 2000. "The Tragedy of the Commoners." In *Agency in Archaeology*, ed. Marcia Anne Dobres and John Robb, 113–29. London: Routledge.

Piperno, Dolores R., Jorge E. Moreno, Jose Iriarte, Irene Holst, Matthew Lachniet, John G. Jones, Anthony J. Ranere, and Ronald Castanzo. 2007. "Late Pleistocene and Holocene Environmental History of the Iguala Valley, Central Balsas Watershed of Mexico." *Proceedings of the National Academy of Sciences of the United States of America* 104, no. 29 (Jul. 17): 11874–81. http://dx.doi.org/10.1073/pnas.0703442104. Medline:17537917.

Pohl, Mary E., Dolores R. Piperno, Kevin O. Pope, and John G. Jones. 2007. "Microfossil Evidence for Pre-Columbian Maize Dispersals in the Neotropics from San Andres, Tabasco, Mexico." *Proceedings of the National Academy of Sciences of the United States of America* 104, no. 16 (Apr. 17): 6870–75. http://dx.doi.org/10.1073/pnas.0701425104. Medline:17426147.

Pool, Christopher A. 1992. "Strangers in a Strange Land: Ethnicity and Ideology at an Enclave Community in Middle Classic Mesoamerica." In *Ancient Images, Ancient Thought: The Archeology of Ideology*, ed. A. Sean Goldsmith, 41–55. Calgary: University of Calgary.

Pool, Christopher A., ed. 2003. *Settlement Archaeology and Political Economy at Tres Zapotes, Veracruz, Mexico*. Los Angeles: Cotsen Institute of Archaeology, University of California.

Pool, Christopher A. 2005. "Contemplating Variation in Olmec Settlement and Polity Using Mississippian Models." In *Gulf Coast Archaeology: The Southeastern U.S. and Mexico*, ed. Nancy White, 223–45. Gainesville: University of Florida Press.

Pool, Christopher A. 2007. *Olmec Archaeology and Early Mesoamerica*. Cambridge: Cambridge University Press. http://dx.doi.org/10.1017/CBO9781139167147.

Pool, Christopher A. 2008. "Architectural Plans, Factionalism, and the Protoclassic-Classic Transition at Tres Zapotes." In *Classic Period Cultural Currents in Southern and Central Veracruz*, ed. Philip J. Arnold and Christopher A. Pool, 121–57. Cambridge, MA: Harvard University Press; Washington, DC: Dumbarton Oaks.

Pool, Christopher A. 2010. "Stone Monuments and Earthen Mounds: Polity and Place-making at Tres Zapotes, Veracruz, Mexico." In *The Place of Sculpture in Mesoamerica's Preclassic Transition*, ed. John E. Clark, Julia Guernsey, and Barbara Arroyo, 97–126. Washington, DC: Dumbarton Oaks

Pool, Christopher A., Charles Knight, and Michael D. Glascock. N.d. "Formative Obsidian Procurement at Tres Zapotes, Veracruz, Mexico." Manuscript in possession of the authors.

Pool, Christopher A., and Michael Loughlin. 2006. "Una vista desde el oeste: Tres Zapotes y el paisaje político olmeca." Paper presented at the 52nd International Congress of Americanists, Seville, Spain.

Pool, Christopher A., and Michael Anthony Ohnersorgen. 2003. "Archaeological Survey and Settlement at Tres Zapotes." In *Settlement Archaeology and Political Economy at Tres Zapotes, Veracruz, Mexico*, ed. Christopher A. Pool, 7–31. Monograph 50. Los Angeles: Cotsen Institute of Archaeology, University of California.

Pool, Christopher A., Ponciano Ortiz Ceballos, María del Carmen Rodríguez Martínez, and Michael L. Loughlin. 2010. "The Early Horizon at Tres Zapotes: Implications for Olmec Interaction." *Ancient Mesoamerica* 21 (1): 95–105. http://dx.doi.org/10.1017/S0956536110000064.

Pope, Kevin O., Mary D. Pohl, John G. Jones, David L. Lentz, Christopher L. von Nagy, Francisco J. Vega, and Irvy R. Quitmyer. 2001. "Origin and Environmental Setting of Ancient Agriculture in the Lowlands of Mesoamerica." *Science* 292, no. 5520 (May 18): 1370–73. http://dx.doi.org/10.1126/science.292.5520.1370. Medline:11359011.

Pyne, Nanette M. 1976. "The Fire-Serpent and the Were-Jaguar in Formative Oaxaca." In *The Early Mesoamerican Village*, ed. Kent V. Flannery, 272–82. New York: Academic Press.

Ranere, Anthony J., Dolores R. Piperno, Irene Holst, Ruth Dickau, and José Iriarte. 2009. "The Cultural and Chronological Context of Early Holocene Maize and Squash Domestication in the Central Balsas River Valley, Mexico." *Proceedings of the National Academy of Sciences of the United States of America* 106, no. 13 (Mar. 31): 5014–18. http://dx.doi.org/10.1073/pnas.0812590106. Medline:19307573.

Redmond, Elsa M. 1983. *A Fuego y Sangre: Early Zapotec Imperialism in the Cuicatlán Cañada, Oaxaca*. Memoirs of the University of Michigan Museum of Anthropology No. 16. Ann Arbor: University of Michigan.

Redmond, Elsa M., and Charles S. Spencer. 2006. "From Raiding to Conquest: Warfare Strategies and Early State Development in Oaxaca, Mexico." In *The Archaeology of Warfare: Prehistories of Raiding and Conquest*, ed. Elizabeth N. Arkush and Mark W. Allen, 336–93. Gainesville: University Press of Florida.

Reilly, F. Kent, III. 1995. "Art, Ritual, and Rulership in the Olmec World." In *The Olmec World: Ritual and Rulership*, ed. Jill Guthrie and Elizabeth P. Benson, 27–45. Princeton, NJ: Art Museum, Princeton University.

Ringle, William M. 1999. "Pre-Classic Cityscapes: Ritual Politics among the Early Lowland Maya." In *Social Patterns in Pre-Classic Mesoamerica*, ed. David C. Grove and Rosemary A. Joyce, 183–224. Washington, DC: Dumbarton Oaks Research Library and Collection.

Rosenswig, Robert M. 2000. "Some Political Processes of Ranked Societies." *Journal of Anthropological Archaeology* 19 (4): 413–60. http://dx.doi.org/10.1006/jaar.2000.0360.

Rust, William F., and Barbara W. Leyden. 1994. "Evidence of Maize Use at Early and Middle Preclassic La Venta Olmec Sites." In *Corn and Culture in the Prehistoric New World*, ed. Sissel Johannessen and Christine A. Hastorf, 181–201. Boulder, CO: Westview Press.

Rust, William F., and Robert J. Sharer. 1988. "Olmec Settlement Data from La Venta, Tabasco, Mexico." *Science* 242, no. 4875 (Oct. 7): 102–4. http://dx.doi.org/10.1126/science.242.4875.102. Medline:17757633.

Sanders, William T. 1981. "Ecological Adaptation in the Basin of Mexico: 23,000 BC to the Present." In *Archaeology*, ed. Jeremey A. Sabloff, 147–97. Supplement to the Handbook of Middle American Indians No. 1. Austin: University of Texas Press.

Sanders, William T., Jeffrey Parsons, and Robert S. Santley. 1979. *The Basin of Mexico: Ecological Processes in the Evolution of a Civilization*. New York: Academic Press.

Santley, Robert S. 2007. *The Prehistory of the Tuxtlas*. Albuquerque: University of New Mexico Press.

Santley, Robert S., and Philip J. Arnold, III. 1996. "Prehispanic Settlement Patterns in the Tuxtla Mountains, Southern Veracruz, Mexico." *Journal of Field Archaeology* 23 (2): 225–49. http://dx.doi.org/10.2307/530505.

Santley, Robert S., and Philip J. Arnold, III. 2004. "El intercambio de obsidiana y la influencia Teotihuacána en la Sierra de las Tuxtlas." In *La Costa del Golfo en tiempos Teotihuacános: Propuestas y perspectivias*, ed. Elena Ruiz Gallut María and Arturo Pascual Soto, 115–38. Mexico City: Instituto Nacional de Antropología e Historia.

Santley, Robert S., Philip J. Arnold, III, and Thomas P. Barrett. 1997. "Formative Period Settlement Patterns in the Tuxtla Mountains." In *Olmec to Aztec: Settlement Patterns in the Ancient Gulf Lowlands*, ed. Barbara L. Stark and Philip J. Arnold, III, 174–205. Tucson: University of Arizona Press.

Santley, Robert S., Thomas P. Barrett, Michael D. Glascock, and Hector Neff. 2001. "Pre-Hispanic Obsidian Procurement in the Tuxtla Mountains, Southern Veracruz, Mexico." *Ancient Mesoamerica* 12 (1): 49–63. http://dx.doi.org/10.1017/S0956536101121036.

Santley, Robert S., Clare Yarborough, and Barbara Hall. 1987. "Enclaves, Ethnicity, and the Archaeological Record at Matacapan." In *Ethnicity and Culture*, ed. Reginald Auger, Margaret F. Glass, Scott MacEncher, and Peter H. McCartney, 85–100. Calgary: Archaeological Association, University of Calgary.

Scott, John F. 1978. *The Danzantes of Monte Albán, Part 1: Text*. Studies in Pre-Columbian Art and Archaeology No. 19. Washington, DC: Dumbarton Oaks.

Shaffer, Gary D. 1993. "An Archaeomagnetic Study of a Wattle-and-Daub Building Collapse." *Journal of Field Archaeology* 20 (1): 59–75.

Sluyter, Andrew, and Gabriela Domínguez. 2006. "Early Maize (*Zea mays* L.) Cultivation in Mexico: Dating Sedimentary Pollen Records and Its Implications." *Proceedings of the National Academy of Sciences of the United States of America* 103, no. 4 (Jan. 24): 1147–51. http://dx.doi.org/10.1073/pnas.0510473103. Medline:16418287.

Smith, Bruce D. 1997. "Reconsidering the Ocampo Caves and the Era of Incipient Cultivation in Mesoamerica." *Latin American Antiquity* 8 (4): 342–83. http://dx.doi.org/10.2307/972107.

Smith, Bruce D. 2000. "Guilá Naquitz Revisited: Agricultural Origins in Oaxaca, Mexico." In *Cultural Evolution: Contemporary Viewpoints*, ed. Gary M. Feinman and Linda Manzanilla, 15–60. New York: Kluwer Academic/Plenum Press.

Smith, Michael E., and Lisa Montiel. 2001. "The Archaeological Study of Empires and Imperialism in Pre-Hispanic Central Mexico." *Journal of Anthropological Archaeology* 20 (3): 245–84. http://dx.doi.org/10.1006/jaar.2000.0372.

Spence, Michael. 1996. "A Comparative Analysis of Ethnic Enclaves." In *Arqueología mesoamericana: Homenaje a William T. Sanders*, vol. 1, ed. Alba Guadalupe Mastache, Jeffrey R. Parsons, Robert S. Santley, and Mari Carmen Serra Puche, 333–53. Mexico City: Instituto Nacional de Antropología e Historia.

Spencer, Charles S. 1998. "Mathematical Model of Primary State Formation." *Cultural Dynamics* 10 (1): 5–20. http://dx.doi.org/10.1177/092137409801000101.

Spencer, Charles S., and Elsa M. Redmond. 2003. "Militarism, Resistance, and Early State Development in Oaxaca, Mexico." *Social Evolution & History* 2: 25–70.

Spencer, Charles S., and Elsa M. Redmond. 2004. "Primary State Formation in Mesoamerica." *Annual Review of Anthropology* 33 (1): 173–99. http://dx.doi.org/10.1146/annurev.anthro.33.070203.143823.

Stark, Barbara L. 1981. "The Rise of Sedentary Life." In *Archaeology: Supplement to the Handbook of Middle American Indians*, vol. 1, ed. Jeremey A. Sabloff, 345–72. Austin: University of Texas Press.

Stark, Barbara L. 1990. "The Gulf Coast and the Central Highlands of Mexico: Alternative Models for Interaction." *Research in Economic Anthropology* 12: 243–85.

Stein, Gil. 1999. *Rethinking World Systems: Diasporas, Colonies, and Interaction in Uruk Mesopotamia*. Tucson: University of Arizona Press.

Stirling, Matthew W. 1943. *Stone Monuments of Southern Mexico*. Bureau of American Ethnology, Bulletin 138. Washington, DC: Bureau of American Ethnology.

Stoner, Wesley D. 2008. "Tepango Valley Archaeological Survey: Tuxtla Mountains, Southern Veracruz, México." Report submitted to Foundation for the Advancement of Mesoamerican Studies, Coral Gables, FL. http://www.famsi.org/reports/07049/index.html.

Sugiyama, Saburo. 2005. *Human Sacrifice, Militarism, and Rulership: Materialization of State Ideology at the Feathered Serpent Pyramid, Teotihuacan*. Cambridge: Cambridge University Press. http://dx.doi.org/10.1017/CBO9780511489563.

Sullivan, Timothy D. 2002. "Landscape of Power: A Spatial Analysis of Civic-Ceremonial Architecture at Tres Zapotes, Veracruz, Mexico." MA thesis, Southern Illinois University, Carbondale.

Symonds, Stacey, Ann Cyphers, and Roberto Lunagómez. 2002. *Asentamiento prehispánico en San Lorenzo Tenochtitlán*. Mexico City: Universidad Nacional Autónoma de México.

Taylor, Sarah R., Arthur A. Joyce, Mathew Sponheimer, and Sarah B. Barber. 2009. Dieta y agricultura en el valle del Río Verde inferior: Basado en análisis de micro-desgaste dental e isótopos estables. In "Estudios alimenticios y de ADN de dientes humanos del valle del Río Verde inferior, Oaxaca, México," ed. Arthur A. Joyce, 3–31. Report submitted to the Consejo de Arqueología, Instituto Nacional de Antropología e Historia, Mexico City.

Umberger, Emily. 1996. "Aztec Presence and Material Remains in the Outer Provinces." In *Aztec Imperial Strategies*, ed. Frances Berdan, Richard Blanton, and Elizabeth Boone, 151–79. Washington, DC: Dumbarton Oaks Research Library and Collection.

Urcid, Javier. 1994. "Mound J at Monte Albán and Zapotec Political Geography during Period II (200 BC–AD 200)." Paper presented at the 59th Annual Meeting of the Society for American Archaeology, Anaheim, CA.

Urcid, Javier. 2005. *The Zapotec Scribal Tradition: Knowledge, Memory, and Society in Ancient Oaxaca*. Coral Gables, FL: Foundation for the Advancement of Mesoamerican Studies. www.famsi.org/zapotecwriting/.

Urcid, Javier. 2008. "The Written Surface as a Cultural Code: A Comparative Perspective of Scribal Traditions from Southwestern Mesoamerica." Paper presented at the symposium Scripts and Notational Systems in Pre-Columbian America, Dumbarton Oaks, Washington, DC.

Urcid, Javier. 2011. "Los oráculos y la guerra: El papel de las narrativas pictóricas en el desarrollo temprano de Monte Albán (500 a.C.–200 d.C.). In *Monte Albán en la encrucijada regional y disciplinaria: Memoria de la quinta mesa redonda de Monte Albán*, ed. Nelly Robles García and Ángel I. Rivera Guzmán, 163–237. Mexico City: Instituto Nacional de Antropología e Historia.

Urcid, Javier, and Arthur Joyce. 2011. "Formative Period Transformations of Monte Albán's Main Plaza and Their Political Implications." Paper presented at the 76th annual meeting of the Society for American Archaeology, Sacramento, CA.

VanDerwarker, Amber. 2003. *Agricultural Intensification and the Emergence of Political Complexity in the Formative Sierra de los Tuxtlas, Southern Veracruz, Mexico*. PhD dissertation, Department of Anthropology, University of North Carolina, Chapel Hill. Ann Arbor, MI: University Microfilms.

VanDerwarker, Amber. 2006. *Farming, Hunting, and Fishing in the Olmec World*. Austin: University of Texas Press.

Venter, Marcie. 2008. *Community Strategies in the Aztec Imperial Frontier: Perspectives from Totogal, Veracruz, Mexico*. PhD dissertation, Department of Anthropology, University of Kentucky, Lexington. Ann Arbor, MI: University Microfilms.

Von Nagy, Christopher L. 1997. "The Geoarchaeology of Settlement in the Grijalva Delta." In *Olmec to Aztec: Settlement Patterns in the Ancient Gulf Lowlands*, ed. Barbara L. Stark and Philip J. Arnold, III, 253–77. Tucson: University of Arizona Press.

Von Nagy, Christopher L. 2003. *Of Meandering Rivers and Shifting Towns: Landscape Evolution and Community within the Grijalva Delta*. PhD dissertation, Department of Anthropology, Tulane University, New Orleans, LA. Ann Arbor, MI: University Microfilms.

Voorhies, Barbara. 1996. "The Transformation from Foraging to Farming in the Lowlands of Mesoamerica." In *The Managed Mosaic: Ancient Maya Agriculture and Resource Use*, ed. Scott Fedick, 17–29. Salt Lake City: University of Utah Press.

Whalen, Michael E. 1981. *Excavations at Santo Domingo Tomaltepec: Evolution of a Formative Community in the Valley of Oaxaca, Mexico.* Prehistory and Human Ecology of the Valley of Oaxaca, vol. 6, Memoirs of the University of Michigan Museum of Anthropology No. 12. Ann Arbor: University of Michigan.

Winter, Marcus. 1989. *Oaxaca: The Archaeological Record.* Mexico: Minutiae Mexicana.

Winter, Marcus. 2001. Palacios, templos y 1300 años de vida urbana en Monte Albán. In *Reconstruyendo la ciudad Maya: El urbanismo en las sociedades antiguas,* ed. Adres Ciudad Ruis, María J. Iglesia Ponce de Leon, and María del Carmen Martínez Martínez, 253–301. Madrid: Sociedad Española de Estudios Mayas.

Winter, Marcus, and Jeffrey P. Blomster. 2008. "Religión e interacción: Oaxaca y los olmecas." In *Olmeca: Balance y perspectivas; Memoria de la primera mesa redonda,* vol. 1, ed. María Teresa Uriarte and Rebecca González Lauck, 205–26. Mexico City: Universidad Nacional Autónoma de México—Instituto de Investigaciones Estéticas and Insituto Nacional de Antropología e Historia.

Workinger, Andrew, and Arthur A. Joyce. 2009. "Reconsidering Warfare in Formative Period Oaxaca." In *Blood and Beauty: Organized Violence in the Art and Archaeology of Mesoamerica and Central America,* ed. Heather Orr and Rex Koontz, 156–71. Los Angeles: Cotsen Institute of Archaeology, University of California.

Zeitlin, Robert N., and Arthur A. Joyce. 1999. "The Zapotec-Imperialism Argument: Insights from the Oaxaca Coast." *Current Anthropology* 40 (3): 383–92. http://dx.doi.org/10.1086/200029.

CONTRIBUTORS

José Aguilar, San Diego State University

Sarah B. Barber, University of Central Florida

Aleksander Borejsza, Universidad Autónoma de San Luis Potosí

Michelle Butler, University of California, Riverside

Michelle Goman, Sonoma State University

Guy David Hepp, University of Colorado at Boulder

Arthur A. Joyce, University of Colorado at Boulder

Marc N. Levine, University of Oklahoma

Arion T. Mayes, San Diego State University

Raymond G. Mueller, Richard Stockton College

Christopher A. Pool, University of Kentucky

Andrew Workinger, University of Tennessee at Chattanooga

INDEX

Page numbers in italics indicate illustrations.